Michael Cranny

Garvin Moles

counterpoints

Exploring Canadian Issues

Contributing Authors

Matthew Christison

Graham Draper

Prentice
Hall

Toronto

National Library of Canada Cataloguing in Publication Data

Cranny, Michael William, 1947-
    Counterpoints: exploring Canadian issues

For use in grade 11.
Includes index.
ISBN 0-13-088877-X

1. Canada - History - 20th century. 2. Canada - Politics and government.
3. Canada - Geography. I. Moles, Garvin, 1943- . II. Title.

FC600.C72 2001   971.06   C2001-930296-7
F1034.2.C72 2001

ISBN 0-13-088877-X

Contributing Authors: Colin M. Bain, Dennis DesRivieres, Peter Flaherty, Donna M. Goodman, Elma Schemenauer, Angus L. Scully
Publisher: Mark Cobham
Product Manager: Anita Borovilos
Managing Editor: Elynor Kagan
Lead Developmental Editor: Jenifer Ludbrook
Developmental Editors: Chelsea Donaldson, Mary Kirley
Production Editor: Francine Geraci
Proofreader: Gail Copeland
Production Coordinator: Zane Kaneps
Art Direction: Alex Li
Design and Page Layout: Monica Kompter/Silver Birch Graphics
Cover Images: Top: Tony Stone 402098-001; Bottom left: CP Picture Archive; Bottom centre: F.R. Kemp/NAC PA-142415; Bottom right: Tony Stone 453797-001.
Illustrations: Maps by Deborah Crowle. All other art by Anthony de Ridder
Photo Research/Permissions: Michaele Sinko, Karen Taylor

The publisher has taken every care to meet or exceed industry specifications for the manufacturing of textbooks. The spine and the endpapers of this sewn book have been reinforced with special fabric for extra binding strength. The cover is a premium polymer-reinforced material designed to provide long life and withstand rugged use. Mylar gloss lamination has been applied for further durability.

Printed and bound in Canada
1 2 3 4 5 F 05 04 03 02 01

Contents

Preface: About This Book

Counterpoints is designed to help students explore contemporary world and Canadian issues. No issue can be understood outside its historical or human context, so that much of *Counterpoints* provides the background needed for an intelligent discussion of selected questions.

The text is divided into three units:

- Canada in the Twentieth Century
- Government and Law
- Geography and Global Issues

Within Unit I, issues in Canadian history between 1913 and the present are covered in a world context.

Two chapters in Unit II consider the structure of Canadian government and the role of the citizen, together with the contemporary issues surrounding these topics. The other two chapters in this unit deal with legal issues and human rights in Canada.

Unit III deals with world human and economic issues from a geographical perspective. These include population growth, world and Canadian disparities in income, urbanization, and environmental stresses on the world's ecosystems.

Within each chapter, issues are raised in context, and one particular issue, called Counterpoints, is explored in depth. Building Your Skills focusses on the fundamentals of skills that are needed to develop proficiency in social studies inquiries.

Activities are embedded in the text, and allow students to check their understanding of concepts and issues. Questions relating to the interpretation of maps, diagrams, tables, charts, photographs, and art works are presented with the visuals and help develop skills. At the end of each chapter a wide range of activities are grouped under three headings, Develop an Understanding, Explore the Issues, and Research and Communicate. These activities focus on understanding main concepts, discussing issues raised within the chapter that are relevant to students today, and researching and communicating ideas.

The final chapter, Looking Forward, challenges students to think about issues and trends that could emerge in the twenty-first century.

Acknowledgements

Garvin Moles would like to thank Gudrun for her support and patience through the many stolen hours devoted to the completion of this book.

We would like to acknowledge Mark Cobham, Anita Borovilos, and Elynor Kagan for their commitment to the project. Special thanks go to Jenifer Ludbrook and Francine Geraci for their creativity, time, and energy in bringing our work to a successful conclusion. The editorial guidance of Mary Kirley, Chelsea Donaldson, and Elma Schemenauer was also much appreciated.

Over 50 teachers and consultants in British Columbia contributed to the development of this text. We would like to thank them all. Special thanks go to the following reviewers:

Cam Murray
Charles Hou
Jan Gladdish
Richard Londsdale

Wayne Axford
Malcolm Bailey
Jim Costley
Bliss Dodd
Rob Griffith
Ed Harrison
James Henham
Michael Kennedy
Fred McCracken
Tom Morton
Ross Norringon
Anne Penner
Greg Roggeveen
Bruce Seney
Darhl Wood

counterpoints

points

Exploring Canadian Issues

UNIT I

Canada in the Twentieth Century

Political Issues

• Did World War I have a positive or negative effect on Canada?

• Did Canada become more or less independent in the 1920s?

• Is the use of weapons of mass destruction ever justified?

• What role should Canada play in U.S.-dominated military alliances?

• How should the Canadian government deal with the issues of western alienation and Quebec separatism?

• Should changes be made to Canada's Constitution to give the provinces more power?

Social Issues

• Should social services be cut to reduce the national debt?

• Should Aboriginal peoples be given more rights and special status in Canada?

Legal Issues

• Is today's government responsible for injustices of the past?

Economic Issues

• How involved should the government be in the economy during a depression?

• Should the federal government negotiate more free trade agreements?

Cultural Issues

• Does Canada need a multiculturalism policy?

• Can the Canadian government protect Canadian culture?

This unit deals with the history of the twentieth century from 1913, and shows how many of the issues that concern Canadians today developed or were already present in much of that century.

In Chapter 1 we look at Canadian society before World War I, and the attitudes and expectations Canadians had for the future. The horrors of World War I marked a turning point for Canadians.

In Chapter 2 we see how the war led to greater confidence and independence from Great Britain.

Chapter 3 looks at the post-war period until the stock market crash of 1929, which marked the beginning of the Depression.

The experiences of Canadians and the government response to the crisis of the Depression is described in Chapter 4, as well as the rise of fascist governments in Europe and Japan. Their rise led to World War II, which is examined in Chapter 5.

Chapters 6, 7, and 8 cover issues in the post-war period between 1945 and 2000. Chapter 6 looks at Canada's role in world affairs, and how it dealt with the problems that arose during the Cold War, the period of nuclear tension that lasted until 1991.

Chapter 7 deals with changes in the society, attitudes, and the economy, while Chapter 8 addresses three continuing themes in the evolution of Canada's national identity: the role of Quebec, immigration, and recognition of the rights of the Aboriginal population.

Why did this photograph become one of the most famous images of Canadians in World War I? ◀

What impact did the "dust bowl" years of the Depression have on Canadian farmers? ▼

What methods did the ▲ Nazi Party use to appeal to the emotions of the German public?

What was the impact on Canadians of the Quebec referendum of 1995? ▶

A Different Canada

FOCUS ON

• What were common attitudes about social behaviour in the early 1900s?

• What were the popular cultural pastimes of Canadians before World War I?

• What was Canada's relationship to Britain at the turn of the century?

• What attitudes did many Canadians have towards Aboriginal peoples and non-Europeans?

• What technological developments benefited Canada's economy during this period?

• What impact did industrial development have on the natural environment?

Counterpoints Issue

• Is today's government responsible for injustices of the past?

Tanoo, Queen Charlotte Islands by Emily Carr, 1913. Carr lived and worked in British Columbia, where many of her paintings were inspired by Aboriginal life and culture.

Expressing ideas What is the mood of this painting? How do you know this is an abandoned settlement? What do you think inspired the painter to record this scene?

Introduction

On a cool October evening in 1904, a tall, dignified man stood in front of a crowd in Toronto's Massey Hall. He was Wilfrid Laurier, Canada's prime minister. Laurier stepped to the podium that night and presented a bold vision of Canada for the new century:

> Let me tell you, my fellow countrymen, that the twentieth century shall be the century of Canada and of Canadian development. For the next seventy-five years, nay for the next 100 years, Canada shall be the star towards which all men who love progress and freedom shall come.

Source: Toronto *Globe*, October 15, 1904.

What was Canada like at the beginning of the twentieth century when Laurier made his bold prediction? The map of Canada in 1905 (Figure 1-1) shows that Manitoba, Ontario, and Quebec were much smaller than they are today. Newfoundland was still a self-governing colony, and the Territory of Nunavut had yet to be created. The census of 1911 reveals that Canada's

1896 Wilfrid Laurier, leader of the Liberals, becomes prime minister.

Klondike Gold Rush begins.

1899 Canada sends volunteers to fight in Boer War in South Africa.

1903 Alaska Boundary dispute is settled.

1905 Alberta and Saskatchewan become provinces.

1906 B.C. Native chiefs take land claim to King Edward VII of England.

1907 Vancouver race riot occurs.

1908 *Anne of Green Gables* is published.

1909 First airplane flight in Canada takes place.

1911 Laurier era ends.

1912 RMS *Titanic* sinks off coast of Newfoundland.

1914 World War I begins.

Passengers on the *Komagata Maru* are refused landing at Vancouver.

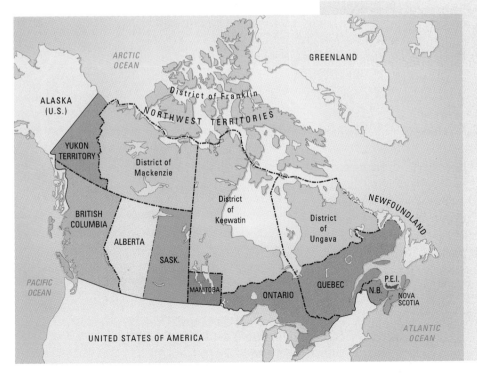

Figure 1-1 Canada in 1905.

Gathering information Which provinces have the same boundaries as today? Which ones have different boundaries?

population was only 7.2 million, less than a quarter of what it would be by the end of the century.

People's attitudes about the role of women, minorities, good manners, and behaviour in general were also different then. In this regard, Canada would have fit the claim that the "past is like a foreign country; they do things differently there." In our study of history, it is important to try to see the world through the eyes of Canadians at that time if we want to understand why they took the actions that they did.

Society and Manners

By the early twentieth century, most Canadians lived on farms or in small villages. It was a minority of English-Canadian middle- and upper-class people, however, who set the standards for morals and manners of the day. These people were greatly influenced by the attitudes of Victorian England. This period—named after Queen Victoria, who was the British monarch from 1837 to 1901—was known for its appearance of moral strictness. Families were expected to attend church regularly; they supported Britain and the monarchy, and believed in honour, virtue, and duty. It was an age in which right and wrong, good and evil seemed clear; they were not seen as issues that needed discussion or debate. Families were expected to take care of their own members, without depending on the assistance of government. Laziness was thought to be the cause of poverty. Those families that couldn't support themselves were often dependent on private charities for food and clothing.

There was little tolerance for those who did not obey the law, and the application of the law could be quite harsh. In 1914, twenty-seven men were sentenced to death for murder. Eleven of the sentences were carried out, with the rest commuted to life imprisonment. Most convictions, however, were for crimes against people's property. Drunkenness was a close second.

For young adults, courtship was a formal affair under the watchful eyes of the community. Once married, women had few rights over property or children, and divorce was rare. Women were not considered persons under the law—unless they committed a crime. Even a woman's salary was legally the property of her husband. Women who worked outside the home, usually before marriage, were employed mainly as servants or factory workers. Some women were teachers and nurses; a few even became doctors.

A group of women, known as **suffragists**, wanted the right to vote. With the vote, women believed they could influence government to address social problems of the day, such as child labour, pollution, and widespread poverty. The suffragists wanted the sale of alcohol prohibited because they believed alcohol was the cause of many of society's problems. Nellie McClung was a well-known suffragist who, together with other women, campaigned for women's rights.

Figure 1-2 The McLean family, 1910. These people exhibit the confidence and proper formality of the typical upper-class, English-Canadian family in the years before World War I.

Gathering information What does the style of dress tell you about the manners of a wealthy family in Victorian society?

Arts and Leisure

As Canada started to become more urbanized, its literature and art became more sentimental, expressing a preference for rural life, simple values, and happy endings. In 1908, Lucy Maud Montgomery published the much-loved novel *Anne of Green Gables*, a rural romance. Stephen Leacock gently mocked small-town Ontario life in his humorous *Sunshine Sketches of a Little Town* (1912). Ernest Thompson Seton wrote moving and realistic stories about animals. Pauline Johnson, daughter of a Mohawk chief and his English wife, read her poems about Mohawk heritage to packed halls and opera houses across the country. Ontario painter Homer Watson gained international recognition with his farm scenes of Ontario. In Quebec, Ozias Leduc painted religious works and landscapes filled with a sense of spirituality.

People enjoyed outdoor entertainment such as distance running, cycling, and rowing. In the summer, trips to the beach were popular despite confining "bathing costumes." In the winter, tobogganing was a must.

Figure 1-3 Bathing was great fun during the long, hot summer of 1914.

Thinking critically In what ways is the bathing attire typically Victorian?

Still a British Nation

At the beginning of the twentieth century, some of Britain's colonies, including Canada, had their own governments, but could not resolve disputes with other countries. This was the responsibility of the British government in London, which did not always have Canada's interests in mind. For example, in a dispute over the Alaska Boundary, the British negotiated an agreement that favoured the United States over Canada. The dispute was over the exact border of the Alaskan "panhandle," a strip of land running down the Pacific Coast between British Columbia and Alaska. Of particular concern was the question of ownership of a fjord called the Lynn Canal. This waterway provided access to the Yukon, where gold had been discovered in 1896.

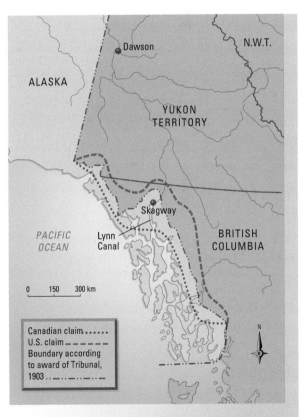

Figure 1-4 The Alaska Boundary dispute.

Using evidence From the map, explain how the Canadian claim would have allowed easier access to Dawson.

In 1903, the matter was finally settled. The British, weary from fighting the Boer War in South Africa and unwilling to become involved in another international conflict, determined that the Lynn Canal was part of Alaska, not British Columbia.

Canadians were angered by this decision. Many believed Britain had sold out Canada's interest in order to keep peace with the United States. However, most English-speaking Canadians were proud to be British subjects, and they shared Britain's dreams of expanding the British Empire throughout the world. These **imperialists** had eagerly supported Britain in the Boer War in 1899.

French-speaking Canadians, however, did not share this enthusiasm for the British Empire. They were the descendants of people who had settled New France more than 200 years earlier, and they saw themselves as *Canadiens* rather than British subjects. French-Canadians tended to be **nationalists**, believing that Canada should be more independent from Britain. For example, nationalist leader Henri Bourassa resigned from Laurier's cabinet when Laurier agreed to send volunteers to fight with the British in South Africa. Bourassa's stand against Canada's involvement in Britain's wars became an even bigger issue during World War I.

Language rights was another issue that divided French-speaking and English-speaking Canadians. After a bitter dispute, French-Canadians lost the right to French-language instruction in Catholic schools first in Manitoba, then in Saskatchewan and Alberta. Henri Bourassa voiced the concerns of many French-Canadians when he suggested that *Canadiens* might have no reason to stay in Canada if their rights as a minority were not protected, as the people of Quebec believed they would be at the time of Confederation.

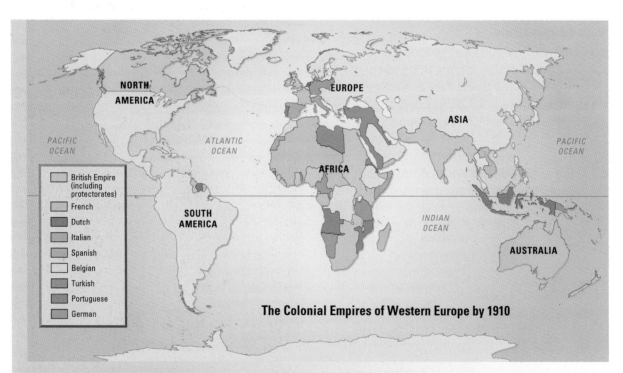

The Colonial Empires of Western Europe by 1910

Legend:
British Empire (including protectorates)
French
Dutch
Italian
Spanish
Belgian
Turkish
Portuguese
German

Figure 1-5 World empires in 1910. Canadians were proud that their country was the senior dominion in the greatest empire since the Roman Empire.

Using evidence The British Empire was the biggest of the European empires that controlled much of the land and people of the world. What does the expression, "the sun never set on the British Empire" mean?

Canada's Changing Population

Soon after Laurier became prime minister, he realized that if Canada were to prosper, it needed many more people, especially in the West. His government circulated posters in the United States and northern and eastern Europe promoting Canada as an attractive place to live. The posters described the Prairies as the "Last Best West," so called to distinguish it from the American West. His government's efforts resulted in an enormous increase in immigration during this period.

Entry into Canada was easy if you were reasonably healthy and had sufficient funds to establish yourself. The federal government offered immigrants willing to farm the Prairies 160 acres (65 ha) of land for only ten dollars. These homesteaders had to build a house and begin cultivating the farm within three years of purchase. Life on the Prairies was often very lonely, and harsh conditions proved too much for some, who moved to urban centres. For those who stayed, however, there were rewards as well as hardships. Cooperation was common in work and play. Community dances and picnics, and church concerts and suppers, gave settlers social lives.

Not Everyone Is Welcomed

Many Canadians did not welcome changes to Canada's ethnic composition. They feared outsiders. Most Canadians were **ethnocentric**, believing their own race or group was superior. As a result, many newcomers to Canada experienced discrimination. Many French-speaking Canadians were also concerned that the arrival of so many immigrants would further reduce the percentage of the population that was Francophone.

Eastern Europeans, particularly the Ukrainians and Poles who settled in the Prairies, were targets of ethnic prejudice. Their language and their dress—embroidered skirts, baggy trousers, long boots, and sheepskin coats—were unfamiliar to Canadians, who often ridiculed and scorned these people and their customs.

Many Chinese, Japanese, and East Indian immigrants settled in British Columbia, where they, too, suffered from discrimination and racism. R.B. Bennett, a future prime minister, reflected popular prejudice when he declared in 1907, "British Columbia must remain a white man's country." As long as Asian immigrants did work that other Canadians considered too unpleasant—such as hauling coal, packing fish, and washing dishes—their cheap labour was generally accepted. But when workers began to fear that Asian immigrants would compete against them for other jobs, they joined in denouncing them.

Figure 1-6 The Darby family in Vulcan, Alberta, 1903. The Darbys were one of the few African-American families allowed to immigrate to Canada from the United States. Mr. Darby was a hotel chef.

Is Today's Government Responsible for Injustices of the Past?

In 1885, because the federal government wanted to discourage Chinese people from coming to Canada, it created the Chinese Immigration Act. Under this act, every Chinese person immigrating to Canada had to pay the government fifty dollars, a fee called a **head tax**. When immigrants continued to arrive, the tax was increased to $100 in 1900, and to $500 in 1903. On July 1, 1923, the Chinese Immigration Act was replaced by the Chinese Exclusion Act—an even stricter act that tried to stop Chinese immigration altogether. Chinese-Canadians refer to this day as Humiliation Day because they felt insulted by this restrictive legislation. It wasn't until 1947 that the act was repealed.

In 1984, the Chinese community in British Columbia asked the federal government to redress—that is, to make up for—past injustices suffered by them. A group of Chinese organizations asked for an apology from the government. The organizations also asked the government to pay $23 million to the Chinese families from whom the head tax was originally collected. The $23 million, they said, was exactly what was collected from 81 000 Chinese immigrants who were forced to pay the tax.

In 1990, the Conservative government of the day apologized to Italian-Canadians who were interned during World War II. The government also apologized to Japanese-Canadians for their internment during the war, and it paid $12 million to Japanese-Canadians whose properties were seized in 1942 (see Chapter 5, pages 126–127).

The Chinese organizations maintained that when the federal government paid out $12 million to Japanese-Canadians, it created a duty to treat other claims for compensation—requests for repayment of money—in a similar way.

In 1993, the Liberal government promised to redress the Chinese community for past injustices. The next year, however, the government rejected the compensation claim for $23 million by Chinese-Canadians, along with claims by six other groups. The minister explained the government's position on claims for compensation in the following way:

> The government must focus on erasing inequality in the future, instead of compensating people for past mistakes. Canadians wish those episodes had never happened. We wish we could rewrite history. We wish we could relive the past. But we cannot. We believe our only choice lies in using limited government resources to create a more equitable society.

Source: Multiculturalism Minister Sheila Finestone in a 1994 letter.

Alan Li, president of the Chinese-Canadian National Council (CCNC), disagreed with the minister's decision. His position was that Chinese-Canadians were asking:

> … for only the return of the $23 million actually taken and [were] willing to forgo any interest benefit that government has received from the money over seventy years. Returning the money is only basic justice. It is a strong statement of principle that a government cannot, and should not, and must not, benefit from racism.

Source: Speech by Alan Li, President of the Chinese-Canadian National Council, 1994.

In 1995, the CCNC asked the United Nations Human Rights Commission in New York to look into the issue. In its submission, the CCNC stated that:

> … after over eleven years, the [Canadian] government has acted in bad faith and without due regard to the … uniqueness of this Chinese-Canadian redress claim. The unconscionable delay in resolving this human rights issue has meant that over half of the approximately 2000 surviving head tax payers in 1984 have now passed away.

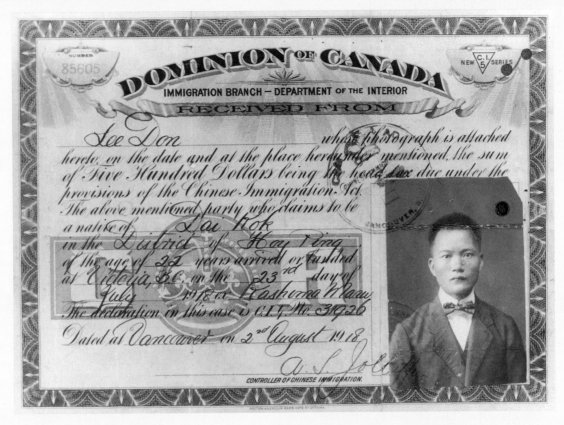

Figure 1-7 Immigration certificate for Lee Don, 1918.

Gathering information How old was Lee Don when he was admitted to Canada? How much was the head tax he had to pay? Where do you think he might have obtained the money to pay the tax?

The CCNC is considering taking the government to court to determine whether the government has a legal duty to redress Chinese-Canadians for the head tax and the Chinese Exclusion Act.

Analysing the Issue

1. Imagine you are a lawyer representing a Chinese-Canadian family whose member paid the head tax. Outline the case you would make to the federal government on behalf of your client.

2. Compare the response of the multiculturalism minister with Alan Li's response. Which position do you agree with? Why?

3. Organize a debate on the topic: *Can we right the wrongs of past generations?*

- 1902   Royal Commission on Oriental Immigration declares that "... further immigration of Chinese to Canada would be injurious to the interests of Canada...."

- 1903   Head tax increased to $500.

- 1923   Head tax on Chinese immigrants replaced by Chinese Exclusion Act.

- 1947   Repeal of Chinese Exclusion Act and enfranchisement of Chinese-Canadians.

- 1958   Douglas Jung becomes first Chinese-Canadian Member of Parliament.

- 1988   David Lam becomes first Chinese-Canadian lieutenant-governor of British Columbia.

- 1996   Jenny Kwan and Ida Chong become British Columbia's first Chinese-Canadian MLAs.

Figure 1-8 The Chinese in Canada.

In response, the federal government tried to limit immigration from Asia by placing a "head tax" on immigrants from China. In 1907, an angry group of whites attacked stores and homes owned by Chinese and Japanese immigrants in Vancouver. This race riot resulted in severe restrictions on Japanese immigration. A year later, there was a virtual ban on East Indian immigration. In the summer of 1914, the *Komagata Maru*, a ship carrying mostly Sikhs, was forced to return to India from Vancouver, when its passengers were refused entry into Canada.

Aboriginal Peoples

As thousands of immigrants settled into the western provinces, the Aboriginal peoples found themselves more and more displaced. Their movements and lives were regulated under the federal Indian Act passed in 1876. By the 1880s, Aboriginal peoples of the Prairies were living on **reserves**, or designated areas of land. The main purpose of reserves was to free the open land for settlers and immigrants from Europe, and to avoid the violent clashes that had taken place between Aboriginal people and settlers in the United States. Once on the reserves, Aboriginal people were supposed to take up farming instead of traditional hunting. But the soil was often unsuitable, equipment was limited, and many people went hungry. As more immigrants arrived, the government allowed sections of reserve lands to be transferred to homesteaders for farming or to companies for mining. Aboriginal leaders protested this incursion by the federal government, but their protests did little to stop the government's actions.

Loss of land wasn't the only problem faced by Aboriginal people. By the early 1900s, their populations were declining. Disease was a major cause. In some **residential schools**, schools for Aboriginal children run by the churches, overcrowded dormitories and unsanitary conditions caused tuberculosis to spread quickly. Most of the Aboriginal population suffered from poor diet and inadequate housing, which also contributed to disease and the decline in population.

Residential schools, reserves, and enforced farming were all part of the federal government's policy of **assimilation**, which was intended to make Aboriginal people abandon their traditional culture and become part of the European way of life. This policy had been in place since 1871. By 1913, an article in *Maclean's* magazine claimed that "the white man of Canada ... is slowly, steadily and surely absorbing his red brother." Aboriginal people did not agree. For many, the struggle to establish land claims and reclaim their culture was just beginning.

Figure 1-9 An Aboriginal man ploughing land on a reserve.

Thinking critically
Aboriginal people had traditionally led a nomadic life, and many survived by hunting, trapping, and fishing. How would farming change their traditional lifestyle? Why would many resist farming?

ACTIVITIES

1. Why did the Canadian government make entry into Canada so easy for most European immigrants?

2. Why were some people upset by the changes to Canada's ethnic composition?

3. Describe the steps taken in British Columbia to restrict Asian immigration.

4. Describe the policies of the federal government that were designed to assimilate Canada's Aboriginal peoples.

Urbanization

While thousands of immigrants were settling farms on the Prairies, thousands more were moving to towns and cities. Some immigrant groups, particularly Jews, who were not allowed to own land in Europe, chose urban life, which was more familiar to them. The population of Canada's western cities exploded in the early 1900s. For example, Winnipeg expanded from 42 340 people in 1901 to 136 035 people in 1911. It called itself, optimistically, the "Chicago of the North."

The growing cities were filled with contrasts between the wealthy and the poor. The rich lived in luxury. They usually had servants; their houses were lit by electricity, warmed by central hot water heating, and had running water. Across town, the working class lived in shacks and overcrowded tenements. Lack of clean water and proper sewers, together with pollution from neighbouring industries, caused widespread health problems. Pneumonia, diphtheria, tuberculosis, and typhoid were common in poorer districts. Still, people flocked to the cities, attracted by jobs as well as by cultural and social opportunities unavailable in rural Canada.

An Economy Transformed

As Canada's population grew, so did its economy. The export of natural resources such as timber, wheat, and minerals was an important part of Canada's economy. Canada's export industries also

Figure 1-10 Top: Wealthy home in Toronto, ca. 1910. Bottom: One-room home in Winnipeg, 1912.

Using evidence Find evidence in these photographs of the contrasts between rich and poor described in the text.

benefited from cheap shipping costs across the Atlantic Ocean. As well, the opening of the Panama Canal in 1914 created a shorter shipping route for Canadian products en route to Europe from the West Coast. Mining, too, contributed to the economic boom in the early 1900s. Prospectors and investors invaded the Yukon and British Columbia after the discovery of gold near the Klondike River in 1896.

The use of electricity in factories was an enormous boost to Canada's industrial growth. With electric power, bigger and better machines could be used to produce many more goods. This industrialization created more jobs in manufacturing. With jobs came an increase in the demand for consumer goods. Canada Dry, Shredded Wheat, Palmolive soap, Heinz ketchup, and other brands became familiar to Canadian shoppers, along with

Innovations

Changing Technologies

▲ Victims of accidents might be taken to a newly built hospital. For centuries hospitals had been places of last resort for the desperate and dying poor. By the turn of the century, however, the invention of *X-rays*, *rubber gloves*, and *face masks* brought many changes. Hospitals became more sterile, staffed with uniformed nurses and specialized doctors and surgeons.

Canadians were experimenting with new ways of getting from place to place. The new craze at the turn of the century was *bicycles*. One in twelve people bought a bicycle. They were much cheaper and cleaner than horses and easier to park.

Canadian Alexander Graham Bell invented the *telephone* in the 1870s. In the early 1900s, however, only a few people had telephones, and they had to share lines and go through an operator to use them.

In 1901, at Signal Hill in Newfoundland, Italian-born inventor Guglielmo Marconi received the first *radio* message sent across a long distance, in this case from Britain. Quebec-born inventor Reginald Fessenden made the first public broadcasts of voice and music in 1906.

Automobiles were one of the newest means of transportation. They were faster than horses, and offered more privacy and personal freedom than trains. Until the 1920s, cars were only for the rich, but many people in cities rode the *electric tram* or *trolley* downtown.

Mechanization was transforming the world of work. West-coast canneries used a new machine for beheading and gutting fish. Fishermen equipped their boats with gas engines, and sent their catch to market in refrigerated railcars. Threshing machines and combines made farmers' work easier, but the long leather belts on these machines and exploding steam boilers made it more dangerous. ▼

For recreation, people could visit the music hall to enjoy the performances of singers and comedians or go to a "*magic lantern*" show (which used an early form of slide projector) to see pictures of foreign places. At home, the *stereoscope* produced three-dimensional images of distant places or romantic subjects.

The Wright Brothers made the first *airplane* flight in the United States in 1903. In Canada, Alexander Graham Bell and Douglas McCurdy also experimented with airplanes. They developed the *Silver Dart*, a gasoline-powered biplane. When McCurdy first flew the airplane in 1909 at Baddeck, Nova Scotia, residents were astounded. ▼

the first five-cent chocolate bar. By 1914, wireless radios were used on board many ships, following their much-publicized role in the rescue of passengers on the ill-fated RMS *Titanic* in 1912. The 1911 census showed that over 300 000 telephones were in use in Canada, and some automobiles were appearing on Canadian streets.

Corporate Giants

Corporations grew larger during this period of industrial expansion. Huge companies, such as Maple Leaf Milling, Dominion Steel, Massey-Harris, and Imperial Oil controlled much of industry. With little competition, employers could set high prices for the goods they produced and pay low wages to their workers. Some workers began to form **trade unions** to press for better pay, reduced hours of work, and better safety conditions. When employers refused to give in to union demands, some unions went on strike. Most employers opposed union demands. As a result, strikes could get violent, and in some cases, the police and military were called in to break up the protests. The coal miners in Nanaimo, for example, were involved in a bitter strike that lasted more than two years. The miners were striking over unsafe working conditions and low pay. This

strike eventually led to the largest mass arrests in Canadian history until the arrest of environmentalist activists at Clayoquot Sound eighty years later.

By 1914, Canada was in a **recession** after almost two decades of rapid growth. Industries cut back on production, and many workers became unemployed. On the Prairies, most farmers were planting the new, higher-yielding Marquis wheat developed by William Saunders and his sons, but the boom was over—the international demand for wheat was down.

Resources and the Environment

For most Canadians in the early 1900s, the destruction of the environment was not the issue it is today. In 1914, however, residents of British Columbia saw how human interference could seriously damage an important natural resource. Workers for the Grand Trunk Railway were blasting a new railway line in the Fraser Canyon when an explosion caused a rockslide at Hell's Gate Canyon. The railway company had been dumping rocks in the canyon throughout the construction of the line, but this rockslide had disastrous effects on the spawning beds of the sockeye salmon. The fallen rocks were massive and partially

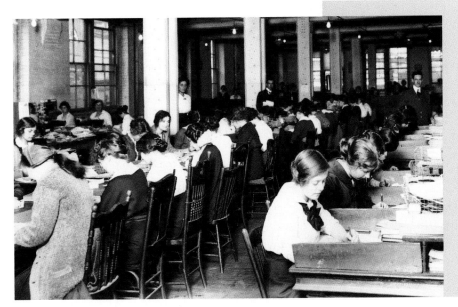

Figure 1-11 Workers at the Robert Simpson Company mail-order office, 1909. Mail-order companies became a popular and practical way for many Canadians to shop.

Expressing ideas Based on the photograph, what would you like and dislike about working in an office like this?

	1914	2000
Population	8 million	32 million
National Anthem	God Save the King	O Canada!
Nationality	British	Canadian
Flag	Union Jack	Maple Leaf
Governor General	Duke of Connaught (British)	Rt. Hon. Adrienne Clarkson (Canadian)
Foreign Affairs	British Foreign Office	Canadian Dept. of Foreign Affairs
Final Court of Appeal	House of Lords	Supreme Court of Canada
House of Commons	221 MPs (all male)	301 MPs (60 women)
Senate	96 Senators (all male)	105 Senators (32 women)
Prime Minister	Robert Borden, Conservative	Jean Chrétien, Liberal
Cabinet Size	8	37
Federal Revenues	$126.1 million	$162 billion
Federal Expenditures	$184.9 million	$158 billion

Figure 1-12 Canada in 1914 and 2000.

Gathering information Select the four changes that you think are most significant, and explain your choices.

blocked the river. This blockage increased the river's current, which prevented many salmon from swimming upstream to spawn. The rocks remained in place for almost thirty years before a fish ladder was constructed to allow the spawning fish to swim up the rapids. Catches of Fraser River salmon, however, would never again equal the twenty-to-thirty million catches of the pre-war years.

The rockslide posed a particular hardship for the Sto:lo, a First Nations people whose livelihood depended on fishing in the Fraser River. As stocks improved, commercial fishers were given a monopoly on fishing to help compensate for their financial losses. The Sto:lo, however, were never given back the allocations they had prior to the Hell's Gate slide.

The federal and provincial governments were also involved in setting aside land for parks. By 1914, British Columbia had three national parks—Mount Revelstoke, Kootenay, and Glacier National Parks. The B.C. government had already set aside Strathcona and Mount Robson as provincial parks in 1913.

War and Change

When Laurier predicted the twentieth century would be the century of Canadian development, he had no way of knowing that before long, Canada would be involved in a devastating war involving many countries throughout the world. He also could not have predicted the events and issues that have shaped Canada's identity during the past century. In the following chapters, you will learn about these events. You can be the judge as to whether or not the twentieth century would really become "Canada's century."

ACTIVITIES

1. Describe the contrasts between rich and poor in cities during this period.

2. What technological changes were taking place in Canada prior to World War I?

3. Explain why employers and unions had stormy relations in these years.

4. Imagine you are a reporter sent to cover the Fraser Canyon rockslide. Send a telegram to your newspaper describing the tragedy. Include a headline.

*T*hroughout this textbook you will be presented with many points of view concerning issues in history, government and law, and geography. You are not expected to agree with these points of view, but to use them to come to your own conclusions. The following guidelines will help you in analysing historical information.

Dealing with Evidence

There are two main categories of evidence: primary and secondary.

Primary sources are sources of information that are created at the time of an event. Eyewitness accounts are the most obvious primary sources. These are often found in diaries, memoirs, minutes from cabinet meetings, government documents, photographs, newspaper articles, and political cartoons.

Secondary sources are accounts created after the event, often describing or analysing it. The perspective of time may provide a more balanced analysis in secondary sources.

Understanding Bias

When you interpret evidence, you cannot help but see it through personal biases. Similarly, primary and secondary sources carry the authors' personal "filters" or biases. Having a bias is not necessarily wrong. It is important, however, to be aware of biases when you analyse evidence. These might include political, religious, racial, ethnic, gender, economic, or vocational biases.

Reliability and Credibility

When you read a document, it is important to determine how reliable a source of information it is. You must ask yourself questions such as:

- Who is the author, and how close was he or she to the event?
- What was the author's motive in recording the event?
- What other sources of information did the author use?

- What are the author's biases or points of view?
- What was the purpose of the document, and who was the intended audience?

Photographs should also be examined closely when they are used as a historical piece of information. The reader should ask: Who took the photo? How was the photograph to be used?

Sources of information must also be credible, that is, they must be accurate and record the truth. One way to determine the credibility and accuracy of a source is to see whether the information can be *corroborated*, or supported by similar sources.

Applying the Skill

Each of the following sources offers a different way of discovering information about the years before World War I. Study these sources of evidence and answer the questions that follow.

Source 1

Rank	Nationality	Number of People	% of Total Immigration
1	U.K.	150 542	37.4
2	U.S.	139 009	34.5
3	Russian	18 623	4.6
4	Ruthenian (Ukrainian)	17 420	4.3
5	Chinese	7 445	1.9
6	Italian	6 601	1.6
7	Jewish	6 304	1.6
8	German	4 938	1.2
9	Bulgarian	4 616	1.1
10	Polish	4 488	1.1
	Other	42 446	10.5
Total		402 432	99.8

Source: *Canada Year Book* 1916.

Figure 1-13 Countries of origin of immigrants coming to Canada in 1913.

Source 2

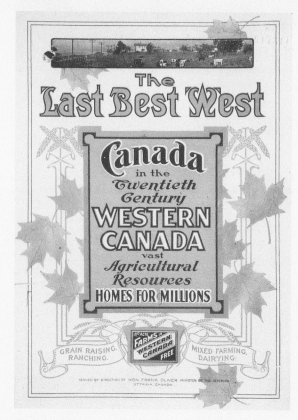

Figure 1-14 Canada as "The Last Best West."

Source 3

Observations of Olga Pawluk, who was eighteen when she and her family moved from Ukraine to Canada:

> I didn't want to go to Canada. I was in school, I was popular.... I didn't know where Canada was really, so I looked at the map. There were hardly any cities there. It looked so wild and isolated somehow and I felt that it would be very difficult to live there.... I felt I was going to a very wild place.

> Source: "Moving Experiences," Living Histories Videos (Toronto: Five Corners Communications, 2000).

Source 4

Conditions in the slums as described by J.S. Woodsworth, a minister and social activist, in a letter to a Winnipeg newspaper in 1913:

Let me tell you of one little foreign girl. She lives in a room in a disreputable old tenement.... Her father has no work.... The place is incredibly filthy. The little girl has been ill for months—all that time living on the bed in which three or four persons must sleep and which also serves the purpose of table and chairs. For weeks this little girl has had an itch which has spread to the children of the surrounding rooms. She has torn the flesh on her arms and legs into great sores which have become poisoned.

> Source: Quoted in Kenneth McNaught, *J. S. Woodsworth* (Toronto: Fitzhenry & Whiteside, 1980), 15.

Source 5

Speech by Prime Minister Laurier after Alaska Boundary dispute was decided in favour of the United States:

> What can I do? I have often regretted ... that we are living beside a great neighbour who, I believe I can say without being deemed unfriendly to them, are very grasping in their national actions and who are determined on every occasion to get the best in any agreement.... While they are a great and powerful nation, we are only a small colony—a growing colony, but still a colony. I have often regretted also that we have not in our hands the treaty making power which would enable us to dispose of our own affairs.... It is important that we should ask the British Parliament for more extensive powers so that if ever we have to deal with matters of similar nature again, we shall deal with them in our own way, in our own fashion, according to the best light that we have.

> Source: *Debates of the House of Commons*, October 23, 1903.

Now answer the following questions:

1. Classify each of the sources as primary or secondary. Explain your choices.
2. How reliable might the statistics in Source 1 be? What are some possible reasons for inaccuracies in population statistics?
3. To whom do you think the poster "The Last Best West" is directed? Explain.

4. Examine the quote in Source 3. What does this document say about some immigrants' perception of Canada at that time? How accurate was Olga in her description of Canada? Upon what was she basing her opinion?

5. How reliable is Source 4 as a source of information? What does it tell us about Winnipeg in 1913?

6. What information does Laurier give us about Canada at the turn of the century in Source 5? According to this document, how did he feel about Canada's relationship with Britain? Who do you think might have shared Laurier's feelings?

7. Assume you are a historian studying this period of history. What picture of Canadian immigration would you form if just the information in these documents was available to you? Make a list of the types of sources you would search out to get a more complete picture of the subject.

LOOKING BACK

Develop an Understanding

1. Select one of the photographs in this chapter. Write a descriptive commentary on the photo, explaining what it illustrates about the pre-World War I period in Canada.

2. Choose three examples from this chapter to explain the statement: *The past is like a foreign country; they do things differently there.*

3. Make a collage of images and words that shows the British influence on Canada prior to World War I.

Explore the Issues

4. Brainstorm with members of your group to create a list of the aspects of British institutions and culture that are still part of Canadian society. Compare the list with the features that are described in this chapter. What differences do you notice? As you continue your study of Canada in the twentieth century, try to explain how these changes occurred.

5. From what you know of Canadian history before 1913 and from what you've learned in this chapter, how was the French-Canadian view of Canada different from the English-Canadian view? What issues were viewed differently by these two groups of people?

6. Racism was not unusual in 1913. Write a statement that would explain to a person in 1913 why the attitudes of the time towards certain immigrants and Aboriginal peoples are not acceptable today.

7. Should historians criticize the people of the past by the standards of the present? Discuss with reference to the immigration policies, treatment of poorer people, and Aboriginal peoples in Canada in 1913.

Research and Communicate

8. Imagine you are a foreign correspondent working in Canada for a European newspaper in 1914. Send a report home on your observations of life in Canada.

9. As a group, research the experiences of one of the ethnic groups that was not welcomed into Canada. Make a list of the difficulties a family from this group would face upon arriving in Canada.

10. Public hearings on complaints by Canada's Aboriginal peoples about their treatment in residential schools have become quite common. Investigate some of their stories. What action do you think the government should take in redressing these injustices?

11. What do you think Laurier meant when he said that Canada would be the star towards which all people who love freedom and progress would come? Rewrite Laurier's speech as though he were giving it before an audience today.

2

Canada and World War I

FOCUS ON
- What caused World War I, and why did Canada become involved?
- How did technological innovations change the way the war was fought?
- What effect did the war have on the status of women?
- What effect did the War Measures Act have on the legal rights of Canadians?
- Why did conscription become a major issue in Quebec?

Counterpoints Issue
- Did the war have a positive or negative effect on Canada?

For What? by Frederick Varley. This sombre painting of Canadian troops uses a devastated landscape and a cart full of dead bodies to reflect the harsh realities of World War I. Many people, excited about the war at first, were traumatized by the massive destruction and the hundreds of thousands of dead and wounded left in the wake of the new weapons of war.

Expressing ideas What is the theme of Varley's painting? Describe the colours and style he used. How do colour and style convey the artist's impressions about the war?

Introduction

In May 1917, Crawford Grier, a young Canadian soldier, lay in an English hospital, recovering from shrapnel wounds he had received while fighting in France. Grier was thankful he was in England, far from the horrors of the trenches and the smell of fear and death, safe from constant bombardment and sniper fire. He was proud of the battle he and other Canadians had won on Vimy Ridge in northern France just a few days earlier.

To Canadian soldiers like Grier, the war had seemed an exciting adventure when it began in the summer of 1914. But by the spring of 1917, Canadians were weary of the awful sacrifices they had to make. Nevertheless, in a letter home, Grier had a sense of hope when he wrote, "The whole thing looks like it's developing into the push that will end the war." Instead, the battles continued until hours before the armistice in 1918, and the effects of "the Great War"—later renamed World War I—were felt for decades to come.

In this chapter, you will learn how a regional conflict in a distant corner of Europe became World War I, and how the lives of Canadians were affected by this conflict. You will see how conscription became a major issue that divided Canadians. You will also learn how Canada gained new influence in international affairs.

1914 Franz Ferdinand, Crown Prince of the Austro-Hungarian Empire, is assassinated by a Serbian nationalist.

Germany invades Belgium and France.

Britain declares war on Germany; Canada is automatically at war.

War Measures Act is passed.

1915 Canadian troops exposed to poisonous gas at Ypres, Belgium.

1916 Women in Manitoba, Saskatchewan, and Alberta gain the right to vote in provincial elections.

The Newfoundland Regiment almost destroyed as Battle of the Somme begins.

1917 Canadian troops capture Vimy Ridge, France.

Women in British Columbia and Ontario gain the right to vote in provincial elections.

Wartime Elections Act gives federal vote to women related to servicemen.

Borden re-elected as head of Union Government.

Canadian troops succeed in muddy battles at Passchendaele in Belgium.

Halifax is flattened by explosion of a French munitions ship in its harbour.

1918 Conscription becomes mandatory.

Armistice declared on the Western Front in Europe.

The Beginning of World War I

On June 28, 1914, Archduke Franz Ferdinand, the Crown Prince of Austria-Hungary, was visiting the city of Sarajevo, Bosnia. Bosnia was part of the Austro-Hungarian Empire, but neighbouring Serbia had claimed it as part of a "Greater Serbia" because the majority of Bosnia's population was Serbian. The Archduke's visit was very controversial, and a Serbian nationalist group called the Black Hand marked him for assassination. A first attempt to blow up his car failed, but as the motor procession sought another route, Gavrilo Princip rushed forward to shoot and mortally wound the Archduke and his wife, Sophie.

The assassination in Sarajevo was the event that brought on World War I. How did this seemingly local event escalate into a global conflict? To understand, we must look beyond the event itself to other developments in Europe.

Background to the War

At the beginning of the twentieth century, much of eastern Europe was dominated by three weak and crumbling empires: the Austro-Hungarian, the Russian, and the Ottoman. Many nationalities within these empires resented being dominated by a foreign power. They wanted to be independent nations, free to determine their own political future and maintain their cultural identity.

When Austria-Hungary took control of Bosnia-Herzegovina, a province in the Balkans, many Serbs were outraged at suddenly being part of the Austro-Hungarian Empire. This sense of **nationalism**, or intense loyalty toward one's own country and culture, was a powerful force throughout Europe.

In an effort to reduce their vulnerability to attack, some countries had formed alliances, agreeing to support one another in the event of an invasion by another country. Germany, Austria-Hungary, and Italy formed the **Triple Alliance**. Then France, feeling isolated and threatened by this power bloc to the east, joined with Russia and Britain in an opposing alliance called the **Triple Entente**. By surrounding Germany, the countries of the Triple Entente hoped to reduce the threat of war. In fact, these alliances had the opposite effect because any one member of an alliance could rely on immediate assistance from its allies if it became involved in a conflict.

Alliances among various countries may have acted as a deterrent to war in the short term, but they failed to stop the massive build-up in armaments and armies, or **militarism**, that was taking place in Europe. Germany, in particular, had been rapidly expanding its army, and other European countries expanded their armies in an effort to maintain the **balance of power**. By the beginning of the twentieth century, Germany had

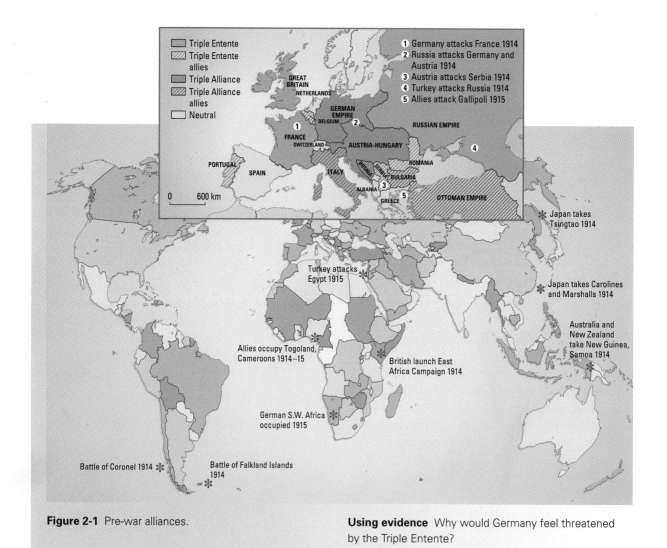

Figure 2-1 Pre-war alliances.

Using evidence Why would Germany feel threatened by the Triple Entente?

Interpreting a Political Cartoon

Political cartoons are a useful source of information about historical or current issues. They simplify an issue by portraying political personalities or events in an exaggerated way and by using symbols to represent ideas. They are a very effective means of convincing a reader to see an issue in a specific way.

Steps in Interpreting a Political Cartoon

1. Read the text and look closely at the drawing.
2. Identify the central issue or event in the cartoon.
3. Identify the devices used by the cartoonist (caricature, analogy, words, symbols, stereotypes, size of figures).
4. Identify the biases of the cartoonist by examining the devices used.
5. Interpret the cartoon.

Applying the Skill

1. Identify the countries represented by the child and the adult who is picking on him. Why is one country shown as a child?
2. The cartoon uses caricatures of speech and clothing to identify European countries. Identify Germany, Britain, France, and Russia. Explain your choice in each case.
3. Use the cartoon to make a list of the countries on either side of the conflict. Compare your list to the map in Figure 2-1.
4. What is the meaning of the title of the cartoon? Could it be interpreted as an ironic or sarcastic title? Explain.
5. Evaluate the cartoon. How effectively does it deliver its message? Explain.

Figure 2-2 The Chain of Friendship. This cartoon highlights some of the main causes of World War I by representing the European countries in 1914 as different characters.

the strongest army and the most powerful arsenal of weapons in Europe. What it wanted next was a strong navy, but it was up against a formidable rival: Great Britain was the undisputed ruler of the seas. When Germany started to expand its navy, Britain responded by building the largest battleship ever, HMS *Dreadnought*. Not to be outdone, Germany built its own dreadnoughts with the result that, by 1914, both countries had amassed huge fleets of warships. A fierce arms race was on.

While nationalist tensions grew across Europe, *imperialism*, the acquisition of overseas territories, was also on the rise. Belgium and Italy had only recently begun to colonize areas in Africa as had Germany, but Germany also sought colonies in Asia and the Pacific. Britain and France were expanding their overseas empires from the colonies they had previously established throughout the world. By the late 1800s, the race to claim territories in Africa, a continent rich in gold, diamonds, and ivory, had become highly competitive. European countries often challenged each other for rights to the overseas territories and their resources.

With this range of background causes, the assassination of Franz Ferdinand was simply the spark that ignited an already tense situation. Austria-Hungary blamed Serbia for Ferdinand's death and eventually declared war on Serbia. As a follow-up to that action, Russia, Serbia's ally, mobilized her troops. Then Germany, as Austria-Hungary's ally, did the same. Within weeks, all the great powers had fielded armies and were at war. Even Britain, which had tried to stay out of European conflicts, declared war on Germany when it invaded Belgium. On the one side were the members of the Triple Entente—Russia, France, and Britain—which became known as the **Allies**. On the other were two of the members of the Triple Alliance that became known as the *Central Powers*—Germany and Austria-Hungary. Italy, an original member of the Triple Alliance, did not join the conflict at first, but eventually many other nations throughout the world became involved in the war.

ACTIVITIES

1. Build a flow diagram that links the following in sequence, noting any that occurred simultaneously: Assassination of Franz Ferdinand and Sophie, Invasion of Belgium, Creation of the Triple Alliance, Britain Declares War on Germany, Russia Mobilizes Troops.

2. List the causes and contributing factors that resulted in the outbreak of war.

3. In a letter to the prime minister of Britain from the prime minister of Canada, explain why you do, or do not, support an alliance between Britain, Russia, and France.

4. Write a well-reasoned argument for the following proposition: "World War I was unnecessary and could have been prevented."

Canada's Response to the War

The assassination in Bosnia was front-page news in Canada, but few Canadians thought much about it. It had been a particularly hot summer, and Prime Minister Robert Borden was vacationing at his cottage when Austria-Hungary declared war on Serbia. Although Canada had become a political union in 1867, Britain still controlled the foreign policy of all its dominions, which meant that when Britain declared war on Germany, Canada, along with the rest of the British Empire, was automatically at war.

Most English-speaking Canadians were of British origin, and they supported the war out of a strong patriotic feeling for Great Britain and the Empire. One Toronto newspaper captured the sense of excitement at the time when it reported:

> Cheer after cheer from the crowds of people who had waited long and anxiously for the announcement of Great Britain's position in the present conflict in Europe greeted the news that the Mother Country had declared war against Germany. Groups of men sang "Rule Britannia," others joined in singing "God Save the King"; some showed their

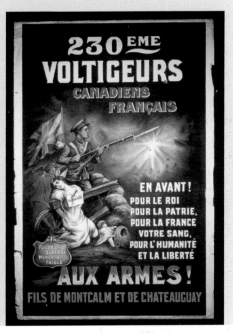

Figure 2-3 Colourful recruiting posters with urgent messages for volunteers appeared across Canada.

Identifying viewpoint
Compare these two posters. What methods does each one use to appeal to different language groups? What image of war does each one present?

sense of the seriousness of the situation by singing "Onward Christian Soldiers"....

Source: Toronto *Mail and Empire*, August 5, 1914.

Wilfrid Laurier, the leader of the Liberals, joined English Canadians in pledging support for Britain and the Empire. Laurier, quoting a famous British naval song, stated that Canadians were "Ready, Aye, Ready" to help.

Prime Minister Borden initially offered Britain 25 000 troops, but more than 30 000 volunteers from across Canada signed up within the first month. Many people volunteered because they believed that the war would be a short one and that they would be home by Christmas. A few months of fighting in Europe could be an exciting adventure—they might even be heroes upon their return. Others signed up because they had no job and the war in Europe meant a chance to escape financial hardships at home. Still others felt the patriotic urge to defend their mother country.

Not all Canadians were welcome to participate in the war. Women were considered too frail and emotional to take part in battle, so they were encouraged to stay at home and support the men who did go. Those women who did join the ser-

vices were limited to activities as nurses and ambulance drivers behind the front lines. Initially the Canadian forces did not accept Aboriginal people, and the forces were also reluctant to take African- and Japanese-Canadians. Volunteers from these groups managed to overcome such racist attitudes and join, but few were promoted within

Figure 2-4 Aboriginal volunteers from Files Hill Reserve, who joined the Saskatchewan 68th Battalion of the CEF, are shown here with family members.

the ranks. Such discrimination didn't prevent these recruits from serving their country well. One Aboriginal recruit, Tom Longboat (Cogwagee), was a well-known athlete and Boston Marathon runner. During the war he became a courier, carrying messages between the trenches in France, a position reserved for the fastest runners in the army.

Training the Troops

Canadian troops had to be made ready for war. The enormous task of training and supplying the troops with clothing and munitions went to Sam Hughes, the minister of militia, who immediately set up a training centre in Valcartier, Quebec. After minimal basic training, 32 000 enthusiastic but rather ill-prepared Canadian and Newfoundland troops set sail for England in thirty-two transport ships.

Before the war, Canada was a patchwork of regions with few of the transportation and communication connections we know today. Canadians in these regions had little contact with one another. Wartime training brought diverse Canadians together as a group, first at Valcartier, then at bases in England. The trials of boot camp built bridges between them and they began to develop a **national identity**, a sense of being Canadian. In the words of one Canadian soldier:

> We were in Witley Camp [in England] and right alongside us was a battalion from French Canada. We didn't speak much French and they didn't speak much English, but they were the finest sports you ever saw.... You met people from Nova Scotia, or from Prince Edward Island, clean through to British Columbia. Very often you didn't take any notice of the fact unless they happened to mention it.
>
> Source: Ben Wagner, quoted in B. Greenhous and S.J. Harris, *Canada and the Battle of Vimy Ridge* (Ottawa: Minister of Supply and Services Canada, 1992), 35.

The army that was formed from these volunteers was known as the Canadian Expeditionary Force (CEF). When the CEF arrived in Britain, British commanders assumed that, as a colonial army, the CEF would be integrated into the larger, more experienced British units. For much of the war, however, the CEF maintained its independence and fought as a separate Canadian unit, another factor that contributed greatly to a growing sense of national identity.

Figure 2-5 The 29th Battalion (Vancouver), CEF, in training in Hastings Park, Vancouver, late 1914.

Using evidence How are these men preparing for war?

Figure 2-6 World War I internment camp near Banff, Alberta.

Gathering information What can you learn about conditions in the internment camp from this photograph?

Canada's Minister of Militia

Sam Hughes was also put in charge of Canada's armament industry. He created the Shell Committee to oversee the manufacturing of shells, and by 1917, Canada was supplying about one-third of the shells used by the British forces. Hughes, however, was a poor administrator and the Ministry of Militia soon became bogged down in patronage, inefficiency, and confusion. By mid-1915, contracts worth about $170 million had been signed with wealthy industrialists, but only $5.5 million in shells had actually been made. Some of the shells were of such poor quality that they exploded before being fired, killing the gun crews. Hughes also took advantage of his position by awarding large government contracts to friends who were *profiteers*, people more interested in making money than in producing quality goods. In one case, soldiers were equipped with boots that fell apart in the rain because the soles had been made of pressed cardboard. Canadian soldiers came to hate the Canadian-made Ross rifle because it tended to jam in rapid fire, so they picked up British-made Lee Enfield rifles from dead infantrymen whenever they could. Hughes was dismissed from his post in 1916 but not before being knighted by King George V.

The War Measures Act

Prime Minister Borden realized that in order for Canada to meet the demands of war, the government would need more control over the country's affairs. Almost immediately after war was declared, Borden introduced the **War Measures Act**, which granted the Canadian government the authority to do everything necessary "for the security, defence, peace, order, and welfare of Canada." The federal government had never been granted such power before. For the first time it could intervene directly in the economy of the country and control transportation, manufacturing, trade, and agricultural production in whatever way it deemed necessary. The act gave the government the power to strip ordinary Canadians of their civil liberties. Mail could be censored, and **habeas corpus**, the right of a person under arrest to be brought before a judge to determine the lawfulness of the arrest, was suspended. This meant police had the power to detain people without laying charges. Anyone suspected of being an enemy alien or a threat to the government could be imprisoned, or deported, or both. Recent immigrants from Germany and the Austro-Hungarian Empire were treated particularly harshly under this act. Over half a million of them had to carry special identity cards and report regularly to registration officers. Another 8579 were held in isolation in **internment camps**.

ACTIVITIES

1. Examine the document on pages 24–25. What does this document say about the attitude of people in Canada towards Britain at this time? How does the document on page 26 demonstrate a growing feeling of Canadian identity among Canadian troops?

2. List the attitudes in Canada in 1914 that led to the exclusion of women and other groups from participating in the war.

3. Why did the government need power to control the economy, transportation, and trade when war was declared?

4. Name the civil liberties that were threatened by the War Measures Act.

New Technology and the War

The muddy trenches and devastated landscape of northern France became symbols of the way the war was being fought. In earlier wars, infantry soldiers had fought in armed units supported by cavalry (soldiers on horses). They charged the enemy across open fields, firing rifles equipped with bayonets. By 1914, however, new weapons were so powerful and deadly that it was suicidal to charge across open ground. Newly developed machine guns fired at unprecedented speed. Airplanes, invented only a decade before the war began, flew over battlefields, allowing pilots to spy on enemy activity; later the planes were equipped with machine guns. By 1916, armoured tanks had been

The War on Land

Before the war began, Germany had developed the Schlieffen Plan, a bold strategy for a two-front war. France to the west was the Western Front, and Russia to the east the Eastern Front. The plan was for the German army to quickly invade Belgium, then France, and capture the capital city of Paris. Once this was accomplished, Germany could turn its attention to Russia. The plan almost worked. By August of 1914, German troops were only 35 km from Paris. They were, however, exhausted by the pace of the Schlieffen Plan. France and Britain rallied to push them back into northern France, where the Germans dug a defensive line of trenches. The Allies dug their own system of trenches, often just a few metres away. Eventually a vast network of trenches stretched from the English Channel to the Swiss border. Between the trenches of the two enemies lay no man's land, a terrible wasteland of corpses, barbed wire, and mud. By Christmas of 1914, the Western Front was locked in a stalemate with neither side able to make advances, yet both sides were unprepared to retreat.

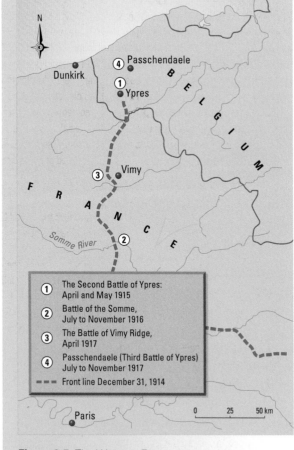

Figure 2-7 The Western Front.

Innovations

War Technology

During World War I, transportation and weapons technology developed rapidly. The result was a war with more casualties than had ever been experienced before.

Germany used *dirigibles*, inflatable airships, for scouting and bombing missions. Ferdinand von Zeppelin built huge rigid dirigibles by covering a light framework of wood or metal with a thin "skin" of waterproof fabric or aluminum. The shell was filled with a lighter-than-air gas such as hydrogen, and the airship was propelled forward by an engine suspended underneath. Britain used smaller frameless dirigibles to protect ships from submarines. ▼

During World War I, bigger *field guns* and *cannon* were developed. Germany's "Big Bertha" artillery could arch shells almost 25 km upward to hit targets up to 120 km away! Giant guns were moved into position on railcars, and worked together in groups called batteries. Often the guns fired shells filled with explosives and *shrapnel*, metal balls or fragments.

▲
At first, *fighter planes* were used to find the enemy; later they were used to attack. There was always a risk that the machine guns used to fire on the enemy would chop off the plane's own wooden propeller, so engineers developed an interrupter system to block the machine gun from firing at the moment the propeller passed in front of it. This safeguard reduced the number of bullets shot, so many pilots used a top-mounted gun that fired above the propeller.

Although the United States and Britain were responsible for much of the development of the early *submarines*, Germany used them most. Their *U-boats* (from *Unterseeboot*, or "under-sea boat") used diesel engines and travelled faster on the surface than most ships. A periscope allowed crew members to view the surface from under water. U-boat crews sank many Allied ships with *torpedoes*, cigar-shaped bombs driven by a propeller. ▼

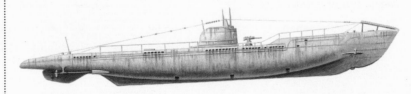

The British developed *tanks* to crush barbed wire and shelter the crew from gunfire while crossing no man's land. Soldiers would follow a wide line of tanks as the tracked vehicles crawled slowly forward. The original tanks were underpowered and very hard to turn. They also often stuck in the mud. By 1917, though, improvements made them important in the Allied ground war. ▼

▲
Both sides used *poison gas* during World War I. Germany was the first to use chemical warfare, releasing clouds of chlorine gas at Ypres in 1915. The gas burned the skin and lungs of the Allied forces, including Canadians. Later, both sides used phosgene gas (invisible but suffocating) and mustard gas (which creates huge skin blisters). One young soldier temporarily blinded in a British gas attack in 1918 was Adolf Hitler, later to lead Germany in World War II. As the use of poisonous gas increased, troops were issued with *anti-gas respirators*.

built to protect crews as they advanced across the battlefield. Using tanks, troops could finally break through the protective wall of barbed wire in front of trenches. The early tanks were crude and often got stuck in the mud, but by the end of the war, they had become a more reliable weapon.

Soldiers may have been using modern weapons on the battlefield, but many of their commanders failed to understand how this new technology demanded new tactics. Over the next three years, hundreds of thousands of soldiers on all sides were slaughtered in the battlefields of France and Belgium as generals stubbornly engaged in a war of attrition, each side repeatedly attacking the other until one was completely exhausted and unable to continue.

Figure 2-8 Many Canadian soldiers lost their lives in the trenches while others suffered psychological disorders and nervous breakdowns.

Gathering information What can you tell about life in the trenches from this photograph? How might these conditions have contributed to psychological problems?

Life in the Trenches

No soldier could ever have been prepared for the horrible conditions of trench warfare. Trenches were cold and damp in the winter and often flooded in a heavy rain. Muddy trenches became stinking cesspools, overrun by rats. Soldiers' clothes were infested with lice, and many men developed trench foot, a painful condition that caused their feet to swell and turn black. An injured limb might require amputation because medical supplies were limited and repair was not possible. Many of those seriously injured in attacks were left to die in no man's land because rescue attempts were too dangerous. Men were in constant fear for their lives, either from deadly sniper fire or from exploding shells. One soldier reported:

> The air is full of shells ... the small ones whistling and shrieking and the heaviest falling silently, followed by a terrific explosion which perforates even the padded eardrums, so that a thin trickle of blood down the neck bears witness that the man is stricken stone-deaf. The solid ground rocks like an express [train] at full speed, and the only comparison possible is to a volcano in eruption with incessant shudder of earthworks and pelting hail of rocks.
>
> Source: Toronto *Globe*, April 15, 1916.

The CEF in Battle

The Second Battle of Ypres

Some of the bloodiest battles of the early war years were fought in and around the Belgian city of Ypres, located in the Flanders district. It was here on April 22, 1915, and again two days later that French and Canadian troops were blinded, burned, or killed when the Germans used chlorine gas even though the use of gas for military purposes had been outlawed by international agreement since 1907. As the clouds of gas drifted low across the battlefield, soldiers tried to escape from the deadly fumes that destroyed their lungs. Many men suffocated or choked to death. Over the next month, neither side gained much advantage in the fields of Flanders though 6000 Canadians were killed, wounded, or captured.

The Battle of the Somme

In July 1916, British and French forces under the command of General Douglas Haig launched a massive attack along a line of low ridges near the Somme River, France. A veteran of cavalry warfare, Haig insisted on using strategies he knew had worked well in previous wars, but they were useless in trench warfare. As wave upon wave of troops were ordered to march across open fields, they were mowed down by German machine guns. Almost 85 per cent of the Royal Newfoundland Regiment, over 700 men including all officers, were killed or wounded within half an hour. When the battle finally drew to a close in November, there were over a million casualties—almost equal numbers on both sides—although Haig claimed victory. Almost 24 000 Canadians were among the casualties, and most soldiers were badly shaken by having witnessed the slaughter. One Canadian soldier, Frank Maheux, recalls the scene:

> I passed the worst fighting here since the war started. We took all kinds of prisoners but God we lost heavy, all my camarades killed or wounded....

Dear Wife, it is worse than hell, the ground is covered for miles with dead corpses all over.... Pray for me dear wife, I need it very bad.... As long as I live I'll remember it.

Source: Quoted in Desmond Morton, *When Your Number's Up* (Toronto: Random House, 1993), 158.

The Battle of Vimy Ridge

Since their first offensive in 1914, the Germans had controlled Vimy Ridge, a strategically important area of land in northern France. The French had tried three times to regain Vimy, but they were unsuccessful. Late in 1916, Canadian troops were chosen to lead a new assault under the command of General Julian Byng, a popular British officer (later appointed a governor general of Canada). Byng developed strategies for attack and trained the troops well, rehearsing their movements thoroughly. From the west side of the ridge, Canadian troops bombarded German positions for over a month. Meanwhile, sappers (army engineers) constructed tunnels to move troops secretly to forward positions. At zero hour on April 9, 1917, Easter Monday and the first day of the attack, Canadian troops moved into position. The weather was cold and snowy, and a strong wind blew snow

Figure 2-9 Lieutenant-Colonel John McCrae, a Canadian surgeon, wrote his famous poem "In Flanders Fields" to commemorate the dead and injured Canadians he treated in Belgium. He wrote the poem in twenty minutes and signed it. Then, dissatisfied with the work, he tossed it aside. A soldier later found it and sent it to a popular British magazine for publication.

Thinking critically How reliable is this poem as a primary source?

Figure 2-10 Canadian soldiers return from Vimy Ridge, May 1917.

Expressing ideas This photograph became one of the most famous images of Canadians in World War I. Why do you think this was so?

into the faces of the enemy on the ridge. The Canadian corps followed their plan of attack with precision and bravery, and in less than two hours they had taken their first objectives. On April 10, they captured Hill 145, the highest point on the ridge, and by April 12 they had taken "the pimple," the last German position. It was a stunning victory. The Canadians had gained more ground, taken more prisoners, and captured more artillery than any previous British offensive in the entire war. Although the cost was high—over 3500 men killed and another 7000 wounded—the losses were significantly fewer than in any previous Allied offensive because of the meticulous planning and training.

The victory at Vimy Ridge marked a Canadian milestone, and Canadians took great pride in the success. Their victory was noted outside Canada as well. An editorial in the New York *Tribune* stated that "every American will feel a thrill of admiration and a touch of honest envy at the achievements of the Canadian troops." Historian Pierre Berton captured these events in simpler terms: "They said it couldn't be done and we did it."

Passchendaele

Byng was promoted for his role at Vimy and his replacement was a Canadian, General Arthur Currie, a former real estate dealer from Victoria, British Columbia. The first Canadian appointed to command Canada's troops, Currie brought an increasingly independent Canadian point of view to the British war effort. Although a disciplined leader and open to new strategies, Currie still took orders from General Haig. In 1917, Currie and the CEF were called upon to retake Passchendaele Ridge in Belgium. Unlike Vimy Ridge, Passchendaele had little strategic value, but General Haig was determined to retake it. His earlier assault on Passchendaele had left massive shell craters in the ground, which the heavy autumn rains turned into a quagmire. Some soldiers and horses actually drowned in these appalling conditions. Currie warned that casualties would be high, but Haig would not change his mind. Currie was right. The Allies won the battle at Passchendaele, but the "victory" cost over 15 000 Canadian lives and nearly half a million soldiers from both sides.

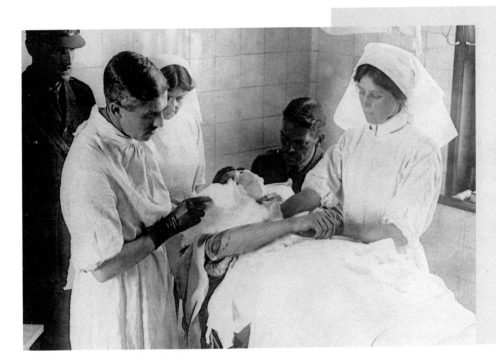

Figure 2-11 Nurses and surgeon in a World War I hospital.

Gathering information How does this scene differ from scenes in modern operating rooms? Identify three elements in the scene that could be sources of infection.

Women on the Western Front

Almost 2500 Canadian women joined the medical and field ambulance corps. Some women served as nurses in the Canadian Army Medical Corps. Affectionately called "Bluebirds" after the colour of their uniforms, the nurses worked in military hospitals in the battle zones as well as in hospitals in Britain. Many were killed or injured by artillery fire, bombs, or poison gas. One nurse, Bertha Merriman, recorded her experiences in letters to her parents in Hamilton, Ontario:

La Panne, Belgium, June 12, 1915

Last night we had a perfectly terrible time. Patients came in in a rush, and were so awfully wounded. My operating room was going all night; I never experienced anything like it.... I am not telling you how many we lost last night, because the censor might not send this letter if I did. We are told not to give details or numbers.

The surgery is more like butchery, but of course it is necessary. They cut away any flesh or bone with which the shell has come in contact, leaving huge holes, and making no attempt at suturing. Then they cleanse the wound with ether, and cover all around with iodine. This radical work is necessary on account of poison and of gas gangrene.

Source: Bertha Merriman, Merriman Family Papers (Ontario Archives).

ACTIVITIES

1. With the aid of a diagram, explain how the failure of the Schlieffen Plan resulted in a stalemate on the Western Front.

2. Write a letter home from the Western Front, either from a soldier's or a nurse's point of view. In your letter, describe conditions where you are. Give your thoughts on leadership.

3. The use of gas as a weapon was outlawed by the 1907 Hague Convention. Discuss whether chemical weapons should be allowed in warfare.

4. Create a series of wartime sketches showing some of the conditions at the front. Include depictions of the air war and field hospitals.

The War in the Air

At the beginning of the war, pilots flew alone in biplanes used mostly for *aerial reconnaissance*, photographing and reporting on enemy troop movements. Soon, however, pilots on both sides were armed and fired pistols and rifles at the enemy below. Within a year, manufacturers for

up close

Billy Bishop

William Avery (Billy) Bishop, from Owen Sound, Ontario, started out as a cavalry officer. In 1916 Bishop transferred to the Royal Flying Corps where he became Canada's top ace with seventy-two "kills." Bishop was the first Canadian pilot awarded the Victoria Cross, a prestigious medal for bravery. He became the toast of Canada because of his success, going on speaking tours to promote the war effort and help sell Victory Bonds. In the following passage from his diary he describes some of his daring adventures:

> I fired on 7 machines on the aerodrome.... One of them took off and I fired 15 rounds at him from close range ... and he crashed. A second one taking off, I opened fire and fired 30 rounds ... he crashed into a tree. Two more were then taking off together. I climbed and engaged one at 1000 feet, finishing my drum [of bullets], and he crashed 300 yards from the aerodrome.... I changed drums and climbed East. A fourth H.A. [hostile aircraft] came after me and I fired one whole drum into him. He flew away....

Source: Quoted in David Barker, *The Man and the Aircraft He Flew* (London: Outline Press, 1990), 15.

But the life of this Canadian legend was less glamorous than it appeared. In a letter home to his wife, Margaret, he wrote:

> I am thoroughly downcast tonight.... Sometimes all of this awful fighting makes you wonder if you have a right to call yourself human. My honey, I am so sick of it all, the killing, the war. All I want is home and you.

Source: Grey County Museum, www.greycounty.on.ca/museum/bishstor.html

Figure 2-12 Thinking critically What does this photograph show you about the skills a pilot needed? Who do you think took the photograph? How might this picture have been used during the war?

Questions

1. Bishop's diary is his personal account of what happened. His "kill" total has sometimes been questioned because his deeds were not always witnessed. Explain why you think Bishop was given credit for the "kills." Is the diary a primary source? Evaluate it as a historical source.

2. Use the two sources presented here to write a character study of Bishop, being careful to note emotions and other aspects of Bishop's personality revealed in his diary.

both the Allies and the Central Powers had built small fighter aircraft with machine guns mounted on the planes. Fighter pilots had to be sharp shooters with nerves of steel and lots of luck. Aerial dogfights were spectacular scenes as pilots used elaborate spins and rolls to shake off attacking planes.

When a pilot could prove that he had shot down five enemy aircraft, he was identified as an **ace**. Because these air aces became heroes in their homelands, they were often withdrawn from active duty overseas to promote fund-raising and recruitment at home. A pilot's life was exciting but there was no escaping the danger. They did not even use parachutes. In 1917, the peak year for aerial dogfights, the average life expectancy for a Royal Flying Corps (RFC) pilot was only three weeks. In all, more than 50 000 pilots and air crew were killed between 1914 and 1918.

Because Canada did not have its own air force, Canadians who wanted to be pilots had to join the British RFC. Nevertheless, Canada produced a number of aces including Billy Bishop, Ray Collishaw, Billy Barker, William May, and Roy Brown, the pilot credited with shooting down the German flying ace, Manfred von Richthofen, the Red Baron.

The War at Sea

Although Germany could not match Britain's navy in size and strength, its U-boat, or submarine, was a dangerous weapon because it could travel under water without being seen or detected. With this advantage, German U-boats were highly successful at disrupting British shipping. When later equipped with torpedoes, they completely destroyed warships or merchant ships. In 1915, a U-boat sank the British passenger liner, the *Lusitania*, killing close to 1200 passengers, including many Canadians and Americans. In April 1917, Germany announced that U-boats would sink any ship within the war zone around Britain, a threat that added one more reason for the United States to enter the war. The effectiveness of the U-boat had hurt the British war effort because Britain had been unable at first to retaliate. Eventually the Allies developed the convoy system and an underwater listening device that helped them locate and destroy U-boats. In the terms of settlement at the end of the war, the Allies forced the Germans to surrender the U-boats they had left, and forbade them to build more.

Prior to the war, Canada's navy consisted of only two warships: the *Rainbow* which patrolled the West Coast, and the *Niobe* stationed in

Figure 2-13 ARTS FOCUS
Troop ships carrying the First Canadian Division and the Newfoundland Regiment to Europe, 1914.

Identifying viewpoint This painting is titled *Canada's Answer*. Why do you think the artist, N. Wilkinson, gave it this title?

Halifax. The strategic location of Halifax and its protected harbour made it a base for the refuelling and repair of Allied warships and the chief departure point for Europe. Canada's **merchant marine** became involved in the dangerous work of ferrying munitions and food to Britain. Although not officially members of the armed forces, many merchant seamen lost their lives during the dangerous crossings of the Atlantic.

The War at Home

When Canada had entered the war, the country was in an economic recession, but by 1916, the economy was booming. After Prime Minister Borden replaced the Shell Committee with the more efficient Imperial Munitions Board, munitions factories started building ships and airplanes as well as shells. Hundreds of thousands of Canadians were employed in these factories to fill the huge orders that poured in from England

and Belgium. The production and export of Canadian goods reached record highs. Resources such as lumber, nickel, copper, and lead were also in high demand, as was Canadian wheat and beef. Because most of what Canada produced was exported to Europe, many goods became scarce within Canada. This scarcity caused the prices to rise. Some Canadian businesses made enormous profits from the inflated prices, but workers became increasingly frustrated by government controls that kept wages low yet allowed prices to rise. Workers' demands for higher wages and better working conditions became a major issue after the war.

Paying for the War

While production levels were at an all-time high, the Canadian government was unable to raise sufficient money to pay for its contribution to the war. New technology and the large number of troops involved made this war a very expensive conflict. The government decided to try to pay its debts through a combination of bonds, taxes, and loans. In a campaign that appealed to patriotism and thrift, Canadians were urged to buy Victory Bonds that they could cash in, with interest, when the war was over.

The government also introduced the income tax—a measure that was supposed to be temporary. Well-off individuals and families had to pay a tax of 3 per cent of their income. The tax of 4 per cent levied on business profits was criticized as too low by many Canadians aware of the enormous incomes earned by some companies during the war. The money from these two initiatives was not enough, and by 1918 a deeply indebted Canadian government was forced to borrow money from other countries, particularly the United States.

The Changing Role of Women

With so many men overseas, women had to take on new roles in wartime Canada. Some organized committees to send food and letters overseas; others became involved in volunteer organizations such as the Red Cross. The most significant

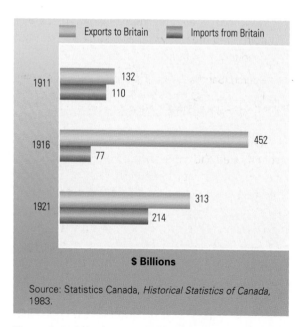

Source: Statistics Canada, *Historical Statistics of Canada,* 1983.

Figure 2-14 Wartime trade with Britain (in $ billions).

Gathering information In which year were Canadian exports to Britain the highest? How significant was the increase from 1911? Why did exports decrease in 1921?

Figure 2-15 About 35 000 Canadian women worked in munitions factories where shells were manufactured, and thousands more drove the delivery trucks.

change, however, was in women's contribution to the labour force. Before 1914 women had been employed at low-skill, low-paying jobs in food and clothing industries, and as domestic servants. When Canada's increased industrial production created a great demand for labour, women were hired for all types of work, from operating fishing boats in Atlantic Canada to running prairie farms. Without the efforts of women on the home front, Canada's wartime economy would have collapsed. Most employers assumed that the women would leave these jobs and return to work in their homes when the war ended.

One Toronto woman volunteered to work filling artillery shells. After the war she described her introduction to the job:

> The foreman [of the munitions factory] met me at the door and he just beckoned to me. The reason why he couldn't say anything was because you couldn't have heard him! I just had to follow him. I went through all these avenues and avenues of clanking, grinding, crashing machines. Some of them were so close together that in order to get to the machines, they'd built a kind of stile—several steps up and then you walked across and went down again.... The foreman ... demonstrated how to do one shell, and then he stood aside and pointed to me.... I was panic-stricken. But I got used to it.

Source: Sandra Gwyn, *Tapestry of War: A Private View of Canadians in the Great War* (Toronto: HarperCollins, 1992), 442–443.

The changing roles of women during the war strengthened the campaign for women's suffrage. The women of Manitoba had been at the forefront of women's struggle to win the right to vote. Conservative Premier Dufferin Roblin refused even to consider allowing women to vote in any election. Then in 1915, the Liberals in Manitoba campaigned in the election with the promise that women would have the right to vote, which they received in January 1916. Alberta and Saskatchewan followed Manitoba's example later that year, and in 1917, women in Ontario and British Columbia also won the right to vote in provincial elections. All Canadian women won the right to vote in federal elections in 1918 in recognition of their patriotic effort during the war.

Propaganda As a Tool of War

During World War I, Canadians, like citizens in the other warring nations, were bombarded with government **propaganda** designed to persuade people to support the war. Propaganda appeared in a variety of media: films, magazine articles, radio programs, political speeches, and posters. Appealing to a sense of patriotism, propaganda encouraged people to join the army, buy savings bonds, use less fuel, eat less meat, and support the government in whatever way necessary. For example, colourful posters that encouraged able-bodied men to enlist contributed to the fact that more than 80 per cent of the Canadians who served in World War I were volunteers.

Propaganda is selective and it often distorts the truth. Reports about conditions on the Western Front were inaccurate; and the number of Allied soldiers killed or wounded was minimized while enemy casualties were exaggerated. British commanders were praised even as they continued to waste lives in futile attacks. When Germany had invaded Belgium in 1914, the Belgian refugees who escaped to England told horrible stories about the invasion. Writers used these stories to portray German troops as "the Huns," a horde of barbarians intent on destroying the civilized world. This portrayal of Germans aroused prejudice against all Germans, including those who had settled in Canada. When a German U-boat sank the *Lusitania* in 1915, some angry mobs attacked innocent German businesses in several Canadian cities.

Residents of the town of Berlin, Ontario, many descended from German immigrants, faced criticism because their town bore the same name as Germany's capital. In response to this criticism, the citizens raised almost $100 000 for the war effort, a huge amount in those days. Nevertheless, in early 1916, unruly soldiers stationed in the city destroyed a German social club, raided German businesses, and attacked people who were said to be pro-German. The city eventually changed its name to Kitchener, after the British War Secretary, Lord Kitchener.

The Halifax Disaster

On December 6, 1917, the horrors of the war in Europe came closer to home. The *Mont Blanc*, a French vessel carrying more than 2500 t of dynamite, was accidentally hit by another ship. The collision caused an explosion so powerful that it devastated Halifax's harbour and much of the city. In all, between 2000 and 3000 people were killed in the explosion or fires that followed, and more than 10 000 were injured.

Figure 2-16 This poster showing a Canadian nurse reminded the public of Edith Cavell, a British nurse at a medical training institute in Belgium. Cavell was executed by the Germans in 1915 for helping Allied soldiers escape the German-occupied countries.

Figure 2-17 Emergency relief poured into Halifax from across Canada, the United States, and Britain, but after three years of war, money was scarce, and many survivors whose homes had been destroyed had to spend the bitter winter living in tents.

ACTIVITIES

1. How was propaganda used during the war? Discuss whether it is appropriate to manipulate information for patriotic purposes during war. What differences, if any, are there between propaganda and advertising?

2. Examine the poster on page 38. All the names that appear in the poster are meant to stand for German atrocities. Edith Cavell was a nurse executed as a spy; the *Lusitania* was sunk by a German U-boat; the ancient library of Louvain, a world heritage treasure, was burned by the Germans. What is the message in this poster? Imagine you are a Canadian of German descent, and write a protest note to the prime minister on the subject of this poster.

3. Explain how women contributed to the war effort, and describe how their status in Canadian society changed as a result.

4. Read the personal account of work in a munitions factory on page 37. Describe working conditions in the factory.

5. Write a letter from the mayor of Halifax asking for aid after the *Mont Blanc* explosion of 1917. Write a second letter from the prime minister explaining why help will be limited.

The Conscription Crisis

When war was declared in 1914, most Canadians expected that it would be over soon. By 1917, however, many thousands of Canadian men had been killed and many thousands more had been seriously wounded. With so many working in industry for the war effort at home, the number of men who volunteered for war was too low to provide replacement troops in Europe.

Prime Minister Borden had promised there would be no **conscription**, compulsory enlistment for military service. However, he was in England at the time of the Canadian victory at Vimy Ridge, and he was shocked to learn how many men had been needed to win that battle. David Lloyd George, the British prime minister, convinced Borden that the war had to be won at all costs and that victory would require many more troops. On his return to Canada, Borden introduced the Military Service Act, a bill that would make enlistment compulsory. At first, the act allowed exemptions (for the disabled, the clergy, those with essential jobs or special skills, and **conscientious objectors**, those who did not believe in the war on religious grounds). Conscription turned out to be a very controversial and emo-

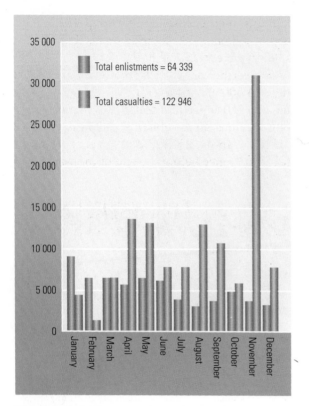

Figure 2-18 Enlistment and casualty rates by month, 1917.

Using evidence In which month did Canada suffer the most casualties? Why were Canadian casualties so high in 1917?

tional issue that divided the country and left lasting scars.

While Canada had a high overall rate of volunteers, the recruitment rates were uneven across the country, with the lowest levels from Quebec. Few French recruits spoke English and few in the officer corps spoke French. There was little attempt to keep French-speaking recruits together as a unit other than the Twenty-second Battalion, the Van Doos. As well, relations between French- and English-speaking Canadians became strained over restrictions in the use of French in schools outside Quebec. The majority of French-Canadians did not feel a patriotic connection to either Britain or France because their ancestors had come to Canada generations before. They saw the Military Service Act as a means of forcing them to fight in a war that they didn't feel was theirs.

Quebec nationalist Henri Bourassa was one of the most outspoken critics of conscription. He argued that Canada had lost enough men and spent enough money on a war that had little to do with this country. Spending even more money and sending even more troops would bankrupt the country and put a strain on Canada's agricultural and industrial production. A weakened economy would eventually threaten Canada's political independence. Perhaps most significantly, he believed that conscription would bitterly divide the nation.

Other groups that opposed conscription included farmers, particularly in the Prairies. They needed their sons, and hired workers, to do the farm work. Industrial workers felt they were already contributing to the war effort and didn't want to give up their jobs to fight overseas. In British Columbia, opposition to conscription was led by the labour movement, in particular, the coal miners of Vancouver Island. They were urged to increase their output, but wages and working conditions did not improve. Workers were already having problems providing for their families, and conscription would mean they would earn less. Resistance to conscription in British Columbia turned violent when labour leader Ginger Goodwin, along with several other union members, hid from the authorities after his application for exemption from service was turned down. He was eventually tracked down and killed by a police constable.

Canada's Most Divisive Election

In the face of such opposition, Prime Minister Borden decided to call an election over the issue of conscription. Prior to announcing the election, he passed two new pieces of legislation designed to ensure his re-election. The first was the Military Voters Act, which allowed the men and women serving overseas to vote. The second was the Wartime Elections Act, which gave the vote to all Canadian women directly related to servicemen. At the same time, the act cancelled the vote for all conscientious objectors and immigrants who had come from enemy countries in the last fifteen years.

Borden had also invited opposition Liberals who favoured conscription to join with him in forming a wartime Union Government. These Liberals were offered important Cabinet positions as an incentive to join the government. Wilfrid Laurier, the Liberal leader, was against conscription. He believed that "The law of the land … declares that no man in Canada shall be subjected to compulsory military service except to repel invasions or for the defence of Canada." The Liberals lost much support in the election outside Quebec because of Laurier's position on conscription.

The Union Government won the election with the strong support of the armed forces and the women related to them, but the anger and resentment stirred up by the conscription debate did not subside. In Québec, people continued to demonstrate against conscription even after the election. Crowds in Montreal marched through the streets shouting "*A bas Borden*" ("Down with Borden"). Canadian troops were pelted with rotten vegetables and stones when they taunted French-Canadians for refusing to enlist. Tensions finally erupted at anti-conscription riots in Quebec City during the Easter weekend of 1918. Four demonstrators were shot dead by soldiers, and ten soldiers were wounded in the riot.

Nevertheless, conscription went ahead. Of the 404 000 men across Canada who were called up, 380 500 applied for exemptions for medical or other reasons. In the end, 130 000 were enlisted, but only about 25 000 conscripted soldiers reached France before the end of the war.

Region	Union Government (Borden)	Liberals (Laurier)
Atlantic Canada	21	10
Quebec	3	62
Ontario	74	8
Western Canada	54	2
Total	152	82

Figure 2-19 Results of the 1917 election by region: Number of seats in Parliament.

Using evidence Find evidence to support the view that this election divided the nation.

Figure 2-20 Prime Minister Borden gave Canadian men and women serving overseas the right to vote in the federal election of 1917. For the women in this photograph, it was their first time voting in a federal election. Borden counted on the support of the military, and the election became known as the "Khaki" Election. What do you think this name meant?

ACTIVITIES

1. Why did Prime Minister Borden believe that conscription was necessary? Why were many people opposed to conscription?

2. Write a letter to the editor of the Toronto *Globe* from Henri Bourassa explaining why conscription was not good for the country.

3. In pairs, create two thumbnail election posters for the Khaki Election, for either political party. Aim your advertising at *two* of the following groups: soldiers, women, French-Canadians, English-Canadians.

4. Why do you think Borden did not allow conscientious objectors or recent Canadian immigrants from enemy countries to vote in the 1917 election? Why did he not give the vote to all women in 1917?

5. By 1917 Canadian soldiers were being used as "shock" troops, leading the attacks in battles. Imagine you are in the position of Robert Borden. Make a list of pros and cons for sending more troops.

The Central Powers Collapse

Two important events in 1917 changed the direction of the war. First, Czar Nicholas of Russia was forced to abdicate in March of 1917 and a provisional Russian government was formed. Second, the United States, angered by the sinking of neutral ships and passenger liners such as the *Lusitania*, declared war on Germany on April 2. In October 1917, revolutionaries, called Bolsheviks, overthrew the provisional government in Russia and, promising the war-weary public "peace and bread," signed a peace treaty with Germany. This truce on the Eastern Front in early 1918 freed German troops for fighting on the Western Front. Germany moved to take advantage of its last chance at victory before large numbers of American troops reached France.

In a last desperate offensive, the German army struck at weak points in the enemy lines and succeeded in driving deep into France. Positions that had been won at great cost in lives were lost in weeks: Ypres, the Somme, Passchendaele, everything but Vimy Ridge. By the summer of 1918,

Figure 2-21 Europe in 1922.

Gathering information
Compare this map with the map of Europe in 1914, on page 22. Describe the changes in national borders, then list the names of the new countries created.

the new front line was only 75 km from Paris. But the Germans had exhausted themselves. They had no reserves, and without fresh troops, food, and supplies, they could not continue. The generals knew the war was over.

During the final months of the war, known as the "Hundred Days," Canada's offensives were among the most successful of all the Allied forces. Canadian troops, under the disciplined command of General Currie, broke through German lines and won important battles at Arras, Cambrai, and Valenciennes. The Central Powers collapsed one by one; the German Kaiser abdicated and fled to Holland. An **armistice**, or truce, was finally signed in a railway car in France, and the war ended at 11:00 a.m., November 11, 1918. An unfortunate Canadian was the last soldier to die on the Western Front—Private George Price was killed by a sniper's bullet just a few minutes before the armistice.

Canada on the World Stage

After the signing of the armistice, the Allies and the new leadership of Germany met in Paris to discuss the terms of a peace agreement. Prime Minister Borden fought successfully for Canada to have its own seat at the **Paris Peace Conference**, and not simply be represented by Britain. He also insisted that he be included among those leaders who signed the **Treaty of Versailles**, the document that eventually set out the terms of the peace agreement in 1919. American President Woodrow Wilson had proposed, early in 1918, a fourteen-point plan for peace that emphasized forgiveness, but the French and Belgian leaders wanted compensation from Germany for the damage their countries suffered during the war. They insisted in the 1919 conference that:

- Germany had to agree to a war "guilt clause," meaning that the country had to accept responsibility for causing the war.
- Germany had to pay war reparations totalling about $30 billion.
- The map of Europe was to be redrawn, reducing Germany's territory and dividing it into two parts so that the newly independent Poland would have a corridor to the sea.
- The German army was to be restricted to 100 000 men; the nation was not to be allowed U-boats or an air force.

The reparation terms were particularly harsh. After the war, Germany's economy, like that of

Figure 2-22 The first Remembrance Day parade.

Identifying viewpoint How do you think these women felt about their sacrifice? Give reasons for your view.

Did the War Have a Positive or Negative Effect on Canada?

World War I brought profound changes to Canada. It changed the way we saw ourselves as a country and a nation. Canadian troops fought well as a united force and their victories, particularly at Vimy and Passchendaele, distinguished them as disciplined and courageous fighters. The need for war munitions had stimulated the economy, resulting in major growth in Canadian industry. Women for the first time achieved the right to vote. Canada gained international status with its participation at the Paris Peace Conference, and Canadians began to see themselves less as colonials in the British Empire and more as citizens of an independent country. World War I marked Canada's coming of age as it moved from a collection of disparate communities to a nation united by a sense of pride and identity.

According to Canadian historian George Woodcock:

… the emergence of Canada … as a nation among nations within the broader world context, caused people to think less of what divided them than of what united them. They shared a single, if immense, geographical terrain, a common historical tradition in which their various pasts intermingled of necessity, and an identity in which the sense of being colonial—and therefore being linked irrevocably to a land far away—metamorphosed into a sense of being Canadian.

Source: George Woodcock, *A Social History of Canada* (Toronto: Penguin, 1988), 297.

But the war also had a very negative effect on Canada. As well as the tragedy of the more than 60 000 dead and thousands more wounded, government measures taken during the war left scars on the nation. The issue of conscription and the bitterness of the debate between English-speaking and French-speaking Canadians have never been completely forgotten. Those who spoke out against conscription were accused of being unpatriotic and labelled cowards and "Hun sympathizers." Such accusations isolated many French-Canadians from the federal government that had broken its promise not to impose conscription. The War Measures Act also caused problems in many communities where immigrants from Eastern European countries suffered racial discrimination even after the war.

The losses both at home and throughout the world were staggering. Approximately thirteen million people were killed during the war, and millions more were psychologically or physically wounded. The economic costs of World War I, in destruction and lost productivity, were also enormous: Canada sent about a billion dollars worth of war materials overseas between 1914 and 1918, a debt that took decades to pay off.

Some historians challenge the belief that World War I marked Canada's coming of age. Historian Jonathan Vance asks, "How could a war that saw the deaths of 60 000 Canadians and the wounding of 170 000 others become a constructive force in the nation's history?" Vance believes that Canadians suffered so much in the war that they needed to attach some greater importance to this event. In his view, Canada's "coming of age" was a myth that developed during the 1920s and 1930s to transform the horrors of the war into a more positive experience. The maturity myth was meant to help heal the country, Vance says, because believing in it meant wartime losses had served a real purpose for Canada.

Analysing the Issue

1. Define "coming of age," and explain how World War I helped bring about Canada's coming of age.

2. Make a PMI chart on the theme of Canadian unity and the effects of World War I.

3. You and a partner have been chosen to be on a radio panel to discuss the impact of World War I on Canada's development. One of you is to defend the position of historian George Woodcock. The other is to defend Jonathan Vance's point of view. Prepare and organize your arguments, then present them to the class for further discussion.

other European countries, was in ruins so it was unable to meet the payments. It also greatly resented the guilt clause, a fact that would come back to haunt the world twenty years later.

Participating in Peace

Prime Minister Borden also fought hard to have Canada became a member of the newly formed League of Nations. The League of Nations was the brainchild of U.S. President Woodrow Wilson. It was established by the Treaty of Versailles.

The League was made up of many nations throughout the world and was based on the principle of **collective security**. If one member state of the League came under attack, all members were to cooperate in suppressing the aggressor.

The idea of a League of Nations was not welcomed by the great powers. Britain and France had doubts about such an organization. They wanted the freedom to pursue their imperialist ambitions. But their leaders realized that Wilson's proposal had good propaganda value—it would gain them publicity and support. As a result, they agreed to the basic concept, in principle at least. Smaller nations, always concerned about becoming victims of the great powers, eagerly looked forward to a new era of peace.

The League's Limitations

Unfortunately, the League of Nations proved to be more an idealistic vision than a practical solution to world problems. It required the nations of the world to cooperate with one another, which was not something they had done very well in the past. The League could punish an aggressive nation by imposing economic **sanctions** against it, thus restricting trade with the offending nation, but the League had no military force of its own to impose its decisions upon aggressor nations.

Figure 2-23 Leaders from around the world gathered in Versailles, outside Paris, to negotiate a peace agreement, which became known as the Treaty of Versailles.

Ironically, the Americans refused to join the League of Nations, even though their own president was responsible for its creation. Wilson had powerful opponents who rejected the principle of collective security. During a heated debate on the issue, the president became ill. Half paralyzed by a stroke, he could no longer campaign for a vote in favour of the United States joining the League, and the motion was defeated. The refusal of the United States to join the League greatly undermined its effectiveness to resolve disputes in the years after World War I.

The Aftermath of War

The armistice of November 11, 1918, did not end people's suffering. During the winter of 1918–1919, people went hungry across large areas of Europe, their crops and transportation systems ruined. At the same time a deadly influenza virus (known as the Spanish Flu) swept across Europe, killing millions, and many returning soldiers carried the virus to North America. Young people were especially susceptible to the virus, which caused the deaths of an estimated 22 million people worldwide, more than the war itself. From 1918 to 1920, approximately 50 000 Canadians died during the epidemic. Schools and public places were closed for months in an effort to stop the spread of the virus, and in some communities, Canadians were required to wear breathing masks in public.

ACTIVITIES

1. With a partner, prepare briefing notes for the Canadian delegation to the Paris Peace Conference. Emphasize Canada's status as a nation, its contributions to the war, and the costs of the war to Canada.

2. Write a medical bulletin on the Spanish Flu of 1918 to be circulated as a warning to all communities and to all Canadian military bases.

3. Research the terms of the Treaty of Versailles. Make a PMI chart on the treaty's terms and their possible consequences.

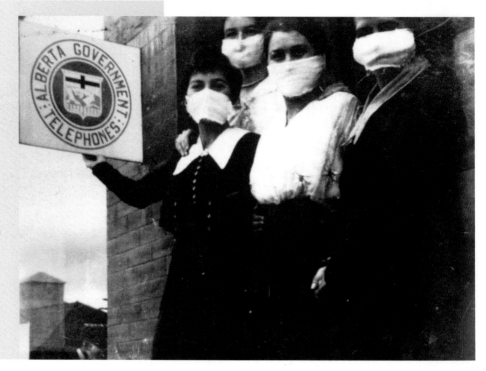

Figure 2-24 After the devastation of World War I, conditions were right for the flu virus to spread rapidly.

Developing understanding Why are these people wearing masks?

LOOKING BACK

Develop an Understanding

1. In your opinion, what is Frederick Varley saying about World War I in his painting on page 20? Based on what you have learned, explain whether you agree or disagree with his interpretation.

2. Some historians have described Europe in 1914 as a "powder keg" waiting for the fuse to be lit. Explain what is meant by this judgement, and give reasons why you agree or disagree with it.

3. Complete the following organizer to show how Canada changed in the four years of World War I.

	August 1914	November 1918
Relations with Britain		
Status of women		
Feelings of national identity		
Role of government		
French–English relations		

4. **a.** Explain what is meant by nationalism.

   b. Give examples from this chapter of the Canadian government's appeal to nationalistic feelings in Canada during the war.

5. Review the descriptions of technology and trench warfare. How would you explain the huge numbers of soldiers killed in World War I?

6. Imagine you and your classmates are workers in a factory making cardboard-soled boots for troops. Discuss together what options you would have to let the public know about this situation without running the risk of losing your jobs.

7. Make a list of points that support the hypothesis that Canada emerged from World War I as an industrial nation.

Explore the Issues

8. During World War I, the women's suffrage movement was very active, and women were arguing for the same rights as men. Write a newspaper column in support of women's rights. For this exercise, it is important that you try to place yourself "in" the Canadian society of 1914–1918.

9. Examine the decisions of the leaders described in this chapter. Write a letter to the government outlining the moral and ethical problems that prevent you from volunteering for the war.

10. **a.** Why was the conscription issue so divisive?

   b. In hindsight, who do you think was right: Henri employers.

11. Reread the section on the conscription crisis. With a partner, write a radio play script on the subject of conscription.

Research and Communicate

12. Research the technique of storyboarding. With a partner, create storyboards for the opening part of a feature-length cartoon on Canadians and World War I. Display your storyboards.

13. Imagine that you have the opportunity to interview either Robert Borden or Henri Bourassa about the conscription issue. Prepare either a program script or make an audiotape or videotape of the interview. Be sure to include questions on the Wartime Elections Act, the Military Service Act, and the election of 1917.

14. Create a newspaper for women during World War I. Include articles on the right to vote, women who worked in non-traditional jobs, children whose fathers and brothers were fighting on the Western Front, and other war-related issues.

15. With a partner, create an advertising poster designed to increase support for the war. Your poster should be aimed at students your age and designed to increase support in all areas of the country. All of your advertising should be based on fact, but you may exaggerate facts for effect as much as you like.

16. Analyse the advertising poster you made in activity 15. What parts of the poster manipulate information? What parts of it use propaganda? Write a summary of your findings and post it next to your advertising display.

3

Canada and the Twenties

FOCUS ON

• Why was there labour unrest after World War I, and how did workers try to improve their working conditions?

• What is regionalism, and how was it expressed in the 1920s?

• How did Canada become more independent from Britain?

• What was the impact of U.S. investment on the Canadian economy?

• How did the growth in Canadian industry affect life in the cities?

• How did new technology influence lifestyles in the 1920s?

Counterpoints Issue

• Did Canada become more or less independent in the 1920s?

October by Clarence Gagnon. This painting was one of a series of Quebec scenes that Gagnon started in the late 1920s to capture a way of life that was rapidly disappearing.

Expressing ideas What does this painting tell you about the way of life in rural Quebec at this time? How might it have been different in other parts of Canada? What aspects of this scene do you think were about to change?

Introduction

The 1920s are generally thought of as a decade of prosperity, fun, and wild living. To some extent this was true. The end of the war released an emotional flood of relief. Prompted by the horror and exhaustion of war, young people in particular tried to sweep away the remnants of the old world. This was the "Jazz Age." Bold new music, shocking fashions, and crazy fads spread quickly across the United States and into Canada. This 1927 editorial from *Canadian Homes and Gardens* may give a false picture of what life was really like for most women, but it certainly catches the optimism of the age:

> There is a certain magic to housekeeping these days—the magic of electricity—over which I confess I never cease to marvel. Your modern housewife leaves the dishes within a machine, pops the dinner into an oven, laundry into a washer, and jumps into a roadster [car] with never a thought except for ... the round of golf which she is away to enjoy for an afternoon. She returns to find the washing done, her china and crystal sparkle, a six course dinner is ready for serving.

> Source: Quoted in V. Strong-Boag, *The New Day Recalled* (Toronto: Copp Clark, 1988), 134.

Life did improve for many people. For many more, however, the prosperity of the twenties was merely an illusion. Life continued as before, filled with discrimination, poverty, and lack of political power.

An Uneasy Adjustment

In November 1918, Canadians celebrated the end of World War I. After four long years of fighting, Canadian soldiers were finally on their way home. Most returned to Canada early in 1919 only to find that there were no steady pensions for veterans, no special medical services for those wounded in the war, and above all, few jobs. To make matters worse, many employers had grown rich during the war. The veterans had made the sacrifices, but it seemed that others were reaping the rewards.

1919   Winnipeg General Strike gives voice to post-war dissatisfaction.

1920   League of Nations established, with Canada as a full member.

British Columbia becomes first province to end Prohibition.

1921   Minority government elected.

Agnes Macphail becomes first woman elected to Parliament.

Frederick Banting and Charles Best discover insulin.

1926   King–Byng crisis focusses on Canada's push for autonomy from Britain.

Imperial Conference leads to publication of the Balfour Report.

1927   Federal government allows for old age pensions, introducing government-run social assistance for the first time in Canada.

1928   Allied Tribes of British Columbia goes to Ottawa to argue for land treaty negotiations.

1929   Persons Case opens the way for Canadian women to be appointed to the Senate.

Stock market crashes.

Many Canadians who had jobs were also dissatisfied. During the war, labour unions had reluctantly agreed to reduced pay as their patriotic duty to the war effort. After the war, the cost of goods soared, and workers suffered. For many families, wages no longer covered the cost of rent and food. Confrontation between workers and employers was inevitable.

Workers Respond

Workers' demands for higher wages, better working conditions, and in some cases, the right to join unions, resulted in numerous strikes in Canada. Many strikes were long and bitter disputes. The coal and steel workers on Cape Breton Island, for example, were hit hard by the closing of wartime industries after the war. Many workers lost their jobs or were forced to accept lower wages. Most communities in the Maritimes, and in Cape Breton in particular, depended on a single employer for jobs, the British Empire Steel Corporation. Unemployment and long strikes

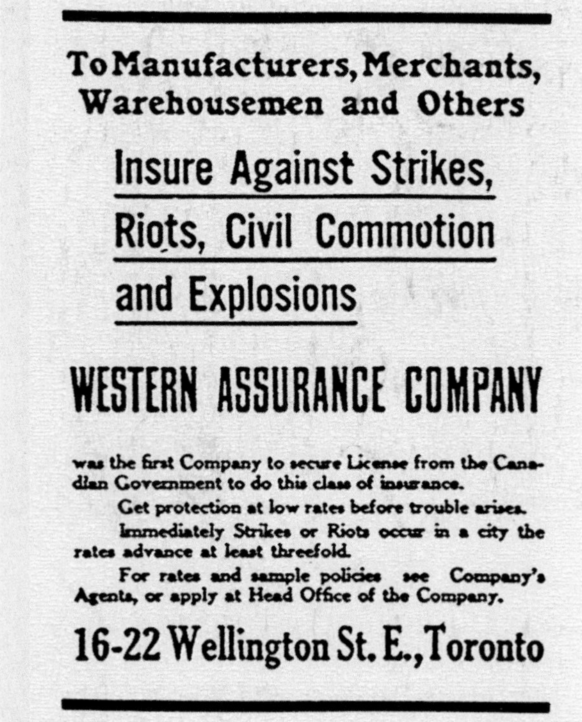

Figure 3-1 One response of business to labour unrest was strike insurance. Businesses could take out a policy that would insure them against damages during strikes.

Identifying viewpoint Who would have placed this advertisement? At whom was it aimed? What attitudes does it reveal?

meant economic hardship for everyone in these single-industry communities. For four years, the union and the steel corporation confronted each other in what became known as the labour wars. When the strikes turned violent, the company called in the provincial police and federal troops to break them up. In 1926, a Royal Commission criticized the labour practices of the British Empire Steel Corporation, but the commission's findings did little to ease the suffering and poverty in the Maritimes.

In western Canada there were also many strikes over wages and working conditions. Western union leaders were more **socialist** in their policies than union leaders on the East Coast, believing ordinary people should have more involvement in government. Some western union leaders were influenced by the 1917 revolution in Russia, where the Bolsheviks had set up a communist regime. Under **communism**, all the means of production (such as factories and farms) and distribution (railways) were publicly owned. There was no private or individual ownership of businesses or land. Unions in eastern Canada didn't always agree with the goals of union leaders in western Canada.

Nevertheless, at the Western Labour Conference in March 1919, union leaders from western Canada succeeded in founding One Big Union (OBU), which would represent all Canadian workers in one organization. The OBU's goal was to help workers establish more control of industry and government through peaceful means. The main weapon would be the *general strike*, a walkout by all employed workers.

The Winnipeg General Strike

All these tensions came together in Winnipeg, the financial centre of western Canada at that time and its largest city. In May 1919, Winnipeg's metal and building workers walked off their jobs. They were demanding higher wages, a shorter working week, and the right to **collective bargaining**. This would allow the union leadership to negotiate with employers on behalf of the union members. The Winnipeg Trades and Labour Council voted for a general strike in support of these principles. Thirty thousand people went out on strike, even though over half were not union members.

Winnipeg was paralyzed. There were no firefighters or postal workers and no telephone or telegraph services. There were no newspapers, streetcars, or deliveries of bread or milk. The union leaders urged strikers to avoid violent confrontations:

> The only thing the workers have to do to win this strike is to do nothing. Just eat, sleep, play, love, laugh and look at the sun. There are those anxious for the workers to do something which would provide an excuse for putting the city under martial [military] law. Therefore, once more, do nothing.

Source: *Western Labour News Strike Bulletin*, May 20, 1919.

Not everyone sympathized with the strikers. Business leaders, politicians, and industrialists formed the **Citizens' Committee of One Thousand**. The committee saw the union leaders as part of a communist conspiracy to overthrow the government. The federal government, fearing that this kind of disruption and protest could spread to other cities, decided to intervene. The Immigration Act was amended to allow foreign-born union leaders to be deported. The mayor of Winnipeg appointed special police, fired many civic workers, and had the strike leaders arrested. On June 21, strikers held a parade to protest the mayor's actions. The parade turned violent when the Royal North West Mounted Police and special police, armed with clubs and pistols, charged into the crowd. The resulting clash became known as Bloody Saturday. One striker died, thirty were injured, and scores were arrested. Defeated, the strikers returned to work. Their protest had lasted forty-three days.

What did the strike achieve? In the short run, there is no doubt that the union movement suffered a setback. Seven of the arrested leaders were convicted of conspiracy to overthrow the government and served between two months and two years in prison. Many striking workers were not rehired; others were taken back only if they signed contracts vowing not to join a union. Distrust and divisions between the working class and businesses grew deeper.

In the long run, the verdict is less clear. A Royal Commission set up to examine the strike found that the workers' grievances were valid. Gradually, much of what they fought for was achieved. Some of those involved in the strike took up political positions in which they could work towards social reform. For example, J.S. Woodsworth, a minister and well-known social reformer who was arrested during the strike, went on to found the Cooperative Commonwealth Federation (CCF), which later became the New Democratic Party (NDP).

ACTIVITIES

1. Explain the following terms: communism; general strike; collective bargaining.

2. **a)** What was the effect of the 1917 Communist (Bolshevik) Revolution in Russia on Canada?

   b) Why was the One Big Union seen as a threat?

3. Write a paragraph to explain the reaction of the Citizens' Committee of One Thousand to the Winnipeg General Strike. Remember the attitudes and values of the time.

4. Write a letter to the editor of a newspaper to explain why you think the Winnipeg strikers were, or were not, justified in their actions.

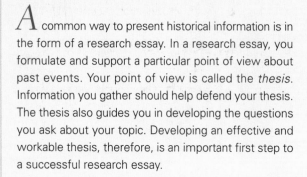

Developing a Thesis for a Research Essay

A common way to present historical information is in the form of a research essay. In a research essay, you formulate and support a particular point of view about past events. Your point of view is called the *thesis*. Information you gather should help defend your thesis. The thesis also guides you in developing the questions you ask about your topic. Developing an effective and workable thesis, therefore, is an important first step to a successful research essay.

Steps in Developing a Thesis Statement

1. Select a topic that is manageable. For instance, the 1920s as an essay topic is too broad, while something like an event in your community in that period may be too narrow.

2. Discover the basic facts about the topic you have chosen by answering the questions: who, what, where, when, why, and how.

3. Use this information to develop the essential question you want to answer about your topic.

4. Refine the question into a thesis statement. Your statement should tell the reader, in one clear sentence, the topic and the viewpoint you will defend in your essay. In your defence, you will have to respond to arguments against your thesis.

Statements on the Winnipeg General Strike

Source 1

... this is not a strike at all, in the ordinary sense of the term—it is a revolution. It is a serious attempt to overturn British institutions in this western country and to supplant them with the Russian Bolshevik system of Soviet rule....

Source: Winnipeg *Citizen*, May 17, 1919.

Source 2

[The] strike has been entirely misrepresented. I know the ... details intimately. Without hesitation I say that there was not a single foreigner in a position of leadership, though foreigners were falsely arrested to give colour to this charge.... In short, it was the biggest hoax that was ever "put over" any people! Government officials and the press were largely responsible....

Source: J.S. Woodsworth, August 25, 1921.

Source 3

It must be remembered that [Winnipeg] is a city of only 200 000, and that 35 000 persons are on strike. Thus it will be seen that the strikers and their relatives must represent at least 50 per cent of the population. In the numerical sense, therefore, it cannot be said that the average citizen is against the strike ... there is no soviet [revolutionary council]. There is little or no terrorism.

Source: W.R. Plewman, journalist, *Toronto Star*, May 23, 1919.

Source 4

... If Capital [business] does not provide enough to assure Labour [workers] a contented existence with full enjoyment of the opportunities of the time for human improvement, then the Government might find it necessary [to step] in and let the state do these things at the expense of Capital.

Source: H.A. Robson, Head of the Royal Commission set up to investigate the strike.

Applying the Skill

1. The sources above provide a number of different views of the Winnipeg General Strike. State each

point of view as a thesis regarding the strike. For each statement, make notes to support the thesis. You may want to read some other accounts of the strike to do this.

2. Using these sources and the information in the text, develop a question you have about the Winnipeg General Strike and formulate a thesis statement that reflects your viewpoint on it.

3. Support your thesis in a short essay using the following format:

a) Introductory paragraph: State your thesis and give the readers enough information to acquaint them with the topic.

b) Body of the essay: Include three paragraphs organized so that each one deals with a significant area of your research. A handy way to organize an analysis of a historical topic is by cause, events, and effects.

c) Conclusion: Summarize the key points in support of your thesis.

4. Share your thesis with others in the class.

New Challenges to Federalism

After the war, Canadian federal politicians were forced to face a growing development in Canadian politics—**regionalism**, or the concern of the various regions of the country with their own local problems.

Regional Protest

During the 1920s, the maritime provinces found their influence in national politics was declining. The population in the Maritimes was small, which meant this region had fewer seats in Parliament. Some businesses and banks were moving to Ontario and Quebec, while others were suffering because their products were no longer in demand.

Figure 3-3 This drawing, entitled *Woman in Mining Town, Glace Bay* by Lauren Harris, was done in 1925.

ARTS FOCUS

Thinking critically What does this drawing tell us about life for some people in the 1920s?

Figure 3-4 Although it gained fewer seats in the 1925 election than in the previous one, the Progressive Party held the balance of power, as neither the Liberals (Grits) nor the Conservatives (Tories) won enough seats to form a majority government. The Liberals won 101 seats, the Conservatives 117, and the Progressive Party 24 seats.

Interpreting a cartoon Is this cartoon effective in representing the situation? Why or why not?

Oil, for example, was gradually replacing coal as the most used fuel for heating and power. The maritime provinces had plenty of coal but no oil. Prominent business and political leaders formed the Maritime Rights Movement, which urged all politicians seeking office to promote policies that would benefit the Maritimes. Soon, however, the movement died away, without having accomplished much.

Other regional challenges came from farmers on the Prairies and in Ontario. Farmers, particularly those in the Prairies, were frustrated by the National Policy, in place since 1878. Under the National Policy, tariffs or duties were placed on foreign goods imported into Canada. Tariffs protected Canadian industries by making foreign goods so expensive that Canadians would choose to buy goods produced in Canada; hence, the Canadian economy would be strengthened. Western farmers felt alienated by this policy because it benefited the manufacturers in central Canada while forcing farmers to buy Canadian-made machinery. Farmers had no such protection, as their agricultural products were sold on the open world market. Farmers wanted free trade, which would abolish tariffs and allow farmers to buy cheaper, U.S.-made machinery. They also wanted lower freight rates and storage fees.

When neither the Liberals nor the Conservatives met their demands, farmers formed their own political parties. By the early 1920s, Ontario and the prairie provinces had all elected members of United Farmers' Parties to their legislatures. In some provinces these parties formed the government. In 1919, the federal Progressive Party was created, led by Thomas Crerar, a former minister of agriculture in Robert Borden's Union Government. The Progressive Party wanted a new National Policy based on free trade and public ownership of the railways. The party contested the 1921 election.

Canadians Choose a New Government

In the 1921 federal election, there were two new leaders as well as a new party in the race. William Lyon Mackenzie King was chosen to lead the Liberals in 1919. King had a reputation as a reformer and was an authority on social and economic issues. Arthur Meighen, a brilliant debater and long-standing Member of Parliament, was chosen to replace Borden as the leader of the Conservatives.

King and Meighen despised each other personally and had very different approaches to politics. King was conciliatory, always seeking the middle path that would offend the least number of people. Meighen believed in principles over compromise, and didn't care who might be offended by his stand on issues.

In the 1921 federal election, the Liberals elected 117 members, the Conservatives elected fifty members, and the Progressives elected an astonishing sixty-four members, mostly in western Canada. The Conservatives didn't win a single seat in western Canada; the Liberals won six. The Independent Labour Party won two seats, and the Labour–Liberals and Independent Liberals each won a seat. This meant that the Liberals were a **minority government** and needed the support of some of the opposition members to pass legislation.

Despite its initial success, the Progressive Party did not last very long. However, it was influential in bringing about changes to Canada's social policy. In 1926, for example, Mackenzie King was challenged by the Progressives to set up an old age pension. The Old Age Pension Act was passed in 1927. The basic pension was not generous, just $240 per year. Nevertheless, the act was an acknowledgement that government had a role to play in providing a network of social services for its citizens.

Canada's Growing Independence

After World War I, Prime Minister Borden had taken a number of important steps that raised Canada's profile internationally. Mackenzie King, once he became prime minister, continued to push for greater independence. In 1922, King refused to support Britain when it announced plans to invade Turkey. The following year, he insisted that Canada be allowed to sign an international treaty without the signature of a British representative. In 1926, he publicly challenged Britain over its influence on Canada's internal politics in what became known as the King–Byng crisis, and he participated in the Imperial Conference that led to the Balfour Report.

The King–Byng Crisis

Following the 1925 election, the Liberals held 101 seats, the Conservatives 116, and the Progressives twenty-four. This meant that the Liberals were forced to seek the support of the Progressive Party in order to stay in power. The following year, however, the Liberals lost the support of the Progressive Party as a result of a liquor-smuggling scandal in the Customs Department. The Conservatives called for a motion of censure—a vote of strong disapproval—against King's government. If the motion of censure had passed, King would have had to resign as prime minister. King immediately asked Governor General Viscount Byng to call another election. Byng refused King's request on the grounds that, constitutionally, the vote of censure had to be completed first. King was furious. Byng was eventually forced to call an election. During the campaign, King appealed to nationalist sentiments by claiming it was undemocratic for an official appointed by Britain to refuse to take the advice of the prime minister, who was elected by Canadians. King won the election. No governor general since has acted against the wishes of an elected prime minister.

The Balfour Report

It was at the Imperial Conference of 1926 that Canada made the greatest progress towards changing Canada's legal dependence on Britain. At this conference, the dominions of the British Empire (Canada, Australia, New Zealand, and South Africa) requested formal recognition of their **autonomy**, the freedom to govern themselves. A

Figure 3-5

Canada's delegation to the League of Nations in Geneva in 1928. Prime Minister King is third from the right.

special committee under the leadership of Lord Balfour, a respected British politician, examined the request. Its findings, published as the Balfour Report, supported the dominions' position:

> ... We refer to the group of self-governing communities composed of Great Britain and the Dominions. Their position and mutual relation may be readily defined. They are autonomous communities within the British Empire, equal in status, in no way subordinate one to another in any aspect of their domestic or external affairs, though united by a common allegiance to the Crown....

The recommendations of the Balfour Report became law in 1931, when the Statute of Westminster was passed by the British government. This statute formally turned the British Empire into the **British Commonwealth**. Canada was now a country equal in status with Britain, entitled to make its own laws. There were, however, two remaining restrictions on Canada's independence. Canada's constitution, the British North America Act (BNA Act), remained in Britain because the Canadian federal and provincial governments could not agree on an **amending formula**—the procedure for changing the act. As well, the judicial court of appeal for Canadians resided in Britain until 1949.

ACTIVITIES

1. What were the reasons for the rise of:

   a) the Maritime Rights Movement?

   b) the Progressive Party?

2. Prior to the 1921 federal election there were two parties (Liberals and Conservatives) represented in Parliament. Since then, three or more parties have arisen. From what you have learned, why do you think this happened?

3. What was the significance of the Old Age Pension Act?

4. You are a Canadian historian writing a biography of Prime Minister Mackenzie King.

   a) Write a paragraph describing how Canada's relationship with Britain changed during the 1920s, and the part King played in this change.

   b) Rewrite this paragraph as an election campaign speech for King.

The Economy Improves

Canada began the 1920s in a state of economic depression. By the middle of the decade, however, the economy started to improve. Wheat remained an important export for Canada, but there was also enormous growth in the exploitation of natural resources and in manufacturing. The demand for Canadian pulp and paper increased, and new mills were built in several provinces. Mining also boomed during these years. Record amounts of lead, zinc, silver, and copper were produced for export. These minerals were being used in the production of consumer goods such as radios and home appliances. The expansion of the forest and mining industries increased demand for hydro-electric power. Several new hydro-generating stations were constructed, providing cheap energy for Canadian industries.

The United States Invests in Canada's Economy

Prior to the war, Canada traded mainly with Britain. After the war, however, Britain was deeply in debt, and the United States emerged as the world's economic leader. During the 1920s, U.S. investment in Canada increased.

U.S. companies invested in pulp and paper mills and mines across Canada. The majority of these resources were then exported to the United States. For example, almost 75 per cent of the newsprint produced in Canada was exported to the United States, and most of the metals mined in Canada were used in U.S.-made products such as automobiles and radios.

Rather than lend money to Canadian businesses the way the British had, most U.S. investors preferred to set up **branch plants**—businesses owned and controlled by companies in the United States, but which operated in Canada. For example, by manufacturing cars in Canada for the Canadian market, U.S. car makers avoided having to pay Canadian tariffs.

By the end of the 1920s, the Canadian auto industry had been taken over by the "Big Three" U.S. automobile companies—General Motors, Ford, and Chrysler. Even the most successful Canadian company, McLaughlin, based in Oshawa, Ontario, had disappeared. U.S. companies also owned a high proportion of Canada's oil business, nearly half the machinery and chemical industries, and over half the rubber and electrical companies.

Figure 3-6 Foreign investment in Canada, 1919–1926.

Reading a graph How much did U.S. investment in Canada increase during the period shown in this bar graph? How much greater was U.S. investment than British investment?

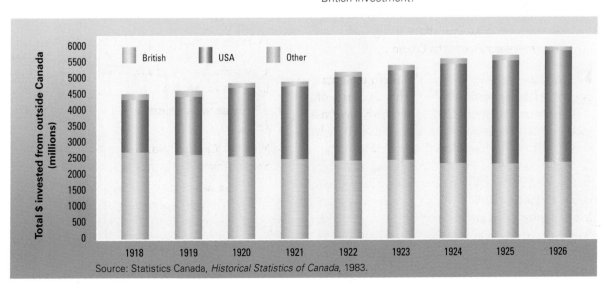

Source: Statistics Canada, *Historical Statistics of Canada*, 1983.

Many Canadians were so pleased with U.S. investment that they did not question what the long-term consequences might be. It was true that the United States enriched Canada's economy by extracting or harvesting raw materials (**primary industries**), but these materials were all transported to the United States for processing and manufacturing (**secondary industries**). It was the U.S. economy that benefited most from this development.

Bootlegging Across the Border

There was one manufacturing product that Canada exported in large quantities to the United States: illegal alcohol. During World War I, the Woman's Christian Temperance Union and similar organizations succeeded in bringing about Prohibition, which banned the manufacture and sale of alcoholic beverages in Canada. Alcohol, however, was still available for those with money, whether obtained as a "tonic" from a doctor, or from a "bootlegger"—someone who sold alcohol illegally, or who made "bathtub gin," homemade alcohol.

By 1920, the provincial governments had to admit that Prohibition was not working: it was too unpopular with most Canadians. War veterans, who were familiar with more relaxed European drinking habits, complained bitterly about the law. From 1921 on, most provincial governments decided to regulate sales of alcohol rather than ban the product. In a series of **plebiscites** (votes on a public issue), Canadians eventually adopted government-controlled liquor outlets.

In the United States, Prohibition continued until 1933. Canadians now had a golden opportunity to supply the United States with illegal liquor. Rum-running—smuggling alcohol into the United States—became a fact of everyday life. Ships from ports in the Maritimes and Quebec, speedboats from Ontario, cars and trucks from the prairie provinces, and salmon trawlers from British Columbia transported alcohol to the United States as fast as they could. There were thousands of tales of daring and wily tricks as the smugglers outwitted the U.S. Customs Bureau.

Rum-running was extremely profitable, and Canadians looked on the rum-runners with tolerance and even admiration for the way they flouted the U.S. authorities. Canadian governments seemed content to close their eyes to the practice. In fact, not all rum-runners were successful. Many got caught or perished during their great adventure.

Figure 3-7 Prohibitionists did not accept the opening of government liquor stores without protest. This ad appeared in British Columbia in 1925. It claimed that, in the previous year, British Columbia had spent just over $9 million on education while the people of the province had spent over $21 million on liquor. "Somebody's boy is required to keep the liquor business operating," it stated. "Shall it be yours?"

Urbanization

Canada's growing manufacturing sector brought more and more people to the cities in search of work in factories. In rural areas, farms were becoming more mechanized, which meant fewer family members and workers were needed to run the farms. This trend towards **urbanization**, which had started at the turn of the century, continued through the 1920s. By 1931, city dwellers outnumbered the rural population for the first time.

It was during this period that the modern Canadian city began to take shape. Businesses and industry often located in the city centre, making this area an undesirable place to live. It was the poor and working-class people who mostly lived in this part of the city, where conditions were crowded and unsanitary. Slums, already an urban problem, became an even bigger one. Smoke from nearby smokestacks polluted the air and contributed to health problems of workers and their families. More affluent families moved to tree-lined residential areas. Automobiles and streetcars made it feasible for them to do so, since they could get from their homes to the business district without difficulty.

Figure 3-8 These photos show the sharp contrast between rural and urban Canada. The gas station at Robson and Seymour streets in Vancouver reflects the growing urban population of Canada. Small farming communities, like this one in Saskatchewan, were still a major part of the Canadian economy.

Thinking critically Identify four differences between rural and urban life, based on these photographs.

The Role of Women

The 1920s was to be a new era for women in Canada. Hopes were high for reforms in health, education, and women's and children's working conditions. The reality, however, did not measure up to the expectations. In the 1921 federal election, only five women ran for office, and only one, Agnes Macphail, won her seat. Macphail was the only woman in the House of Commons until 1935. The four western provinces elected nine women to their legislatures, but the federal and provincial governments remained firmly male dominated.

The principal role of women was as wives and mothers. New labour-saving devices—such as the refrigerator, vacuum cleaner, washing machine, and electric iron—became more affordable to middle-class women, but this often meant that women were expected to maintain higher standards of cleanliness in the home. Many families still couldn't afford these modern consumer goods. Married women were expected to stay at home and raise a family. Those who weren't married had limited opportunities in careers. The professions of nursing and teaching were open to women, but these paid very poorly. A few women became doctors, lawyers, professors, or engineers, but most women who worked in business or industry held jobs as secretaries, telephone operators, or sales clerks.

Figure 3-9 As the first woman elected to the House of Commons, Agnes Macphail was under tremendous pressure. Her every move and word were scrutinized. She eventually started eating away from Parliament rather than face the stares in the House of Commons.

The Persons Case

The Persons Case of 1929 brought the issue of female political participation to a head. Emily Murphy, a well-known suffragist, was appointed a magistrate in Alberta. Her appointment was challenged on the basis that only "persons" could hold this office under the BNA Act, and that women were not "persons" in the eyes of the law. The Supreme Court of Alberta ruled that Murphy did, indeed, have the right to be a judge, but the matter did not stop there. Emily Murphy and four other women activists challenged Prime Minister Mackenzie King to appoint a woman senator and to clarify the definition of "persons." In April 1928, the Supreme Court of Canada decided that women were not "persons" under the Constitution. Murphy and her associates, nicknamed the "Famous Five," appealed to the Judicial Committee of the Privy Council in Britain. On October 18, 1929, the Judicial Committee declared its support for the women:

> The exclusion of women from all public offices is a relic of days more barbaric than ours.... To those who ask why the word ["person"] should include females the obvious answer is why should it not?

ACTIVITIES

1. What was the difference between U.S. and British investment in Canada?

2. a) Explain how tariffs imposed by the Canadian government on imported manufactured goods encouraged U.S. branch plants to locate in Canada.

   b) Most of the manufacturing branch plants were set up in Ontario and Quebec, as these provinces were closest to the manufacturing centres in the United States. How do you think this affected the trend towards regionalism in Canada? Explain your answer.

3. What have you learned about the attitude towards women in positions of authority in Canada during the 1920s?

A New Prosperity

The upswing in the economy meant that many Canadians had enough income to participate in the style of life that caused the decade to be known as the "Roaring Twenties." People bought cars and radios and went to the movies. Fads from the United States spread quickly to Canada. College students took to swallowing live goldfish, and six-day bicycle races were all the rage. Songs like "Happy Days Are Here Again" and "I'm Sitting on Top of the World" flooded the airwaves. Young people scandalized their parents with dances such as the Charleston, the Shimmy, and the Turkey Trot. American tourists drove to Canada in their newly acquired cars, and the tourism industry flourished. Jobs increased as people found work in services such as railways, hotels, and holiday resorts. Merchants welcomed affluent Americans. In 1929, four million Americans spent $300 million vacationing in Canada.

Tourists from the United States brought more than their money to Canada. Canadians were influenced by the newest fashions these tourists were wearing. For men, straw hats, form-fitting double-breasted suits, bell-bottom pants, bow ties, and slicked-down hair (in imitation of screen idols such as Rudolph Valentino) were popular. The "flapper" look dominated women's fashion. "Bobbed" hair, hemlines above the knees, silk stockings, and dresses that promoted the flat-chested look outraged the older generations.

Figure 3-10 These flappers were right in style and were considered the "bee's knees" by other young people.

Thinking critically Compare this photo with Figure 1-2 on page 6. How would you explain the drastic change in women's fashion from 1910 to 1925? Is fashion a valid indicator of social change?

Increased Mobility

In the 1920s, the automobile was beginning to change the landscape of the country, much as the railway had done earlier. The invention of the assembly line in 1913 by Henry Ford meant that cars could be mass produced inexpensively and quickly. The most popular automobile was the Model T Ford. One came off the assembly line every three minutes; all were identical and cost less than $300. As Henry Ford said, "You can have any colour you like, as long as it's black." Ford paid his workers five dollars a day, far above the average for those days. In return he wanted no unions in his factories.

In 1920, Canada had only 1600 km of top-rated highways, a figure that increased tenfold by the end of the decade. The Canadian Shield and the Rocky Mountains were physical barriers that delayed the construction of the Trans-Canada Highway. As a result, most of the better roads ran south to the United States. These closer north–south connections led British Columbia to change from driving on the left-hand side of the road (the British system) to the right-hand side (the U.S. system) in 1927. Another U.S. innovation linked to the automobile arrived in Vancouver in 1928 when the hamburger chain White Spot opened the first drive-in restaurant in Canada.

Aviation also expanded in the years after the war. Many veteran pilots became "bush pilots" who flew geologists and prospectors into remote areas to explore mining opportunities. The first aerial mineral exploration in Canada was in the Telegraph Creek area of northwestern British Columbia in 1925. Bush pilots helped make the rugged coast of British Columbia more accessible. Many pilots started businesses flying supplies to lumber camps up the coast.

One daring mission was made by Wilfrid "Wop" May, the World War I Canadian flying ace. May and fellow pilot Vic Horner volunteered to deliver an antitoxin to treat a diphtheria outbreak in a northern Alberta community. It was New Year's Day, 1929. After a harrowing flight through a blizzard in an open cockpit, they landed without skis on a snow-covered lake. The engine had to be thawed with a blowtorch before they could take off again. They returned to a heroes' welcome in Edmonton.

May also assisted the RCMP in one of the greatest manhunts in Canadian history, the hunt for Albert Johnson. Johnson, nicknamed the Mad Trapper of Rat River, was suspected of wounding an RCMP constable who was investigating trap lines. Following a shoot-out in the northern Yukon that left Johnson and one Mountie dead, May flew another seriously wounded Mountie to Aklavik.

Figure 3-11 Traffic accident in Toronto, 1929.

Thinking critically Give three possible causes of this traffic accident.

Improved Communications

By the 1920s, the telephone had become a standard household appliance. Telephone lines were shared by many neighbours, which meant anyone could eavesdrop—listen in on everyone else's conversations. Eavesdropping became daily entertainment.

Widespread use of the radio began to break down the isolation between far-flung communities. It soon became a necessity, bringing popular culture and entertainment into Canadian homes across the country. For farm families and other isolated communities, this was a revolutionary development. Smaller Canadian stations, however, soon found it difficult to compete with bigger, more powerful U.S. ones. By the end of the twenties, nearly 300 000 Canadians were tuning into U.S. stations for their entertainment.

Soon radio entertainment was rivalled by moving pictures—the movies. At first, movies were silent. An orchestra or piano player would provide sound effects to accompany the silent screen, while subtitles conveyed the messages and dialogue. The "talkies" arrived in 1927 with comedians such as Laurel and Hardy and the Marx Brothers.

Movies about Canada were made here during the early days, but Canadian-made films could not compete with productions from the big U.S. studios. Eventually Hollywood came to dominate the industry. In the absence of a home-grown industry, many Canadian actors, writers, and technicians were drawn to the glitter and glamour of Hollywood. Many were very successful. Movie star Mary Pickford, born in Toronto, became known as "America's Sweetheart."

Figure 3-12 The Mounties were a favourite topic with Hollywood. Mounties always caught the villain and got the girl.

Using evidence What stereotypes are used in this photo to portray the RCMP?

Innovations

Canadian Inventions, Innovations, and Inventors

During the 1920s, Canadians witnessed rapid changes in technology that had an effect on everyday life. *Electric washing machines*, *refrigerators*, and *neon signs* began to appear in Canadian cities. *Telephones* came into widespread use, with links to Europe in place by 1927. By 1929, three out of four families had a telephone, up from one in four in 1921. *Linoleum* covered wood floors and *aluminum* replaced iron for pots and pans. *Bobby pins* were invented in 1926 for the shorter hair styles.

U.S. automobiles came to dominate the Canadian market during these years. However, Canadian cars such as the *Durant*, a low-cost, four-cylinder "Star," managed to survive until 1928.

Frederick Banting was a medical doctor in London, Ontario. At the University of Western Ontario he developed a technique that eventually led to the isolation of the antidiabetic component of the pancreas. In the winter of 1921–1922, he and Charles Best were part of a team of scientists who discovered *insulin*. The discovery helped millions of people suffering from diabetes. In 1923, Banting won the Nobel Prize for medicine. ▼

In 1925, Ted Rogers from Toronto created the alternating-current *radio tube* which replaced the noisy, battery-operated model. In 1928, Morse Robb of Ontario invented the first electronic church organ. A more significant discovery, perhaps, given Canada's harsh climate, was the invention of the first *snowblower* by Arthur Sicard of Montreal, in 1927.

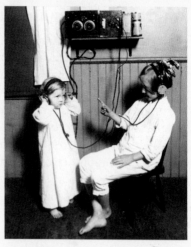

Early radios were crude. Listeners used earphones and strained to hear broadcasts made only 150 km away. Before long, radios were encased in handsome cabinets with speakers, so that earphones were not needed.

Armand Bombardier of Valcourt, Quebec, developed the *snowmobile* in 1922, when he was just sixteen. From 1926 to 1935, he improved on the first machine, designing vehicles that could travel on snow-covered roads, helping people in rural and remote areas to overcome the isolation of winter.
▼

Reginald Fessenden has been called "Canada's great forgotten inventor." He made the first public broadcast of music and voice in 1906. He redesigned Thomas Edison's light bulb, giving it the shape and material we use today. Fessenden also invented the *depth sounder*, which was used by sea vessels in the 1920s to indicate the depth of the ocean floor. The depth finder emitted a short burst of sound underwater. The time it took the echo to come back indicated the depth of the bottom of the ocean.

A New Canadian Art

The increased U.S. influence on Canada's culture coincided with the development of a new Canadian art movement. In 1920, the **Group of Seven** held an exhibition in Toronto that broke with traditional Canadian art. These painters were in tune with the new post-war national confidence. Rather than imitate realistic classical styles, members of the group sought to interpret Canada's rugged landscape as they saw it, using broad, bold strokes and brilliant colours. Although criticized by some critics in the early years as the school of "hot mush painting," they had gained wide acceptance by the end of the 1920s.

Emily Carr

On the Pacific coast, the best-known painter was Emily Carr of Victoria. She painted scenes of West Coast forests and Aboriginal life. At first, she gained little recognition for her work. She had almost abandoned hope of making a living from her painting when the National Museum in Ottawa organized a showing of West Coast art built around her work.

While she was in Ottawa, Emily Carr first saw the work of the Group of Seven. She was immediately moved by their bright, powerful images. Carr eventually had a show at the Vancouver Art Gallery and in eastern Canada. She also wrote, winning a Governor-General's Literary Award for *Klee Wyck*, a collection of stories of her life with British Columbia Aboriginal people.

Of the reaction to her painting, Carr said:

Local people hated and ridiculed my newer work.... Whenever I could afford it I went up to the North, among the ... woods and forgot all about everything in the joy of those lonely wonderful places. I decided to try and get as good a representative collection of those old villages and wonderful totem poles as I could.... Whether anybody liked them or not I did not care a bean. I painted them to please myself in my own way.... Of course nobody wanted to buy my pictures.

Source: Quoted in J. Russell Harper, *Three Centuries of Canadian Painting* (Toronto: Oxford, 1973), 29.

Sports as Popular Entertainment

The thirst for entertainment led to tremendous interest in spectator sports. Baseball became important to Canadians who were delighted to spend Saturday afternoon listening to the radio, following their favourite players. Professional boxing and rugby football were also popular, as were curling and golf. Hockey came into Canadian homes across the country when sportswriter Foster Hewitt made the first hockey radio broadcast in 1923.

Canadian athletes also excelled on the international stage. Vancouver's Percy Williams won two gold medals at the 1928 Olympics in sprinting events, and Ethel Catherwood, nicknamed "the Saskatoon Lily," won the gold medal in the women's high jump event, clearing 1.59 m. Canadian hockey teams won gold medals by lopsided scores at every Olympics, with the exception of 1936, during the inter-war period. Charles Gorman held seven world speed skating records before he retired in 1928, and John Myles set a new record for the Boston Marathon in 1926.

ACTIVITIES

1. Our economy is fuelled by consumers spending money on various items. What evidence is there in this chapter that the 1920s were the beginning of the modern "consumer age"?

2. a) List the technological developments that made the 1920s a period of great change in communications.

   b) Beside each development, make short notes on how the change affected society.

3. What does the interest in professional sports tell you about leisure time and the standard of living for Canadians in this period?

4. Go to the library and find a painting you like by Emily Carr or one of the Group of Seven. Explain why you think the painting you chose is "Canadian."

Did Canada Become More or Less Independent in the 1920s?

After World War I, Canada took a number of steps to lessen its political dependence on Britain. At the Imperial Conference in 1923, Prime Minister Mackenzie King reflected the growing support for Canadian autonomy when he said:

> The decision of Canada on any important issue, domestic or foreign, we believe should be made by the people of Canada, their representatives in Parliament, and the Government responsible to that Parliament.

In the arts as well, there was a growing sense of independence. The Group of Seven painted Canadian scenes that celebrated Canada's wilderness. In a review in the *Mail and Empire,* art critic Fred Jacob wrote of an exhibition by the Group of Seven, "In their work the spirit of young Canada has found itself."

Canadian magazines and literature also reflected a growing sense of national identity. The political magazine, *Canadian Forum,* first appeared in 1920. Political debates and works of Canadian poets and writers appeared regularly on its pages. As well, *Maclean's* magazine published Canadian stories and articles from across the country, being careful to use only Canadian spelling. Canadian novelists such as R.J.C. Stead, F.P. Grove, Martha Ostenso, and Morley Callaghan wrote novels about Canadians and their experiences. And poets such as A.J. Smith and Frank Scott wrote passionately about Canada and Canadian issues.

But while Canada had gained greater political independence from Britain, it was developing much closer ties to the United States economically. In 1922, U.S. investment in Canada topped that of Britain's investment for the first time. By 1929, nearly 60 per cent of foreign investment in Canada was from the United States. During the same period, close to a million Canadians moved to the United States in search of better jobs and higher pay.

Despite a developing Canadian cultural industry, most Canadians listened to U.S. radio stations, read U.S. magazines, watched the latest films from Hollywood at their cinemas, and drove home in their American-designed Model T Fords. Fashion from the United States became Canadian fashion. American service clubs, such as the Rotary, the Lions, and the Kiwanis also became popular in Canada. Even Canadian sports teams were being bought up by U.S. interests. The National Hockey League became Americanized as smaller Canadian cities were unable to compete following the inclusion of U.S. teams.

One historian described the close ties that developed between Canada and the United States in the 1920s:

> … in the immediate aftermath of the war, the United States had a … depression and Canada had a … depression too. Coal strikes broke out in the United States; coal strikes broke out in Canada. The United States embarked on prohibition; so … did almost all the provinces of Canada. The United States spawned the prohibition gangster; Canada spawned the prohibition rum-runner to keep him supplied.

Source: Ralph Allen, *Ordeal By Fire: Canada, 1910–1945* (Toronto: Doubleday Canada, 1961), 221–222.

So, was Canada more or less independent by the end of the 1920s? Had the United States simply replaced Britain as the country that controlled Canada's development? On the one hand, Canada's economy was very dependent on that of the United States. Canada was also awash in U.S. popular culture. How much the exposure to U.S. entertainment diminished a sense of Canadian identity during those years is difficult to measure. For example, the people of Quebec remained relatively untouched by the increase in U.S. culture in Canada. A different language and a fiercely protective church helped to ensure that most *Canadiens* remained outside the sphere of U.S. influence.

On the other hand, concern about U.S. cultural and economic domination made some Canadians even more determined to protect their identity. A Royal Commission in 1928 recommended that the Canadian government regulate private radio to ensure that Canadian content

Figure 3-13 *Solemn Land* (sketch), ca. 1918–1919, by J.E.H. MacDonald.

Expressing ideas In what ways does this painting represent a landscape that is distinctly Canadian?

remained on the airwaves. Although Canadians benefited from having a larger, more prosperous neighbour to the south, they never showed interest in becoming part of the United States. A British correspondent in Canada during the 1920s, J.A. Stephenson, observed:

> The people of Canada are imbued with ... a passion to maintain their own separate identity. They cherish the rooted belief that they enjoy in their existing political and social order certain manifest advantages over their neighbours.

> Source: Quoted in J.H. Thompson & A. Seager, *Canada 1922–1939* (Toronto: McClelland & Stewart, 1985), 191.

Analysing the Issue

1. How did new technology contribute to the spread of American popular culture in Canada?

2. In a speech in Vancouver in 1923, U.S. President Warren Harding made the following statement about the interdependence of Canada and the United States: "We think the same thoughts, live the same lives, and cherish the same aspirations...." Why do you think many Canadians listening to this speech would have agreed with Harding?

3. In a letter to the editor of a Vancouver newspaper, explain why you agree or disagree with President Harding's statement. Give examples of Canada's dependence or independence to support your argument.

up close

Two Canadian Sports Heroes

Lionel Conacher grew up in a deprived area of Toronto, one of ten children. He began his sporting career as a wrestler, but went on to become a baseball player, a star at lacrosse, a football player, and an NHL all-star.

Nicknamed the "Big Train," Conacher was known for his power, stamina, and speed. In the 1921 Grey Cup, he led the Toronto Argonauts to victory with a score of 23–0 over Edmonton. Conacher had scored fifteen of the points himself! On occasion, Conacher played in more than one championship game a day. One day in 1922, he hit a triple in the last inning of a baseball game, winning the championship for his team. Later the same day, he scored four times and assisted once in lacrosse, bringing victory to that team as well. As a hockey professional, Conacher played for several U.S. teams, as well as for the Montreal Maroons. In 1950, he was named the best Canadian male athlete for the first half-century.

Figure 3-14 Bobbie Rosenfeld (No. 677). At the Amsterdam Olympics she won a silver medal for the 100-m dash and was lead runner for the women's relay team that won gold. Rosenfeld was also joint holder of the world record for the 100-yard dash, which she ran in eleven seconds.

Bobbie Rosenfeld was born in Russia, but came to Canada as a baby and grew up in Ontario. At the age of thirteen, she beat the reigning Canadian champion in the 100-yard sprint. Later, she worked in a chocolate factory, but spent her spare time practising various sports. Rosenfeld went on to become a star at basketball, softball, hockey, and tennis, as well as track and field. In the 1928 Olympic Games in Amsterdam, she won a gold and a silver medal for Canada, becoming a national hero and the best-known Canadian woman of her time. Rosenfeld went on to become a sportswriter. In 1949, she was elected to Canada's Sports Hall of Fame. A year later, a poll of sportswriters named her the best Canadian female athlete for the first half-century.

Questions

1. What is the role of the sports hero in society? Give examples from this chapter and your own experience to support your opinion.

2. Compare and contrast Bobbie Rosenfeld's and Lionel Conacher's achievements as athletes with those of popular sports heroes of today. How would you account for the differences?

Missing the Roar

While economic and social conditions generally improved during the 1920s, many Canadians still battled discrimination, lack of political representation, and poverty.

Aboriginal Nations

Aboriginal nations saw little of the good life in the twenties. Veterans returning from the battlefields of Europe found that their contribution to the war effort did little to change their situation at home. Aboriginal people were still not classified as "persons" under the law. They could not vote in provincial or federal elections. In British Columbia, Aboriginal people didn't win the right to vote in provincial elections until 1949. It wasn't until 1960 that Aboriginal people across Canada could vote in federal elections.

Social and economic conditions on reserves were poor, and many who sought employment in the cities faced discrimination and hostility. Residential schools were a particularly difficult experience for many young Aboriginal students and their families. Although the people running the schools were often well-meaning, many students were traumatized by the separation from their families, the foreign surroundings, and—in some cases—the physical and emotional abuse they suffered in these schools. Some students adapted to the new way of life they were taught, but many more were unsuccessful in finding work or being accepted into Canada's European-based culture. Villages were also instructed by the government to replace traditional or family leaders with graduates of residential schools. This practice often divided the community between those who supported traditional leaders and those who sought to replace them.

In the early 1920s, the Aboriginal people in British Columbia challenged the federal and provincial governments on three issues: the *potlatch ceremony*, *cut-off lands*, and *Aboriginal title*.

The potlatch was an important cultural ceremony among certain peoples of the Pacific coast. At this ceremony, births, deaths, marriages, and other significant events were recorded in an oral tradition. The potlatch was a carefully planned event that involved families and even entire villages. It was also a way of establishing status in tribes.

Figure 3-15 Stoney Indians line up in 1929 to receive their first royalties on oil found on reserve lands. When oil was discovered on reserves, bands were legally entitled to a portion of the oil revenue, but few bands actually benefited. On the Stoney reserve, for example, each member received ten dollars. In total, the Stoney nation received just 12 per cent of the net profits per year.

Missionaries and the government saw it as an obstacle to assimilation, and the practice was forbidden in 1884. The following newspaper article shows a common attitude towards the potlatch ceremony at that time:

> The feasts were followed by wild rites, and devil-dances, at which the demon-scaring masks, huge helmets of cedar sculpture with grotesque carvings were worn.... The dark influences of the medicine men is still stronger than that of the missionaries. The ancient fetishism [reverence for objects believed to have magic powers] is still stronger than the gentle religion taught by the missionaries.
>
> Source: Vancouver *Sun*, August 29, 1913.

However, the government began to enforce the ban vigorously only after World War I. When the Kwagiulth people decided to hold several potlatch ceremonies in 1920, the provincial government arrested the chiefs responsible, and many were sentenced to jail terms.

Land claims, or **Aboriginal title**, was another major issue for Aboriginal people. British Columbia was unique in Canada in that only a few First Nations on Vancouver Island had negotiated land treaties. This meant that most of the land in the province had not been signed away to the government. Although large tracts of land had been set aside as reserves for Aboriginal people, the federal government had been taking land from reserves without the consent of the Aboriginal bands involved. These were known as **cut-off lands**. Aboriginal leaders wanted their claims to the land recognized by the federal government. In 1906, for example, Joe Capilano, a chief of the Squamish people, made the long journey to London, England, to present a land claim petition to King Edward VII. Several years later, the Allied Tribes of British Columbia, an organization made up of several tribes, appealed the federal government's actions. They claimed the removal of this land was contrary to the Indian Act, which regulated relations between the federal government and the Aboriginal peoples. The federal government responded by changing the Indian Act so that Aboriginal consent was not required for the transfer of reserve lands.

Under the leadership of Andrew Paull and Peter Kelly, the Allied Tribes of British Columbia continued to petition the government to begin treaty negotiations. It appeared before a joint committee of the House of Commons and Senate in 1927 and argued that the government should engage in treaty negotiations as they had with Indians in the rest of Canada. The Department of Indian Affairs defended the government's actions, stating that money spent on Aboriginal people had compensated them for the land they lost. The parliamentary committee agreed with the government and recommended that there was no need for treaties in British Columbia. The Indian Act was amended to forbid the raising or acceptance of money to pursue land claims.

For the governments of Canada and British Columbia, these issues were closed. For the Native peoples of British Columbia, however, they were far from resolved.

African-Canadians: Undisguised Racism

The entry of African-Americans into Canada had been discouraged during the heyday of immigration before World War I. Those who managed to move to Canada found that discrimination against minority groups was blatant. In Nova Scotia, the Education Act of 1918 provided for separate schools for "blacks" and "Europeans," a policy that remained unchanged until 1954. Racial segregation was openly practised and, in some instances, supported by the courts. In 1921, the Superior Court of Quebec ruled in favour of racially segregated seating in Montreal theatres, and in 1929, a black delegation to a World Baptist Convention in Toronto was denied hotel rooms.

There were also instances of tolerance. In 1924, Edmonton City Council refused to support an attempt to ban African-Canadians from public parks and swimming pools. In 1919, the Brotherhood of Railway Workers accepted black porters as members, becoming the first Canadian union to abolish racial discrimination.

Figure 3-16 The Ku Klux Klan, a secret fraternity founded in the United States, promoted fanatical racial and religious hatred against non-Protestants and non-whites. In the 1920s, the Klan established short-lived local branches in Canada, like this one in Vancouver in 1925.

Thinking critically What does the existence of this group in Canada say about attitudes at this time?

Immigrants

The war had increased tensions among various groups of Canadians. Immigrants from Russia and Eastern Europe were often accused of being socialist revolutionaries, and the government was constantly petitioned to deport them. The government adopted immigration restrictions, giving preference to applicants from Britain and the United States. Some Canadians didn't want restrictions on immigration for selfish reasons. Farmers, railway owners, and some other businesses welcomed immigrants because they would work for low wages in jobs that Canadian workers didn't want. Labour groups, however, supported the restrictions because unions saw the willingness of some immigrants to work long hours for low wages as "unfair competition."

Restrictions on Asian immigrants were particularly severe. In 1923, the federal government passed a law that virtually excluded Chinese immigrants to Canada until 1947 (see Counterpoints, Chapter 1). A Canada–Japan agreement in 1922 restricted immigration from Japan to 150 servants and labourers a year.

In 1925, when the economy improved, the government relaxed restrictions on immigration from many countries. The goal was to increase the population so that businesses would have a larger domestic market for their goods. Thousands of immigrants landed monthly at Canada's ports looking for jobs. Many found themselves in company towns or city slums, where they were forced to work in terrible conditions for pitiful wages.

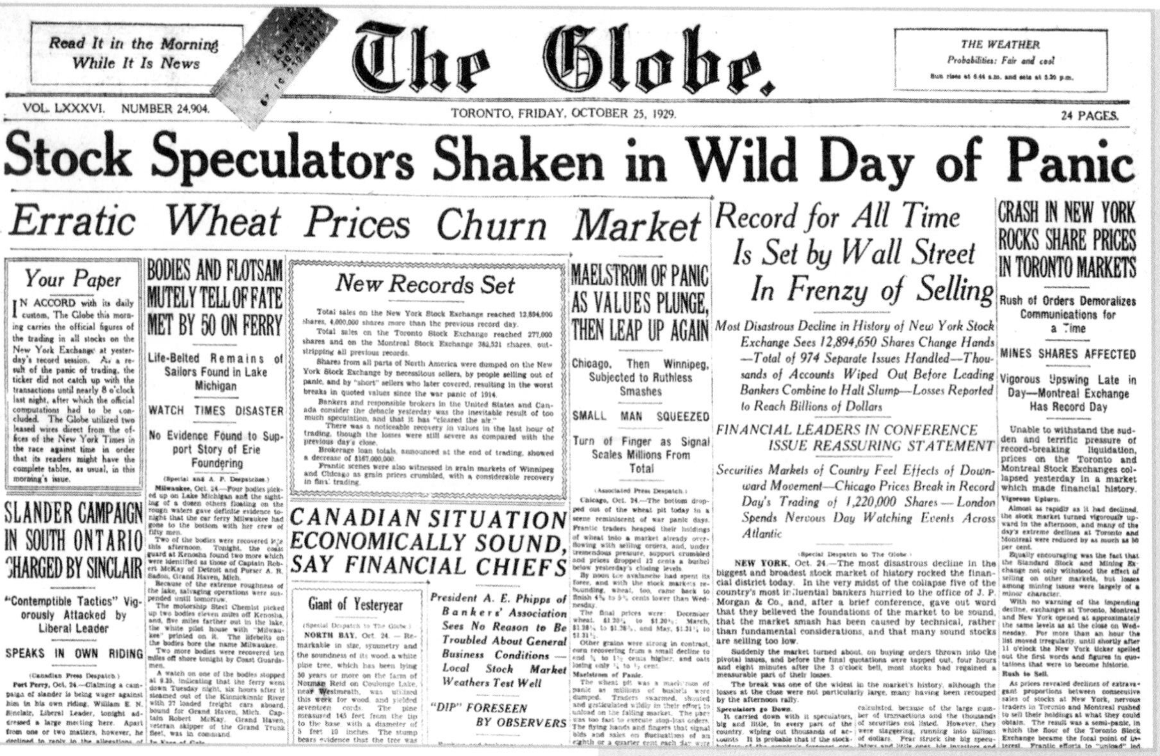

Read It in the Morning While It Is News

The Globe.

THE WEATHER
Probabilities: Fair and cool

VOL. LXXXVI. NUMBER 24,904. TORONTO, FRIDAY, OCTOBER 25, 1929. 24 PAGES.

Stock Speculators Shaken in Wild Day of Panic

Erratic Wheat Prices Churn Market

Your Paper

IN ACCORD with its daily custom, The Globe this morning carries the official figures of the trading in all stocks on the New York Exchange at yesterday's record session. As a result of the panic of trading, the ticker did not catch up with the transactions until nearly 8 o'clock last night, after which the official computations had to be concluded. The Globe utilized two leased wires direct from the offices of the New York Times in the race against time in order that its readers might have the complete tables, as usual, in this morning's issue.

BODIES AND FLOTSAM MUTELY TELL OF FATE MET BY 50 ON FERRY

Life-Belted Remains of Sailors Found in Lake Michigan

WATCH TIMES DISASTER

No Evidence Found to Support Story of Erie Foundering

(Special and A. P. Despatches.)

Milwaukee, Oct. 24.—Four bodies picked up on Lake Michigan and the sighting of a dozen others floating on the rough waters gave definite evidence tonight that the car ferry Milwaukee had gone to the bottom with her crew of fifty men.

Two of the bodies were recovered late this afternoon. Tonight, the coast guard at Kenosha found two more which were identified as those of Captain Robert McKay of Detroit and Purser A. R. Sadon, Grand Haven, Mich.

Because of the extreme roughness of the lake, salvaging operations were suspended until tomorrow.

The motorship Steel Chemist picked up two bodies eleven miles off Kenosha, and, five miles farther out in the lake, the white pilot house with "Milwaukee" printed on it. The lifebelts on the bodies bore the name Milwaukee.

Two more bodies were recovered ten miles off shore tonight by Coast Guardsmen.

A watch on one of the bodies stopped at 9.35, indicating that the ferry went down Tuesday night, six hours after it steamed out of the Kinnickinnic River with 27 loaded freight cars aboard, bound for Grand Haven, Mich. Captain Robert McKay, Grand Haven, veteran skipper of the Grand Trunk fleet, was in command.

New Records Set

Total sales on the New York Stock Exchange reached 12,894,000 shares, 4,000,000 shares more than the previous record day.

Total sales on the Toronto Stock Exchange reached 277,000 shares and on the Montreal Stock Exchange 382,521 shares, outstripping all previous records.

Shares from all parts of North America were dumped on the New York Stock Exchange by necessitous sellers, by people selling out of panic, and by "short" sellers who later covered, resulting in the worst breaks in quoted values since the war panic of 1914.

Bankers and responsible brokers in the United States and Canada consider the debacle yesterday was the inevitable result of too much speculation, and that it has "cleared the air."

There was a noticeable recovery in values in the last hour of trading, though the losses were still severe as compared with the previous day's close.

Brokerage loan totals, announced at the end of trading, showed a decrease of $167,000,000.

Frantic scenes were also witnessed in grain markets of Winnipeg and Chicago as grain prices crumbled, with a considerable recovery in final trading.

SLANDER CAMPAIGN IN SOUTH ONTARIO CHARGED BY SINCLAIR

"Contemptible Tactics" Vigorously Attacked by Liberal Leader

SPEAKS IN OWN RIDING

(Canadian Press Despatch.)

Port Perry, Oct. 24.—Claiming a campaign of slander is being wager against him in his own riding, William E. N. Sinclair, Liberal Leader, tonight addressed a large meeting here. Apart from one or two matters, however, he declined to reply to the allegations of

CANADIAN SITUATION ECONOMICALLY SOUND, SAY FINANCIAL CHIEFS

Giant of Yesteryear

(Special Despatch to The Globe.)

NORTH BAY, Oct. 24.—Remarkable in size, symmetry and the soundness of its wood, a white pine tree, which has been lying 50 years or more on the farm of Norman Reid on Coulonge Lake, near Westmeath, was utilized this week for wood, and yielded seventeen cords. The pine measured 145 feet from the tip to the base, with a diameter of 5 feet 10 inches. The stump bears evidence that the tree was

President A. E. Phipps of Bankers' Association Sees No Reason to Be Troubled About General Business Conditions — Local Stock Market Weathers Test Well

"DIP" FORESEEN BY OBSERVERS

MAELSTROM OF PANIC AS VALUES PLUNGE, THEN LEAP UP AGAIN

Chicago, Then Winnipeg, Subjected to Ruthless Smashes

SMALL MAN SQUEEZED

Turn of Finger as Signal Scales Millions From Total

(Associated Press Despatch.)

Chicago, Oct. 24.—The bottom dropped out of the wheat pit today in a scene reminiscent of war panic days. Frantic traders heaped their holdings of wheat into a market already overflowing with selling orders, and, under tremendous pressure, support crumbled and prices dropped 12 cents a bushel below yesterday's closing levels.

By noon the avalanche had spent its force, and with the stock markets rebounding, wheat, too, came back to finish 4⅝ to 5½ cents lower than Wednesday.

Maelstrom of Panic.

The wheat pit was a maelstrom of panic as millions of bushels were dumped. Traders swarmed, shouted and gesticulated wildly in their effort to unload on the falling market. The pace was too fast to execute stop-loss orders. The flying hands and fingers that signal bids and sales on fluctuations of an eighth or a quarter cent each day were

Record for All Time Is Set by Wall Street In Frenzy of Selling

Most Disastrous Decline in History of New York Stock Exchange Sees 12,894,650 Shares Change Hands —Total of 974 Separate Issues Handled—Thousands of Accounts Wiped Out Before Leading Bankers Combine to Halt Slump—Losses Reported to Reach Billions of Dollars

FINANCIAL LEADERS IN CONFERENCE ISSUE REASSURING STATEMENT

Securities Markets of Country Feel Effects of Downward Movement—Chicago Prices Break in Record Day's Trading of 1,220,000 Shares — London Spends Nervous Day Watching Events Across Atlantic

(Special Despatch to The Globe.)

NEW YORK, Oct. 24.—The most disastrous decline in the biggest and broadest stock market of history rocked the financial district today. In the very midst of the collapse five of the country's most influential bankers hurried to the office of J. P. Morgan & Co., and, after a brief conference, gave out word that they believed the foundations of the market to be sound, that the market smash has been caused by technical, rather than fundamental considerations, and that many sound stocks are selling too low.

Suddenly the market turned about, on buying orders thrown into the pivotal issues, and before the final quotations were tapped out, four hours and eight minutes after the 3 o'clock bell, most stocks had regained a measurable part of their losses.

The break was one of the widest in the market's history, although the losses at the close were not particularly large, many having been recouped by the afternoon rally.

Speculators go Down.

It carried down with it speculators, big and little, in every part of the country, wiping out thousands of accounts. It is probable that if the stock-

CRASH IN NEW YORK ROCKS SHARE PRICES IN TORONTO MARKETS

Rush of Orders Demoralizes Communications for a Time

MINES SHARES AFFECTED

Vigorous Upswing Late in Day—Montreal Exchange Has Record Day

Unable to withstand the sudden and terrific pressure of record-breaking liquidation, prices on the Toronto and Montreal Stock Exchanges collapsed yesterday in a market which made financial history.

Vigorous Upturn.

Almost as rapidly as it had declined, the stock market turned vigorously upward in the afternoon, and many of the day's extreme declines at Toronto and Montreal were reduced by as much as 50 per cent.

Equally encouraging was the fact that the Standard Stock and Mining Exchange not only withstood the effect of selling on other markets, but losses among mining issues were largely of a minor character.

With no warning of the impending decline, exchanges at Toronto, Montreal and New York opened at approximately the same levels as at the close on Wednesday. For more than an hour the list moved irregularly, until shortly after 11 o'clock the New York ticker spelled out the first words and figures in quotations that were to become historic.

Rush to Sell.

As prices revealed declines of extravagant proportions between consecutive sales of stocks at New York, nervous traders in Toronto and Montreal rushed to sell their holdings at what they could obtain. The result was a semi-panic, in which the floor of the Toronto Stock Exchange became the focal point of interest.

Figure 3-17 Front page of the Toronto *Globe* just days before the stock market crash.

Using evidence How does this front page show the different opinions on the state of the stock market prior to the crash? What words express concern? Confidence?

The Stock Market Crash

In the latter half of the 1920s, the North American economy was booming. In 1929, the president of the Vancouver Board of Trade, Robert McKee, reflected the sense of optimism in the financial community when he told a business audience that "prosperity was so broad, so sound, [and] so hopeful" that it inspired confidence in the future. And Canada's richest man at the time, Sir Herbert Holt, was calling for unending economic growth.

The prosperity, however, soon came crashing to an end. On Tuesday, October 29, 1929, the New York Stock Exchange collapsed. On that day, prices of all stocks fell quickly. The order to traders was to "Sell, sell, sell!" More than twenty-three million shares changed hands, but prices continued to fall. Everyone knew a disaster had occurred. As you will see in the next chapter, the stock market crash marked a shift from the prosperity of the 1920s to the crushing poverty of the **Depression** of the 1930s.

ACTIVITIES

1. Give examples to show that the federal government was pursuing a policy of cultural assimilation of Aboriginal peoples.
2. What responses from the Aboriginal peoples show that they were prepared to defend their rights?
3. What do the immigration policy, Aboriginal policy, and treatment of African-Canadians reveal about the attitudes and values of Canadian authorities in the 1920s?
4. Many immigrants and families from non–English-speaking areas "anglicized" their names in this period. From what you have learned, why do you think they did this?

LOOKING BACK

Develop an Understanding

1. Discuss why the decade of the 1920s is described as the "Roaring Twenties." Do you agree with this name? Explain your answer. If you do not agree, decide on another name.

2. Write a paragraph to explain how these events showed discontent with the situation in Canada after World War I:

   a. the Winnipeg General Strike

   b. rise of the Progressive Party.

3. List the advantages and disadvantages of foreign investment and branch plants in Canada. Use your list to create an illustration (e.g., a flow chart) showing the positive and negative impacts of foreign investment and a branch-plant economy.

4. Make a two-column organizer. In the first column, list the steps towards equality of women during this decade. In the second column, list the areas in which women still lacked equality.

5. Describe the effects of the new technology of the 1920s on the lives of Canadians.

Explore the Issues

6. Organize a class debate on the following topic: *Resolved—The 1920s "roared" for only the few.*

7. With a partner, write and record a number of thirty-second radio commercials designed to acquaint Canadians with the policies and grievances of the Progressive Party.

8. Imagine you are Agnes Macphail. Write a speech she might give in the House of Commons supporting the cause of women's rights. Include her experiences as the only woman in Parliament.

9. Your group has been hired by the Liberal government of the 1920s to report to them in confidence on the extent and impact of U.S. investment in Canada. Prime Minister King wishes you to conclude the report with three recommendations on how the government should deal with the issue.

Research and Communicate

10. Research one Canadian athlete or team of the 1920s and design a poster to show their accomplishments. Make a case for why Canadians should be more aware of their sports heroes.

11. A film is organized around a storyboard that illustrates and describes scenes in the order in which they will be seen. Construct a storyboard of five to ten scenes for a film about the Persons Case.

12. In a poll of historians in 1999, Mackenzie King was declared to be the best Canadian prime minister. Research the life of Mackenzie King and evaluate his position as "number one."

13. Research the dances, fashions, and behaviour of young people in the 1920s and the reaction of the older generations. Act out a scene in which a group of "flappers" and escorts is confronted by older people who are not amused by their dress or by their antics.

14. Research the role of J.S. Woodsworth in the Winnipeg General Strike. Include an account of his ideas for change for workers and society.

15. Imagine you are a soldier who was a factory worker before the war, or a nurse returning to Canada in 1919 after four years of war. Write a journal entry that expresses your hopes for a better life, and your reactions to the situation in Canada in 1919. Mention any changes you see.

4

The Thirties: A Decade of Despair

FOCUS ON

• What was the federal government's immediate response to the economic crisis of the 1930s?

• Which parts of Canada suffered most from the Depression?

• What remedies did the federal and provincial governments use to try to deal with the Depression?

• What were the programs of new political parties that arose in response to the Depression?

• What steps did the government take to try to protect Canadian culture?

• What events led to World War II?

Counterpoints Issue

• How involved should the government be in the economy during a depression?

Recluse by Bertram Brooker. Brooker was born in England and moved to Canada at the age of seventeen. He lived in Manitoba and Saskatchewan before moving to Toronto in 1921. *Recluse* was painted in 1939.

Expressing ideas What does Brooker's painting say about life in the Depression? How does the title relate to social and economic conditions in the 1930s?

Introduction

James Gray was a young man at the beginning of the Depression. This account of his family's struggle to survive those difficult years is a vivid picture of the hardships endured by ordinary Canadians in the bleakest decade of the twentieth century:

> For two months, half a million farm people huddled around stoves and thought only of keeping warm. If food supplies ran low they ate less. Only when fuel reached the vanished point would they venture to town for a load of relief coal.... Winter ended with a thaw ... and presently we were into summer which was much worse.... There was no escape from the heat and wind and dust of the summer of 1936.... From Calgary to Winnipeg there was almost nothing but dust, in a bowl that extended clear down to Texas. Within the bowl was stifling heat, as if someone had left all the furnace doors open and the blowers on.

> Source: James Gray, *The Winter Years* (Toronto: Macmillan, 1966, 1976), 108–111.

Falling Off the Economic Edge

The end of the economic boom came as a surprise to many Canadians. With only 4.2 per cent unemployment in 1929, it looked as if the good times would continue far into the future. Activity on the U.S. and Canadian stock exchanges was feverish. Between 1922 and 1926, Canadian companies issued new shares to a value of $700 million. Virtually every company's profits went up in these years, and share values went up too. Many investors were buying "on margin," that is, buying shares with only a 10 per cent down payment. It was assumed that when the prices of the stocks increased, as they had for ten years, the remaining 90 per cent would be paid. Loans for stocks were easy to obtain, and the rush to get rich quickly had driven the price of stocks up beyond their real value.

- 1929 N.Y. Stock Market crashes on Wall Street.
- 1930 R.B. Bennett becomes prime minister.
- 1931 Severe drought devastates the Prairies.

  City dwellers outnumber rural population for the first time in Canada.

  Japan invades Manchuria.
- 1932 Cooperative Commonwealth Federation (CCF) established.
- 1933 Unemployment hits highest level.

  Federal relief camps established.

  Hitler comes to power in Germany.
- 1935 On-to-Ottawa Trek occurs.

  Mackenzie King is elected prime minister.

  Italy invades Abyssinia (Ethiopia).
- 1936 Canadian Broadcasting Corporation established.

  Germany sends troops into the Rhineland.
- 1937 Royal Commission on Dominion Provincial Relations created.
- 1938 *Kristallnacht* takes place in Germany, as Nazi followers attack Jewish businesses.

  Germany annexes Austria.
- 1939 Germany invades Czechoslovakia.

  Germany and Soviet Union sign non-aggression treaty.

  Germany invades Poland.

When some cautious investors started selling their stocks in order to cash in on high profits, other investors rushed to follow their lead. Sellers panicked as the value of stocks fell dramatically. On October 29, 1929, the New York Stock Market collapsed, followed by the Toronto and Montreal stock markets. The effects of the collapse were devastating. Investors who had borrowed heavily to buy shares went bankrupt in a single day. The collapse of the stock market was the beginning of the **Depression**, a period of severe economic and social hardship, massive unemployment, and terrible suffering. The stock market crash contributed to the severity of the Depression, but it did not cause it. There were several reasons for the Depression.

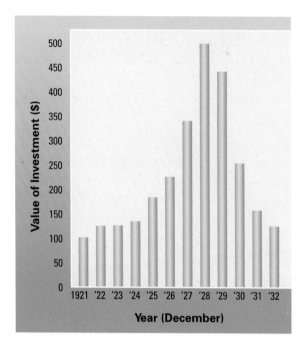

Figure 4-1 Value of $100 investment in industrial companies' stock, Canada, 1921–1932. Note that most Canadians bought shares after 1927.

Using evidence Suggest why most Canadians bought shares after 1927. Why would people who had bought shares later in the decade have suffered more than those who bought shares before 1927?

Leading Up to the Depression

One sign that the North American economy was in trouble appeared in 1927 when the price of wheat on the world market began to fall. More wheat was being produced than was being sold. Canadian and U.S. wheat farmers had depended on foreign markets, but many countries were producing their own wheat. As sales decreased, the income of farmers dropped. Soon many were unable to meet their mortgage and loan payments.

Many industries in the United States and Canada were experiencing a similar problem of overproduction. More goods were being produced than were being sold. At first, manufacturers continued to stockpile goods; then, they began cutting back on the goods they were producing.

This decrease in production led to layoffs in factories, which meant less income for families, and less spending on consumer goods.

To make matters worse, the United States had imposed high tariffs on foreign goods coming into the country. These tariffs were meant to protect the U.S. domestic market by making foreign items more expensive. However, this **protectionism** had harmful effects, as other countries imposed their own tariffs in response to the United States' actions. Tariffs caused a slowdown in world trade as opportunities for export shrank.

Another factor that contributed to the Depression was Germany's inability to meet its financial obligations under the 1919 peace agreement. After World War I, Germany's economy was in ruins. The enormous reparations—payments it was obligated to make to Great Britain and France to compensate for war damages—stunted its ability to recover even more. At the same time, France and Great Britain counted on German reparations to pay back their own war debts owed to the United States. Britain and France also borrowed from the United States after the war, and the United States was demanding repayment of these loans as well.

Canada and the Depression

The Depression illustrated a major weakness in the Canadian economy: its dependency on the export of primary resources. Two exports in particular—wheat from the prairie provinces, and newsprint from British Columbia, Ontario, and Quebec—made Canada extremely vulnerable to changes in world markets. Canada supplied 40 per cent of the world demand for wheat and 65 per cent of the demand for newsprint.

As international markets reduced their demand for these products, people in Canada's wheat and paper industries lost their jobs. Without jobs, they could no longer afford to buy such items as cars, radios, or telephones. Without customers, the people who worked in the factories producing these goods also lost their jobs. Within a year, millions of Canadians were out of work.

Canada's economy was hit particularly hard because of its close ties to the U.S. economy. The

Figure 4-2
Unemployed men of all ages line up at a soup kitchen in Vancouver, for food provided by a private charity.

Thinking critically Do you think the men in this photograph are accustomed to this situation? How would you describe this scene?

United States had become Canada's biggest trading partner and largest investor. Consequently, when the U.S. economy "crashed," Canada's economy was bound to feel the effects.

Desperate Years

While some wealthy and middle-class Canadians with secure jobs noticed little change in their lifestyle, many people working in factories lost their jobs. One by one, factories and businesses closed their doors. People were evicted from their homes because they couldn't afford to pay rent. The loss of a job also meant the loss of respect, as this one man explained in an interview years later:

> I never so much as stole a dime, a loaf of bread, a gallon of gas, but in those days I was treated like a criminal. By the twist in some men's minds, men in high places, it became a criminal act just to be poor, and this percolated down through the whole structure until it reached the town cop or railway "bull" and if you were without a job, on the roads, wandering, you automatically became a criminal. It was the temper of the times.

Source: Barry Broadfoot, *Ten Lost Years, 1929–1939* (Toronto: Doubleday, 1973), 17.

Thousands existed on "pogey"—government relief payments given to those who had no alternative source of income. The government did not make getting relief easy. People had to wait in line for hours and then publicly declare their financial failure. They also had to swear that they did not own anything of value and prove that they were being evicted from their home. If the applicants met these requirements, they received vouchers that could be used to buy food. The vouchers were never enough to cover expenses, and obtaining them was always a humiliating experience.

Private charities also helped those who were desperate, providing used clothing and meals. Soup kitchens were set up to help the hungry and homeless. But for some people, the economic hardships were too much to bear. One Winnipeg man returned home to discover that his wife, who had been living on relief, had drowned their son, strangled their daughter, and poisoned herself. The note she left said, "I owe the drugstore forty-four cents. Farewell."

Figure 4-3 As the Depression grew worse, more and more people found themselves out of work and destitute.

Developing understanding Why was unemployment a humiliating experience for Canadians? What does the sign in this photo mean?

As economic growth drained away, the Depression deepened. By the winter of 1933, more than one-quarter of Canada's workforce was unemployed. The country was filled with young, jobless, homeless men drifting from one place to another, looking for work that was never there. Penniless, they travelled across the country by "hopping" freight trains. Some men even rode on the roof or clung to the rods underneath the train.

After "riding the rods," the men would stay a day or two in the many shanty towns that sprung up in and around cities. These sprawling shanty towns were often referred to as "jungles." Sydney Hutcheson, a young unemployed man in the summer of 1932, recalls what life was like during these years:

> ...I made Kamloops my headquarters as there were hundreds of men in the jungles on the north side of the Thompson River right across from town.... I made three round trips across Canada that summer by boxcar.... I carried my packsack with a change of clothes, razor, a five pound pail and a collapsible frying pan that a man made for me in the jungles in Kamloops in exchange for a pair of socks. I also had a little food with me at all times such as bacon ends, flour, salt, baking powder and anything else I could get my hands on.

Source: Sydney Hutcheson, *Depression Stories* (Vancouver: New Star Books, 1976), 64–65.

Drought on the Prairies

The Depression affected the entire country, but conditions in the prairie provinces were particularly severe. The collapse of the wheat market had left families struggling to survive. At the same time, the Prairies were hit by a disastrous drought that started in 1928 and lasted almost eight years. In 1930, the winds began; by mid-spring of 1931, there were almost constant dust storms. Millions of hectares of fertile topsoil blew away. Dust sifted in everywhere. It piled in little drifts on window sills, and got into cupboards and closets. In a bad windstorm, people could not see the other side of the street. The semi-arid area in southern Alberta and Saskatchewan, known as Palliser's Triangle, was especially badly hit.

As if this were not enough, a plague of grasshoppers descended on the Prairies. They stalled trains and buses, clogged car radiators, and almost choked a dental patient to death while he had his mouth open.

In 1935, the federal government passed the Prairie Farm Rehabilitation Administration Act, which helped farmers build irrigation systems and reservoirs. But by this time, drought and poverty had forced many families to leave their farms and move elsewhere.

Figure 4-4 Windstorms like this one turned the Prairies into a "dust bowl" during the Depression years. Overcultivation of fields and poor land-use practices prior to the 1930s contributed to the erosion of the soil.

Using evidence What does this photograph tell you about life on the Prairies in the 1930s?

ACTIVITIES

1. **a)** What factors contributed to the Depression?

   b) Show how a reduction in consumer spending can result in a slowdown in the economy.

2. Why was the Depression so severe in Canada? What part of the country was hardest hit? Why?

3. Reread James Gray's description of the 1930s. Write a first-person account of the summer of 1936 on the Prairies.

The Disadvantaged

Canadians who had difficulty earning a decent wage when times were good suffered even more during the Depression. For women, there were few jobs other than domestic work, which paid just a few dollars a week. Some critics believed working women actually contributed to the Depression. In an article in *Chatelaine* magazine, one man argued that the Depression had two causes:

> …overproduction and the employment of women. Starting some Monday morning, every woman gainfully employed shall stay home and permit her nearest male relative to take over her job and her pay.

Aboriginal families on relief got only five dollars a month. They were expected to "live off the land," even though conditions on the reserves were so poor that they had been unable to do so for decades. In Vancouver, the Chinese population suffered greatly and by 1932, many were starving. One author writes:

Using Statistics in History

S tatistics are a primary source of evidence that historians rely upon to provide a picture of the past. Analysing statistics can help us understand the terrible hardships people suffered during the Depression. Analysis allows us to compare data and see how situations changed over a certain period of time, or from place to place. Statistics can tell us how many Canadians were jobless in different years, how much income was reduced over time, or how different parts of the country were affected by the Depression.

Examine the four sets of statistics below to get a better understanding of Canada in those years. Then, answer the questions that follow.

Source 1

Annual Unemployment Rate, Canada, 1928–1939

Year	Per Cent	Year	Per Cent
1928	2.6	1934	20.6
1929	4.2	1935	19.1
1930	12.9	1936	16.7
1931	17.4	1937	12.5
1932	26.0	1938	15.1
1933	26.6	1939	14.1

Source: J.H. Thompson and Allen Seager, *Canada 1922–1939* (Toronto: McClelland & Stewart, 1985), 350.

Source 2

Total Relief Expenditures, 1930–1937

Year	Relief ($ millions)	Percentage National Income
1930	18.4	2.2
1931	96.5	4.9
1932	95.0	6.0
1933	97.9	6.6
1934	158.5	8.4
1935	172.9	8.4
1936	160.3	7.6
1937	165.1	7.3

Source: Rowell–Sirois Report, Book 1, 174.

By [1932] destitute Chinese men, most of them elderly, were begging in the street.... The first ... Chinese deaths from starvation finally forced the provincial government to show some concern. It funded the Anglican Church Mission's soup kitchen..., but it expected a Chinese to be fed at half of what it cost to feed a white man on relief. Some destitute Chinese said they'd rather starve than accept relief.

Source: Denise Chong, *The Concubine's Children* (Toronto: Penguin, 1994), 61–62.

Immigrants were viewed with hostility when they competed for scarce jobs. Jews in particular were targeted, and they suffered from anti-Semitism—prejudice specifically against Jews. Many professions were closed to them, and employers often posted signs forbidding them to apply. In cities, many clubs and organizations forbade Jewish membership. Almost 10 000 immigrants were deported from Canada in the first half of the Depression. In 1931, the government put a complete stop to immigration.

Decline in Provincial per Capita Incomes, from 1928–1929 to 1932

	1928–29 Average $ per Capita	1932 $ per Capita	Percentage Decrease
Canada	471	247	48
Saskatchewan	478	135	72
Alberta	548	212	61
Manitoba	466	240	49
British Columbia	594	314	47
Prince Edward Island	278	154	45
Ontario	549	310	44
Quebec	391	220	44
New Brunswick	292	180	39
Nova Scotia	322	207	36

Source: Michael Horn, *The Dirty Thirties* (Toronto: Copp Clark, 1972), 175.

Source 4

Canadian Wheat Price per Bushel, 1925–1937

Year	Price	Year	Price
1925	$1.43	1932	$0.35
1926	$1.09	1933	$0.49
1927	$1.00	1934	$0.61
1928	$0.80	1935	$0.61
1929	$1.05	1936	$0.94
1930	$0.49	1937	$1.02
1931	$0.38		

Source: A.E. Safarian, *The Canadian Economy in the Depression* (Toronto: McClelland & Stewart, 1970), 196.

Applying the Skill

1. a) Which years had unemployment rates of over 15 per cent?

   b) Which three years had the highest expenditure on relief?

2. With a partner, calculate the total national income for 1930–1937. What happened to the national income between 1931–1935? 1935–1937?

3. Use the tables to help you determine the two worst years of the Depression. List and explain the evidence you used in reaching your decision.

4. Which province do you consider was hardest hit by the Depression? Explain.

Responding to the Depression

Prime Minister Mackenzie King was totally unprepared to deal with a crisis on the scale of the Depression. He believed the situation was temporary and that, in time, the economy would recover. When desperate Canadians turned to the federal government for financial help, King told them this was the responsibility of municipal and provincial governments. The financial strain of the Depression, however, had bankrupted many municipalities. When asked by the Conservative opposition why some provincial governments were not being helped by the federal government, King said he wouldn't contribute "a five-cent piece" to a Tory provincial government.

King never lived down this impulsive remark. He failed to understand that unemployment was a major issue for Canadian voters. King's attitude cost him the election of 1930. He lost to R.B. Bennett, leader of the Conservatives.

Bennett's Response

Prime Minister Bennett was no more in favour of government relief than Mackenzie King had been. He once told a group of students that "one of the greatest assets a man can have on entering life's struggle is poverty." Nevertheless, his government gave the provinces $20 million for work-creation programs. In spite of this spending, the economy did not improve.

Bennett had pledged to "use tariffs to blast a way" into world markets and out of the Depression. Bennett's "blast" was to raise tariffs by 50 per cent to protect Canadian industries. This enormous increase in tariffs did provide protection for some Canadian businesses, but in the long run, it did more harm than good, as other nations, in turn, erected trade barriers against Canada.

As the situation in Canada grew worse, Prime Minister Bennett became a target for people's anger and frustration. A deserted prairie farm was called a "Bennett barnyard"; a newspaper was a "Bennett blanket." Roasted wheat was "Bennett coffee," and "eggs Bennett" referred to boiled chestnuts.

The growing number of jobless, homeless men drifting across the country frightened many middle-class Canadians. Prime Minister Bennett also feared these men would come under the influence of the Communist Party. In 1931, the government banned the Communist Party and arrested several of its leaders, including Tim Buck, the party's general secretary.

The federal government also decided to create work camps for unemployed, single men. In British Columbia, the provincial government had already established work camps, and these were absorbed into the federal ones.

Working for Twenty Cents a Day

Work camps were usually located deep in the woods, so the men were completely isolated. Men

Figure 4-5 High tariffs were meant to protect a country's domestic market.

Interpreting a cartoon
What is this cartoon saying about Canada's protective tariffs? How did tariffs contribute to the stockpiling of goods? To the slowdown in world trade?

worked on projects such as building roads, clearing land, and digging drainage ditches. They were paid twenty cents a day and given room and board. The food was terrible, and the bunks were often bug-infested. Over 170 000 men spent some time in these camps. Red Walsh was one of those men. He described the conditions of the camp this way:

> We lived in a bunkhouse. So many men to a bunkhouse. Tar-paper shacks. Hard-board beds without a mattress. No sheets, just blankets. And the meals were very poor. The food itself we were eating could not be sold over the counter in a store…. There was nothing to do. You'd work your eight hours a day every day. There was nothing else. No recreation. No sports. Nothing like that.
>
> Source: Red Walsh, "On to Ottawa." In Gloria Montero, *We Stood Together* (Toronto: Lorimer, 1979), 24–25.

The On-to-Ottawa Trek

In 1935, over a thousand men left the camps in the interior of British Columbia in protest against camp conditions. They congregated in Vancouver. Under the leadership of their union, the Relief Camp Workers Union, the men decided to take their complaints to Ottawa. Thus began a protest that became known as the On-to-Ottawa Trek.

Crowding into and on top of freight cars, the trekkers rode through the Prairies, picking up more and more supporters along the way. When the protesters reached Regina, the RCMP confined them in a local stadium, allowing only the leaders to proceed to Ottawa.

The union leaders who met with Prime Minister Bennett had great hopes of being heard, but Bennett made his position clear immediately. He attacked the leaders as radicals and troublemakers. When he called one leader, Slim Evans, a "criminal and a thief," Evans shouted back, "And you're a liar, Bennett, and what is more, you're not fit to run … a great country like Canada." The delegation was hustled out of the prime minister's office at once.

Back in Regina, the RCMP were ordered to clear all the trekkers from the stadium. The trekkers resisted, battling the RCMP and the local police for two hours. One man was killed, many were injured, and 130 men were arrested.

Figure 4-6 The On-to-Ottawa Trekkers.

Gathering information Write three questions you could ask to find out more about the scene shown here.

How Involved Should the Government Be in the Economy During a Depression?

Before the Depression, North American governments kept their involvement in the economy to a minimum. This policy was known as **laissez-faire**. During the 1930s, however, governments were overwhelmed by the economic crisis of the Depression. They came under increasing pressure by the public to create work programs for the unemployed as well as to provide money to help those who were unable to help themselves: the poor, the sick, and the elderly.

John Maynard Keynes was a leading British economist who believed that, during a depression, the government needed to "jump start" the economy by spending money on programs that would put people back to work. Once working, people would spend money on consumer goods, which would increase the demand for these goods. Increased demand would mean people would be hired to produce goods, thus creating more jobs, more spending, and so on. Relief payments to the poor and destitute would also be beneficial, as this money would work its way back into the economy.

The U.S. president, Franklin Roosevelt, supported Keynes's theory. After he took office in 1933, Roosevelt introduced a "New Deal" that created numerous public work programs for the unemployed and for farmers. His most drastic action was the introduction of the Social Security Act. This act provided several social assistance programs, such as old age pensions for workers sixty-five years of age and older, unemployment insurance, and financial assistance for dependent mothers and children.

Under the New Deal, the U.S. federal government spent billions of dollars to get the economy working again. Roosevelt's easy-going manner appealed to voters, and in a series of radio talks known as "fireside chats," he built up their confidence in the U.S. economy. The New Deal didn't pull the United States out of the Depression. It did, however, help millions to survive, and it gave hope for the future in a time of national despair.

Not everyone agreed with Roosevelt's actions. The Republican Party, for example, criticized Roosevelt's New Deal:

> The New Deal Administration ... has been guilty of frightful waste and extravagance, using public funds for partisan political purposes.... It has created a vast multitude of new offices, filled them with its favorites, set up a centralized bureaucracy, and sent out swarms of inspectors to harass our people. It has bred fear and hesitation in commerce and industry, thus discouraging new enterprises, preventing employment and prolonging the Depression....

Source: Quoted in N. Barber, *A New Nation: The American Experience* (Toronto: McGraw-Hill Ryerson, 1989), 278.

To these critics, the New Deal meant a bigger and more intrusive government, higher taxes, and unnecessary restrictions on business activities. Most significant, perhaps, was the criticism that the New Deal was a waste of taxpayers' money and that the debt would be left to future generations to pay down.

Prime Minister Mackenzie King did not support increased government spending during the Depression, believing that, in time, the economy would improve on its own. King also felt that spending money on social programs during a depression did not make economic sense, that it was better to wait until the economy was strong before introducing these expensive programs. As he said in a radio interview in 1935:

> A house is not built from the top down. It is constructed from the ground up. The foundation must be well and truly laid, or the whole edifice will crumble. To seek to erect an ambitious program of social services upon a stationary or diminishing national income is like building a house upon the sands.

Source: Quoted in R.C. Brown and M.E. Prang, *Confederation to 1949* (Toronto: Prentice Hall, 1966, vol. 3), 249.

Figure 4-7 Roosevelt priming the New Deal pump.

Thinking critically What is the message of this cartoon? Why has the cartoonist chosen the image of priming a pump to describe Roosevelt's New Deal?

Prime Minister Bennett, as well, did not support Keynes's theory of government spending during a depression. Bennett was convinced that "…government is not here to subsidize idleness."

In a series of radio addresses leading up to the 1935 election campaign, however, Bennett surprised listeners, and his Cabinet colleagues, by coming up with his own version of a New Deal:

> …In my mind, reform means Government intervention. It means Government control and regulation. It means an end of laissez-faire.
>
> * * *
>
> In what way and to what extent must the government intervene? That is a difficult question. All I can tell you is that we will go just as far as necessary to reform the system and to make it effectively work again.

Source: Quoted in R.C. Brown and M.E. Prang, *Confederation to 1949* (Toronto: Prentice Hall, 1966, vol. 3), 244, 245.

Bennett promised Canadians a fairer tax system, unemployment insurance, workplace reforms, revised old age pensions, and support for farmers. Many voters regarded Bennett's change in policy as a desperate attempt to win more votes and not as a shift in his view of the role of government in the economy.

Since the Depression, the role of the government in Canada's economy has been an important debate. Some Canadians believe that, even if the country is not experiencing a depression, it is the government's duty to provide basic services such as education, health, unemployment benefits, and other kinds of social assistance to those who need it. These people believe in a *welfare state*, where the government should actively look after the well-being of its citizens. Other Canadians support a *competitive state*, where the role of government is to create an atmosphere of healthy competition for businesses by cutting spending on social programs and reducing taxes. Most Canadians believe in a *mixed economy* where the role of government is to provide a certain level of social services, yet not be overly intrusive in planning and running the economy.

Analysing the Issue

1. Draw a flow chart to illustrate Keynes's theory of how government spending could lift a country out of a depression.

2. In a two-column organizer, summarize the arguments for and against government intervention in the economy:

   a) in a period of economic slowdown

   b) in a period of economic growth.

3. How did Roosevelt's New Deal reflect Keynes's theories? Bennett's "new deal"?

4. What did Bennett mean by "the government is not here to subsidize idleness"?

5. Canadian governments spent the 1990s trying to reduce government spending and cut national and provincial debts. Research the view of the major political parties on the issue of government spending. Decide which party you might be inclined to support on this issue, and list your reasons for doing so. Share your findings with the class.

Trouble in Vancouver

One of the last protests by the unemployed during the Depression was in Vancouver. When the federal government closed relief camps in 1937 and the provincial government reduced relief payments, many men were left destitute. In protest against the lack of government support, these men would conduct "sit-ins" at various buildings until the government responded to their complaints. In April, 1600 protesters occupied the Vancouver Art Gallery, the main post office, and the Georgia Hotel. Most of the protesters were convinced to end their sit-in without incident. At the post office, however, the men refused to leave; they were eventually evicted with tear gas. For the next two days there were battles between police and the "sitdowners," causing much damage to storefronts in the area.

Figure 4-8 Relief camps like this one in British Columbia were established by the federal government between 1932 and 1936.

ACTIVITIES

1. What seemed to be the government's attitude towards those people who had lost their jobs? Why do you think this was the case? Do you think this attitude exists today towards the unemployed?

2. What did people have to do to qualify for "pogey"? Why do you think people were given vouchers instead of cash?

3. Why did Mackenzie King fail to win the election in 1930? Write a press release from the prime minister's office explaining why Prime Minister King is not in favour of relief payments. Include initiatives his government has taken to fight employment.

4. Write a paragraph describing conditions in Vancouver's Chinese district during the Depression. Explain why conditions were so harsh. Include information you have learned from earlier chapters.

Politics of Protest

As Ottawa struggled to find ways of coping with the Depression, some Canadians looked to alternative parties for solutions. One party formed in the West in 1932 was the Cooperative Commonwealth Federation (CCF). It appealed to a wide variety of Canadians who were dissatisfied with the government's response to the Depression. They included farmers, labourers, socialists, intellectuals, and discontented Liberals. Their leader was J.S. Woodsworth.

The CCF was a socialist party. In its platform, the Regina Manifesto, the party stated its support for public ownership of key industries. It also supported social programs to assist people in need of money: the elderly, the unemployed, the homeless, the sick, and other citizens unable to support themselves. Woodsworth also urged the government to spend money on public works in order to create employment. The CCF did not win many seats in the 1930s, but it did provide a clear alternative to the policies of the mainstream

Speech bubble: WE PROPOSE TO TAKE OUR FIRST, DEFINITE STEP TOWARD THE ESTABLISHMENT OF SOCIAL CREDIT

Figure 4-9 William Aberhart came to power based on the popularity of his theory of social credit.

Interpreting a cartoon What is this cartoonist's opinion of the soundness of social credit?

parties. The CCF was the forerunner of the New Democratic Party.

In the 1935 election in Alberta, the Social Credit Party, led by William Aberhart, won a landslide victory. "Bible Bill" Aberhart was a charismatic preacher and high school teacher in Calgary. He publicized the social credit theory in his weekly radio program, "Voices of the Prairies." Social credit was based on the belief that capitalism was a wasteful economic system. Under capitalism, banks hoarded money, preventing customers from buying the abundant goods that capitalism produced. Aberhart felt that the government should release money into the economy so that people could spend it. The theory of social credit appealed to many people from Alberta because the Depression had devastated their economy and they resented the power and control of the banks in Central Canada.

Aberhart promised each citizen a "basic dividend" of twenty-five dollars a month to buy necessities. The federal government challenged the right of a province to issue its own currency, and social credit was disallowed by the Supreme Court. Despite this setback, the popularity of the Social Credit Party never dimmed. It remained in power in Alberta until 1971 under Aberhart's successors, Ernest Manning and Harry Strom.

Provincial Solutions

During the Depression, many voters expressed their dissatisfaction with government inaction by voting out ruling provincial parties. In Ontario, the provincial Liberals came to power in 1934, the first time in twenty-nine years. The Liberal leader was a populist farmer, Mitch Hepburn, who won wide support by championing the causes of "the little man." He railed against big business and was fond of flamboyant gestures, such as the sale of the provincial fleet of automobiles. Hepburn was at heart a conservative, however, and did little for the unemployed. He was also involved in the ruthless suppression of strikes.

In Quebec, Maurice Duplessis, a former Conservative, brought the newly formed Union Nationale party to power in 1936. The Union Nationale was a nationalistic French-Canadian party that relied upon the support of the Roman Catholic Church and rural voters. Duplessis blamed many of Quebec's social and economic problems on the English minority in Quebec, which controlled the province's economy. During his first term, however, Duplessis's promises of reform evaporated, and he did little to improve economic and social conditions in Quebec. With one interruption, he remained premier until 1959.

In British Columbia, Premier Dufferin Pattullo, a Liberal, was elected in 1933. Pattullo, too, was a strong believer in greater provincial spending power. He promised voters a "Little New Deal," based on the New Deal in the United States. He introduced reforms to shorten the work day, increase the minimum wage, and increase relief payments by 20 per cent. Public works projects were launched, most notably the Fraser River bridge at New Westminster and a new city hall for Vancouver. Pattullo's projects were short lived, however, as the federal government challenged his authority to introduce programs that were considered to be in the federal domain.

A Change in Government

By 1935, voters were fed up with Bennett's inability to deal with the crisis of the Depression. In the federal election, they returned Mackenzie King to power. Five years in opposition did little to change King's stand on government intervention in

Figure 4-10 Vancouver's city hall was built as part of a public works project.

up close

Mackenzie King and R.B. Bennett

William Lyon Mackenzie King was one of the most dominant political leaders in Canadian history. He was prime minister of Canada for twenty-two years, from 1921 to 1930, save for a few months in 1926, and from 1935 to 1948. King was a highly educated man who had studied political economy at Harvard University.

In his day, King was notorious for dull and ambiguous speeches that blurred the issues and seemed to promise everything to everyone. These speeches infuriated many listeners. In fact, King was a skilled negotiator who wanted desperately to keep Canada united—French and English, the different regions, social classes—and his vague manner was a deliberate technique to try to please everyone. King was Canada's prime minister during World War II; his friendships with British Prime Minister Winston Churchill and U.S. President Franklin Roosevelt helped strengthen the relationship among the Allies.

After King's death, it was discovered that this apparently colourless man had led a secret life. He had kept a detailed personal diary from his student days in the 1890s to his death in 1950. His diaries revealed that King was a believer in spiritualism. He held seances in which he spoke to the dead, especially to his mother and his dog Pat.

Richard Bedford Bennett, Canada's prime minister during the darkest days of the Depression, was a millionaire. Like King, he too was a bachelor; he made his home in Ottawa in a suite occupying a whole floor of the luxurious Château Laurier Hotel. It was small wonder that poverty-stricken Canadians felt little affection for him.

Bennett was hated by many for his failure to find a solution to the bad times. After his death, however, proof of his compassion appeared. Thousands of desperate Canadians had written to the prime minister asking for help, with letters like the following:

Figure 4-11 Mackenzie King and his dog Pat.

Figure 4-12 R.B. Bennett.

Dear Sir, — I am a girl thirteen years old and I have to go to school every day its very cold now already and I haven't got a coat to put on. My parents can't afford to buy me anything for this winter. I have to walk to school four and a half miles every morning and night and I'm awfully cold every day. Would you be so kind to send me enough money so I could get one.

Secretly, Bennett sent many of these people five dollars of his own money—a significant sum in those days. His generosity was uncovered in his private papers only after he died.

Questions

1. Do you think King's interest in spiritualism affected his ability to function as prime minister? Is it necessary to know such private details to evaluate his role in Canadian history?

2. How was Bennett perceived by Canadians during the Depression? Do you think this image of him was justified? Explain your answer.

the economy. His views clashed with the findings of a commission he had set up to examine the state of unemployment in Canada in 1936. The National Employment Commission found that unemployment was a national problem, and it recommended the federal government spend millions of dollars on job creation and training programs. King ended up spending only a fraction of what the commission had recommended on job-creation schemes.

Increased Tension in Federal–Provincial Relations

King created another Royal Commission in 1937. The Rowell–Sirois Commission, named after its two chairpersons, was to examine the thorny issue of federal–provincial relations.

The unemployment crisis of the Depression had caused a great deal of tension between the federal and provincial governments. There was disagreement over which government had the right to collect tax money and which government should pay for social and employment assistance. The Rowell–Sirois Commission recommended that the federal government have more control over taxation. The federal government would then give the poorer provinces grants or **equalization payments** to ensure that every province was able to offer its citizens the same level of services. The Commission also recommended that the federal government bear the responsibility of unemployment insurance and other social benefits such as pensions.

The wealthier provinces did not like the idea of equalization payments because they did not want their tax dollars going to other provinces. The provinces also felt that many of the Commission's recommendations would mean a loss of provincial power. By the time the Commission made its report, the economy had started to turn around. More people were finding jobs, and there was a mood of cautious optimism throughout the country. Canada's involvement in World War II meant most of the Commission's recommendations were either pushed aside indefinitely or adopted many years later.

ACTIVITIES

1. List the political parties that were started during the Depression. State who were the parties' supporters; their leaders; and their policies.
2. How did federal–provincial relations make it difficult for provincial governments to deal with the problems of the Depression? Give examples from British Columbia and Alberta.
3. What were the main recommendations of the Rowell–Sirois Commission? Why did the wealthier provinces dislike these recommendations?

Distractions from Despair

Through the Depression, there was one aspect of life that changed little: entertainment. Movies, magazines, and the radio remained enormously popular. They provided romance, adventure, and glamour to millions of people whose lives had become a series of hardships.

Radio was particularly popular during the Depression. Initially, Canadian audiences preferred syndicated U.S. shows, such as a western entitled "The Lone Ranger" and big-band entertainment programs, because they were more sophisticated than Canadian programs at that time. In an effort to win over Canadian listeners, the federal government created a public radio service, which became the Canadian Broadcasting Corporation (CBC) in 1936. The CBC ran Canadian-produced music and entertainment programs in French and English. French programming in Quebec was very popular, but many English-speaking listeners still tuned in to popular U.S. shows.

In 1934, the birth of the Dionne quintuplets brought a welcome distraction from the grim realities of the Depression. Born in Corbeil, northern Ontario, they quickly became an international sensation. When their poverty-stricken parents were judged incapable of looking after the "miracle babies," the five girls were taken into the care of the Ontario government.

The Dionne girls were put on display to the public, and over three million people visited the

Figure 4-13 The establishment of a public radio service provided an opportunity for Canadian talent to develop. One particularly popular program was "The Happy Gang," a variety show that was broadcast from coast to coast from 1937 to 1959.

specially built hospital where they were raised. Visitors could watch the daily lives of the quints behind a one-way screen. The Ontario government earned millions of dollars from this tourist attraction. Hollywood fictionalized the Dionnes' story in three different movies, and hundreds of businesses used images of the quints to endorse their products. Decades later, it became clear that the quints had been denied normal lives and had seen little of the money the government had supposedly set aside for them.

The conservationist Grey Owl was another Canadian figure who achieved popularity and world fame. When he died in Saskatchewan in 1938, however, the secret of his life became known: the famous "Apache" naturalist was actually an Englishman named Archie Belaney. He had moved to Canada at age seventeen in 1906 and took on the identity of a Canadian Aboriginal. He wore buckskin clothing, darkened his skin, and married an Iroquois woman, one of a number of women he married in his lifetime.

Grey Owl devoted the latter part of his life to the preservation of the northern Canadian forests and the disappearing beaver. His writings and speaking tours promoting conservation made him

Figure 4-14 Grey Owl credited his wife, Anahareo, with convincing him to stop trapping and work for the preservation of the beaver and the wilderness that was its habitat.

the most famous Canadian of his day. His books, such as *The Adventures of Sajo and Her Beaver People*, became best-sellers. He made movies, and dined with prime ministers and royalty.

The Rise of Dictatorships

As Canada and the United States struggled to cope with economic hardship during the Depression, other countries were experiencing enormous political and social upheaval. The economies of most European countries never recovered from World War I, and the Depression made matters even worse. Unemployment was high, food was often scarce, and lawlessness became a major problem. People became divided over how these problems should be solved. Some believed communism was the only solution to the economic and social suffering. Others abhorred the idea of public ownership, believing a strong military was needed to restore law and order. The result was the rise of several leaders who, once in power, proved to be powerful dictators who suppressed all forms of opposition and dissension.

In the Soviet Union, Josef Stalin took over as leader of the Communist Party after the death of Lenin, the leader of the 1917 Revolution. Stalin, "the man of steel," was a ruthless and cruel leader whose agricultural and economic policies caused the death of millions of Soviet workers. Under his leadership, the Soviet Union became a **totalitarian state**, with every aspect of people's lives controlled by the Communist Party.

In Italy, Benito Mussolini, or Il Duce ("the leader") came to power in 1922. Mussolini created a **fascist** government. Fascist governments are opposed to democracy, are extremely nationalistic, and rely on military and police power to maintain absolute control. They control all media, and use propaganda to promote the ideals of the state. Soon, there were fascist parties based on Mussolini's system in many countries. The most powerful fascist party, however, was the German National Socialist party, or Nazi Party, under the leadership of Adolf Hitler.

Germany After the War

Since the end of World War I, Germany had grown increasingly unhappy with the terms of the Treaty of Versailles. It bitterly resented the "war guilt" clause that required it to make reparations to other countries. The German economy had been ruined by the war; in order to make reparations, the government had begun printing large amounts of money in the early 1920s. As a result, the value of the German currency declined and inflation spiralled. In other words, German money became worth less and less, while the prices of basic goods increased rapidly.

To control this inflation, Britain, France, and the United States agreed to give better terms for Germany's reparation payments. Germany made a modest recovery. When world stock markets collapsed in 1929, however, the weakened German economy was affected more than most countries.

Figure 4-15 This photograph, taken in 1923, shows a German woman using several million marks to fuel her stove.

Using evidence What can you conclude about the value of German currency from this photograph?

Hitler Comes to Power

Since 1923, Hitler and his followers had been gathering support by criticizing the weak German government and the humiliating terms of the Treaty of Versailles. It was the Depression, however, that provided the conditions for his rise to power. Hitler and his Nazi Party claimed they had the solutions to bring Germany out of the Depression and make it a great nation again. In January 1933, Hitler became Chancellor of Germany, and by March, his party had won control of the German parliament. Once in power, the Nazi government defied the terms of the Treaty of Versailles by stopping all reparation payments. It also started a massive expansion of the armed forces, an action that violated the terms of the peace treaty. Hitler subsidized farmers to help rebuild their farms, and poured money into public projects such as the building of the *Autobahn*, a network of expressways running across the country. To the delight of

the German people, unemployment went down and the economy started to improve.

At the same time, the Nazis abolished all other political parties in the country. Trade unions were banned. Hitler became known as *der Führer* ("the leader"). Like Stalin and Mussolini, Hitler was a ruthless dictator who ruled his country through intimidation and fear. Not all Germans supported him, but no one was free to oppose him or his party without risking severe punishment.

The Nazi Party was deeply racist. Its members believed that the German people were a

Figure 4-16 The Nazis were brilliant propagandists, presenting selected information and using symbolism and pageantry to appeal to the emotions of the public.

Gathering information What methods did the Nazis use at their rallies? What atmosphere or mood do you think they were trying to create?

"master race" composed of Aryans, a supposedly "pure" race of northern Europeans. Non-Aryans, who included Jews, Roma (Gypsies), and Slavs, were considered to be inferior. People with mental or physical disabilities were despised because they destroyed the image of the "master race." The Nazis persecuted these groups. Communists and homosexuals were also targeted. For example, the government prohibited these people from teaching or attending schools and universities, holding government office, practising professions, or writing books. The Nazis also encouraged mobs to assault members of these groups and destroy their property.

One of the most notable of these occasions was November 9, 1938, when Nazi mobs attacked Jewish businesses across Germany. Afterwards, sidewalks in many parts of the country were covered with broken glass from windows, giving the attack the name *Kristallnacht* or "Crystal Night." The Nazis also set up concentration camps to imprison and isolate non-Aryans from German society. Eventually, they decided to purge their nation altogether of people they considered undesirable in the **Holocaust** (see Chapter 5).

On the Road to War

In 1931, Japan invaded the Chinese industrial province of Manchuria. The Chinese government appealed to the League of Nations to take punitive action against Japan. The League, established by the Treaty of Versailles, was supposed to help maintain world peace, but it proved a much weaker body than originally intended. It condemned Japan's action and tried to negotiate, but Japan responded by withdrawing its membership from the League.

In the spring of 1935, Italy attacked Abyssinia (now Ethiopia). Ethiopia was one of the few independent African nations. The Ethiopians, who had never been colonized, fought hard against the Italian invasion and won support around the world. This time the League immediately voted to impose trade sanctions against Italy. Oil, a crucial import for Italy, was not included in the sanctions.

Italy had no oil of its own, and had it been unable to import oil, its war machine would have run down very quickly. France and Great Britain were reluctant to punish Italy, however, as they wanted Italy's support in case of a new war with Germany.

Germany on the Offensive

In 1936, Hitler ordered his troops into the Rhineland, an area along Germany's western border that was demilitarized by the Treaty of Versailles. Hitler counted on little resistance from world leaders to this occupation, and he believed his actions would go unpunished by the League of Nations. He was right.

That same year, General Francisco Franco and his Falange (fascist) followers led an attack on Spain's government. The result was a civil war between the elected socialist government and the rebel forces of General Franco. Franco, with military support from Hitler and Mussolini, won the war and became the ruler of Spain. The democratic governments around the world chose not to get involved in the conflict, although socialist supporters from several countries went to Spain to join in the fight against Franco and fascism. Canadian volunteers, called the Mackenzie–Papineau Battalion (the Mac-Paps), numbered over 1200. One of the volunteers was Dr. Norman Bethune, a surgeon and political activist from Ontario.

The Policy of Appeasement

Throughout the 1930s, Western democracies adopted a policy of **appeasement** in response to Germany's aggression. Because no one wanted to fight another war, many leaders were willing to make concessions to Hitler to maintain peace. Appeasement, however, simply made Hitler bolder. In March 1938, he took over neighbouring Austria, a German-speaking country. He then demanded the right to take over the Sudetenland, the German-speaking region in western Czechoslovakia. In September 1938, at a conference in Munich, Britain and France agreed to this demand. In turn, Hitler pledged that this would be his last territorial claim.

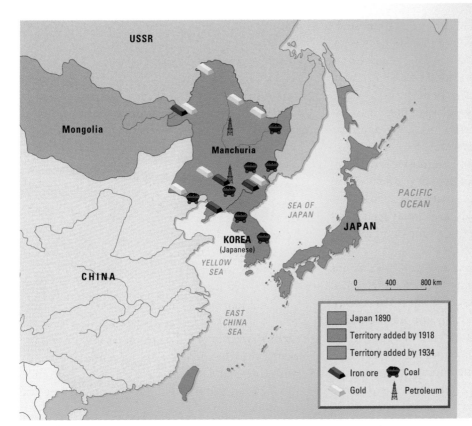

Figure 4-17 Japan's aggression by 1934. In 1931, Japanese troops invaded China's resource-rich province of Manchuria. Japan needed these resources in order to expand its empire. By 1934, the invasion of Manchuria was complete.

Reading a map What resources did Japan acquire after its invasion of Manchuria? How would the invasion of Manchuria assist Japan in its later invasion of China?

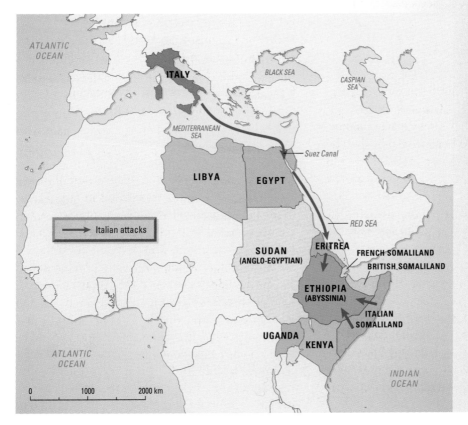

Figure 4-18 Route of Italian troops invading Ethiopia, 1935. Mussolini wanted to create his own empire and in 1935 he invaded the country of Ethiopia (Abyssinia).

Thinking critically With the invasion of Ethiopia, what advantage would Italy have should war break out in northern Africa?

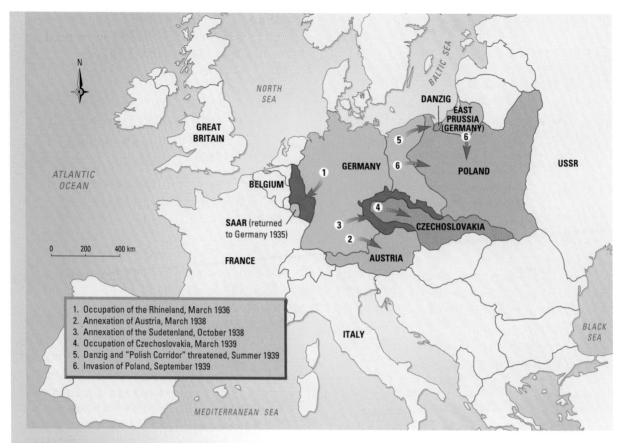

Figure 4-19 Hitler's aggression in Europe, 1936–1939.

1. Occupation of the Rhineland, March 1936
2. Annexation of Austria, March 1938
3. Annexation of the Sudetenland, October 1938
4. Occupation of Czechoslovakia, March 1939
5. Danzig and "Polish Corridor" threatened, Summer 1939
6. Invasion of Poland, September 1939

Thinking critically Which countries might have felt threatened by Germany's actions? Why? Italy, also ruled by a fascist government at the time, was Germany's ally. What difference might this alliance have made to the countries of Europe?

Then, in March 1939, Hitler ignored his pledge to Britain and France and took over the rest of Czechoslovakia. Western leaders were beginning to fear that only war would stop Hitler. The final blow came in 1939, when Hitler invaded Poland.

For some months, Hitler had been making warlike speeches against Poland. He wanted to regain an area of Poland that had been taken away from Germany in the peace agreement of 1919. But first, Hitler had a problem to solve. If

Germany invaded Poland, it was likely that the Soviet Union would regard Germany's actions as a threat to its own security and declare war on Germany. In August 1939, Hitler stunned the world by concluding a non-aggression pact with Joseph Stalin, leader of the Soviet Union. Both countries pledged not to fight each other if one of them went to war, and they agreed to divide Poland between them. Germany was now free to make its move. On September 1, 1939, German troops invaded Poland, and bitter fighting followed.

Britain and France ordered Germany out of Poland by September 3, 1939. When Germany ignored this deadline, Britain and France declared war on Germany. For the second time in just twenty-five years, the countries of the world were embroiled in a global conflict.

Canada's Response to Growing Tensions

Throughout the events of the 1930s, Canadians, including Prime Minister Mackenzie King, remained **isolationists**, uninterested in affairs outside their borders. Besides, many Canadians believed the Treaty of Versailles had been too harsh. Others, remembering the 60 000 Canadians who had died in World War I, adopted a pacifist position. As events escalated in Germany, many Canadians asked why Canadian lives should be risked in another European war when Canada itself was not threatened.

Prime Minister King was anxious to find out for himself what Hitler's intentions were. In 1937, he went to Germany and visited the German leader. Completely taken in by what he saw, King came away sure that Hitler had no warlike intentions. In his diary he wrote, naively:

> [Hitler] smiled very pleasantly and indeed had a sort of appealing and affectionate look in his eyes. My sizing up of the man as I saw and talked with him was that he was the sort who truly loves his fellow man....

While King knew that the Nazis were persecuting Jews and other groups, he saw no need for Canada to become involved or to accept Jewish refugees. In 1938, he wrote in his diary:

> We must ... seek to keep this part of the Continent free from unrest.... Nothing can be gained by creating an internal problem in an effort to meet an international one.

Canada's Secretary of State, Pierre Rinfret, had other reasons for rejecting Jewish refugees. In 1939, he told a meeting of his supporters that "despite all sentiments of humanity, so long as Canada has an unemployment problem, there will be no 'open door' policy to political refugees here."

After the *Kristallnacht* incident, Thomas Crerar, who was now a Liberal cabinet member, made a recommendation that 10 000 Jews be allowed to emigrate to Canada. The Cabinet refused Crerar's suggestion. Immigration director Fred Blair was against Jews coming to Canada, maintaining that "none is too many." Canada's policy had tragic consequences in 1939 when the ocean liner, the *St. Louis*, with over 900 Jewish refugees on board, was refused permission to dock when it appeared off the east coast of Canada.

Figure 4-20 Prime Minister Mackenzie King in Germany.

Using evidence What symbols of the Nazi Party are evident in this photograph?

Figure 4-21 Passengers aboard the *St. Louis* looked to the Canadian government to accept them as refugees.

The ship was forced to return to Europe, where many of the passengers later died in concentration camps.

Many Canadians did not share the government's anti-Semitic views. In 1938, there were 165 000 Jewish people living in Canada, the vast majority of whom were citizens. Rallies were held in many parts of the country in support of a more humane immigration policy. When the *St. Louis* was turned away, and its passengers sent back to Nazi Germany, newspaper editorials also lashed out at the government:

> This country still has the bars up and the refugee who gets into Canada has to pass some mighty stiff obstacles—deliberately placed there by the government.... Immigration bars ... are undesirable.... We are deliberately keeping out of this country [people] and money who would greatly add to our productive revenues. We are cutting off our nose to spite our face.

Source: *Winnipeg Free Press*, July 19, 1939.

ACTIVITIES

1. Explain these terms in the context of events described in this chapter: totalitarian state; fascist government; appeasement.

2. What factors contributed to the rise of dictators after World War I?

3. How did the Treaty of Versailles help the rise of the Nazi Party in Germany?

4. **a)** Why was the League of Nations unable to stop the aggression of Japan and Italy?

   b) How did this failure encourage Hitler?

5. Write a brief summary of Canada's response to the plight of Jewish refugees prior to World War II.

LOOKING BACK

Develop an Understanding

1. Explain the title of this chapter. Do you consider it appropriate? Why or why not?

2. What were the major weaknesses in the Canadian economy from 1919 to 1939? Does the Canadian economy still suffer from any of these weaknesses? Explain.

3. **a.** How did the social policies of the federal and provincial governments respond to the crisis of the Depression?

    b. What does this response say about the values that were held by the society at the time? Use the personal reminiscences in this chapter to support your answer.

4. Why were Aboriginal people, Asian men, and women in a particularly desperate situation in the 1930s? What might account for the attitude of many Canadians and the government towards Jews in the 1930s?

5. In your view, which political party would each of the following have supported during the Depression? Explain your choice.

    a. owner of small business

    b. single unemployed person

    c. farm wife

    d. hourly paid worker

6. What major events led to World War II?

Explore the Issues

7. In an organizer, compare the responses of the democratic and totalitarian states to the problems of the Depression. Use the information to speculate on why Canada and the United States never resorted to totalitarian governments.

8. Make a timeline showing Germany's acts of aggression during the 1930s. For each act, state whether you think it was worth going to war over this issue, and give reasons for your view.

9. Imagine you are an adviser to the federal government in the 1930s. Write a report advising the prime minister on steps that he could take to lessen the effects of the Depression. Remember to include

    a. your analysis of the sources of income for the government

    b. your opinions on federal–provincial relations

    c. your opinion of Roosevelt's New Deal.

10. What lessons do you think we can learn from the handling of the Depression by federal and provincial governments?

Research and Communicate

11. View a film or read a novel set in the Depression, such as *The Grapes of Wrath*. Research the film or novel of your choice. Write a report describing how it was received at the time, and its effectiveness today.

12. With a partner or in a small group, imagine you are the founding members of a new political party. Yours is a party dedicated to solving the economic and social problems of the Depression. On a single page, write your party's name, a summary of the country's major problems, and a five- to ten-point declaration of your party's program. Include a catchy slogan or statement that sums up what your party stands for.

13. Statistics Canada's Web site at **<www.statcan.ca>** gives on-line access to Canadian statistics. Visit the site and gather statistics and information on Canadian employment, average incomes, and other data that allow you to judge the standard of living of Canadians today. Compare these data with similar information on the Depression.

14. Some historians maintain that World War II could have been avoided if Britain and France and their allies had stood up to Hitler's demands earlier than they did. In one sentence, formulate a thesis on this idea, and use it for a class debate.

15. Use the school library or the Internet to find out more about what was happening in Canada in the summer of 1939. What was popular in **a)** the movies, **b)** music, **c)** sports, **d)** fashions, **e)** any other aspects of everyday life? How had Canada changed since World War I? Prepare a short report or visual display of your findings.

5

Canada and World War II

FOCUS ON

• Why did Canada take part in World War II?

• What effect did the war have on Canada's economy?

• What were the main campaigns in World War II?

• What role did Canadian armed forces play in the war?

• How did the war change Canadians' perception of themselves?

Counterpoints Issue

• Is the use of weapons of mass destruction ever justified?

Maintenance Jobs in the Hangar by Paraskeva Clark. Once the Canadian government declared war on Germany, it committed the country to "total war," with all Canadians and sectors of the economy contributing to the war effort. Paraskeva Clark (1898–1986) was a feminist whose paintings conveyed a strong social message.

Expressing ideas How does this painting illustrate Canada's commitment to total war? What other message(s) does it convey?

Introduction

On the clear, balmy Sunday of Labour Day weekend in 1939, Mary Peate was walking home from church. There were rumours of war, but the Montreal neighbourhood where she lived had never looked more peaceful. At home, she joined her family for lunch in the dining room. Everyone ate half-heartedly while listening to a special radio broadcast from London, England. King George VI was speaking:

> For the second time in the lives of most of us, we are at war. Over and over again, we have tried to find a peaceful way out of the differences between ourselves and those who are now our enemies; but it has been in vain.
>
> We have been forced into a conflict, for we are called, with our allies, to meet the challenge of a principle which, if it were to prevail, would be fatal to any civilized order in the world.

Once again, the world was on the brink of war. What would war mean to Mary and her family? How would Canadians respond to the message issued by the King? In this chapter, you will learn about the events of World War II and the contributions made by hundreds of thousands of Canadians during its course.

Canada Declares War

In 1938, British Prime Minister Neville Chamberlain optimistically announced to the world that he had managed to secure "peace for our time" with the Munich Agreement. This agreement let Hitler take over part of Czechoslovakia on the promise that he would cease his aggression. In March 1939, however, Hitler ignored the terms of the agreement, and his troops marched through the rest of Czechoslovakia. War seemed inevitable.

In May, Britain's King George VI and Queen Elizabeth visited Canada, the first time a reigning monarch had ever visited this country. The purpose of their visit was to rally support for Britain in these tense times. Crowds of cheering Canadians did just that, lining the streets wherever the royal couple appeared across the country. When the King and Queen left Halifax on June 15, they could be satisfied that the bonds of friendship between Canada and the former "mother country" remained very strong.

But Prime Minister Mackenzie King did not want Canada to become involved in another world conflict. He had desperately hoped that Britain's policy of appeasement towards Hitler would be successful. The scars of World War I, fought less than twenty-five years earlier, were still fresh for

Figure 5-1 King George VI and Queen Elizabeth on their visit to Canada in May 1939.

The World at War

1939

September 1: Germany invades Poland.

September 3: Britain and France declare war on Germany.

September 10: Canada declares war on Germany.

1940

April: Germany invades Denmark and Norway.

May: Germany invades Netherlands, Belgium, Luxembourg, and France.

May–June: Evacuation of Dunkirk.

June: National Resource Mobilization Act allows conscription of Canadians for home defence.

June 22: France surrenders to Hitler.

July: German air force begins bombing Britain ("the Battle of Britain").

1940–1944

Battle of the Atlantic is fought.

1941

June 22: Germany invades USSR.

December 7: Japan bombs Pearl Harbour.

December 8: United States declares war on Japan.

December 25: Canadian soldiers defeated in Japan's invasion of Hong Kong.

1942

February: Japanese-Canadians sent to internment camps.

April: Canadians vote in plebiscite to support conscription.

August: Raid on French port of Dieppe by Canadian and other Allied forces.

1943–1945

Allies bomb German cities.

1943

July: Canadian troops participate in invasion of Sicily and mainland Italy.

December: Canadians win Battle of Ortona, Italy.

1944

June 6: D-Day; Canadian troops join British and Americans in Allied invasion of Normandy in northern France.

1945

Spring: Canadian troops help liberate the Netherlands from German military control.

May 7: Germany surrenders.

August 6: United States drops atomic bomb on Hiroshima.

August 9: United States drops atomic bomb on Nagasaki.

August 15: Japan surrenders.

Figure 5-2 Canadian nurses arrive at the beachhead in Normandy, July 1944, shortly after the Allied invasion. These women worked under very difficult circumstances, close to the fighting.

Figure 5-3 German troops surrender to Canadian soldiers in France, 1944.

many Canadians. That war had deeply divided Canada on the issue of conscription. King knew that if he imposed conscription in this war, he and the Liberal Party would lose support in Quebec. Besides, Canada was just starting to come out of the dark years of the Depression. The economy was slowly improving, and King didn't want the country plunged back into debt.

But on September 1, Germany invaded Poland. Two days later, Britain and France declared war on Germany. In World War I, when Britain declared war on Germany, Canada was automatically at war with Germany, as well. Now, Canada was an independent country, and had to decide for itself whether it would go to war again. King knew that once Britain become involved in such a major conflict, Canada would not stand by idly. Still, it was important that the decision to join the war be a Canadian one, decided by Canada's Parliament.

On September 8, Prime Minister King called a special session of Parliament to decide Canada's response. King gave a strong speech in favour of declaring war. His minister of justice, Ernest Lapointe from Quebec, also spoke in favour of the war, which helped convince Quebec voters that Canada's involvement in the war was necessary. But Lapointe spoke bluntly about what conscription would do to Liberal supporters in Quebec. "I am authorized by my colleagues in the cabinet from Quebec," he informed Parliament, "to say that we will never agree to conscription and will never be members or supporters of a government that will try to enforce it."

King assured Parliament, and Quebec, that "So long as this government may be in power, no such measure [conscription] shall be enacted." King's position on joining the war was supported by the opposition Conservative Party. Only J.S. Woodsworth, leader of the Commonwealth Cooperative Federation (CCF), argued against going to war. On September 10, Canada declared war on Germany.

Mobilizing Canada's Resources

Despite its willingness to join the war, Canada was not prepared for it in 1939. Army, air force, and navy troops were small in number, and most of Canada's equipment was outdated and unfit for combat. For example, the army had only 4500 troops, a few dozen anti-tank guns, sixteen tanks, and no modern artillery. The air force and the navy also had outdated equipment and only a small number of recruits.

Unlike World War I, there were no crowds cheering on the streets when Canada declared war on Germany. Many Canadians remembered only too well the suffering and horrors of the last world conflict, and they were unwilling to become involved in another. Still, Canada had no trouble finding volunteers. In September alone, over 58 330 people volunteered for service. As in World War I, Aboriginal people volunteered at a higher percentage of their population than any other group in Canada. Among them was Thomas Prince, who was to become one of Canada's most decorated soldiers. The Canadian army initially rejected African-Canadian volunteers because of racist attitudes towards people of non-European origin. As the war continued, however, African-Canadians were accepted into the regular army and the officer corps.

After years of the Depression, some Canadians were attracted by the private's pay of $1.30 a day plus sixty dollars a month for a dependent spouse and thirty dollars a month for each child. Yet many still felt strong ties with Britain and volunteered from a sense of duty. Others came forward from a sense of new-found national pride. The first Canadian troops sailed from Halifax on December 10, 1939.

The British Commonwealth Air Training Plan

In the early months of the war, Mackenzie King hoped Canada's contribution to the war effort would remain, as much as possible, at home. This way, the issue of conscription could be avoided. The British Commonwealth Air Training Plan (BCATP) seemed to offer Canada this possibility. In December 1939, Canada agreed to host and administer a training plan in which British instructors would train pilots and other flight personnel from all over the Commonwealth in Canada. Canada's open skies, its climate, and its distance from enemy aircraft made it an ideal training location. Air fields were built on the Prairies and in other locations near small towns and villages, and old aircraft were refitted and returned to service. The program was a major Canadian contribution to the war effort. The BCATP trained over 130 000 pilots, navigators, flight engineers, and ground staff. The total cost was over $2.2 billion, of which Canada paid over 70 per cent. Contrary to King's hopes, however, Canada's role in the war would go much beyond its involvement in the BCATP.

Figure 5-4 Troops departing from Winnipeg.

Using evidence From this photograph, how do you think most Canadians felt about going to war? Consider the feelings of those who were staying home, as well as those who were going to fight.

Total War

With the declaration of war, the Canadian government immediately became much more involved in the planning and control of the economy. In April 1940, the government established the Department of Munitions and Supplies, and King appointed C.D. Howe as its minister. Howe was given extraordinary authority to do whatever it took to gear up the economy to meet wartime demands. He told industries what to produce and how to produce it. In his direct, impatient manner, he convinced business leaders to manufacture goods they had never made before. Soon Vancouver was building ships for the navy,

Figure 5-5 Student pilots and instructors wait to board their Tiger Moths at an Oshawa BCATP training school.

Gathering information From this photograph, what can you tell about the following: the scale of the BCATP; the aircraft used; training methods?

Figure 5-6 A poster issued by the Vancouver Board of Trade. It was meant to show workers in the lumber industry how they were contributing to the war effort by supplying lumber to Britain.

Expressing ideas How would this poster encourage the policy of total war?

Montreal was constructing new planes and bombers such as the Lancaster, and Canada's car industries were producing military vehicles and tanks. Munitions factories opened in Ontario and Quebec. If the private sector was unable to produce what Howe wanted, he created **Crown corporations** to do the job. Even farmers were told to produce more wheat, beef, dairy products, and other foods. Under Howe's leadership, the government ran telephone companies, refined fuel, stockpiled silk for parachutes, mined uranium, and controlled food production. This was the policy of *total war*, with Canadians willing to do whatever it took to defeat the enemy.

ACTIVITIES

1. What assurance did Mackenzie King give Canadians during the debate on Canada's involvement in the war? Why did he do this?

2. What was the British Commonwealth Air Training Plan? Why was Canada chosen to host it? Why did Mackenzie King support the plan?

3. Compare Canadians' reaction to the announcement of World War I with that of World War II. Why did many people volunteer?

4. How did Canada's policy of total war change the economy? Why was the policy necessary?

The War in Europe

With the declaration of war, the *Allies* (Britain, France, Commonwealth countries including Canada, Australia, and New Zealand) raced to get their forces organized and prepared for battle. The alliance of Germany, Italy (1939), and Japan (1940) became known as the **Axis**. Allied troops were quickly stationed along France's border with Germany, where they waited for Germany's next move—but for seven months, nothing happened. This period became known as the "phoney war," and many people started to believe there might not be a war.

These illusions were shattered, however, when Germany renewed its *blitzkrieg* ("lightening war"), attacking Denmark and Norway in April 1940. The blitzkrieg was a powerful and extremely successful war tactic: in surprise attacks and with lightening speed, German panzers (tanks) would crash through enemy lines, driving forward as far as they could. At the same time, war planes would roar through the skies, constantly bombing the enemy below. German soldiers would also parachute into enemy territory, destroying vital communication and transportation links. The attacks were swift and thorough, and left the defending army confused and, eventually, surrounded.

Evacuation at Dunkirk

It took Germany just hours to conquer Denmark and only two months to subdue Norway. Then, on May 10, the German *Wehrmacht* (armed forces) began its invasion of the Netherlands. The German forces moved quickly through Belgium, and finally into France. Within days of arriving in France, German panzers had reached the English Channel. The Allied forces were soon surrounded in the French port of Dunkirk. They had to escape before the Germans captured the town. They decided to try an evacuation by sea. On learning of the Allied plan, the British navy rounded up every boat capable of navigating the English Channel. Hundreds of fishing boats, pleasure crafts, and ferries joined naval and merchant ships as they headed across the Channel for the beaches of Dunkirk. The evacuation began on May 26.

Figure 5-7 The Allies' evacuation at Dunkirk.

Thinking critically Why were the Allies forced to retreat to Dunkirk? What was their only chance of escape?

Two days later, the German *Luftwaffe* (air force) bombed the port of Dunkirk, making the escape by the Allies even more difficult, but the evacuation continued. On June 4, the evacuation was finally completed. It had been a dramatic rescue. Nearly 340 000 Allied soldiers, thousands more than originally anticipated, were brought to safety in Britain.

The German army continued its sweep through France. The French army was no match for the powerful German troops, and on June 22, 1940, France surrendered. Britain and the Commonwealth now stood alone against Germany.

The Battle of Britain

Hitler's next goal was "Operation Sea Lion," the invasion of Britain. First, however, Germany planned to destroy Britain's air power. On July 10, 1940, the German *Luftwaffe* started a massive bombing campaign, aimed at destroying harbours and shipping facilities in southern England. In August, the bombing raids targeted air fields and aircraft fac-

tories. By September, the German strategy shifted to bombing civilian targets, and for fifty-five consecutive nights, German planes bombed London and other cities, terrifying and killing civilians and destroying buildings and streets. These raids became known as "the Blitz." The Germans had more fighter aircraft than the British but, even after months of bombing, they were unable to defeat the British air force. One reason was that the British had a very sophisticated radar system that gave them early warnings of German air raids. The British also used Spitfires and Hurricanes, two fighter planes that, although limited in number, were extremely effective defence planes. And the British pilots were not alone. They were joined by many pilots from Commonwealth countries, including some eighty Canadian fighter pilots.

Eventually the British air force was having more and more success in shooting down German bombers, and in May 1941, Hitler finally gave up on his plans to invade Britain. Although Germany lost the Battle of Britain, more than 23 000 people were killed in the Blitz, mostly British civilians.

The War Spreads

Shortly after Germany's defeat in the Battle of Britain, Hitler turned his attention eastward: he launched "Operation Barbarossa" ("red beard"), the invasion of the USSR. Even though Germany and the Soviet Union had agreed, in 1939, not to invade each other, Hitler never let go of his original plan to take over the USSR when the time was right. Hitler needed to conquer the USSR in order to fulfil his long-term plans of a German Empire. He planned the invasion for later in the war, but when the Soviet Union took over part of the Balkans in 1940, Hitler became suspicious of the motives of the Soviet leader, Joseph Stalin. Hitler decided the time was right to invade. This decision turned out to be a major miscalculation on Hitler's part.

The Soviets were surprised and unprepared for the attack. At first, the German troops were able to push the Soviet army deeper and deeper into the Soviet Union. By autumn, the Germans had managed to reach the outskirts of Moscow and Leningrad (now St. Petersburg). But the

German troops were ill-equipped for the long and bitterly cold Soviet winter, and soon lost their advantage. In 1942, Germany launched another offensive in the USSR, hoping to capture the rich oil fields in the south. This time, the German troops got as far as Stalingrad, but once again were stopped by the severe winter. Their situation grew desperate and, after suffering more than 300 000 casualties, the German army surrendered in early 1943. Taking advantage of this victory, the Soviet army went on the offensive, retaking much of the territory they had lost earlier. By early 1944, the Soviets were advancing into Eastern Europe, towards Germany.

The War in the Pacific

Japan was an Axis power, but it was not involved in the war in Europe. By 1941, it was prepared to invade U.S. and European colonies in Southeast Asia, which were rich in valuable resources such as oil, rubber, and tin.

On December 7, 1941, Japanese planes bombed the U.S. naval base in Pearl Harbour, on the island of Hawaii, destroying half the fleet. Then they bombed the Philippines. The surprise bombings stunned the Americans; the next day, the U.S. government declared war on Japan. Japan's allies—Germany and Italy—then declared war on the United States. Japan continued its invasion of most of Southeast Asia and Burma (Myanmar), and the Netherlands East Indies (Indonesia), heading towards Australia. The whole world was now at war.

Only hours after Japanese planes bombed Pearl Harbour, Japanese troops began their surprise invasion of the British colony of Hong Kong. By Christmas Day, 1941, Hong Kong had fallen to the Japanese. Canada had sent troops to Hong Kong only months earlier, and all 1975 Canadians were either killed or taken prisoner by the Japanese. Of the 555 who perished, nearly half died as prisoners during the three and a half years they were imprisoned. Canadians at home were horrified to learn of the fate of the Canadians and angry that troops had been sent to Hong Kong.

Figure 5-9 This recruitment poster was issued after Canadian forces were defeated at Hong Kong.

Expressing ideas How do the images and words on this poster help to convey its message?

Canada's Role in Europe

By the middle of 1942, the Soviet Union, now one of the Allied powers, had lost close to a million soldiers in its desperate fight against invading German troops. Soviet leaders wanted the Allies to invade Europe from the west, a move that would weaken the German army by forcing it to fight the war on two fronts.

The Dieppe Raid

The Allies were not prepared for a full invasion of Europe, but they felt ready for a trial run. A smaller raid would give them an opportunity to test new techniques and equipment, as well as serve as a reconnaissance mission for a future invasion. Canadian troops had seen little action since coming to England. Until 1942, most of the war had been fought in Africa, and Canadians training in Britain were anxious to participate. The Second Canadian Division was chosen to be the main force of attack in an experimental raid on the French port of Dieppe, under German occupation. Four pre-dawn attacks along the coast were to be followed by one main attack on the town of Dieppe half an hour later. Allied troops were to be covered by air force bombers, and tanks were to be landed at the town.

From the very beginning of the raid, however, things went wrong. On the morning of August 19, 1942, one of the ships carrying Canadian soldiers to Dieppe unexpectedly met a small German convoy. The two sides engaged in a brief sea battle, but the noise alerted German troops on shore. To make matters worse, the Canadians were to disembark before dawn, but the ships were delayed,

and as Canadian soldiers leapt ashore in the early daylight, they were easily machine-gunned by the waiting German soldiers. Communication between the ships and troops on land was poor, and commanders sent more reinforcements ashore, believing the first wave of soldiers had reached the town. These troops, too, became trapped on the beaches, unable to retreat or advance, making them easy targets for the German soldiers positioned in the cliffs along the coastline. As the day wore on, the situation got worse. Allied tanks couldn't get enough traction on the pebbled beach, and many were left immobile.

The raid was a terrible failure. Ross Munro, the Canadian war correspondent who accompa-

Figure 5-10 Planned and actual movements of Allied troops in raid on Dieppe, August 19, 1942.

Reading a map What information does the legend of this map give? What were the planned movements of the Allies? What were the actual movements? What physical barriers did the Allies face?

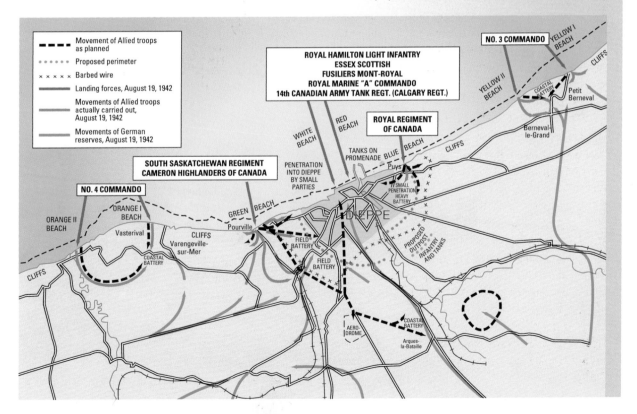

nied the troops to Dieppe, described the raid and its devastating results:

> Our planes were overhead.... German flak [anti-aircraft fire] spouted from Dieppe, and the sky was a spectacular... chandelier of coloured lights and flashes. Searchlights fingered the sky. There were a dozen sharp flashes of bursting bombs. Now I could see the long stone pier at Dieppe, a red navigation light burning at the end....
>
> The men in our boat crouched low. Then the ramp went down and the first infantrymen poured out. They plunged into about two feet [60 cm] of water and machine-gun bullets laced into them. Bodies piled up on the ramp. Some men staggered to the beach....
>
> Orders were to land the troops, then pull back to sea. It was useless to remain a sitting target. Everyone who had tried to leave the boat had been cut down. Our naval officer ordered the craft off the beach.... Through an opening in the stern I got my last look at the grimmest beach of the Dieppe raid. It was khaki with the bodies of Canadian boys....
>
> Some boys had been hit a dozen times. Nobody had counted on casualties like this....

Source: *The Canadians at War, 1939–1945*
(Montreal: Reader's Digest Association [Canada], 1969), 180–181.

Casualties were high. In all, 907 Canadians were killed during the nine-hour battle, more than any other day of the war. Another 586 were wounded and 1874 taken prisoner.

Was the raid on Dieppe worth the price? Did the Allies learn anything from it? Opinion is divided on whether Dieppe was a valuable learning experience or a complete disaster. Some historians claim that the Allies were later able to launch a successful invasion based on what they had learned at Dieppe. Others maintain that the raid was badly planned and taught the Germans more than it taught the Allies.

ACTIVITIES

1. Explain why, for tactical purposes, German forces needed to invade Britain if they were to hold Western Europe. What efforts did they make to do this?

2. **a)** Do you think it was an error on Germany's part to invade the USSR? Explain.

   b) The German defeat at Stalingrad is considered by some historians to be the point at which the defeat of Germany became inevitable. Why?

3. **a)** What was the purpose of the Dieppe raid?

   b) Why were Canadian troops chosen for the raid?

   c) Why did the raid fail?

   d) What useful information might have been learned from the raid?

Figure 5-11 Dead Canadian soldiers and tanks on Dieppe beach, August 19, 1942.

Using evidence
Canadian troops were supported by tanks, but most never advanced far from the shoreline. Find evidence in this photograph to suggest why vehicles with caterpillar tracks were useless during the attack.

Canadians at Sea

When war broke out, the Royal Canadian Navy (RCN) rushed into a massive building and training program. With only thirteen ships and 1819 sailors, Canada's navy was desperately short of equipment and trained manpower. By 1941, the **Battle of the Atlantic** was in full force, and Canada's contribution was much needed. Britain was almost completely dependent on food and military supplies from Canada and the United States, but the Allied merchant ships bound for England were being sunk by "wolf packs" of German U-boats patrolling the Atlantic. Germany was trying to starve Britain by cutting off vital shipping routes to the island.

In order to protect supply ships from being sunk by German torpedoes, Allies sailed in *convoys*: warships escorted vessels carrying vital supplies, protecting them. But even convoys didn't stop the attacks. German U-boats continued to destroy hundreds of supply ships, sinking millions of tonnes of cargo. Canada started building small warships, called *corvettes*, to escort convoys across the ocean. The corvette was quick, small, and ma-noeuvred well, but it was not a very seaworthy vessel. Some sailors claimed the corvette would "roll on wet grass," it was so unsteady. Nevertheless, the corvette was the best ship that could be built in such short time.

Until the winter of 1942–1943, it seemed that the Allies would lose the Battle of the Atlantic. German submarines continued to pound the convoys, sinking ships at a rapid pace. Some German submarines even sailed into the Gulf of St. Lawrence and up the St. Lawrence River to attack ships there. Gradually, however, the situation started to turn around. By May 1942, the British had cracked the German naval code, which meant the Allies could track German submarine movements more easily. In December, the British cracked a second German code. As well, the Allies were reaching the point where more ships were being built than were being destroyed. Better training of RCN personnel and more sophisticated equipment also contributed to the Allies' success. And the corvettes were helped by long-range Liberator bombers, which could fly far enough from bases in Britain and Canada to protect much of the convoy's route.

Figure 5-12 A convoy gathered in Bedford Basin, Halifax, 1942.

Thinking critically Locate ships that appear to be smaller. What might be the nature and function of these vessels?

Innovations

War Technology

Submarines became much more efficient. The Germans invented a snorkel that brought air into a submarine. Surfacing to recharge its battery made a submarine vulnerable to attack. With the snorkel, batteries could be recharged below the surface.

Great advances were made in *radar* (radio detection and ranging), an electronic system that uses radio waves to detect objects beyond the range of vision. Radar can provide information about the distance, position, size, shape, direction, and speed of an object. Radar was used to detect approaching aircraft and naval vessels. ▼

The United States developed the *atomic bomb*. In this weapon, a sphere about the size of a baseball was equal in power to over 20 000 t of TNT. A single atomic bomb could cripple an entire medium-sized city. The nature of warfare was permanently changed.

The German *V-2 rocket* was a powerful new weapon. With a range of 350 km, the V-2s were used with deadly accuracy against London in the closing days of the war but had no impact on the war's outcome. Wernher von Braun, the designer of the V-2, moved to the United States after the war. After becoming a U.S. citizen, he designed the Gemini and Apollo rockets that eventually led to the U.S. moon landing in 1969.

The Germans developed a *coding machine*, known as "Enigma," which converted radio messages into code so that they could not be understood by the enemy. This machine spurred the development of an early computer that could decode German signals.

The first *jet-propelled airplanes* were used in World War II. Because jets could fly higher and faster than propeller-driven planes, both the Axis powers and the Allies worked around the clock to produce as many jets as they could. However, jets were not perfected until after 1945, and not enough were produced to affect the outcome of the war.

Because of the war, some natural raw materials were no longer available, so scientists developed *synthetics* to replace them. Synthetic rubber was stronger than natural rubber and more resistant to heat. Nylon became a substitute for Japanese silk in parachutes. Aircraft windows were made from perspex, a clear plastic that was superior to glass because it did not shatter. Heat-resistant polyethylene was used to improve radar equipment, and other plastics were used to waterproof tanks.

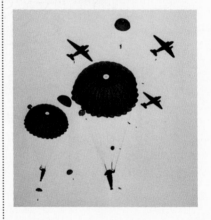

Great advances were made in *medical technology*, as doctors tried to repair the hideous wounds of war. Penicillin, an antibiotic, was first isolated in 1929 by British scientist Alexander Fleming, but was not used to treat infections in humans until 1941. It contributed to a 95 per cent recovery rate for wounded Allied soldiers. Plastic surgeons performed thousands of operations, using innovative techniques to restore hands, feet, and faces. ▶

Figure 5-13 The Women's Royal Canadian Naval Service was created in 1942. Most "WRENs" were limited to shore-based jobs, working as wireless operators, coders, drivers, and operational plotters. This WREN was one of the few to be posted overseas.

Canadians in the Air

Like the RCN, the Royal Canadian Air Force (RCAF) grew quickly after the war began and played a variety of important roles. Altogether, almost 250 000 Canadians joined the RCAF during the war years. At one point, there were forty-eight Canadian squadrons posted overseas. Canadian air crews participated in bombing raids in Britain, North Africa, Italy, Northwest Europe, and Southeast Asia. They also participated in one of the most controversial missions of the war: night bombings over Germany. By mid-1943, the Allies had started a series of bombing raids aimed at destroying German industry. Night after night, British and Canadian bombers pounded German cities; U.S. bombers attacked during the day. One of the worst attacks was on the German city of Hamburg. Relentless bombing by the Allies created a firestorm below, and the city was engulfed in flames driven by fierce winds. Canadian bomber ace Johnnie Fauquier later described those missions:

> There were sights you can't forget. Fire bombs, which set off as many as a hundred individual fires when they exploded, did the most damage. When

By 1943, Germany's U-boat fleet had suffered serious losses, and many more Allied convoys were reaching their destination. British Prime Minister Winston Churchill recognized the importance of this outcome:

> The only thing that ever really frightened me was the U-boat peril.... The Battle of the Atlantic was the dominating factor all through the war. Never for one moment could we forget that everything happening elsewhere—on land, at sea or in the air—depended ultimately on its outcome, and amid all other cares we viewed its changing fortunes day by day with hope or apprehension.

Canada's navy grew significantly during the war. By 1945, it had 400 vessels and over 100 000 sailors: 99 688 men and 6500 women. The RCN is credited with having provided about half the escorts across the Atlantic.

Figure 5-14 Quebec's George "Buzz" Beurling was Canada's greatest flying ace during World War II. He preferred to fly alone and always recorded his hits on the side of his plane.

you dropped thousands of them, the city looked like a vast pot of boiling lead.

We were after military objectives: the seaport, armament works and so on. But there was another policy at work: demoralize the people, don't let them sleep, make them homeless, break their will. It's not a thing we bragged about. But those people were at war with us and they were very serious about it.

Source: Quoted in *The Canadians at War, 1939–1945* (vol. 2) (Montreal: Reader's Digest Association [Canada], 1969), 382.

The casualty rate among air crew was very high. Nearly 10 000 Canadian bomber crew lost their lives in the war, a quarter of the total number of Canadians killed in World War II. One graduate of the BCATP put it simply: "There were forty-three of us graduated, forty-three of us went to England. There were only three survivors. I am one of the lucky guys who lived."

In 1941, the RCAF formed the Women's Division (WD) to support the war effort. Women were trained as clerks, cooks, hospital assistants, drivers, telephone operators, welders, instrument mechanics, and engine mechanics. There were women pilots in Canada at the time who were frustrated by the RCAF's refusal to let them fly. Only later in the war were women allowed to fly bomber planes on flights to deliver them to Britain. Women never took part in combat.

building your skills

Reading a Historical Map

*H*istorical maps are useful documents that give specific information. They are a visual way of conveying facts as well as concepts. As with other historical documents, the information included in these maps is selective, so you must examine them carefully.

Steps in Reading a Historical Map

1. Look at the title and legend of the map. These should tell you the historical period of the map, its main purpose, and the other kinds of information that the map is meant to convey.

2. Examine the names (or symbols) closely. Look for patterns in the information. Why, for example, are some names bigger or bolder than others? Certain colours may be used to illustrate similarities in or differences between regions.

3. Now read the map by analysing the information. Ask yourself: What is this map about? How is the information being communicated? What conclusions can be drawn from this map?

Applying the Skill

As you read about the events that occurred in Europe between 1942 and 1945, refer to Figure 5-15. Go through the three steps in reading a historical map, and answer the questions below.

1. What is this map about? What are the six pieces of information given in the legend?

2. The cartographer (map maker) has shown a limited number of cities. How would you explain the choice of Dunkirk, Stalingrad, and Palermo?

3. What ideas does this map convey about:

   a) the importance of the success of the North African campaign to the Allies?

   b) the role of the USSR in the defeat of Germany?

   c) the problems of the Allies in establishing a second front in Western Europe?

   d) the importance of supremacy in naval forces for the Allies?

   e) the importance of an effective air force?

ACTIVITIES

1. Define: Battle of the Atlantic; convoys; corvettes; Women's Division of the RCAF.

2. Give at least three reasons for the growth of technology and industry during World War II. How was radar used in the war? Why was coding important?

3. What did Winston Churchill mean when he said everything in the war depended on the outcome of the Battle of the Atlantic?

4. A TV film produced by the CBC in the 1990s implied that the firebombing of German cities by Allied forces was a war crime. The film aroused great controversy. What would be your opinion? Explain.

The Tide Turns

In 1942, the tide of the war finally began to turn. The Allies gained strength when the United States entered the conflict in December 1941. They began to win the Battle of the Atlantic and made important advances in the Pacific. By 1943, the Allies had cleared North Africa of Axis forces and could, once again, turn their attention to the invasion of Europe.

The Invasion of Italy

British Prime Minister Winston Churchill felt that the best way for the Allies to recapture Europe was through what he called the "soft un-

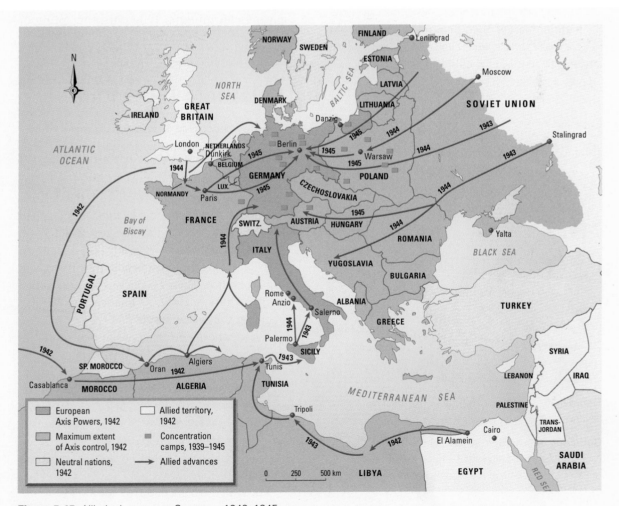

Figure 5-15 Allied advances on Germany, 1942–1945.

derbelly" of Europe—Italy and Sicily. The invasion ended up lasting almost two years, cost thousands of lives, and proved anything but soft.

On July 10, 1943, Canadian soldiers participated in the Allies' invasion of Sicily. After two weeks of fierce fighting, the Allies were successful. In September, they moved to mainland Italy where the rugged terrain, muddy conditions, and cold, rainy weather reminded many Canadian soldiers of the horrible conditions of World War I. Advances were slow; battles were often fought house by house and street by street. In the battle over one medieval coastal town, Ortona, Canadians fought for a month and lost 1372 soldiers before the Germans withdrew.

Canadian war correspondent Matthew Halton captured the drama of the fighting in this radio report from Ortona:

> Soaking wet, in a morass of mud, against an enemy fighting harder than he's fought before, the Canadians attack, attack and attack. The enemy is now fighting like the devil to hold us. He brings in more and more guns, more and more troops. The hillsides and farmlands and orchards are a ghastly brew of fire, and our roads [six kilometres] behind the [enemy] infantry are under heavy shelling....
>
> We have fire superiority, we have wonderful soldiers—there's a dogged fierceness about the Canadians now—but the enemy is well disciplined and cunning, and he knows all the tricks.... Some of his troops surrender to attacking Canadians. As the Canadian platoon advanced to take the surrender, they were mowed down by flanking machine guns. They were trapped and murdered—just one of the many treacheries....

Source: Quoted in *The Canadians at War, 1939–1945* (Montreal: Reader's Digest [Canada], 1969), 362.

The Allies' advance through Italy was difficult, but on June 4, 1944, they finally took Rome. Fighting continued in Italy until the spring of 1945.

Figure 5-16 Streets of Ortona after the Canadian advance.

Gathering information What might have been the cause of the devastation shown here? What can you tell about the effects of the fighting on the town and its residents?

D-Day and Liberation

The Allies' success in Rome was followed immediately by the biggest Allied invasion of the war. On June 6, 1944, "D-Day," the Allies launched "Operation Overlord"—a full-scale invasion of Europe. The Allies had learned from the disaster at Dieppe, and this time the invasion was planned and rehearsed down to the smallest detail.

There were to be five landing points along an eighty-kilometre stretch of beach in Normandy in northern France. These beaches were code-named "Sword," "Juno," "Gold," "Omaha," and "Utah." Attacks on the beaches were preceded by massive air attacks, and paratroopers were parachuted in behind the German lines. On the morning of June 6, over 30 000 Canadians soldiers arrived at "Juno" Beach (see inset map, Figure 5-17) as part of the first wave of the attack. The task was daunting: they had to make their way past the concrete barriers the Germans had erected, through barbed wire and other obstacles, in order to work their way inland.

The Allied troops had two advantages. First, they had massive air and naval support, with the

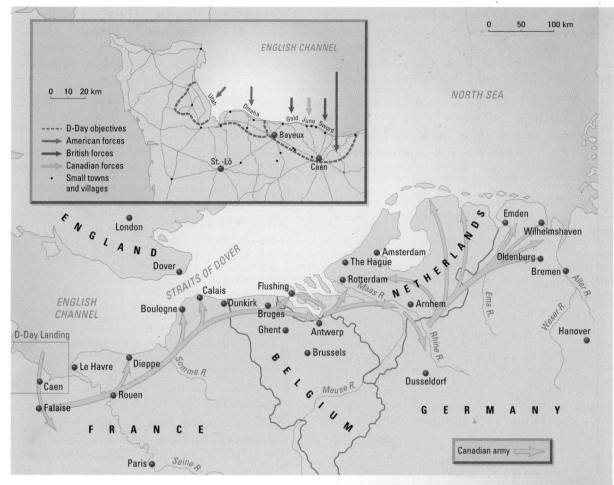

Figure 5-17 D-Day. The Allies landed on a stretch of French coast over 80 km long. Canadians landed at "Juno" Beach; they were divided into different units, each responsible for a specific area. From Normandy, the Allies pushed through France, Belgium, the Netherlands, and into Germany.

Reading a map What route did the Canadians use in their attack on the Netherlands? Why were Canadian troops hailed as heroes there?

ability to land more than a million troops within two or three weeks of the initial landing. Second, they had managed to keep the details of the attack a secret from the Germans. The weather had been stormy leading up to the invasion, and although the Germans had anticipated an attack, their meteorologists concluded that the Allies would not attempt a landing in bad weather. As a result, the German defence was poorly coordinated. Even so, casualties from that day were high—359 Canadians died and 715 were wounded. But these figures were lower than had been expected.

It took the Allies weeks of constant fighting to work their way inland. Then, they began an eleven-month advance through France and Belgium, towards Germany. The campaign was exhausting, brutal, and dangerous, but there were also moving moments in which the Allies were welcomed as the liberators of Europe. In September, for example, Canadians marched triumphantly through the streets of Dieppe, where only two years earlier they had suffered a terrible defeat. Once again, Canadian correspondent Ross Munro was there:

I reached Dieppe in a scout car, my mind flooded with emotions.... I thought of the men who had died there [in 1942], who were wounded, who were taken prisoner when they could fight no longer....

As I drove through the extravagant happiness of the crowds, the flowers, the memories, an old lady tottered up to my scout car with a bouquet of flowers.... A hundred people crushed around, wanting to shake our hands, to kiss us, to tell us how welcome we were.

Source: Quoted in *The Canadians at War, 1939–1945* (vol. 2) (Montreal: Reader's Digest [Canada], 1969), 522.

In March 1945, Allied forces attacked Germany. The Canadians were given a separate task: the liberation of the Netherlands. This was a difficult job. An earlier Allied attempt to liberate Holland in 1944 had failed; German troops had retaliated by destroying much of the port cities of Amsterdam and Rotterdam, and by flooding much of the countryside. By the end of 1944, food and fuel supplies to the Dutch had been cut off, and many were starving to death. The bitter winter of 1944–1945 made difficult conditions even worse for civilians. One Red Cross worker in the Netherlands described the desperation: "In the struggle for existence, men even eat flower bulbs. Horses killed in bombardments are immediately cut up [for food] by passersby."

In early April, Canadian troops began their attack on the Netherlands. The fighting was slow, and, as in Italy only months earlier, battles were often fought house by house. Casualties were high: over 6300 Canadians were killed in the operation. By April 17, the Canadians had defeated the German army in the northern city of Groningen. They then worked their way south to the city of Zwolle, while other Canadian troops fought their way to the cities of Arnhem and Apeldoorn. By May 4, the German troops in the Netherlands were surrounded, and they surrendered. Even before the German surrender, Canadians had begun air drops of food over parts of the Netherlands. These air drops were followed by convoys of trucks carrying food and fuel. Eventually, Canadian army trucks were delivering thousands of tonnes of food a day to the civilian population. Canadians were hailed as heroes in victory parades throughout the Netherlands. Wim Alings, Jr., who was a boy in the Netherlands during the war, recalls when the Canadian troops entered his town:

Early the next morning I was awakened by shouts in the house: "They will be here in an hour!" They came in jeeps, tanks and trucks—fellows in funny uniforms. They waved. Everybody waved. Now and then the column [procession] was held up and people jumped on the cars, but the children were

Figure 5-18
Celebrating the liberation of the Netherlands by Canadian troops in the Dutch city of Delden, April 1945.

not so daring that first morning. It was hours before we began to run after them, shouting, hoping to draw the attention of just one Canadian, or to catch just one of the cigarettes they were throwing by handfuls into the streets.... That same week we got bread and chocolate and chewing gum....

Source: Quoted in *The Canadians at War, 1939–1945* (vol. 2) (Montreal: Reader's Digest [Canada], 1969), 650.

While the Allies invaded Germany from the west, the Soviet Union attacked from the east. Facing certain defeat, Germany surrendered on May 7, 1945. Earlier, Hitler, together with his wife Eva Braun, had committed suicide in a bunker in Berlin rather than submit to the Allies.

The Holocaust Discovered

At the end of the war, as the Allies pressed closer to Germany, they discovered the extent of Nazi atrocities. Millions of people had been murdered, and the piles of corpses and starving people the Allies found in the concentration camps horrified them. The following letter was written by a Canadian soldier at Bergen-Belsen.

Tonight I am a different man. I have spent the last two days in Belsen concentration camp, the most horrible festering scab there has ever been on the face of humanity.... It makes me sick to my stomach even to imagine the smell, and I want to weep

Figure 5-19 Survivors from Buchenwald concentration camp in Jena, near Germany. Right: Author Elie Wiesel wrote about his experiences during the Holocaust in his book, *Night*. Wiesel was later awarded the Nobel Peace Prize. He is also shown in the photo above, the farthest face on the right in the centre bunk.

and go out in the streets and kill every Nazi I see when I think of what they have done....

You have seen pictures in the papers but they cannot tell the story. You have to smell it and feel it and keep a stern look on your face while your heart tears itself into pieces and tears of compassion drench your soul....

Source: PR Officer King Whyte, Department of Psychological Warfare, Canadian First Army Source.

The anti-Semitic and racist views of Hitler and the Nazi government were well known in the 1930s. By 1941, the Nazi government adopted the "Final Solution"—a grisly and horrifying plan

counterpoints

Is the Use of Weapons of Mass Destruction Ever Justified?

During World War II, both the United States and Germany were secretly working on developing a new kind of weapon to win the war. It was a race to see who could develop the technology first. On July 16, 1945, a group of U.S. scientists succeeded in testing the most powerful bomb that had ever been built: the atomic bomb. By this time, the Allied powers were desperate to end the war. Millions of people had died in World War II, and billions of dollars of damage had been caused worldwide. Still, the team of scientists who had developed the bomb and witnessed the test were awestruck by the power of the weapon they had created:

We knew the world would not be the same. A few people laughed. A few people cried. Most were silent. I remembered the line from the Hindu scripture—the Bhagavad-Gita. Vishnu is trying to persuade the prince that he should do his duty and to impress him, takes on his multi-armed form and says, "Now I am become Death, the destroyer of the worlds." I suppose we all felt that, one way or another.

Source: Robert Oppenheimer, leader of the scientific team at Los Alamos; quoted in Gwynne Dyer, *War* (New York: Crown Publishers, 1985), 96.

The atomic bomb ended the war against Japan, but the controversy surrounding its use continues. Was it necessary to use such a deadly weapon? Even before the bomb was dropped, there were those who believed the use of such a weapon could never be justified.

Admiral William Leahy, an adviser to U.S. President Truman, opposed the use of the bombs. In 1944, he argued with Truman's predecessor, Franklin Roosevelt, advising him not to use the bomb. Leahy later wrote:

Personally I recoiled at the idea and said to Roosevelt: "Mr. President, this would violate every Christian ethic I have ever heard of and all known laws of war. It would be an attack on the noncombatant population of the enemy...."

It was my opinion that the use of this barbarous weapon at Hiroshima and Nagasaki was of no material assistance in our war.... The Japanese were already defeated and ready to surrender.... My own feeling was that in being the first to use it, we had adopted an ethical standard common to the barbarians of the Dark Ages. I was not taught to make war in that fashion, and wars cannot be won by destroying women and children....

Source: Memoirs of Admiral Willam D. Leahy, <www.peacewire.org.hironecessary.html>.

Colonel Paul Tibbets, commander of the air force squadron that dropped the bombs on Japan and pilot of the plane that dropped the bomb on Hiroshima, rejects such criticism, which, he feels, fails to take into consideration the "context of the times":

As for the missions flown against Japan on the 6th and 9th of August, 1945, I would remind you, we were at war. Our job was to win. Once the targets

to rid their society of all people they considered undesirable. Death camps were built in a number of places, including Bergen-Belsen and Buchenwald in Germany and Auschwitz and Treblinka in Poland. German scientists experimented with the most efficient ways of killing large numbers of people.

Jews from all over Europe were shipped to the death camps. On arrival, they were stripped of their clothes and valuables, their heads were shaved, and families were separated. The weak, the old, and the young were sent immediately to the "showers," which spurted not water, but deadly Zyklon-B gas. The strong and healthy were put to

---

were named and presidential approval received, we were to deliver the weapons as expeditiously as possible, consistent with good tactics. The objective was to stop the fighting, thereby saving further loss of life on both sides. The urgency of the situation demanded that we use the weapons first— before the technology could be used against us.

Source: Statement on accepting Air Force Sergeants Association's Freedom Award, <www.glue.umd.edu/~enola/vets/tibbets.html>.

For almost 200 years, war strategists (planners of war) have been influenced by the writings of Karl von Clausewitz, a Prussian general who supported the idea of total war. He believed a country's entire resources had to be used to ensure victory:

To introduce into a philosophy of war a principle of moderation would be an absurdity. War is an act of violence pushed to its utmost bounds.

Source: Karl von Clausewitz, 1819; quoted by Gwynne Dyer, *War* (New York: Crown Publishers, 1985), 75.

Once scientists discovered how to make atomic weapons, however, von Clausewitz's theory of total war had to be re-evaluated. Suddenly, weapons existed that could destroy all of humanity. Since the end of World War II, nuclear weapons have been built that are a hundred times more powerful than the bombs dropped on Japan. Biological weapons that spread deadly microorganisms, such as anthrax and smallpox, have also been developed, as well as deadly chemical weapons such as nerve gas. Von Clausewitz could never have envisioned destruction on such a scale.

Many nations have agreed to treaties that limit the testing of nuclear weapons. The Strategic Arms Limitation Treaty (SALT) between the United States and the Soviet Union was ratified in 1972. A second treaty on arms limitation was signed in 1979, although it was never ratified. Other agreements to reduce the arsenal of nuclear weapons were signed: one in 1988 between the United States and the Soviet Union, and another in 1991 between the United States and the Soviet Union. Despite these various agreements, both the United States and Russia still have the capability of destroying the world several times over.

In spite of international agreements that ban the use of biological and chemical weapons, there is strong evidence that Iraq used chemical weapons on its Kurdish population in 1988, according to the international human rights organization Human Rights Watch. It is also conceivable that such weapons could be used by a rogue state—a country that ignores international agreements and takes actions for its own gain to the detriment of other nations.

Analysing the Issue

1. What reasons did Admiral Leahy give against using the atomic bomb?

2. What three arguments did Colonel Paul Tibbets give to support the use of the atomic bomb on Japan?

3. What do you think Robert Oppenheimer meant when he said, "We knew the world would not be the same"?

4. Do you think there are any circumstances in which weapons of mass destruction could ever be justified? Explain your answer.

work. Their turn at the "showers" came when over-work, starvation, and disease had weakened them. By 1945, the Germans had murdered more than six million Jews, Roma (Gypsies), Slavs, and other people they considered inferior, in what has come to be known as the **Holocaust**.

Japan Surrenders

After the Allied victory in Europe, the war in the Pacific intensified. By mid-1945, most of the Japanese air force and navy had been destroyed, but the army was still strong. The Japanese had demonstrated that they would "fight to the last person." In response, the U.S. government decided to use the atomic bomb—a completely new kind of weapon, equal in power to over 20 000 t of TNT.

For some time, U.S. and British scientists had been working on the Manhattan Project, a top-secret plan to develop a nuclear bomb. In 1942, Canada was made aware of the project. Uranium was an important component of the bomb, and the Eldorado mine at Great Bear Lake, NWT, produced uranium. The Canadian government secretly bought the mine.

On August 6, 1945, a U.S. bomber (nick-named the "Enola Gay," after the pilot's mother) dropped an atomic bomb over the Japanese city of Hiroshima. The destruction unleashed by the bomb had never been experienced before. Some 70 000 residents of Hiroshima were killed. The explosion was so powerful that some people were instantly vaporized, with only the imprint of their shadows left on the streets. Another 130 000 were wounded, many of them severely burned by radiation or injured by collapsing buildings.

Three days after the bombing of Hiroshima, a second atomic bomb was dropped on Nagasaki, killing 40 000 people. The Japanese, realizing that they could not withstand the power of the new U.S. weapon, surrendered. World War II was over.

ACTIVITIES

1. What was D-Day? Why was it necessary? How did the D-Day invasion differ from the raid on Dieppe? What role did Canadian troops play in these invasions?

2. In your own words, explain the situation in the Netherlands in the spring of 1945. Why were Canadian troops hailed as heroes in the Netherlands?

3. Working with a partner, read Matthew Halton's description of the battle of Ortona. List examples of descriptive language and of images he uses. What characteristics do you think are needed to be a good war correspondent? Together with your partner, write a radio report of Canada's role in the D-Day invasion.

4. Since World War II, Canada and many other nations have enacted laws that protect their citizens' human rights, including laws to protect them against discrimination based on race. How do you think the Holocaust contributed to this movement?

The War at Home

The roles played by Canadians at home were just as important in winning the war as were the actions of the armed forces. Under the policy of total war, Canadian factories were producing more goods than ever before. Workers put in long hours, many working seven days a week. Before long, there was a shortage of labour. As in World War I, women were mobilized to take men's places, and they began working as welders, drillers, punch-press operators, and machine operators. "Rosie the Riveter" became a popular nickname for these working women.

Single women were in high demand as factory workers as they often had limited family obligations and could work long hours. But married women also found factory work, and in Ontario and Quebec, where most munitions factories were located, the provincial governments began to provide money for day care facilities. Many workers, especially single women, moved from rural areas to the industrial cities. Companies built dormitories to house them close to the factories, and the government helped subsidize the food and rent in the dormitories.

Canada's Wartime Economy

With so much increased production and employment, people suddenly had more money to spend. But there were also fewer goods to buy, as most of what was being produced was being shipped to Britain. Prime Minister King wanted to avoid the problem of **inflation**, in which "too many dollars were chasing too few goods." King also wished to prevent the massive debt problem that had burdened Canada after the last war.

King chose James Ilsley, a former lawyer from Nova Scotia, to address these concerns. As minister of finance, Ilsley enthusiastically set about encouraging Canadians to buy Victory Bonds, as they had during World War I. By selling bonds, the government would ensure that Canadians saved money, which would help solve the problem of inflation. The government would then use the money from the bonds to help finance the war. Ilsley also increased income taxes, which helped the government's revenue.

Ilsley was successful in raising funds for the government, but his actions did not prevent prices from rising, and this increased inflation. In 1941, the Wartime Prices and Trade Board took the drastic step of freezing all wages and prices as a way to prevent inflation. Then, in 1942, King introduced food rationing, which meant Canadians were allowed only a limited amount of certain goods per week. For example, each Canadian adult was limited to a weekly ration of about 1 kg of meat, 220 g of sugar, 250 g of butter, and about 115 g of coffee. Canadian rations were generous compared with those in England and the United States.

Figure 5-21 The Canadian government used posters to remind Canadians of the need for everyone to play a part in the war effort, including being aware of possible spies.

Identifying viewpoint How serious does the danger of spying and sabotage appear to be from this poster? What course of action does it suggest citizens take? What techniques does it use to create an impact on the viewer?

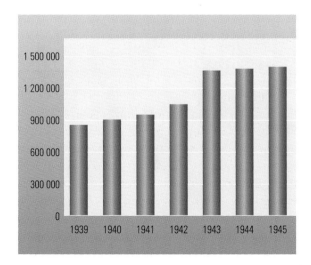

Figure 5-20 Women with jobs, 1939–1945.

The Growing Demand for Social Change

During the war, the federal government also tried to restrict or prevent strikes by unions. The power of trade unions was limited also with the introduction of wage and price controls. The acute shortage of labour, however, often worked to the unions' advantage, and many ignored restrictions on the right to strike. Workers wanted higher wages, but they were also demanding the right to bargain. Canada's Minister of Munitions and Supply, C.D. Howe, was strongly anti-union, but his harsh stand against organized labour didn't stop steel workers in Nova Scotia and coal miners in Alberta and British Columbia from going on strike in 1943. In 1944, the federal government softened its policy, allowing workers the right to join a union and forcing employers to recognize unions chosen by their workers.

The war brought changes to the role of government, as well. The wartime government had been involved in almost every aspect of Canadians' lives, and many Canadians wanted some of this involvement to continue. The CCF party and its platform of social reform was becoming increasingly popular at both the national and provincial levels, a fact that was not lost on Prime Minister King. In 1943, the CCF made up the opposition in Ontario; in 1944, it formed the government in Saskatchewan under T.C. "Tommy" Douglas. Prime Minister King had already brought in an unemployment insurance program in 1940. In 1945, he expanded Canada's social assistance programs by bringing in the Family Allowance program, which helped families cover the cost of child maintenance. Canada's policy of "cradle to grave" social security had begun.

The Conscription Crisis

Even though Mackenzie King had promised there would be no conscription, the speed with which the Germans occupied Europe in 1940 stunned Canadians. Many Canadians, including the opposition Conservative Party, demanded more government action. In response to these demands, King's government quickly brought in the National Resources Mobilization Act (NRMA). This act gave the government special emergency powers to mobilize all the resources in the nation to defeat the enemy. Most significantly, the NRMA allowed for conscription, but only for home defence.

As the war progressed, however, King continued to come under pressure from the

Figure 5-22 Anti-conscription rally in Montreal, 1939.

Gathering information
From this photograph, who do you think attended this rally? Why might the rally draw these people to attend?

Conservative opposition to adopt overseas conscription. King decided to hold a plebiscite to get people's views on the issue. On April 27, 1942, voters were asked whether they would release the government from its promise not to send conscripts overseas. In all provinces except Quebec, the majority voted "yes." Once again, the issue of conscription had divided the nation. In an amendment to the National Resources Mobilization Act in August 1942, King finally permitted overseas conscription, even though conscripts were not sent until 1944. Quebec felt betrayed by King's actions. King tried to smooth over the conflict with the slogan, "Not necessarily conscription, but conscription if necessary." His strategy didn't work; the slogan failed to satisfy either side. Frustrated by King's inaction, the Minister of Defence, J.L. Ralston, resigned. Ralston later changed his mind and stayed in his position, but King kept Ralston's letter of resignation. For the next two years, King managed to avoid the issue of overseas conscription.

In the 1944 invasion of Europe, however, Canada had lost almost 23 000 soldiers, and there was now a severe shortage of trained infantry. Ralston journeyed to Europe to see for himself whether more Canadian troops were needed to help win the war. He concluded that they definitely were. But King refused to be convinced. In a move that stunned his Cabinet, King announced Ralston's resignation, two years after it had been submitted. King then replaced Ralston with General Andrew McNaughton, commander of the Canadian army in Europe from 1939 until 1943. King believed that, as a military man, McNaughton would be able to convince the men conscripted under the NRMA to volunteer for duty overseas. But McNaughton failed to do so, and King finally had to agree to send conscripts overseas. In the final months of the war, some 12 000 NRMA conscripts were sent to Europe. Not all went peacefully. Conscripts in British Columbia refused to leave at first, and there were riots in Montreal to protest King's decision. The Quebec legislature passed a motion condemning the federal government's actions. In the end, only 2463 Canadian conscripts ever reached the front.

ACTIVITIES

1. What three initiatives did the Canadian government undertake to prevent inflation and pay for the war? How successful were these initiatives?

2. What social changes were taking place in Canada during the war? What demands were unions making?

3. Explain how Mackenzie King managed to avoid sending conscripts overseas during the war. Why did he eventually have to send troops overseas?

What the War Meant to Canada

Under its policy of total war, Canada provided major military and economic support to the Allies. The value of goods it produced rose from $5.6 billion in 1939 to $11.8 billion in 1945. During the course of the war, financial aid given by Canada to the Allies amounted to $3.4 billion. By the end of the war, Canada was known as the "arsenal [military storehouse] of democracy."

Virtually every sector of the economy boomed. There was a rapid increase in the production of aluminum, the strong, rust-proof, and light metal used in the manufacture of aircraft. Paper production rose, too, because Germany had occupied Norway and Sweden, and was preventing paper products from reaching Germany's enemies. There was also a great increase in demand for petroleum products to fuel wartime tanks, trucks, and airplanes. A wave of exploration led to major discoveries of oil fields in Alberta. Many new jobs were created, not just in production but also in transportation, processing, and providing services for the new industries.

All this activity had a dramatic effect on Canada's economy. One measure of a nation's output is its **gross domestic product** (GDP). This figure is the value of all the goods (such as food, cars, and airplanes) and services (such as nursing, insurance, and education) produced in a country in one year. Figure 5-25 on page 128 shows how Canada's GDP increased during the war years.

up close

Japanese-Canadians in the War

As the war in the Pacific heated up, many Canadians, particularly those in British Columbia, feared that Canada itself might be attacked. After the Japanese bombed Pearl Harbour and invaded Hong Kong, many west coast communities in Canada "blacked out" their areas at night, turning off all their lights so that their location would not be obvious to airborne attackers. Japanese-Canadians living in British Columbia became a special target of public suspicion. If the Japanese attacked Canada, it was thought, local residents of Japanese descent might assist them. Some people became convinced there were Japanese spies in their midst. These suspicions were strengthened by local editorials, gossip, and years of racism towards Canada's Japanese population.

By 1941, there were over 23 000 Japanese-Canadians living in Canada, 22 000 in British Columbia. There was no evidence to suggest that any of these people supported Japan rather than Canada. Indeed, some had served in the Canadian armed forces during World War I. For this service, they had been promised the right to vote in 1918, but by the outbreak of World War II, this promise had still not been fulfilled.

Neither the government nor the Mounties considered the Japanese-Canadians a security risk. But as anti-Japanese sentiment grew into hysteria, the federal government caved in to public pressure. In early 1942, under the War Measures Act, all Japanese-Canadians living near the British Columbia coast were "invited" to move to the Okanagan Valley, where they would be settled in temporary camps known as "relocation centres." In the wake of anti-Japanese marches in Vancouver, about 750 people moved voluntarily. Soon all Japanese-Canadians, regardless of how long they had been living in Canada, were forced to leave the coast.

Families were separated, and many were sent to isolated **internment camps** in the interior of British Columbia, where they were detained without trial until the end of the war. Some families chose to go, instead, to Alberta or Manitoba, where they laboured on beet farms. These locations were farther away from their homes, but at least families were permitted to stay together.

In January 1943, the Custodian of Enemy Property, a federal government official, was given the power to confiscate and sell Japanese-Canadian property. People who had been relocated inland lost everything: their houses, cars, shops, fishing boats, and other property. All their possessions were sold at fire-sale prices, and the owners received virtually nothing.

The persecution did not end when the war did, in 1945. At that point, the federal government offered

Figure 5-23 Victory Bond poster.

Identifying viewpoint
Who do the rats in this poster represent? What is the apparent purpose of this poster? What other effects might it have had?

If they over-run Canada your money'll be useless...

Buy VICTORY BONDS Now

UNDERWOOD ELLIOTT FISHER LIMITED *makers of* UNDERWOOD TYPEWRITERS

Figure 5-24 Part of a Japanese-Canadian family awaits relocation from Vancouver, 1942. Many families were separated, with men being interned separately.

Japanese-Canadians a terrible choice. They could apply for repatriation to Japan, which had been devastated by war, or they could agree to settle permanently east of the Rocky Mountains. Canada's right to deport its own citizens who were innocent of wrongdoing was challenged, but the Supreme Court, in a close vote, upheld the government's position. In all, 3964 Japanese-Canadians were repatriated. Of these, over 2600 were Canadian citizens, of whom 1979 had been born in Canada. Thousands of others were relocated to other parts of Canada.

In 1947, the government bowed to public pressure and cancelled the repatriation order. It was not until 1988, however, that the federal government apologized for its actions. As compensation, it agreed to pay the 1400 people who were affected by the policy and were still living $21 000 each. It also agreed to restore Canadian citizenship to any person who had lost it through repatriation to Japan.

Questions

1. **a)** What attitudes do you think contributed to support for the evacuation of Japanese-Canadians during World War II? Give evidence from this account.

   b) How would posters such as the ones shown on pages 123 and 126 contribute to these attitudes?

2. Do you think Japanese-Canadians should have been given

   a) compensation earlier?

   b) more compensation?

   c) no compensation?

3. The veterans from Hong Kong who were imprisoned in Japan were not given compensation for maltreatment, starvation, or being used as slave labour in Japanese factories, all of which were in violation of the rules of war. People often cite the compensation given to Japanese-Canadians as a reason why the Canadian government should negotiate with the Japanese for compensation for these veterans. Do you agree with this reasoning? Why or why not?

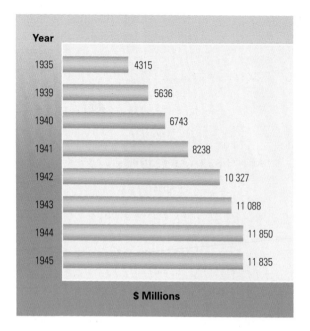

Year	$ Millions
1935	4315
1939	5636
1940	6743
1941	8238
1942	10 327
1943	11 088
1944	11 850
1945	11 835

Figure 5-25 Value of Canada's gross domestic product (total value of all goods and services produced), 1935–1945.

Reading a graph What is the difference in the gross domestic product from 1935 to 1945? What accounted for the increase?

The wartime boom brought another important change to the Canadian economy. Agriculture, once the most important sector of Canada's economy, was overtaken by industry. Manufacturing was now much more important. Huge investments were made in mining, production, transportation, and service industries. Canadian cities and the industrial areas around them became much more important contributors to the economy. They attracted a massive wave of post-war immigration that eventually led to the multicultural society we know today. There is probably no other ten-year period when there was more change to Canada's economy than in the period from 1939 to 1949. Canada had become a modern industrial nation.

Building an Identity

Canada's enormous contribution to the war, in both human and economic terms, gave it a new role on the world stage. Just a few years before, Canada had been a colony in the British Empire; now, Canadians were major players in the global conflict. They had built the world's third-largest navy and fourth-largest air force.

Although many Canadians were killed, wounded, or captured, World War II became a defining event in the development of Canada's identity:

> It was a good war. I'm not talking about a good war from the standpoint of a high moral purpose. If going out and killing millions of [Germans] to get Hitler off his ... pedestal is a high moral purpose, then I'm all for it.
>
> But it was a good war for Canada too, because it made us a great nation. I mean ... it showed us what we could do. We just weren't a bunch of wheat farmers and Nova Scotia fishermen and lumbermen in B.C. We were a nation. A big and tough and strong nation.

Source: Quoted in Barry Broadfoot, *Six War Years, 1939–1945: Memories of Canadians at Home and Abroad* (Toronto: Doubleday, 1974), 11.

ACTIVITIES

1. **a)** How did the war end the Depression?

   b) What were the major changes in Canada's economy during this period?

2. **a)** Why do you think the CCF made gains during the war?

   b) What was the federal government's response to these gains?

3. Why do you think there was opposition to conscription in Canada?

4. Do you agree that "It was a good war"? Explain your viewpoint.

LOOKING BACK

Develop an Understanding

1. Write four statements explaining how the character of Canada was changed by World War II.

2. In your own words, summarize Canada's contribution to World War II.

3. The table below shows the losses of both the German U-boats and the Allied ships during the Battle of the Atlantic. Examine the table closely and, in your own words, describe this battle, using figures to explain the pattern of fighting.

Year	U-boats Active	U-boats Sunk	Allied Ships Sunk
1940	42	22	435
1941	110	35	410
1942	300	87	1015
1943	330	237	435

4. Write a series of five headlines about key events described in this chapter. Be sure to focus on events and aspects of those events that would have been most significant at the time.

Explore the Issues

5. Could war have been avoided if Britain, France, and their allies had stood up to Hitler's demands earlier than they did? Formulate a resolution based on this idea and use it for a class debate.

6. Why do you think the RCAF allowed the Women's Division only a small number of military roles in the war? In your opinion, what roles should women play in military life today?

7. The moral question raised by the Americans dropping atomic bombs on Japan to bring the war to an end has become an issue of debate. The Germans were developing the technology to build a similar bomb. Does this change your views on this issue? Why or why not?

8. Do you think the war had a "high moral purpose," as suggested on page 128? Choose three events in the war that raised moral questions, and explain why you chose these.

Research and Communicate

9. Assume you are the editor of a national newspaper. Prepare an editorial that might have been published the day after Mackenzie King and J.S. Woodsworth spoke in the House of Commons to give their opinion on a declaration of war. In the editorial, state where, when, and why the speeches were made. Summarize King's and Woodsworth's positions. Then state your newspaper's position, together with its reasons for taking this view.

10. Work with a partner. Assume you are a radio journalist who has the opportunity to interview Prime Minister King on September 11, 1939, the day after Canada has declared war on Germany. Prepare a ten-question interview, taking care to ask a range of questions from simple factual questions to more speculative ones. Role-play your interview for the class.

11. Go to the Web site for the *Encyclopedia Britannica* at **<www.britannica.com>**. Find information on the Nuremberg war crimes trials. What was the purpose of these trials? What was the outcome? Prepare a written or oral report on your findings.

12. Assume you are a veteran of World War I. Write a letter to your son or daughter who wants to volunteer for duty in World War II. In the letter, give reasons why you either support this decision or why you want him or her to reconsider it.

13. Contact the Canadian Legion in your area and ask if there are any veterans from World War II who would be willing to visit your school and share their experiences with the class. If you have any relatives who remember the war, interview them about their experiences. Videotape the interview and show it to the class.

14. The Japanese committed atrocities in China ("the rape of Nanking") and abused Chinese and Korean women as so-called "comfort women" during the war. Investigate the treaties made with Japan to find out how the war crimes investigations in Japan were different from the Nuremberg trials, and why.

Canada in the Post-War World

6

FOCUS ON

• What was the Cold War, and what was Canada's role in it?

• Why was globalization of the economy an issue by the end of the twentieth century?

• What were Canada's post-war relations with the United States and with the developing world?

• How did Canada's involvement in U.N. peacekeeping, NORAD, and NATO affect the way Canadians saw themselves as a nation?

Counterpoints Issue

• What role should Canada play in U.S.-dominated military alliances?

Horse and Train by Alex Colville. The end of World War II did not bring world peace, as many had hoped. Tension between the United States and the Soviet Union increased, and the threat of nuclear war was ever present. The sense of confrontation in this painting reflects the tensions of the post-war period.

Expressing ideas Alex Colville painted *Horse and Train* in 1954, when it was clear to everyone that the so-called Cold War was underway. Why do you think Colville chose a horse and train as his subjects? How would you describe the mood of this painting?

Introduction

On a hot evening in September 1945, Igor Gouzenko, a Russian clerk at the Soviet embassy in Ottawa, left work with several documents hidden under his clothes. These papers proved that a Soviet spy ring was operating within the Canadian government. Gouzenko was enjoying life in Ottawa, and he had decided to defect from the Soviet Union to Canada.

Gouzenko took the documents to the *Ottawa Journal* and tried to convince the newspaper of the Soviet spies' existence. No one paid attention. The next day, fearing for his life, and with his pregnant wife and child in tow, Gouzenko tried again. This time, he went to the offices of the RCMP, the department of justice, and the prime minister's office. Again, his efforts were in vain. Only when Soviet agents broke into Gouzenko's apartment did the Ottawa police finally listen to his story. Shocked Canadian officials secretly informed the British and U.S. governments that a Soviet spy ring had been operating in Canada.

On a grey February dawn in 1946, the RCMP rounded up several people suspected of being Soviet spies. They kept the suspects in isolation, without charge, and without legal counsel. Eventually, eighteen people were brought to trial; eight were found guilty and imprisoned.

The spy ring was likely trying to discover the secrets of the atomic bomb, but it appeared that the Soviets had learned very little. The Gouzenko affair did, however, startle Canadians into the new era of foreign affairs.

During World War II, the United States and the Soviet Union had been allies. Nevertheless, they had little in common except for their opposition to the Axis powers. Once the war was over, tensions between the two countries surfaced. The two powers were soon openly hostile towards each other, though they were careful not to start a new war. Instead, they used espionage (spies) and helped their allies in "little wars" and revolutions. Both East and West built stockpiles of conventional arms, powerful nuclear weapons, biological and chemical weapons, long-range bombers, missiles, and atomic submarines.

Post-war tensions between the Soviet Union and the United States forced Canada to align itself closely with U.S. interests. At the same time, Canada tried to remain true to the goals and aspirations of Canadians—no easy task. Through the early part of the twentieth century, Canada had achieved independence from Britain; in the

Figure 6-1 Igor Gouzenko and his family were given new identities and settled in Ontario. Gouzenko wrote a book about his experiences and occasionally appeared in public, as in this television interview. He always wore a hood for fear that the KGB, the Soviet Secret Service, would kill him if they discovered his new identity.

latter half, it struggled to keep U.S. influences from weakening its national identity. In this chapter, you will examine the various ways Canada tried to fulfil its commitment to international organizations while maintaining sovereignty over its policies.

1945 World War II ends.

United Nations is created.

1949 United States, Canada, and ten Western countries form NATO.

Communists take over China.

1950 North Korea invades South Korea; Korean War begins.

1955 Soviet Union and many Eastern European countries form Warsaw Pact.

1956 Lester Pearson, as Canada's Minister of External Affairs, works to defuse the Suez crisis.

1957 Progressive Conservative leader John Diefenbaker becomes prime minister.

1961–1975 Vietnam War is fought.

1961 Berlin Wall is built, dividing Berlin into east and west.

1962 Cuban missile crisis threatens world peace.

1963 Liberal leader Lester Pearson defeats Diefenbaker and becomes prime minister.

1979 USSR invades Afghanistan.

1989 Berlin Wall is destroyed, marking symbolic end of Cold War.

Canada–U.S. Free Trade Agreement is implemented.

1991 Canada participates in the Gulf War.

1994 Canada joins NAFTA.

1999 Canadian air force joins NATO attacks on Yugoslavia.

The Cold War Begins

While Canadians and other allied countries celebrated the end of World War II, they soon realized that the world was about to become involved in another kind of war. The military strength of the Soviet Union and the United States made them **superpowers**, each capable of inflicting massive destruction. As a result of this destructive capability, the two superpowers did not fight a direct war between themselves. To do so would have meant nuclear annihilation. Instead, they competed for political influence in other parts of the world, especially in developing nations that were poorer and less politically stable than themselves. This rivalry between the two superpowers was called the **Cold War** because it did not erupt into an open war. It was to last over forty years.

The roots of the Cold War lay in the differing views these two countries had on political and economic systems. The Soviet Union was communist; the government controlled all industry and commerce. Under communism, no political opposition was tolerated. The United States and most Western countries were **capitalist**. Their economies were based on private enterprise, with individuals investing in business for profit. Citizens had basic freedoms such a free press and freedom of speech.

Western countries were suspicious of communism. As in earlier decades, they feared that communists aimed to overthrow Western societies in a world revolution. The Soviet Union, for its part, was suspicious of its previous allies. It believed that the Western countries might try to invade Soviet territory through Europe, particularly through East Germany.

To create a buffer between the USSR and Western Europe, the Soviets took over the countries of Eastern Europe and established communist governments there. Then communists took over China in 1949, and the former government fled to Taiwan. The United States took drastic action to stop any spread of communism on its home front. The U.S. Congress established a Committee on Un-American Activities to root out communists from all areas of public life. This committee was chaired by Senator Joseph McCarthy, who terrified the nation with secret lists of supposed communists in government, universities, the entertainment industry, and even the Girl Scouts. Anyone suspected of being a communist could be persecuted, fired, and blacklisted (prevented from finding another job).

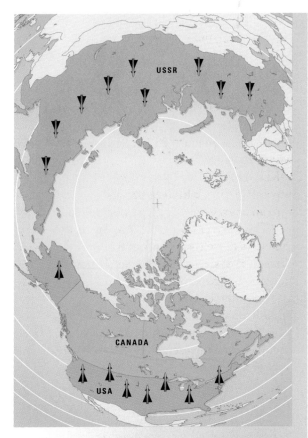

Figure 6-2 The United States and the Soviet Union both stockpiled weapons in the years following World War II.

Gathering information Where is Canada on this polar projection? In what way does the polar projection clarify the threat to Canada?

The Cold War at Home

While Canadians saw little of the hysteria and "witch-hunting" that took place during the McCarthy era in the United States, they were shocked to learn that a communist spy ring had been operating in Canada during the war.

In 1949, the leader of the Conservative Party tried to make the spread of communism, or the "red menace"—the term used to describe the Soviets—an issue. He accused the government of harbouring communists in the civil service. Prime Minister Louis St. Laurent, however, refused to outlaw communism. He reminded Canadians that such tactics were the trademarks of dictatorships, not democracies.

Nevertheless, some Canadians continued to fear the spread of communism. Union leaders who fought for better conditions for workers came under suspicion. Defence industries secretly sent lists of their employees to Ottawa for screening. Workers suspected of communist sympathies found themselves dismissed for no apparent reason. The RCMP Special Branch watched those who "might be or might become" a security risk, including artists, peace activists, union leaders, and intellectuals who were seen in any way to criticize the Canadian government. In Quebec, Premier Maurice Duplessis took a strong stand against communism. Police raided offices and private homes in search of "revolutionary" material. The Padlock Law was used to shut down suspected organizations and newspapers. When a poorly constructed bridge collapsed in Trois-Rivières in 1951, Duplessis blamed communist sabotage.

NATO and the Warsaw Pact

The United States took the lead in founding a new alliance aimed at protecting Western countries from the threat of invasion by the Soviet Union. In 1949, Canada joined the United States, Great Britain, and other Western European nations in a military alliance—the **North Atlantic Treaty Organization** (NATO). Any attack on one NATO member was to be treated as an attack on all. NATO members agreed that, if conventional weapons were not sufficient, they would use tactical nuclear weapons—atomic bombs and artillery shells. As a last resort, they would be prepared to wage total nuclear war.

When NATO admitted West Germany as a member, the Soviet Union felt threatened by NATO countries, and it established the **Warsaw Pact** in 1955. This alliance, made up of Eastern European countries, was to protect these countries and the Soviet Union from attack. A large

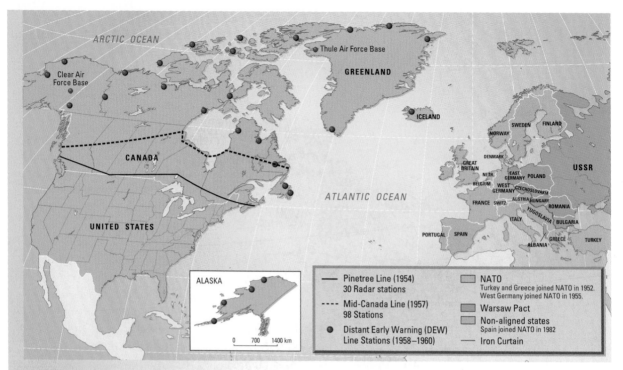

Figure 6-3 Countries of NATO and the Warsaw Pact. The dividing line between the Western European and communist countries was known as the "Iron Curtain," and movement of people and information from one side to the other was tightly restricted.

Thinking critically Why would countries in Western Europe feel threatened by the countries of the Warsaw Pact?

Canada's Commitment to NATO

Prime Minister Mackenzie King defended Canada's decision to join a military alliance in a time of peace. In a 1948 speech to the House of Commons, he stated:

> Where force threatens, it can be kept at bay by superior force. So long as communism remains a menace to the free world, it is vital to the defence of freedom to maintain ... military strength on the side of freedom, and to ensure the degree of unity among the nations which will ensure that they cannot be defeated one by one.
>
> Force has not in itself the power to create better conditions. But a measure of security is the first essential. If properly organized, the force required to provide security would have the power to save from destruction those who have at heart the aim of creating better conditions....

Canada made a serious commitment when it joined NATO. It agreed to keep a full army brigade and several air squadrons in Europe. It built and supplied military bases overseas. Canadian ships and aircraft tracked the movements of Soviet sub-

part of the northern hemisphere was now effectively divided into two hostile camps. Armies constantly practised for war, and countries continually added to their arsenals of weapons. Everywhere, spies and counterspies probed for weaknesses in their enemy's security, searching for secrets and carrying out assassinations and murders, promoting revolutions and counter-revolutions. In 1956, Soviet troops brutally crushed a revolution in Hungary. In 1961, communist-controlled East Germany built a wall around West Berlin to keep East Berliners in and West Berliners out. The Berlin Wall became a powerful symbol of the Cold War and the tensions that divided East from West.

Figure 6-4 Canadian sailors watch from the deck of HMCS *St. John's* as a Dutch refuelling ship prepares for an open-sea refuelling practice during NATO exercises in the Adriatic Sea, October 1998.

Thinking critically
Why were these kinds of activities necessary in the late 1990s?

marines. Canadian forces participated regularly in military exercises with Canada's allies. And perhaps most significantly, by joining NATO, Canada had to adapt its defence policy to those of its allies.

ACTIVITIES

1. **a)** What groups of Canadians came under suspicion of being communists? What actions were taken against some of these people?

   b) How was communism considered a threat to democracy?

2. What was the Cold War? Why did the Soviet Union want to have a buffer of countries between it and Western Europe?

3. What is NATO? Why was it formed? What did Prime Minister King mean when he said, "it is vital to the defence of freedom to maintain ... military strength on the side of freedom"?

4. What commitments did Canada make as a member of NATO? How did membership in NATO affect Canada's foreign policy?

The Issue of North American Defence

At first it seemed that, if hostilities broke out, Europe would be the battleground. However, when long-range bombers were developed to carry warheads to distant targets, North America also became vulnerable.

To protect against direct Soviet attack from the air, the United States built three lines of radar stations across Canada. The Pinetree Line, the Mid-Canada Line, and—in the Arctic—the DEW (Distant Early Warning) Line were constructed between 1950 and 1957. These stations were designed to detect a surprise Soviet attack over the North Pole, giving the United States time to launch a counterattack.

For the first time, U.S. military personnel were stationed on Canadian soil. Some Canadians felt that this defence system compromised their country's independence. To visit the DEW Line, for example, Canadian members of Parliament and journalists had to fly first to New York and gain security clearance from U.S. authorities. Most Canadians, however, accepted this loss of independence as the price of added security against an attack from the Soviet Union.

Their peace of mind was short-lived. Soon, the superpowers had developed intercontinental ballistic missiles, armed with nuclear warheads. Missiles launched from the USSR could reach North American cities within thirty minutes. The radar stations in Canada would not be able to detect them in time for anything to be done.

To meet the possible threat of Soviet attack on North America, Canada and the United States agreed, in 1957, to establish an integrated North American Air Defence agreement (NORAD). It would include fighter forces, missile bases, and air-defence radar, all controlled by a central command station built deep within Cheyenne Mountain, Colorado. NORAD had a force of one thousand bombers at its disposal at one time, some of which were always in the air, armed with nuclear weapons. A separate Canadian command post, under joint control, was established deep inside tunnels at North Bay, Ontario.

Civil Defence: The Home Front in the Cold War

Canadians feared that an open war between the USSR and the United States would result in a rain of nuclear bombs and missiles on their cities. The federal government developed civil defence plans, and cities prepared to protect their populations. Some cities had nuclear shelters in deep basements or subway lines. If an attack were to occur, sirens would sound a warning and people would try to find shelter. Schools ran drills to teach students to "duck and cover" (hide under desks) or to lie in ditches. *Scientific American* magazine declared that fallout shelter programs were a hoax—none of these shelters could provide real protection in case of nuclear attack. Nevertheless, the fear of a nuclear World War III was very real. Ironically, the existence of nuclear weapons—and the threat of mass destruction—probably prevented an all-out war between the superpowers.

Figure 6-5 Radar station at Hall Beach in Canada's Eastern Arctic. Northern radar stations made up the Distant Early Warning (DEW) Line.

Developing understanding How would you describe this location? Why do you think this location was chosen by NORAD?

Planning for Peace: The United Nations

Despite the growing tensions at the end of World War II, world leaders began making plans for an international agency that would prevent another global conflict. In April 1945, delegates from fifty-one countries, including Canada, drew up a charter for the United Nations. The United Nations was based on the idea of collective security, as the League of Nations before it had been. This time, however, the nations of the world were ready to support the idea.

The General Assembly of the United Nations provides a forum in which member nations can debate issues of concern. Each member is given a seat and the right to vote on issues. The United Nations was given three powers it could use against aggressor nations. It can:

- condemn the aggressor through speeches and resolutions;
- use economic sanctions, urging members not to trade with the aggressor; and
- respond militarily by sending in an armed force.

Over the decades, these measures have had only limited success.

The Security Council is the body of the United Nations that is responsible for maintaining peace and security. The Council has five permanent members—the "Big Five" powers—Britain, France, the United States, Russia (formerly the Soviet Union), and China (represented by the government in Taiwan until 1971). There are also ten other non-permanent members, each holding a two-year term. Decisions need the consent of nine members, but each of the five permanent members has the power of veto—the right to reject actions with which they disagree. The use of the veto has often prevented the United Nations from taking decisive action. Up to 1955, as the Cold War escalated, the veto was used seventy-eight times, seventy-five of them by the Soviet Union. When permanent members agree on a course of action, however, the United Nations has the potential to be a great power.

The founders of the United Nations also pledged to abolish disease and famine and to protect human rights. To achieve these goals, they created various agencies such as the World Health Organization and UNICEF (United Nations

Figure 6-6 The Security Council is responsible for keeping peace. It issues calls for ceasefires and creates peacekeeping forces. Canada has had a seat on the Security Council in every decade since the United Natations was formed.

Thinking critically Judging by this photo, how would you describe debate and proceedings at the United Nations?

Figure 6-7 The World Health Organization (WHO) tests wells and undertakes other initiatives to help reduce illness from water pollution. This girl in Peru is pumping water from a well whose water has been declared safe.

Children's Fund). The United Nations also established the **International Monetary Fund** to stabilize the world economy by helping countries that face great debt and the collapse of their currencies. The United Nations has benefited millions of people worldwide, especially through its social and economic agencies and peacekeeping operations.

Canada has been a strong supporter of the United Nations since its creation. Through a variety of U.N. agencies, Canada has aided refugees from war or natural disasters and worked on development projects in various countries—for example, by helping to build schools, dams, and roads. By 1999, Canadian peacekeepers had been involved in every U.N. operation since the start of these missions in 1956.

The Korean Conflict

Though the threat of nuclear annihilation kept the major powers from open war, both sides had allies in the developing world, where wars did occur. World War II left the Asian country of Korea divided. In the north was a communist state, supported by the USSR and communist China. In the south was a fragile democracy backed by the United States. In 1950, war broke out as North Korea tried to invade South Korea.

A U.N. force, composed largely of Americans, tried to force the invaders to retreat. Encouraged by the United States, Canada sent thousands of troops and three naval destroyers to Korea. At the United Nations, Lester Pearson, Canada's Minister of External Affairs, urged all sides to

Figure 6-8 Lester Pearson, with his wife, Maryon, displays his Nobel Peace Prize medal. He helped defuse the Suez crisis.

agree to a ceasefire. At one point, the United States considered using the atomic bomb, but luckily, calmer heads prevailed. Although a ceasefire was reached in 1953, the war had increased tensions between the West and the communist nations.

The Suez Crisis

In 1956, a crisis over the Suez Canal, in Egypt, gave Canada a chance to take a leading role at the United Nations.

The Suez Canal links the Mediterranean and Red seas, and provides the shortest sea route from Europe to the Indian Ocean. It was built in the late 1800s, and was privately owned by British and French investors. In 1956, Egypt's president, Gamal Abdel Nasser, on behalf of the Egyptian

government took over the canal. The neighbouring state of Israel was frightened by what it saw as Egyptian aggression, as Egypt threatened to bar ships to and from Israel from using the canal. Britain and France were quick to support an Israeli invasion. Ignoring a U.N. Security Council resolution to cease hostilities, they landed troops in the canal zone. The Soviet Union immediately offered Egypt financial aid and missiles.

The United States was angry at its allies, Britain, France, and Israel, who had not consulted the U.S. government before attacking Egypt. Nevertheless, the United States threatened retaliation against any Soviet involvement.

Canadian public opinion on the crisis was divided. The Conservative Party and many other Canadians felt it was their duty to support Britain. Liberal Prime Minister Louis St. Laurent, however, denounced the British and French intervention and, like the United States, refused to support them. Once again, Lester Pearson went to the United Nations to try to work towards a solution.

Pearson proposed that a United Nations Emergency Force be sent to the Suez Canal to separate and mediate between the rival armies. The U.N. agreed. The force, under the command of a Canadian general, was chosen from countries not directly involved in the conflict. For his efforts in defusing the crisis, Lester Pearson was awarded the Nobel Peace Prize.

ACTIVITIES

1. Identify: **a)** the United Nations; **b)** NORAD; **c)** the DEW Line; **d)** WHO.

2. Why was Canada willing to enter an air defence agreement with the United States?

3. **a)** What is the purpose of the U.N. General Assembly?

   b) Why were the five permanent members of the Security Council given veto powers? How did this power create a stalemate in the United Nations?

4. What caused the Korean War? How did Canada participate?

5. What important roles did Canada play in the Suez crisis?

Towards a More Independent Defence Policy

As the Cold War intensified, tensions developed between Canada and the United States during the early 1960s. Personal relations between Prime Minister John Diefenbaker and U.S. President John Kennedy were strained. The men had very different styles, and they took a strong dislike to each other. These differences were particularly obvious during the most serious crisis of the Cold War: the Cuban missile crisis, which took the world to the brink of nuclear war.

The Cuban Missile Crisis

In 1959, Cuban rebels under the leadership of Fidel Castro overthrew Cuba's pro-U.S. leader in a revolution. The United States reacted angrily by imposing trade and economic sanctions on Cuba. In 1961, the United States backed an invasion of the island by a group of anti-Castro Cubans. The invasion was a failure, but it encouraged Cuba to turn to the USSR for support.

In October 1962, U.S. planes took photographs showing that the USSR was installing offensive nuclear missile bases in Cuba. Missiles launched from these sites were a direct threat to U.S. security (see Figure 6-9). President Kennedy announced a naval and air blockade of Cuba. U.S. forces and NORAD were readied for war. Aircraft loaded with bombs were constantly in the air. The world was poised on the brink of war.

Soviet Premier Nikita Khrushchev at first refused to remove the missiles. The armed forces of the USSR were put on full alert. Soviet ships steamed towards the U.S. ships that were blockading the island. At the last minute, Khrushchev agreed to dismantle the missile bases in exchange for a promise that the United States would not

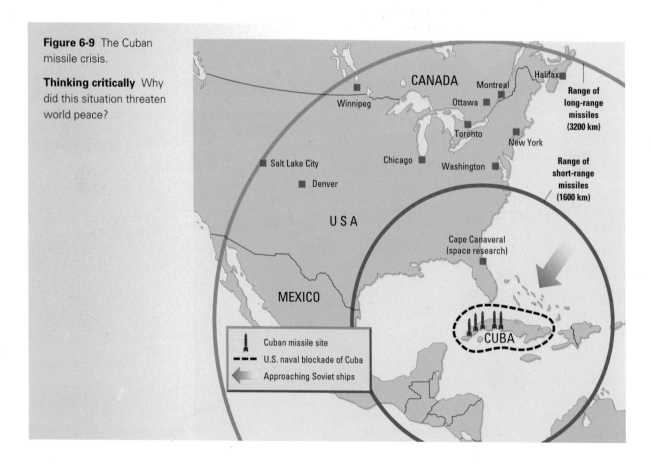

Figure 6-9 The Cuban missile crisis.

Thinking critically Why did this situation threaten world peace?

Range of long-range missiles (3200 km)

Range of short-range missiles (1600 km)

CANADA

Winnipeg   Montreal   Halifax
Ottawa
Toronto
New York
Salt Lake City   Chicago   Washington
Denver

USA

Cape Canaveral (space research)

MEXICO

CUBA

⬛ Cuban missile site
▬ ▬ ▬ U.S. naval blockade of Cuba
⬅ Approaching Soviet ships

The Avro Arrow

As part of its military program in the 1950s, Canada and the A.V. Row (Avro) Company developed the Arrow, a state-of-the-art supersonic jet aircraft. In 1959, the project was cancelled by the Diefenbaker government. The existing planes were cut up for scrap, and most of Avro's designers and engineers moved to the United States. However, the memory of the Avro Arrow remains. Canadians, looking back, often feel that they lost an opportunity to establish their country as a technological leader.

Why was the Avro Arrow cancelled? Opinions vary. In 1997, one newspaper summarized a view so popular that it has become a Canadian myth, kept alive by a TV movie:

Avro's dauntless little band of aircraft engineers ... worked out the highly original design for the new fighter.... But this hardy band of Canadians were bucking the odds. Senior American officials, including [the] President, conspired to kill the project. Why? Because if they could not build so grand a fighter, Canada couldn't have one either!

[In the TV movie] ... the Americans—who declare ... that Canadians should stick to building canoes, not warplanes—find a gullible ally when John Diefenbaker is elected Prime Minister.... Dief and his ministers hate the Arrow because it is a Liberal-initiated project.

Source: *Financial Post*, January 18, 1997.

The reality was different, say several historians:

Everyone in authority knew that the Arrow had to go—costs had soared, there were no foreign orders, A.V. Row Canada was a ramshackle, disorganized company....

Source: Michael Bliss, *Right Honourable Men* (Toronto: HarperCollins, 1994), 204.

The Arrow cost six times more to produce than its American counterpart.... No one, not even the Canadian Air Force, wanted to buy it.

Source: A. Finkel and M. Conrad, *History of the Canadian Peoples* (Toronto: Copp Clark Pitman, 1993).

Questions

1. What opportunity do some people feel Canada lost when it cancelled the Avro Arrow project?
2. What are the different points of view surrounding the cancellation of the Avro Arrow?

Figure 6-10 The Avro Arrow. When the superpowers developed long-range missiles, interceptor fighter planes like the Arrow seemed obsolete.

invade Cuba. The Americans had won a game of "nuclear chicken."

During the crisis, the United States expected Canada—its partner in NORAD—to provide unconditional support of its policies. Prime Minister Diefenbaker, however, preferred that the United Nations send a fact-finding mission to Cuba, and implied that he did not believe the U.S. photographs. Diefenbaker was reluctant to have Canada drawn into a major conflict that seemed largely rooted in U.S. policy and interests. At first, the Canadian government refused to place Canada's NORAD forces on alert. Nor did it allow U.S. planes with atomic weapons to land at Canadian bases. The Americans were furious.

Diefenbaker believed he was defending Canada's independence, but a poll later showed that 80 per cent of Canadians thought he was wrong. Eventually, Diefenbaker did put Canadian troops on alert, but damage to Canada–U.S. relations had already been done.

The Nuclear Issue in Canada

The Cuban missile crisis caused a debate about Canada's defence policy and the country's stand on nuclear weapons. Should Canada accept nuclear weapons on its territory, as the United States wished? When the Avro Arrow was scrapped, Canada had agreed to accept U.S. Bomarc mis-

When photographers cover events, they don't just point their cameras and shoot. They have points of view. What they choose to photograph and how they present their subject can have different impacts on the viewer.

For example, a close-up view of a person's face can bring the viewer closer to that person, emotionally if not physically. A wider view of an event can make the viewer feel more involved in the action. A black-and-white photograph may create a certain mood that the photographer wants to convey. Painters also have points of view. The angle of the subject, the colours used, and the details that are included are important clues to the message the artist is trying to communicate. When you look at a photograph or painting, it is

a)

Figure 6-11 a) Canadian artillery firing on enemy positions in Korea.

b) *Contact* by Korean War artist Edward F. Zuber.

c) A Korean child accidentally burned by napalm (a jelly-like substance used in fire bombs and flame throwers). He is showing soldiers his burns.

siles, which were capable of carrying nuclear warheads. The years that passed before the missiles were actually installed, however, allowed time for second thoughts.

Many people were starting to realize that nuclear war amounted to global suicide. In 1963, the ruling Conservative Party was divided on the issue. The minister of external affairs felt Canada should be a non-nuclear nation. He argued that it was hypocritical to urge the United Nations to work for disarmament while accepting nuclear weapons. The defence minister, in contrast, insisted that nuclear weapons were vital in protecting Canada against communist aggression.

Meanwhile, the anti-nuclear movement was growing among ordinary Canadian citizens.

During the election campaign of 1963, the Liberals, under the leadership of Lester Pearson, proposed that Canadian forces accept nuclear weapons under certain conditions. Prime Minister Diefenbaker and the Conservatives, on the other hand, appealed to Canadian nationalism, including Canada's right to decide for itself on international matters. Many business leaders and influential newspapers supported the Liberals, fearing that Diefenbaker's anti-Americanism would injure trade and investment from the United States. The nuclear issue split the country and reflected uncertainty in the minds of Canadians.

b)

c)

important to "read" the work and try to interpret the viewpoint of the photographer or artist.

Examine the three figures, then answer the questions that follow.

Applying the Skill

1. What do you think the people in figure (a) might be saying? Does the photographer have a particular point of view? If so, what is it? How do you think this viewpoint differs from that in figure (b)? In figure (c)?

2. What emotions do you associate with figure (b)? What viewpoint do you think the artist wants to convey?

3. Why do you think artists and photographers were sent to record scenes of the war? Should we view their pictures as primary or secondary information sources?

4. Choose another photograph or painting from this book or another source. Interpret it, applying the skills you have learned.

Figure 6-12 In 1961, Canadian activist Thérèse Casgrain helped form the Quebec chapter of the Voice of Women. VOW was an organization set up to lobby government and educate the public to promote peace and nuclear disarmament. Its members used political demonstrations before these became a popular method of protest.

Diefenbaker was narrowly defeated in the election of 1963, and the Liberals formed a minority government. This federal election was the first since 1911 to be fought over Canada–U.S. relations.

The Vietnam War

The war in Vietnam was a major conflict in the Cold War. Like Korea, Vietnam was divided into two. The north was communist-controlled. The government in the south, although more a dictatorship than a democracy, was supported by the United States. The Americans felt that if the south should fall to communism, then other Asian states would fall, one after another, like a set of dominoes. At first the United States offered only military advice and economic help to the South Vietnamese, but by the 1960s it was sending U.S. troops as well.

In 1965, U.S. President Lyndon Johnson increased the number of U.S. troops and authorized the bombing of North Vietnam. By 1966, there were 190 000 U.S. soldiers in Vietnam, and the number kept growing. At the same time, the USSR and communist China supplied weapons and help to North Vietnam.

Vietnam was the first war recorded by television cameras. As Americans watched Vietnamese villages being bombed—and their own young men returning home disabled or in body bags—some began questioning their involvement. Anti-war protests were held across the country, as more and more Americans disagreed with their government's actions. In 1968, the public learned that U.S. soldiers had massacred women and children in the village of My Lai. Then, the North Vietnamese launched the Tet Offensive, simultaneously attacking cities throughout South Vietnam and briefly seizing the United States embassy in the city of Saigon. Despite their superior weapons, U.S. troops were unable to win the war.

In 1969, a new U.S. president, Richard Nixon, took office, pledging to pull U.S. troops out of Southeast Asia. The last U.S. combat forces left South Vietnam in 1973. Less than two years later, a North Vietnamese offensive crushed the South Vietnamese army. Vietnam, a nation ravaged by decades of war and destruction, was unified under communist rule. Many anti-communist Vietnamese fled their country. They took to the seas in crowded boats. These people made their way to sprawling refugee camps in Malaysia and Hong Kong, where they applied for refugee status. Thousands were accepted into Canada.

Figure 6-13 This cartoon recalls the incident described by author Lawrence Martin.

Interpreting a cartoon How is Lester Pearson portrayed in this cartoon? What is the cartoonist telling us about Pearson? About Canada?

Canada's Reaction to the War

Canadians were at first divided over the war in Vietnam. Some benefited from the war. Canadian firms sold goods such as berets, boots, airplane engines, and explosives to the U.S. Defense Department. And most people still saw communism as a real threat to Western security. All the same, many were not sure that the peasants of Vietnam were "better dead than Red (communist)," as a popular saying of the time claimed. Prime Minister Pearson shared the growing doubts that many Canadians had about the war. In 1965, he criticized Operation Rolling Thunder—the name of the U.S. bombing campaign of North Vietnam—in a speech at a university in Philadelphia. Pearson later joined President Johnson for lunch at his retreat at nearby Camp David. The president was enraged that the Canadian leader had dared to criticize him in his own country. As one observer later reported:

As the luncheon dragged mercilessly on, Pearson finally chose to throw the raw meat on the table. "Well," he offered daintily, "What did you think of my speech?" LBJ's growl was audible. "Awwwful." He stretched his large hand across the table, clutched the prime minister by the upper arm, and led him on to the terrace where there was room for wrath. Striding the porch, his arms sawing the air, his sulphurous vocabulary contaminating it, Johnson ripped into Pearson full-voltage. The prime minister had betrayed the president. He had joined the ranks of ignorant liberals, "those know-nothing do gooders"....

For more than an hour he tore on until ultimately, ... he moved beyond the realm of words. Having pinned the much smaller Pearson against the railing, the president of the United States grabbed him by the shirt collar, twisted it and lifted the shaken prime minister by the neck. The verbal abuse continued in a venomous torrent.

Source: Lawrence Martin, *The Presidents and the Prime Ministers* (Toronto: Doubleday, 1982), 1–2.

Trudeau's Foreign Policy

In 1968, Pierre Elliott Trudeau, a Liberal, was elected prime minister. As you will see in Chapter 7, he reflected many changing attitudes in Canada at that time. One of his goals was to chart a course in foreign policy that was less dependent on U.S. approval. This intention was clearly signalled in 1970, when Canada officially recognized the communist government of the People's Republic of China. Even though Trudeau had defied U.S. pressure to withhold this recognition, his decision made sense to most Canadians. Mainland China was clearly a great power. Also, as a major purchaser of Canadian wheat and other goods, it was an important trading partner.

At the same time, Trudeau had no wish to anger the United States. Neither did he think Canada could act on foreign affairs without considering the U.S. government to some extent. He explained his views in one of his most famous speeches:

> Let me say that it should not be surprising if our policies in many instances either reflect or take into account the proximity of the United States. Living next to you is in some ways like sleeping with an elephant. No matter how friendly and even-

Figure 6-14 In 1976, Trudeau became the first leader of a NATO country to pay a state visit to Fidel Castro's communist Cuba. At the end of one speech, he surprised and delighted his audience by proclaiming "Viva Fidel Castro."

Expressing ideas How do you think U.S. officials would have reacted to this photograph? Why?

tempered is the beast, one is affected by every twitch and grunt.

Source: Pierre Trudeau, speech to the National Press Club, Washington, DC, March 1969.

Trudeau's approach to national defence was a departure from previous policies. He wanted to scale back Canada's participation in the nuclear arms race with the Soviet Union in the hope that this would ease Cold War tensions. From 1970 to 1972, nuclear missiles were removed from Canada's NATO forces in Europe. Bomarc missile sites that Pearson had accepted in 1963 were dismantled. In 1984, the last nuclear warheads were removed from Canadian soil. Trudeau also cut the national defence budget and reduced Canada's NATO contingent in Europe to half its former strength, in spite of protests from military officers, diplomats, and the U.S. embassy. Canada did, however, continue to participate in NATO and NORAD.

Canada as a Middle Power

Throughout Trudeau's period in office, the Cold War dominated international affairs. The world remained divided between the West (the United States and its allies) and the East (communist China, the Soviet Union, and countries friendly to it).

Outside the two rival power blocs, however, most of the world's people lived in countries not officially allied with either superpower. Indeed, the new African and Asian nations that had emerged from colonial rule after World War II tried to remain detached from Cold War rivalries. But other divisions were emerging. Most of the new nations were located in the southern hemisphere. They were also, for the most part, far less industrialized than countries in the northern hemisphere. So, while the Cold War split the world politically between East and West, a huge economic gap separated the rich North from the poor South.

The Trudeau government aimed to bridge both gaps in order to promote world peace and understanding among nations. Canada had become a "middle power," building links between East and West and North and South. Trudeau's efforts to reduce nuclear weapons and to establish trade and sporting links with communist states were part of this plan. Trudeau called for more aid for the poor countries of the world. He believed that the prosperous nations of the North should be helping the poverty-stricken countries of the South to develop their economies and

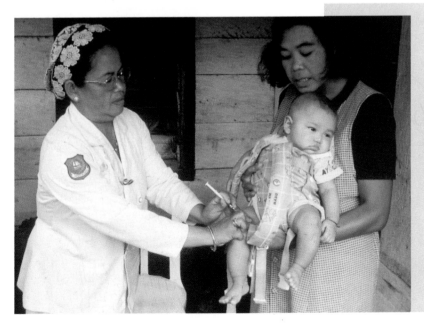

Figure 6-15 Canadian-sponsored immunization program in the Philippines.

Developing understanding How would Canadian programs such as immunization improve living conditions for less developed countries? How would improved living conditions promote peace?

Innovations

Advances in Science and Technology

Even a famous science fiction writer could not begin to guess the extent to which technology would transform life in the decades after World War II. H.G. Wells, author of books such as *The Time Machine* and *The Shape of Things to Come*, predicted that by 1950 soldiers would wage war from bicycles and drop bombs from balloons. In reality, by this time, the atomic bomb had demonstrated the awesome power of science. The following inventions were just a few of those that transformed military technology and everyday life.

July 21, 1969, marked the first manned *moon landing*. U.S. astronauts from the Apollo XI spacecraft landed on the moon in the lunar module Eagle 5. The first person to set foot on the moon's surface was Neil Armstrong. As millions of people around the world watched the historic event live on television, Armstrong proclaimed he was taking "one small step for man, one giant leap for mankind." ▼

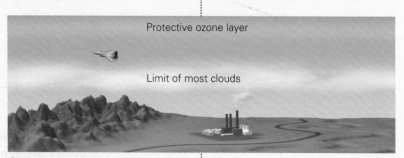

In 1976, scientists discovered damage to the *ozone layer*, the part of the Earth's upper atmosphere that protects the planet from ultraviolet rays coming from the sun. The damage was caused by freon and chlorofluorocarbons (CFCs), chemicals used by industry, and in refrigerators and spray cans. As concern about the damage grew, Canada and other countries passed legislation restricting the manufacture and sale of products containing freon and CFCs.

The U.S. Defense Department and four U.S. universities linked their computers in a network in 1969. They called their new link the *ARPANET* (Advanced Research Projects Agency Network). Its aim was to decentralize the Defense Department's computer system and make it less vulnerable to attack by the Soviet Union. It was the first step in the creation of what would later become the Internet. Other networks slowly began to appear and link to each other. ▶

The first *nuclear reactor* built by Canadian scientists was switched on at Chalk River in September 1945. In 1967, Ontario Hydro completed the first CANDU nuclear reactor, and began a program by which nuclear fission would supply about one-half of Ontario's electricity.

The first *Canadarm* was designed and built by Spar Aerospace in 1981. The remote arm is attached to NASA's space shuttles. It allows crews to launch satellites into precise positions in orbit, and to recapture satellites to return to Earth for servicing. Without this technology, much of the world's satellite communication would be impossible.

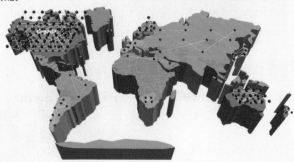

improve living conditions for their people. This policy of **trade and aid** became the cornerstone of Trudeau's foreign policy in bridging the *North–South gap*.

In 1968, a new government body known as the Canadian International Development Agency (CIDA) was formed. CIDA's responsibility was to boost foreign aid to less industrialized countries. Countries receiving aid would have to agree to use it to buy products manufactured in Canada. In this way, Canada would benefit, as well. This was known as "tied aid," and it made up over half the total development aid Canada extended to less industrialized nations. During Trudeau's administration, the total amount of aid Canada extended to developing countries increased from $277 million in 1969 to over $2 billion in 1984.

The Commonwealth and la Francophonie

Canada was in a good position to build bridges between North and South because of its membership in two organizations, the Commonwealth and la Francophonie. The Commonwealth was made up of several countries that had once belonged to the British Empire. La Francophonie was an organization of French-speaking states, many former colonies of France. Both organizations had many members that were less industrialized, and both offered a forum for discussing solutions to the North–South gap. In 1950, Commonwealth countries, including Canada, established the *Colombo Plan* to provide money and aid to less developed countries in the organization. Canada contributed in a number of ways, for example, by inviting overseas students to study in Canada, and by sending Canadian experts overseas to give technical assistance. Most Canadian aid under the Colombo Plan went to India and Pakistan.

The Cold War Renewed

While Trudeau was trying to bridge the economic gap among countries during the early 1970s, tension between the United States and the Soviet Union also eased, and they agreed to reduce the number of their nuclear weapons. They signed the Strategic Arms Limitation Treaty (SALT I) in 1972. This agreement was a breakthrough in relations between the two superpowers. In 1979, however, the Soviet Union invaded Afghanistan. At the same time, the USSR sent new medium-range missiles to Eastern Europe. In response, NATO announced that it, too, was deploying new, more advanced missiles in Europe. A second round of SALT talks on the issue of further disarmament was halted. In protest against the Soviet occupation of Afghanistan, many Western nations, including Canada, boycotted the 1980 Olympic Games held in Moscow. In 1981, the U.S. government announced a massive increase in defence spending, with most of the money to be spent on modernizing the U.S. nuclear arsenal.

In September 1983, Soviet jets shot down a Korean passenger jet that had strayed into Soviet air space. A month later, U.S. forces invaded the

Figure 6-16 Paul Henderson of the Montreal Canadiens after scoring the winning goal in the Canada–USSR hockey series in 1972. This popular sporting event was one of the steps taken by Canada in a new approach to foreign affairs.

Gathering information How would you describe Henderson's reaction to his goal? Why do you think this victory was particularly thrilling for Canadians?

Caribbean nation of Grenada and deposed a pro-Soviet government. The United States carried on a covert (secret) war against the left-wing Sandinista regime in Nicaragua. Each superpower accused the other of provoking war, and watched nervously for any sign of attack. The world seemed closer to nuclear war than at any time since the Cuban missile crisis.

Prime Minister Trudeau appealed to the United States and the Soviet Union to show more restraint. He made a special tour of a number of world capitals to enlist other political leaders in his campaign to mediate between the superpowers. In February 1984, he summed up his peace initiative in a speech to Parliament:

> Let it be said of Canada and of Canadians, that we saw the crisis, that we did act; that we took risks; that we were loyal to our friends and open with our adversaries; that we have lived up to our ideals; and that we have done what we could to lift the shadow of war.

But Trudeau was growing tired of politics. He felt he had played his part. On the evening of February 29, 1984, he left his official residence at 24 Sussex Drive in Ottawa for a walk through the snowy streets of the capital. It was then that he decided to retire from politics. The Trudeau era had come to an end.

ACTIVITIES

1. What did Trudeau mean when he said living next to the United States was like sleeping next to an elephant?

2. How did Trudeau's leadership change Canada's relations with:
   a) communist countries?
   b) the United States?
   c) new nations in the southern hemisphere?

3. How did Trudeau try to bridge the gap between rich and poor countries?

4. In what areas of the world did Cold War tensions increase from 1979 through 1984? What was Canada's response?

The Mulroney Era: Closer Ties with the United States

Conservative leader Brian Mulroney became Canada's prime minister in September 1984. His approach to international relations was in many ways the opposite of Trudeau's. While Trudeau had tried to separate Canadian from U.S. interests, Prime Minister Mulroney worked to forge closer links. He developed a close personal relationship with U.S. President Ronald Reagan, with whom he shared a similar conservative philosophy.

In 1985, the U.S. government unveiled an ambitious plan to create a defence shield, part of which would orbit the Earth. This Strategic Defence Initiative (SDI), nicknamed "Star Wars," had an enormous budget. Canada belonged to the North American Aerospace Defence Command (formerly NORAD). Did this membership commit it to becoming involved? Across Canada, anti-nuclear groups protested Canada's possible involvement. These groups believed that Star Wars would provoke other nations to develop similar weapons. Prime Minister Mulroney finally said no to Canada's official participation. However, the door was left open for private Canadian companies to bid on Star Wars contracts if they wished.

At the same time, the Mulroney government tightened other links with the United States. Over the years, some Canadians had continued to express concern that U.S. companies controlled so much of the Canadian economy. Some measures had been put in place to limit U.S. investment. In 1973, the Trudeau government had formed the Foreign Investment Review Agency (FIRA) to block any foreign investment that seemed not to be in Canada's interest. Now Mulroney announced that Canada was "open for business." He dismantled FIRA and replaced it with Investment Canada, a body that would encourage suitable foreign investment. Then, in 1987, he started negotiations that led Canada into the **Free Trade Agreement** (FTA) with the United

States. The agreement removed tariffs on goods crossing the border, and opened Canada to U.S. investment as well as opening the United States to Canadian investment.

Free trade proved to be a very controversial issue for Canadians. Those who supported free trade argued that, by eliminating tariffs, Canada would attract more U.S. investment—which would help Canadian industry grow and benefit the whole economy. Free trade would also provide access to the larger U.S. market, which would increase Canada's productivity and growth. With larger production runs, Canadian products could be sold at lower prices to compete effectively with imports. A free trade agreement would also attract U.S. firms to Canada to take advantage of our natural resources, skilled workers, and well-planned transportation system.

Many people did not support the Canada–U.S. Free Trade Agreement, however. These groups argued that once protective tariffs were removed, those U.S. branch plants operating in Canada to avoid paying tariffs would simply return to the United States, thus eliminating hundreds of thousands of jobs in Canada. This would mean that free trade would increase unemployment and de-industrialize Canada. Canadian businesses would be unable to compete against giant U.S. companies, which were able to flood the Canadian market with cheap goods and services. Perhaps most significantly, opponents of the deal argued that free trade threatened Canada's independence—that economic union would lead to pressure for political union, as well.

After much heated debate, the FTA was established in 1989. In 1992, the Mulroney government expanded the free trade zone by signing the **North American Free Trade Agreement** (NAFTA), which included free trade with Mexico. This agreement, too, proved to be controversial. The major fear of NAFTA's opponents was that companies operating in Canada would move to Mexico to take advantage of the low wages and less strict anti-pollution laws. Those who supported NAFTA argued that while a few compa-

Figure 6-17 Canadian Prime Minister Brian Mulroney, on the left, sings "When Irish Eyes Are Smiling" with U.S. President Ronald Reagan. Mulroney was Canada's prime minister from 1984 to 1993.

Developing understanding What does this photograph tell you about Canada's relations with the United States during this period?

nies might move to Mexico, most would remain in Canada, preferring better educated and better skilled Canadian workers. Canada had other attractions, such as transportation and communication systems, social services, and social stability.

Amid protests, the Liberal government under Jean Chrétien signed the North American Free Trade Agreement, which came into effect in 1994. Although the Conservatives had been defeated in 1993, their policies had linked Canada's political and economic fortunes much more closely to those of the United States.

The End of the Cold War

The Cold War ended astonishingly quickly. Soviet leader Mikhail Gorbachev realized that the Soviet Union could no longer afford its costly arms race with the United States. He proposed massive cuts in the arsenal of both superpowers. Gorbachev then began a series of sweeping economic, social, and political reforms that would help the communist countries run more efficiently and create better conditions for their citizens. He also loosened censorship and allowed greater freedom of speech. These policies, called *perestroika* (reconstruction) and *glasnost* (openness), encouraged people of East Germany, Czechoslovakia, Poland, Hungary, and Romania to demand similar reforms in their countries. In November 1989, East German border guards, who earlier would have shot anyone crossing the Berlin Wall, watched people from East and West demolish it. Even the powerful Soviet Union fell apart, as member states became independent countries. The Cold War in Europe was over.

Communist China, too, experimented with a kind of *perestroika*, allowing capitalism to flourish in many areas of the economy. Many Chinese people demanded political freedom, as well. Their hopes were brutally dashed, however, in Tiananmen Square in June 1989. Red Army soldiers and tanks attacked students involved in the democracy movement, killing hundreds, perhaps thousands.

In the end, few of the world's communist governments survived. With the dissolution of the Soviet Union in 1991, the great division between East and West—between the communist and noncommunist world—had gone.

Figure 6-18 In November 1989, Canadians joined television viewers around the world in watching the fall of the Berlin Wall.

Expressing ideas How were these people's actions symbolic of what was happening in East–West relations?

The New World Order

Many thought the end of the Cold War might bring a new age of world peace. However, this was not the case. There were numerous regional conflicts and ethnic rivalries, most notably in the Persian Gulf, the former Yugoslavia, and Africa.

In August 1990, Iraqi troops invaded the oil-rich country of Kuwait. Almost immediately, the United Nations demanded that Iraq withdraw from Kuwait, and threatened economic sanctions if it refused. The United States began to demand that military force be used as a last resort to oust Iraqi forces from the country. For the first time since the Korean War, the United Nations was poised to lead a multinational force against an aggressor nation. And as in Korea, the United States would take the lead. The Americans were joined by a coalition of forces from twenty-seven other countries.

In January 1991, when the U.N. deadline for an Iraqi withdrawal from Kuwait came and went, U.S. and coalition forces began bombarding targets from the air and sea. Canada participated with a squadron of CF-18 fighter bombers, units of the Canadian Army, and ships from the Canadian Navy patrolling the Persian Gulf. "Operation Desert Storm" had begun.

The Gulf War destroyed the Iraqi fighting force and much of the country's infrastructure. The use of "smart" weapons, such as laser-guided bombs and cruise missiles launched many kilometres from their targets, changed the nature of war.

After victory in the Gulf War, U.S. President George Bush proclaimed a "new world order." From now on, the United Nations would take a much more active role as a global police force. In the past, the United Nations had been dedicated to *peacekeeping*—negotiating settlements and keeping warring factions apart. Now it would have more of a peacemaking role: it would, where necessary, use force to punish aggression. Military action would preserve long-term peace and security. And the United Nations would undertake this role under the guidance of the United States. As the only superpower remaining after the collapse

Figure 6-19 Canadian members of the United Nations force in the Persian Gulf.

Using evidence How does this photo demonstrate a change in the peacekeeping policy of the United Nations?

of the Soviet Union, the United States was left to dominate world affairs.

Somalia

In 1992, the United Nations launched "Operation Restore Hope" in Somalia, an east African nation that had been ravaged by years of civil war and starvation. The mission was directed by the United States, but Canadian forces joined those from other countries in distributing food and other essential supplies to the desperate local population.

The mission resulted in a crisis in Canada's armed forces. One night, members of the Canadian Airborne Regiment arrested a Somali

What Role Should Canada Play in U.S.-Dominated Military Alliances?

In 1991, ethnic wars broke out in the former Yugoslavia. Slobodan Milosevic, leader of the Federal Republic of Yugoslavia, began to talk about establishing a greater Serbia by uniting all the Serbian population from surrounding states into one country. By 1992, fighting had spread to the Republic of Bosnia-Herzegovina, which formed part of Yugoslavia. Bosnia-Herzegovina was inhabited by Croats, Serbs, and Muslims. U.N. peacekeeping missions were sent in to try to keep the sides from fighting. Canadian forces were the first U.N. peacekeepers to arrive inside Bosnia-Herzegovina, but neither they nor any other U.N. peacekeeping mission were able to keep peace. Frustrated by the failure of the United Nations to control the situation, the countries of NATO threatened to take steps to end the fighting.

In 1995, NATO forces launched a series of air strikes against the mainly Serbian forces of the Yugoslav army, which was perceived as the aggressor. The warring factions eventually agreed to a ceasefire, and U.S. troops were sent to bolster the U.N. peacekeeping forces on the ground.

In 1998, Serbian forces moved into the province of Kosovo to ensure it would remain under Serbian control. The majority of the population in Kosovo were Albanian Muslims. In spring 1999, after prolonged diplomatic efforts failed to stop the Serbian operations, the U.S.-dominated NATO alliance launched its first-ever military operation against an independent country. It began bombing the Federal Republic of Yugoslavia. Canada, as a NATO member, engaged in the controversial air strikes. The stated purpose of the air strikes was to force the Yugoslav president, Milosevic, to stop

Serbs from persecuting, murdering, and displacing Albanians in Kosovo.

Canada's participation in the bombings was the subject of heated debate at home. Some Canadians supported NATO's bombings, insisting that NATO was obligated to act to prevent the Serbian–Albanian conflict from spreading to neighbouring countries. Critics of the bombing argued that NATO should never have interfered in the domestic affairs of a sovereign nation, and that its involvement had escalated the conflict. They thought the United Nations should have pursued peace through its own channels.

Canadians began to question NATO's role in the "new world order" and Canada's role in NATO. Should NATO force be used to prevent or intervene in international conflicts, acting as a kind of North American and European police force?

Perhaps the most important issue for Canadians is: What role should Canada play in U.S.-dominated alliances such as NATO and the North American Aerospace Defence Command (formerly NORAD)? Should we play a role at all? These questions were brought into sharp focus again in 2001, when it seemed likely that the United States would renew its 1985 Star Wars initiative. The new U.S. national missile defence (NMD) project would involve spending billions to protect the United States from nuclear attack.

For and Against

What views do the following excerpts present on Canada's involvement in U.S.-dominated military alliances?

Source 1

Canada has been a member of NATO for the last half century and as a result would have been protected if attacked by another country. This is important because the Canadian military is *not capable of defending this country!* Our military has been bled to the point that it would be impossible to defend ourselves if China, Russia or North Korea for that matter, decides to invade Canada. Therefore we have depended and continue to depend on NATO for our protection and consequently we must *live up to our obligations* to the alliance.

Regardless of what you think of the Kosovo situation, do not be critical of our government or

Figure 6-20 A young Muslim girl pats a Canadian peacekeeper on the head as he walks by the front gate of the Canadian base in Visoco, Bosnia, in 1994.

eign policy independent of the United States. There are already welcome signs of this, including ... Canada's advocacy role in trying to establish a world ban on the use of land mines.... There is much to recommend the long-standing relationship between Americans and Canadians across the longest undefended border in the world, but lockstep adherence to U.S. foreign (military) policy is not one of them. (A recent example of this kind of concern was provided on the CBC National News..., when the Minister of Defence, Mr. Art Eggleton, ... opined that Canada should consider contributing to the resurgent, ultimately destabilizing and doomed-to-failure U.S. "Star Wars" missile defence program.)

In this way [by redefining its independence on the world stage], Canada will recover the world respect it deserves from an earlier time, and rediscover its mandate to provide a much needed forum of sober second thought, a necessary counter-measure to those "great powers" too often inebriated by their own self-righteous views....

Source: Prof. Donald Fleming, University of British Columbia, "Kosovo and Canada's participation in NATO's war." Letter to Bill Graham, Chair, Standing Committee on Foreign Affairs and International Trade, April 21, 2000.

military for its involvement. There could come a day when NATO will be there when we most need it.

Source: L. Ryan, a former peacekeeper in Bosnia from Newfoundland, in a letter dated April 19, 1999. In *Canada on the Attack: The Debate*, "Letters from Canadians and Others Outside Yugoslavia." From the Canadian Broadcasting Corporation Web site: <http:cbc.ca/news/indepth>.

Source 2

Canada MUST redefine its independence on the world stage, and in particular set a course in for-

Analysing the Issue

1. What key ideas does Source 1 express? How do they contrast with those of Source 2?

2. Do you think it is possible for Canada to "set a course in foreign policy independent of the United States"? In what way? Explain your answer.

3. What do you think Canada's role in NATO should be?

4. Should Canada participate in the development of "Star Wars"? What could be the military and economic benefits? What could be the disadvantages?

teenager found wandering in the Canadian base camp. During the night, the teen was tortured and beaten to death. At first, a military inquiry found that only a few low-ranking officers had committed this terrible, racist crime. As more evidence came to light, however, it became clear that there had been a high-level attempt to cover up the incident. Canadians were shocked by these events. In 1995, the Airborne Regiment was disbanded. A serious shadow had been cast upon the reputation of Canada's armed forces.

Rwanda

Canadians were also active in the central African country of Rwanda. This small nation was torn apart by ethnic rivalries. France and Belgium, the former colonial forces in the area, sent troops to try to control the slaughter. A small detachment of U.N. peacekeepers was also sent under the command of Canadian Major General Roméo Dallaire.

When Dallaire realized the extent of the planned killings, he sent a series of urgent appeals to U.N. headquarters in New York. He outlined an ambitious military plan to halt the killing. As he saw it, the United Nations needed to send a huge multinational force to disarm the warring factions. For the plan to work, two things were required: speed and the support of the United States, the only country that could provide enough troops at short notice. Unfortunately, the response from the United Nations and Washington was unenthusiastic. The United States feared a defeat similar to that in Somalia. In April 1994, the world was horrified to learn of a massive wave of killing in Rwanda. Within a few weeks, close to a million people had died, including many women, old people, and babies.

With the failure of the U.N. efforts to keep the peace in the Persian Gulf, the former Yugoslavia, and Africa, many observers wondered what the future of the organization would be.

Figure 6-21 The United Nations had greater success in Haiti than in Somalia or Rwanda. Canadian peacekeepers assumed a major role in policing this Caribbean country as it recovered from a brutal dictatorship. RCMP officers also helped to train a new Haitian police force in the newly democratic society.

ACTIVITIES

1. Contrast Prime Minister Brian Mulroney's approach to foreign affairs with that of Prime Minister Pierre Trudeau. Present your information in the form of a diagram, chart, paragraph, poem, or other representation.

2. List at least four reasons for the end of the Cold War. Which reason(s) would you classify as economic? How would you classify your other reasons?

3. What are some areas in which military conflicts have occurred since the end of the Cold War? How and why have Canadians participated?

4. What did President Bush mean when he proclaimed a "new world order"?

5. What is the difference between peacekeeping and peacemaking?

A New Era of Globalization

When the Liberals came to power in 1993, one of Prime Minister Jean Chrétien's priorities was to expand Canada's trading opportunities with other countries. He enthusiastically organized "Team Canada" trade missions to Asia and Latin America to secure deals for Canadian investment and exports. The Canadian government has signed free trade agreements with Chile and Israel. Canada also joined APEC (the Asia–Pacific Economic Cooperation Group) to promote freer trade among Pacific countries.

These trade initiatives were part of a trend sweeping the world by the end of the twentieth century. The trend was **globalization**—a vast network of business, communications, and cultural links among countries. Globalization was partly the result of rapid changes in communications technology and the fall of communism. Countries around the world were now "open for business." Goods could be easily shipped around the world, and the Internet made it possible to do business on-line in almost any part of the globe.

Globalization as an Issue

Many people in Canada and around the world believe globalization is a powerful trend that cannot be stopped. They maintain that globalization will raise living standards for everyone, rich and poor. Large corporations will invest in less industrialized countries, creating jobs for many more people and raising standards of living. On the other hand, some observers doubt these optimistic predictions. The booming economies of the Philippines, Malaysia, and other "Asian tigers" had been held up as examples of how global trade could result in

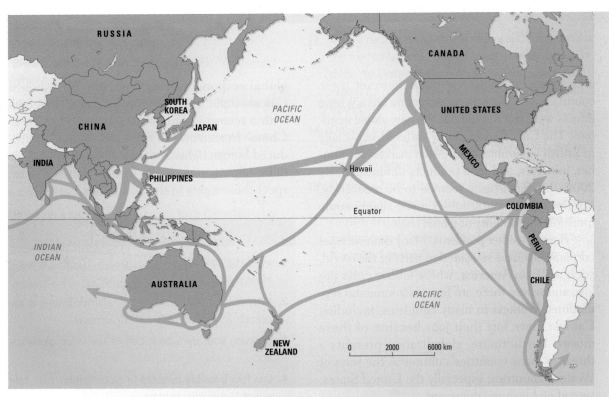

Figure 6-22 The Pacific Rim trading area, including major ocean trading routes.

Expressing ideas Why is the Pacific Rim trading area especially important to British Columbia?

Coming Home

The veterans returning to Canada were eager to come home but anxious about the future. Would they find jobs? Many had enlisted in the armed forces right out of high school, or had been unemployed during the Depression. To ease their transition back into society, the Canadian government passed special legislation. Veterans who wanted their old jobs back were given them, and the years that they had been away at war were counted as years of service on the job. Veterans and war widows were given hiring preference for government jobs. Those who wished to attend university or trade school received free tuition and living allowances. The Veterans' Land Act was passed, enabling veterans to obtain mortgages at preferential rates.

The New Face of Canada

Going home after the war was not a possibility for the wave of immigrants to post-war Canada. At the end of the war, millions of refugees languished in camps across Europe. The United Nations called these refugees *displaced persons*. They included concentration camp survivors and others uprooted by the war. These people had no homes, possessions, or hope for the future. Canada accepted 165 000 displaced persons, settling them in communities across the country. Speaking no English and unable to practise their former trades or professions, these newcomers often had a hard time in Canada. Nevertheless, refugee children absorbed English quickly at school, and their parents found that a job—any job—opened up new opportunities.

Other families who were exhausted by war, or simply looking for a new life, also found Canada attractive. Many sailed to Halifax or Montreal as new immigrants. Altogether, 2.5 million newcomers arrived in Canada between 1945 and 1967.

Unlike immigrants before World War I, who had settled largely on farms in western Canada, the newcomers now settled mostly in the cities of central Canada. This wave of immigrants changed the face of the country. Their cultures, viewpoints, and hard work enriched Canada in many ways. The older areas of cities, vacated as veterans and their families moved to the suburbs, became home to vibrant new communities.

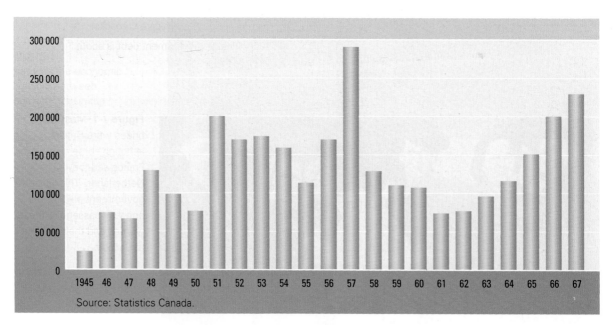

Source: Statistics Canada.

Figure 7-2 Immigrant arrivals in Canada, 1945–1967. The dramatic rise in 1957 was caused by a wave of refugees from Hungary, where Soviet tanks crushed an uprising in 1956.

The Rise of the Suburbs

With the expansion in Canada's population, there was a tremendous demand for housing in the years after the war. To help address this need, developers began building thousands of new homes. Many new housing developments were in the outlying areas of cities, the *suburbs*, where land was cheaper. In time, many subdivisions became "bedroom communities" to which commuters returned at the end of the working day. These communities had their own schools, parks, and places of worship.

Suburban Values

The suburbs were not just a place to live; they brought a new set of values. These values centred on the traditional family, with the stay-at-home mother at its heart. Women, who had made up one-third of the workforce during the war, were let go to create jobs for returning veterans. Popular women's magazines denounced working mothers as the cause of delinquent children. The fashions of the day emphasized traditional femininity: long, full skirts; narrow waists; high heels; and red lips. New gadgets such as electric floor polishers, pop-up toasters, and electric food mixers made house-

Figure 7-3 The post-war boom in housing gave rise to many suburban developments like this one. Cheap land encouraged the building of low-density units on large lots surrounded by manicured lawns; backyard patios; and long, curving side streets with few or no sidewalks.

Using evidence Based on this photograph, suggest two direct effects that suburban living would have had on people's lifestyle.

work seem less like drudgery. The father's role was to be the breadwinner, supporting the family on his paycheque.

Families were larger in the post-war years than they are today. The increase in the birth rate in the post-war period until 1960 became known as the **baby boom**. For a time, Canada's birth rate was the highest in the industrial world, peaking in 1959. Average families had three or four children. In all, 6.7 million children were born in Canada between 1946 and 1961, after which the birth rate began to decline.

Because the "boomer" generation is the largest age group in Canada, its influence has been felt throughout our culture and economy. The sheer numbers of the boom reshaped many institutions. Boy Scouts, Girl Guides, and junior hockey flourished. Schools, too, had to be built at an unprecedented rate. Manufacturers began to make a whole range of new products for the baby boomers.

The Age of the Automobile

In the 1950s, Canadians fell in love with cars and bought 3.5 million of them. For people living in the suburbs, a car was a necessity. While suburban houses of the fifties and sixties were usually plain and functional, cars grew steadily longer and fancier, graced with fins and fancy tail lights.

Automobile culture changed Canada's neighbourhoods. Corner grocery stores shut down as large new supermarkets appeared. The shopping mall, where a bewildering variety of consumer goods could be purchased, became the hub of suburban life. It replaced the front porch, the village green, and the corner store as a gathering place. The opening of a mall was a community event.

The automobile represented all the elements of the post-war era: fascination with technology, progress, security, and personal freedom. However, it also exacted costs. As car makers hurried to install enormous V-8 engines, few thought about gas consumption or atmospheric pollution. Nor did people think much about safety, even though automobile accidents were becoming a leading cause of death. Seat belts were non-existent in

Figure 7-4 Throughout the 1950s, cars grew longer, lower, and wider. Manufacturers unveiled new models every autumn, with improvements such as this easy-to-manage convertible roof.

Using evidence What does this design suggest about the importance of the automobile at the time?

the 1950s, and drinking "one for the road" was common in an era when the cocktail party was regarded as chic evening entertainment.

Television and the Consumer Society

By the late 1950s, most Canadians had access to television—although there were only one or two channels, and the programs were in black and white. Television magnified every cultural trend. It created attractive images and an appealing, if artificial, lifestyle. Television encouraged people to buy more products, fostering a **consumer society**. Youngsters soon demanded sweetened cereals, Barbie dolls, Davy Crockett hats, and many other advertised goods. Thousands of new gadgets and inventions were introduced: ballpoint pens, photocopiers, Polaroid cameras, long-playing records, spray cans, Frisbees, and refrigerator magnets. Shopping became a national pastime.

Teen Culture

Baby boomers spent more time in school than earlier generations. Before the war, the average Canadian child received only eight years of schooling. Only one in ten students finished high school. After the war, Canada's economy flourished. There were no wars or economic hardship to force boomer students out of school. The result was the invention of the *teenager*.

With ample leisure time, and more money to spend from part-time jobs, teenagers had an independence that had not been available to young people before. Businesses began catering to them, and teens adopted their own styles that set them apart from the adult world. Girls wore their hair in poodle cuts, pony tails, or beehives. They dressed in saddle shoes or penny loafers, poodle skirts, crinolines, and cardigans. They wore strapless gowns to their proms. Boys had crew-cut or duck-tail hairstyles and dressed in white socks, blue jeans or dress pants, and V-necked sweaters, black leather jackets, or sports coats.

Rock 'n' roll, a musical style developed in the mid-1950s, soon became the favourite of many teenagers. The roots of rock 'n' roll were in African-American music from the southern United States, adapted for other audiences by Elvis Presley and many other musicians. Rock 'n' roll's strong rhythms and sometimes rebellious teen-centred lyrics shocked the older generation. It was banned in many places.

With the new music came new dances. TV's *American Bandstand* and local Canadian teen dance shows popularized dances including the Jive, the Monster Mash, the Watusi, the Mashed Potato, and the Twist. Canada produced its share of international music stars. Paul Anka and, later, Buffy Sainte-Marie, Neil Young, Joni Mitchell, and The Guess Who were among the most famous.

Figure 7-5 Paul Anka's hit song "Diana" is one of the biggest-selling records in history. An Ottawa-born Canadian of Lebanese descent, Anka was only fifteen when "Diana" became a hit in 1956. Anka's other hits included "Lonely Boy" and "Puppy Love."

Canada the Good

While television and popular music were bringing new trends to teenagers, most Canadians were still very conservative. In English Canada, no newspapers were published on Sundays, nor could people go to the movies. No large stores opened on Sundays anywhere. Movies and books—both popular paperbacks and serious literature—were strictly censored. Many towns were "dry," prohibiting the sale of liquor. Women were discouraged from going to taverns alone. It was not until the 1960s, when many baby boomers were in their teens, that such restrictions were relaxed.

Canadians were not so sedate, however, when it came to spectator sports. Hockey was a favourite. The rival Montreal Canadiens and Toronto Maple Leafs dominated the six-team National Hockey League. From 1945 to 1967, the Leafs and Canadiens each won nine Stanley

Figure 7-6 Barbara Ann Scott was a celebrity who brought a sense of pride to Canadians.

Cups. The superstars of all six teams were Canadian. When one of the greatest, Maurice "Rocket" Richard of the Canadiens, was suspended during the 1955 season, a riot erupted at the Montreal Forum. Bottles and rotten eggs were thrown at the NHL president. In the street, store windows and telephone booths were destroyed, and thirty-seven people were injured.

Canada's "fairy-tale princess" of the post-war period was Barbara Ann Scott, who won the world figure skating championship in 1947 and the Olympic gold medal in 1948. In the mid-1950s, teenager Marilyn Bell became an instant legend when she became the first person to swim across Lake Ontario and the youngest person to conquer the English Channel. In 1957, she swam the Strait of Juan de Fuca, from Port Angeles, Washington, to Victoria, British Columbia.

Protecting Canadian Culture

While many sports heroes were Canadian, other figures who had an influence were not. Hollywood stars enthralled Canadians, who followed the actors on screen and in the U.S. movie magazines that flooded the newsstands.

As early as 1949, the federal government established the Massey Commission to investigate the state of Canadian culture. Reporting in 1951, the Commission suggested that Canadian culture needed to be protected from U.S. influences. It recommended that the National Film Board, established in 1939, be strengthened and that the federal government become involved in funding universities and the arts. As a result, the Canada Council was established in 1957 to award tax-funded grants to writers, artists, and theatres. New institutions such as the Royal Winnipeg Ballet and the National Ballet were soon winning international acclaim and making Canadians proud. Canadian literature, which was not well known before the war, could now boast authors such as Robertson Davies, Margaret Laurence, and W.O. Mitchell.

The Massey Commission also worried about television, which had come to the United States by 1951, but had not yet spread to Canada. In the United States, television was designed for entertainment. It was a commercial enterprise, operated to create profit for station owners and advertisers. The Commission recommended that TV in Canada be used instead for national com-

Figure 7-7 U.S. shows on television promoted the fairy tale of the perfect, traditional, and wholesome family. People who were not white and middle-class could find little to reflect their world on television.

Identifying viewpoint What values are evident in this still from *Father Knows Best*?

munication and for cultural education in drama and music. The CBC, which had already created a national radio network, was put in charge of the development of television. It opened the first two stations in Toronto and Montreal in 1952. Two years later, four more cities were included. By 1960, 90 per cent of Canadian homes had television—more than had telephones.

It soon became clear, however, that the concerns of the Massey Commission were well-founded. U.S. programs topped the list of Canadian television favourites. Kids tuned in to *Howdy Doody, Roy Rogers, Lassie*, and the *Mickey Mouse Club*. Families chuckled at *I Love Lucy* and first saw Elvis and the Beatles on the Sunday evening *Ed Sullivan Show*. As the years passed, Canadian children grew up knowing more about U.S. culture and values than any generation before them. In 1968, the federal government established the Canadian Radio-television and Telecommunications Commission (CRTC). This agency would regulate the amount of foreign material broadcast over the airwaves and impose rules requiring Canadian content.

ACTIVITIES

1. Make a web diagram showing social changes in Canada after World War II. Be sure to include the following, and show relationships among them, where possible: war brides, immigration, the baby boom, suburbs, youth culture.

2. How did the automobile culture change neighbourhoods? What businesses developed because of the automobile culture?

3. What effect did television have on many people's buying habits in the post-war period? What effect do you think it has today?

4. What was life like for many teenagers in the post-war period? Present your answer under the following headings: **a)** independence **b)** styles **c)** music **d)** teenagers as a "target market."

5. Describe the roles of women and men in the 1950s. Discuss reasons why you think many accepted these roles.

6. What is the role of the CRTC? Do you think the agency is necessary? Write a short paragraph explaining your views.

Making an Oral Presentation

*I*n recent years, the term "baby boom echo" has been used to refer to children of baby boomers—children born between 1981 and 1996. Some analysts think the "echo" is having almost as great an impact on the economy and buying habits as the original boom did:

> The arrival of the echo kids, the largest group of teens since the boomers themselves, is an important new factor in the retail marketplace. ...Because of the echo kids, frozen pizza, metallic nail polish, and name-brand sweatshirts have been growth industries. ...Companies that just a few years ago were focussed on figuring out what the boomers wanted now had to ask themselves a second question: "What do the boomers' kids want?"
>
> The answer, of course, is that they want the same things teenagers have always wanted—music and clothing their parents disapprove of and lots of unhealthy food. But there is a significant difference...: these kids have more money to spend. ...When the boomers were young, they had to compete for their parents' money with two or three siblings because, at the peak of the boom, the average Canadian woman was producing four children. The boomers themselves, however, produced [an average of] only 1.7 children per family; that means that two-income boomer households have more money to lavish on each [child]. ...What some marketers call the "six-pocket" phenomenon—kids getting cash from two parents and four grandparents—explains why many echo boomers can afford to spend $50 for a Nike sweatshirt when a similar garment without the trademark can be had for only $15.
>
> The brand name is increasingly important. Echo kids have been saturated in television since birth and, as a result, they are the most brand-conscious cohort [group] in the history of the planet.

Source: David K. Foot, *Boom, Bust & Echo 2000* (Toronto: Macfarlane Walter & Ross, 1998), 120–121 (abridged).

As an "echo kid," you might have a strong reaction to this description. If you were to explain your views in an oral presentation, where would you start?

Steps in Preparing an Oral Presentation

1. In point form, outline this author's main arguments.
2. Decide what your own opinions are on this topic, and write them down in point form.
3. Develop your opinions and organize them in a written outline that is easy to follow, with one idea leading logically into the next one.
4. Prepare an introduction that will get the audience interested in your topic. Write it out and practise presenting it.
5. Prepare a concluding statement that will leave your audience thinking about what you have said.
6. Practise making your presentation. If it helps, write out the whole speech and practise delivering it, using a tape recorder. Do you speak clearly? Too quickly? Do you emphasize the right points? Pause for effect when you should? (Remember: Always look at the audience when you speak.)

Applying the Skill

1. Watch an oral presentation such as a news report on television. Make notes on the speaker's presentation, including ways in which the presentation is or is not effective, and why.
2. Working alone or with others, prepare an oral presentation on the topic "What it means to be an 'echo kid.'" Your presentation might take the form of a speech, interview, or panel discussion.

Post-War Prosperity

At the end of World War II, the Canadian government needed to find ways to ease the transition from a wartime to a peacetime economy. The government had learned from its lack of preparedness in 1918, when high unemployment and other social problems had led to the Winnipeg Strike. This time, planning began even before the war ended.

After years of hardship during the Depression, Canadians had become used to being employed. Now, a million people who had worked in war-production industries and close to a half-million in the armed services were about to lose their jobs. On August 6, 1945, Prime Minister Mackenzie King called a meeting of the provincial premiers to discuss the transition to a peacetime economy. The premiers were told that the Canadian people wanted "security and stability." During the war, the provinces had transferred their powers to manage the economy to the federal government. King recommended that this change become permanent. This would allow Ottawa to increase or decrease government spending to help solve problems such as unemployment and inflation.

The prime minister's proposals were not well received. The provinces, especially Ontario and Quebec, were not willing to give up the powers given to them at Confederation. King went back to the drawing board. The Minister of Reconstruction, Trade, and Commerce, C.D. Howe, presented a new strategy: private industry would handle the transition to a peacetime economy, with the help of government incentives. Generous tax breaks would be given to companies that agreed to produce consumer goods or invest in new plants. Government Crown corporations were auctioned off to private companies, often at very low prices. Soon, factories were humming—producing washing machines, automobiles, and other items that were in demand. Canada's economy was booming.

Despite Howe's solution, the question of federal–provincial relations did not go away. During the war, Canadians had become accustomed to social programs such as unemployment insurance and family allowances, which offered protection from the grinding poverty of the past. It was clear that Canadians wanted social support programs to continue. How could Ottawa ensure that similar social services were available in all parts of the country, even in provinces that were not rich enough to provide them?

The answer was for the provinces to transfer taxation powers to the federal government. In return, the provinces would receive government

Figure 7-8 After the war, resource industries boomed. The Kemano aluminum smelting project created the boom town of Kitimat, British Columbia, in the 1950s.

grants to provide social services such as health care and education. Through a system of "equalization" or "transfer" payments, the federal government would then transfer to the poorer provinces some of the taxes collected in the richer provinces. In this way, Ottawa succeeded in gaining most of the powers that the provinces refused to give up in 1945. The nature of Confederation changed. The federal government gained power at the expense of the provinces, especially over social programs.

Rich Resources and New Industries

Much of Canada's new wealth came from industries that developed in the post-war years. Some of the new products, including plastics and pesticides, grew out of inventions made during the war. Above all, the economic boom was fostered by the development of natural resources such as metals and other minerals. One of the most important developments was the discovery of oil at Leduc, Alberta, in 1947.

Where new mines and wells developed, *boom towns* were carved out of the wilderness. In some places, airlifts brought in heavy equipment, construction material, and automobiles. Tents, trailers, and temporary shanties were made to serve as offices and homes. Although they were prosperous, many workers in these boom towns were lonely: most were single men, and there were few women.

While resource industries developed in frontier areas, southern Ontario thrived as a centre of manufacturing. By the 1950s, more than half of the nation's factories and plants and 99 per cent of its automobile industry were located in Ontario. In later decades, when resource industries in other parts of the country were not prospering, Ontario would be resented by the other provinces for its domination of industry.

In later decades, also, Canadians would realize that many of the new industries were having a profound effect on the environment, as they dumped wastes that polluted the ground, air, and water systems.

Giant Projects for a Giant Land

As towns across Canada grew, the government recognized the need to improve the country's roads, sewer systems, power plants, schools, and hospitals. Taxes from business and workers in the booming economy would provide the money to pay for these services. Furthermore, the money paid out to construction companies would create more jobs and stimulate the economy as workers spent their wages. Inspired by this thinking, the federal government enthusiastically undertook several **megaprojects** that changed the face of the Canadian landscape.

In 1950, work intensified on the Trans-Canada Highway, which was to stretch from St. John's, Newfoundland, to Victoria, British Columbia. Building the 7821-km road was expensive and difficult, especially through moun-

Figure 7-9 An ore carrier enters St. Lambert Lock on the St. Lawrence Seaway.

tainous sections such as Revelstoke and Golden, British Columbia. When finally completed in 1970, the Trans-Canada was the longest national highway in the world.

The St. Lawrence Seaway was also built, to link the Atlantic Ocean with the Great Lakes and open the heart of the continent to large ocean-going ships. The joint Canada–United States project began in 1954 and was completed in 1959. A complex system of locks, dams, canals, and channels, the Seaway was a major feat of engineering. Long stretches of rapids were dynamited, islands were destroyed or created, and whole communities were moved to make way for the Seaway.

Another giant project was the Trans-Canada Pipeline. Abundant supplies of natural gas had been discovered in Alberta. The pipeline was built to transport gas cheaply from the West to the industrial centres of central Canada.

American Investment: A Continuing Issue

The United States, like Canada, had a booming economy in the post-war years. When it began to run short of raw materials, it looked to Canada as a vast storehouse of minerals and other natural resources. Canadians, for their part, recognized that they needed investment to extract newly discovered resources such as oil, uranium, and iron ore. By 1956, 68 per cent of the oil industry in Canada was U.S.-owned; by 1967, foreign ownership of this resource had risen to 88 per cent. In addition, U.S. companies had opened numerous branch plants in Canada. By 1956, U.S. firms controlled more than half of all manufacturing in Canada.

Canadians regularly debated this situation. Was Canada becoming the "forty-ninth state"? There were advantages and disadvantages to U.S. investment. Branch plants provided many Canadians with good jobs in manufacturing, and Canadian industries benefited from U.S. technology. On the other hand, profits from the branch plants went back to the parent corporations in the United States. To many critics, it looked as though Canada was losing control of its economy. The debate would continue for decades, until the Free

Trade Agreement brought about a new economic relationship (see Chapter 6).

Canadian Owners and Workers

The wealth of Canada was not entirely in the hands of others. Canadian tycoons built up commercial empires that commanded vast resources and employed many people. On the west coast, H.R. MacMillan put together one of the world's largest forestry companies. In New Brunswick, K.C. Irving became one of the world's richest men, with businesses ranging from gas stations to timber and newspapers. In central Canada, E.P. Taylor and the Bronfman family controlled the production of many consumer goods and the stores that sold them.

At the same time, members of trade unions fought for a greater share of the country's prosperity. In 1946 and 1947, seven million workdays were lost to strikes as workers fought for the right to form unions and pressed for wages that would support a family. As a result, wages rose—for example, from sixty-nine cents per hour in 1945 to ninety-one cents per hour in 1948. Workers won a major victory in establishing the five-day, forty-hour work week, and increased fringe benefits such as paid vacations. This meant Canadian workers had more money and more leisure time to enjoy it. Business benefited as well, because consumer spending rose. Non-industrial unions grew rapidly, including organizations for teachers, nurses, civil servants, postal workers, and police.

The Limits of Prosperity

Some groups did not share the prosperity of the times. The working poor in cities—including many immigrants—washed dishes, cleaned offices, sweated in meat-packing plants, or toiled at sewing machines under miserable conditions. Women who could not afford to be stay-at-home wives and mothers were at a particular disadvantage. They were made to feel guilty by a society that condemned mothers who went out to work. Women were legally discriminated against by their employers, who paid them less than men even if they did the same work.

Figure 7-10
Public service employees striking in Montreal, 1972.

Using evidence
Which of the signs can you read? What do they indicate about the employees' demands?

	National	Aboriginal
Average per capita salaries and wages	$3500	$1600
Access to credit and loans per person (including farm improvement and housing)	$255	$1
Total per capita investment in housing	$90	$21
Population receiving general assistance	3.5%	36%
Houses with septic tank or sewer services	92%	9%
Houses with running water	92%	13%
Houses with indoor bath	84%	7%
Houses with electricity	99%	44%
Average age of death, including deaths in year one of infancy:		
For females:	64.1	34.71
For males:	60.5	33.31

Source: W. Rudnicki, "The Big Picture: Indian Affairs Branch Statement for Federal-Provincial Conference on Poverty," November 1965.

Figure 7-11 Profile of Aboriginal poverty, 1963.

Interpreting statistics Based on these figures, what general statement can you make about the living conditions of Aboriginal people in Canada in 1963?

Those who fared worst, however, were Canada's First Nations. They suffered the most from environmental damage caused by resource industries. For example, mercury poisoning from a pulp and paper mill contaminated the fish caught and eaten at the White Dog Reserve at Grassy Narrows, Ontario. The development of mines, highways, pipelines, and boom towns disrupted the hunting grounds and way of life of other First Nations.

ACTIVITIES

1. What are transfer or equalization payments? What was the purpose of these payments? How did the start of transfer payments mark a change in the nature of Confederation?

2. Why did the government believe it was necessary to provide Canadians with a system of social services?

3. Why did Canada's economy grow in the post-war years? Give at least three reasons.

4. List at least three gains that trade unions made in post-war years. How did they affect Canadian workers and businesses?

5. Megaprojects, resource development, and industrialization brought many benefits, but there were also costs, such as pollution and urban sprawl. Were the gains worth the costs? Argue your view.

Post-War Politics

The Nation Expands

Prime Minister King's last task in office was to expand the nation from sea to sea. Until 1932, Newfoundland had been an independent, self-governing dominion within the British Empire. During the Depression, however, the island had suffered so badly that its government had gone bankrupt; Britain set up a special commission to govern it. After World War II, the islanders were given the opportunity to vote on their political future in a **referendum**. They were offered three options: to continue under the existing government by commission, to return to the status of a self-governing dominion, or to join Canada.

One man took the lead in persuading the islanders to join Canada. J.R. "Joey" Smallwood was a skilful politician who argued that union with Canada would bring modernization and higher living standards to Newfoundland. Yet, many Newfoundlanders believed the benefits could not make up for the higher taxes and loss of identity that Confederation would bring them. Some would have preferred economic union with the United States.

In a referendum in June 1948, only 41 per cent of Newfoundlanders favoured Confederation. A larger number, 44.6 per cent, voted in favour of returning to the self-governing dominion status, while 14 per cent preferred government by commission. As no option won a clear majority, another vote was scheduled for late July. This time, the commission option was dropped, and the Confederation option won 52 per cent of the vote. On March 31, 1949, Newfoundland became part of Canada.

The Changing Face of Politics

Mackenzie King had been in power longer than any Canadian prime minister before him. In 1948, at the age of seventy-three, he retired. He was succeeded by Louis St. Laurent, and a new age of politics was born.

King had governed in the days before television. The media in those days did not pry into the private lives of politicians. By the early 1950s, the media were playing a much larger role in Canadian life. St. Laurent was a Quebec lawyer who entered politics late in life. When a reporter noticed, on the campaign trail, that he seemed to like children, the Liberal advertising agency made sure the nickname "Uncle Louis" stuck to him. The media thus created the image of a kindly relative. In reality, St. Laurent was an aloof man with a rich lifestyle. Nevertheless, most Canadians saw him differently. The media had become the makers of public image. From this time on, they would play a large role in Canadian politics.

By 1957, television showed the seventy-five-year-old Laurent looking tired and depressed. In comparison, the new Progressive Conservative leader, John Diefenbaker, was electrifying. Used to public speaking as a defence attorney in

Figure 7-12 St. Laurent on the campaign trail.

Expressing ideas What impression does this photograph give of St. Laurent? What elements in the photo suggest that it was carefully posed?

Saskatchewan, "Dief" proved to be a great campaigner and a witty orator. Television carried his image across the nation, and he led his party to an election victory, the first westerner to become prime minister. The defeated Liberals chose a new leader, the diplomat Lester "Mike" Pearson.

Dief versus Mike

For the next decade, Diefenbaker and Pearson dominated Canadian politics, taking turns at being prime minister and leader of the opposition. The two men had different styles and visions of Canada. They were bitter rivals, fighting five national elections in ten years.

Of German extraction, Diefenbaker was the first Canadian prime minister whose father was of neither English nor French background. He saw himself as a Prairies populist, one who spoke for and listened to ordinary people. Ordinary people, in turn, responded to him. A colleague recalled the 1958 campaign: "I saw people kneel and kiss his coat. Not one, but many. People were in tears. People were delirious."

Diefenbaker was passionately committed to what he called "unhyphenated Canadianism"—a belief in the equality of all Canadians, whatever their heritage. A staunch nationalist, he also believed in preserving Canada's British connections and standing up to the Americans. In addition, he championed human rights. He was the first prime minister to include a woman in his Cabinet and to appoint an Aboriginal senator. He gave Canada's **status Indians** living on reserves the right to vote in federal elections. It was also Diefenbaker who introduced the Canadian Bill of Rights (see Chapter 12).

While Diefenbaker's beliefs made him popular among many Canadians, they were also the source of his problems. In particular, French-Canadians, who saw their culture as distinct, did not appreciate Diefenbaker's version of "unhyphenated Canadianism."

Pearson and his Liberals appealed to younger and urban voters, especially in central Canada. Pearson's vision of Canada was based on two founding peoples, French and English. He believed that, in the long run, the British connec-

Figure 7-13 Diefenbaker was by nature theatrical. He was a lawyer before he became a politician, and "once, in the British Columbia Supreme Court, he fell to the floor, clutching his throat, to show how a murder had been committed, until a horrified judge rebuked him." He was also a talented mimic: "The repertoire was varied and endless. Striding up and down his little office..., Diefenbaker would people it with the entire Parliament, from the Speaker to the page boys." (B. Hutchison, *Mr. Prime Minister*, 1964, 319.)

tion to Canada would be severed. In his view, Canada needed an identity that would be meaningful to all Canadians, including the two million people who had immigrated since World War II.

Pearson was responsible for many features of modern Canada. His government introduced a trial abolition of capital punishment and easier divorce laws. Above all, he is remembered for introducing Canada's flag (see Chapter 8) and for improving Canada's social welfare system.

Social Welfare

Pearson's government continued to build on the social welfare programs started by Mackenzie King. During the war, King was looking for a way to keep the support of voters who remembered the hardships of the Depression and were attracted by the CCF (Cooperative Commonwealth Federation), the political party that stood for social benefits. As a result, he introduced unemployment insurance in 1940 and the family allowance, or "baby bonus," in 1944. In 1966, Pearson's government began the Canada Pension Plan, which improved on existing pension schemes. It also introduced the Canada Assistance Plan to help the provinces finance social assistance programs for all needy people. In the same year, Pearson introduced Canada's system of *medicare*.

The struggle for government-funded medical care had started many years earlier in Saskatchewan. At that time, Canadians who fell seriously ill could see their life savings wiped out on medical care. They had to depend on charity or face debt or bankruptcy to pay medical bills. Despite bitter opposition from doctors, Saskatchewan Premier T.C. "Tommy" Douglas introduced a complete medicare program that allowed all people in the province to seek medical treatment without paying directly out of their own pockets. When the bill was finally passed in Saskatchewan in 1962, it proved to the rest of the nation that a medicare system was possible.

In the same year, Tommy Douglas left provincial politics to become leader of the New Democratic Party (NDP), formed from the CCF. Fearing that the NDP might capture votes with a campaign for national medicare, the Liberals

Figure 7-14 Pearson's period of government was plagued by scandals, and the prime minister often seemed bumbling. Nevertheless, his achievements were considerable.

Interpreting a cartoon Both this cartoon and the one in Figure 7-13 were done by noted Canadian cartoonist Duncan Macpherson. Compare the cartoons. What are the similarities and differences in the way the prime ministers are presented? What do the cartoons say about each prime minister? What do they say about politicians at the time?

added health care to their party platform. As a result, the national **Medical Care Act** was passed in 1966. This bill meant that federal and provincial governments would now share the cost of medical care by doctors and hospitals for all Canadians, with funding coming from taxes.

Medicare was, and continues to be, a controversial social program. It is very costly, and some critics are dissatisfied with the government's role in the provision of health care. In poll after poll, however, Canadians identify medicare as the social program they value most.

Figure 7-15 Polio survivor Jeff Cranny as a "Timmy"— poster child for children with disabilities—in the 1950s. Polio is an infectious disease that causes temporary or permanent paralysis or death. Polio epidemics struck each summer in the early 1950s. To stop the spread of infection, swimming pools, movie theatres, and sometimes even schools were closed. It was an enormous relief when, in 1954, a U.S. doctor, Jonas Salk, developed a polio vaccine.

1967: Canada Turns 100

In 1967, towns and cities throughout the country celebrated Canada's centennial, or one-hundredth birthday. The celebrations reached a peak in Montreal, the site of Expo 67, an international fair that brought the world to Canada. Expo 67 was a triumph. The glamour and excitement of the fair seemed to define a new and positive spirit of Canadians as they celebrated 100 years as a nation.

As the centennial year drew to a close, the end was also approaching for Diefenbaker and Pearson, who had led the nation in its tenth decade. Both leaders seemed out of touch with the times, especially in comparison with the image of political leaders set by the dynamic, youthful U.S. President John Kennedy and his glamorous wife, Jacqueline. Diefenbaker was defeated in a leadership convention of the Progressive Conservative Party in September 1967. Pearson made the decision to step down and allow his party to choose a new face and leadership style to take the country into its second century.

ACTIVITIES

1. **a)** Why did Newfoundlanders disagree about joining Canada?

   b) Only 52 per cent of Newfoundlanders voted to join Canada. Do you think this was enough of a margin to warrant such a huge political change? Should it have been necessary for a greater percentage to support the change? Give reasons for your view.

2. **a)** Define social welfare.

   b) Why did most Canadians support the introduction of medicare and other social welfare programs?

3. To have a social conscience is to care for all people in society and try to improve their lives. How did Diefenbaker, Pearson, and Douglas all demonstrate a social conscience?

4. There was intense rivalry among Diefenbaker, Pearson, and Douglas. Did this rivalry benefit Canada? Give reasons for your view.

The Trudeau Era

Pearson's successor was Pierre Elliott Trudeau, a new kind of political figure for Canadians. Previous leaders had seemed formal and serious, but Trudeau was relaxed and irreverent. He scandalized members of Parliament by arriving at the House of Commons in a flashy sports car and wearing sandals and an open-necked shirt. A bachelor until 1971, he dated celebrities like Canadian guitarist Liona Boyd and U.S. actor Barbra Streisand. He delighted in joking with reporters, sliding down banisters, and pirouetting behind the Queen's back before the cameras.

Canadians were thrilled. Trudeau captured their imagination like no other politician before or since. Crowds of admiring followers swarmed him at his public appearances. Young people responded to him as though he were a rock star. "Trudeaumania" gripped the nation.

Glamorous and charismatic, Trudeau also had a clear vision of what he thought Canada should be. He used the expression "**just society**" to describe the kind of country he wanted to build. He believed firmly that government had a duty to protect the rights and freedoms of people, and to foster their social and economic well-being. At the same time, he was a strong advocate of individual freedom, and believed that governments should not interfere with personal liberties.

Towards Social Change

Trudeau was a man of his times. In the late 1960s, many Canadians were calling for change. Some took to the streets to make their protests heard. Among the most vocal of the groups were the student movement, the women's movement, and the environmental movement.

The "Youthquake"

By the early 1960s, adults were beginning to accept the teen culture that had evolved after World War II. After all, as a result of the baby boom, over half the population of North American was under the age of twenty-five by 1965. However, the adults' sense of comfort was short-lived. From the mid-1960s, the sheer numbers of young people in North America and western Europe created a more powerful youth culture of protest—a "**youthquake.**"

Figure 7-16 Pierre Trudeau stands before a crowd during an official visit to Grand Bank, Newfoundland, in 1971.

Expressing ideas Why do you think this image would have appealed to many Canadians?

Four Who Made a Difference

Most of the pressure for change came from groups in the 1960s and 1970s. Nevertheless, many individuals stood out, and helped to make a difference in a variety of ways. The following profiles tell the stories of just four.

Irene Murdoch

Irene Murdoch was an Alberta farmer who worked alongside her husband on their family ranch. For five months each year she was in charge of the farm while her husband found work elsewhere. In 1968, Murdoch decided to divorce her husband, who had been abusive. She claimed a share of the ranch on the basis of her contributions to it. The case went all the way to the Supreme Court of Canada, but Murdoch was denied her claim. In the opinion of the majority of judges, Irene Murdoch's work was only what would have been expected from a farmer's wife, and it did not entitle her to any claim to a partnership with her husband in the ranch.

Canadian feminists were outraged at the court's ruling, and decided to present the case to the "wider court" of Canadian public opinion. They publicized the case across the country. In 1973, Irene Murdoch was finally granted a payment. Her case helped bring about many changes in family law during the 1970s. The Ontario Family Law Reform Act of 1978, for example, stated that child care, household management, and finances were the joint responsibility of both husband and wife. It also required that both parties be entitled to an equal division of the family assets in the event of divorce.

Rosemary Brown

Rosemary Brown achieved many "firsts" in Canadian political life. Born in Jamaica in 1930, she came to Canada to study at McGill University in Montreal. She later moved to Vancouver, and in 1972, won a seat in British Columbia's NDP government, the first black woman to be elected to a legislature in Canada. In 1975, she ran for the federal leadership of the NDP. Although she lost the race, she was, again, a trailblazer for women and minority groups in Canada as the first woman and first Canadian of African heritage ever to contest the leadership of a major political party.

When she retired from political life, she served in a number of public positions. In 1996, Brown was named an officer in the Order of Canada in recognition of her many important contributions to public life.

Figure 7-17 Rosemary Brown.

David Suzuki

Scientist David Suzuki became internationally famous for his commitment to the environment. Suzuki was born in Vancouver in 1936. During World War II, he and his family were interned with thousands of other Japanese-Canadians. His internment camp was located in a deserted mining town in the Slocan Valley, and it was here that Suzuki discovered his love of nature. Later, Suzuki trained as a geneticist, but he has also applied his scientific knowledge to many environmental issues. He has contributed to a growing awareness of environmental issues in Canada and other countries through his popular books and radio and television programs.

Figure 7-18 David Suzuki.

Terry Fox

In 1980, twenty-two-year-old Terry Fox, who had lost a leg to cancer, inspired Canadians with his "Marathon of Hope," a run across Canada to raise money for cancer research. He ran from St. John's to Thunder Bay, stopping only when cancer was discovered in his lungs. In a massive and emotional response to his story, Canadians donated almost $25 million to his fund. Fox died in 1981 in his home town of New Westminster, British Columbia. Thousands of people participate annually in a fund-raising run named after him.

Figure 7-19 Terry Fox.

Questions

1. How did Irene Murdoch, Rosemary Brown, David Suzuki, and Terry Fox make a difference? Make a chart summarizing the impact of each of these figures. Use headings such as Problems Faced, Reaction to Setback, Achievements.

2. Select at least two other Canadians whom you consider "made a difference" during this period. Explain why you selected these people.

The transition began with the "British invasion," led by four long-haired young men from Liverpool, the Beatles. Boys' hair became longer, girls' skirts shorter. "Psychedelic" fashions became popular for both sexes. This was the start of the "hippie" phenomenon. Large numbers of young people embraced rock music, long hair, bizarre clothing, sexual promiscuity, and experimentation with drugs as a protest against mainstream society. With slogans such as "Make love, not war" and "Turn on, tune in, drop out," they strove to be different from earlier generations. For many of their parents, the world seemed to be coming apart.

Some young people had more serious aims. Many students had strong political beliefs, and rejected the consumerism of post-war society in the hope that the world would be changed for the better. Some became involved in the women's, environmental, and Aboriginal movements. Many joined in protests against the war in Vietnam, hoping to persuade Canadian leaders to take a stronger stand against the war.

Popular music of the day reflected these concerns. Protest songs decried racism, war, and the devastation of the environment. Protest singers like Americans Bob Dylan and Joan Baez attracted a wide following. Rock groups like the Beatles, the Rolling Stones, and The Who captured the mood with songs like "Revolution," "Street-Fighting Man," and "Talkin' 'bout My Generation."

The youthquake showed Canadian governments that young people were becoming more politically aware. Soon, politicians began making an effort to appeal to them. Governments began spending more money to provide employment and activity for youth. In 1972, the voting age for federal elections was lowered from twenty-one to eighteen, after most provinces had already lowered theirs. Hoping to decrease the appeal of illegal drugs, most provinces lowered the legal drinking age to eighteen at the same time.

It was only as the 1980s approached that baby boomers began moving away from their radical political opinions and lifestyles. They were entering the workforce and forming families. Financial concerns replaced youthful idealism. Their desire for wealth led some to nickname them the "Me Generation," a group fixated on

Figure 7-20 Although many young people had serious aims, their appearance and behaviour shocked the older generation.

Expressing ideas Why do you think some members of the older generation disapproved of scenes such as this?

self-satisfaction. The social protest movement had all but disappeared.

The Women's Movement

During the social protests of the 1960s, **feminism** emerged as a significant force. Many women had come to resent the expectations of the post-war period. They felt isolated in the suburbs and trapped by roles that did not allow them to develop their potential. Those who did work were streamed into lower-paying jobs such as waitressing, hairdressing, secretarial work, and retail sales. As you have seen, employers could legally discriminate against them in both wages and benefits.

Responding to pressure from feminists, the government set up the Royal Commission on the Status of Women in 1967 to examine women's place in Canadian society. The Commission reached several important conclusions:

- Women should have the right to choose to work outside the home.
- Society in general, as well as parents, should take some responsibility for children; therefore, day care services should be provided.
- Women should be entitled to paid maternity leave from their jobs.
- The federal government should do all it can to help overcome discrimination against women in society.

But would the federal and provincial governments follow these recommendations? Several women's groups joined forces to form the National Action Committee on the Status of Women (NAC) in 1971. This **pressure group** began to lobby both federal and provincial governments to act quickly on the Commission's recommendations. One of NAC's key victories was the inclusion of a clause guaranteeing the equality of women in Canada's Charter of Rights and Freedoms, which came into force in 1982 (see Chapter 12).

Canadian feminists also demanded that women be promoted to positions of responsibility in government, business, education, and the civil service. They argued against the stereotyping of women and the kinds of work they do, and pressed for changes in schools, where girls were not encouraged to excel in math and sciences, subjects more likely to lead to a well-paying job.

By the 1980s, more Canadian women were becoming engineers, doctors, politicians, and company presidents—pursuing careers in which they had previously been underrepresented. There were still barriers to overcome, but the women's movement had made a lasting difference to Canadian society.

The Environmental Movement

In 1962, a U.S. writer, Rachel Carson, published *Silent Spring*. This book warned the public that terrible damage was being done to the Earth's air, water, and land. Gradually, organizations were established to lobby the government to control industrial pollution.

At first, business and governments resisted any attempts to limit pollution, but public concern over the environment rose dramatically. Eventually, the federal government and many provinces passed laws requiring companies to prove that their projects and plants would not harm their immediate environment. Recycling in homes and in industry also became an issue, and automobile companies were pressured to make vehicles that were more fuel-efficient and produced less pollution.

Of all the environmental groups that were formed during this time, Greenpeace was the most famous. It was created in 1970 by a small group of activists in British Columbia. They were concerned about the testing of a nuclear bomb off the coast of Alaska. Greenpeace organizers took a small boat into the test area to protest the explosion, and refused to leave until the test was cancelled.

Since then, Greenpeace has used other dramatic tactics to draw attention to environmental issues. The organization has attracted a great deal of support, and a great deal of criticism for its tactics. No one doubts, however, its ability to attract attention. Today, the organization is based in Amsterdam, but a number of Canadians remain among its leaders.

Economic Challenges

When the Trudeau era began, Canadians could look back on nearly two decades of economic prosperity. People old enough to remember the dark days of the Depression were amazed by the wealth they were enjoying. Many Canadians believed that the post-war boom would continue indefinitely. Severe unemployment and poverty were surely problems of the past, never to be seen again. But within just a few years, this optimism was badly shaken.

The Problem of Inflation

A variety of factors caused the economic crisis, but one of the most important was an oil embargo imposed in 1973 by the Organization of Petroleum Exporting Countries (OPEC). In that year, war broke out in the Middle East between Israel and its Arab neighbours. Many Western countries, including Canada, supported Israel. In retaliation, OPEC, which included many Arab countries, refused to sell oil to these countries. Almost overnight, oil and gas prices jumped about 400 per cent!

The huge increase in oil prices started a round of inflation that would last most of the 1970s. The prices of all manufactured products went up sharply, and Canadians found that the purchasing power of their dollar fell steadily. Suddenly, they were heading for tough economic times.

As prices rose, Canadian workers began to demand higher wages; but as their wages increased, so did prices, and inflation spiralled. At the same time, businesses were failing. Their costs for energy and labour had soared, but the demand for their products was down. Unemployment in Canada soon rose to its highest level since the 1930s.

For the average Canadian family, the 1970s were unsettling times. Inflation stretched household budgets and increased the need for women to enter the workforce. Dual-income families, with two wage earners, became common. By 1978, the average family's buying power had fallen for the first time since the end of World War II. With few exceptions, it has continued to do so ever since.

Regionalism

To make matters worse, two economic problems that had plagued Canada in the past resurfaced. Both were the result of regionalism. The first of these problems was **regional disparity**, or the economic gap between the poorer and more prosperous regions of Canada. As in the Depression of the 1930s, industries based on natural resources were hit the hardest in the recession of the 1970s. The fishing industry in Atlantic Canada and the forestry, mining, and fishing industries in British Columbia suffered massive layoffs. Ontario and Quebec did not seem to suffer from as much of an economic downturn, and the other provinces resented them.

It was in western Canada that this sense of grievance against the central provinces reached its highest pitch. This was the second of the regional problems—**western alienation**. Ever since the prairie provinces had entered Confederation, western alienation had been a concern. People in the Prairies had long believed that many of Ottawa's policies favoured central Canada at the expense of the West. In the 1970s, the West found a particular cause for grievance. In response to the oil crisis, the federal government froze the price of domestic oil and gas. It also imposed a tax on petroleum that was exported from western Canada. The money raised by the tax would be used to subsidize the cost of imported oil in the East. These actions infuriated Albertans who, along with their premier, Peter Lougheed, felt that Alberta had the right to charge world prices for its oil:

> The Fathers of Confederation decided that the natural resources within provincial boundaries would be owned by the citizens through their provincial governments, rather than through the federal government....
>
> We view the federal export tax on Alberta as contrary to both the spirit and the intent of Confederation. We object to it in principle because it is discriminatory. It is not just an export tax—it is also a price freeze on all of Alberta's oil production at immense cost to Albertans....
>
> [For] the federal government to have taken such a major step unilaterally, without first even consulting with the producing provinces, is unfortunately firmly implanted in the minds of Albertans in terms of Ottawa's attitude towards the West.

Source: Peter Lougheed, Federal–Provincial Conference on Energy, Ottawa, January 22, 1974.

To help deal with unemployment and regional disparity, the Trudeau government increased transfer payments to the provinces to be used for social services. It also spent millions of dollars on regional projects to help economic development in certain areas, especially the Atlantic provinces.

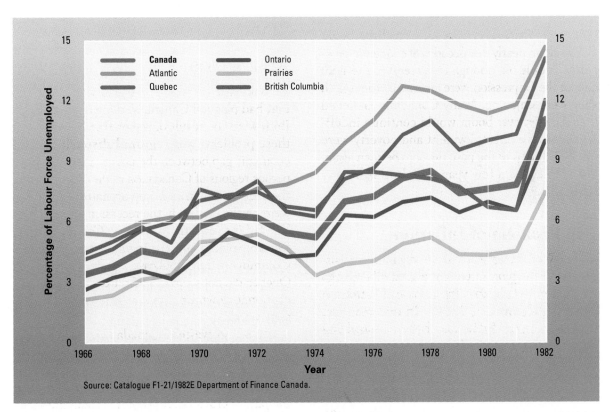

Source: Catalogue F1-21/1982E Department of Finance Canada.

Figure 7-21 Regional unemployment rates, 1966–1982.

Reading a graph Which regions had the highest unemployment? Which had the lowest? How did the rate in British Columbia vary in relation to the other provinces? How might you account for this change?

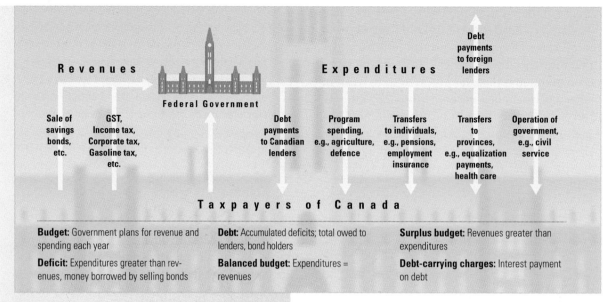

Figure 7-22 Government finances.

Gathering information What are some of the sources of government revenue? What are some of its expenditures?

To deal with a renewed oil crisis and rising gas prices, the Liberals also brought in the National Energy Program (NEP). The NEP had three aims: to reduce consumption of oil, to protect Canadians from rising oil prices, and to make Canada self-sufficient in oil. The program provided funding to Canadian petroleum companies to drill for oil in promising sites in the Arctic and off the coast of Newfoundland. It also took steps such as encouraging consumers to switch from oil to gas and electric sources of power. Alberta, once again, reacted angrily. By 1984, oil prices had fallen and the NEP had been dismantled, but the bitterness it caused in the West would linger for years to come.

The Debt Crisis

All these moves to protect the economic well-being of Canada and its people were proving expensive. Social services cost more than anyone had envisioned. Government was operating at a **deficit**: expenditures (amount of money spent) were far greater than revenues (money taken in,

especially through taxes). When businesses failed and people lost their jobs, the government collected fewer taxes but had to spend more on welfare and unemployment insurance. As a result, it had to borrow money to pay for its programs. By the time Trudeau left office in 1984, the federal government was almost $160 billion in debt.

Mulroney and the Debt

Brian Mulroney's Progressive Conservatives swept to power in 1984 with a promise to address Canada's economic problems. The Conservatives were inspired by events in the United States and Britain. In both countries, conservative governments were cutting back on the role of government in the economy. In the United States, President Ronald Reagan thought the solution to economic problems lay in the hands of corporations and wealthy citizens. If they were given large tax breaks, he believed, they would reinvest in the economy and create new jobs for everyone else. In Britain, Conservative Prime Minister Margaret Thatcher took a similar line. She lowered taxes and drastically cut spending on social benefits. People would have more incentive to work, she claimed, if the state did not take so much care of them.

Figure 7-23 Prime Minister Chrétien listens to Paul Martin defending his budget, 1995.

Mulroney planned to use this approach to cut the debt. He would save money by trimming social programs. The savings would help to pay off the debt. He would stimulate the economy by cutting the rate of taxes. The Free Trade Agreement with the United States would cause businesses to thrive, and people would be employed. In this way, government revenues would actually increase.

But the plan did not work. Canada was hit by recession in 1990. Once again, businesses failed and workers lost their jobs. Once again, fewer people paid taxes but more needed welfare and unemployment insurance. Instead of falling, the debt increased. The government was forced to increase, rather than cut, taxes. Its failure to tackle the debt contributed to the disastrous defeat of the Conservatives in 1993, when only two Tories won seats in the federal election.

The Liberals and the Debt

When Jean Chrétien and the Liberals came to power in 1993, they inherited a staggering national debt of close to $466 billion. Their solution was to inject more money into the economy. These projects would create jobs, and workers would then spend their earnings and boost the economy.

The Liberal government spent $6 billion on public works such as road repairs and new bridges.

Chrétien's Liberals had little opportunity to judge the effectiveness of their policy. At the end of 1994, interest rates shot up. Finance Minister Paul Martin calculated that interest alone would force the annual debt-carrying charges up to $60 billion within five years. Considering this a crisis, Martin announced that Canada could no longer afford "big government." It could not afford to continue spending on social services as it had in the past.

Martin began cutting federal government spending. He rejected the suggestion that he raise taxes as a solution. Instead, he cut $25.3 billion in spending over three years. More than 40 000 jobs in the federal civil service were done away with. Transfers to provinces for post-secondary education, health care, and welfare were substantially cut. Subsidies to businesses were removed. And the deficit grew smaller year by year.

The government was achieving its aim, but Canadians paid a high price. The federal government did less for them. For example, universities and colleges had to raise their tuition fees. The health care system suffered badly. Through the 1980s and 1990s, health care costs had risen

Should Social Services Be Cut to Reduce the National Debt ?

Paul Martin's policy of deficit reduction cut away at Canada's social services. Nevertheless, the Liberals were re-elected in 1997, partly because they had attacked government spending. By 1998, they had a **surplus**. This meant that revenues exceeded expenditures: the government was spending less than it took in. It did not mean that the debt had been paid off. The government still owed money it had borrowed over the years.

The surplus ignited a debate about the role of government in the economy. The government had four main options:

- Use the surplus to reduce the debt.
- Use the surplus to restore spending on social programs, such as health care.
- Reduce taxes to eliminate surpluses in coming years.
- Use parts of the surplus for each of the above.

Provincial premiers called upon the federal government to increase transfers to provinces for health care and other social programs. Groups concerned with welfare issues supported this view. They argued that the government was paying too much attention to deficit and debt reduction. It was more important to help those in need, many of whom were in no position to help themselves. Some also maintained that Canada's social programs gave the nation its identity, keeping it distinct from the United States, where few social services are provided by government.

Opposition parties pointed out that the debt was still very high, and that the government was still paying interest on its loans. If the government did not pay off what it owed, they argued, it would simply get further and further into debt. They wanted the surplus used to reduce the debt. These critics also called for a reduction in taxes, which they believed would boost the economy. Some returned to the arguments of the

Figure 7-24 Nurses on strike in Saskatchewan, 1999. They were protesting health care cutbacks, arguing that the safety of patients was at stake.

Mulroney era, saying that it would actually be better in the long run for Canadians to be more self-sufficient and less dependent on government support.

The government chose to repay some of the debt and also to increase social spending to some extent. But in trying to satisfy both sides, it seemed to please neither. The debate over social services and the debt continued to be a central issue for many Canadians.

Analysing the Issue

1. Make a comparison organizer listing arguments for and against deficit reduction as described in the text.

2. If you had been finance minister in 1998, what would you have done with the surplus, faced with the four options listed?

3. In 2000, the national debt was about $576 billion. Much of this debt was owned by Canadians themselves. For example, if you or your family members have Canada Savings Bonds, or provincial or municipal bonds, you own part of the debt. What difference do you think this makes to the seriousness of the debt problem?

4. What do you think Canadian governments should do about spending, debt, and social services in the future? Give reasons for your view.

rapidly. New drugs and technologies were expensive, and an aging population meant increased use of the system. At the same time, as the federal government cut transfer payments to the provinces, less money was available for health care. Hospital wards were closed; staffs were reduced; registered nurses were replaced by aides having much less training; and the length of hospital stays was reduced. Canadians were alarmed. Some patients went to the United States for treatment because the services they needed were not available in Canada. There were even reports of people dying because the Canadian system could not provide medical attention soon enough or at all.

There were other problems. Rising numbers of Canadians were homeless, and many had to rely on food banks. Thousands of Canadian children were living in poverty. Yet, at the beginning of the new millennium, the future of Canada's social services was uncertain.

Canada and New Technology

World War II spurred a wave of new technology, as you saw earlier in this chapter. By the 1970s, this wave had grown tremendously, and was picking up speed. Computers and other communications technologies were revolutionizing the way Canadians worked, played, and communicated. Canada had entered the "information age."

As the speed of air journeys increased and the cost fell, Canadians became world travellers. With satellite broadcasting, they had access to hundreds of television stations. Satellite links also allowed for cheap long-distance telephone calls, making it far easier for Canadians to communicate with family or friends and businesses abroad.

In the early 1980s, it was possible to own a personal computer, one with limited power. At the beginning of the twenty-first century, more than half of Canadian homes had computers. Many of these computers were used for Internet access, and a range of information and consumer services were available on-line. Some Canadians began to "telecommute": to work from their home or car, keeping in touch with the office via computer. In some industries, robots—computer-programmed machines—replaced humans, working at a fraction of their cost. A "new economy" emerged, in which knowledge, skills, and the ability to adapt to new situations became more important than ever before.

You will learn more about the impact of new technology and its implications for the future in Chapter 18.

ACTIVITIES

1. What economic problems did Brian Mulroney inherit? How did he propose to deal with them? What was the outcome?

2. How did the Liberals propose to deal with Canada's economic problems when they came to power in 1993? Why did they change their approach? What steps did they take, and what was the outcome?

3. What would be the effect of high inflation on:

   a) people on fixed incomes and pensions?

   b) workers who were not in unions?

   c) lenders who had agreed on a low interest rate for a loan to be paid back over five years?

   d) a family seeking a mortgage loan to buy a house?

4. How did the problems of this period influence the growth of:

   a) regionalism?

   b) western alienation?

5. What did Paul Martin mean when he said Canada could no longer afford "big government"?

Innovations

The Technology Explosion

In the 1950s and 1960s, *television* was the dominant technology that transformed the way Canadians were entertained and educated. *Vinyl* also had a huge impact. It was invented between the wars by the chemist who also discovered bubble gum. Fire-resistant, waterproof, malleable, and cheap, this synthetic product was used to make a host of products, including long-playing records, garden hoses, and shower curtains.

Cheaper plastics also made the *ballpoint pen* readily available after the war. It was denounced by schoolteachers, who felt that the old straight pen and ink bottle produced better handwriting.

In 1948, Bell Telephone announced the invention of the *transistor*, an electronic device for amplifying and switching that is durable, small, and inexpensive. In 1955, Sony Corporation sold the first transistor radios, and over the next decades the radios grew smaller and more portable. Radio, which was predicted to die out in the age of TV, was revived, as teens could now take their ▶ music with them wherever they went.

The *birth control pill* became available in 1960 and the first *disposable diapers* were introduced in the mid-sixties. Both products contributed to the increase in the number of women working outside the home.

Technology was also transforming medicine. In 1951, the first heart *pacemaker* (below) and artificial heart valves extended the lives of people who, just years before, would not have survived. Artificial kidneys (*dialysis machines*) and kidney transplants also saved lives. The first successful heart transplant took place in 1967. In 1978, the first "*test-tube baby*" was born, and in 1997, scientists announced the first *cloning* of a mammal, a sheep named Dolly.

Video-cassette recorders (VCRs), *microwave ovens*, and *cable television* all became widespread in the 1980s. The *compact disk* was introduced in 1984; it soon displaced vinyl records and became a common way of storing information.

The first computer *microchip* was invented in 1971, and went on to revolutionize computer technology. Computers had been in use since the end of World War II, but they were very big and slow in processing information. The microchip made computers smaller, more portable, and cheaper. The first home computers appeared on the market by the mid-1970s, but were not yet common in the early 1980s.

The *Commodore 64* computer (1982) had no hard drive, a very slow 4-MHz processor, and limited software. Nevertheless, it showed that desktop computers in homes were practical. By 1993, the *Internet* allowed for cheap and almost instant communication between personal computers, and for enormous amounts of information stored in databases around the world. ▼

The *Global Positioning System* (GPS) became widely available in 1994. This satellite system allows users to plot their position on the globe with great accuracy. Soon commercial airliners, private yachters, and wilderness campers were all using GPS.

LOOKING BACK

Develop an Understanding

1. Summarize social and economic changes that occurred during the decades following World War II. You might do this in point form, or in a timeline or short essay.

2. List some effects of the baby boom. Use information from the text, and brainstorm suggestions of your own.

3. Define *consumer society*. Give three examples indicating that Canada developed a consumer society after World War II.

4. Working in a group:

   a. identify three major causes of change described in this chapter

   b. make a cause-and-effect chart showing the impact of these forces of change on Canadian society.

Explore the Issues

5. In the 1950s, the president of General Motors called Canada "a vast storehouse of agricultural and mineral wealth waiting for further development." What did he mean? Use his statement as the basis for a PMI chart titled "U.S. investment in Canada in the post-war period."

6. Which groups do you think benefited most from the economic boom after the war? Which groups did not benefit? Why do you think this was so?

7. a. Identify what you think are the three most significant technological developments mentioned in this chapter.

   b. Explain why you have chosen these items.

   c. Suggest how your life might be different today if these developments had never been made.

8. How do you think the issue of western alienation should be dealt with by the federal government? Explain your reasoning.

Research and Communicate

9. Interview your parents, grandparents, or other family members about their memories of the post-war years. Present your findings in the form of a report or wall display.

10. Prepare an audio-visual presentation using slides, tapes, and/or computer technology to present the fashions and music from a period of time covered in this chapter—for example, 1945 to 1965, 1965 to 1985, or 1985 to 2000.

11. As part of a group, research a major economic project of the 1950s, 1960s, or 1970s. The Trans-Canada Highway, St. Lawrence Seaway, Trans-Canada Pipeline, Kemano Project, and Columbia River Project are examples. Prepare an illustrated presentation covering the costs, benefits, environmental impacts, and other relevant factors. Present your report to the class.

12. Compare the lyrics of a song from the 1960s with one from the 1980s or 1990s. Present your findings to the class. If possible, play the songs for your classmates.

13. In 1967, a famous Canadian communications theorist, Marshall McLuhan, wrote a book called *The Medium Is the Message*, in which he claimed that the form our information takes can be more important than the actual message it carries. McLuhan was writing mainly about television. Find out more about Marshall McLuhan. Present your findings in the form of a short report. Include your own ideas about how McLuhan's ideas might be applied to more recent forms of communication, such as the Internet.

The Canadian Identity: One, Two, or Many Nations?

8

FOCUS ON

• How did French–English relations shape Canadian identity in the second half of the twentieth century?

• How has immigration shaped the Canadian identity since World War II?

• What constitutional changes occurred during the 1980s and 1990s?

• How did Aboriginal peoples contribute to Canadian culture in the late twentieth century?

Counterpoints Issue

• Does Canada need a multiculturalism policy?

*I*n the decades following World War II, various groups in Canada became concerned about their identity and their role within the nation. This painting, *Unity Rally III, Montreal* by Evangeline Murray, focusses on French–English relations, but Aboriginal concerns and multiculturalism also became important issues.

Expressing ideas From the title, explain what is happening in this painting. What is the significance of the flags? What impression is given by the balloons?

Introduction

During the night of March 7, 1963, three Canadian army buildings in Montreal were bombed with Molotov cocktails (homemade fire-bombs). The mysterious letters "FLQ" were painted on the walls. The next day, a document from an organization claiming responsibility for the bombings was delivered to the news media:

> The Front de libération du Québec is a revolutionary movement of volunteers ready to die for the political and economic independence of Quebec.
>
> The suicide-commandos of the FLQ have as their principal mission the complete destruction, by systematic sabotage of:
>
> all colonial [federal] symbols and institutions, in particular the RCMP and the armed forces; ...
>
> all commercial establishments and enterprises which practise discrimination against Quebeckers, which do not use French as the first language, which advertises in the colonial language [English];
>
> all plants and factories which discriminate against French-speaking workers.
>
> ... INDEPENDENCE OR DEATH

The age of terrorism had arrived in Canada.

How did this new crisis emerge? What had happened between English- and French-Canadians to make the relationship so strained? How could the crisis be resolved?

In this chapter, you will learn about the impact of Quebec nationalism in the latter part of the twentieth century. You will also see how growing multiculturalism and the struggle of Aboriginal peoples for their rights changed the nation.

The Roots of Quebec Nationalism

The Duplessis Era

From 1936 to 1939, and again from 1944 to 1959, Quebec was controlled by Premier Maurice Duplessis and his party, the Union Nationale. Duplessis was a strong Quebec nationalist who was devoted to the idea of Quebec as a distinctive

- 1960   Quiet Revolution begins in Quebec.
- 1965   Canada's maple leaf flag flies for first time.
- 1967   Canadian immigration policy becomes officially "colour-blind."
- 1968   National Indian Brotherhood formed.
- 1970   FLQ crisis in Quebec leads Prime Minister Trudeau to invoke War Measures Act.
- 1971   Federal government introduces multiculturalism policy.
- 1980   Quebec holds a referendum on sovereignty-association.
- 1982   Constitution patriated without Quebec's agreement.
- 1990s   Asian countries become major sources of immigration.
- 1990   Meech Lake Accord dies.
- 1992   Charlottetown Accord rejected in referendum.
- 1993   B.C. Treaty Commission established.
- 1995   Second referendum on Quebec sovereignty is held.
- 1999   Nunavut created.
- 2000   Nisga'a Treaty given royal assent.

society, a "nation" rather than just another Canadian province. To emphasize his province's difference from English-speaking Canada, he introduced a new flag for Quebec bearing the French symbol, the *fleur-de-lis*. He fiercely opposed the growing powers of the federal government in the post-war years.

Under Duplessis, the Roman Catholic Church was the main defender of Quebec culture. Priests urged people in Quebec to turn their backs on the materialism of English-speaking North America. The Church praised the old Quebec traditions of farm, faith, and family. It ran Quebec's hospitals and schools, where most children received only a basic education. Religion played a role in every part of the curriculum, and the schools taught children to accept authority. The elite few who attended high school and university received a fine education, but the emphasis was on traditional subjects such as classical

Figure 8-1 Duplessis associated labour unions with communism, and he did not hesitate to call in the provincial police to crush strikes. This photograph was taken in 1949 during a strike by Quebec asbestos miners.

Using evidence What do you think is happening in this photograph? Who do you think these men are? Give reasons for your view.

languages and philosophy. As a result, Quebec produced many priests, lawyers, and politicians but few scientists, engineers, or business people.

While Duplessis tried to keep out the influence of foreign culture, he encouraged foreign investment in Quebec. Businesses and industries from Ontario and the United States were attracted by what Quebec had to offer. The province guaranteed cheap labour, since union activity was either discouraged or banned. It also promised low taxes. Quebec would benefit from the new investment, but so would Duplessis. In return for favourable business conditions, companies were expected to contribute generously to the Union Nationale. Bribery and corruption became the trademarks of the Duplessis regime. In return for government jobs or licences, businesses were expected to give "kickbacks" or gifts to the Union Nationale.

The Quiet Revolution

In 1960, after Duplessis died, Jean Lesage and the Liberals came to power with an election slogan that announced it was "Time for a change." Once in power, Lesage's first step was to stamp out corruption. Government jobs and contracts were now awarded according to merit. Wages and pensions were raised, and restrictions on trade unionism were removed.

The government also began a peaceful but dramatic movement to modernize the province's economy, politics, education, and culture. It took control of social services and the education system. Students were now required to take more science and technology courses to prepare them for the new Quebec. Above all, Quebeckers were encouraged to think of themselves as citizens of the twentieth century. As new attitudes began to take hold, the influence of the Roman Catholic Church declined. This wave of change became known as the Quiet Revolution, and it transformed the face of Quebec.

In the 1962 election, the Liberals went one step further. They campaigned, and won, with the motto *Maîtres chez nous*, "Masters in our own house." The aim now would be to strengthen Quebec's control of its own economy. Among other steps, the government nationalized (bought out) several hydro companies and turned them into a large, provincially owned power monopoly, Hydro-Québec.

Figure 8-2 A Canadian Army engineer lies injured in Montreal after an FLQ bomb, which he had removed from a mail box, exploded in his hands. On May 17, 1963, a total of seventeen bombs were placed in mail boxes in the Montreal suburb of Westmount.

The Birth of Separatism

As Francophone Quebeckers became proud of their achievements, they became angrier at what they perceived as injustices at the hands of English-speaking Canadians. Why was Ottawa, the national capital, so overwhelmingly English-speaking? Why did federal politicians from Quebec seldom hold key Cabinet posts? Why did French-Canadians not have the right to their own schools and hospitals in the rest of Canada, even though English-Canadians enjoyed those rights in Quebec? And why was Quebec's Francophone majority expected to speak English in stores or at work?

For some, the only solution lay in a Quebec controlled entirely by Quebeckers—in separation from Canada. Some young radicals with extreme views joined terrorist groups such as the FLQ (Front de libération du Québec) and fought in the name of le Québec libre—a "free" Quebec. As you read in the introduction to this chapter, these groups used firebombs and explosives to attack symbols of English-Canadian power in Quebec. For example, in the early 1960s, Royal Mail boxes and downtown office towers belonging to Canadian National Railways were attacked.

While most Quebec nationalists disapproved of such tactics, there were signs of general discontent in the province. In 1967, the influential Quebec cabinet minister René Lévesque left the Liberal Party and, a year later, formed the Parti Québécois (PQ). Lévesque believed that Quebec and Canada would do better to divorce peacefully than to continue a marriage of two cultures that, to many Quebeckers, was no longer workable.

Ottawa's Response

Lester Pearson became prime minister in the midst of the Quiet Revolution. He was convinced that Canada would face a grave crisis unless the French were made to feel more at home in Canada. He appointed the Royal Commission on Bilingualism and Biculturalism (the "Bi and Bi Commission") to investigate some solutions. The commission recommended that Canada should become officially bilingual.

In 1964, Pearson acted on a long-standing complaint in Quebec that Canada's symbols were too British. He suggested that Canada should have a new flag to replace those in use—the British Union Jack and the Red Ensign, which had the

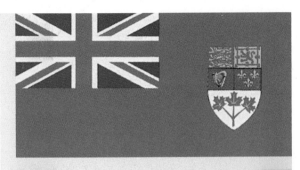

Figure 8-3 Diefenbaker and the Conservatives wanted to keep the old Red Ensign (top), with its traditional links to Britain, while the Liberals favoured a design using the three maple leaves of the Canadian coat of arms (bottom).

Expressing ideas Compare these two flags with the flag that was finally chosen. Consider the use of symbols and colour. Which of the three flags do you think is best, and why?

Trudeau and Quebec

When Pierre Trudeau succeeded Pearson as prime minister in 1968, he was determined that the federal government should do more to persuade people from Quebec that their future lay with Canada. In 1969, he acted on the advice of the "Bi and Bi Commission." His government passed the Official Languages Act, making Canada an officially bilingual country. Now, all federal government agencies across the country were required to provide services in both languages. English-speaking civil servants had to take French-language training courses, and more French-Canadians were appointed to senior federal government positions. Trudeau also called on all Canadians, especially young people, to increase their understanding of the other national culture.

Trudeau's moves met with mixed reviews. Many Canadians embraced the idea of bilingual-

Union Jack in the upper corner. Pearson chose the maple leaf as a symbol for the new flag because it seemed to represent all Canadians. Unfortunately, rather than bringing Canadians closer together, the new flag increased the tensions between French and English Canada.

Many Canadians opposed any new flag because they felt that Pearson was pandering to Quebec. An emotional debate split the country. Finally, after hundreds of suggestions from across Canada, the red-and-white maple leaf design was chosen. On February 15, 1965, Canada's new flag was raised on Parliament Hill for the first time. Ironically, English-Canadians have come to regard the flag with pride and affection, while people from Quebec, disillusioned by the bitter debate, continued to fly primarily the *fleur-de-lis*.

BILINGUAL PACKAGING! IN FRENCH!

BILINGUAL PACKAGING! IN ENGLISH!

...same old AMERICAN CONTENT...

Kanada's CORN FLAKES

Figure 8-4 This 1976 cartoon shows B.C. Premier Bill Vander Zalm, Prime Minister Trudeau, and Quebec Premier René Lévesque. Many people in British Columbia, farthest from Quebec geographically, opposed the Official Languages Act.

Interpreting a cartoon What is happening in the cartoon? What does this cartoon say about western Canada's reaction to bilingualism? About regionalism in Canada? About Pierre Trudeau's views?

ism with enthusiasm and enrolled their children in French immersion classes. But others, western Canadians especially, felt that the federal government was forcing French on them. Some also believed that Ottawa was focussing all its attention on Quebec, while the West and its concerns were largely ignored. Francophones in Quebec were also unimpressed. Trudeau was not doing enough, they felt. They wanted "special status" for Quebec in Confederation. Trudeau, however, insisted that Quebec was a province just like any of the others.

The October Crisis

In October 1970, events in Quebec made headlines across the nation and around the world. On October 5, members of the FLQ kidnapped James Cross, a British diplomat, from his Montreal home. In exchange for Cross's safe release, the FLQ made several demands, including the release of FLQ members serving prison sentences for previous criminal acts.

While both federal and Quebec authorities agreed to most of the demands, they refused to release any FLQ prisoners from jail. In response, on October 10, the FLQ kidnapped Quebec labour minister Pierre Laporte. Alarmed that the situation in Quebec was getting out of control, Trudeau decided to take drastic action.

Claiming that Quebec was on the verge of a violent revolution, Trudeau asked Parliament to impose the War Measures Act. This sweeping piece of legislation had only ever been used during the two world wars. Under the act, civil rights were suspended. Anyone could be arrested and detained without being charged with an offence. Membership in the FLQ became a crime. When asked by a reporter just how far he would go to defeat the FLQ, Trudeau brushed aside concerns about the measures he was taking and replied, "Just watch me."

On October 16, federal troops were sent in to patrol the streets of Ottawa and Montreal. Hundreds of pro-separatist Quebeckers were arrested and held without charge. While critics both inside and outside Parliament questioned the wisdom of these moves, Trudeau stated such action was necessary in order to combat FLQ terrorism and help free the hostages unharmed.

One day later, police made a horrifying discovery: they found the body of Pierre Laporte in the trunk of a car. He had been strangled. His murder shocked Canadians and increased the pressure on the government to crack down on the FLQ and find the remaining hostage, James Cross.

Two months later, the Montreal police tracked the group holding Cross in a Montreal house. In return for the captive's release, the kidnappers were permitted safe passage to Cuba, where they would be granted political asylum. Those detained under the War Measures Act were released. Of the 450 people held in detention under the act, only twenty-five were ever charged. The October crisis was over.

Figure 8-5 Soldiers with semi-automatic rifles patrol the streets of Montreal.

Expressing ideas How do you think you might have reacted to this image in 1970?

The PQ in Power

In 1976, Quebec voters chose the Parti Québécois as their next provincial government. It was a stunning victory for René Lévesque and his party. In the 1970 election, the PQ had won only seven of the 110 seats in the provincial legislature. During the 1976 election campaign, Lévesque had reassured Quebeckers that a vote for the PQ would not automatically mean separation. He promised that he would hold a province-wide referendum before making any moves towards independence. With this reassurance, Quebeckers had voted in, for the first time, a party dedicated to the ultimate goal of separation from Canada.

The top priority of the new government was strengthening the status of the French language. Shortly after taking office, the PQ government

Figure 8-6 Quebec Premier René Lévesque hushes supporters at a PQ rally following his party's victory over the Liberal party of Robert Bourassa in the provincial election.

Assessing Viewpoints

The use of the War Measures Act by Prime Minister Trudeau remains controversial. Was he justified in invoking such powerful legislation?

The following four documents give different points of view. Read the documents. For each, identify who made the statement, the circumstances under which the statement was made, and what position was taken.

Source 1

The kidnapping in broad daylight of a Quebec cabinet minister [Laporte] in front of his own ... residence had a dramatic effect on [the government's] view of the crisis we were facing. We began to believe that perhaps the FLQ was not just a bunch of pamphlet-waving, bomb-planting zealots after all; perhaps they were in fact members of a powerful network capable of endangering public safety, and of bringing other fringe groups—of which there were a large number at the time—into the picture, which would lead to untold violence. If all these groups coalesced [came together], the crisis could go on for a very long time, with tragic consequences for the entire country.

Source: Pierre Trudeau, *Memoirs* (Toronto: McClelland & Stewart, 1993), 136.

Source 2

...[T]he list of people arrested, without warrant, on the strength of suspicions, prejudice, or pure idiocy, exceeded the incredible number of four hundred.... Deprived of all their rights, beginning with habeas corpus [see Chapter 2], a great many of them were to remain in custody for days and weeks. As much as, if not more than in 1917, when there was at least the excuse ... of a real world war, the whole of Quebec found itself behind bars as Trudeau and company now attempted to justify their act before Parliament, the existence of which they seemed just to have remembered.

Source: René Lévesque, *Memoirs* (Toronto: McClelland & Stewart, 1986), 247.

Source 3

...[T]here were no fine distinctions drawn between separatism and terrorism in the general round-up in October 1970.... After the crisis had passed, rather than issuing an apology for such overzealous police work, the Prime Minister boasted that separatism was "dead." Other ... Liberals agreed: the FLQ crisis had been an opportunity to "smash separatism" and the government had taken it.

Source: J.L. Finlay and D.N. Sprague, *The Structure of Canadian History* (Toronto: Prentice Hall, 1984), 444.

Source 4

As for the objection that Trudeau was acting to squash separatism and ... the Parti Québécois, we have the statements of both the Prime Minister and one of his supporters ... during the crisis. On October 17, [Bryce] Mackasey stressed to the House of Commons that the Parti Québécois was "a legitimate political party. It wants to bring an end to this country through democratic means, but that is the privilege of that party." Trudeau ... made the same point in November to an interviewer.

Source: Robert Bothwell, Ian Drummond, and John English, *Canada Since 1945: Power, Politics, and Provincialism* (Toronto: University of Toronto Press, 1989), 394.

Applying the Skill

1. Are these documents primary sources or secondary sources? Explain in each case.
2. Summarize each document's main argument.
3. Which documents support Lévesque's claims?
4. Which documents do you consider to be the most credible sources? Justify your choice.
5. Write one or two paragraphs giving your view on whether the use of the War Measures Act was justified. Support your view with details from the text and the documents above.

passed Bill 101, sometimes referred to the "Charter of the French Language." This law made French the only official language of the province. Quebec government employees had to work in French. Commercial outdoor signs would have to be in French only, and children of immigrants would be required to attend French rather than English schools.

Francophone Quebeckers welcomed the language law. Many felt their culture and language were endangered. The birth rate in Quebec had fallen to its lowest level in history, and while immigration had increased, most new immigrants preferred to educate their children in English. To non-Francophone Quebeckers, however, Bill 101 was a symbol of oppression. In the rest of Canada, as well, many people felt that the PQ's policies were too extreme. They looked to the federal government to stand up to the separatist challenge and find a way to preserve Canadian unity.

The 1980 Referendum

In 1980, the Lévesque government called a referendum, as promised, to determine Quebec's political future. Lévesque asked Quebeckers to vote "yes" to giving his government a mandate to negotiate a new agreement with Canada based on **sovereignty-association**. He proposed that Quebec become politically independent, yet maintain a close economic association with Canada. At rally after rally, Lévesque inspired his listeners to seize the opportunity to become "*maîtres chez nous.*"

Prime Minister Trudeau also made impassioned speeches urging the people of Quebec to remain part of a strong, united, and forward-looking Canada. During the campaign, Trudeau promised to negotiate a new Constitution should the "no" side win. This promise proved popular among Quebeckers. They wanted a Constitution that recognized Quebec as an equal partner in Confederation and as a distinct society within Canada. Trudeau's promise helped to swing many Quebec votes to the "no" camp.

In the referendum, 40 per cent of Quebeckers voted "yes" to sovereignty-association; 60 per cent voted "no." In front of thousands of distraught supporters, a visibly upset René Lévesque accepted defeat. Yet, he also promised his followers that their dream of a sovereign Quebec would triumph one day.

Figure 8-7 This cartoon showing Prime Minister Trudeau and Premier Lévesque offers one view of sovereignty-association.

Interpreting a cartoon According to the cartoonist, how did sovereignty-association differ from separation? What was this cartoonist's view of Lévesque? How do you know?

NOW REMEMBER, I'VE CHANGED THE OPERATION FROM COMPLETE SEPARATION TO SOVEREIGNTY ASSOCIATION... THAT MEANS WE'LL BE COMPLETELY SEPARATE ... EXCEPT FOR WHERE I'M ATTACHED TO YOUR WALLET...

The Canadianese Twins

Patriating the Constitution

True to his word, Trudeau announced plans to revise Canada's Constitution. The British North America (BNA) Act had been Canada's Constitution since 1867. The act set out the powers of the federal and provincial governments and guaranteed the language and education rights of Quebec's French-speaking majority. Since the BNA Act fell under British jurisdiction, no changes could be made without the British Parliament's approval.

Trudeau wanted to patriate the Constitution (bring it home to Canada), where the Canadian government would have the authority to make changes. Trudeau wanted this authority because he hoped, above all, to include a Charter of Rights and Freedoms, a clear statement of the basic rights to which all Canadians were entitled. Before he could make any changes, however, he had to have the approval of the provinces.

As a first step, Trudeau needed to come up with an **amending formula**. How many provinces would have to be in agreement for a change in the Constitution to be made? Should Quebec, as the French-speaking partner in Confederation, be given veto power? These were difficult issues to resolve. Quebec was not the only province pushing for more power; the western provinces also saw this as an opportunity to have more say over affairs that affected them. Furthermore, most of the provincial premiers were opposed to the Charter. In English-speaking Canada, premiers

Figure 8-8 Queen Elizabeth II arrives at Parliament to sign Canada's new Constitution Act, April 17, 1982.

Using evidence From this photograph, what would you say was the mood of the occasion?

felt that the Charter would make the courts more powerful than their legislatures. In Quebec, Lévesque feared that the Charter could be used to override his language laws—or any other legislation that might be passed to protect Quebec's distinct society.

A series of meetings failed to resolve these issues. In a last-ditch attempt to reach agreement, the prime minister and the ten premiers met in Ottawa on November 4, 1981. Over late-night cups of coffee in the kitchen of the National Conference Centre, federal Justice Minister Jean Chrétien and the justice ministers from Saskatchewan and Ontario hammered out what came to be called the "Kitchen Compromise." Nine of the ten provincial premiers were awakened in their rooms at the Château Laurier Hotel and asked to approve the deal.

The premiers agreed to accept the Charter if an escape clause were added. This was the **"notwithstanding clause,"** which allowed the federal government or any of the provinces to opt out of some of the clauses in the Charter. This meant that a provincial law that was contrary to a specific Charter guarantee could be passed, despite anything the Charter contains (see also Chapter 12). An agreement on the amending formula was also reached. Changes to the Constitution could be made only with the agreement of "seven out of ten provinces representing 50 per cent of Canada's population." This meant, in effect, that Quebec could be excluded as long as Ontario was included.

Only René Lévesque, who was staying at another hotel, was not included in the Kitchen Compromise. The next day, he argued against the deal. Nevertheless, Trudeau accepted the compromise. He maintained that the federal government had so many members from Quebec that it could speak for that province. Lévesque and the people of Quebec felt betrayed. They believed that the federal government and the English-speaking premiers had ganged up on Lévesque in order to deny Quebec recognition of its distinct status. The Quebec provincial government refused to sign the proposed new Constitution.

Without Quebec's agreement, Trudeau went ahead. On April 17, 1982, the new Constitution Act was signed into law by Queen Elizabeth II and Prime Minister Trudeau outside the Parliament Buildings in Ottawa. The Canadian Constitution had officially come home. The last step towards making Canada a completely independent nation had been taken. As the rest of Canada celebrated, flags in Quebec flew at half-mast, and Premier Lévesque led an angry demonstration through the streets of Quebec City.

The last step towards making Canada a completely independent nation had been taken. But the process had revealed cracks in national unity that would continue to trouble Canadians in the years that followed.

ACTIVITIES

1. Do you think the Official Languages Act was an effective way to address dissatisfaction in Quebec? Explain.

2. Make a timeline of events during the October crisis. Identify events that you think were most significant. Give reasons for your choices.

3. In Quebec elections, the Parti Québécois won 23.5 per cent of votes in 1970, over 30 per cent in 1973, and 41 per cent of votes in the 1976 election. What do you think accounted for these results in each case? Find evidence from the text.

4. Would you describe Lévesque's plan for sovereignty-association as separation from Canada? Why or why not?

5. Explain:
   a) amending formula
   b) patriation
   c) Charter of Rights and Freedoms
   d) Constitution Act of 1982.

6. Make a chart with two columns: "Attitude to Patriating Constitution" and "Reasons." Complete the chart with information from the text for Trudeau, Quebec, and Other Provinces.

7. a) Do you think Lévesque was betrayed by the Kitchen Compromise? Explain.
   b) Role-play a conversation between Lévesque and Trudeau on the Kitchen Compomise.

The Constitution Debate

By 1984, most Canadians outside Quebec felt that the issues of the Constitution and Canadian unity had been settled. Their greatest concern was the worsening economy. Yet, when John Turner, Trudeau's replacement as prime minister, called an election later that year, Brian Mulroney, the leader of the Progressive Conservatives, returned to the issue of the Constitution. To build support from separatists in Quebec during the election campaign, Mulroney promised to repair the damage of 1982 by obtaining Quebec's consent to the Constitution "with honour and enthusiasm."

Once elected, Mulroney looked for an opportunity to follow up on his promise. The time seemed right when René Lévesque retired and the pro-federalist Liberal Party, led by Robert Bourassa, took office in Quebec. Mulroney began negotiations. His first priority was to reach an agreement by which Quebec would sign the Constitution, but by now, other provinces had their own demands. For example, Newfoundland and Alberta wanted more control of their own resources—Newfoundland of the fisheries, and Alberta of its oil industries.

Western alienation, which had grown through the oil crisis of the 1970s, had come to a head once again over a government contract to repair air force jets. Ottawa awarded the multibillion-dollar contract to the Bombardier company of Montreal, even though Bristol Aerospace of Winnipeg had made a better proposal. Westerners were outraged. They were convinced that the contract went to Bombardier just to "buy" Conservative votes in Quebec. In response, the Reform Party was formed in 1987 to be the voice of western Canada. As well, both Alberta and Newfoundland demanded reforms to the Senate that would give their provinces a stronger voice in Ottawa. (Senate reform is discussed in Chapter 9.)

The Meech Lake Accord

In 1987, Prime Minister Mulroney called the premiers to a conference at Meech Lake, where he proposed a package of amendments to the Constitution. Among other provisions, the Meech Lake Accord offered to recognize Quebec as a distinct society. It also proposed giving more power

Figure 8-9 Some critics thought Mulroney had made a bad mistake in reopening the Constitution debate.

Interpreting a cartoon
Who are the characters shown in this cartoon? What is happening to them? Do you find this cartoon effective? Explain.

to the other provinces. All provinces, for example, would have the power to veto constitutional change. Quebec supported the accord. Premier Bourassa announced:

> The Meech ... Accord is an unprecedented historic attempt to maintain and consolidate the unity of our country, Canada. For Quebeckers, Canada is the first choice, and I would like it to remain that way.

However, there were many critics. The most vocal of these was Pierre Trudeau. He argued that the designation of Quebec as a distinct society would create "two solitudes" in Canada. It would, he said, simply isolate the Francophones of Quebec. It would make them less rather than more a part of Confederation. Other critics disliked the "distinct-society" clause. Quebeckers saw this clause as a way of protecting French culture and language, but opponents worried that it might be used in Quebec to override the Charter and deprive specific groups of their rights. Aboriginal peoples pointed out that they, too, had a distinct society that needed to be recognized and protected. And other critics argued that the citizens of Canada had not been given enough opportunity to have their say on the crucial issue of the Constitution.

Two provinces, Manitoba and Newfoundland, withheld their support; as a result, the Meech Lake Accord disintegrated in June 1990. Quebeckers were dismayed. The failure of the accord was seen as a rejection of Quebec itself, even a "humiliation." By late 1990, support in Quebec for separation had soared to 64 per cent. Lucien Bouchard, a powerful Quebec member of Mulroney's Cabinet, resigned in protest and formed the **Bloc Québécois**. This political party would run in federal elections to support the aim of Quebec separation.

The Charlottetown Accord

Prime Minister Mulroney believed he had to continue with the Constitution debate. Anxious to avoid previous mistakes, his government appointed a special "Citizen's Forum"—a committee that travelled across the nation to hear the views of Canadians on the future of the Constitution. Eventually, Mulroney and the premiers came up with another package of proposed constitutional amendments. This was the **Charlottetown Accord**, which answered Quebec's concerns in ways similar to the Meech Accord. Now, other interests were also addressed. The Charlottetown Accord proposed reforming the Senate, making it an elected body with equal representation from all parts of the country, as the western provinces wanted. It also supported Aboriginal self-government to draw the support of the First Nations.

The Charlottetown Accord was put to a national referendum in October 1992. Mulroney warned that rejection of the accord would endanger the very future of the nation. Yet, 54.5 per cent of Canadian voters rejected it. The

Figure 8-10 Elijah Harper, a Cree NDP member of the Manitoba legislature, shown here holding an eagle feather for spiritual strength, opposed the Meech Lake Accord because it did not recognize Canada's Aboriginal nations as a distinct society. He started procedural delays that prevented final ratification of the accord by the provincial legislatures.

Charlottetown Accord had so many clauses, each designed to please a different group, that it was easy to find fault.

The greatest opposition was in British Columbia, the fastest-growing province, where 68.3 per cent voted "no." B.C. voters felt that the accord gave Quebec too much power. They objected particularly to the guarantee that Quebec would always have 25 per cent of the seats in the House of Commons, regardless of the size of its population. Voters in Quebec generally believed that the Charlottetown Accord did not give them enough power because most of the Senate seats had been given up to the West. They also feared Aboriginal self-government, because it would affect a large portion of northern Quebec.

Referendum of 1995 and After

Angered by events in the Constitution debates, Quebeckers again elected the separatist Parti Québécois in the 1994 provincial election. The following year, Premier Jacques Parizeau called a provincial referendum on full sovereignty—the separation of Quebec from the rest of Canada. The "yes" forces reminded Quebeckers to remember their "humiliation" in the rejection of the Meech Lake Accord. On the night of October 30, 1995, as the referendum votes were counted, the nation held its breath. When the results were in, 49.4 per cent of Quebeckers had voted "yes" to sovereignty; 50.6 per cent had voted "no."

The vote was so close that the country was in a state of shock. The "no" side had won by a slim margin of just over 1 per cent. In the aftermath of the referendum, some politicians continued to believe that Canada could change the Constitution to satisfy at least some of Quebec's demands. Others thought it was time to take a hard line with the separatists. By the end of the century, no permanent settlement was clear. Lucien Bouchard became Quebec premier and talked periodically of a new referendum on sovereignty. Meanwhile, Prime Minister Jean Chrétien began working on guidelines for a future vote on sovereignty in Quebec. He stressed that, should the province ever opt for sovereignty, the costs for Quebeckers would be high.

Following the narrow margin of victory in the 1995 referendum, the federal government moved to ensure that a future referendum would follow a clear process. Prime Minister Chrétien sent the question of how Quebec might separate to the Supreme Court of Canada. Then, he followed up on the court's ruling with his controversial "clarity bill," which set down in law, for the first time, Ottawa's insistence on a clear question in any future referendum and a substantial "yes" majority

Figure 8-11 People from across Canada took planes, buses, cars, and trains to Montreal to tell the people of Quebec that they wanted them to stay in Canada.

Using evidence How does this photograph demonstrate support for the "no" side?

before Quebec's exit from Confederation would be negotiated.

As the century closed, support for separatism appeared to be declining in Quebec. Liberal gains in Quebec in the 2000 federal election and the resignation of Premier Bouchard seemed to support the tough stand towards separation that had been adopted by Prime Minister Chrétien. The new premier of Quebec, Bernard Landry, remains committed to a restructuring of Canadian confederation into something resembling the European Union. The "clarity bill" may soon be tested.

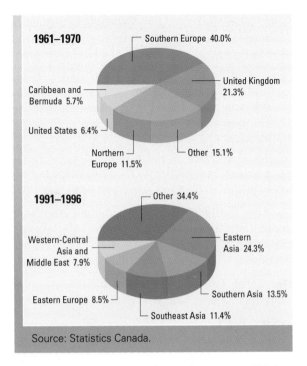

Source: Statistics Canada.

Figure 8-12 Immigration to Canada by country of birth (five leading regions).

Using evidence Based on these graphs, find evidence to support the following conclusion: *The sources of Canadian immigration changed almost completely between the two periods shown.*

ACTIVITIES

1. **a)** Why did Brian Mulroney reopen the Constitution debate?

   b) Do you think he made a mistake in doing so? Support your answer with evidence from the text.

2. List the criticisms of the Meech Lake Accord. Why did it fail?

3. Why did the Charlottetown Accord fail?

4. How did the Quebec referendum of 1995 differ from that of 1980?

5. Why did the results of the 1995 Quebec referendum shock the country?

A Multicultural Nation

As Anglophone and Francophone Canada attempted to define their country's nature, another force was developing that would have an impact on Canadian society: Canada was becoming more multicultural.

Immigration and Multiculturalism

From the end of World War I until the 1960s, Canada had a somewhat restrictive **immigration policy**. Immigrants of British and European origins, especially northern Europeans, were preferred because it was thought they would adapt the most easily to the Canadian way of life.

Immigrants of other origins did arrive, but the government limited their numbers in various ways.

By the 1960s, Canadians had a more open attitude towards people of other cultures and countries. In 1962, new regulations removed most limits on immigrants of Asian, African, and other origins. In 1967, legislation made Canada's immigration policy officially "colour-blind." Since the Canadian economy required people with training and specific skills, immigrants were to be chosen by a point system based on education and employment prospects. National and racial origins were no longer factors.

In 1971, Prime Minister Trudeau also introduced an official policy of **multiculturalism**. Trudeau claimed that the policy would:

> ... support and encourage the various cultures and ethnic groups that give structure and vitality to our

Birthplace	Toronto* Population	Vancouver* Population
Canada	60.2%	66.5%
Europe	16.2%	10.1%
Asia	14.5%	18.7%
Caribbean and Bermuda	3.5%	0.3%
Central and South America	2.8%	0.9%
Other	2.8%	3.5%

*These figures refer to the Toronto and Vancouver Census Metropolitan Areas, whose 1996 populations were: Toronto 4.4447 million, Vancouver 1.8914 million.

Source: Statistics Canada.

Figure 8-13 Birthplace of populations, Toronto and Vancouver, 1996, by selected regions (in percentages).

Interpreting statistics Using information from this table, write two or three sentences comparing and contrasting the compostion of the populations of Toronto and Vancouver based on place of birth.

society. They will be encouraged to share their cultural expressions and values with other Canadians and so contribute to a richer life for us all.

The policy of multiculturalism encouraged the country's different ethnic groups to express their cultures. Multicultural activities were organized across the country. For example, heritage language classes were provided to help children learn the language of their parents. Festivals were held for cultural communities to share their music, dances, foods, games, arts, crafts, and stories. Various programs were designed to make all residents feel at home in Canada, regardless of their origins. These programs were also intended to prevent racism by promoting respect for all cultures.

In 1976, immigration regulations changed again, this time to allow immigration of family members with relatives already in Canada. From the late 1960s on, more allowance was also made for refugees fleeing persecution in their homelands. For example, some 11 000 refugees came to Canada in 1968, after the Soviet Union invaded Czechoslovakia. In 1972, about 7000 people of Asian background, many of them highly trained, came from Uganda after their country's dictator, Idi Amin, singled them out for ill treatment. During the 1980s, immigration policy especially encouraged immigrants having the money and business skills to create jobs by investing in existing companies or starting new ones.

During the 1980s, Canada became more multicultural than ever before. Figure 8-12 shows how the sources of immigration continued to change into the 1990s. The biggest increase was in immigration from Asian countries. Canada's cities also continued to draw most of the new immigrants and to develop as lively multicultural centres (see Figure 8-13).

Multiculturalism Becomes an Issue

The federal government recognized the growth of Canada's multicultural communities by establishing the Department of Multiculturalism and Citizenship in 1988. This department continued to promote multiculturalism in all areas of government policy. Despite these initiatives, however, Canadian attitudes towards multiculturalism were complex. Many Canadians believed that the policy benefited Canada. It allowed people of all ethnic, racial, religious, and cultural backgrounds to feel welcome here, and to play a positive role in the development of the nation. Supporters say the policy also helped strengthen national unity by drawing all Canadians closer together in mutual respect.

But through the 1980s and 1990s, it became clear that not everyone agreed with this position. Some Canadians argued that the policy of multiculturalism was preventing Canada's communities from developing a common Canadian identity. Canada's model of multiculturalism was like a mosaic, where groups maintained their own identity. It would be better, they said, to follow the "melting-pot" model of the United States, where cultural groups were encouraged to assimilate— that is, to give up their identities and take on the mainstream culture to a greater extent.

As new cultures took root in British Columbia, other issues were raised. For example, traditional Canadian holidays such as Easter and Christmas are rooted in the Christian faith and culture. These holidays presented a challenge for schools with large multicultural populations. One solution was to highlight the festivals of groups represented in sufficient numbers in the school. For example, Chinese New Year, the Muslim holy month of Ramadan, and Sikh holy days such as Baisakhi were celebrated in some schools. These festivals offered students a better understanding of the beliefs and customs of Canada's multicultural society.

ACTIVITIES

1. How did Canadian immigration policies and patterns develop between 1960 and 2000? Present your answer in the form of a timeline or chart.

2. Why did the federal government introduce an official multiculturalism policy in 1971?

3. Do you think the policy has had its intended effect? Support your view with examples.

4. Explain how the Canadian model of a "cultural mosaic" differs from the U.S. model of a "melting pot."

5. Quebec has long pressed for a greater share of immigrants to Canada and a greater say on who can enter. Why do you think this is so?

counterpoints

Does Canada Need a Multiculturalism Policy?

Canada's official multiculturalism policy has fierce defenders and critics. Many Canadians believe the policy benefits Canada. They feel multiculturalism plays a positive role in the nation's development, and that it helps create national unity, as Pierre Trudeau claimed it would in 1971. Supporters also feel that multiculturalism gives Canadians an awareness of other cultures, an asset when dealing with problems that may arise in various communities. Furthermore, they say the policy helps promote values such as tolerance, equality, and support of diversity.

Opponents claim that it is not good for the country to promote differences in cultures. They say this approach weakens the country's unity. Some critics feel that ethnic groups should maintain their own cultures in Canada if they wish, but that the government should not provide financial support to these groups—rather, it should support Canadian culture. Critics also point to

countries such as Rwanda and Yugoslavia, where ethnic diversity has ripped communities and families apart.

For and Against

The Honorable Hedy Fry, who is also the member of Parliament for Vancouver Centre and an immigrant to Canada, has expressed the following view:

Multiculturalism is the key to Canadian unity. We must understand that people of different races can have a strong sense of belonging to one nation while maintaining their original cultural identities.... Multiculturalism and respect for our differences are important reasons why this country has been ranked as the best nation in the world by the United Nations.

Source: Gary Engler, "Dr. Fry defends her job and policies." *Vancouver Sun*, November 19, 1997.

Neil Bissoondath, an author and also an immigrant to Canada, has a different view:

Anyone critical of multicultural policy ... is immediately branded a racist. And if one happens to be, as I am, a "person of colour," one is then graced with words such as "sell-out," "traitor" ... from "ethnic" defenders with a stake in the system.... Many are they in this country who fear a serious

Figure 8-14 Hedy Fry responds to questions in the House of Commons, March 1999.

examination of multiculturalism, its policies and its consequences.

Source: Neil Bissoondath, *Selling Illusions: The Cult of Multiculturalism in Canada* (Toronto: Penguin, 1994), 5.

Rais Khan, a University of Winnipeg political science professor and immigrant to Canada, is also critical of the multiculturalism policy:

Immigrants come here to become Canadians; to be productive and contributing members of their chosen society. I am one of them. I did not come here to be labelled as an ethnic or a member of the multicultural community, or to be coddled with preferential treatment, nurtured with special grants, and then to sit on the sidelines and watch the world go by. I came here to be a member of the mainstream of the Canadian society.... I do not desire special consideration; I wish to be treated equally.... Whether or not I preserve my cultural background is my personal choice....

Source: Rais Khan, presentation to the Reform Party, quoted in Preston Manning, *The New Canada* (Toronto: Macmillan Canada, 1992), 316–317.

Myrna Kostash, an Alberta author with an Eastern European background, has responded to Neil Bissoondath:

It is precisely the policy of multiculturalism that has brought ethnic minorities out of the so-called ghettoes into the mainstream of our public culture....

Bissoondath takes great satisfaction from his successful acculturation into Canada, having arrived some twenty years ago from Trinidad. He spurns identification with the "ethnic bastions" of ex-Trinidadians in Canada. Fair enough. But he should acknowledge the experience of those Canadians for whom multiculturalism emerged after decades of a less salubrious [agreeable] history in a far less culturally accommodating society than the one Bissoondath joined. For a real experience of ghettoization [being kept apart as a group], he should have come to Canada before the Multiculturalism Act....

Source: Myrna Kostash, reviewing Neil Bissoondath's book *Selling Illusions* in the *Toronto Star*, October 22, 1994, F17.

Analysing the Issue

1. In a group, survey a variety of Canadian newspapers, magazines, and television progams to determine the extent to which they reflect Canada's multicultural nature. Use a three-column chart to record your findings, according to the media types surveyed. Summarize your findings, and present them to the class.

2. Both Hedy Fry and Neil Bissoondath are from Trinidad. Why do you think their views on multiculturalism differ?

3. Imagine you are the federal minister responsible for multiculturalism. Prepare a speech announcing that you are going to either **a)** continue the policy of multiculturalism or **b)** make changes to it. Justify your decision, taking possible consequences into account.

Aboriginal Nations

By the latter half of the twentieth century, Canada was becoming a bilingual but multicultural country. Yet, its roots were even more diverse, including the First Nations that were its original residents.

When Aboriginal people living on reserves won the right to vote in 1960, it did little to improve their living conditions. They continued to suffer from serious problems, including poverty, poor health, and inadequate housing and education. For those who left to try their luck in the large cities, life was often worse. Lacking education, job skills, and the ability to adapt to urban life, many faced hostility and discrimination.

By the late 1960s, First Nations were organizing to pressure Ottawa and the provincial governments to deal with the crisis they were facing. The National Indian Brotherhood was formed in 1968 to lobby on behalf of Aboriginal people living on reserves. In response to their growing demands, Pierre Trudeau's Liberal government proposed a policy outlined in the White Paper of 1969. A white paper is a document that a government puts forth for discussion. If it is accepted, it may be passed into law. The 1969 White Paper called for an end to what Trudeau viewed as the overly protective attitude that had previously marked government policy in dealing with Aboriginal peoples.

Trudeau and his Indian Affairs Minister, Jean Chrétien, suggested that Aboriginal peoples should be treated exactly like other citizens. Any special rights they had on the reserves, such as not having to pay income tax, would be abolished. At the same time, more would be done to encourage them to leave the reserves and seek jobs in the cities. In this way, they would become part of mainstream Canadian society. This kind of assimilation would supposedly bring an end to their problems.

Aboriginal people were furious. They saw the White Paper as an attack on their right to maintain their unique identity. Harold Cardinal, an Alberta Cree leader, explained their response:

> Ironically, the White Paper concludes by ... calling upon Indian organizations ... to assist [in the process it recommends].... It is difficult to envision any responsible Indian organization willing to participate in a proposal that promises to take the rights of all Indians away and attempts to ... legislate Indians out of existence. It is a strange government and a strange mentality that would have the gall to ask the Indian to help implement its plan to perpetrate cultural genocide on the Indians of Canada. It is like asking the doomed man on the gallows if he would mind pulling the lever that trips the trap.

Source: Harold Cardinal, *The Unjust Society: The Tragedy of Canada's Indians* (Vancouver: Douglas & McIntyre, 1999), 137.

The National Indian Brotherhood led the attack on the White Paper. Instead of assimilation into "white" (non-Aboriginal) society, they demanded **self-government** and control over their own affairs. When they presented their paper, called *Citizens Plus*, or the "Red Paper," a surprised Jean Chrétien announced he was shelving the White Paper. However, he offered no new policy in its place.

Educational Concerns

Gradually, First Nations began to take some control in areas that concerned them most. One of these was education. The system of residential schools was finally abandoned in 1969. In following years, many First Nations took over the education of their children, and "band schools" emerged in various parts of the country. At band schools, Aboriginal children could study their own languages and learn about their own cultures and traditions. However, the lack of secondary schools near the reserves meant that most Aboriginal children were forced to leave home at a much younger age than other Canadian children. As part of a government-run "boarding home program," some high school students were sent to live with families and attend school in cities such as Vancouver and New Westminster, British Columbia. But they were far from home, and loneliness drove some to return before graduating from high school.

Although the residential school system was dismantled, its legacy continued to haunt many who had lived through it. In 1990, a prominent

Figure 8-15 Phanuelie Palluq performs a drum dance in 1999 before Minister of Indian Affairs Jane Stewart and Natural Resources Minister Ralph Goodale at the Ottawa ceremony in which the government offered an apology for the cruel treatment of Aboriginal children in residential schools.

Aboriginal chief and lawyer, Phil Fontaine, spoke out about how he was mistreated at school. Others soon came forward with horrifying stories of abuse. In 1998, the federal government apologized for its part in the problem and announced a $350 million healing fund.

Environmental Concerns

Aboriginal peoples also began taking control over another area of concern: the environment. Canadian industries were expanding, sometimes in and around reserves. Many Aboriginal groups were concerned that hydroelectric and natural gas projects would endanger their traditional activities of hunting, fishing, and trapping.

Probably the most significant Aboriginal victory during the 1970s was won by the Inuit, Métis, and Indian Brotherhood (later Dene) of the Yukon and Northwest Territories. They were struggling to halt the construction of oil and natural gas pipelines that were to run through their lands in the Mackenzie Valley. The pipelines were to deliver energy from Alaska and the Arctic to Alberta. The three Aboriginal groups lobbied to stop construction of the pipeline. They demanded a study to determine its impact on their lands and the environment.

Figure 8-16 An eloquent spokesperson for the Aboriginal cause was Teswahno, also known as Dan George. He was Chief of the Squamish Band of Burrard Inlet, British Columbia, from 1951 to 1963. At age sixty, he became an actor committed to portraying Aboriginal characters in a positive light. He helped the movie industry move away from its stereotyped views of Aboriginal people. Chief George had roles in a number of Hollywood films, including *Little Big Man* (1970) and *The Outlaw Josey Wales* (1975). Also a poet and essayist, he died in 1981.

The federal government agreed to create a commission to investigate the issue. The Berger Commission conducted hearings all over the North, listening carefully to Aboriginal concerns. In 1977, the commission recommended that construction of the Mackenzie Valley pipeline be suspended for ten years pending an in-depth environmental study and negotiations with the Aboriginal peoples about financial compensation, self-government, and other issues. In fact, construction was suspended for much longer. By 2000, however, Aboriginal groups were open to the idea of building the pipeline. At the same time, they stressed that they wanted control and some ownership of the project.

In Quebec, after a long dispute in the 1980s and 1990s, Cree residents of the North managed to halt construction of two new phases of the huge James Bay Hydro Project, which threatened to flood a large part of their ancestral territories.

The Path to Self-Government

In 1980, Canadian Aboriginal peoples formed the Assembly of First Nations to represent them in their dealings with the federal government. During the constitutional negotiations, the Assembly of First Nations pressured the country's political leaders for legal recognition of Aboriginal rights. As a result, Aboriginal rights were entrenched in the Charter of Rights and Freedoms. In 1985, Parliament also passed Bill C-31, which gave Aboriginal band councils the power to decide who had the right to live on Aboriginal reserves. Previous decisions of this sort had been made by the federal government's Department of Indian Affairs.

The increase in band council powers raised the question, "What other powers should be transferred from the federal government to the band councils?" The stage was set for discussions about self-government. Aboriginal peoples said self-government would give them the right to manage resources and gain control of their education, culture, and justice systems. Control of resources would also allow them to tackle social and health concerns in their communities.

But how would self-government work in practice? Should Indian reserves be run as municipal or town governments by the band members? Or would Aboriginal lands and reserves across Canada eventually join together to form something like a province? Furthermore, how could Aboriginal nations lay claim to lands that they considered to be theirs?

Aboriginal land claims have been of two types. **Specific claims** have arisen in areas where treaties between Aboriginal peoples and the federal government have been signed, but their terms have not been kept. For example, the agreed-upon size of a reserve may have decreased as land was taken away for the building of a highway or other development. **Comprehensive claims** have questioned the ownership of land in large parts of Canada that were never surrendered by treaty.

The Oka Confrontation

By the end of the 1980s, scores of specific claims were slowly making their way through the courts, as members of reserves demanded additional land or compensation for lands they had lost. Few Canadians paid much attention, however, until the summer of 1990, when events in the Quebec town of Oka made headlines across the nation. The Oka town council decided to expand a golf course into land that Mohawks at the nearby Kanesatake reserve considered sacred. The ownership of the land had long been disputed.

The Mohawk warrior society decided to stop construction of the golf course by blockading the land. In response, the mayor of Oka called in the Quebec Provincial Police to remove the blockade. On July 11, the police advanced on the Mohawk lines, gunfire broke out, and an officer was killed. It was not clear which side fired the fatal shot. From that point, events snowballed. The police blockaded Kanesatake. Mohawks from the nearby Kahnawake reserve barricaded the road to a bridge which ran through their reserve, blocking access to part of Montreal. There were nightly violent confrontations involving the population of nearby Quebec communities, the police, and the Mohawks. Across Canada, other Aboriginal groups demonstrated their support by blockading highways and railway tracks that ran through their reserves.

As the tense stand-off continued, Quebec Premier Robert Bourassa called in the Canadian Forces for help. Troops with heavy weapons moved into the area. Negotiations to end the crisis were tense. Towards the end of September, members of other bands persuaded the Mohawks of Kanesatake to end the stand-off. Eventually, the disputed land was purchased by the federal government and given to Kanesatake. The crisis passed, but the point made by the confrontation hit home. Oka was a wake-up call to the government and people of Canada. Canada's First Nations had demonstrated that they were prepared to fight for their rights.

Figure 8-17 This image of the Oka confrontation became famous around the world.

Expressing ideas
What did this image say about relations between Canada and Aboriginal communities?

As the visibility of Aboriginal people in Canada's political life has increased, so too has their presence in Canadian art and culture. Aboriginal writers and artists have won acclaim around the world. Giving voice to their culture, they have enriched the Canadian identity.

Tomson Highway (born 1951) is a Cree from Manitoba. After studying music and literature in Ontario and in England, he joined a performing arts company. He is a well-known playwright whose works include *Dry Lips Oughta Move to Kapuskasing* and *The Rez Sisters*. He became Artistic Director of Native Earth Performing Arts in Toronto, one of only a few Aboriginal theatre groups in North America.

Daphne Odjig was born in 1919 on Manitoulin Island, Ontario. Her grandfather was a stone-carver who told her, as a child, about the history and legends of her people. Odjig later moved to British Columbia, where her paintings were inspired by the landscape of the B.C. interior and the West Coast islands. She published her memoirs, *Paintbrush in My Hand*, in 1992 and in 1998 received an Achievement Award in Arts and Culture from the National Aboriginal Achievement Foundation.

Figure 8-18 *The Indian in Transition* by Daphne Odjig. This mural hangs in the National Arts Centre in Ottawa. Painted in the late 1970s, it outlines the history of Aboriginal people in Canada.

Rita Joe (born 1932) is from the Eskasoni First Nation reserve on Cape Breton Island, Nova Scotia. As a foster child, she moved many times from family to family and from reserve to reserve. Many of her poems deal with the pain of her people, once proud and self-sufficient, and serve as a plea for better understanding between cultural groups. When she was made a Member of the Order of Canada in 1990, she accepted the award in recognition not just of herself but of her people as well. The poem below records her experience of residential school.

I Lost My Talk

I lost my talk
The talk you took away
When I was a little girl
At Shubenacadie school.
　　You snatched it away;
　　I speak like you
　　I think like you
　　I create like you
　　The scrambled ballad, about my word.
Two ways I talk
Both ways I say,
Your way is more powerful.
　　So gently I offer my hand and ask,
　　Let me find my talk
　　So I can teach you about me.

Douglas Cardinal (born 1934) is from Calgary, Alberta. A distinguished architect, he is best known for his design of the Canadian Museum of Civilization in Hull, Quebec. As he described it, the Museum was designed to speak "of the emergence of man from the melting glaciers; of man and woman living in harmony with the forces of nature and evolving with them."

Figure 8-19 The Canadian Museum of Civilization in Hull, Quebec, designed by Douglas Cardinal.

Bill Reid (1920–1998) came from mixed parentage in British Columbia. It was not until he was in his teens that he discovered that his mother was Haida. He soon became interested in traditional Haida carving techniques, and began to create wooden masks and poles. Many of these techniques were on the verge of extinction, and Reid's work inspired other Aboriginal artists to return to traditional art forms.

Figure 8-20 One of Bill Reid's most famous works, *The Spirit of the Haida Gwai*, sits in the foyer of the Canadian Embassy in Washington.

John Kim Bell was born on the Kahnawake Mohawk reserve in Quebec. He studied violin and piano as a youth. In 1980, he was appointed apprentice conductor of the Toronto Symphony Orchestra, and went on to devote his time to promoting opportunities for Aboriginal artists. In 1993, he established the National Aboriginal Achievement Awards. Between 1993 and 1998, over $5 million in educational awards was given to over 800 Aboriginal students pursuing studies in the arts, business, medicine, and the sciences.

Susan Aglukark (born 1967) was raised in Arviat, now part of Nunavut. She has developed a distinctive musical style, fusing traditional Inuit chants with modern pop melodies. But she is more than a pop star. She does social work as well, and is the national spokesperson for the Aboriginal Division of the National Alcohol and Drug Prevention Program.

Questions

1. What themes and concerns are evident in the works of Rita Joe, Bill Reid, and Daphne Odjig included here?

2. Summarize the contributions of Aboriginal artists to Canadian society.

Land Claims in British Columbia

Most land claims in British Columbia have been comprehensive, as Aboriginal nations never officially gave up their claims to most of what is now British Columbia. In addition, when the British took over Canada, the Royal Proclamation of 1763 declared that "any lands whatever, which, not having been ceded to or purchased by us, … are reserved to the … Indians." Treaties were not signed except in a few areas, such as the province's northeast corner and parts of Vancouver Island.

Opponents of comprehensive claims argue otherwise. They deny that the 1763 proclamation can be valid in parts of Canada, such as the North and British Columbia, that were not known to the British at that time. They assert that Canada exercised the traditional rights of "discoverers and conquerors." The land ceased long ago to belong to the First Nations. In any case, without written records, it is difficult for some First Nations to prove continuous occupation of the land.

The history of Aboriginal land claims in British Columbia goes back more than a century. In 1887, the Nisga'a, the original occupants of the Nass Valley in the northwest, began asserting their land rights. In 1912, they became the first group to make a land claim against the Canadian government. Even when the Indian Act made it illegal for them to raise funds for land claims, they continued their struggle.

Figure 8-21 The overlapping claims of the forty-two Aboriginal groups claiming land in British Columbia. Together, they amount to 110 per cent of the province. The B.C. government has stated that it favours a total land settlement of approximately 5 per cent, reflecting the Aboriginal percentage of the B.C. population.

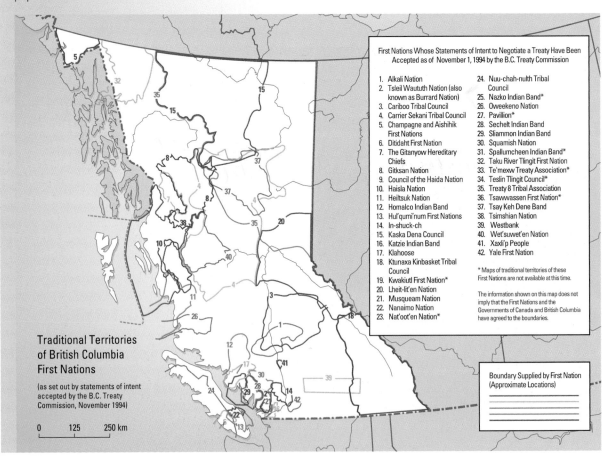

First Nations Whose Statements of Intent to Negotiate a Treaty Have Been Accepted as of November 1, 1994 by the B.C. Treaty Commission

1. Alkali Nation
2. Tsleil Waututh Nation (also known as Burrard Nation)
3. Cariboo Tribal Council
4. Carrier Sekani Tribal Council
5. Champagne and Aishihik First Nations
6. Ditidaht First Nation
7. The Gitanyow Hereditary Chiefs
8. Gitksan Nation
9. Council of the Haida Nation
10. Haisla Nation
11. Heiltsuk Nation
12. Homalco Indian Band
13. Hul'qumi'num First Nations
14. In-shuck-ch
15. Kaska Dena Council
16. Katzie Indian Band
17. Klahoose
18. Ktunaxa Kinbasket Tribal Council
19. Kwakiutl First Nation*
20. Lheit-lit'en Nation
21. Musqueam Nation
22. Nanaimo Nation
23. Nat'oot'en Nation*
24. Nuu-chah-nulth Tribal Council
25. Nazko Indian Band*
26. Oweekeno Nation
27. Pavillion*
28. Sechelt Indian Band
29. Sliammon Indian Band
30. Squamish Nation
31. Spallumcheen Indian Band*
32. Taku River Tlingit First Nation
33. Te'mexw Treaty Association*
34. Teslin Tlingit Council*
35. Treaty 8 Tribal Association
36. Tsawwassen First Nation*
37. Tsay Keh Dene Band
38. Tsimshian Nation
39. Westbank
40. Wet'suwet'en Nation
41. Xaxli'p People
42. Yale First Nation

* Maps of traditional territories of these First Nations are not available at this time.

The information shown on this map does not imply that the First Nations and the Governments of Canada and British Columbia have agreed to the boundaries.

Traditional Territories of British Columbia First Nations

(as set out by statements of intent accepted by the B.C. Treaty Commission, November 1994)

0   125   250 km

Boundary Supplied by First Nation (Approximate Locations)

In 1993, the Nisga'a won a partial victory when some justices of the Supreme Court of Canada acknowledged that the concept of Aboriginal title (right to land) did indeed exist. Then, two neighbouring nations, the Gitksan and Wet'suwet'en, took their land claim to court. Their claim became known as the Delgamuluukw case, named after one of the people who made the claim.

Both the Nisga'a and those involved in the Delgamuluukw case persevered until they met with success. In the mid-1990s, the governments of Canada and British Columbia decided that the time had come to settle rather than dispute the Nisga'a claims. In 1996, the Nisga'a were offered a settlement that entitled them to 8 per cent of their original claimed land, ownership of the forests, and partial profits from salmon fisheries and hydro development. The Nisga'a also won the right to develop their own municipal government and policing. The government offered to pay the Nisga'a $190 million over fifteen years, in compensation for lost land. The Nisga'a agreed to become taxpayers, giving up their tax-exempt status under the Indian Act.

In 1998, ruling on the Delgamuluukw case, the Supreme Court of Canada defined "Aboriginal title." It ruled that Aboriginal groups could claim ownership of land if they can prove that they occupied the land before the Canadian government claimed sovereignty, and that they occupied it continuously and exclusively. This was a landmark ruling that would have application in other parts of the country.

The Nisga'a settlement and Delgamuluukw decisions stirred up controversy. Some businesses feared future court cases over ownership of the land. They began to halt their investments, and jobs were lost in British Columbia. Opponents of the Nisga'a deal argued that there would be further

Figure 8-22 Prime Minister Jean Chrétien congratulates Joseph Gosnell, president of the Nisga'a Tribal Council, on the passage of the Nisga'a Treaty bill in Commons. Assembly of First Nations Chief Phil Fontaine (second from right) and Indian Affairs Minister Robert Nault look on.

Figure 8-23 Celebrating the creation of Nunavut in Iqaluit, the territory's capital, in April 1999.

expensive disputes over land and self-government. They demanded that the province hold a referendum on the deal. The B.C. government refused a vote by all the population, arguing that the rights of a minority can never be fairly decided by a vote of the majority. In the closing days of 1999, the Parliament of Canada passed the Nisga'a deal over the strong objections of the opposition Reform Party. When the treaty was given royal assent, Nisga'a Chief Joseph Gosnell announced:

> Today, the Nisga'a people become full-fledged Canadians as we step out from under the Indian Act—forever. Finally, after a struggle of more than 130 years, the government of this country clearly recognizes that the Nisga'a were a self-governing people since well before European contact. We remain self-governing today, and we are proud to say that this inherent right is now clearly recognized and protected in the Constitution of Canada.
>
> Source: Federal government press release, April 13, 2000.

A Powerful Force for Change

Self-government and land claims continued to be important issues in many other parts of Canada. The creation of the territory of Nunavut in 1999 resulted from the largest treaty ever negotiated in Canada. It gave the Inuit of this northern area political control of some 1.6 million square kilometres on the eastern Arctic. It suggested that Aboriginal land claims and self-government will continue to be a powerful force for change in shaping the nation into the twenty-first century.

ACTIVITIES

1. Explain the importance of the following in the development of Aboriginal identity:

   a) the 1969 White Paper and *Citizens Plus*

   b) the Mackenzie Valley Pipeline and the Berger Commission.

2. a) Define assimilation.

   b) Give examples of the federal government's attempts to assimilate Aboriginal people into Canadian society.

3. What was the government's response to demands that it acknowledge its part in the ill treatment of Aboriginal children in residential schools? Do you think this response was adequate? Give reasons.

4. Explain the importance of:

   a) the Assembly of First Nations

   b) specific land claims

   c) comprehensive land claims

   d) the Nisga'a Treaty

   e) the Delgamuluukw decision.

5. What percentage of B.C. land do Aboriginal groups claim? What Aboriginal land settlement percentage does the B.C. government favour? What issues do these percentages raise?

6. a) Why do you think the creation of Nunavut is significant?

   b) What challenges do you think are posed for Nunavut by having 29 000 people politically control 1.6 million square kilometres of land? How do you think e-mail and other modern technologies can help?

LOOKING BACK

Develop an Understanding

1. Make a three-column chart with the following headings: "Key People," "Key Events," and "Key Ideas." List examples from this chapter under the appropriate headings. Include a brief explanation of each.

2. Choose at least seven events from this chapter's sections on French–English relations. Devise a way to present them in order to illustrate the evolution of relations between Quebec and the rest of Canada from the 1940s to the present.

3. Make a PMI chart in which you list the effects of Canada's multiculturalism policy.

4. How have Canadian Aboriginal peoples made their voices heard since 1945? What key events have contributed to their affirmation of their identity and position in society? Make a timeline including at least five events. Write brief notes on why you chose them.

5. Look back at the photographs in the sections dealing with Aboriginal nations. What do they tell you about how Aboriginal people have given voice to their culture? How do you think this has helped shape the Canadian identity?

Explore the Issues

6. a) Do you think Quebec has a distinct society? Why or why not?

   b) In view of your answer, how should the rest of Canada respond to Quebec?

7. Pierre Trudeau hoped to create a strong, unified country that was bilingual and multicultural. Did he succeed? Did his policies address the major concerns in all parts of the country? Work in a group to formulate a debate topic based on these questions. Then, debate your topic in class.

8. Hold a class debate or small-group discussion on one of the following topics:

   a) Is Quebec a distinct society?

   b) Would a distinct-society clause in the Constitution hurt Canada as a country, or hurt Canadians?

   c) Should further constitutional talks be attempted while there is a Parti Québécois government in Quebec?

   d) Is the constitutional debate over?

9. Review Chapters 6, 7, and 8. Using information in those chapters, make a "report card" to comment on the state of Canadian identity at the end of the twentieth century. Consider such criteria as Role in the World, Economic Growth, Caring Society, Technology, French–English Relations, Multicultural Relations, and Aboriginal Issues. Be sure to include a section on Areas for Improvement.

Research and Communicate

10. With a partner, script and tape a message you would like to broadcast from British Columbia to Quebeckers on the day before a referendum on sovereignty.

11. Some immigrants have achieved high honours in Canada. List the names of at least three, and provide descriptions of their main accomplishments. If necessary, do research in sources such as encyclopedias, almanacs, and Web sites.

12. In 2000, Matthew Coon Come was elected chief of the Assembly of First Nations. How has he contributed to the affirmation of Aboriginal identity in Canadian society? Do research and write a biographical article about him.

13. Most of British Columbia is involved in Aboriginal land claims disputes. Research and report on an Aboriginal land claim in your area.

14. In groups, conduct a poll on the present status of land claim negotiations in British Columbia. Construct your questions so that people can express their opinions on Aboriginal title, compensation, fishing rights, and other issues. Compile and analyse your results.

15. Research the status of Aboriginal rights in another country such as Brazil, Australia, or New Zealand. Compare your findings with the situation in Canada.

UNIT II

Government and Law

We live in a country that affords us many rights and privileges. People from all over the world envy Canadians' standard of living, democratic government, and the relative fairness of our legal system. But our government can function well only with the active involvement of its citizens. To participate effectively in society, you need to understand how the system works and what your rights and responsibilities are.

In Chapter 9, we examine the structure of our government, how laws are passed, and who makes decisions on our behalf.

Chapter 10 focusses on how citizens can influence government decisions.

Chapters 11 and 12 look at the operation of the justice system, and how it has changed since the Charter of Rights and Freedoms was passed. We also look at some special provisions that are in place to protect the more vulnerable members of our society and the world.

How did the amendment of Canada's Constitution in 1982 affect the rights of its citizens?
◄

What are some of the ways in which citizens in a ▲ democratic society can influence the decisions of government?

What factors contribute to the incidence of ▲ child poverty in Canada?

9

The Structure of Canada's Government

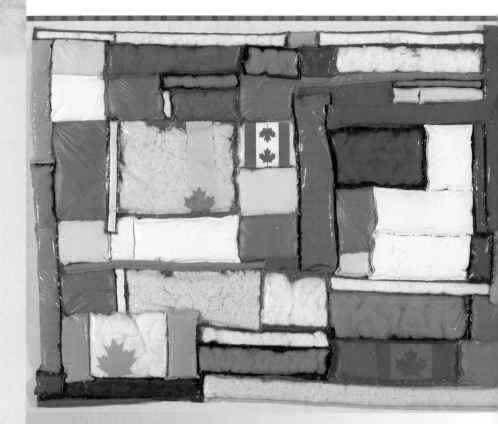

ARTS FOCUS

Confedspread by Joyce Wieland (1967). Joyce Wieland composed this work of clear plastic compartments filled with different-coloured fabrics as a salute to 100 years of Confederation in 1967.

Expressing ideas What does Wieland's choice of medium and materials tell you about her view of Canada?

Introduction

It sometimes seems as if life would be much simpler without the restrictions placed on us daily by government regulations. Yet, if you were free to run all aspects of your own life, how would you provide health care for yourself? Or organize a method of trading with foreign countries? Or protect yourself from acts of aggression by others? Or obtain the skills and training necessary to enter a career of your choice? Expecting each individual to handle all these aspects of life alone would be unrealistic. Therefore, our nation, like other societies, has created a formal system of decision making to assist us. This decision-making system is called *government*.

Our government acts, for the most part, according to established rules and procedures, which over time become *traditions*. The bodies or groups responsible for carrying out specific aspects of the government's work are called *institutions*, such as the military, the post office, police forces, and schools. Each of these institutions provides services that address the needs of Canadians. Institutions also help to unify people—to promote what is common to all people of the nation.

In this chapter, you will learn about the main features of Canada's federal and representative system of government. We will look at the origins of our system, and at how it works today. We will also look at some of the more controversial aspects of government, such as the campaign to reform the Senate.

Foundations of Our Government

Before the appearance of Europeans, Aboriginal peoples used many methods of decision making and power sharing. Each First Nation had its own system of governance. Some relied upon hereditary leaders whose positions were handed down through a clan or family; others chose leaders based on their wisdom, strength, and other abilities. Still others made decisions in open community discussions. All these methods of decision making relied on participation by members of the community and were carried on from one generation to the next. These traditions were not formally recorded or written into documents. Rather,

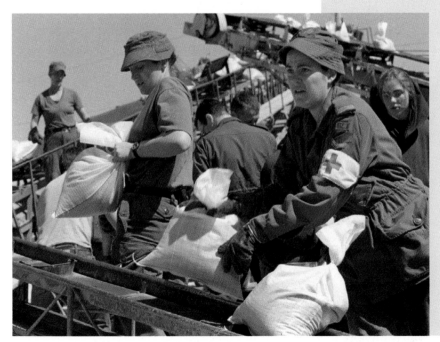

Figure 9-1 Members of the Canadian Forces make sandbags in the town of St. Germain, Manitoba, south of Winnipeg, in 1997. The Red River flooded during the spring thaw, threatening to swamp many communities.

Gathering information The military is one example of a government institution. What other institutions can you think of?

they were a part of the oral (spoken) traditions of Canada's First Nations.

Our formal methods of decision making, including written laws and institutions such as elections, have their roots in the traditions of the nation states of Europe. European colonists brought their forms of government with them to North America. In Canada, the British parliamentary tradition became the basis for our national and provincial governments. The principal features of this tradition are representative democracy and constitutional monarchy.

Representative Democracy

Canada operates on democratic principles. **Democracy**, which means "rule by the people," was first practised by the ancient Greeks. In the Greek city states, every eligible citizen participated directly by voting in all the decisions that affected society. This was called **direct democracy**. In modern societies, our large populations make this much involvement by each individual impractical. Instead, citizens in **representative** **democracies** such as Canada allow elected representatives to make decisions on their behalf.

Constitutional Monarchy

Canada has strong historical ties to Great Britain, and has adopted many British political institutions and traditions. One of these is **constitutional monarchy**—the recognition of a monarch (king or queen) as head of state. The current monarch of Canada is Queen Elizabeth II, who is also the monarch of the United Kingdom and sixteen other nations that have some form of British political tradition. In Canada, the monarch is represented by the governor general.

Queen Elizabeth does not actually rule Canada—or any other nation—alone. She is not involved in the everyday affairs of governing the nation. For example, although royal assent is necessary before a proposed law is passed, this assent is rarely, if ever, withheld.

However, the presence of the monarch represents a crucial safeguard for our democracy. This is because she holds the powers of the

Figure 9-2 Democracy was established in Athens around 500 BCE. Citizens were guaranteed the right to membership in the Assembly, freedom of speech, and equality before the law. The Greek concept of "citizen" was limited to free men (not slaves or women) who owned property.

Thinking critically
What qualifications do you think should be required for a person to be considered a "citizen"?

Figure 9-3 Queen Elizabeth signs Canada's constitutional proclamation in Ottawa on April 17, 1982, as Prime Minister Pierre Trudeau looks on.

Thinking critically Some people think we should cut our ties to the British monarchy. How would this change the structure of our government? Do you think this is a good idea? Why or why not?

Crown. The Crown has ultimate power, beyond that held by any particular government at any particular time. Under our current system, the powers of the Crown are vested in the queen, and in the governor general as her representative.

For example, if the prime minister were to decide not to call an election within five years as required by law, the governor general could order him or her to do so—in the name of the Crown. If the prime minister refused, the governor general could call on the army to force the election. This ultimate authority ensures that no one, not even the leader of the nation, can ignore the law. This is the power of the Crown.

The powers and responsibilities of the monarch and the governor general, as well as those of citizens, elected representatives, and others who make up our government, have developed over time. The specific details are set out in the Canadian Constitution, a legal document that outlines who should have the power to make various decisions. Our Constitution is the supreme law of the land. It outlines the structure of our government and defines and limits the government's power. Canada is called a *constitutional* monarchy because the powers and responsibilities of the monarch are subject to the laws set forth in the Constitution. Not even the monarch is exempt from following these laws.

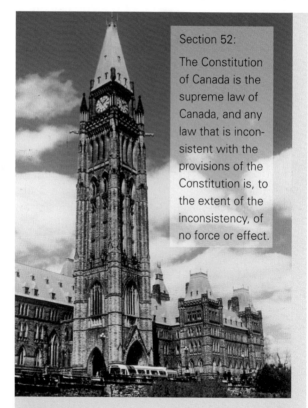

Section 52:

The Constitution of Canada is the supreme law of Canada, and any law that is inconsistent with the provisions of the Constitution is, to the extent of the inconsistency, of no force or effect.

Figure 9-4 An excerpt from the Canadian Constitution.

Identifying viewpoint What view of power and responsibility is evident in this excerpt? What does this indicate about our system of government?

The Written Constitution

Canada has both a written and an unwritten constitution. Most of the written part, drafted in 1867 during Confederation, was originally called the British North America (BNA) Act. The powers of the representatives of the citizens, the federal and provincial governments, and the monarch were set out in this act. Since its amendment in 1982, Canada's written Constitution now has three main parts:

- a description of the powers of provincial legislatures and Parliament, as well as their parts and authority
- a Charter of Rights and Freedoms that outlines the basic rights and responsibilities that all Canadians possess
- an amending formula, which sets out ways in which the Constitution may be changed or altered. This formula requires that the federal government and seven of the ten provinces agree on the proposed amendment or change. The seven provinces must make up at least one-half of the total population of Canada.

The Unwritten Constitution

There are other rules and practices concerning the roles and functions of Parliament and provincial legislatures that are unwritten. These are based on the thousand years of parliamentary tradition that we have inherited from Britain. These traditions, along with the written Constitution, provide the basis for the sharing of power between rulers and the people.

Numerous customs, laws, and statutes that are a part of the British tradition make up the unwritten part of our Constitution. For example, there is no mention of political parties in the Constitution Act, yet they are an important part of how we govern ourselves (see Chapter 10).

The Federal System

At the time of Confederation, the colonies of Canada East and Canada West (which became Quebec and Ontario, respectively), New Brunswick, and Nova Scotia were united to form the nation of Canada. Unity would allow the once-separate colonies to pool their resources for defence, trade, and other common goals. However, none were willing to give up their autonomy completely to a central government. As a compromise, the Fathers of Confederation chose to unite these provinces under a *federal system*—an organization of regional governments (provinces), each acting on behalf of its own residents, with a central government in Ottawa responsible for matters vital to the nation as a whole. This system is sometimes referred to as *federalism*.

Areas that require a consistent national policy such as defence, currency, and the postal system were made a federal (or central) responsibility. The provincial governments were given jurisdiction over areas "best handled locally," such as education. There are also areas of shared powers: for example, both the federal and provincial governments can create laws regarding agriculture, immigration, and the environment.

The Fathers of Confederation assigned all new areas of decision making that did not yet exist or were not listed in 1867 to the federal government as **residual** (leftover) **powers**. This is why the federal government is responsible for laws regarding telecommunications and information

Federal Responsibilities	Shared Responsibilities	Provincial Responsibilities
National Defence	Immigration	Education
Foreign Policy	Agriculture	Charities
Aboriginal Affairs	Health Care	Health Services & Hospitals
Postal Services	Natural Resources	Licences
Banking System	Environmental Issues	Highways
Marriage & Divorce Law		Provincial Court System
Criminal Law		Provincial Police & Prisons
Federal Prisons		

Figure 9-5 Some federal, provincial, and shared responsibilities.

Figure 9-6 The environment is one area of overlapping powers between the federal and provincial governments. For example, the Lakeview coal-fired power station in Ontario is a major emitter of nitrogen oxide, which pollutes the air in Canada and the United States. The federal government has the responsibility to negotiate smog reduction limits with the United States, but cannot force the Ontario government to reduce that province's emissions.

Thinking critically What are the disadvantages of shared powers with regard to the environment?

services such as cable television stations, computers, modems, and faxes. The Fathers of Confederation could not have predicted such advances in technology, yet they had the foresight to provide for the control of "unknown possibilities." Still other federal responsibilities include issues related to debt and social security reform.

Soon after Confederation, the provinces began challenging the powers of the federal government. At that time, the judicial committee of the Privy Council in Britain was the court that dealt with constitutional matters, and its decisions consistently favoured the provinces. Today, the Privy Council no longer makes these decisions for us, but the division of powers between federal and provincial governments is still a contentious issue. The separatist movement in Quebec is one example of this tension, but not the only one. Provinces in Canada's West and East feel that the policies of the federal government have always favoured the populous central provinces of Ontario and Quebec. The Reform Party started in 1987

in the western provinces as a response to this feeling of lack of power and alienation from decision making. In 2000, the Reform Party attracted disaffected members of the Progressive Conservative Party and became the Canadian Alliance Party. The Canadian Alliance was elected as the official opposition in November 2000. As we saw in Chapter 3, eastern provinces have also tried to form alliances in order to increase their power.

The Creation of Municipal Governments

The local, or *municipal*, level of government has the greatest amount of contact with individual citizens. The essential services that municipalities provide include garbage collection and disposal, sewage treatment, fire protection, water supply, and establishment of schools. However, municipal governments do not have the same level of autonomy as provincial or territorial governments. Under the Canadian Constitution, provincial governments decide what form municipal governments take, their powers, and their responsibilities.

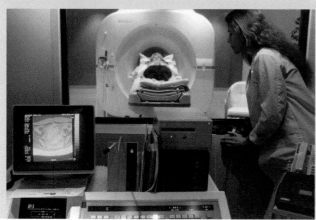

Figure 9-7 (Left, top:) Commuters in Montreal; **(left, bottom:)** a magnetic imaging clinic in Richmond, B.C.; **(below)** artist Peter Ka-Kin Poon beside his design for a new twenty-five-cent coin, one of twelve designs issued in 1999.

Using evidence Which level of government do you think is responsible for each of the activities shown in these pictures? Give reasons for your answers.

ACTIVITIES

1. Brainstorm how government has affected you since you woke up this morning.

2. Create a web diagram showing your connections to groups and organizations in Canadian society, including family, friends, institutions, and government. Explain the connections in terms of what is shared between you and others.

3. What is the difference between direct democracy and representative democracy?

4. What organizations do you belong to that have a constitution? Why is a constitution necessary in a complex organization?

5. Use a two-column chart to summarize the advantages and disadvantages of the monarchy.

6. What forces hold Canada together today? Consider interests or concerns that people across the country share. What forces are pulling us apart? Consider issues that separate provinces or regions.

The Parliamentary System

In Canada, the powers of government are divided into three branches: legislative, executive, and judicial.

The **executive power** of government is the power to make decisions and administer them (through the civil service). For example, at the municipal level, governments may inspect businesses and restaurants. At the provincial level, governments decide on the number of examinations high school students must write. At the federal level, the government may decide to purchase helicopters for national defence.

Legislative power is the power to make laws. All three levels of government—federal, provincial, and municipal—have the power to make and amend laws, many of which have a direct impact on your life. For example, the federal government in Ottawa makes laws in Parliament concerning funding for the armed forces; your provincial government establishes the taxation rate for educa-

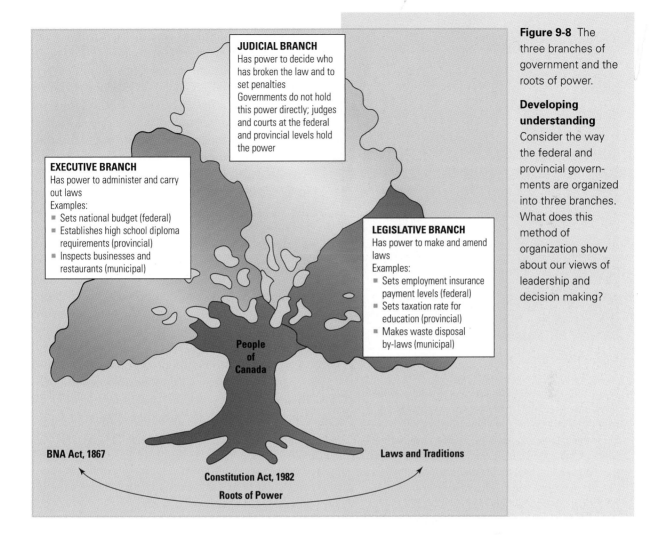

JUDICIAL BRANCH
Has power to decide who has broken the law and to set penalties
Governments do not hold this power directly; judges and courts at the federal and provincial levels hold the power

EXECUTIVE BRANCH
Has power to administer and carry out laws
Examples:
- Sets national budget (federal)
- Establishes high school diploma requirements (provincial)
- Inspects businesses and restaurants (municipal)

LEGISLATIVE BRANCH
Has power to make and amend laws
Examples:
- Sets employment insurance payment levels (federal)
- Sets taxation rate for education (provincial)
- Makes waste disposal by-laws (municipal)

People of Canada

BNA Act, 1867

Laws and Traditions

Constitution Act, 1982

Roots of Power

Figure 9-8 The three branches of government and the roots of power.

Developing understanding
Consider the way the federal and provincial governments are organized into three branches. What does this method of organization show about our views of leadership and decision making?

tion; and your town or city council may pass by-laws to determine how to dispose of local garbage.

Judicial power is the power to interpret and administer the law. Governments do not hold this power directly. In democracies such as Canada, the *judiciary* is separate from the other two branches of the government to ensure that the government acts within the boundaries of the Constitution and the laws of the land. Judicial power rests with the courts and judges, who act as both referees of private rights and interpreters of the Constitution. Chapter 11 looks at the justice system in more detail.

The Federal Government

The Legislative Branch

The legislative branch of the federal government is composed of the governor general, the House of Commons, and the Senate. These parts of the legislative branch make up *Parliament*.

Parliament must meet at least once a year in what is called a *session*. In each session, Parliament passes new laws, amends or repeals (removes) others, and debates issues of concern to Canadians. (The process for passing laws is described later in this chapter.) During question period, opposition parties challenge the government's actions and raise issues they feel the government needs to address. Individual members of Parliament may bring

Figure 9-9 Speaker of the House Gilbert Parent looks on during question period in November 1999, as Prime Minister Jean Chrétien defends his decision to introduce the clarity bill setting ground rules in the event of a referendum on Quebec secession. Exchanges during question period are often heated. Many of the sound bites (short video or audio clips) that you see and hear on the news are from question period. You can watch question period in its entirety on the cable Parliamentary channel (CPAC).

Developing understanding What purpose(s) do the exchanges during question period serve in the democratic process?

stituencies. Eligible voters in each riding elect one candidate to represent them in Parliament. Together, the elected representatives, or members of Parliament (MPs), make up the Lower House.

The total number of seats in the House of Commons is determined by the population of Canada. This means that as our population increases, the number of seats in the Commons may increase. In 2000, there were 301 seats (up from 282 in 1986); of this number, 178 came from the more populous provinces of Ontario and Quebec.

Debates in the House of Commons are controlled by the speaker of the House. The speaker (who is also an elected MP) is elected by the other members of Parliament and has a range of duties to perform. Most importantly, he or she oversees the impartial operation of the House, applying the rules of Parliament fairly and firmly to all members, including the prime minister.

In the House of Commons, members sit with their party. Opposite the government party (the group with the largest number of elected representatives) sit the opposition parties. The opposition is made up of all the MPs from parties other than the party in power. The leader of the second-largest party in the House usually becomes the official leader of the opposition.

The opposition's job is to scrutinize the actions of the government. This close examination is an important part of the governing process. It helps to ensure that the views of all Canadians are represented. Many of the laws that are passed in Parliament do so with full support of the opposition.

up issues that their constituents have raised with them. Usually, a Cabinet minister or the prime minister will respond to the questions, explaining the government's position on the issue.

The House of Commons

The House of Commons, or Lower House, is the only part of the legislative branch that has elected members. Elections for seats in the Commons must occur every five years, unless the prime minister calls an election at an earlier date. Canada is divided into areas that are roughly equal in population (100 000 citizens) called *ridings* or con-

How Do MPs Vote?

Each political party having elected representatives holds private meetings called a **caucus**. In these meetings, elected party members have an opportunity to discuss concerns and to express opinions freely. Party leaders explain their programs, policies, and actions. These discussions may become heated, as each member is allowed to disagree or challenge the party's position. Once a decision is made in caucus, however, tradition holds that all MPs are expected to vote in favour of the party's position in the House of Commons.

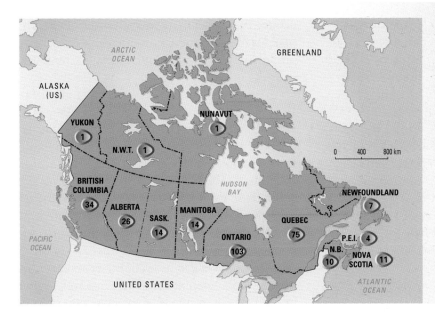

Figure 9-10 Seats in the House of Commons, 2001.

Thinking critically Why do some provinces have more seats than others? Explain how this seat distribution might contribute to the feeling that Ontario and Quebec dominate decision making in Canada.

Figure 9-11 The House of Commons. The speaker of the House sits on the dais between the rows of MPs. He or she controls the debate and announces the results of votes. The prime minister, Cabinet, and the ruling party sit on the speaker's right, while opposition MPs sit on the speaker's left, facing them.

Thinking critically How does this seating arrangement reflect the way our government works?

Some question whether representatives should vote as expected by their party or according to the desires of their constituents. This places elected representatives in a difficult position. What are MPs expected to do when the communities they represent want them to vote against a proposal put forth by their own party? Where does an MP's first loyalty lie? One method used to address this situation is the *free vote*, which allows members of the legislature to vote according to what they believe is best, rather than following the party position. Free votes are used relatively rarely, however, and usually on moral issues.

The Senate

The Senate, or Upper House of Parliament, is independent of the House of Commons. It appoints its own speaker and runs its own affairs. The governor general appoints senators on the recommendation of the prime minister. Members of the Senate must be Canadian citizens, at least thirty years of age, and living in the province or territory that they represent. In addition, they must own at least $4000 worth of property. Senators may serve until they are seventy-five years of age.

The Senate's main role is to provide a final check on the legislation passed in the House of Commons. The Senate may also introduce bills (proposed laws), debate them, pass them, and send them to the Commons, although this rarely happens.

In addition to giving "sober second thought" to all bills, the Senate is meant to provide regional representation, serving as a forum for the discussion of regional issues. Senate seats are allotted regionally on the basis of population, so provinces with greater populations have more senators. In 2001, there were 105 seats in the Senate. Figure 9-12 shows how these seats were distributed.

The Senate often undertakes investigations into issues with which the House of Commons cannot or will not get involved. For example, it was a Senate committee that initiated an investigation into euthanasia, as the elected body felt it was too sensitive a topic to raise. In addition, senators may work on committees and task forces, and perform diplomatic services for the government.

Prime ministers often fill vacant Senate seats with supporters of their own party, as a form of **patronage** (reward) for their individual loyalty or support. This practice has led to accusations that Senate positions have been handed to people who have found favour with the political leader, rather than to those who are best qualified.

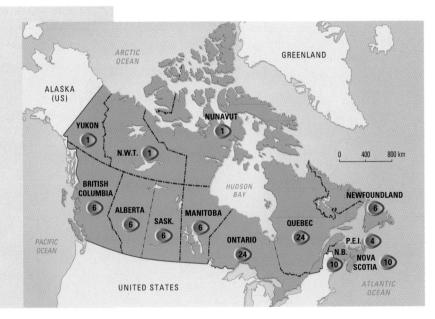

Figure 9-12 Seats in the Senate, 2001.

Reading a map How many Senate seats are held by the western provinces? The Atlantic provinces? Ontario and Quebec? Compare this with the seat allotment for the House of Commons (Figure 9-10).

This charge of patronage also explains why some people claim that the Senate is not truly representative. In addition, while close to 20 per cent of senators are female, almost all members of the Senate come from middle or upper levels of society. Some people feel that senators represent their party rather than their province or region.

Provinces and territories believe they should have a greater say in who represents their concerns in the Senate. Therefore, in 1987, an amendment to the Constitution was passed to allow recommendations for senators to come from the provinces. However, these changes to the selection of Senate members were not significant enough for many Canadians.

ACTIVITIES

1. Draw three diagrams to illustrate executive powers, legislative powers, and judicial powers in Canadian government. Compare your understanding with two other students. What ideas do you share? What ideas are unique to your summary?

2. Explain the role of the following in our representative democracy:

   a) caucus

   b) the opposition.

3. What qualities does the speaker of the House need to do the job well? Watch a session of question period on the cable Parliamentary channel to see the speaker at work.

counterpoints

Is the Senate Worth Keeping?

Patronage is not the only criticism that is levelled against the Senate. Dissatisfaction with its present structure takes several forms, from calls for its complete abolition to various proposals designed to increase its role in the operations of government.

Option 1: Abolish the Senate

Some people feel that the Senate should simply be abolished. They feel it is outdated, unnecessary, and undemocratic. They argue that patronage has effectively destroyed any role the Senate may have had as a representative of the regions, and that it is too costly to justify keeping—in any form. Instead, more power should be vested in elected members of the House of Commons:

> ...[T]he Senate can never be reformed. The Reform Party members have said that the Senate costs us

$60 million and that they want to reform it. They want an elected Senate which will cost Canadians $120 million or more every year to operate. If we put this question to a referendum and asked Canadians if the Senate should be abolished, my sense is that they, in a unanimous way—probably around 80% to 90%—would support the abolition if the alternative, as the Reform has said, will cost twice as much money.

> ...[W]e are already overgoverned in this country. We have municipal governments, urban hamlets, towns and villages, rural municipalities, counties, school boards, hospital boards, provincial governments, the federal House of Commons, and the Senate. We have more governments than people want to pay for. They are asking us to downsize the number of politicians, not to increase the number of politicians.

Source: Hon. John Solomon, NDP member for Regina-Lumsden-Lake Centre, *Debates of the House of Commons*, February 24, 2000.

Option 2: Reform the Senate

Others, however, feel that the Upper House has some value, but needs renewal. Support for reforming the Senate is strongest in Alberta, where many people feel

Okay, now let's all think **asymmetrical** Triple-E ...
Everything Ontario wants they get,
Everything Quebec wants they get,
Everyone else gets whatever is left over ...

CONSTITUTIONAL
CONFERENCE
CALGARY

SENATE REFORM

Figure 9-13

Interpreting a cartoon What view of the Senate does each of these cartoonists hold? Do you agree with either of their views? Explain your reasons.

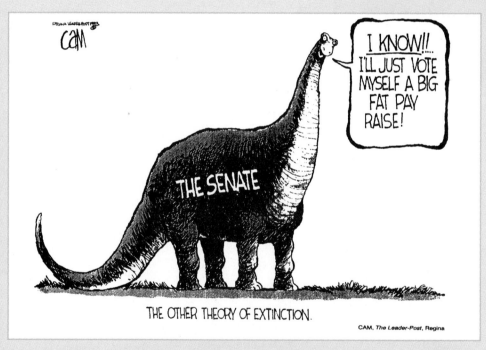

THE SENATE

I KNOW!!... I'LL JUST VOTE MYSELF A BIG FAT PAY RAISE!

THE OTHER THEORY OF EXTINCTION.

CAM, *The Leader-Post*, Regina

that the number of seats held by Ontario and Quebec gives the central provinces too much power at the expense of smaller provinces.

Some seeking major revisions to the Senate and its role in the legislative branch advocate the creation of a "triple-E" senate (elected, equal, and effective).

This proposal was originally put forward by Preston Manning, leader of the former Reform Party:

Many people have approached me and said the Senate should simply be abolished—that it is a waste of money. I agree that the current Senate arrangement is not serving Canadians. But, if we abolish the Senate, Canadians outside of Ontario and Quebec will continue to be at the mercy of Central Canadian influence. The Senate has the potential to provide a more balanced regional representation to protect less populous areas of the country. In addition, the Senate should act as a chamber of sober second thought on government legislation. While an elected Senate is the first step to achieving true representation, it is only one-third of what is needed to ensure Canadians are truly equal. The answer is a "triple-E" Senate:

Effective: Under current legislation the Senate has the power to be effective in representing regional interests and sober second thought. However, because the Senate is not elected and represents the worst of partisan, political patronage, it lacks all legitimacy. It is unaccountable to Canadian taxpayers.

Equal: Although Senators frequently say that they will take on regional interests, when push comes to shove they invariably vote along party lines. If they were elected they would be accountable to the regions they represent.

Elected: The starting point of Senate reform so that Canadians will have a lawmaking system that reflects the needs of this great country is with the election of Senators. The Senate and its important functions will never be a legitimate part of the lawmaking body, unless its members are accountable to the people of Canada through a democratic election process.

Option 3: Keep the Senate As Is

But others feel that we should not rush to move from the present model. They note the benefits of having a body that is not subject to the whims of the public, and point to the unnoticed contributions and vast experience of Senate members:

An elected Upper House would naturally end up challenging the House of Commons. In our system, it is the Commons that determines key elements of government and social policy. The present Senate regularly improves legislation so that it does what it was meant to do, to safeguard minority or general human rights. However, although it has wide powers under the Constitution, the Senate

rarely defeats a basic policy the government has approved. Australia's experience suggests that an elected Senate holding these same powers might not be so scrupulous.

Source: Adapted from Senator Joan Fraser, "Senator Fraser Defends the Red Chamber," *National Post*, February 29, 2000, A19.

…The Senate is truly a chamber of sober second thought. To perform that role properly, this chamber should be above the partisan factions of the day. This chamber is supposed to be above the day's fads and fantasies, and it is supposed to be independent….

I venture to say that the experience accumulated in this chamber exceeds that of any task force, commission, or advisory group ever established by a government. It would cost substantially more than the cost of operating this place if this group charged the government for its services and advice at rates available to them in the private sector.

Source: Senator William M. Kelly, *Senate Debates*, December 15, 1997.

Analysing the Issue

1. In your own words, explain the main arguments in each of the quotations above.

2. Which provinces stand to gain the most from the "triple-E" proposal? Which stand to lose? Prepare an advertising campaign that provinces in favour of the triple-E senate might use to convince voters in other provinces to support a triple-E proposal.

3. Some groups feel that the Senate should be made more representative of women and minorities. Brainstorm ideas for reform that would help to meet this criterion.

4. Present your own view of what should (or should not) happen to the Senate. You may choose one of the options discussed above, or another idea of your own. You may want to do some more research before you present your proposal.

The Executive Branch

The executive branch of the federal government includes the governor general, the prime minister, the Cabinet, and the public service.

The Governor General

As the monarch's representative, the governor general gives *formal assent* (agreement) to a bill before it becomes law, performs ceremonial functions, and acts as an adviser to the government to ensure it abides by the Constitution. Although the Constitution Act of 1867 declares the monarch holds executive power and authority,

it is the prime minister and the Cabinet who run the daily affairs of the federal government.

The Prime Minister

In Canada, citizens do not directly choose the leader of their nation. Instead, the leader of the political party with the most elected representatives in the House of Commons is usually asked by the governor general to become prime minister. A *political party* is an organization of individuals who support a common set of goals and beliefs (see Chapter 10). Each political party elects its own leader and has candidates who run for office during federal elections.

The leader of the federal government has several important roles to play—as the head of government, the leader of the nation, and the leader of a national party.

As the *head of government*, the prime minister asks the governor general to name new judges and senators; decides on the best time to ask the governor general to call an election; chooses and changes Cabinet members to reflect the needs of

Figure 9-14 Governor General Adrienne Clarkson (right) shares a cup of iceberg tea with a Nunavut elder during a visit to celebrate the territory's first anniversary in 2000. In 1999, Clarkson became the first immigrant to hold the post of governor general. She came to Canada as a refugee from Hong Kong when Japan invaded the former British colony in 1942.

Thinking critically What kind of person do you think would make a good governor general?

the ruling government; and has the final say in creating the policies of the government in power.

As the *national leader*, the prime minister addresses Canadians on issues of national concern and explains the goals of the ruling party; represents Canada on trips to other nations; speaks on behalf of all Canadians at international meetings; and works with provincial premiers to coordinate and share responsibilities.

As a *party leader,* the prime minister acts as spokesperson for his or her party; gives out patronage appointments, rewarding loyal supporters with positions in the Senate, diplomatic corps, or government-operated businesses; and leads other party members in Parliament.

The Cabinet

The **Cabinet** is made up of elected party members chosen by the prime minister. Usually, the prime minister designates each member of the Cabinet as a minister responsible for a particular government department, such as defence or finance, or as a more junior secretary of state. The task of selecting a Cabinet is very difficult and extremely important to maintaining support for the ruling government. The prime minister attempts to select ministers who reflect the cultural, linguistic, and social diversity of the nation.

An ideal federal Cabinet would include equal numbers of men and women, as well as representatives from all the regions and major ethnic groups that make up the country. Of course, such a perfect balance is never really achieved.

Cabinet ministers are responsible for their department's efficient and effective operation and finances, as well as the actions of their staff. They also speak on behalf of their department in Parliament and in public. However, ministers usually rely heavily on the advice of their department's staff in drawing up proposals for new legislation, and seek staff counsel regarding specific problems that Cabinet is examining.

In Cabinet meetings, which are held in private, members may express their views frankly, and even question the leadership of the prime minister. Publicly, however, Cabinet members must display full support for their leader and the decisions of the government. This show of strength is called **cabinet solidarity**, and is important as

Figure 9-15 The federal Cabinet with Prime Minister Jean Chrétien, 2000.

Using evidence How representative of the diversity of the people of Canada does this Cabinet appear to be? What is the significance of the prime minister's position in the photograph? The governor general's?

a demonstration to the public that the government is united and confident in its plans. Cabinet ministers who are unable to accept the decisions of the government are usually expected to resign.

Solidarity is so important that parties usually elect one member to act as *party whip*. The whip's role is to ensure that members are present in Parliament to support party bills and vote in the legislature. Occasionally, party whips discipline members who do not behave as expected by their party. In 1996, Liberal MP John Nunziata was forced to resign for speaking out against a policy of his own party. He later ran as an independent, not affiliated with any party, and won his seat.

The powers of the prime minister and the Cabinet extend beyond the executive level. Because they introduce bills that eventually become laws, the prime minister and Cabinet also hold legislative power. This is why it is so important that the Cabinet be representative of the entire nation and that the prime minister and Cabinet act in the interests of all Canadians.

The Public Service

The public service is often referred to as the civil service or the bureaucracy. It is a group of permanent employees who perform the ongoing business of government. Civil servants are often the only direct contact that most of us have with our government. As such, they are the "face" of government for many people.

Public servants provide a vast range of services. They gather statistics, write details for new laws, and represent Canada in other countries. Other public servants carry out the laws; they collect taxes, monitor the flow of imported goods, and inspect food. Still others process passports, deliver the mail, answer questions for citizens regarding government programs and policies, and fulfil thousands of other tasks necessary for a government to run effectively.

Senior civil servants advise ministers and help draft new laws. These high-level bureaucrats can wield a great deal of influence over public policy. They hold hidden power through the influence and controls they exert over how the government responds to the needs and requests of citizens.

How a Bill Becomes Law

Any member of the House of Commons or Senate may introduce a bill. If the member is not in the Cabinet, the bill is referred to as a *private member's bill*. However, few private member's bills pass into law. The procedure for making a law is complex and requires a great deal of sup-

Figure 9-16 Public servants are employed by all three levels of government. Firefighters work at the municipal level, teachers at the provincial level, and food inspectors at the federal level.

Gathering information How many other civil service careers can you think of?

port from other members of the House to be successful. Therefore, the Cabinet usually controls which bills are introduced. Figure 9-17 illustrates the passage of a government bill into law.

Figure 9-17 How a bill becomes a law.

Thinking critically Why are there so many steps in the process of making laws? Why do we use such a lengthy process?

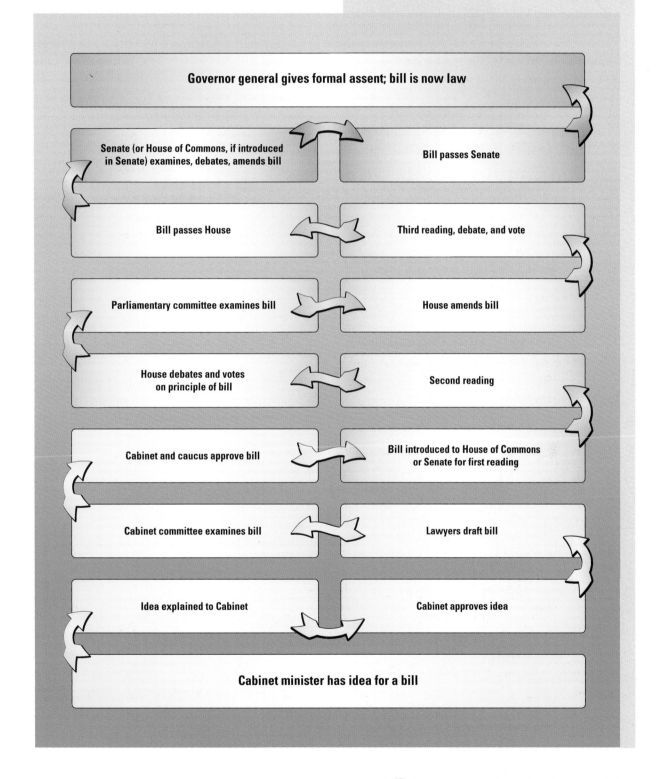

Governor general gives formal assent; bill is now law

Senate (or House of Commons, if introduced in Senate) examines, debates, amends bill

Bill passes Senate

Bill passes House

Third reading, debate, and vote

Parliamentary committee examines bill

House amends bill

House debates and votes on principle of bill

Second reading

Cabinet and caucus approve bill

Bill introduced to House of Commons or Senate for first reading

Cabinet committee examines bill

Lawyers draft bill

Idea explained to Cabinet

Cabinet approves idea

Cabinet minister has idea for a bill

Cabinet decides on which matters require new legislation. Specialists in the government department concerned investigate policies and alternatives and report to the minister in charge. The minister then reports to Cabinet, where a decision to change the existing law, or to create a new one, may be made. After Cabinet has decided how to change the law, government lawyers draft a bill that puts into legal language what the government wants. The caucus of the governing party meets, and the bill is discussed in private. Any objections or suggestions by the other (non-Cabinet) party members are dealt with here. The bill is then ready to be brought to the legislature for debate and, ultimately, passage into law.

A federal bill must pass three readings in both the House of Commons and the Senate before it can be signed into law. The *first reading* is just a

building your skills

Evaluating Newspaper Sources

*T*he news media—newspapers, magazines, television, radio, and the Internet—are an important aspect of democracy. Governments use the media as a way of communicating policies and decisions to citizens. The media also comment on various aspects of government, reflecting the concerns of citizens back to their elected representatives. It is therefore important that the information in the news media be accurate and objective. It is also important for you to know how to evaluate its accuracy and objectivity.

Three Sources of Newspaper Stories

Only about half of the stories in a typical newspaper are *direct reports* written by a reporter who works for the paper. Others come from *news agencies*, also known as wire services, which write stories and send them to newspapers across the country that subscribe to their service. The newspapers may pick up the story as is, or modify it slightly.

How can you tell if a story originated with a news agency? Check the opening line: if it names an agency such as Canadian Press (CP) or Reuters, it was not written by a journalist at the newspaper, but by someone working for a large newswire service.

A third source of stories for newspapers is *press releases*. These are written in the style and format of a news article, but give the perspective of a particular group on an issue or event. Special-interest groups send press releases to news editors in the hope that their group will get publicity for their ideas, events, or viewpoints. Federal and provincial ministries issue press releases giving information on new programs and recently passed legislation. Other groups may issue press releases that report on these same events from a different perspective.

Press releases sound objective because they are written in the form of news stories, but they do not provide a balanced view, especially of controversial issues. It is up to the news reporter to check the facts, and to supplement the information with quotes or arguments for the opposing point of view.

Applying the Skill

1. Scan the news section of three daily newspapers to find out what percentage of articles are based on newswire stories. Why do you think newspapers use news agencies? What problems can you see with this practice from the point of view of the reader?

2. Clip major news articles by individual reporters, all writing on the same political event, from three separate newspapers. Do not use stories from a news agency. Compare the articles, noting similarities and differences. How would you account for the differences?

3. Find a recent news article that reports an announcement by a government department. Identify the department, and check its Web site for a press release about the announcement. Compare the press release and the news report. Did the reporter use the press re-

formality. The bill is introduced without debate. This reading allows the opposition parties to see what is in the proposal so that they may prepare for later debates. It also allows the media to notify the public about controversial legislation.

Second reading is where the principle (idea) behind the bill is debated. For example, if the government wanted to introduce a system of gun reg-istration, the debate would be about whether reg-istering guns was a good thing to do.

If the bill passes second reading, a multiparty standing committee is assigned to study the bill clause by clause to work out the details. This committee stage often allows the public to have a say in the formal legislative process. Committees may hold hearings at which concerned citizens or groups suggest improvements to a bill. The com-

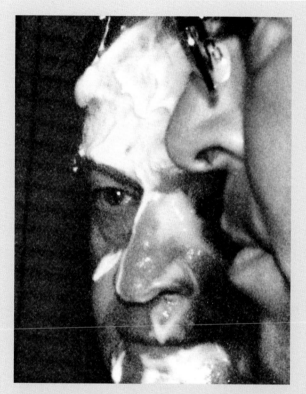

lease as a source? How can you tell? What similarities do you see? What differences? To what extent did the reporter quote directly from the press release?

4. How important is it to recognize the sources of news reports? What are the benefits and drawbacks of the three sources (direct reports, news agency stories, and press releases) mentioned here? Explain your answer.

5. Compare the front pages of three daily newspapers published on the same day in terms of the photographs and lead articles chosen. As a group, discuss and account for the similarities and differences.

Figure 9-18 Left: Prime Minister Jean Chrétien accepts a petition from pre-schoolers asking for more child care during a protest in the foyer of the House of Commons. "Photo opportunities" such as this are one vehicle for government to reach the public.

Right: The Prime Minister, photographed after receiving a pie in the face from a student who disagreed with some of the government's policies.

Developing understanding What criteria do you think news editors use in choosing a "newsworthy" photograph? How might they decide on the photographs to be used on the front page?

mittee then makes its final recommendations on how to amend the bill. In addition, citizens can make their views known through letters to the editors of newspapers and magazines, e-mails or faxes to their MP, radio phone-in shows, or organized protests or demonstrations.

In the *third reading*, the House accepts or rejects the amended bill, usually without too much debate. If accepted, it is then sent to the Senate, where it goes through the same process of three readings. The Senate rarely rejects a bill that has been passed in the House of Commons; however, it may recommend further changes.

If a bill passes all three readings, it is sent to the governor general to be signed. Once signed, the bill becomes law.

ACTIVITIES

1. Prepare a job advertisement for the position of Canada's prime minister. Include a brief job description, including the personal qualities and experience you think are necessary for the job.

2. **a)** What is cabinet solidarity?

   b) As a class, discuss some situations in which a Cabinet minister may not wish to follow cabinet solidarity.

3. How important is it that Cabinet reflect the diversity of population as well as regions of the country? Give three reasons to support your view.

4. **a)** At what stage do members of the public have an official opportunity to have input into a bill that is presented in the legislature?

   b) Explain why few private member's bills are passed in legislatures.

   c) If you were an MP or MLA introducing a private member's bill, whom would you want to support the bill before introducing it?

5. If you were a member of a federal or provincial cabinet, what bill would you try to get passed? Choose an issue that is important to you, and give a brief speech to your class in support of your bill. Highlight arguments in favour of the bill that demonstrate how it will benefit various segments of society.

Provincial/Territorial Governments

Like the federal government, provincial and territorial governments have three branches: the executive, legislative, and judicial, which are very similar in structure to their federal counterparts. In the provincial executive, the *premier* takes the role of the prime minister, and the monarch is represented by a *lieutenant-governor.* Provinces and territories have only one house, called the legislature, which is equivalent to the House of Commons (in Quebec, it is called the National Assembly). There is no provincial equivalent of the Senate. Members elected to sit in provincial legislatures are called either MLAs (members of the legislative assembly) or MPPs (members of the provincial parliament), depending on which province they serve in. Bills that pass three readings in a provincial legislature are ready to be proclaimed into law by the lieutenant-governor.

Provincial and territorial governments play a direct role in the lives of citizens in each region of Canada. Tensions inevitably arise between the federal and provincial governments, especially where their interests coincide or overlap. Leaders of a provincial government may also find their policies and interests are not the same as those of other provincial governments.

As you learned earlier in this chapter, provincial governments have responsibilities in areas that include education, the environment, health and social services, transportation, and negotiations with the federal government.

Education

Canadians expect a great deal from the educational system, in part because of the need for specialized training and employment skills. In addition, our schools share responsibility with family and society as a whole for helping students acquire the basic skills required to be productive citizens in a democracy.

The costs of education are rising as our expectations increase. Responsible governments attempt to balance the expectations of their citizens

Federal Government	Role	Provincial/Territorial Governments
Governor General	Representative of the monarchy	Lieutenant-Governor
Prime Minister	Leader of the government and party in power	Premier
Cabinet	Ministers responsible for departments, as chosen by the leader of the government	Cabinet
House of Commons (Lower House)	Part of legislative branch of government, where elected representatives make and change laws	Legislative or National Assembly
Senate (Upper House)	At the federal level, provides "sober second thought" to actions of Parliament	[No equivalent]
Public Service	Civil service or bureaucracy: non-elected people who conduct the daily business of government	Public Service

Figure 9-19 Parallel roles in federal and provincial governments.

Thinking critically Suggest reasons why the Fathers of Confederation did not think a body like the Senate was necessary at the provincial level.

with the need to spend money responsibly. Provincial governments must provide for the needs of their citizens without creating burdensome debts for future generations.

Environment

Provincial governments are responsible for the policies and laws that determine how resources will be used in a province. These governments must consider the current demands for resources by industry and citizens, as well as the need to conserve resources for future generations. They must try to find a balance between present and future use that will not have a negative impact on economic growth, employment, and the development of vital industries. For example, the logging and paper production industries in British Columbia employ thousands of workers, directly and indirectly. The forests must be carefully managed and cared for to ensure that tree cutting does not damage the environment or destroy natural habitats.

Health Care and Social Welfare

Health care is a shared responsibility, with the federal government providing some funding from its budget to the provinces and territories in ex-

change for national standards of health care. These regional governments then decide how to spend the money to provide the services and care their citizens require. Hospitals, testing, long-term care, and other forms of health care are established and maintained by provinces and territories.

Canada's population is aging, with more people over the age of fifty than under twenty. As people age, they require more health services. These services are costly and in greater demand each year. Health care is usually the largest item in provincial budgets.

To help cut costs, most provincial and territorial governments are moving towards more community-based care, focussing on prevention and on keeping patients in their own homes as much as possible. Patients and their families are being asked to pay for more of the services they receive, and hospitals have been forced to cut back drastically on services.

But as waiting periods for expensive hospital treatments grow, some patients are choosing to travel south to the United States, where they can pay for more immediate medical care. This has raised concerns that a "two-tier" medical system is emerging, in which those who can afford to pay receive better care than those who can't.

Figure 9-20 Dorothy Gawenda paid $10 000 for surgery in Seattle after doctors told her she might lose the use of her arm. She decided to get off the surgical waiting list in British Columbia after waiting seven months for surgery in Canada.

In the late 1990s, the federal government cut over $4 billion from its transfer payments to the provinces for health care. This made it difficult for the federal government to insist that provinces not charge fees for some services, or not privatize some parts of their health care system.

Transportation

As urban areas grow, the importance of transportation also increases. While the provinces have primary responsibility for transportation, they must work closely with the federal government to coordinate the development of railways, public transit, and airports.

Negotiation with the Federal Government

You have seen that the federal and provincial governments share jurisdictions in certain areas, such as the environment. As well, through equalization and transfer payments, they share the costs of trying to ensure that Canadians enjoy a similar level of services across the country.

As you learned in Chapter 8, relations between the federal government and the provincial government of Quebec have been seriously strained since 1982. Discontent in the West—the feeling that the interests of central Canada dominate federal policy decisions—has been a problem since the 1870s. For example, the western oil-producing provinces were not consulted during the oil crisis of the 1970s and early 1980s, when world oil prices soared, and the federal government legislated a National Energy Program to control domestic oil prices and so protect eastern consumers. The rise of the Reform Party was a response to this lack of consultation, as a way for western interests to be heard.

The two levels of government, federal and provincial, continually work to redefine their balance of powers. Conflicts sometimes occur over which level should provide specific services, and the amount of revenue each should receive—for example, from taxes and sales of natural resources such as lumber, oil, and gas. If a dispute remains unresolved, the Supreme Court of Canada may be asked to make a decision. The Court's decision is final and binding for both federal and provincial governments.

up close

Dennis Streifel

Dennis Streifel is a former backbench MLA in the B.C. Legislature who also held a number of cabinet positions, including Minister of Forests, Minister of Social Services, Minister of Human Resources, and Minister of Fisheries. He lost his seat in the turn-around election in 2001 when the Liberal Party swept to power, winning 77 of the 79 seats in the legislature.

What was a typical week like for you?
There are two parts to an MLA's life: when the Legislature is sitting, and when it isn't. When we were in session, I spent four days a week in Victoria at the Legislature, dealing with government business. I attended meetings, worked on committees, and attended sessions of the Legislature.

When we weren't in session, I was usually at my constituency office in Mission, or attending functions in the community. I met with a lot of community groups—arts groups, representatives of business or industry, citizens' groups—and individual citizens who wanted my help with a whole range of issues. Sometimes people only needed information about government departments or programs. Other times they wanted me to intercede directly.

MLAs work extremely hard. A citizen's committee that reviewed MLAs' compensation found that most MLAs put in about seventy hours a week, including evenings and weekends. They spend a lot of time travelling. When we were in session, I used to drive to Victoria on Sunday and return home on Friday. It took about ten hours to do the round trip every week. When we weren't in session, I was in Victoria about two to three days a week.

How would you compare the job of a backbench MLA with that of a cabinet minister?
When I was a backbencher, I thought there was no way I could possibly do more than I was doing. But then I became a member of cabinet, and I found out that cabinet ministers are twice as busy as backbenchers! You get one extra staff member in the contituency office when you're in cabinet, and that person has to represent you at a lot of local functions, because there's no way you could fulfil all those obligations and still do your job in the ministry. Your staff must keep you informed of what's happening, which can mean phone calls in the middle of the night and on weekends, if necessary.

Another difference: when you're in charge of a ministry, you *are* the government; when you're a backbencher, you're primarily a community representative. That means that at times you may disagree with decisions your government makes because they don't correspond with the wishes of your constituents. In that sense, your job is no different from that of the opposition, although there are different ways to go about expressing your dissent. If your own government decides not to build a school in your community, you have to let your views be known publicly—but diplomatically. Then you work behind the scenes, making phone calls, lobbying other MLAs and ministers, to try to change that decision. Sometimes you're successful, sometimes you aren't.

Figure 9-21 B.C. Minister of Fisheries Dennis Streifel (centre) confers with colleagues before a meeting of the federal Commons Committee on Fisheries and Oceans, Ottawa, November 1999. Streifel and the NDP government were defeated in the 2001 election.

What changes would you like to see in the way government works?

I'd like to see sitting times for the Legislature, and a set election slate, rather than leaving these to the whim of the government. I also think like the process could be more open to citizens. Perhaps the government needs to extend question period, and invite both backbenchers and members of the public to ask their questions directly to the government and opposition. I also think the idea behind a bill should be debated in public before it's debated in the House—for example, in public hearings and meetings with concerned groups.

Questions

1. List the educational qualifications and personal characteristics that you think would be most helpful to someone wishing to make a career as an MLA or an MP. Discuss your list in a small group, and make any additions or changes to your list that you feel are warranted.

2. Does this career interest you? Why or why not?

Local Governments

The simplest form of local or municipal government is the town council. The leader of the council may be called a mayor, reeve, chairperson, overseer, or warden. This is an elected position, and this person is accountable to local citizens such as yourself. Other elected members of the council are usually called councillors, alderpersons, or controllers. Councillors are elected to represent their own ward, or area of the municipality.

When Canada was formed, only about one of every ten citizens lived in a city with over 10 000

Figure 9-22 In the 1990s, homelessness and poverty became a growing problem in large Canadian cities. Food banks like this one in Toronto were started in the 1980s to collect and distribute food to the poor.

Thinking critically Who do you think should be mainly responsible for providing shelter and food to the homeless and poor: the federal government, provincial governments, municipalities, or charities? Give reasons for your answer.

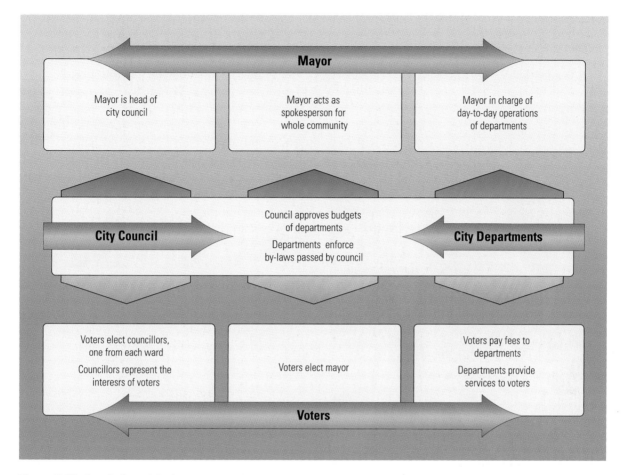

Mayor

| Mayor is head of city council | Mayor acts as spokesperson for whole community | Mayor in charge of day-to-day operations of departments |

City Council — Council approves budgets of departments / Departments enforce by-laws passed by council — **City Departments**

| Voters elect councillors, one from each ward. Councillors represent the interesrs of voters | Voters elect mayor | Voters pay fees to departments. Departments provide services to voters |

Voters

Figure 9-23 A typical municipal government structure.

Gathering information Find out how your local government is organized, and compare it to the model above. What do the similarities and differences indicate about local views of government?

people. The local governments that existed provided only a few basic services, such as firefighting, police protection, and road maintenance. Presently, more than seven out of ten Canadians live in urban settings. Municipalities must provide more and more services to more and more residents.

If you have ever travelled to a mall and been frustrated looking for parking, or have been caught in a traffic jam, you have experienced some of the problems associated with the growth of cities. The services provided by local governments are expensive. Revenues from property taxes, licensing fees, and grants may not cover all of the costs—especially since provincial and federal government grants to municipalities have been decreasing, rather than increasing. In addition, many provincial governments now expect local governments to assume responsibility for areas that have traditionally been under direct provincial control, such as social housing, highways, and road construction.

Faced with this squeeze, local governments have two basic choices: provide fewer services, or generate more money to pay for the services. Some governments have compromised by reducing some services while charging more money for others.

Cities like Toronto and Vancouver now have more people than some provinces, yet the decisions that their governments make can still be overruled by the provincial government. Municipal councils would like more power to be passed down to them, to correspond with the greater responsibilities they are now taking on.

Aboriginal Self-Government

Many Aboriginal communities have local governments that provide for the needs of their people using band councils or elders. The leader of this type of local government is a chief, who is responsible to the people in much the same way as a mayor or a reeve. However, band councils and chiefs may have more dealings with both the premier of the province and federal ministers than a mayor or reeve would. The chief must negotiate with the higher levels of government regarding issues such as licences, access to highways that cross band lands, and education. Many Aboriginal communities are in the process of negotiating increased powers and control over the governing of their own affairs.

Figure 9-24 Rod Robinson, executive director of the Nisga'a Tribal Council, carries the sacred Talking Stick as he leads a procession of elders into a 1996 general assembly in New Aiyansh, B.C.

ACTIVITIES

1. List four powers of the provincial government that have had an effect on your life in the last year. Consider what aspects of your life are linked to services or programs controlled by the provincial government.

2. Consider the local area in which you live. If your local government were to approve the list of developments below, what changes would occur in your life and the lives of people in your area? Which of those changes, in your opinion, would be positive? Which would be negative? Which would be both positive and negative?

   ▪ A shopping mall with over 200 stores and services
   ▪ An industrial park, with businesses that burn waste materials and receive raw materials by transport truck
   ▪ A multiple-sports arena, including ice rink, swimming pool, gymnasium, and baseball diamond
   ▪ A senior citizens' complex and shuttle bus service
   ▪ A major hotel and convention centre complex.

3. If you were to become head of the local government tomorrow, what four problems or issues would you address immediately, and why?

4. What five challenges does your community face over the next ten years? What plans would you make as leader of the executive branch of your local government to deal with those five challenges?

LOOKING BACK

Develop an Understanding

1. Explain the terms *constitutional monarchy*, *representative democracy*, and *federal system* in relation to Canada's system of government.

2. Create a diagram that shows the relationship among federal, provincial, and municipal governments.

3. Describe the main purpose of each of the three readings of a bill during its passage into law.

4. Which level of government would you say has the most direct effect on your day-to-day life? Provide three examples to support your response.

Explore the Issues

5. Should Cabinet members be chosen to represent many regions and groups in Canada, or should members be chosen on ability alone? For example, should a brilliant, capable MP be left out of a Cabinet because his or her region is already represented by more senior party members? If there is only one MP from a particular region, should that person automatically be chosen for the Cabinet? Explain how you would choose your Cabinet in each of the situations described above if you were prime minister.

6. What could you do to be a part of the passing of a new law? How would you show your support for, or opposition to, a proposed law? Write a brief description of your concern, actions, and intentions.

7. The United States has a Senate that elects two representatives from each state. The power of the U.S. Senate is equal to that of the U.S. House of Representatives, which is the equivalent of the Canadian House of Commons. If we had a U.S.-style senate in Canada, would it qualify as a triple-E senate? Why or why not?

8. Working in groups of three, imagine you are members of the cabinet of British Columbia. Which three concerns would you make top priorities for your government? How would you ensure support from citizens for the changes you and your government would make?

9. Should municipal governments be given autonomy from the provinces, including the power to set their own taxes?

Research and Communicate

10. Who are the key people in your local government? Create a chart with names, titles, and brief profiles of each individual (background, number of years in office, major achievements, etc.) for display in your school.

11. Select one of Canada's governors general and investigate that person's life as a private citizen and as a representative of the monarchy. Compile a biography that includes information about his or her background, duties as governor general, and other information you consider important. You will find the Parliamentary Web site useful: **http://www.parl.gc.ca**

12. Follow the course of a provincial bill that was recently passed into law in your province. Use newspaper articles, Web sites, and government publications to prepare a timeline that illustrates the highlights of the process, from first reading (or before) to the proclamation of a new act of provincial parliament.

13. Invite a local politician to speak to your class about his or her role in local government. Prepare your questions in advance.

14. Research how the elections and decision-making methods used in Nunavut differ from those of your provincial legislature. Which of these differences, if any, would you like to see implemented in your province? Explain your answer.

15. Research the structure of the U.S. government and identify three important ways in which it differs from ours. How does each of these differences affect the way our two governments operate?

10

The Citizen and Government

FOCUS ON

• What roles do political parties play in Canadian politics and decision making?

• Is our first-past-the-post electoral system fair?

• How do lobby and pressure groups influence government decisions?

• How can individuals influence political decision makers?

• What role do the media play in influencing policy decisions?

Counterpoints Issue

• Should citizens have more input in the processes of government?

Clayoquot Protest, 1993, one of nine panels by Ian Wallace. The panels show the artist's impression of a protest by about 12 000 people against logging of old-growth rainforest in the Clayoquot Sound area on the west coast of Vancouver Island in 1993. They objected to an agreement between the B.C. provincial government and the logging industry to open a large percentage of the area for logging. The forest industry is a mainstay of the B.C. economy, and the protest split communities.

Expressing ideas In the course of the protest, 859 people were arrested and charged with breaking the law. What do you think is the artist's opinion about this act of civil disobedience?

Introduction

Let's say you live on a busy street. Cars speed past your home every day, and you worry that someone will be injured. It seems to you that some form of traffic calming, such as narrowing the road, installing crosswalks or speed bumps, or handing out more speeding tickets, is called for. How would you get your ideas put into action?

Or suppose you feel strongly that the voting age for elections should be lowered. How could you work to make that aim a reality? Would letters to the editor of a widely read newspaper accomplish anything? Or should you speak to somebody who works in a government department? Should you join the youth wing of a political party, or join a group that is pressuring the government to change the voting age?

An important aspect of citizenship is working to make changes that you feel will improve your community, region, or the country as a whole.

Figure 10-1 Students protest cuts to education funding.

Developing understanding How effective do you think protest demonstrations are for getting decision makers to pay attention to a cause? Why is media attention important to these demonstrators? How else can students such as you make their voices heard by government?

In order to be effective, you need to know how to direct your efforts. You need to know who is responsible for making decisions, and who can help you achieve your goals. How can citizens get their views and opinions heard? What opportunities are there for unelected citizens to influence decision making? In this chapter, you will explore answers to these questions.

Choosing the Government

Canadians have a democratic government. All voters have an equal opportunity to choose their representatives, and the freedom to express their views freely. As you have seen, we live in a representative democracy, and the way that most Canadians take part in political decisions is to vote in elections for the representative of their choice.

Elections

If you are over eighteen years of age and a Canadian citizen, you are eligible to cast a ballot. Elections are held at least every five years for federal and provincial parliaments. Municipal elections usually occur more frequently—often every two to three years. In British Columbia, municipal elections are held on the same day every three years.

Voting in elections is perhaps the most widely used method for citizens to influence government. Provincial voter participation varies from election to election and from province to province. Participation in municipal elections also varies considerably, but is usually lower than in provincial or federal elections—and the difference of a few votes often determines the winner. Depending on the size of the municipality and the election issues, voter turnout can range from 20 to 70 per cent.

Those who choose not to vote make the votes of others more influential. For example, imagine that fewer than half of the eligible citizens in your municipality cast ballots in a mayoralty election. The person who is elected mayor may not have the support of the majority of citizens because

Federal Voting Participation

Year	Percentage
1980	69
1984	75
1988	75
1993	70
1997	67
2000	63

Source: *Reports of the Chief Electoral Officer.*

Figure 10-2 The percentage of eligible voters who voted in Canadian federal elections, 1980–2000.

Thinking critically What is the average voter turnout in federal elections for this period? The voting average for provincial elections and for municipal elections is lower than this average. How would you explain this? Why do you think voter participation has dropped so drastically since 1988?

only a minority bothered to vote. In this case, each vote cast was of greater influence than if every eligible citizen voted.

Election Campaigns

When the prime minister decides it is time to call an election, he or she asks the governor general to dissolve Parliament. Usually, the prime minister chooses a time near the end of his or her five-year term when public opinion polls show that the ruling party is popular. However, sometimes the government will call an early election to test whether it still has the support of the people. For example, in 1979, Prime Minister Joe Clark, who was leading a minority government, had to call an election because a key policy, his budget, was defeated in the House of Commons. In 2000, Prime Minister Jean Chrétien called an election less than three and a half years into his term—before the new, untried leader of the Canadian Alliance, Stockwell Day, could garner wide public support.

Most candidates in federal and provincial elections are members of political parties, although some run as independents. Usually, local party members choose candidates, although sometimes the leader of a party will select a candidate to run. The names of all candidates, including any independents, go onto the ballot. A candidate needs money and plenty of volunteers to run an election campaign. This is when some citizens are most actively involved in politics. They answer phones, distribute campaign literature, put up signs, canvass for support from door to door, drive voters to the polling station, and raise money.

Political parties usually solicit donations from individuals and businesses to pay for their campaigns. The costs of campaigning have become an issue of concern to many people, including those involved in political parties. Some candi-

Rules of the Election Expenses Act

Rule	Reason
Political parties' campaign spending is limited by the number of eligible voters in a riding.	To prevent parties from launching massive campaigns against opponents in smaller ridings.
The source of all donations of more than $200 to a political party in a single year must be made public.	To hold the parties accountable for the money they receive and to make public any particularly large contributions by a single company or group.
When they register to run in the election, all candidates must pay a deposit, which is returned when they submit their expense records. Candidates who receive more than 15% of valid votes are reimbursed for 50% of election expenses.	To help candidates with fewer funds to campaign, and to discourage candidates who are not serious from campaigning.

Figure 10-3 These rules are part of the Elections Expenses Act, 1974.

Thinking critically Why is it important to have rules governing election spending? What other rules would you like to see imposed on election campaigns?

Figure 10-4 Volunteers on the campaign trail, 2000 (clockwise from top left): A poster crusade aimed at getting voters to the polls; a worker delivering campaign signs; "down time" for an exhausted volunteer on election night.

dates have a great deal of money to spend, while others do not. This can distort the election process, giving an advantage to the candidate who can pay for an image or presentation that attracts voters. Others believe that expensive advertising and other campaign tactics divert attention away from the examination of real issues and problems.

Public Opinion Polls

During elections, public opinion on projected voting behaviour is constantly surveyed and the results reported by the media. Political parties seek public opinion throughout the year, but particularly during elections. Parties typically spend 15 per cent of their election budgets on polling. Polling companies hired by political parties contact a cross-section of the population that is believed to represent the views and opinions of Canadians in general. The people are asked questions about voting preferences and their opinions regarding political leaders, parties, and issues. The answers collected from the polls are tabulated and given to campaign organizers, who often alter the speeches of candidates to emphasize issues of importance to voters. Television commercials, debate responses, and even candidates' appearance may be altered to reflect the findings of the polls.

Some commentators are concerned that public opinion polls published during election campaigns affect voters' choices. If a party is shown to have a large lead in popular support just prior to an election, for example, some voters may believe their vote is unnecessary, or wasted if they plan to vote for an alternative party. This is one reason why public opinion polls showing the level of voter

Figure 10-5 Less than a month before the 2000 federal election was called, Canadian Alliance leader Stockwell Day arrived at a news conference on a personal watercraft.

Thinking critically How important do you think the appearance of political leaders is to their success? Explain your answer.

Figure 10-6 Before the advent of the secret ballot in 1874, Canadian voters used to have to declare their vote in public.

Developing understanding What are the disadvantages of voting publicly, as shown in this picture?

support for parties are not allowed to be published in the twenty-four hours immediately prior to an election.

On election day, polling stations are set up in every riding. Schools and places of worship are often used as polling stations. The names of all eligible voters who have registered are listed at each poll, and a polling officer crosses off the name of each individual as he or she votes. Voting takes place in private, behind a small screen, and no campaign signs or literature are allowed at or around the polling station.

Figure 10-7 Today, voting is done by secret ballot. Citizens mark their choice behind a screen, and place their ballot in a closed box. Counting of ballots, which is done by hand, is strictly scrutinized.

1. In some countries, like Australia, voting in elections is compulsory for eligible voters. Do you think Canada should adopt this system? Why or why not?

2. Because of the size of the country and the number of time zones, results of federal elections in the East are announced half an hour before voting stations are closed in British Columbia. Some people argue that this can influence the way people in the West vote. Do you consider this a problem that should be addressed? Why or why not?

3. Do you think the voting age should be lowered to seventeen? Prepare a letter to send to your member of Parliament to explain your opinion.

4. An election, it is often said, is won on the backs of the volunteers. What types of jobs are done to help get someone elected in Canadian elections? How important do you think volunteers are in running election campaigns? Why might people volunteer to work in a campaign?

5. Research how public opinion polls are conducted. What are their drawbacks? How reliable to you think they are in reflecting public opinion?

Candidate	Votes
Herb Dhaliwal, Liberal	17 705
Ron Jack, Canadian Alliance	15 384
Herschel Hardin, New Democratic Party	3 848
Dan Tidball, Progressive Conservative	2 649
Others	1 880

Figure 10-8 The results of the federal election of 2000 in the riding of Vancouver–Burnaby.

Thinking critically Did Herb Dhaliwal win 50 per cent or more of the votes? Should a candidate or a government have to win 50 per cent or more of votes cast? Explain your opinion.

The Electoral System

When the polls close, the votes are counted and the candidate with the most votes in each riding is announced the winner. This is called the **first-past-the-post system**. The winner does not necessarily have to win a majority of the votes cast; he or she simply has to win more votes than any of the other candidates. This system has the virtue of being simple and straightforward. Its supporters also argue that it means there is usually a clear winner of elections and that minority governments do not often happen. However, the result does not always represent the wishes of the majority of voters (see Figure 10-8).

First-past-the-post is so named because a candidate has only to win more votes than his nearest competitor to take the riding, not an absolute majority of the votes cast. The most direct conse-

quence is to exaggerate the majority enjoyed by the winning party, often grotesquely: with less than half the popular vote, governments have been formed with nearly all of the seats…. [I]t produces results that are increasingly at odds with voters' desires.

Source: Andrew Coyne, *Toronto Star*, October 17, 1996.

For this reason, some people advocate a switch to some form of **proportional representation** (PR). PR systems are used in countries such as Israel, Holland, and Italy. Each political party puts forward a list of all its candidates. Voters support a candidate on the basis of the party he or she represents. The number of seats a party wins in the legislature is based on the total number of votes it receives. For example, in a 100-seat legislature, a party that received 38 per cent of the popular vote would have thirty-eight seats in the legislature. The candidates who got the most votes from the party's list would fill the thirty-eight seats.

One objection is that this kind of PR system would mean that local representation—having an MP allocated to each riding—would disappear, or change. Another is that, since most elections using PR do not give one party a majority, parties often have to create coalitions, or alliances, to form a government. The experience in some other countries appears to be that these coalitions often cannot be maintained for very long.

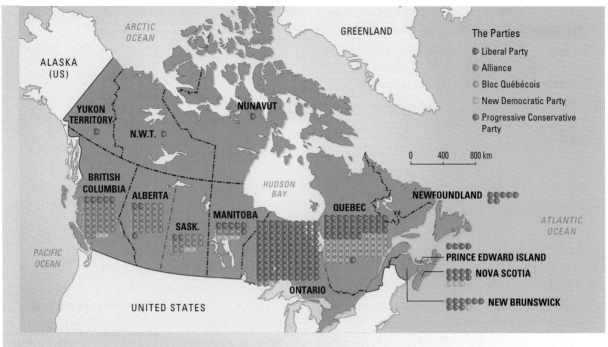

Figure 10-9 Results of the 2000 election by province.

Reading a map

1. How does this map support the view that the Bloc Québécois and Canadian Alliance are regional parties?

2. The Liberal Party claims to be the only party that can call itself a "national" party. How does this map support that claim? How does it not?

Figure 10-10 In 2000, a simple majority in Parliament required 151 seats.

Reading a table

1. In which year did the governing party win 50 per cent of the vote?

2. Explain how the Liberal Party formed the government in 1997 with less than 40 per cent of the vote.

3. Explain how in 1993 the Bloc Québécois became the opposition party when the Reform party gained a larger number of votes.

4. Why do you think the present system of voting causes regional dissent in Canada? Explain your answer.

Party	1984	1988	1993	1997	2000
Bloc Québécois					
% of votes			13.5	10.7	11
Number of seats			54	44	38
Reform/Canadian Alliance					
% of votes		n/a	18.7	19.4	26
Number of seats		1	52	59	66
Liberal					
% of votes	28	32	41.3	38.4	41
Number of seats	40	83	**177**	**156**	**172**
New Democratic Party					
% of votes	19	20	6.9	11.1	n/a
Number of seats	30	43	9	21	13
Progressive Conservative					
% of votes	50	43	16	18.9	n/a
Number of seats	**211**	**169**	2	19	12
Others					
% of vote	3	5	3.6	1.5	0
Number of seats	1	2	1	2	0
Total seats	282	295	295	301	301

n/a = not available
Governing parties are indicated in bold type.

This increases the number of elections and diminishes the stability of the government. Some countries, however, such as Germany and New Zealand, have developed systems that combine elements of PR and first-past-the-post, and these appear to work very well.

An important argument favouring a change in the first-past-the-post system for Canada is that the present system accentuates regionalism in Canada. For example, although the Canadian Alliance won all but three seats in Alberta in the 2000 federal election, 25 per cent of voters in that province voted Liberal. In Ontario, a large number of voters supported the Canadian Alliance, but the party won only two seats there. The same problem exists at a provincial level. In Prince Edward Island, the opposition in 2001 consisted of one member, even though his party won more than 40 per cent of the vote.

Political Parties

Most elected representatives at the federal and provincial level belong to one of the political parties. Political parties act as a way of representing the views of Canadians in the decision-making process. Members of a political party share a common set of beliefs. These beliefs together are called an *ideology*. The ideology of a party provides a framework for its decisions and policies. One way of describing the ideology of a party is to describe it as generally left wing, centre, or right wing, as shown in Figure 10-11.

From 1867 to 1988, two long-established political parties were dominant in Canada: the Progressive Conservative Party and the Liberal Party. In the federal election of 1988, as you saw in Figure 10-10, the Progressive Conservative Party lost a massive number of seats. Two new parties took their seats: the Reform Party, which became the Canadian Alliance in 2000, and the Bloc Québécois.

The Canadian Alliance, like its predecessor, the Reform Party, gets most of its support from the western provinces. It grew out of feelings of western alienation—the conviction among many westerners that the federal government in Ottawa favoured the central provinces of Ontario and Quebec, and that western voices were not being heard. The party hopes to extend its appeal to voters in other provinces who would like to see substantial changes in the way government operates, particularly how the federal government responds to the concerns of various regions in Canada.

As you saw in Chapter 8, the Bloc Québécois formed after the failure of the Meech Lake Accord, and became the official opposition after the election of 1993. Its support comes entirely from Quebec.

Left-Wing	Centre	Right-Wing
Support change in order to improve the welfare of all citizens.	Tradition is important, but change must be supported if most people want it.	Tradition is important; change should be treated with caution.
Governments should play a larger role in people's lives, especially in providing social services.	Governments should play a role only when it improves the lives of citizens.	Governments should play a small role. Private businesses should ensure needs of citizens are met.
Law and order are important to protect the rights of all citizens fairly and equally.	Law and order are important to encourage and protect the rights of individuals.	Emphasizes law and order to protect society and its traditions.

Figure 10-11 The political spectrum in Canada. People who study politics sometimes use a political "spectrum" to explain the range of beliefs and views on a civic issue. In this political spectrum, beliefs and views are categorized "left-wing," "centre," or "right-wing." Often, political parties are linked with these categories.

Identifying viewpoint What words or phrases would you use to summarize the three ideologies shown in the political spectrum? Which of the positions on the spectrum is most attractive to you? Explain.

Joining a Political Party

Those who choose to join a political party can nominate and vote for the candidates who will run in their riding. To join a political party, you need to be eighteen years of age. However, most of the major political parties have special youth wings that allow young people to have their say regarding policies and future directions for the party. Youth wings often have considerable influence over party policies, as parties are anxious to get young people involved to ensure the party's survival in the future.

Why do people join political parties? Some wish to improve the quality of life in their community, region, or nation. Others believe strongly in the ideology of the political party and act on their beliefs. Still others are attracted to the power

up close
Jenny Kwan: Politics with Passion

Jenny Kwan's political career is full of firsts. At the age of twenty-seven she became the youngest person ever elected to Vancouver City Council. Then, at thirty, she and Ida Chong were the first Chinese-Canadian women to sit in the British Columbia Legislative Assembly. In 1998 she became the first Chinese-Canadian cabinet minister in B.C. history, when she was appointed minister of Municipal Affairs. Since then she has held two more provincial cabinet posts, first as Minister of Women's Equality and then as Minister of Community Development, Co-operatives, and Volunteers. Here is what she has to say about how and why she entered politics.

"When people ask me how I got politicized, I think back to my childhood. My family arrived in Vancouver in 1975, when I was nine. I had childlike expectations, and the reality shocked me. My mother had to work for $10 a day in the farms outside Vancouver. We lived in worse accommodation than we had in Hong Kong. There were six kids and my parents, living in a tiny two-bedroom basement suite.

"At school I was made fun of by other children. I remember one incident in the washroom. Two girls started to call me Chink. I locked myself in a stall, but they climbed over each side.... I grew up wishing that I wasn't Chinese. As a child, I had full command of the language, but I made myself forget it. It's ironic because now I spend a lot of time trying to relearn the language and culture.

"When I was twenty-one, I was asking myself soul-searching questions about life and purpose. I decided to answer them by going back to Hong Kong and China. I talked to people in the villages who all wanted to go to more progressive places. I grew to love China, but the more I saw, the more I realized it was up to me to take advantage of the opportunities in Canada.

"I went back to Vancouver and worked for an advocacy group called the Downtown Eastside Residents' Association. On the first day, I knew I had found my calling. All kinds of people came to see us. Some had been wrongfully evicted by a landlord. Many were immigrants. Most were poor. We helped them exercise their rights. Housing is fundamental to providing stability in people's lives....

"My career goal had always involved ensuring there is equality and justice for everyone. When I was approached to run for City Council, I thought it might allow me to achieve my goals. But when I was elected, I was the only representative of my party, the Coalition of Progressive Electors, and the youngest person on Council. It was the toughest three years of my career....

"That time on Council got me ready for the fight of running provincially. I went door knocking for a whole month. The residents of the riding took me into their homes. They wanted to discuss crime and safety.

and influence of politics. Many influential people in politics today got their start by joining a political party.

Perhaps the real question is why do so few people—only about 2 per cent of the population—join political parties. Individuals are far more likely to seek change by participating in a special-interest group or a **non-governmental organization** (NGO) than by joining a party.

NGOs are non-profit organizations that work to improve some aspect of people's lives. Many NGOs work internationally, providing services and lobbying governments to change unfair laws or policies. Examples of some NGOs are the United Way, the Canadian Red Cross, Doctors Without Borders, Oxfam, and the Western Canada Wilderness Committee.

Figure 10-12 Jenny Kwan, member of the British Columbia legislature for Vancouver–Mount Pleasant.

Employment. Poverty. Education. Just like my parents, these residents wanted a better quality of life for their children.

"When Ida Chong and I got elected to the legislature, it sent a strong message: we all have a legitimate role to play in our democratic society. We should never forget that the Asian community didn't have the vote until 1948. That wasn't long ago.

"People say I'm too idealistic, but I take it as a compliment. Women campaigned to get the vote and were criticized for being idealists. Well, thank God they were because otherwise I wouldn't be here as an elected official. I have a saying: if I get up in the morning and know not what I want to achieve, then what is the purpose of getting up? I believe in my ideals so strongly, I'm willing to fight for them."

Questions

1. Jenny Kwan has worked for change both as part of an advocacy group and as an elected representative. What do you think are the pros and cons of each of these forms of political involvement?

2. Why is it important to encourage people from all ethnic backgrounds to participate in politics? What barriers might immigrants such as Jenny Kwan face in pursuing a political career? What can we do as a society to overcome those barriers?

3. What qualities do you think are needed to be an effective politician? What educational background do you think would be a good preparation for such a career? Does this career choice interest you at all? Why or why not?

Figure 10-13 The logos of the main political parties in 2001.

ACTIVITIES

1. **a)** What is considered to be the strength of the first-past-the-post system? What is the major disadvantage of this system?

   b) What problems associated with first-past-the-post would proportional representation (PR) address? What new problems might PR create?

2. Why do you think politicians are reluctant to change the system of first-past-the-post?

3. Choose one of the political parties shown in Figure 10-13, and research its policies and ideologies. Then decide where on the political spectrum shown in Figure 10-11 you would place it. Explain your decision.

4. **a)** What reasons would you give to explain why so few people join political parties in Canada?

   b) What advice would you give to party organizations to help them recruit members from your age group?

Influencing Government

Between elections, individuals can and do influence their government by contacting their MP, MLA, or alderperson to express their view, or simply to request information, assistance, or intervention. Canadians also communicate with public servants, who conduct the daily business of the government. Letters to the editor and radio phone-in shows are another way that citizens communicate their thoughts and ideas to government.

While individual contact between citizens and government can make a difference, especially at the local level, and is welcomed by most elected representatives, it is not the most effective way to initiate change. Individual action may also be slow and too time-consuming and expensive.

Pressure Groups and Lobbyists

Groups who seek to influence government policies and decisions are called interest groups or **pressure groups**. A pressure group is made up of people who share a certain viewpoint and want to change or influence government policy in order to promote their common interest. There are two kinds of pressure groups. *Institutionalized pressure groups* are well established and have formal organizations. Examples of these groups are shown in Figure 10-14. *Issue-oriented groups* are less permanent. People form these groups to accomplish limited aims, and disband after they have accomplished their aim. A group that lobbies a local

Figure 10-14 Some institutionalized pressure groups in Canada.

Area	Group
Economics	Business Council on National Issues Canadian Manufacturers Association Canadian Labour Congress Consumers' Association of Canada
Religion	Canadian Council of Churches Canadian Jewish Congress
Health	Canadian Medical Association Canadian Cancer Society
Gender, race, or ethnicity	National Council of Women Black Action Defence Committee Arab Palestinian Association Canadian Polish Congress
Environment	Greenpeace Sierra Club
Human rights	Amnesty International Free the Children

Figure 10-15 Pressure groups in action, clockwise from top left: environmentalists stage a sit-in at an MP's office; a lobby group for the disabled protests cuts to provincial services; a poster campaign targets young people; petitioners gather signatures; an issue-based protest march.

government to have a traffic light installed would be an example of this kind of pressure group.

Over the years, pressure groups have persuaded the government to write new legislation, move airports and industries, establish parks and wildlife reserves, reduce taxes for certain industries, control or not control pollution, and provide more government funding for research and development of certain products and services.

Free the Children: Young People in Action

One pressure group that has been remarkably successful on an international level is Free the Children. Craig Kielburger started the group when he was just twelve years old. Its goal was to end child labour around the world. The group began by writing letters, circulating a petition, and speaking out in their school and community about the issue. They gained a reputation as passionate and convincing speakers. A trip to South Asia gave Craig an opportunity to witness the conditions of child labourers first hand. It also helped the group to gain media attention, as Prime Minister Jean Chrétien, who was visiting the region on a trade mission, agreed to meet with Craig to discuss the issue of child labour.

Since its beginnings in 1995, Free the Children has raised awareness of children's rights, and has grown from a small group of friends to an international organization operating in over twenty countries. The group's members

...have become international spokespersons for children's rights. They have built schools, created

building your skills

Conducting an Interview

*C*onducting an interview is an important skill if you want to collect opinions and information from individuals. What kind of preparation should an interviewer do before an interview? Here is how one journalist interviewed Craig Kielburger about his visit to India and Pakistan in 1996 and the aims of his pressure group.

Q: *How did you first become interested in the issue of child labour?*

A: In April 1995, I read about Iqbal Masid, the young Pakistani rug weaver who was killed because he spoke out against child labour. I was horrified. I did more research on the issue and found out that over 200 million children worldwide have to work, many under conditions of terrible exploitation. I made a presentation on the topic to my class and, after that, a few of us decided to form Free the Children, a group dedicated to ending child labour. Since then, our group has grown to over two hundred members all across Canada, and we're still growing.

Q: *Why do you think that Canadians in general, and especially young people, should be concerned about this issue?*

A: Canadians should be concerned about issues that affect them, either directly or indirectly. Children under the age of eighteen have rights that are internationally recognized. Among these is the right to an education. Young people in Canada can identify with children in other countries who are being mistreated and abused. It is our moral responsibility to speak out against this situation. We should learn more about the issue, and work to bring child labour to an end by pressuring governments and businesses to take action.

Q: *What led you to go on your own fact-finding trip to Asia?*

A: My visit was organized by a branch of the International Labour Organization dedicated to the elimination of child labour. For seven weeks, I visited a number of Asian countries, gathering information.... During

Figure 10-16 Craig Kielburger, meeting with the press in India in 1996.

Using evidence How does this photograph support the view that Kielburger was skilful in getting his view across to the media?

my trip, I learned that the Team Canada trade mission was going to be arriving in Asia. A press conference was organized, where I was asked if I was going to be meeting with Prime Minister Chrétien. I said that I would like to discuss the issue with him, and ask him to talk about it with the leaders he was going to meet. [Later I did meet with him, and he] promised me that he would do this.

Q: *Do you think that your meeting with Prime Minister Chrétien accomplished anything positive?*

A: Yes, I think it did. He raised the issue with the leaders of India and Pakistan, two countries where child labour is quite common, especially in the rug-making trade. Government and business leaders also promised that they would follow up on the issue by making Canadians more aware of it. Education is the key to getting people more involved and active in trying to end child labour.

Q: *What do you say to adults who think that young people like yourself lack the knowledge and maturity to speak out on issues like trade and human rights?*

A: Young people have a special interest in working to end social injustice around the world. It's our future we're concerned about, and practices like child labour really have no place in society today. Despite our youth, we care a lot about the things that are going on in the world, and with knowledge, enthusiasm, and teamwork, we can bring about some positive changes.

Q: *What do you say to young people who think that it's pointless to try to change things, and that they're wasting their time doing so?*

A: I would say to them that they should think about the potential power that young people have. Imagine if thousands of teenagers from across Canada put pressure on governments and businesses to stop importing products made by child labour. Young people have the energy, enthusiasm, and dedication to make changes. What we need is more education and the opportunity to form groups that can get the job done. That's what we're trying to do with Free the Children, and we seem to be making our point to the people in power.

Applying the Skill

1. Read the questions that the journalist asked Craig Kielburger. Make up three further questions that you would add to find out more about how to organize a pressure group like Free the Children.

2. Make up a list of questions that you would like to ask Jenny Kwan to find out more about her aims and how she became involved in political life.

3. Arrange an interview with a politically active individual in your community. Your goal is to find out more about why this person is politically active, and what strategies his or her group has found to be successful in initiating change. Summarize what you have learned about political activism during the interview in a report to the class.

alternative sources of income for poor families, led campaigns against sweatshop and child labor, convinced governments to stiffen laws to charge tourists who sexually exploit children, are raising funds to build a peace center and have created an international network of children helping children.

Source: Free the Children Web site, www.freethechildren.org/info/Whatisftc1b.htm

One of the goals of Free the Children is to encourage young people to exercise their rights and become politically active. Children set the policies of the group; adults play a supportive role as secretaries and advisers, but cannot vote on major decisions.

counterpoints

Should Citizens Have More Input in the Processes of Government?

In Chapter 9, you saw that the caucus of the governing political party and the Cabinet approve policies and new legislation before they are introduced to the legislature. Sometimes these policies are based on the party platform—the promises that the leader and candidates made when they ran for election. By electing the governing party, electors (although usually not the majority) have given approval for these policies. Other times, the policies are new initiatives introduced by the government without input from the general public.

Prime ministers, who have the most control over the direction government will take, have two bodies to advise them on policy: the Privy Council Office (PCO), which is made up of senior public servants, and the Prime Minister's Office (PMO), which is made up of party members who are trusted by the prime minister. Members of the PMO are not elected, and have special access to the leader of the government. Provincial premiers have similar unelected advisers. The number of people serving in the PMO has risen dramatically since 1968, and with it, the body's power. In Ontario in the late 1990s, even elected members of the governing

party complained about the power that the people in the premier's office wielded in policy making.

So, it is not surprising that many people feel they have little say in government policies. Elected officials sometimes seem inaccessible to the ordinary citizen. The levers of power seem to be firmly in the hands of bureaucrats, advisers, and pressure groups that do not always represent the views of the majority.

What avenues are there for the citizen who is not involved in the political system to be heard? People can contact members of Parliament and voice their opinions, join a pressure group or political party, protest in a public demonstration, phone in to talk shows, or write letters to newspapers. If they are more persistent, they can prepare submissions to present to standing committees if these are held when legislation is being passed, although there is no guarantee their concerns will be addressed. Still, many Canadians feel that their governments do not hear them. Should steps be taken to allow the general public to have more say in policies and decision making?

Dennis Streifel (see Chapter 9, page 243) has two suggestions to allow more public input: that the public be allowed to ask questions in question period, and that legislation should be publicly debated before it is introduced. Electronic mail and other forms of rapid communication make it easier for people's opinions to be known. The Canadian Alliance want to include more use of referendums, so that the public can vote on accepting or rejecting proposals for legislation. They also favour the recall of representatives who do not follow the electors' wishes. All these suggestions are aimed at increasing the level of citizen participation.

However, Canada has a representative democracy. With over 30 million people in the country, it is impossible to have direct democracy. We elect people to act

Applying Pressure

How do pressure groups try to achieve their aims? One way to influence government is by providing research, polls, reports, and advice to government ministries. The government often seeks out the technical expertise of such groups. These resources provide the government with clear and accessible information that they can use in making decisions. However, it also gives the group more influence over decisions made by the government, and in some cases presents the group with a conflict of interest, in which the goals of the interest group are likely to prevail. For example, the minister of finance routinely consults with business groups in setting tax policy. While these consultants' knowledge of the market can be on our behalf. They belong to political parties, and in order to have a stable government, the party members vote as one on legislation, even if some may disagree with a policy. If a member disagrees continually, or on an important issue, he or she must resign from the party. These members usually continue to sit in the legislature, and the voters can decide whether to reelect them in the next election. Some political commentators feel that party discipline is too strict, and that there should be more free votes; but on major policy initiatives, this is unlikely.

The federal government has held very few referendums in its history, the most recent being the one on the Charlottetown Accord in 1992. Voters were given the opportunity to vote on whether or not they accepted the Accord. The Accord was rejected, but the vote illustrates some of the problems with referendums. Voters have to respond with a simple "yes" or "no" to complex issues. Even a seemingly simple question like, "Should Canada adopt capital punishment?" is more complex than it seems. What crimes should be punishable by capital punishment? Who will make this decision?

Direct democracy assumes that the people will be actively engaged in learning about legislation and policies. Usually, issues in politics are complex, with many compromises to be made for agreement to be reached. Yet surveys show that most voters are too busy with their families and working lives to spend much time on political issues. Only 2 per cent actually join political parties; sometimes more than 30 per cent do not vote in federal elections. What percentage of the population would be prepared to spend the time to be properly informed about issues, and convey their thoughts to the government? Lack of participation by a large number of voters would mean that those who make the effort to be heard have more influence than those who are silent.

The era of electronic communication certainly makes it easier to convey individual voters' opinions on issues, but not everyone has access to these tools. A system that asked for more citizen participation would have to ensure that each person's voice is heard only once on an issue. We have careful supervision of voting in elections to make sure that there is no pressure applied to people, and that counting of votes is carefully scrutinized. A similar system would have to apply to public input on policy decisions and voting on legislation. No such system is in place.

Analysing the Issue

1. Suppose that the government is proposing to introduce a bill or policy that you disagree with. Outline three steps that you could take to show your opposition. Rank them in order of effectiveness.

2. a) Should members of Parliament be able to ask questions from the general public in question period? Why or why not?

   b) Draw up a plan for allowing citizens' questions to be asked in question period. For example, who would choose the questions? How many citizen questions should be asked? Should the governing party be made aware of the questions beforehand? Do you think this reform would make governing parties more responsive to citizens' concerns? Why or why not?

3. Prepare an organizer to show the pros and cons of each of the reforms suggested in this feature.

4. Do you think that citizens should have more say in deciding on government policies? Explain your answer.

helpful to the government, these groups have a vested interest in the outcome of such policies, and cannot be expected to give objective advice.

Institutionalized groups often use **lobbyists**. A lobbyist is someone who is paid to represent the interests of a particular group to key decision makers, such as high-level bureaucrats in the public service or politicians. They often have expertise in the field of the pressure group. Some professional lobbyists are former high-ranking members of the public service and maintain contact with their former colleagues, such as deputy ministers, Cabinet ministers, other key government officials, and the opposition. Outside the government, lobbyists may target other pressure groups, the media, and important party members.

The danger with lobbying is that people with special influence can persuade governments to put in place policies that favour their group but are not necessarily in the public interest. An example is the tobacco company lobby, which has fought government efforts to limit advertising for tobacco products. In 1989, when people were very concerned about the power of lobbyists in influencing decisions, a bill was passed requiring lobbyists to register. Public servants who resigned from their jobs could not work as lobbyists until a year had passed since their resignations.

Another avenue that groups can use is the courts. For example, in 1988 Canada's law prohibiting abortion was struck down by the Supreme Court. The case was backed by a coalition of pro-choice groups. However, court cases can cost a lot of money, and the outcome is not guaranteed. Also, while courts can strike down a law, they cannot order that it be replaced by something else. That is up to the government. For those pressure groups who are hoping to convince the government to create new laws or policies, the best the courts can do is to make governments aware that a law may be needed.

One aspect of pressure group activity that causes some concern is funding. Some groups are large enough to be self-financing. However, public interest groups are often dependent on funds from government. While receiving government funds can help give a group a voice in policy making, it can also limit the effectiveness of the group.

The National Action Committee on the Status of Women (NACSW) began receiving operational grants from the government in 1973. However, its funding was drastically cut in 1988 by the Progressive Conservative government, after the NACSW spoke out against government policies.

Some critics argue that if pressure groups are too successful, then democracy is put at risk. They argue that if government is influenced too greatly by well-organized minority interest groups, then the wishes of the majority may not be heard—or even sought. They are critical of the influence that certain pressure groups seem to have over government, particularly those well-funded and highly organized groups with professional lobbyists.

ACTIVITIES

1. Explain in your own words the meaning of the terms *pressure group* and *lobbyist*.

2. **a)** Make a list of the steps that Craig Kielburger used to organize political action.

   b) What organizations helped him apply political pressure? What role did the media play in his success?

   c) Do you agree with Kielburger that young Canadians have a responsibility to speak out about injustices in other countries? Give reasons for your views.

3. Identify an issue that is important to you. How would you like to influence the government on this issue? Write a letter to your MP, MLA, or local representative explaining your position.

4. Develop a code of ethics for professional lobbyists to use in dealing with government and other officials. For example, is it acceptable for a lobbyist to take an official to lunch? Contribute to a politician's election campaign or political party? Buy an official gifts?

Role of the Mass Media

The mass media include television, radio, newspapers, and magazines. They are the chief methods of communicating ideas and information in our society. Citizens get most of their day-to-day information about government actions from media reports. Journalists are free to criticize government actions, or to question the decisions made by elected representatives and officials. As well, the media report on public opinion polls. This gives the government feedback on what people think about its policies. For these reasons, the media are very important in the political process.

The influence of the media goes beyond the role of go-between. In many ways, the media can actually influence government—and citizens' attitudes towards it. Issues that receive large amounts of media coverage often get more attention from government. Since there are always more stories to report on than there is space to report them, editors must make choices about what they think is important. In this way, the media can actually change the direction of government policy.

Yet what makes a good media story is not always what is most deserving of attention. Sometimes important issues are not given any attention by the media. Activist groups know that simply making a statement about an issue is unlikely to get them much attention in the media, but organizing an event of some kind—a protest rally, for example—may be more successful. Sometimes crowds march in silence until the television cameras appear. Then, organizers encourage the marchers to shout slogans and chant so their message will appear in the news.

Media Concentration

In recent years, media ownership has become more and more concentrated in the hands of a few corporations. For example, between 1989 and 1999, the number of daily papers that were run independently of a large newspaper chain dropped from twenty-three to seven. Two or three large chains, such as Southam/Thomson, Hollinger, or CanWest Global, owned most of the remaining papers.

This concentration means that the news read by significant numbers of Canadians is from limited sources, rather than from a variety of sources. At some point, critics argue, if ownership is in the hands of a very small group, it will go against the intent of diversity and plurality in a democracy. Like a powerful pressure group, media owned by

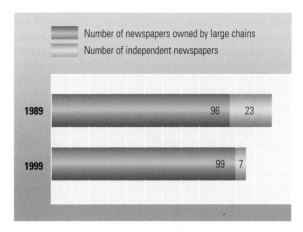

Figure 10-17 Describe the trends in newspaper ownership in Canada shown by this graph.

Figure 10-18 Finance Minister Paul Martin is surrounded by reporters outside the House of Commons in the wake of concern over Canada's response to a crisis in the global economy, 1998.

Developing understanding Why do politicians usually welcome attention from the media? What problems might they have if they refuse to talk to the media when the public wants answers to an issue?

a small group will come into conflict with the public interest while promoting its own interests. Questions about bias arise. Can the views of Canadians be represented accurately and fairly by a select and powerful group?

Civil Disobedience

There are numerous ways for citizens to make their voices heard in Canada: through the vote, through individual actions such as letter writing, and through joining pressure groups and using the media. Yet, they may not be successful in changing the policies and actions of governments, because governments must balance the needs and wants of many different segments of society.

Suppose you feel that the actions of the government are actually unethical or undemocratic. Is it ever acceptable to break the law as a way of protesting government actions?

Civil disobedience is the act of intentionally breaking, or refusing to keep, laws one considers unjust. The term was coined by a nineteenth-century U.S. writer, Henry Thoreau. He felt that the basic democratic principle of majority rule existed not because the majority was always right but because it was more powerful and could force the minority to comply. "If the machinery of government is unjust," Thoreau said, "break the law. Let your life be a counter friction to stop the machine."

This form of protest has been used by some of the greatest moral leaders of our time—including the U.S. civil rights activist Martin Luther King and the Indian politician Mohandas Gandhi.

Figure 10-20 The Rev. Martin Luther King, Jr. waves to the crowd before his "I have a dream" speech during the March on Washington, DC, August 28, 1963. The march was organized to support proposed civil rights legislation and to end segregation in the U.S. South.

Both these men embraced non-violent civil disobedience in their quest for justice, and both ultimately died for their cause.

If everyone in society disobeyed laws with which they personally disagreed, we might have no effective order. Different people would be living by a variety of rules, and the result would be chaos. Imagine your classroom if every student could choose which rules he or she would obey. Great thinkers such as Gandhi and King agree that civil disobedience is warranted only when there is significant harm from the law itself. Relatively trivial matters do not merit breaking the law, as the harm to society of that violation could be greater than the benefit. As well, those who choose to practise civil disobedience should be willing to face the consequences of their actions. Running away from this responsibility would diminish the moral authority being demonstrated.

---

1. Civil disobedience should not involve violence.

2. Civil disobedience should be directed against laws that are seriously harmful.

3. Civil disobedience requires taking responsibility for one's actions. Willingness to face punishment shows the strength of one's beliefs.

Figure 10-19 The principles of civil disobedience.

Figure 10-21 The 1993 protests against logging in the Clayoquot Valley brought the largest mass arrests in British Columbia's history.

Clayoquot Sound

Acts of civil disobedience—blocking logging roads near Clayoquot Sound, British Columbia—brought the issue of clear-cut logging to public attention in 1993. The provincial government had been faced with a difficult decision about the future of the area. It opted for compromise. It set aside 34 per cent of the area as protected lands, and allowed selective and environmentally sensitive logging of another 21 per cent. The area available for general logging was reduced from 80 per cent to 40 per cent. The government claimed that opinion polls showed a majority of the population was in favour of the solution.

However, opposition to the compromise was vocal, and led to the largest example of civil disobedience in Canadian history. Protesters organized blockade after blockade, sitting in groups in the middle of the road to prevent loggers from entering the forest. Police had to drag each individual from the road. Most protesters offered no resistance, other than to refuse to move. Over 800 people were arrested in the summer of 1993 alone.

Most received warnings, fines of up to $500, or jail sentences. Since that time, the issue of logging practices in the area has been monitored, and all decisions regarding the clear-cutting of old-growth forest are closely examined.

ACTIVITIES

1. Do you think it is dangerous to allow newspaper ownership to be concentrated in the hands of a small group? Explain your response. What are the potential benefits of such concentration?

2. Working in a small group, think of an issue or cause you would like to bring to the media's attention. Then brainstorm a list of events you could stage in order to gain some media attention for the issue. Remember that, especially for television, your event needs to provide opportunities for interesting visuals, as well as getting your message across.

3. Explain the three basic guidelines for practising civil disobedience. Why are these guidelines an important part of this approach to changing government policies?

LOOKING BACK

Develop an Understanding

1. Explain how each of the following allows you to influence the government of Canada:

   a. voting in an election

   b. joining a pressure group

   c. membership in a political party

   Use mind maps, ideas webs, flow charts, or other graphics to clarify your written explanations.

2. Describe the role of the media in the democratic process. Give examples to illustrate each aspect of the media's role.

3. Explain the following terms and their possible role in political decision making: professional lobbyists; pressure groups; the Prime Minister's Office; public opinion poll.

4. List three statements that Craig Kielburger makes in his interview that particularly impressed you. Explain why these statements had an impact on you.

Explore the Issues

5. A pressure group called Fair Vote Canada formed after the 2000 federal election. Members want to reform the electoral system so that the distortions caused by the first-past-the-post system are lessened.

   a. How would you advise this pressure group to organize?

   b. Whom would you suggest they target with their ideas?

6. What advice would you give to political party organizers who want to increase membership in their party?

7. a. In your own words, describe the difference between a left-wing and a right-wing ideology for a political party.

   b. Where on the ideological spectrum do your own beliefs fall? Why?

8. You have just formed a new provincial (or federal) party, the Youth Party of British Columbia (or Canada). Develop policy statements covering at least three different areas of government. What issues would you want to see on the political agenda?

Research and Communicate

9. Make a collage from newspaper clippings and other illustrations of your choosing that show the importance of citizens influencing government.

10. Create a poster that shows your view of how individuals and groups can affect government decision making. Consider how to get your message across to other students and concerned citizens.

11. Examine your local newspaper, listen to a news broadcast on a local radio station, and watch a news report on television, paying attention to editorials and letters to the editor in the newspaper. Working with one, two, or three other students, analyse the editorials and news reports by answering the following questions.

    a. What news reports about government are emphasized in each medium? Does each medium concentrate on the same stories, or is a variety of stories presented? Why do you think this is so?

    b. What is the general tone of the reports—critical, supportive, or both?

    c. If the news reports express opinions about the government, do they present more than one side of an issue? Do the reporters express a personal preference in the issues?

    d. How do different stations or papers cover the same event? Why do you think this occurs?

    e. Write a paragraph to present your opinion about the influence of the media in politics. Provide reasons and examples to support your view of the role of the media in the making of political decisions.

12. Investigate the recent changes in South Africa and its voting laws. Black South Africans—the majority of citizens—have only recently gained the right to vote. How did these changes come about? What were the results of the first election in which blacks could vote? Why are the changes to the voting laws in South Africa so important for the future of that country?

13. Investigate the voting patterns of Canadians in either provincial or federal elections. The Web site for Elections Canada at **<www.elections.ca>** is a useful source. Choose one of the following topics to focus on, or create one of your own.

   a. Do voters who live in rural areas tend to support the same party as urban voters?

   b. Are there certain regions that are more likely to support a particular party, regardless of the leader or the issues?

   c. Do certain areas of your own province tend to be dominated by particular parties or ideologies?

   d. Are people more likely to vote in municipal, provincial, or federal elections?

What conclusions can you draw about the voting patterns of Canadians? Present your findings on maps, charts, or graphs, as well as in written form.

14. Organize a list of suggestions for increasing voter turnout in federal and provincial elections. How might you persuade students to vote in school elections? Would you use similar or different techniques to promote increased voter turnout?

15. Select one of the pressure groups mentioned in this chapter (or another group of your choosing) and investigate its history, political activity, membership numbers, and goals. Try to evaluate the influence of the group on government policy and decision making.

11

Canada's Legal System

FOCUS ON

- What is the principle of the rule of law?
- What is the difference between civil law and criminal law?
- What are the origins of Canadian law?
- What are Canadians' legal rights under the Charter of Rights and Freedoms?
- How is the Canadian legal system structured, and how does it function?
- What is the purpose of the Canadian penal system?
- How may Aboriginal Canadians' problems with the justice system be addressed?
- What are the major provisions of legislation regarding youth crime?
- What are some of the most critical legal issues facing Canadians today?

Counterpoints Issue

- Should Canada reinstate the death penalty for murder?

The Supremes, by Charles Pachter, 1986. This serigraph (silkscreen lithograph) is the artist's vision of judges in the highest courts in the land. Pachter is a painter, sculptor, printmaker, designer, lecturer, and historian. He is renowned for producing art that is contemporary and witty yet serious.

Expressing ideas What is your opinion of the title for this piece? What do you think the artist is saying about Supreme Court judges?

Introduction

Laws influence almost everything we do in our daily lives. For example, they affect our education, the foods we eat, the entertainment we see, the minimum wage we must be paid at a job, and our conditions of work. Laws also regulate business conduct, trade, immigration, and even the government itself.

Laws spell out the rights, privileges, and powers we enjoy as citizens and balance them with the duties expected of us. They protect our lives and property from criminal conduct. We, in turn, must agree to behave responsibly towards other citizens and towards society. In other words, along with our rights come responsibilities. For example, if we did not all agree to drive at about the same speed on the right-hand side of the road and obey traffic signs, we would soon have chaos on our roads. Without responsibilities, we would soon have no rights.

Canadian laws also reflect the values that we hold in common. As a society, we choose to have laws that protect children, workers on the job, the aged, and minorities. Our laws also recognize and protect basic rights and freedoms. Perhaps most important, we have the right to oppose laws that we feel are unjust and to work to change the law by legal means.

Laws have to be made, enforced, and applied. For this we have legislatures to make the laws (as we saw in Chapter 9), police forces to enforce them, a system of courts to interpret them, and prisons to carry out the sentences of the courts. Together, these make up the Canadian justice system. In this chapter, we will look at the justice system, as well as examine the debate over capital punishment. We will also look closely at some of the alternatives to incarceration for less serious crimes. We will examine issues surrounding legislation aimed at young offenders, and then consider how the new information technologies have affected the justice system.

Figure 11-1 These headlines are examples of the role of the legal system in everyday life in Canada. Newspapers across Canada report daily on legal decisions and instances where laws and regulations have been broken. For our society to function as it does, we require citizens to know that certain laws exist, and that to break these laws can result in action by the state.

Expressing ideas Which of these headlines report on instances of law-breaking? Why do newspapers report on these instances? Which of these headlines report on actions of law enforcers?

The Rule of Law

We are lucky to live in a country that observes the **rule of law**. This means that we are governed by a fixed set of laws that apply to all people equally, regardless of their position in society. What's more, police can only charge an individual for a specific offence, and then only by following proper legal procedures.

A great symbol of the rule of law is the Magna Carta. King John of England signed this document, dated 1215, under pressure from the British barons. Later generations applied the Magna Carta to guarantee many rights for British citizens, including trial by jury and habeas corpus (the right to be brought before a court soon after arrest and released if the judge finds there is no legal charge).

The legal protections Canadians enjoy are in short supply in many places in the world. Some countries have harsh and unfair laws, with police or the army handing out punishments as they see fit. There, citizens cannot expect a fair trial, or perhaps any trial at all. They may not even be told why they are being held in custody.

Those who make the laws are also subject to the rule of law. The Constitution of Canada is the supreme law of Canada. It defines and limits the legal powers of the lawmakers. As part of the Constitution, the Charter of Rights and Freedoms takes precedence over any laws passed by any government in Canada. It protects the fundamental freedoms of Canadians and guarantees their democratic, mobility, legal, equality, and language rights. The Charter does recognize, however, that these rights and freedoms have limits. Section 1 states that they are subject "to such reasonable limits as can be justified in a free and democratic society."

The Main Categories of Law

The two main types of law in Canada are civil law and criminal law. **Civil law** deals with relationships between individuals or groups. **Criminal law** deals with matters that affect society as a

Criminal Law	Civil Law
Murder	Defamation of character
Assault	Trespassing
Kidnapping	Contracts
Theft	Tenant and landlord disputes
Riots	Injuries occurring on private property
Firearms	
Hijacking	Product warranties
Sexual offences	Advertising
Youth offences	Compensation for injuries
Drug offences	Divorce and child custody
	Sales contracts

Figure 11-2 Examples of criminal and civil law issues.

whole. Criminal acts are considered to be committed against the state, not just against individual victims.

Civil Law

Civil law cases usually involve disputes over contracts, property, or personal relationships. Property can be physical (possessions), intellectual (ideas), or creative (artwork). Civil suits can arise over such things as neighbours disagreeing over property damage, accident victims seeking compensation for injuries, or child custody in a divorce case. The person who claims to have suffered harm, loss, or injury to self or property is called the *plaintiff*. He or she sues the alleged wrongdoer, called the *defendant*.

Deciding on the ownership of a physical possession is often difficult. But it can be even harder to assess ownership of creative property, as the following case demonstrates.

Case 1

Neudorf versus McLachlan

The well-known singer Sarah McLachlan was sued in Vancouver in 1998 for copyright infringement and breach of contract. The case was brought by Darryl Neudorf, the former drummer with the band 54-40, who claimed that he co-wrote four of the songs on McLachlan's best-selling 1988 debut album, *Touch*. The album was originally expected to sell only a few thousand copies, but over 600 000 have since been sold. Neudorf told the court that McLachlan "took all the credit for herself; my feelings were hurt." He was credited on the album for preproduction, coordination, production assistance, and inspiration. He wanted credit and payments for what he claimed were collaborations.

McLachlan testified that Nettwerk Studios in Vancouver had brought in Neudorf and others to provide technical assistance and speed up the development of the album. She said he imposed discipline on her schedule and helped her to focus. However, she claimed his job was not to co-write songs: "That was never brought up." McLachlan acknowledged that

Neudorf contributed suggestions to simplify or enhance existing tunes, but denies he ever co-wrote with her. Songwriting, testified McLachlan, is a lonely process that "involves playing for hours and hours, working out things in my head and singing ideas to myself." After hearing all the evidence, the judge ruled in McLachlan's favour.

ACTIVITIES

1. Make a list of what you consider your "rights." Alongside each right, describe a responsibility that right entails. For example, the right to free speech entails the responsibility of not spreading unflattering lies about other people. (This is called slander, and it is against the law.)

2. Imagine you are writing a letter to a friend in another country. Explain the meaning of "the rule of law," and give examples of aspects of our system that show we are governed by the rule of law.

3. **a)** How does Case 1 illustrate the difficulties of giving credit for creative collaboration?

   b) With a partner, discuss what criteria you think should determine ownership of creative property such as songs. At what point should someone be credited as a co-writer? Make a list of questions that could be used as guidelines in such decisions.

Figure 11-3 An optimistic Sarah McLachlan leaves a Vancouver courthouse during her civil trial.

Criminal Law

Most criminal laws are contained in the Criminal Code of Canada, which was passed by federal Parliament in 1892. The Code has been amended many times but remains essentially in its original form to this day.

Breaking a criminal law is considered to be a wrong against Canadian society. For this reason, criminal cases are carried out in the name of the Crown (identified as *R* or *Regina*, the Latin word for queen). Lawyers representing the Crown are called the *prosecution*; those representing the accused person are called the *defence*. Only the federal government can make criminal laws, although the provincial governments help to administer them.

1. Presumption of Innocence

Anyone charged with a criminal offence is presumed to be innocent until proven guilty. The prosecution must prove guilt; the defence does not need to establish innocence.

2. The Criminal Act

In order to prove guilt, the prosecution must establish that the accused has committed an act that is considered a crime under Canadian law.

3. Mens Rea

The prosecution must show that the accused intended to commit a criminal act. This is called *mens rea*, or "the guilty mind."

Figure 11-4 The three basic elements of criminal law.

Figure 11-5 A statue depicting Justice.

Developing understanding Why would artists choose to portray Justice with a blindfold and scales? With a sword? As a woman?

The following criminal case was heard in the British Columbia Supreme Court, in 1999.

Case 2
Regina versus Julia Campagna

On May 30, 1998, an American woman named Julia Campagna smashed her car into another car in Canada near the Peace Arch border crossing. The driver and passenger in the other car, Monique Ishikawa, nineteen, and Kimberley Brooks, eighteen, died instantly in the accident. Campagna was charged with driving dangerously and causing the deaths of the two teenagers.

Campagna admitted to crashing into the car, but claimed that she was not criminally responsible. She had been taking an over-the-counter hunger-suppressant drug called Xenadrine at the time of the accident, which she claimed made her suffer from delusional symptoms.

The prosecution argued that she should be found guilty of manslaughter. Furthermore, they claimed that because of a history of mental illness within her family, Campagna could suffer a mental relapse and once again pose a danger to others.

Justice T.M. Singh found Campagna to be mentally unstable at the time of the accident. However, he gave her an absolute discharge without conditions. Justice Singh cited a Supreme Court ruling from June 1999, which states that people found not criminally responsible because of a mental disorder should not be restricted or punished unless the evidence suggests they pose a danger to society. As he believed that the accused was not a risk to society, Judge Singh did not even require Campagna to visit a psychiatrist for two years, as the Crown had requested.

Canada's Legal Tradition

Except for Quebec, where the civil law is based on the French *Code Napoléon*, Canada's criminal and civil law have their origins in English common law and statutory law. The **common law** was based on the decisions of judges in the British royal courts. It is a system of rules based on past decisions, or *precedent*. The fact that it exists only in past decisions makes common law unique. However, this approach also makes it flexible and adaptable to changing circumstances. Common law is used in most countries that were once part of the British Empire.

Statutory law is set out in acts of Parliament. While most of our criminal laws are in the Criminal Code, other federal acts also outline criminal laws. Some examples include the Narcotics Control Act, the Fisheries Act, and the Youth Criminal Justice Act.

The civil law system used in Quebec comes from a quite different legal tradition and applies only to that province. It is based on Roman law, which codified (arranged) laws into a single book to avoid confusion. Courts in Quebec first look to the Quebec Civil Code, and then refer to previous decisions for consistency.

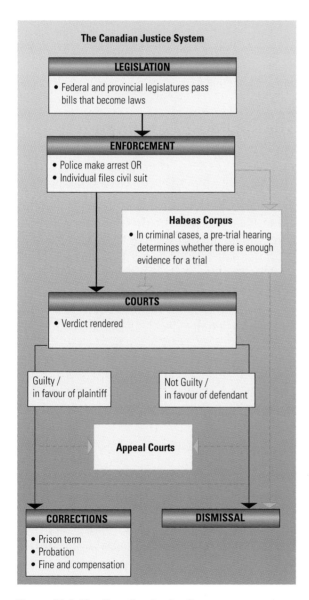

Figure 11-6 The Canadian Justice System.

ACTIVITIES

1. How do criminal and civil law differ? What are the benefits of dividing the law in this way? Select two examples of civil laws. Explain why you think each should or should not be a civil law.

2. **a)** Name the three basic elements of criminal law in Canada, and explain how each protects the rights of the accused.

   b) Explain how each of the three basic elements of criminal law figured in the case of *R v. Campagna*. Which of the three do you think led to controversy about the judgement in this case? Explain your answer.

   c) Some people felt that the sentence in this case was not just. With a partner, role-play a discussion between a person who agrees with Justice Singh and a person who disagrees. In your dialogue, explore the difference between the emotional concept of "justice" and the more rigid concept of "the law."

3. Explain how common law works. What is the main advantage of this system?

The Charter of Rights and Freedoms

Legal Rights of the Individual

Canadians have their legal rights guaranteed by sections 7 to 14 of the Charter of Rights and Freedoms. These rights cannot be taken away without a proper legal process. Many of the Charter cases before the courts are attempts to settle situations where the Criminal Code conflicts with individual rights and freedoms. A landmark case in protecting the legal rights of the accused occurred in 1986, shortly after the Charter came into effect.

7. Everyone has the right to life, liberty, and security of the person.

8. Everyone has the right to be secure against unreasonable search and seizure.

9. Everyone has the right not to be arbitrarily detained or imprisoned.

10. Everyone has a right on arrest or detention:

    a) to be informed promptly of the reasons

    b) to retain and instruct counsel without delay and to be informed of that right

    c) to have the validity of detention validated by way of habeas corpus.

11. Any person charged with an offence has the right:

    a) to be informed without unreasonable delay of the offence

    b) to be tried within a reasonable time

    c) to be presumed innocent until proven guilty

    d) not be denied reasonable bail

    e) to the benefit of trial by jury for maximum punishments of five years or more

    f) if finally acquitted of an offence, not to be tried for it again.

12. Everyone has the right not to be subjected to any cruel or unusual punishment.

13. A witness who testifies in any proceedings has the right not to have any incriminating evidence so given used to incriminate that witness in any other proceedings, except in a prosecution for perjury or for the giving of contradictory evidence. [Evidence that a witness gives in one case cannot be used against that witness in another case, unless the witness lies or contradicts the evidence.]

14. A party or witness in any proceedings who does not understand or speak the language in which the proceedings are conducted or who is deaf has the right to the assistance of an interpreter.

Figure 11-7 Legal rights of Canadians under the Charter of Rights and Freedoms.

Case 3

Regina versus Oakes

David Oakes was convicted in court of possession of narcotics. After his conviction, Oakes brought a motion challenging section 8 of the Narcotics Control Act. That section says that if someone is charged with possession of a narcotic, the onus is on the accused person to prove that he or she was not intending to sell it. If the accused fails to do so, the court assumes that he or she is guilty of trafficking. Oakes claimed that the law as it stood violated his right under section 11(c) of the Charter to be presumed innocent until proven guilty.

Eventually, the case came to the Supreme Court, which ultimately agreed with Oakes. The court declared section 8 of the Narcotics Control Act unconstitutional, which meant that section could no longer be enforced.

The Rights of Law Enforcers

The powers of police to arrest and question suspects, seize evidence, and conduct searches have been steadily reduced since the introduction of the Charter in 1982. Some people argue that this is necessary to protect the rights of citizens. Others maintain that it severely restricts the ability of the police to carry out their duties.

The courts have also strongly upheld the rights of those held or arrested by the police. Prisoners have the right to know the reason for their arrest and to have a judge decide if they are being held legally. They also have the right to contact a lawyer, and the right to a speedy trial. To make sure that accused people are fully aware of their rights, police officers carefully read them the following statement when they are arrested:

> I am arresting you for.... It is my duty to inform you that you have the right to retain and instruct counsel in private, without delay. You may call any lawyer you want. There is a twenty-four-hour telephone service available which provides a legal aid duty lawyer who can give you legal advice in private. This advice is given without charge, and the lawyer can explain the legal aid plan to you. If you wish to contact a legal aid duty lawyer, I can provide you with a telephone number. Do you understand? Do you want to call a lawyer?

Figure 11-8 The police have primary responsibility for enforcing the laws of Canada. In British Columbia, centres such as Vancouver, Victoria, and some smaller communities have municipal police forces, while the RCMP patrols the rest of the province. This arrangement is similar to that in most provinces, although Ontario and Quebec maintain their own provincial police forces.

ACTIVITIES

1. Which three legal rights protected in sections 7 to 14 of the Charter do you think are the most important? Defend your choices.

2. Imagine you are writing the headline for a newspaper about the Oakes case. Ensure that your headline (and any subheading) conveys to the reader the basic information about the case and its importance.

3. In what areas have the powers of the police been restricted since the introduction of the Charter? How would you respond to those who argue that these restrictions interfere with the ability of law enforcement officers to carry out their duty?

4. List reasons for and against setting up a British Columbia provincial police force.

The Court System

Provincial Courts

The provinces are responsible for the administration of justice in Canada. As a result, court systems vary from province to province. In general, provincial supreme courts handle more serious cases, called **indictable offences**, while less serious **summary offences** are handled by lower courts.

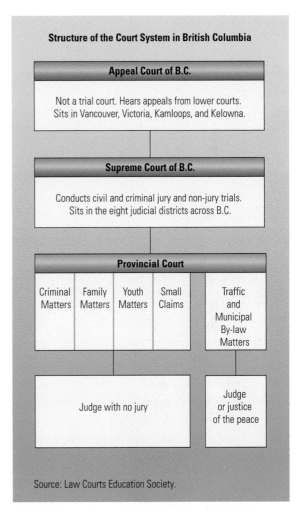

Figure 11-9 The British Columbia court system has three levels. Less serious criminal and civil cases are heard in provincial courts in many communities throughout the province. More serious cases come before the Supreme Court of British Columbia. The Appeal Court of British Columbia is the highest court of appeal in the province.

Once an individual is arrested by the police, the court system takes over. Trials in the lower courts are generally heard by a *judge* or by a *justice of the peace*. Justices of the peace are civil servants who are given some limited powers to hear and judge specific cases such as traffic offences.

In the Supreme Court of British Columbia, the accused is tried by either a judge or a judge and jury. A *jury* is made up of adult citizens called at random from the community. It is a moral and legal duty to serve on a jury if you are called. To be tried in an open court by a jury of our fellow citizens is one of the fundamental legal safeguards we enjoy as Canadians.

Another safeguard in our system is that we can appeal the decisions of lower courts to a higher court. The grounds for appeal are usually that an error of law was made in the conduct of

Innovations

DNA: *Changing the Nature of Evidence*

◀ Since the discovery of the technique in the 1980s, *DNA matching* has become standard procedure for Canadian police forces. Deoxyribonucleic acid (DNA) contains an individual's genetic code. It is present in even small amounts of skin, hair, blood, or other bodily fluids, and acts like a genetic fingerprint. Apart from identical twins, the chances of two people having the same DNA are ten billion to one. DNA can give investigators the evidence they need to link a person to a crime scene.

DNA evidence has helped to solve previously unsolved crimes and free those who have been falsely accused or convicted. For example, almost thirty years after two young mothers were found shot to death in their homes in separate killings, a DNA sample that matched evidence from the crime scenes resulted in first-degree murder charges against one man. These 1970 murders were two of the oldest unsolved cases to come to trial in Canada.

Some criticism has been directed at the ways police can obtain DNA samples for evidence and the processing of those samples. Canada now has a law regulating how DNA should be obtained and handled.

The law gives the police certain powers to obtain DNA samples from suspects in violent crimes but has not allowed them to develop a national DNA bank, as they have requested.

Some people worry that juries may be so awed by the scientific nature of DNA testing that they ignore other evidence. There have already been cases where mistakes made in the laboratory have led to false evidence. And as investigators find more uses for DNA in solving crimes, forensic laboratories are finding they have increased workloads, which may cause them to rush procedures and make errors.

A jubilant Guy Paul Morin is shown here, after his acquittal in the murder of a nine-year-old girl. He spent several years in jail before being cleared by a DNA test. ▼

the trial. The highest court of appeal for criminal matters is the Supreme Court of Canada; however, the Supreme Court does not agree to hear every case that is brought before it.

Judges have the responsibility for interpreting and applying the laws of Canada. In British Columbia, the provincial cabinet, on the recommendations of the attorney general, appoints judges of the Provincial Court. Judges of the Supreme Court of British Columbia and the Court of Appeal are appointed by the federal Cabinet, on advice from the minister of justice.

Judges are expected to avoid commenting publicly on politics and controversial issues. To ensure that they can give unbiased judgements, our laws ensure that judges are free from government interference or influence. For this reason, judges can be removed from the bench only by votes in both the House of Commons and the Senate. Many Canadians do not agree with this system. A controversial comment by a judge, or the release of a prisoner who later commits a crime, usually brings a flood of criticism of the present system and calls for reform. The alternatives most often suggested are for a more open selection process, fixed terms of office, or the election of judges.

The Supreme Court of Canada

The Supreme Court of Canada has been the highest court for all legal issues in Canada since 1949. It decides on constitutional issues and acts as the final court of appeal for some criminal cases. The governor general, on the advice of the prime minister, appoints the nine members of the Supreme Court. The minister of justice encourages lawyers and other judges to recommend appointees. The Canadian Bar Association's national judiciary committee assesses the names put before them, and makes recommendations for suitable candidates, based on their service to the legal system and to the people of Canada.

Three of the nine justices must be from Quebec. Traditionally, three others come from Ontario, one from the Maritimes, and the remaining two from the western provinces. Of these nine, the prime minister chooses one to act as

Figure 11-10 In 1982, Bertha Wilson (top) became the first woman to be named to the Supreme Court of Canada. Eighteen years later, Beverley McLachlin (bottom) became the first female chief justice.

chief justice. Beverley McLachlin, appointed to the post in 2000, is the first woman to hold that position. Born in Alberta, Chief Justice McLachlin became a lawyer before being appointed to the Supreme Court of British Columbia. In 1994, she was appointed to the Supreme Court of Canada. "Growing up," Chief Justice McLachlin has said, "I had no sense that there were limitations on me because I happened to be a woman."

The importance of the Supreme Court in the everyday lives of Canadians has grown since the introduction of the Charter of Rights and Freedoms. The Court's decisions set precedents that are defining our rights and, in some cases, changing our legal system. No one can alter the decisions of the Supreme Court, unless Parliament passes a constitutional amendment. Seven provinces, totalling at least 50 per cent of the population of all provinces, must approve such an amendment.

Today the media regularly report Charter decisions made by the Supreme Court. Since 1982, some of the Court's most newsworthy judgements have included decisions to strike down a government abortion law, uphold cruise missile testing, condemn unfair treatment on the basis of pregnancy, affirm Aboriginal rights, and grant survivor benefits to same-sex couples.

The Supreme Court has a number of options when enforcing rights and freedoms in its decisions. It can indicate that the law no longer applies to anyone, or that it doesn't apply in the case in question. The Court often goes beyond merely giving a judgement. It may also provide for a way to right the wrong. For example, in the case of a person denied access because of a disability, it will instruct that the access must be provided.

The entrenching of the Charter in the Constitution has made the decisions of the Supreme Court more important. Should these judgements be based solely on legal interpretations? Or should the Court take social, political, and economic questions relating to the case into account? Does it have the right to amend existing laws unilaterally, without consulting Parliament?

The Supreme Court's recent decisions regarding Aboriginal rights have been among its most controversial in this regard. In several instances, the Court has gone beyond looking at legal precedents. In its decisions, it has also considered the historical mistreatment of Aboriginal groups and their existing social and cultural needs. Supporters have praised this more liberal approach in cases such as Delgamuukw (see Chapter 8).

However, critics claim the Supreme Court has sometimes gone too far. Some of the decisions it has brought down have required that laws actually be rewritten, without benefit of bills, debates, or the input of elected representatives:

> Some judges [of the Supreme Court] love the exercise of legislative power through the bench, believing that the courts are the last repository of social conscience and [that they] should use the Charter to make bad things good. These judges proudly go beyond their duty to strike down laws that unreasonably offend Charter rights, and amend laws.... Supreme Court judges are appointed by the prime minister, with no public consultation. We simply must insist that this change so that we can determine the judicial philosophy of qualified candidates and weigh in on what kind of court we are creating.
>
> Source: William Thorsell, "How to keep the Supreme Court from fishing off Parliament's dock," *Globe and Mail*, October 16, 1999.

ACTIVITIES

1. What are the advantages and disadvantages of the jury system for an individual accused of a crime? Why is the right to trial by jury considered such an important part of democracy?

2. What safeguards are taken to ensure that Canadian judges are free from interference? What might be some of the drawbacks of these safeguards?

3. Explain how the Charter of Rights has changed the role of the Supreme Court in the lives of Canadians. What problems are associated with this new role?

Problem Solving

When an issue is controversial, it often arouses strong emotions, which makes it hard to evaluate the most effective solution. This is where a formal, step-by-step problem-solving process can be helpful. Try using this approach to determine the most effective way to choose judges in Canada. Look over the steps below. Then, answer the questions that follow in order to practise your skills in problem solving.

Steps in Problem Solving

1. *Identify the problem.* Make sure you have a clear understanding of the issue you wish to examine. Write the problem in the form of a question that you will try to answer.

2. *Gather information about the issue.* Take particular note of possible solutions offered by others.

3. *List options or solutions.* Include those you have read about as well as any original ideas you come up with.

4. *Consider the advantages and disadvantages* of each option, and choose the one you think is the best.

5. *Evaluate the effectiveness* of your solution.

Applying the Skill

1. The chart below lists some of the most frequently suggested alternatives to the present system of selecting judges. Do research in magazines, newspapers, textbooks, and on the Internet to find out more about each option. As you read, note any other solutions you hear about or think of on your own. Copy the chart and add these solutions to it. Consider methods used in other countries, such as the United States, France, or Germany. For each option, list the advantages and disadvantages in the appropriate columns.

2. Use the information in your chart to decide on the solution that you think is preferable. Then write a paragraph explaining the reasons for your choice.

3. Test your ideas by talking to an informed person who can give you an opinion on whether they would work. You might invite a guest from the legal community to address the class and evaluate your proposals.

4. What does Thorsell mean by "judicial philosophy"? Which option do you think he favours?

How Should Canada's Judges Be Chosen?

Option	Advantages	Disadvantages
Judges chosen by members of the government in power, holding office until retirement (existing system in Canada)		
Judges chosen by government in power for a fixed term		
Potential judges scrutinized by Parliament before being appointed		
Judges elected for a fixed term		

The Penal System

When people are convicted of a crime, the judge has a number of options for sentencing. In some cases, he or she can order that the guilty person be given a complete discharge. More often, the judge may sentence the offender to one of the following:

pay a fine to the court; make some kind of restitution to the victim; perform a number of hours of community service; or serve time in prison. In instances such as a first offence, where a jail term may not be appropriate, the judge may place the offender on *probation*. For a set period of time the offender must follow the conditions determined by

counterpoints

Should Canada Reinstate the Death Penalty for Murder?

In 1976, Canada abolished the death penalty by a majority of just six votes. In 1987, a motion to reinstate capital punishment was defeated by eleven votes. In both cases, members of Parliament were given the freedom to vote according to their conscience, rather than in accordance with official policies of their parties.

Here is how Prime Minister Pierre Trudeau expressed his stand in favour of abolishing capital punishment in the 1976 debate:

> My primary concern here is not compassion for the murderer. My concern is for the society which adopts vengeance as an acceptable motive for collective behaviour. Vengeance and violence damage and destroy those who adopt them.... Respect for human life is absolutely vital for the rights and freedom we all enjoy. Even the life of the most hardened criminal must be accorded some degree of respect in a free society. If we take that life without proven purpose ... we weaken dangerously one of the fundamental principles which allows us to live together in peace and harmony, and mutual respect.

The historian Jacques Barzun, Dean of Columbia University, presented another point of view when he wrote in favour of retaining the death penalty in the United States:

> The propaganda for abolition [of the death penalty] speaks in hushed tones on the sanctity of human life, as if the mere statement of it as an absolute should silence all opponents who have any moral sense. But most of the abolitionists belong to nations that spend half their annual income on weapons of war and that honor research to perfect means of killing.
>
> ...[Sanctity of life] should inspire a comparative judgment: there are hundreds and indeed thousands whom, in our concern with the horrors of execution, we forget: the victims of violence....

For and Against

Those in favour of capital punishment claim it will cut down on the number of murders—first, by stopping those who have murdered from ever doing so again, and second, by persuading other would-be murderers not to commit the crime. Those against capital punishment claim it has no positive effect on the murder rate. They point to studies in Texas, California, and the midwestern United States, where the death penalty is still in force, that found the number of executions was unrelated to murder rates. Furthermore, they note that in the ten years following the abolition of the death penalty in Canada, the crime rate went down but convictions for first-degree murder doubled, from 10 to 20 per cent. One possible reason for this may be that juries are more likely to find someone guilty of murder if they know their decision is not a matter of life or death.

Another common argument against capital punishment is that mistakes can be made. Eight Canadians convicted of murder have had their life sentences overturned in recent years. If Canada still had the death the court and report regularly to a probation officer, who makes sure the individual is following the terms of the probation.

Even when a jail term is deemed necessary, the judge has some flexibility in imposing a sentence. However, in general the maximum sentence is life in prison. In Canada this means twenty-five years without *parole*, the right to early release for good behaviour. Life sentences are reserved for particularly serious crimes, such as murder. A person who is convicted of many serious offences and shows no sign of change can be declared a dangerous offender and be kept in prison indefinitely.

penalty, some of these falsely convicted people might now be dead. But supporters of the death penalty counter that in many cases there is no room for doubt, and in such instances judges should have the option of sentencing the offender to either life in prison or the death penalty.

Let the People Decide?

Public opinion in Canada on the issue has remained fairly consistent over the last twenty-five years, with about 70 per cent of Canadians in favour of capital punishment for first-degree (planned) murder. Should politicians, then, abide by the wishes of the general public and reinstate capital punishment in Canada?

In 1996, a member of the Reform Party (now the Canadian Alliance Party), Bob Ringma, introduced a private member's bill. It advocated that a national referendum be held on the following question: "Do you agree that if a person is found guilty of first-degree murder the judge or jury should have the option of sentencing the person to life imprisonment or the death penalty?" Ringma claimed that it was the duty of elected representatives to carry out the will of the people, not act on their own conscience:

> Who should decide this question, our leaders, our elites, or the people? The resistance out there to even asking the question tells me two things. First, our leaders and our elites in this country do not trust the judgement of ordinary people. Second, the elites think they know best. More than that, they are absolutely convinced they know best.

Those speaking against the bill, such as Michel Bellehumeur, Bloc Québécois MP for Berthier-Montcalm, countered this argument by claiming that:

> [w]e do not have to hold a referendum on every issue on which we believe that the public may have a different view or ... simply to wash our hands of it. We have been given the mandate, each one of us in our respective ridings, to represent our constituents and express the opinion which we believe to be the majority's.

Others who oppose a referendum point out that although national polls consistently show a majority favour reinstatement of capital punishment, this support tends to decrease when the issue is looked at in more depth in the media. Support for the death penalty decreased from 73 per cent to 61 per cent when the issue was being debated in the media and in Parliament in 1987. And in 1998, one survey found that the percentage of Canadians in favour of reinstatement dropped to an all-time low of 48 per cent, with 47 per cent opposed. The pollsters suggested that the drop was at least partly a result of publicity surrounding a Canadian prisoner, Stanley Faulder, who was on death row in a Texas jail at the time.

Analysing the Issue

1. Organize a debate on the following proposition: *Resolved—That Canada should reinstate the death penalty for first-degree (planned) murder.*

2. Canadian society considers murder our most serious crime. Assuming the death penalty is not an option, what sentence do you think is appropriate for those convicted of first-degree murder?

3. Do you think politicians should vote according to their conscience on moral issues such as the reinstatement of capital punishment, even if this goes against the wishes of their constituents? Give reasons for your answer.

Figure 11-11 David Milgaard (left) and Donald Marshall (right) were both falsely convicted of murder and served long prison sentences for crimes they did not commit. In both cases, evidence favourable to the defence had been hidden.

Thinking critically Should the cases of Milgaard and Marshall have any bearing on the way we deal with people convicted of crimes? Why or why not?

Prisoners serving sentences of under two years go to provincial prisons; those with longer sentences serve them in federal institutions. Prisons may be minimum-, medium-, or maximum-security institutions, according to the level of threat the inmates pose to society and other inmates.

The purpose of the corrections system in Canada is to protect society by controlling dangerous individuals and helping offenders to become law-abiding citizens. Our corrections system is based in part on the principle of *rehabilitation*, the belief that inmates can be brought back into society as useful citizens. Many Canadians support a system that is designed to rehabilitate the prisoner by providing educational and vocational programs.

However, others wish to see the guilty punished and complain that conditions in prisons—particularly at minimum-security institutions—are too comfortable. Critics of the present system claim that it has gone too far in promoting rehabilitation and has neglected the need to punish wrongdoers. They feel that the parole system, which allows prisoners with good behaviour to apply for early release after serving only one-third of their sentence, is too lenient.

Figure 11-12 In 1999, the federal solicitor general announced the closing of the Kingston Prison for Women. Overcrowding and poor facilities led to criticism of its lack of success in rehabilitating inmates. "P4W," as prisoners called it, will be replaced by smaller regional facilities that will try to be more effective in rehabilitation and will also allow the women to be closer to their families.

An Alternative to Prison: Restorative Justice

David Milgaard spent twenty-three years in prison before the Supreme Court of Canada ordered his release. He is critical of a prison system that has "people sit inside prisons and do nothing with their lives…. A perfect justice system would be fair, not punishment oriented." Milgaard speaks for many people who think prison sentences are inappropriate when the accused poses no danger to the public.

Canada has one of the highest rates of imprisonment, or *incarceration*, in the Western world. In 1998, the incarceration rate in Canada was 129 per 100 000 people. By contrast, Norway had only fifty-three prisoners per 100 000. It costs more than $60 000 a year to keep an inmate in custody, and a little more than $10 000 to supervise him or her on release. Those who want longer prison terms see them as a way to stop people from breaking the law. However, as the prison population in Canada continues to grow, the justice system has begun to look for alternatives to prison.

In many Canadian communities, *restorative justice* is being used as an alternative to incarcer-

ation for first-time offenders or for people who commit less serious crimes. Rather than focussing on punishment, restorative justice tries to repair the damage that has been done. Victims, offenders, and other people in the community work together to find ways for the offender to make amends directly to the victim.

In one British Columbia case, an elderly woman who found it hard to get around after being hit by a speeding driver accepted that the young man was genuinely sorry and approved a plan for restorative justice. After apologizing to her, the youth was required to do chores for the woman, take on the volunteer work she could no longer carry out, and help her get around as she recovered from her injuries. The court agreed to accept a guilty plea and postpone sentencing until it could review the young man's efforts to undo the damage he had caused.

Restorative justice does not work for all offenders, and not all victims are willing to accept community-sentencing forums instead of court action. However, while this may not be the only solution to the problem of administering justice, it does provide one alternative to prison.

Justice for Aboriginal Peoples

Twelve per cent of male and 17 per cent of female convicts in federal prisons are Aboriginal, although Aboriginal people make up only 3 per cent of Canada's general population. A combination of discrimination and cultural differences are often cited as reasons for this overrepresentation.

The high number of Aboriginal offenders in the prison system makes it important for the courts to look at alternative sentencing methods. In 1999, the Supreme Court of Canada suggested that judges look at restorative justice measures when dealing with Aboriginal offenders. Formal restorative justice programs are already practised in many Aboriginal communities in Canada. The offender is brought before a *healing circle* that includes the victim, elders, and other community members, as well as a judge and lawyers. Together, members of the circle try to come up with sentences that will help the victim heal his or her wounds and the offender make amends. In one northern community, a young man accused of assault was required to spend time on a remote island as his ancestors had done to reflect on his misdeed and be spiritually cleansed.

Even more far-reaching is the belief that First Nations should have their own justice systems. The Nisga'a Treaty in British Columbia provides for Nisga'a control of the justice system on their own lands, but in accordance with the laws of Canada. Opponents argue that all Canadians should be treated equally under the law. They object to what they see as a system of justice that is beyond the control of Parliament.

A number of reserves also have Aboriginal police forces. Since 1991, the federal government has been helping Aboriginal communities establish police services that respond to their cultural needs. Sometimes, First Nations choose self-administered police services, such as the Nishnawbe-Aski Police Service (NAPS) in northern Ontario. The NAPS has thirty-three officers, the majority of whom are Aboriginal. They are responsible for policing many First Nations communities in northern Ontario. Other communities have chosen the RCMP's First Nations Community Policing Service (FNCPS). The Nuu-chah-nulth community of Ahousaht on the west coast of Vancouver Island established the first all-Aboriginal detachment of the RCMP–FNCPS in Canada.

Questions

1. What measures have been adopted to improve the functioning of the justice system in relation to Aboriginal people?

2. Why do you think Aboriginal police officers might be more effective in dealing with Aboriginal offenders?

3. What general principles about the effective operation of a justice system can be learned from the example of Aboriginal people in Canada?

Figure 11-13 The healing circle brings together all those concerned about the wrongdoer and involved with the offence. Aboriginal elders, the families involved, police, and a judge attempt to reach agreement on the most appropriate consequence for a wrongful act.

Youth and the Law

Government, schools, and social agencies are greatly concerned over the problem of youth crime. People dealing with juveniles who commit crimes, and so become involved with the justice system, want to ensure that youths get a second chance. Yet few Canadians are aware that the incarceration rate for young offenders in Canada is even higher than in the United States—approximately one-third of juvenile offenders are sentenced to time in custody. The problem is complicated by a lack of community support networks that would allow for alternative sentences.

High-profile cases of youth crime that are reported in the media usually lead to debate on a range of related issues: Under what circumstances should youths be tried in adult court? At what age is one too young to be charged with an offence? How long should the maximum sentence be for juveniles? Should any record of crimes remain on their files after they become adults?

Historical Background

Before the twentieth century in Canada, youths received no special treatment when they broke the law. Both boys and girls were sentenced to prison terms, and sentences were often harsh. One ten-year-old boy, committed in 1845 to a seven-year term, was publicly lashed fifty-seven times in the space of eight and a half months. His offences were staring and laughing. Once in prison, young people were subject to the same rules as adults—and to the foul conditions typical of nineteenth-century prisons. The emphasis was on punishment and strict discipline, not on reforming the prisoner.

By the end of the nineteenth century, attitudes towards young offenders began to change. There was a growing movement to reform the justice system and treat young people differently from adults. People who belonged to the movement thought youths should be treated not as criminals needing punishment, but as young people requiring help and understanding. Gradually, the justice system began to adopt these principles. The emphasis on rehabilitating and reinte-

1892 Criminal Code of Canada states that no one under the age of seven years can be convicted for an offence, and any persons under the age of fourteen must know the nature and consequences of their conduct and appreciate that it was wrong.

1893 Youthful Offenders Act separates youthful offenders from older offenders and advocates reform and rehabilitation.

1908 Juvenile Delinquency Act marks a turning point, proclaiming that "every juvenile delinquent shall be treated, not as a criminal, but as a misdirected and misguided child."

Youth courts established to provide young offenders with help and guidance. These courts are slow to be established; by the 1920s there are only twenty in all of Canada.

1929 Juvenile Delinquency Act is amended to allow judges to impose probation, fines, or detention for sixteen- to eighteen-year-olds accused of crimes, rather than treating them as adults. Act remains in effect until the 1980s.

1984 Young Offenders Act applies to all young people from twelve to eighteen years of age and deals with all offences in the Criminal Code. It makes jail sentences more lenient, setting the maximum sentence for a young offender at three years.

1985 Young Offenders Act is amended to allow naming of a youth who is considered dangerous.

1992 Sentences under Young Offenders Act are lengthened to allow a maximum prison sentence of five years for a young offender convicted of murder.

2000 Youth Criminal Justice Act is passed, distinguishing between violent and non-violent crimes. Harsher measures are in place for violent offenders. Also strengthens efforts to rehabilitate young people who commit crimes, and encourages alternatives to custody for non-violent youth.

Figure 11-14 Legislation relating to young offenders.

grating young offenders into society has guided most legislation to this day.

However, the passage of the Young Offenders Act in 1984 caused much debate as to whether the system had now become too lenient towards young offenders. Many people felt that the moderate penalties included in the act were no longer tough enough to stop young people from committing serious crimes. More recent laws, including the Youth Criminal Justice Act, passed in 2000, represent a move towards harsher penalties, especially for more serious crimes committed by youths.

Many people still defend the basic philosophy of reform that has guided past legislation. They argue that individuals should not be burdened throughout their lives for mistakes made in their youth. They point to the need for more social programs and community resources to help young people in trouble with the law. In Quebec, which has the lowest youth crime rate in Canada, the emphasis is on dealing with youth crime through restorative justice programs, in which young offenders meet face-to-face with their victims.

Rights of Young Offenders

Youths between the ages of twelve and seventeen who are charged with a crime are guaranteed the same legal rights under the Charter as any other Canadian citizen, including the right to a lawyer and the right to a fair trial. In addition, they are granted special rights because of their age. Details of their trial may be reported, but most young offenders charged with or convicted of a crime cannot be named, nor can any other young person involved in the proceedings. Police and court records relating to the crime remain confidential and will be destroyed when the youth becomes an adult. Exceptions to this rule include cases involving youths aged fourteen or older who commit serious crimes, such as violent assault, aggravated sexual assault, or murder.

In addition, cases involving young offenders are usually dealt with in a separate youth court. A judge alone hears the case and decides on a sentence. In youth court, a sentence is called a *disposition*. A disposition can vary from a jail term, to a fine, to community service. The maximum jail term for a young offender is five years. However, youths as young as fourteen who are charged with

serious crimes such as murder or violent assault can be transferred to adult court to face the same penalties as an adult. A pattern of serious violent offences will also result in adult sentences.

Youth Court Dispositions

- Absolute discharge
- Conditional discharge (depending on circumstances)
- Fine of up to $1000
- Payment of costs of the crime up to 240 h of community service
- Report to a probation officer regularly for up to two years
- Open or secure custody for up to five years

Figure 11-15 Sentences a youth court judge can order.

Expressing ideas How might sentences for youths convicted of crimes be made more effective in preventing repeat offences? Explain your reasoning.

ACTIVITIES

1. **a)** What is the main purpose of prisons in the Canadian justice system? What is the main criticism levelled against this approach?

   b) Explain the benefits, drawbacks, and limitations of restorative justice programs as an alternative to imprisonment.

2. You are a lawyer who is helping a young person accused of a crime. Briefly explain his or her rights as a young offender.

3. Find and evaluate recent examples of the media's treatment of youth crime. In your opinion, do the examples support the contention that the media sensationalize youth crime? Explain your answer.

4. Describe three changes you would make in the law respecting young offenders if you were the federal justice minister. Give reasons for each recommendation.

Information Technologies and the Law

The pace of change in the twentieth century was staggering, and shows no sign of slowing down. Great changes in information technology are racing ahead of the ability of the justice system to regulate them. Is the justice system flexible enough to respond to these new challenges?

Copyright Laws and the Internet

The new information technologies are challenging traditional copyright laws. For example, what does it mean for the music industry if anyone can download high-quality recordings from the Internet without ever leaving home—or paying a cent to the artist or recording company? New music recording technologies have shaken the music industry, leading to numerous civil suits in the United States against companies that sell file-trading applications and provide services that allow the downloading and trading of digital music files.

On the other hand, some musicians believe that the legal uses of the new technologies are a boon. They offer lesser-known musicians a way of making their music available to a huge audience at virtually no cost, and without the need for an agent or the backing of a record label. Many more established artists have used the same technology to increase sales of their albums, by allowing fans to download previews and buy them on-line.

Technology-Assisted Crime

The Internet has also provided a whole new arena for more serious crimes. Web sites offering gambling, pornography, fraudulent schemes, and information from hate groups abound. If a site originates in a country where such activities are legal, then there is little Canadian police or courts can do to stop them.

The difficulty of regulating the Internet was recognized by the *Canadian Radio-television and Telecommunications Commission* (CRTC), the body responsible for regulating communications in Canada, when it decided not to try to control Internet sites as it does radio and television broadcasting in Canada. The Commission ruled that general laws governing hate propaganda, pornography, and other questionable material were sufficient to protect Canadians.

Figure 11-16 In 1998, the band Metallica sued the music Web site Napster over copyright issues. Napster was selling software that allowed users to download music files from the Internet illegally.

Thinking critically
Who stands to gain from file-downloading technology such as this? Who stands to lose?

Figure 11-17 While computers have created many new problems for law enforcement, they have also opened up new opportunities for crime prevention. Most police departments are linked to the Canadian Police Information Centre (CPIC), which is in turn linked to the International Criminal Police Organization (Interpol). Both these agencies have central databases that can provide Canadian police with up-to-date information.

Even electronic mail (e-mail) can be used to commit crimes. Despite precautions, large computer systems can be attacked by deliberately planted computer viruses—self-replicating programs designed to destroy data or infect e-mail. Tracing these crimes back to their source is a difficult and time-consuming process.

With the amount of sensitive information now stored on computers, issues of privacy and security are crucial. Amateur programmers, called hackers, can break into computer systems illegally and steal information without ever leaving their homes. With no actual crime scene to examine, police have had to adapt to the new reality of "cyber crime."

Meanwhile, efforts are increasing to give officers the means to deal with criminals who take advantage of the improvements in information technology. The *Canadian Centre for Information Technology Security* (CCITS) is a joint initiative of the University of British Columbia and the Police Academy at the Justice Institute of British

Columbia. The goal of the CCITS is to help police deal effectively with technology-assisted crime and threats to information security.

ACTIVITIES

1. With a partner, make a two-column organizer listing reasons to support and reasons to oppose the regulation of the Internet. Use the information from the organizer to defend your viewpoint in a summary paragraph.

2. Think of a slogan for an advertising campaign with the goal of stopping the illegal downloading of music recordings from the Internet. The campaign should be aimed at teenagers.

3. List ways that the Internet and information technologies could be seen as a positive development for law enforcement. Do you think these benefits outweigh the problems, or vice versa? Defend your opinion.

LOOKING BACK

Develop an Understanding

1. Imagine you are presenting a summary of the Canadian justice system for a brochure aimed at new immigrants. What features of our system would you emphasize? Why?

2. "If one man can be allowed to determine for himself what is law, every man can. That means first chaos, then tyranny. Legal process is an essential part of the democratic process." In your own words, explain what the speaker means. Give reasons why you agree or disagree with this statement.

3. The right to be presumed innocent until proven guilty is one of the foundations of Canada's system of justice. Imagine what might happen if the reverse were true, and you were presumed to be guilty as soon as you were charged with a crime. Draw a cartoon or describe a scene that illustrates the difficulties such a fundamental change might cause.

4. Why do you think criminal law is under federal jurisdiction? Assess the benefits and drawbacks for Canadians if the provinces were allowed to make criminal law.

Explore the Issues

5. Discuss any circumstances in which you think young offenders should be treated the same as adults, and the circumstances in which they should be treated differently.

6. Review the measures taken by the government during the 1970 October Crisis. (See Chapter 8.) Assess the possibility of imposing such measures today in the face of the safeguards provided by the Charter of Rights and Freedoms.

7. Imagine you have been hired by the attorney general to develop strategies to reduce the number of Aboriginal people in the prison system. Outline your suggestions, and include the benefits and drawbacks of changing to the new system.

8. Prepare notes for a discussion of the following issues:

   a. Does the Supreme Court of Canada exercise too much power in its decisions?

   b. At what age should a young person be tried in adult court?

   c. To what degree should retribution be part of the purpose of our penal system?

   d. What are the alternatives to incarceration for lawbreakers, and how effective do you consider each of these in preventing the lawbreakers from re-offending?

9. In a group, brainstorm five essential points that should be taken into account in reforming the Canadian penal system.

10. Look through local newspapers for articles on criminal and civil cases. Explain the points of law discussed in each article. Estimate what percentage of the paper is devoted to reporting criminal acts. Evaluate its impact on the public's perception of crime rates in Canada.

Research and Communicate

11. Invite a police officer to address the class on a topic related to crime or the justice system in British Columbia.

12. The Canadian system of justice differs significantly from that in some other countries. In a group, research the justice system in a country that does not follow the British tradition, such as Switzerland, France, Egypt, India, Russia, or Japan. Present your findings in a display comparing and contrasting these legal systems with Canada's.

13. As a class, conduct a poll on one or more of the issues in this chapter, such as the death penalty, computer crime, or youth and the law. Report your conclusions using graphs, charts, or other means.

14. Research one of the following careers: police officer, court worker, lawyer, or parole officer. Present your findings in a colourful brochure aimed at students who are considering a career in this area.

15. In a group, brainstorm a list of technological advances in the last 100 years that have helped the police fight crime. How would you rank DNA matching as a tool?

12

The Era of Human Rights

*I*n the latter part of the twentieth century, various groups in Canada became increasingly concerned with establishing and protecting their rights. Cree artist Jane Ash Poitras investigated some of the issues that lay at the heart of Aboriginal concerns about human rights in works such as *Diluted Indians Ride Across History* (1990), shown here.

Expressing ideas What traditional symbols can you identify in this painting? Why do you think Poitras chose this title? How might the views expressed in this painting have influenced views about human rights?

Introduction

"I'm sorry, we have no more one-bedrooms available."

"But yesterday when I was here, you said..."

"I'm sorry. They're all gone."

The woman was puzzled. Just yesterday, when she had come to inquire about renting one of these suites in the Fraser Valley, the caretaker had seemed friendly and helpful. Now she had come back with her husband, and the caretaker seemed suddenly cold.

After a lot of persuading, the caretaker did agree to show them one of the more expensive two-bedroom units. Despite the higher price, the couple decided to take it. However, while they were in the process of filling out the application, the caretaker took the paper from them and refused to return it. The building superintendent later turned down their incomplete application, and the suite went to someone else.

The couple were convinced that they had been the victims of discrimination. The woman who first spoke to the caretaker was fair-skinned, while her husband was of Indo-Canadian descent. It was only when the husband showed up that the caretaker became so cold and unhelpful.

Human rights abuses such as this one occur frequently across the country. Fortunately for the couple in question, they could seek help from the legal system. The British Columbia Human Rights Tribunal heard their case and agreed that they had been victims of racial discrimination. Because the suite they finally rented was more expensive than the original unit, they were awarded compensation for extra rental expenses. They also received $2000 as compensation for injury to their dignity and self-respect.

In this chapter, you will explore what human rights are, and how they are defined by the United Nations. You will learn about Canada's efforts to guarantee human rights through the Charter and other laws. The chapter also examines the human rights status of particular members of Canadian society, including Aboriginal people, women, and children.

Figure 12-1 In 1990, the Canadian government agreed to allow Sikh RCMP Constable Baltej Singh Dhillon to wear his turban in place of the traditional Royal Canadian Mounted Police hat. Sikhs are required by their religion to wear the turban in public at all times. The decision caused an uproar among some Canadians who felt that this was an unnecessary break with the tradition of the RCMP.

Expressing ideas In what way was the government's decision a matter of human rights? Do you think such a decision would cause the same uproar today as it did over a decade ago? Why or why not?

What Are Human Rights?

The term *human rights* is used so frequently, and in so many different situations, that a simple definition is hard to find. According to one dictionary, human rights are rights that are "considered basic to life in any human society." They include the rights to adequate food and shelter, and protection from abuses such as torture. But we often use the term "human rights" to describe other rights—such as freedom of speech, thought, expression, and religion, or the legal protections outlined in Chapter 11. Other people would add to the list the rights to adequate health care, a basic education, and freedom from economic bondage.

The concept of human rights can vary from culture to culture. For example, some Muslim societies require women to be completely covered when in public and to remain separated from men, except in the privacy of their home. Is this an infringement of their human rights? To some people, cultural practices such as this seem unfair; yet members of this culture would argue that our society places too much emphasis on the individual and not enough on society as a whole.

Despite these different points of view, many people believe that some moral values are, or should be, universal. These are the foundation for human rights around the world.

The Global Movement for Human Rights

Concern for the protection of human rights became a worldwide issue in the twentieth century. Some terrible abuses of human rights had occurred—including the deaths of millions of Africans in the Belgian colony of the Congo before

Figure 12-2 One of the most famous organizations concerned with the protection of human rights is Amnesty International. It monitors human rights violations throughout the world, particularly violations of freedom of speech and religion and the imprisonment and torture of those who speak out against their government.

Expressing ideas What does the candle wrapped in barbed wire symbolize? Why were these colours chosen for the poster?

World War I, the Holocaust of World War II, the torture and death of millions of Cambodians under the dictatorship of Pol Pot, and the mass killings of fellow citizens by rival tribes in Rwanda in the 1990s.

These and other atrocities have strengthened the resolve of the United Nations and human rights organizations to protect the basic rights of all people, regardless of where they live. This global movement for human rights has become increasingly influential in bringing about change in some countries. For example, pressure from human rights organizations helped bring down the racist system of *apartheid* in South Africa. Human rights organizations have also helped expose the issue of child labour in many countries. Even governments have started including human rights abuses as topics for discussion with other governments. In 1989, after the Chinese government brutally suppressed students who were demonstrating for greater democracy, the Canadian government introduced the topic of

human rights in some of its trade talks, hoping to persuade some of its trading partners to increase human rights in their countries.

The Universal Declaration of Human Rights

The Universal Declaration of Human Rights was proclaimed at the United Nations General Assembly in 1948. The Declaration is based on the belief that "all human beings are born free and equal in dignity and rights," and it condemns the "barbarous acts which have outraged the conscience of mankind." This is a reference to the horrors of the Holocaust of World War II. This document is significant because it was the first international statement to recognize that all human beings have specific rights and freedoms.

The Declaration states that:

■ everyone has the right to life, liberty, and security of the person

Figure 12-3 In the last week of May 1989, Chinese students staged a demonstration in Beijing's Tiananmen Square, erecting this statue (left), which they called "The Goddess of Democracy." In the early-morning hours of June 5, government tanks bore down upon the demonstrators camped in the square (top), dispersing the crowd and effectively putting an end to China's fledgling pro-democracy movement. Hundreds of protesters were killed, and many more were jailed.

- no one should be held in slavery, and the slave trade should be prohibited
- no one should be subjected to torture or cruel, inhuman, or degrading treatment
- everyone has the right to recognition everywhere as a person before the law
- no one should be subjected to arbitrary arrest or detention
- everyone is entitled to a fair and public hearing by an impartial tribunal in the case of any criminal charge against him or her
- everyone has the right to freedom of movement and residence.

The Declaration was adopted unanimously by U.N. member states. The Canadian federal government and all the provinces have signed and ratified the Declaration, and it is now binding upon Canada in international law. This means that individuals in Canada can complain to the Human Rights Committee of the United Nations if they believe the Canadian government is not meeting U.N. standards.

up close

An International Criminal Court

Would an international criminal court contribute to a more humane world? Many agencies, including Amnesty International, have called for the creation of a permanent international court to deal with human rights abuses on a global scale. The United Nations International Court of Justice at The Hague in the Netherlands can hear disputes between states only if both sides agree to ask for its help. Temporary courts, or *tribunals*, have sometimes been established to deal with specific events. A famous example of a tribunal court is the Nuremberg Trials, which dealt with atrocities committed during World War II in Germany. At the end of the 1990s, tribunals were set up to investigate war crimes in the former Yugoslavia and the genocide in Rwanda.

In 1998, ninety-eight countries agreed to the establishment of a permanent International Criminal Court (ICC) that would have the power to investigate and prosecute individuals, including political leaders, who commit the following types of crimes:

- **war crimes**, such as the killing, torture, and hostage-taking of civilian populations, or the deliberate and extensive destruction of their property
- **genocide**, or the deliberate mass killing of a national, ethnic, or religious group

- **crimes against humanity**, such as widespread attacks against civilians, including murder, enslavement, deportation, and torture.

The ICC will begin its work once all ninety-eight countries have signed and ratified the U.N. agreement. Some countries, such as the United States and China, are against the creation of a permanent international criminal court. Opponents say they are not willing to let an international body interfere in areas of law affecting their citizens.

Even if these countries can be persuaded to sign the agreement, some observers wonder how effective the ICC would be in prosecuting war criminals. According to the most recent agreement on the ICC—the Rome Agreement of 1998—any member of the U.N. Security Council with a veto would have the ability to stop or postpone an investigation by the court. Furthermore, the ICC could not investigate an incident if the country in question were to say it is already investigating that incident. This means the ICC would have very little power over tyrants who commit crimes against their own people. Some critics fear that peacekeepers, or those involved in humanitarian missions in areas of conflict, might be subject to politically motivated prosecutions by their host country. Countries or

The United Nations has been successful in getting most countries to agree with the general principles of the Universal Declaration of Human Rights. Non-governmental organizations—independent non-profit organizations working to improve people's lives—have also played a large role in promoting acceptance of the U.N. Declaration in developing countries. Yet, the only power the United Nations has to enforce the provisions of the Declaration is to draw world attention to abuses in an effort to bring pressure on the offending countries.

ACTIVITIES

1. In your own words, define human rights.

2. Explain which of the human rights listed in this section were violated in the case of the couple trying to rent the apartment.

3. Why did the members of the United Nations feel it was necessary to prepare the Universal Declaration of Human Rights? What are the problems of enforcing the Declaration?

Figure 12-4 Louise Arbour is a Canadian judge who was appointed as the chief United Nations war crimes prosecutor at the International Court of Justice in The Hague. Here she tours Bosnia as part of her investigation into war crimes in the former Yugoslavia.

Using evidence What kind of evidence do you think Louise Arbour looked for in her investigations into war crimes?

warring factions might fabricate incidents of atrocities in order to discredit their opponents.

Supporters of the ICC argue that the existence of an international criminal court sends a message to the world that a recognized international code of conduct exists, and that those who violate this code will be prosecuted. In this way, the ICC would act as a deterrent to those who are thinking about committing war crimes. Even if accused leaders cannot be arrested, the court would be able to issue international warrants to restrict their movements.

Questions

1. Make a two-column organizer listing points for and against the establishment of the International Criminal Court.

2. What other tools do nations have in order to deal with large-scale human rights abuses? What are the drawbacks of these methods?

Human Rights Legislation in Canada

Before World War II, there were few protections for human rights under Canadian law apart from some individual property, criminal, and civil laws. However, attitudes began to change after 1945, and the rights of minority groups in particular gradually improved. An order-in-council that allowed the federal government to deport any Japanese to Japan, including any children who had been born in Canada, was revoked in 1947. That same year, Canadians of Chinese and East Indian descent won the vote, and the Chinese Immigration Act was repealed, allowing Chinese wives and children to join husbands and fathers who were already Canadian citizens. In 1949, Canadians of Japanese origin who had been relocated during World War II to other parts of Canada were allowed to return to the West Coast and were given the vote. But it was 1960 before Aboriginal people who lived on reserves were allowed to vote in federal elections.

Gaining the right to vote, however, didn't solve the problem of racism and discrimination. The attitude towards Canadians of non-European descent by some Canadians had changed very little:

> The postwar trend in Chinatown was for anyone who could afford better accommodation to move out. Like other Canadian families, Chinese families had aspirations to own their own homes. However, they did not necessarily have their choice of neighborhood. Mr. Gee had put down a deposit on a house in Kitsilano, a crowded middle-class neighborhood that rose up the slope from English Bay. When white neighbors got wind that a Chinese family wanted to move in, they amassed a petition against him. He walked away, losing his deposit.
>
> Source: Denise Chong, *The Concubine's Children* (Toronto: Penguin, 1994), 173.

Prime Minister John Diefenbaker, long a crusader for human rights, made the passing of a bill of rights a priority when he became head of the government. In 1960, his government passed the

Figure 12-5 A Chinese couple vote in the 1963 general election, when for the first time, the federal franchise was free of racial and religious discrimination.

Canadian Bill of Rights. This bill formally recognized and outlined rights already held by Canadians under common law. However, as an act of Parliament, the bill could be amended (changed) like any other piece of legislation, and it did not override other federal or provincial laws. Human rights in Canada weren't solidly entrenched into our legal system until 1982, when the Charter of Rights and Freedoms became part of the new Canadian Constitution.

Human Rights in the Charter

Since 1982, Canadians have had the right to challenge in court any law they believe violates their rights as specified in the Charter. Of course, the courts do not always agree with the challenges made, but Canadians have generally come to believe that the Charter offers them a chance to stand up for their rights, even against powerful governments.

Fundamental Freedoms

Section 2 of the Charter protects the fundamental freedoms of conscience, religion, thought, belief, expression, peaceful assembly, and association. In the past, the federal government has restricted or denied these freedoms. For example, in 1907 it passed the Lord's Day Act, which restricted activities such as shopping on Sundays. This act was overturned in 1985 as contrary to freedom of religion. In 1970, during the October Crisis, the government invoked the War Measures Act, the first time this had happened in peacetime, restricting people's freedom of assembly, association, and expression.

Equality Rights

Section 15 of the Charter guarantees equality "before and under the law." "Before the law" means every individual must have access to the courts. For this reason, we have legal aid programs to make sure that those who cannot afford a lawyer are represented fairly. "Under the law" means that laws passed by the government must treat every individual equally. The courts cannot favour the rights of one group of people over another. Section 15 prohibits anyone, including the justice system or any other branch of government, from discriminating against individuals on the basis of race, national or ethnic origin, colour, religion, sex, age, or mental or physical disability. Some exceptions are allowed that are aimed at improving the conditions of "disadvantaged individuals or groups."

Figure 12-6 This touch-feedback computer technology called TouchWeb allows people who are blind to access the Internet. Wheelchair ramps and other modifications to public buildings and transit systems can enable people with reduced mobility to live more active and productive lives. Section 15 of the Charter prohibits discrimination of the basis of physical disability.

Case 1

Eldridge et al. versus Attorney General of British Columbia, 1995

When John and Linda Warren, who are both deaf, were in the hospital during the birth of their twin daughters, they had no interpreters to explain the birth process. During the delivery, a nurse indicated through hand gestures that something was wrong with the heart rate of one of the babies. Later, the babies were taken away and the parents were given only a note, which said their babies were fine. The Warrens claimed the experience was frightening for both of them. They claimed that the lack of sign interpreters was a violation of their rights under section 15 of the Charter.

Both the Supreme Court of British Columbia and the British Columbia Court of Appeal rejected the Warrens' claim. However, the Supreme Court of Canada found in favour of the plaintiffs. The Court ruled that effective communication is essential for the proper delivery of medical services. They found that failure to provide sign interpreters in certain situations was a violation of section 15. It denies deaf persons equal benefit of the law and therefore discriminates against them. The Court ordered the government of British Columbia to provide deaf persons with interpreters when necessary for effective communication.

ACTIVITIES

1. Section 1 of the Charter states that "The Canadian Charter of Rights and Freedoms guarantees the rights and freedoms set out in it subject only to such reasonable limits prescribed by law as can be demonstrably justified in a free and democratic society." You are one of the British Columbia judges who rejected the Warrens' claim. Write your decision, based on section 1 of the Charter.

2. According to the Supreme Court, were the Warrens being denied equality before the law, or under the law? Explain.

3. List the effects this decision would have on those providing health care. What other groups might find themselves included in this ruling, and with what results?

The Notwithstanding Clause

Section 33 of the Charter gives the federal Parliament or provincial legislatures an escape clause, the **notwithstanding clause**. This clause allows these governments to pass a law, even if that law violates a specific freedom or right guaranteed in the Charter. The use of the notwithstanding clause expires five years after it is invoked, but it may be renewed. The notwithstanding clause was a compromise. Some provincial politicians felt that the Charter, which would be interpreted by judges, would weaken their power as elected lawmakers. The clause gave some power back to them. Critics of the notwithstanding clause claim that it weakens the Charter unnecessarily.

Saskatchewan and Quebec are the only two governments to have used the notwithstanding clause. Saskatchewan used it to protect a law that ordered striking workers back to work. The Supreme Court of Canada later ruled that the back-to-work legislation did not violate the Charter anyway, so the notwithstanding clause was not strictly necessary.

Of greater significance was its use by the Quebec government. In 1976, the Parti Québécois passed Bill 101, sometimes referred to as the

Figure 12-7 A veteran in Montreal responds to Bill 101.

"Charter of the French Language." This law made French the only official language of the province. All employees of the Quebec government would have to perform their work in French. Commercial outdoor signs would all have to be in French, and children of immigrants would be required to attend French, rather than English, schools. Quebec used the notwithstanding clause to override a 1989 Supreme Court decision that declared Bill 101 unconstitutional.

Federal and Provincial Human Rights Legislation

The federal and provincial governments have passed specific laws to deal with particular cases of discrimination. These laws are administered by human rights commissions. The Canadian Human Rights Act covers all federally regulated businesses and agencies including banks, the major airlines, Canada Post, and the national media. The Canadian Human Rights Commission deals with federal human rights complaints. Provincial human rights codes clarify people's rights in areas such as employment, tenancy, and institutions, and are interpreted by provincial bodies.

The B.C. Human Rights Code

Most human rights complaints in British Columbia fall under the British Columbia Human Rights Code. The B.C. Human Rights Code protects you against discrimination on the grounds of age (nineteen to sixty-five), ancestry, colour, family or marital status, physical or mental disability, place of origin, political belief, race, religion, sex, or sexual orientation.

The Code covers employment; tenancy and property purchases; accommodation, services, and facilities customarily available to the public; and hate propaganda.

■ *Employment.* Unfair employment practices are by far the most common complaint heard by the B.C. Human Rights Commission. You cannot be refused work or a promotion because of your age or any of the other grounds listed in the Code. Employers cannot refuse to hire an applicant because of a criminal record if the crime is unrelated to the job. Employment advertisements cannot exclude any category of persons except on the basis of occupational requirements. The Code also requires equal pay for work that is substantially similar.

Figure 12-8 Demonstrators march outside a motel in Toronto in 1997 to protest the arrival of Czech Roma (Gypsies) in Canada. The Roma were applying for refugee status, claiming they were persecuted in their native land. Many had seen a television program describing Canada's human rights legislation.

Thinking critically Is this protester's sign a violation of human rights? Explain your answer.

Tenancy. The Code protects tenants in the same way as employees. As well, a landlord cannot refuse to rent to you (or impose any extra conditions on you) based on your source of income. A landlord can determine whether you can afford to pay the rent, except in the case of older people and those with disabilities.

Accommodation, service, or use of facilities. You cannot be unfairly denied accommodation, service, or use of a public facility. There are two exceptions to this rule. Discrimination on the basis of sex is allowed in matters of public decency (public washrooms and change rooms, for example, can be designated for males or females only). And insurance

counterpoints

Should There Be Limits on Freedom of the Press?

In 1997, the British Columbia Human Rights Tribunal heard a landmark case. It involved a conflict between the right to freedom of expression and the right to live in a society that is free from discrimination. It was the first time a journalist had been investigated by a human rights commission for remarks made in print.

The Canadian Jewish Congress (CJC) filed a complaint against Doug Collins and the *North Shore News* over an article Collins wrote, titled "Hollywood Propaganda." In his article, Collins claimed that the number of Jews who died in World War II was grossly exaggerated and that the media, in supporting the accepted figure of six million, were part of a Jewish propaganda plot. Collins was accused by the CJC of a hate crime for denying in print that the Holocaust really happened. The CJC claimed that Collins's views discriminated against and exposed Jewish persons to hatred, contrary to section 7 of the British Columbia Human Rights Code:

> 7 (1) A person must not publish, issue or display, or cause to be published, issued or displayed, any statement, publication, notice, sign, symbol, emblem or other representation that (b) is likely to ex-

pose a person or a group or class of persons to hatred or contempt because of the race, colour, ancestry, place of origin, religion, marital status, family status, physical or mental disability, sex, sexual orientation or age of that person or that group or class of persons.

In its defence, the newspaper claimed that section 7 (1)(b) of the provincial code restricted freedom of speech and was therefore unconstitutional.

The Tribunal disagreed with the newspaper's claim that the regulation was unconstitutional. It pointed out that section 1 of the Charter of Rights states that a right is subject to "reasonable limits." The court also found that, while the newspaper article was anti-Semitic, offensive, and hurtful to Jewish people, it was not hurtful enough to violate the Code. The Tribunal dismissed the case.

The CJC launched another complaint in 1998 when some of Doug Collins's articles were featured in a Victoria newspaper. This time, the Tribunal, under a different chairperson, found the *North Shore News* and Doug Collins guilty of violating section 7 of the Code. The new Tribunal chairperson put the articles in a social and historical context. He concluded that "through a repetition of anti-Semitic themes the columns ... take on a vicious tone that taps into a centuries-old pattern of persecution and slander of Jews. They perpetuate the most damaging stereotype of Jews."

Clash of Opinions

Public opinion was divided over the outcome of these hearings. Many groups and individuals were upset that companies are allowed to take your sex and physical and mental health into account when calculating insurance costs.

■ *Hate propaganda.* People are also protected against hate propaganda, which means a person cannot publish or display any notice, sign, symbol, emblem, or other representation that is likely to expose a person or class of persons to hatred or contempt.

The British Columbia Human Rights Commission deals with complaints. If it feels the complaint is justified, the Commission may refer cases on to the B.C. Human Rights Tribunal for a hearing.

the first tribunal did not equate anti-Semitism with hate. They also supported the Canadian Jewish Congress's claim that the second decision demonstrated that a citizen could "seek relief for serious grievances under section 7 of the Code while at the same time balancing the interests of free speech." These groups believed the previous decision by the Tribunal was too academic in its interpretation, and they applauded the second Tribunal's common-sense approach to interpreting section 7 of the Code.

Other groups, Canadian press organizations in particular, were concerned about the effect the Tribunal's decision would have on freedom of the press. David Frum, a columnist, took issue with the Tribunal's entire approach:

It is often said ... that a free press is indispensable to a free society. I wholeheartedly agree. Make no mistake: the investigation of Doug Collins is a terrifying attack on our liberties. Collins, unlike James Keegstra and Malcolm Ross (who propounded similar poisonous views), is not entrusted with the education of the young. So long as he avoids libeling anyone, using obscene words, or falling into one of the other small and well-established exceptions to the rule of free speech, he ought to be free to say what he likes, no matter how repulsive or even lunatic. And if he can find a publisher whose standards are low enough, he should be free to publish those views.

Source: *Financial Post*, May 24, 1997.

By contrast, the CJC's position on the media and free speech recognizes the huge influence the media can have on public opinion:

CJC has long recognized the importance of the media's role in reporting and disseminating information in a free and democratic society. While supporting the fostering and protection of individual freedoms, CJC is mindful of the unprecedented power and influence wielded by the media and especially aware of the consequences and the impact that unfair and unbalanced reporting has on minorities in Canada.

Source: CJC Pacific Region Initiatives and Programs, 1995–1998.

Analysing the Issue

1. Write a letter to the editor of a newspaper outlining your views on Doug Collins's claim to the right of free speech. Include your opinion of the decisions reached by the first and second hearings.

2. How credible are the viewpoints of the CJC and David Frum? Can you find evidence of bias in these articles that might affect their credibility? Explain your answer.

3. In his article, David Frum implies that Collins should be treated differently from Keegstra and Ross, who were teachers. What is your opinion of Frum's view? Should different groups have different standards for freedom of speech because of their profession? Consider other groups whom you think should have more or less freedom of speech because of their position in society.

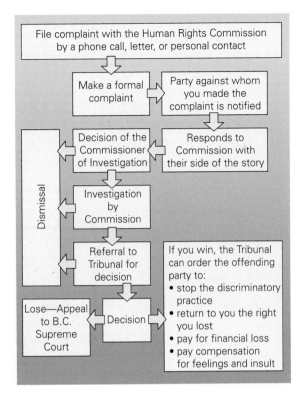

Figure 12-9 How to make a complaint to the B.C. Human Rights Commission.

Interpreting a diagram In your own words, describe the process of making a human rights complaint in British Columbia.

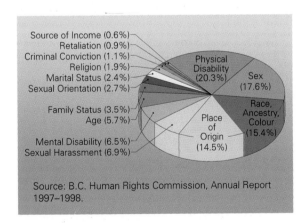

Source: B.C. Human Rights Commission, Annual Report 1997–1998.

Figure 12-10 Complaints to the B.C. Human Rights Commission, 1998.

Reading a graph Do any of the data surprise you? Why? How do you account for the greater number of complaints relating to sex, race, and physical disability?

1. Both the Charter of Rights and Freedoms and the B.C. Human Rights Code restrict age discrimination to those between nineteen and sixty-five. Describe some problems that might occur if this age restriction were removed.

2. Determine which of the following situations contain human rights violations, and under which category they might fall in the B.C. Human Rights Code:

   a) A person in a wheelchair is denied access to a sporting event because the wheelchair can't fit in the space designated for wheelchairs.

   b) A woman working on an all-male crew is annoyed by suggestive remarks made by her co-workers.

   c) A landlord refuses to rent a suite to a group of young people aged sixteen to eighteen years of age because he is afraid they will cause damage and make too much noise.

   d) A group puts up posters for a dance that include some racist lyrics from the songs that will be played.

   e) A woman is refused an interview for a job as a security guard in a mall because the company says it finds men are more effective at controlling groups of young people.

   f) An advertisement for a house rental says that only non-smoking women need apply.

3. Do you consider the notwithstanding clause a necessary addition to the Charter of Rights and Freedoms? Explain your answer.

Aboriginal Rights

As you have seen in earlier chapters, rights taken for granted by most Canadians were only slowly granted to Aboriginal groups. While most of the legal restrictions that had been placed on First Nations are now gone, Aboriginal groups still suffer from serious problems including poverty, poor health, and inadequate housing and education (see also Chapter 14).

Phil Fontaine, a former National Chief of the Assembly of First Nations, expressed the opinion of many First Nations people when he said:

A major part of Canadian history is the story of Canada's dysfunctional relationship with First Nations. The two societies never shared a common perspective on their relationship, but instead of trying to accommodate the differences, Canada … tried to forcibly displace our perspective with the values and culture of Western society.

In July 2000, Canadian Aboriginal leaders presented their case for human rights violations against Canada at the U.N. Working Group on Indigenous Populations. Ashley Iserhoff, a James Bay Cree, told hundreds of diplomats:

> Our experience with Canada is an ongoing violation of our people's fundamental human rights…. Our people are still confined to tiny portions of Canada's land mass, with few or no resources…. Our peoples still mostly live in desolate communities with unsafe drinking water and inadequate sanitation. Our people are still crowded into unsafe and unhealthy dwellings or live homeless on the streets of big cities.

The Charter of Rights and Freedoms has helped to eliminate some of the injustices that existed in law prior to 1982. The case of Jeannette Corbière Lavell is one such example.

Figure 12-11 Jeannette Corbière Lavell with her husband.

Case 2

Lavell versus Regina

Under the Indian Act, an Aboriginal woman who married a non-Aboriginal was no longer considered to be a **status Indian**. Nor were her children. This meant that the woman could no longer live on the reserve, nor receive any of the treaty benefits designated to the band or nation. She was not allowed to participate in band councils. As a final indignity, she was no longer eligible to be buried with her ancestors. None of these rules applied to Aboriginal men who married non-Aboriginal women. In those cases, the non-Aboriginal wives gained Indian status for themselves and for any children born to the marriage.

In 1970, Jeannette Corbière, a member of the Anishnawbe nation in Ontario, married a non-Aboriginal, David Lavell. Once married, she lost her Indian status. Lavell decided to challenge the law. Her case was the first case under the 1960 Canadian Bill of Rights that claimed discrimination on the basis of sex. Lavell lost her case in County Court, but appealed it to the Federal Court of Appeal, which ruled in her favour. The Crown, however, chose to appeal the decision to the Supreme Court of Canada.

In 1973, the Supreme Court on appeal ruled against Lavell. The Court found that, as she was being treated in the same manner as other Aboriginal women who had married non-Aboriginals, she had not been discriminated against. It dismissed the argument that treating Aboriginal women differently from Aboriginal men was discriminatory.

However, Lavell did eventually triumph. When the Charter of Rights and Freedoms was passed, it expanded the equality provisions in the Bill of Rights. The Charter also contained a provision that Aboriginal and treaty rights must be applied equally to men and women. These changes meant that the regulations in the Indian Act were now unconstitutional. In 1985, this part of the act was changed to allow Aboriginal women to maintain their status when they married outside the reserve.

Gender Equity in the Workplace

For several years the United Nations, using measurements based on health, education, and income, has ranked Canada as having the best quality of life of any country in the world. However, it is less impressed with our efforts to deal with gender equality. In this area, Canada ranked only ninth. This finding encouraged efforts to enforce the gender equity provisions of section 15 of the Charter.

Section 15 of the Charter provides guarantees against discrimination based on sex, but this guarantee does not mean that attitudes change quickly. While most Canadians believe in the idea of equity

and fairness, opinions differ as to how to achieve these goals, particularly in the workplace. Women have been and continue to be underrepresented in many traditionally male disciplines, and they are often paid less than men when they perform the same or an equivalent amount of work.

As the table in Figure 12-13 shows, the average earnings of women have been rising, perhaps partly because the number of women in the labour force has increased. However, working women account for nearly 70 per cent of part-time workers. Part-time work generally provides fewer benefits, such as pensions, health coverage, and life insurance.

Section 15 of the Charter allows for special initiatives, such as affirmative action programs, that would improve the situation of those people who traditionally have been discriminated against in the workplace. These include people who have been discriminated against because of "race, national or ethnic origin, colour, religion, sex, age, or mental or physical disability."

But just how far should this principle be extended? Two practices designed to improve employment equity still cause debate: the principle of equal pay for work of equal value, and the use of preferential hiring practices.

Figure 12-12 This cartoon appeared in a national newspaper after the release of a United Nations study ranking Canada as the number one place to live in the world.

Interpreting a cartoon What comment is the cartoonist making about the U.N. findings? How is Canada represented? Why is it represented in this manner?

Year	Women's Earnings	Men's Earnings	Women's Earnings as a % of Men's (1998$)
1989	19 965	33 826	59.0
1990	19 969	33 413	59.8
1993	20 413	31 761	64.3
1996	20 879	32 336	64.6
1998	21 999	34 171	64.0

Source: Statistics Canada, Labour Force Characteristics.

Figure 12-13 Average earnings by sex, full- and part-time.

Equal Pay for Work of Equal Value

One problem that women face in the workplace is the prospect of not being hired for work outside the traditional "job ghettoes," occupations that usually pay poorly and are dominated by female workers. For example, secretarial and nursing positions were once overwhelmingly held by female workers, and as a result the average wages were lower than for equivalent positions held by males:

> Studies have shown that the values attached to various types of work often reflect attitudes based on stereotypes of who does what kind of work and a frequent assumption that the work performed mainly by men is more valuable than work performed mainly by women.
>
> Source: Public Service Alliance Canada Pay Equity Bulletin #42, June 28, 2000.

In order to avoid this form of discrimination, the Canadian Human Rights Act, 1986, states:

> (1) It is a discriminatory practice for an employer to establish or maintain differences between male and female employees employed in the same establishment performing work of equal value.
>
> (2) In assessing the value of work performed by employees employed in the same establishment, the criterion to be applied is the composite of the skill, effort and responsibility in the performance of the work and the conditions under which the work is performed.

Most people agree that female teachers, police officers, and postal workers should be paid at the same rate as their male colleagues (equal pay for equal work). However, some critics claim that it is virtually impossible to compare the value of jobs, especially when those jobs are as different as clerk and plumber, for example.

Preferential Hiring Policies

"Universities hiring, but white males need not apply." So read the headline in a Vancouver newspaper in the summer of 1999. At issue were the employment advertisements of a number of Canadian universities, which clearly expressed a preference for equity groups—meaning female, minority, or disabled candidates. The universities said they were trying to hire instructors who would more accurately reflect the mix of students in university. In order to receive federal government funding, universities were required to set equity hiring targets that reflected the number of higher degrees earned by equity groups.

Employment equity policies have become quite controversial. Some critics argue that they amount to reverse discrimination and are unfair to qualified applicants who cannot be considered for some positions. Critics feel these hiring policies are unnecessary because existing inequities will correct themselves in time.

Case 3

B.C. Public Services Employee Relations Commission versus B.C. Government Service Employee's Union

In 1995, Tawney Meiorin lost her job as a forest firefighter because she took 49.4 s too long to finish a 2.5-km run. She had been doing the job for three years before she failed the new test, which required her to run the 2.5 km in eleven minutes. The test standards were based on the aerobic capacity of several dozen elite male firefighters. Ms. Meiorin's union brought the case to the courts after a B.C. labour arbitrator's decision was overturned by the B.C. Court of Appeal. At issue was whether the running test was a reasonable occupational requirement.

The Supreme Court of Canada, in a unanimous decision, ruled that although the province apparently developed its aerobics test in good faith, it failed to take into account the differing physiology of males and females. It was too easy, the Court stated, for employers to develop difficult standards that could end up excluding particular groups. Madame Justice Beverley McLachlin wrote: "If men and women do not have equal ability to meet the excessive standard, the effect may be to exclude qualified female candidates from employment for no reason but their gender."

The Court said that employers can discriminate in hiring standards only if not doing so would impose "undue hardship" on the employer, and if the standards reflect a legitimate occupational requirement. It ordered the province of British Columbia to compensate Ms. Meiorin for lost wages and benefits.

This ruling was supported by those who saw it as a major step in eliminating one kind of discrimination that had stopped women from being hired for jobs traditionally dominated by men. They pointed out that at one time all police officers had to be exactly 1.78 m tall. By relaxing such restrictions, they said, we gain access to a larger pool of applicants who better reflect the diversity of Canadians.

Critics of the judgement claimed that it would compromise safety standards in the name of political correctness. One editorial claimed that "More people will die in burning buildings in order to ensure that more women can become firefighters."

Figure 12-14 Tawney Meiorin, shown here with her lawyer, smiles as she leaves the Supreme Court of Canada.

ACTIVITIES

1. Summarize the arguments given in Tawney Meiorin's case.

2. What occupations do you think would be justified in imposing discriminatory hiring standards, based on the Supreme Court's requirement of "undue hardship" on the employer? What would the standards be?

3. Define the terms: preferential hiring policy; equity group; employment equity.

4. In a brief essay, explain why preferential hiring programs are controversial.

5. **a)** In a group, brainstorm areas in Canadian society where the laws could still be changed to improve equality in the workplace.

   b) What methods, other than using decisions from the human rights commissions, could be used to promote equality in the workplace?

Children's Rights

A century that began with children having virtually no rights is ending with children having the most powerful legal instrument that not only recognizes but protects their human right.

Source: Carol Bellamy, UNICEF Executive Director.

In 1989, the United Nations General Assembly unanimously adopted the Convention on the Rights of the Child. This Convention is the first legally binding international agreement to include children's civil and political rights. As well, it includes their economic, social, and cultural rights, giving all rights equal emphasis. Work on drafting this Convention began in 1979, the International Year of the Child. This Convention is the most widely ratified human rights treaty in history. Countries that ratify the Convention have a legal and moral obligation to advance the cause of children's rights through administrative, legislative, judicial, and other measures.

As well as the general principles (Figure 12-16), the Convention document also states that:

- children have the right to freedom of expression, thought, conscience, and religion, subject to appropriate parental guidance
- children should not be separated from their parents, unless this is deemed to be in the child's best interests
- every child has a right to the highest attainable standard of health
- children have a right to education, and the State is responsible for providing free primary education. Discipline in school should respect the child's dignity; and the aims of education should be geared towards developing children's personalities as well as their mental and physical abilities to the fullest extent.

The Convention also includes the following protections:

5. *Special protection measures*
a) In situations of armed conflict States ensure that children under fifteen years of age take no direct part in hostilities and that no child below fifteen is recruited into the armed forces.

Figure 12-15 A young student in the Maldives writes on a sand slate. Nearly half the population of this island republic in the Indian Ocean are under the age of fifteen.

Non-Discrimination

States shall ensure each child enjoys full rights without discrimination or distinctions of any kind.

Best Interests of the Child

The child's best interests shall be a primary consideration in all actions concerning children whether undertaken by public or private social institutions, courts, administrative authorities or legislative bodies.

Survival and Development

Every child has an inherent right to life and States shall ensure, to the maximum extent possible, child survival and development.

Participation

Children have the right to be heard.

Figure 12-16 The four guiding principles of the Convention on the Rights of the Child.

b) Children who come in conflict with the law have the right to treatment that promotes their dignity and self-worth.

c) In situations of exploitation children have the right to be protected from economic exploitation and from work that threatens their health, education or development. States shall set minimum ages for employment and regulating working conditions—particularly in line with standards set forth by the International Labour Organization. The State shall protect children from sexual exploitation and abuse, including prostitution and involvement in pornography. The Convention stipulates that it is the State's obligation to make every effort to prevent the sale, trafficking, and abduction of children.

d) Children of minority communities and indigenous populations have the right to enjoy their own culture and to practise their own religion and language.

Figure 12-17 This poster was produced by the relief organization Oxfam.

Thinking critically What does the information on this poster tell us about the rights of some children today?

Children's Rights in Canada

Canada has taken a number of steps to protect the rights of children. The British Columbia government has established a ministry to protect the rights of children and youth. Its stated mission is to serve "the people of British Columbia by ensuring a child-centred, integrated approach that promotes and protects the healthy development of children and youth while recognizing their life-long attachment to family and community." Children's rights are considered paramount and social workers have the power—and the obligation—to remove them from unsafe environments.

Canadian Coalition for the Rights of the Child

Shortly after the adoption of the Convention on the Rights of the Child in 1989, several Canadian organizations decided to form the Canadian Coalition for the Rights of the Child. This organization, which consists of over fifty federal, provincial, and non-governmental organizations, conducts research into how well Canada fulfils its international obligation according to the U.N. Convention on the Rights of the Child. The coalition has looked into such issues as child abuse and neglect in Canada, refugee children, education and health care, and other basic rights and freedoms of Canadian children.

Child Poverty

Perhaps the single biggest issue in regard to children's rights in Canada is that of child poverty. In 1989, the House of Commons passed a resolution "to seek to achieve the goal of eliminating poverty among Canadian children by the year 2000." Yet, by 2000 the number of children in Canada living below the Statistics Canada Low-Income Cut-Off (LICO) actually increased by 49 per cent. A family was defined as living below the LICO if it spent more than 55 per cent of its income on food, clothing, and shelter. According to that measure, nearly half a million, or one in five, children in Canada were poor in 2000.

While Canadians agree on the principle of eliminating child poverty, there is significant disagreement about how achieve this goal. Some

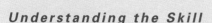
Understanding the Skill

In Chapter 3, you practised the skill of stating a thesis and developing it in a short essay. Social studies essay topics generally require you to respond to a set question containing a *command* (key) word. To respond effectively to questions, you need to understand what these command words mean. The following is a list of standard command words used in social studies essay questions:

Assess: To determine the value or significance of the subject in relation to other factors.

Example: Assess the degree to which preferential hiring policies are justified.

Compare/Contrast: To show the similarities and differences between one idea or issue and another.

Example: Compare the human rights protections in Canada with those in Afghanistan.

Describe: To give a detailed account of a topic.

Example: Describe protections available to Canadian children in both U.N. and Canadian legislation.

Discuss: To examine the topic from a number of points of view. Points of view should be supported or challenged.

Example: Discuss the claim that the B.C. Human Rights Tribunal has too much power.

Evaluate: To examine and judge carefully the value of a statement and its significance.

Example: The Supreme Court of Canada has been the greatest ally in the advancement of Aboriginal rights in Canada. Evaluate this statement.

Explain: To make a topic plain and offer reasons for, or causes of, an event or action.

Example: Explain the growth of human rights legislation in the years following World War II.

Justify/Support: To defend and give points of view that are in favour of a topic.

Example: The Charter of Rights and Freedoms protects the basic human rights of Canadians. Support this statement.

Introduction

- Indicate the general topic you are dealing with in your essay
- State your thesis
- Outline the topic areas you will deal with to develop the thesis

Body of the Essay

- Use a separate paragraph for each of the topic areas you explore
- Ensure each paragraph has a topic sentence and supporting facts
- Make sure your facts relate back to the thesis

Conclusion

- Summarize the key points in support of the thesis
- Describe any questions raised by the findings of your essay

Figure 12-18 Guidelines for writing an expository essay.

Applying the Skill

1. Which of the examples given in the list of command words already contain a thesis statement? Provide thesis statements for the remaining examples.

2. Choose one of the theses and write an outline for that topic, using the guidelines.

3. Write a rough draft of the essay.

4. Ask a classmate to edit your rough draft.

5. Write a final good copy of the essay.

Figure 12-19 A homeless teenager panhandles for spare change on a street in Victoria, B.C.

Developing understanding
What are some of the factors that might account for the numbers of young people living on the streets of Canadian cities?

activists feel that the best way to help children living in poverty is to cut taxes, thereby lessening the tax burden for parents with low incomes. This would give parents more income, which would, in turn, give them and their families a better standard of living. Others emphasize the need for governments to invest directly in programs and services for poor children and their families, such as good-quality and affordable child care, housing supplements, and allowances such as the Child Tax Benefit Program, paid directly to low- and middle-income families.

ACTIVITIES

1. With a partner, create a poster that effectively presents the rights issues outlined in the U.N. Convention on the Rights of the Child.

2. Is child poverty a human rights issue? Explain your viewpoint with reference to the U.N. Convention on the Rights of the Child.

3. Do you agree with the definition of poverty used by Statistics Canada in LICO? In a two-column organizer, list the benefits and drawbacks of using such a definition as a way of helping children in poverty in Canada.

LOOKING BACK

Develop an Understanding

1. Use the information in this chapter and elsewhere in the text to make a timeline of events since 1945 that have helped to advance the cause of human rights in Canada and throughout the world. Beside each event, provide a brief summary of its importance.

2. What is the significance of the Universal Declaration of Human Rights?

3. What would be the purpose of an International Criminal Court?

4. Explain, using examples from this text or other examples that you are familiar with, how the Charter of Rights and Freedoms protects human rights in Canada.

Explore the Issues

5. Is a universally acceptable human rights code possible? Consider the many different cultures and religions in the world, and explain your views.

6. Make a list of exceptions to the equality rights in section 15 of the Canadian Charter of Rights and Freedoms that you would consider reasonable under the age category. Compare your list with others in the class, and discuss areas of disagreement.

7. Landlords sometimes complain that their property rights are not given the same attention as the rights of tenants. With a partner, write and act out a discussion between a landlord and a tenant, each of whom thinks his or her rights are more important than those of the other person.

8. Organize a class debate on the following topic: *Resolved—That Canada's international trade agreements should be linked to human rights issues.*

9. Should women and other underrepresented groups be given hiring priority for government and/or private-sector jobs? Write a Counterpoints on this issue.

10. In a group, create a students' bill of rights for your school, based on the various human rights declarations in this chapter and your own ideas.

Research and Communicate

11. Work in a group to present a script for a thirty-second public service announcement on the issue of preferential hiring policies for equity groups.

12. Research the state of human rights in one of the following countries: Indonesia, China, Chile, Colombia, Iran, Afghanistan, Myanmar, or Sierra Leone. Design a campaign to make others in your school aware of the human rights issues people in these countries face.

13. Conduct a survey in your community to determine how public facilities ensure that they can provide services for people with physical disabilities.

14. Investigate the life of someone who actively supported human rights. You could choose from one of these well-known examples: Rosemary Brown or John Diefenbaker in Canada, Rosa Parks or Eleanor Roosevelt in the USA, Mohandas Gandhi in India, Aung San Suu Kyi in Myanmar, Nelson Mandela in South Africa, or the Sakharovs in Soviet Russia.

15. As a class, use your library and other facilities to research findings of the B.C. Human Rights Commission in each of the following categories:
    a. employment
    b. tenancy
    c. accommodation, service, or use of facilities
    d. hate propaganda.

    Organize a classroom bulletin board to display the results of the research. The display should summarize the findings and significance of each of the cases investigated. The Human Rights Commission's Web site is a good place to start: **www.bchrc.gov.bc.ca**

16. Imagine you are writing a letter to a friend in a country that does not have the basic human rights protections enjoyed by Canadians. Summarize the protections that you as a Canadian have before and under the law.

UNIT III

Geography and Global Issues

Environmental Issues

• Has the rate of population growth outstripped the capacity of the world to support world population?

• Should there be land use controls around cities to control urban sprawl?

• What policies should Canada adopt to live up to its commitment to the Kyoto Protocol?

• What should Canadians and Canadian governments do to protect air and water quality?

Political Issues

• Should Canada link its foreign aid to human rights?

• Should Canada be encouraging more immigration to deal with the growing dependency ratio as the population ages?

Social Issues

• Will technology widen the gap between the "haves" and the "have nots"?

• How would Canadian cities have to change to become sustainable?

• Should equalization payments be used to solve Canada's regional disparities?

Economic Issues

• How do we measure standards of living?

• Why are there regional disparities in Canada and countries around the world?

• Should Canada treat water as a resource to be traded?

• Is ecotourism a sustainable solution for preserving ecosystems?

Cultural Issues

• Should the international community do more to improve the status of women around the world?

Many of the world issues that confront us today cannot be understood without studying our relationship to the planet on which we live — in other words, without knowing some geography.

Chapter 13 examines the reasons behind the huge growth in world population in the twentieth century, and what this means for the future.

As population has increased, the gap in living standards between rich and poor has widened, and this trend is looked at in Chapter 14.

Increasingly in the twentieth century people moved into cities, especially in developing countries. Chapter 15 deals with the reasons behind this trend, and the problems of urbanization.

Chapter 16 looks at the geographic and economic factors that lead to growth and prosperity in some areas and not in others.

Chapter 17 describes the impact on the environment of all the issues outlined in previous chapters, and identifies the most pressing threats to the planet's ecosystems.

How will today's family planning campaigns affect ▲ people's quality of life in the future?

314

How have governments responded ▲
to the growing awareness of the
fragility of Earth's ecosystems?

What are the factors that contribute
to the growth of urban shanty
towns?
◄

315

Population Rates—Go Figure!

Demographers are most interested in statistics that help them predict and explain changes in society. For instance, the number of working women in a society will have an effect on the birth rate. It may also influence the diet of families, increasing the amount of packaged and pre-prepared foods they eat.

The components of population change are:

- how many people are born,
- how many die, and
- how many move in or out of an area.

Expressed in an equation, these are:

Births – deaths + immigrants – emigrants = increase or decrease in population

It is not very useful to compare births and deaths of countries that have widely differing population sizes. To know that each day slightly more than 1000 children are born in Canada, 4200 in India, and ninety-four in Gabon is not very useful unless the total populations of the countries are considered. What really matters is comparing the relationship between the number of births and the size of the population in each country. Demographers do this by using measurements called *birth rates* and *death rates*.

Demographers use rates per thousand when figuring population change. The **crude birth rate** is calculated by dividing the number of births in one year by the population and then multiplying the result by 1000. The same method is used to calculate the **crude death rate**. Subtracting deaths from births gives the rate of **natural increase**.

Canada's annual crude birth rate is about eleven per thousand, and the crude death rate is about seven per thousand. The natural increase of the Canadian population for a given year is six per thousand. This is usually expressed as 0.6 per cent. This figure does not include the increase that comes from immigrants. In countries like Gabon, where there are few immigrants, the annual growth rate of 1.5 per cent is made up entirely of natural increase.

Country	Population	Births per 1000 per Year	Birth Rate (%)
India	982 223 000	25	2.5
Russia	147 434 000	10	1.0
Canada	30 563 000	11	1.1
Gabon	1 167 000	37	3.7

Figure 13-3 Comparing birth rates of selected countries, 1999.

Interpreting statistics Calculate the approximate number of births for 1999 for each country by multiplying the total population by the percentage birth rate, and dividing the answers by 100. How would this information allow you to predict the population in 2000?

The Rule of Seventy

Human populations have the potential to grow at an ever-increasing rate. Suppose that a couple has four children, and each of these grows up to produce four children. By the third generation the couple will have sixteen descendants. This is called an **exponential rate** of increase. A regular arithmetic rate of 1, 2, 3, 4, and so on is quickly overtaken by an exponential rate which increases by 1, 2, 4, 8. Each generation builds on previous generations in a compound fashion.

A convenient way to express exponential population growth is to use the length of time it would take for a population to double in size. One way of calculating this is to apply the "rule of seventy," which states that **doubling time** is approximately equal to seventy divided by the growth rate (in per cent) per year. For example, Gabon at the present rate of natural increase has a doubling time of approximately forty-seven years:

70 divided by 1.5 (per cent growth per year) = 46.7 years

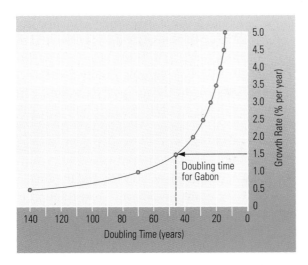

Figure 13-4 Population growth rate and doubling times.

Reading a graph Canada's rate of natural increase is 0.6 per cent. How many years would it take Canada's population to double if we did not take in immigrants?

The Effect of Migrations

Population increase in some countries, particularly Canada, depends on immigrants. As well, emigrants leave the country each year, which affects the demography. The **immigration rates** and **emigration rates** are calculated in a similar manner to birth and death rates. The difference between the two gives the **net migration rate**. Net migration rate is given as a rate per thousand. A combination of the birth rate, the death rate, and the net migration rate gives a complete picture of the annual change in the Canadian population:

Birth Rate – Death Rate ±
(BR)   (DR)

Net Migration Rate =
(NMR)

Population Growth Rate

Canada, the United States, and Australia are some of the few countries in which immigration is a significant factor in the growth of their populations. Most immigrants to Canada come as economic migrants from developing nations, wanting to better their standard of living. Others come as

Figure 13-5 The differing circumstances of migrants. Top: These illegal Chinese migrants await immigration processing after being dumped off the coast of British Columbia in 1999. In spite of the perils of the journey, many Chinese are attracted by the promise of improved living standards in the land of the "Golden Mountain."

Bottom: Displaced women line up at a food distribution centre in western Ethiopia. The drought and famine that struck the east African country in the late 1990s caused many people to migrate in search of food, water, and other essentials of life.

refugees seeking to escape persecution in their home country.

Large-scale mass migrations affect the structure of population by age and sex. Most immigrants are young and generally single males. This gives the host countries a younger population that will eventually result in a higher birth rate. The country losing population experiences the reverse effect. For instance, the migration from Communist-controlled East Germany to the West after World War II until the Berlin Wall was built gave East Germany a population with a disproportionate number of older people.

The multicultural populations of Canada and the United States are the result of migrations. During the last decades of the twentieth century, "visible minorities" in Canada increased dramatically with immigration from Asia and the Caribbean. Canada and the United States have also become home to many Spanish-speaking migrants from Latin America.

ACTIVITIES

1. Define demography; emigration; immigration; migration.

2. **a)** What are the main components of population change?

   b) What is meant by an exponential rate of growth? The rule of seventy?

3. Imagine you want to open a sports store. What demographic information would you want to know about your target market? Describe how you would use the information to choose the type of sports products that you would hope to sell.

4. Statistics Canada has refused to transfer any data collected since the 1901 census to the National Archives in Ottawa, claiming it would be an invasion of privacy. As a group, do a PMI chart on this issue. Summarize your findings.

The Demographic Revolution

For most of human history, birth rates have been high. Yet, the population grew slowly before the 1700s because death rates were also very high, particularly among infants and young children. Except for a small elite life was, as Thomas Hobbes described it in 1651, "poor, nasty, brutish, and short."

People had a **life expectancy**—the average number of years that an individual is expected to live—of little more than thirty years. (Today in Canada life expectancy is over seventy-five years.) Disease, poor medical care, poor nutrition, and unsanitary living conditions contributed to the high death rate. Families needed to have many children to ensure a few survived. Larger families were needed also to help farm the land, from which most people made a living, and to provide security for parents in old age. This situation is still common today in many developing countries.

The rapid increases in population growth after 1750 were mainly due to falling death rates. Beginning in Europe, then spreading to North America, and then to developing countries, death rates fell much more rapidly than birth rates. The agricultural revolution increased food production, so that people had better diets. Hygiene and medical knowledge improved. For example, clean drinking water, a more varied and nutritious diet, and vaccination against infectious diseases meant that far more children survived to become parents themselves. Birth rates remained high for a number of years, producing a wide gap between birth and death rates and a rapid growth in population.

The falling death rate was finally matched by a decline in the birth rate. Not all demographers agree on the reasons for this decline. Three likely reasons are economic development, the move to cities, and rising standards of living. The fact that the world's most economically developed nations now have the lowest population growth rates would seem to support this conclusion.

After World War II, the World Health Organization (WHO) and aid programs made improved health measures available to all countries. Death rates fell, but birth rates are still high in many developing countries. This explains the rapid population growth in areas of the world, such as Africa, that do not have significant economic development. These countries are not equipped to deal with the huge growth in their populations, particularly in the number of young dependents and youths ready for the labour force (see Chapter 14).

Life Expectancy in Years

Country	1900 Males	1900 Females	1950 Males	1950 Females	2000 Males	2000 Females
India	22.6	23.3	39.4	38.0	62.5	64.3
Japan	42.4	43.7	62.1	69.5	77.0	83.4
Uganda	n/a	n/a	n/a	n/a	42.2	43.9
Canada	43.2	45.3	63.2	68.7	76.1	82.8
Argentina	n/a	n/a	n/a	n/a	71.1	78.6

Source: Adapted from Statistics Canada, Population Reference Bureau, *World Population Beyond Six Billion*, 1999.
n/a = not available

Figure 13-6 Life expectancy at birth in selected countries for 1900, 1950, and 2000.

Interpreting statistics Why has there been a dramatic increase in life expectancy in all these countries? Suggest why there are differences in life expectancy. How could a demographer use the statistics for Japan and Canada in 1900 to argue that these were developing countries at that time?

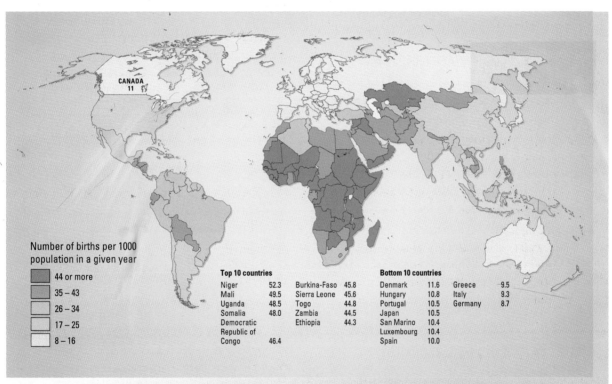

Number of births per 1000 population in a given year
- 44 or more
- 35 – 43
- 26 – 34
- 17 – 25
- 8 – 16

CANADA 11

Top 10 countries		Bottom 10 countries	
Niger	52.3	Denmark	11.6
Mali	49.5	Hungary	10.8
Uganda	48.5	Portugal	10.5
Somalia	48.0	Japan	10.5
Democratic Republic of Congo	46.4	San Marino	10.4
Burkina-Faso	45.8	Luxembourg	10.4
Sierra Leone	45.6	Spain	10.0
Togo	44.8	Greece	9.5
Zambia	44.5	Italy	9.3
Ethiopia	44.3	Germany	8.7

Figure 13-7 World map of birth rates, 1997.

Reading a map

1. Which continents of the world have the highest birth rates? Suggest three reasons that might account for these high rates. Review your reasons as you read further in this and the next chapter.

2. Which continents have the lowest birth rates? Suggest three reasons that might account for these low rates. Review your reasons as you read further in this and the next chapter.

3. With a partner, brainstorm a list of problems that might result for countries experiencing **(a)** very high birth rates; **(b)** very low birth rates.

The Demographic Transition Model

Geographers sometimes use *models* to represent reality or a theory. A model simplifies information so as to make it understandable. Models must strike a balance between detail and useful generalization.

One useful way of explaining population change is the **demographic transition** model. It shows changes over a period of time in three elements: birth rates, death rates, and trends in overall population numbers. The model assumes that in any country high birth rates and high death rates (Stage 1) will gradually fall (Stages 2 and 3). Because the model is based on what has happened in developed countries, it assumes that countries will pass through periods of industrialization and urbanization on the way to reduced birth and death rates. The model is useful in showing how the population growth rates of countries that are industrializing are in a state of transition. It seems that this transition period is unlikely in some countries, particularly in Africa, and so the model must be used with caution.

ACTIVITIES

1. **a)** Why was world population growth so slow before the 1800s?

   b) What improvements in living conditions led to increasing population growth?

2. How did declines in birth rates differ between the developed and the developing world?

3. With a partner, design an illustrated flow chart that depicts the general trend in life expectancy in the twentieth century.

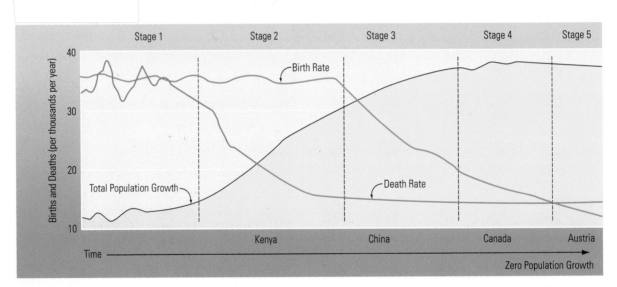

Figure 13-8 The demographic transition model, showing examples of countries in various stages of demographic transition.

Stage 1 High birth rates and high fluctuating death rates result in small population growth. Plagues, diseases, and poor nutrition keep mortality high.

Stage 2 Improved health care, sanitation, and increased food supplies lead to a rapid fall in death rates. Birth rates are still high, so there is a rapid increase in population numbers.

Stage 3 Population growth begins to decline. Birth rates begin to fall. Industrialization, urbanization, and improved living standards lead to less desire for large families.

Stage 4 The transition is complete to a low growth rate with low birth rates and death rates. The birth rate may fluctuate in special circumstances, such as in the post-war "baby boom."

Stage 5 Birth rates drop below death rates. This is happening in some European countries and in Japan. It is not known if this trend will extend to other regions.

Figure 13-9 (a) The population of Canada, 1900–2000; **(b)** The population of India, 1900–2000.

Reading a graph

1. In which years was the natural increase greatest in each country?

2. Based on the demographic transition model, what stages are **(a)** Canada and **(b)** India in at present?

3. Predict what will likely happen to India and Canada in the next five decades. Explain your answer.

4. With a partner, write a report to the United Nations making them aware of three problems you have noted as a result of your study of the information on India in the graph.

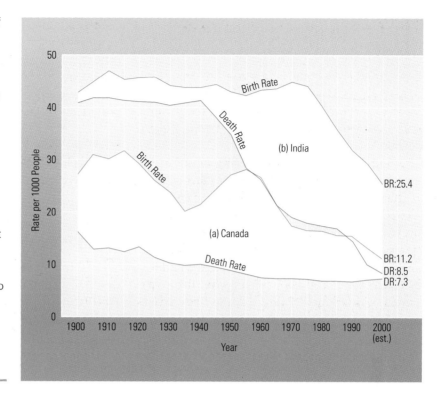

The Age Structure of Populations

The **age structure** of a population helps us understand the reasons for changes in population. Demographers divide populations into three age groups: children up to the age of fifteen; working adults from ages sixteen to sixty-four; and adults sixty-five years and older. This gives the **dependency ratio**, that is, the proportion of the population that is being supported by the working age group.

Children and older people put pressure on society for medical, education, housing, and other services. In the 1996 census, Canada's population included 21 per cent children and 12 per cent adults sixty-five years and older, giving it a dependency load of 33 per cent. A country like Bangladesh has a dependency load of 53 per cent, made up of 47 per cent children and 6 per cent adults aged sixty-five years and older. The age structure can give us insights into problems that

could arise in the future resulting from a predominantly old or young population.

Population Pyramids

A **population pyramid** is a graph that shows the age and sex structure of a population. A series of horizontal bar graphs for the male and female populations are placed back to back at age intervals of five years, called **cohorts**. Population pyramids make it easier to see the structure of a population. They are also useful in comparing the population structures of different countries. As the examples in Figure 13-10 show, countries with high birth rates have many children and an *expanding population*. A *stable population* will have birth rates and death rates in balance, and a *contracting population* will have a growth rate below replacement level. In general, the expanding pyramids are representative of developing countries, while the stable and contracting pyramids represent developed countries.

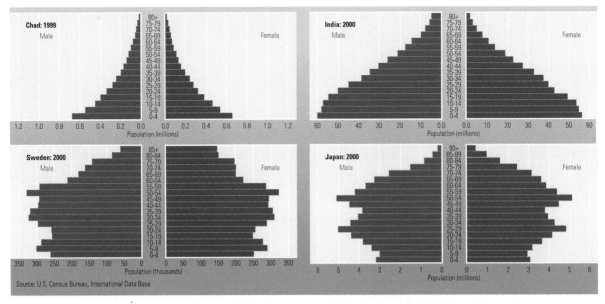

Source: U.S. Census Bureau, International Data Base

Figure 13-10 Population pyramids for selected countries.

Thinking critically

1. What evidence is there that the pyramid for Chad has a very high birth rate? What per cent of the population would you estimate is under the age of fifteen?

2. What does the shape of the pyramid for India tell you about trends in infant mortality and death rates in the country? How does India compare with Chad and Sweden in this regard?

3. What does the pyramid for Sweden tell you about the future population numbers in the country?

4. Suggest a number of problems Japan may face as a result of the age structure of its population.

5. In what stage of the demographic transition model is each of the pyramids? Explain each choice.

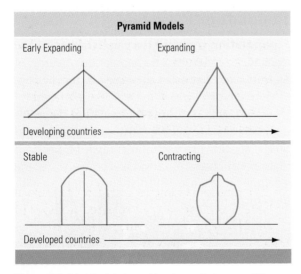

Figure 13-11 Model pyramids of populations at different stages of population development.

Interpreting a diagram Match these models with the population pyramids shown in Figure 13-10.

Canada's Population: The Past and the Future

Canada's birth rate and death rate have been dropping steadily in the past thirty years. This means the population is getting older. In 1951, one in ten Canadians was over sixty-five years of age. In 2020, one in five will be over that age. Life expectancy in Canada increased from an average of forty-five years in 1900 to sixty-five by 1950 and to seventy-nine by the year 2000. This trend is the same for most developed countries.

The increasing numbers of elderly people put immense strains on social and medical services. There are fewer children to look after aging parents. This has put pressure on the health care system to provide more long-term care for the elderly. The cost of health services for the aged continues to rise as medical technology becomes ever more complex.

	Planned No. of Immigrants	Actual No. of Immigrants
1989	150 000–160 000	192 001
1990	165 000–170 000	214 030
1991	220 000	232 760
1992	250 000	254 864
1993	250 000	256 575
1994	250 000	224 372
1995	250 000	212 845
1996	195 000–220 000	226 050
1997	195 000–220 000	216 044
1998	200 000–225 000	174 100
1999	220 000–225 000	180 000
2000	220 000–225 000	n/a
Source: Citizenship and Immigration Canada.		

Figure 13-12 Canada's immigration levels, planned and actual, 1989–1999.

Interpreting statistics What patterns can you see in this table? Suggest three factors that could explain differences between planned and actual immigration.

The age structure of Canada's population is one of the main factors the federal government considers when deciding on the number of immigrants Canada should accept each year. Without immigration between 1991 and 1996, our population would have shrunk by almost 750 000 instead of increasing by more than 1 600 000. The average age of the Canadian population would have increased rapidly.

The number of immigrants entering Canada fluctuates above or below the 200 000 level. This is far from the federal government's goal, which is to have annual immigration equal 1 per cent of the population. The difference between planned and actual immigration levels is shown in Figure 13-12. Immigration numbers have never come near the record level of 402 432 immigrants in 1913, which represented 5.5 per cent of a population of 7.3 million. The main difficulty the government faces is in attracting young, skilled workers and entrepreneurs to offset the aging workforce.

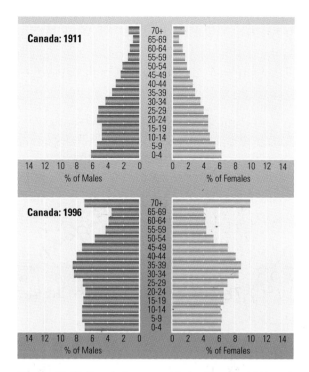

Figure 13-13 Population pyramids for Canada, 1911 and 1996.

Reading a graph

1. Refer to Figure 13-11. At what stage of development—expanding, contracting, or stable—would you place each of the pyramids?

2. What impact will the increasing number of dependents in 1996 have on the dependency load?

3. In the 1996 pyramid, which age group has significantly more females than males? Give possible reasons for this pattern.

4. What other information can be found by analysing these pyramids? Give examples of how government and business might use these pyramids to deal with present and future trends.

The number of refugees accepted into Canada in 1999 was close to the projected number of 22 000. The single largest group of refugees came from China. More money is now spent on handling refugee claims than on processing regular immigration. Critics have pointed to cuts in the 1990s to the budget of the federal immigration department and the greater attention paid to refugees than to regular immigration for the failure to reach immigration targets.

Dependency: Too Young Or Too Old

There has been a major change in the age structure of the world's population as the numbers of people have increased. There have never been so many people in the dependent category. This change will put increasing pressure on the financial resources of countries. In Japan, for example, the life expectancy is eighty-one years for males and eighty-four for females, the highest in the world. The government has declared the aging population to be its greatest future challenge. If present trends continue, one-quarter of the Japanese population will be over sixty-five by the year 2025. Years of exceptionally low birth rates mean there are fewer workers to care for them. How and whether Japan can maintain its economic position in the face of these problems remains to be seen.

At the other end of the scale, some developing countries have young dependents under the age of fifteen making up half their population. Any fall in birth rates in these areas has been offset by a greater number of women who can bear children, even if families are smaller. These countries remain in a cycle of poverty, as their limited resources and attempts to improve development are swallowed up by young populations. India and sub-Saharan Africa, with a combined population of over two billion people, face a daunting task of providing employment for the increasing numbers of young people entering the labour market. Young men in particular grow restless as they reach working age and find few opportunities to improve their standard of living. This results in an underemployed generation that could threaten the stability of entire regions.

Figure 13-14 Top: Masai children in Kenya stand in front of their village school. Currently, some 44 per cent of Kenyans are under the age of fifteen; only 3 per cent are sixty-five years or older.

Bottom: A group of Japanese seniors pose for a photographer in Yokohama, Japan. Fifteen per cent of Japanese are under the age of fifteen, while 16 per cent are sixty-five or older.

ACTIVITIES

1. Describe the connection between the age structure of a population and its rate of population growth.

2. **a)** What is the dependency ratio? Why is it important for a country to know this figure for future planning?

   b) Why does an aging population present a serious problem in the developed world?

3. **a)** What information does a population pyramid show about a population?

   b) What information can you discover about a country's past and future by analysing a population pyramid?

4. **a)** What effects do migrations have on the structure of the receiving country's population?

   b) How would the age structure of the population in Canada be different if there had been no immigration?

CASE STUDY

The One-Child Policy: China's Solution

Nearly one-fifth of the world's population lives in China. Even with growth rates below the world average, China adds twenty million children to its population each year. These are twenty million more mouths to feed in a country that depends on agriculture, yet where less than 15 per cent of the land is suitable for cultivation. Although it is one of the largest countries in the world, half of China's area is composed of mountains, hills, and deserts.

China's present population problem goes back to the policies adopted by the newly established Communist government in 1949. The leader, Mao Zedong, encouraged increases in the population of 540 million. He saw this as a way to make China into a great power. When challenged to explain how China would feed the growing population, Mao pointed out that "every stomach comes with two hands attached." By 1972, the population had swelled to 852 million. Dealing with growth rates reaching 2.85 per cent was using up over half the output of China's economy. The govern-

ment reacted with a publicity campaign in the 1970s that encouraged people to limit their family to two children. This had the effect of reducing the growth rate to 1.57 per cent, still too high for a population approaching 900 million.

The death of Mao Zedong in 1976 opened the way for a major effort to control population growth. In 1980, the Chinese government launched a policy of one child per family, a challenge for a culture that valued large families. Cash rewards, free medical care, and improved educational and housing opportunities were offered as incentives for those who had one child. People who did not cooperate with the policy were fined for each child after the first-born, and lost many medical and educational privileges. Pressure to be sterilized and have abortions was common at the height of the program in the mid-1980s.

By 1980, China's birth rate had been halved. The success of the one-child policy was greater in urban than in rural areas, which could not be as tightly controlled. Sons were valued as labourers on the farms, and they were expected to look after their parents in their old age. This, and reports of forced abortions and infanticide if the first-born was a girl, led the government to relax the policy in the late 1980s. A second child was allowed in rural areas if the first-born was a girl or was born with a disability.

Figure 13-15 A crowded Sunday market in Menghun, Yunnan Province, China.

Figure 13-16 A poster advertising the one-child policy in China.

Thinking critically Chinese culture traditionally favours male babies over females. Use information from this case study to suggest why this poster shows a little girl.

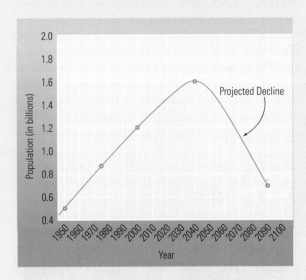

Figure 13-17 China's projected population in the twenty-first century.

Reading a graph

1. In what year is China's population expected to peak? What will be the total population at that point?

2. What is China's population estimated to be by 2090?

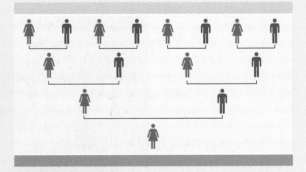

Figure 13-18 The effect of China's one-child policy on the extended family.

Thinking critically Traditionally, Chinese society was structured around the extended family, with each child having many brothers and sisters, aunts, uncles, nieces, nephews, and cousins. How might the one-child policy affect family values in China?

Figure 13-19 These Chinese children will grow up in a country with an aging population. Identify the social costs these children will have to carry when they become working adults.

Today, China's one-child policy is firmly established in the cities. City dwellers realize that one child gives them the financial means to take advantage of the luxuries available in most cities. Still, China began to face a baby boom in the 1990s, with hundreds of millions of rural peasants apparently ignoring the policy. A visit in 1999 to central China by a Canadian reporter found people who wanted to have as many children as possible. He quoted a Chinese demographer, who said, "The one-child policy has long been more slogan than reality."

The results of the one-child policy on Chinese society are now beginning to be felt. The growth in the rural population is putting more pressure on farmland. This may lead to a migration of massive proportions by the younger rural population to cities. Another problem is the aging of the people who were born after the 1949 revolution. Increased life expectancy means that the 400 million Chinese born before introduction of the one-child policy will have fewer young people working to support them. Will these young people want to help their aging fellow citizens? What has been called the "Little Emperor Syndrome" has been reported widely. These are the children who have been raised in single-child families and feel no sense of obligation to their families or society at large.

Present estimates indicate that the program has been successful in reducing the rate of growth of the population. The number of the Chinese population will only be known when the results of the 2000 census are announced, although the figures may be in doubt because of the huge task of counting that many people, many in remote areas.

The effects of population growth in China are important for the world. Growth rates in a population comprising over a sixth of humankind are a concern to all people. Canadians particularly have felt the immediate effects of population pressure in southern China with the arrival of smuggled Chinese migrants on Canada's West Coast. And if a controlled society like China has such difficulty in limiting population increase, what hope is there for India, which will eventually outstrip China to have the world's largest population?

Questions

1. Examine maps of the physical geography (landforms, climate, natural vegetation, and soils) of China in your atlas and other resources. Describe the geographical limitations that exist in China for the support of an expanding population.

2. Describe the situation in 1980 that led the government to impose a one-child policy.

3. Do a PMI analysis on outcomes of China's one-child policy. Summarize your results as a justification or a condemnation of the policy.

4. With a partner, write a series of short letters between a young Chinese couple and their parents who are pressuring them to have more than one child.

5. Organize a debate on the topic of a government's right to control people's right to have children. Is such a policy ever justified? Explain.

Where Do Six Billion People Live?

Population distribution refers to the way people are spaced over the Earth's surface. The Greek fathers of geography studied population distribution. They called their part of the world **ecumene**, and we now use this word to describe permanently inhabited places.

Approximately 35 per cent of the world's land area is not good for settlement. Over half the population lives on only 5 per cent of the land, and 90 per cent of people live on 20 per cent of the land. Two-thirds of people live within 500 km of the ocean.

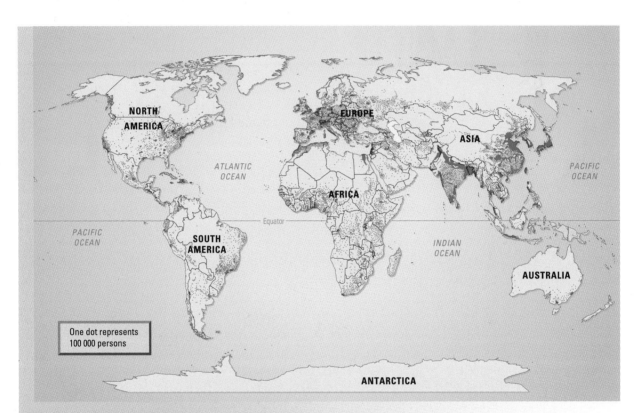

One dot represents 100 000 persons

Figure 13-20 World population distribution. Why do you think the dot method is used in preference to methods such as shading for distribution maps?

Reading a map

1. Are the most densely populated areas north or south of the equator?

2. Which two continents are most densely populated?

3. Compare this map with a map showing world landforms or relief. What relationship do you see between:

   a) densely populated areas and lowlands?

   b) sparsely populated areas and highlands? Identify two highland areas that are densely populated.

4. Compare this map with a map showing climate. What is the relationship between population distribution and areas that are:

   a) very cold throughout the year?

   b) very dry?

5. Identify two very dry areas that are densely populated. Refer again to the relief map, and give an explanation for this population density.

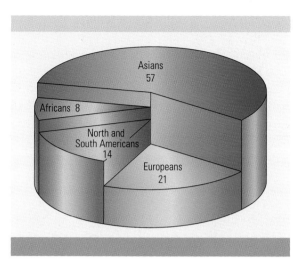

Figure 13-21 If we could shrink the Earth's population to a village of precisely 100 people, it would look something like this.

Population density describes the number of people in a given area. Population densities for the countries of the world are shown in Figure 13-22. These are **crude densities**. They are calculated by dividing the population of a country by its area. These figures are useful for general comparisons, but do not take into account the wide variations that exist within larger countries. For example, most Canadians and Chinese live at far higher densities than those indicated for Canada and China on the map. Rural and urban densities also differ dramatically in most countries. There are many explanations for the different population densities found in countries. The web in Figure 13-23 shows some of the major physical and human factors affecting population density.

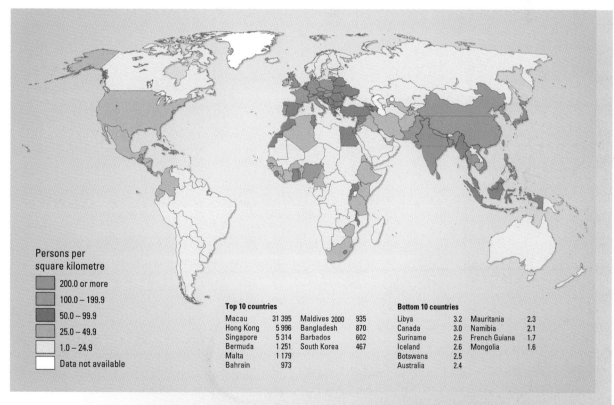

Persons per
square kilometre

- 200.0 or more
- 100.0 – 199.9
- 50.0 – 99.9
- 25.0 – 49.9
- 1.0 – 24.9
- Data not available

Top 10 countries

Macau	31 395	Maldives 2000	935
Hong Kong	5 996	Bangladesh	870
Singapore	5 314	Barbados	602
Bermuda	1 251	South Korea	467
Malta	1 179		
Bahrain	973		

Bottom 10 countries

Libya	3.2	Mauritania	2.3
Canada	3.0	Namibia	2.1
Suriname	2.6	French Guiana	1.7
Iceland	2.6	Mongolia	1.6
Botswana	2.5		
Australia	2.4		

Figure 13-22 Population density of the countries of the world, 1997.

Reading a map

1. Which two areas of the world have the highest population densities?

2. List a number of uses for a map like this.

3. How does the map reinforce the information in Figure 13-21?

Physical Factors

Climate — Areas that are very dry or very cold generally have lower densities.

Landscape — Lowlands near the rims of continents have the highest densities.

Resources — Areas rich in a variety of resources will attract higher densities.

Soils — Rich river valley and lowland soils result in higher densities.

Vegetation — Areas of very dense vegetation, such as rainforests, have low densities. In temperate zones, former forested areas and grasslands have high densities.

Water — A reliable water supply from rainfall or rivers is necessary for higher densities.

Accessibility — Areas that are easier to reach by land or sea will increase in population.

Human Factors

Communications — Areas that are easier to reach by land or sea will increase in population.

Culture — Nomadic or agricultural cultures may determine the level of density.

Development — Areas with a highly developed economy will have higher densities.

Disease — Areas of high incidence of disease will have low densities.

Government policies — May encourage settlement in remote areas, as in the case of Brazil and the Amazon basin or in Communist USSR, where settlement was forced.

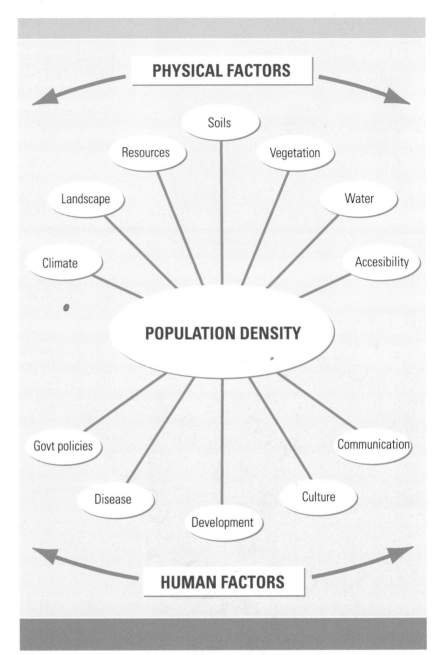

Figure 13-23 Major factors affecting population density.

Interpreting a diagram

1. The density of most countries is determined by a combination of some of the factors shown in the ideas web. Which factors apply best to Canada? Which to British Columbia? For each area, rank the factors in order, starting with those having the greatest effect.

2. Working with a partner or in small groups, choose a country from each of the categories in the legend of Figure 13-22. Use the ideas web to give reasons for each country's being in the category.

What Are the Limits of Population Growth?

"A finite world can support only a finite population; therefore population growth must eventually equal zero."

—Garrett Hardin, ecologist, author, *The Tragedy of the Commons*

Figure 13-24 Albrecht Dürer, the German Renaissance artist, depicted the Four Horsemen of Apocalypse—Conquest, War, Famine, and Death.

Thinking critically Describe, or draw, an illustration on the same theme that would be appropriate for the twenty-first century.

The idea that there are limits to the number of people that the Earth's resources can support is not a new one. In 1798, at the beginning of the Industrial Revolution in Britain, a British economist, Thomas Malthus, published *Essay on the Principles of Population*. At the time the population of Britain was seven million. The country was in Stage 2 of the demographic transition, so the population was growing very quickly. Malthus predicted that the numbers of people would be checked by diseases and famine at under fourteen million as the population outstripped the food supply. He pointed out that population increases exponentially (2, 4, 8, 16...) while food supplies increase arithmetically (1, 2, 3, 4...). Eventually, the growth in population would be checked.

By 1999, Britain's population of about fifty-seven million and a world population of over six billion had made a mockery of this prediction. Malthus was not able to foresee the improvements in agriculture, transportation, hygiene, and medicine that would make larger populations possible. Also, in the nineteenth century, migrations of millions opened up new farmlands in North and South America, Asiatic Russia, and Australia. These eased population pressure.

Some thinkers, called neo-Malthusians, predict that in the long term, Malthus was right. Disaster will overtake populations in the world's poorest developing countries in the next fifty years. They predict increasing shortages of **arable** land to grow enough food, conflicts over fresh water, declining fish stocks, and the spread of AIDS or other diseases. Africa will be most vulnerable to these threats.

Neo-Malthusians claim that migrations, technology, and new farming lands cannot solve the problems in the poorest developing countries. A leading neo-Malthusian, Lester Brown of the Worldwatch Institute, says that millions of people will die while the population in the developing world tries to return to a balance with the environment's ability to provide food. He points to shortages of water in India and cropland in China, countries with more than a third of the world's population, as indicators of impending disaster. By 2050 the population of countries like Nigeria and Pakistan are projected to triple in size; Ethiopia, with sixty-five million people, will reach a population of over 210 million, and the Congo will rise to 165 million. Only Nigeria has significant resources that may allow it to deal with this challenge. The others, unless there are profound changes, will see their population increases checked by famine, disease, and war. The latest ammunition for neo-Malthusians comes from studies by William Rees and Mathias Wackernagel of the University of British Columbia. They point out that if everyone were to live at the North American standard of living, the resources of three Earths would be required.

Central to these ideas that there are limits to growth is the concept of the **carrying capacity** of the land. This is the idea that land can produce only so much in the way of food or goods given the technology of the time. As population increases, it reaches a point beyond which the land cannot support that number of people. This is when the carrying capacity of the land is exceeded. As population outstrips food supplies, it is reduced by checks such as famine and disease until it stabilizes close to the land's carrying capacity (Figure 13-25).

Not everyone agrees with the neo-Malthusians. Organizations such as the United Nations, the World Bank, and most international aid agencies are more positive in their outlook. They claim technological developments, increased trade, and more efficient ways of

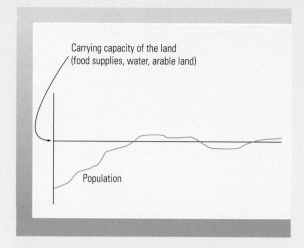

Figure 13-25 Carrying capacity of land and population. Unless new ways of increasing the carrying capacity of the land are found, population, after reaching a certain level, fluctuates above and below carrying capacity.

Thinking critically What technological changes in the twentieth century increased the carrying capacity of farmland in Canada? What other changes might increase or decrease carrying capacity in the future?

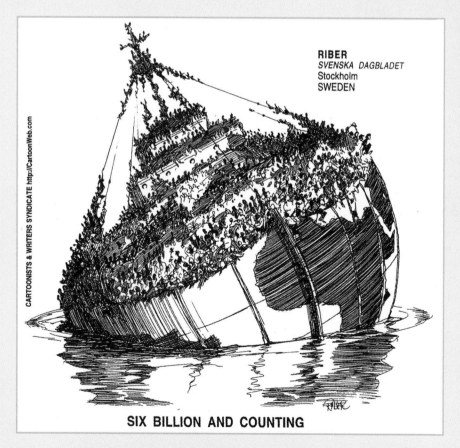

RIBER
SVENSKA DAGBLADET
Stockholm
SWEDEN

SIX BILLION AND COUNTING

Figure 13-26

Interpreting a cartoon
What is the point of view of the cartoonist regarding present world population figures? Is the cartoonist a neo-Malthusian or not? Explain

sharing the Earth's resources will ease the problems of developing nations. They point to the rapid increases in population in the twentieth century that were always matched by increased food production. Food production has increased by 25 per cent since the 1960s. New developments in genetic engineering of crops and animals could repeat this success. The optimists point to the best-seller by noted ecologist Paul Ehrlich, *The Population Bomb*, published in the 1960s. It argued that an exploding population would plunge large parts of the world into famine as early as the 1970s. None of its dire predictions happened.

Those with a positive outlook claim that educational programs will increase awareness of the benefits of population control. They point out that enough food is produced to feed everyone adequately, and it is the distribution system that causes malnutrition in some countries. Increased globalization, they believe, will help to create a more equal distribution of food and resources. Raising the standard of living of people around the world, they say, will cause population growth to level off. Alexander Cockburn, a critic of neo-Malthusians,

accuses them of holding out no hope and believing "that the Third World [developing countries] is incapable of reform and improvement, and efforts to assist it are useless."

Analysing the Issue

1. Explain the concept of carrying capacity.

2. Briefly summarize the viewpoint of each of the following on trends of world population: Malthus, Brown, Rees and Wackernagel, Ehrlich, and Cockburn. Which do you find most credible? Why?

3. With a partner, use a three-column organizer to compare and contrast the views of neo-Malthusians and the optimists on the effects of future population growth. Then use the information to script and perform a dialogue between supporters of the two viewpoints.

4. With a partner, design a visually appealing poster that effectively illustrates the problem of carrying capacity and population in an area of the developing world where people live at subsistence levels.

Nutritional Density

There are great differences in the productivity of farmlands in different parts of the world. For example, the Fraser Valley in southern British Columbia has exceptionally rich agricultural soils, but its output is restricted by a short growing season. Canadian farms cannot match the output of areas like southern China, where rich soils and ideal climate produce three crops a year. This means that a square kilometre of farmland in southern China can produce far more food for people than a similar area in the Fraser Valley. **Nutritional density** of land is a measure of how much nutrition in calories can be produced from the land. The nutritional density column in Figure 13-27 shows the average nutritional densities for the countries listed.

Country	Densities in km²	
	Crude	**Nutritional**
Australia	2	37
Canada	3	60
China	122	1192
Egypt	6	2203
Japan	334	2629

Figure 13-27 Crude population densities and nutritional densities for selected countries, 1997.

Interpreting statistics Why are the differences between crude and nutritional densities for Canada and Australia lower than for the other three countries? Use a climate map in an atlas to help explain why the nutritional density in China, Egypt, and Japan is so much higher than the crude density.

Earth's Crowded Future

The world's population will continue to grow in the twenty-first century. What is not certain is how fast it will grow. Given their large populations, China and India's success in bringing their population growth under control are important considerations in the size of the overall world population.

Age structure is an important factor in determining how fast a population will increase. Developing countries with high numbers of young dependents will likely experience greater population growth than developed countries. The number of developing countries that will improve their standards of living to a point where birth rates begin to fall cannot be predicted.

Changes in birth rates in the developed world also cannot be foretold. For example, it's possible that a major cultural change in Canada and the United States could change fertility rates and bring about another baby boom.

Birth rates will continue to decline worldwide, but the large base in countries like India means increases will continue to be too high for the population to be sustained without environmental damage. The future will be determined by the youth of developing nations. The age at which they choose to marry, and the number of children they have, may be the most important decisions of the twenty-first century.

LOOKING BACK

Develop an Understanding

1. Compare the typical shapes of population pyramids for developing nations and developed nations. Describe the differing dependency problems for these nations.

2. Using countries from different regions of the world as examples, explain how population density figures for countries can often be deceiving.

3. Construct imaginary population pyramids for populations that are:

   a. expanding rapidly following a lengthy war

   b. expanding after experiencing a devastating famine

   c. stable with an aging population

   d. experiencing a negative growth rate.

   Match your pyramids with the population pyramids of actual countries today.

4. Do a PMI analysis on the results of an influx of young migrants into British Columbia. Summarize and compare your findings with others.

Explore the Issues

5. Define the term *overpopulation*. Use your definition to suggest the optimum level of population the world can sustain today. Support your choice, and compare it with others in the class.

6. Debate the motion: *The ideas of Malthus are more relevant today than ever before.*

7. As a group, write a policy statement for the minister of immigration. Suggest amendments to the Immigration Act that would make it more responsive to the changing demographics of the Canadian labour force.

8. With a partner, create a map of the Canadian or British Columbian ecumene. Around the map, explain significant patterns that are evident and the impact these have on Canadians.

9. Imagine it is twenty-five years in the future. Write the population entry for your region or community for the *Encyclopedia of British Columbia* to be printed that year.

Research and Communicate

10. With a partner, write and deliver a "news fact" broadcast on the topic of population growth over the past two thousand years. Focus on the rate of change, absolute numbers, and the situation today.

11. With a partner, make a collage of images that depict the impact of the changing demographic structure of the Canadian population.

12. Write and record a number of thirty-second radio commercials informing people of the importance of Canada's five-year census counts.

13. As a group, make a poster showing world, or Canadian, population growth in the twentieth century. Illustrate the poster with images depicting the impact of this growth on people in various parts of the world at different times.

14. With two other students, research a complete demographic profile of a country from each of the developed, developing, and least developed worlds. Use a poster format to compare and contrast the countries.

15. Imagine it is 2025. Describe the changes you will experience as a result of changes in the Canadian population.

16. With a partner, do some research on the effects the aging population will have on the workforce in British Columbia, and any measures being taken to deal with shortages. Make a presentation to your classmates on career choices that they might consider as a result of your findings.

17. Use the Internet to investigate and classify the population pyramids of four different countries.

18. Conduct a poll in your community to determine the level of understanding of issues surrounding world population growth. Take care in framing the questions so that they are clear and cover the main themes of this chapter.

19. With a partner, write and perform a question-and-answer dialogue between a radio interviewer and a demographer. Focus the interview on the numbers of elderly people in the world and the problems facing society because of the increasing number of older dependents.

20. Imagine you are a staff member with the Canadian embassy in a developing African country. Write a memorandum to the Canadian Secretary of State for External Affairs on the problems that country might face as a result of the increase in young dependents. Suggest some steps Canada might take to help.

21. Use Figure 13-26 as a model to draw a cartoon that might appear in a future year, as shown in the U.N. estimates of future growth given in Figure 13-1.

14

Living Standards

FOCUS ON

• What are the different ways of measuring a country's development?

• How does improving the status of women improve a country's level of economic development?

• Why are the mortality rates of some countries increasing?

• What is the relationship between the levels of health of populations and their economic development?

• What is the impact of population growth on a country's standard of living?

• What role does Canada play in aiding developing countries?

• What problems are created by the indebtedness of developing countries?

• How do we determine the success of aid programs in assisting developing countries?

Counterpoints Issue

• Should Canada link its foreign aid to human rights?

(Left) A woman returns from market carrying her supplies alongside an open sewage drain in Port-au-Prince, Haiti.

(Right) Shoppers browse at County Arcade, a showcase pedestrian mall in Leeds, England.

Imagine living with no running water in your one-room home, being sent to beg on the streets or work long hours at the age of seven, never knowing if you will go to bed hungry, and never having the opportunity to learn to read or write. These are the conditions that millions of people around the world live in. This gap in living standards between these people and people living in countries like Canada could become the most important issue in the twenty-first century.

Expressing ideas What is your reaction to this contrast in living conditions?

Introduction

Each year the United Nations publishes a Human Development Report. The report contains an index that ranks its member countries according to three measures: adult literacy (people who can read); life expectancy; and the **per capita GDP**. (GDP, or *gross domestic product*, is the total value of all goods and services produced in a country in one year. If you divide this number by the number of people in the country, you get the average GDP per person, or per capita.) For each of the last six years of the twentieth century, Canada ranked first overall on the Human Development Index.

The purpose of the U.N. index is to give a crude indication of different levels of economic and social development among the countries of the world. As you can see from Figure 14-1, there is a huge gap between the ten countries at the bottom of the index and the ten at the top. The 1999 report focussed on this continuing gap between rich and poor countries, and between rich and poor people in those countries. It showed that people in eighty-five countries were worse off than they were in the 1980s. In more than twenty countries, life expectancy at birth was still under fifty years, a full thirty years less than in Canada. Yet the wealth of the 200 richest people in the world—over a thousand billion dollars in 1998—was greater than the combined income of 41 per cent of the world's population.

Rank	Country	Life Expectancy at Birth (Years)	Adult Literacy Rate (%)	GDP Per Capita ($U.S.)
1.	Canada	79.0	99.0	22 480
2.	Norway	78.1	99.0	24 450
3.	United States	76.7	99.0	29 010
4.	Japan	80.0	99.0	24 070
5.	Belgium	77.2	99.0	22 750
6.	Sweden	78.5	99.0	19 790
7.	Australia	78.2	99.0	20 210
8.	Netherlands	77.9	99.0	21 120
9.	Iceland	79.0	99.0	22 497
10.	United Kingdom	77.2	99.0	20 730
* * *				
165.	Central African Rep.	44.9	42.4	1 330
166.	Mali	53.3	35.5	740
167.	Eritrea	50.8	25.0	820
168.	Guinea-Bissau	45.0	33.6	861
169.	Mozambique	45.2	40.5	740
170.	Burundi	42.4	44.6	630
171.	Burkina Faso	44.4	20.7	1 010
172.	Ethiopia	43.3	35.4	510
173.	Niger	48.5	14.3	850
174.	Sierra Leone	37.2	33.3	410

Source: United Nations Human Development Report, 1998.

Figure 14-1 Top ten and bottom ten countries, U.N. Human Development Index, 1998.

Thinking critically
Which two continents contain most of the top countries? In which continent are all the bottom countries? From what you learned in Chapter 13, what are the characteristics of the birth, death, and infant mortality rates in the top countries and the bottom countries? Do you think these three measures are adequate to show human development in a country? Explain your answer.

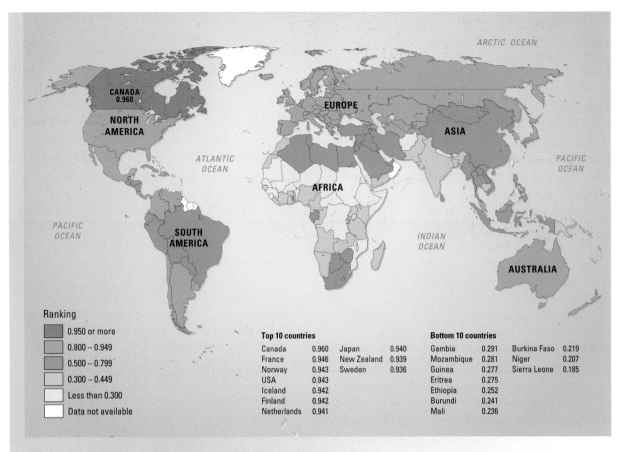

Ranking

Color	Value
	0.950 or more
	0.800 – 0.949
	0.500 – 0.799
	0.300 – 0.449
	Less than 0.300
	Data not available

Top 10 countries

Country	Value	Country	Value
Canada	0.960	Japan	0.940
France	0.946	New Zealand	0.939
Norway	0.943	Sweden	0.936
USA	0.943		
Iceland	0.942		
Finland	0.942		
Netherlands	0.941		

Bottom 10 countries

Country	Value	Country	Value
Gambia	0.291	Burkina Faso	0.219
Mozambique	0.281	Niger	0.207
Guinea	0.277	Sierra Leone	0.185
Eritrea	0.275		
Ethiopia	0.252		
Burundi	0.241		
Mali	0.236		

Figure 14-2 The U.N. Human Development Index for 1995. The minimum score is 0; the maximum, 1.0.

Reading a map

1. Which continents have a majority of countries in the highest category of human development? The lowest category? The 0.500 to 0.949 categories?

2. The world is often described as a developed North and a developing South. How does the map support this description? How does it not?

3. Which continent has the widest range of countries in all categories? How might you account for this?

4. Compare this map with the map of birth rates in Figure 13-7 (page 323). Write a short paragraph to summarize the similarities and differences that you can see.

5. Compare the list of countries in this 1995 map with the 1998 list in Figure 14-1. Which countries that appear in the top ten 1995 list no longer appear in the 1998 list? Which countries appear in 1998 that did not appear in 1995?

Efforts have been made to close the gap. Still it continues to grow, despite the efforts of organizations such as the United Nations, aid from government agencies, and non-governmental organizations (NGOs) such as Save the Children or Oxfam. In this chapter you will explore standards of living in various developed and developing countries, and consider the problems in comparing standards of living. How and what do we measure? Why is there such a huge gap between the wealth of the "have" and "have-not" countries? What is Canada's policy with regard to this gap?

Figure 14-3 The horn of plenty represents the bounty of food that Canadians enjoy at Thanksgiving.

Interpreting a cartoon
Discuss why the cartoonist showed the starving child on television. Write a caption suitable for the cartoon.

The Divided Planet

In 1949, President Truman of the United States referred to a world of "developed" and "underdeveloped" nations. By this he meant that some countries were industrialized, with their people well-housed, healthy, and educated. Their **infrastructure**—such things as transportation and communications links, electric-power distribution systems, schools, and hospitals—was well-developed. The "underdeveloped" countries had few schools, doctors, and hospitals; roads were mainly unpaved; there were few railways; few people had telephones; and only the cities had electrical power.

For a time, the "developed" countries were called the First World, and the "underdeveloped" the Third World. The countries between these two categories were called the Second World. In the mid-1970s, the geographical location of countries in each category led some to refer to the industrialized countries as the North and the countries with lower incomes as the South. Now the accepted terms are **developed countries** for the most wealthy countries, **newly industrializing countries** for places like Indonesia that are building up their industries and infrastructure, and **developing countries** for countries that do not have a modern infrastructure or many industries. Most of the countries at the bottom of the U.N. Human Development Index are in debt to the developed nations, and they are now being called **highly indebted poor countries** (HIPCs).

Comparing Living Standards

Levels of economic development are hard to measure accurately. The developed world has accounting systems that can determine such things as the level of industrialization, value of services, and exports and imports. It is much harder to measure these things in developing countries.

What to measure is another problem in trying to compare levels of development. Developing economies have many people who make goods at home and trade them in local communities. Money may not be used in these transactions. This makes it impossible to measure this output. This kind of production is not included in the countries' accounting systems.

If the wealth of the country is not shared among the people, the average income figure does not reflect the standard of living for the majority. In Saudi Arabia, for example, the average per capita income is $9000 (U.S.) because of the income from the sale of oil resources. However, the wealth from these sales is concentrated in the hands of a few very wealthy families.

Standards of living are not only measured in incomes people earn. The quality of life includes such things as health, levels of nutrition, life expectancy, literacy, and the status of women and

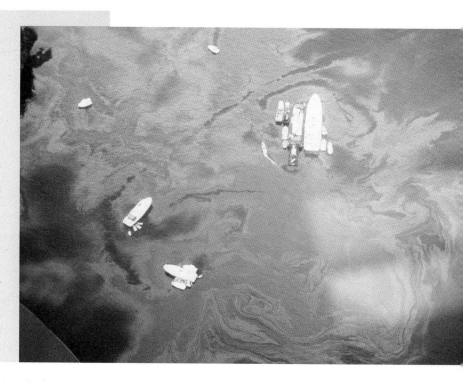

Figure 14-4 On March 24, 1989, the fully loaded oil tanker, *Exxon Valdez*, hit a reef in Prince William Sound, Alaska. Forty million litres of oil was spilled. Over 6000 sea otters died, as well as over half a million birds. Over 1500 km of shoreline was contaminated. Yet, the accident contributed to a rise in GDP because of the costs of clean-up, fees paid to lawyers, and other income it generated.

Thinking critically How might a car accident in which people are critically injured add to the GDP? How does this example and the *Exxon Valdez* accident illustrate the limitatiuons of GDP as a measure of quality of life and standards of living?

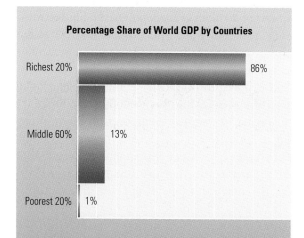

Percentage Share of World GDP by Countries

Richest 20%   86%

Middle 60%   13%

Poorest 20%   1%

As a result of this disparity, the richest 20% also:

- eat 45% of all meat and fish
- use 58% of total energy
- have 74% of all phone lines
- own 82% of the world's motorized vehicles
- use 84% of all paper
- account for 86% of all private consumption of goods and services purchased for private use by individuals.

Source: United Nations Human Development Report, 1998.

Figure 14-5 Disparities between rich and poor countries, 1998.

children. A person living in poverty in Canada has access to health care, education, and other services. There are government programs and private agencies that provide a safety net of services that do not exist for most of the poor people in developing countries. A very poor family in a city there is likely to live in a dwelling made from scrap materials with no electricity, sanitation, or access to safe water. Getting water and basic food-stuffs may take women many hours of the day. The people also may be in debt to a local money-lender whose high interest rates seldom allow them to pay off the original debt. Figure 14-5 shows some of the economic disparities between the richest and poorest countries in the world.

Measuring Poverty

Poverty is also measured differently in developed and developing countries. One measure sets the absolute poverty line in developing countries at less than one dollar per person per day. Using this measure, the World Bank—an international lending agency—estimates that 1.3 billion people live below the poverty line. Yet there are people who earn two, three, or even five dollars a day in these countries who remain poverty-stricken. Critics of

Figure 14-6 Single-parent families headed by females are among those most likely to live below the poverty line in Canada. Others falling below Statistics Canada's low-income cut-off include the elderly, particularly women.

the World Bank measurement prefer to look at individual countries and determine at what level people are unable to afford a minimum of food, clothing, shelter, health care, and education services. This is closer to the way poverty is measured in Canada and the United States.

Until recently in Canada, a set income figure was used to measure poverty. This figure did not take into account the differences in cost of living across the country. A 1999 report by the National Council of Welfare, a federal government agency, redefined living in poverty as spending more than 56 per cent of a person's or family's income on the necessities of life, such as food, shelter, and clothing. Using this figure, the report found that 17.2 per cent of Canadians, or 5.1 million people, lived below the poverty line in 1998. In the United States, poverty is measured against the "cost of a minimum adequate diet multiplied by three to allow for other expenses." In 1998, this translated into an approximate per capita income of eleven dollars (U.S.) per day.

The quality of life also depends on freedom of expression, economic freedom, and the right to a safe and clean environment. For example, advocates for the poor in Canada are free to promote their cause. In some developing countries, the homeless and the illiterate may be denied the

vote, or may be intimidated by government-hired thugs if they try to improve their conditions. Even in countries that are recognized as democracies, the illiterate may have no way of confirming that their vote is recorded as requested.

ACTIVITIES

1. What is the purpose of the Human Development Index? How effective is it in highlighting the differences between rich and poor countries?

2. List a number of characteristics, apart from those used in the Human Development Index, that would be common to the top ten countries.

3. What are the limitations of measuring development in a country by the gross domestic product? What are the advantages?

4. **a)** How is poverty defined in Canada?

   b) What difficulties are there in comparing poverty in Canada with poverty in developing countries?

5. **a)** How useful do you think the terms *developed* and *developing* are in describing the differences in standards of living between countries? Explain.

   b) Brainstorm with your group to think of other terms to describe the differences in standards of living in countries.

Using Scatter Graphs to Compare Statistics

When comparing living standards of countries it is useful to see the relationship between various factors. For example, the U.N. Human Development Index (Figure 14-1) shows that there is a relationship between GDP per capita, life expectancy at birth, and adult literacy rates. Scatter graphs help us to see clearly any relationship between two factors. One set of figures is plotted on the horizontal axis and the other is set on the vertical axis.

	Life Expectancy (years)	GDP per Capita ($U.S.)
Mexico	72.1	6769
Brazil	66.6	5928
Botswana	51.7	611
Gabon	54.5	3766

Figure 14-7 compares the life expectancy in years and the real GDP per capita of countries using the 1998 Human Development Index (HDI) figures. It shows that the top ten countries from the HDI countries with a high GDP per capita also have a longer life expectancy. Conversely, there seems to be a relationship between low GDP per capita and lower life expectancy. Gabon,

Botswana, Brazil, and Mexico have been included on the graph for comparison.

Applying the Skill

Country	Secondary School Enrolment (% female)	Birth Rate /1000
Afghanistan	8	52
Australia	86	13
Benin	7	41
Bhutan	2	39
Burkina Faso	6	46
Canada	100	11
Germany	100	9
Italy	82	9
Japan	97	10
Mali	6	47
Mexico	58	24
Mozambique	6	43
Nepal	23	34
Niger	4	48
Pakistan	13	36
Russia	91	10
Sierra Leone	12	46
Somalia	5	52
U.K.	94	12
USA	97	14

Figure 14-8

Making a scatter graph

1. Use the statistics in the table to make a scatter graph showing the relationship between the two columns of information.

2. a) Describe the pattern shown on your graph.

   b) What relationship between secondary school enrolment and birth rates does your graph indicate?

3. a) How would you describe the development level of countries with low secondary school enrolments? With high enrolments?

   b) What other pairs of factors would show a relationship that highlights the differences between developed and developing countries?

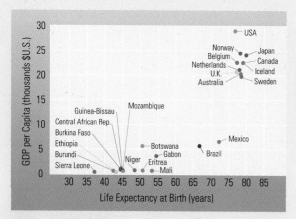

Figure 14-7 Scatter graph of GDP per capita ($U.S.) and life expectancy, 1998.

The Poverty Trap

It is estimated that almost 800 million people in developing countries are starving or malnourished. Yet, the world produces enough food to feed all six billion people an adequate diet. For many of the poor, the problem is not being able to purchase the food that is available. Farmers who do not own their own land and migrant labourers are the first to feel the effects of droughts, crop failures, or economic downturns.

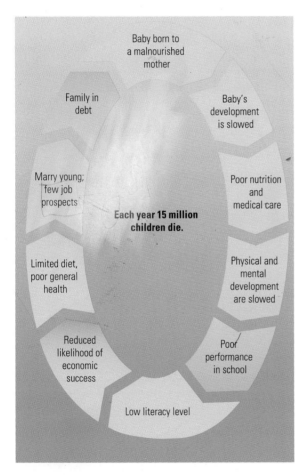

Figure 14-9 The cycle of poverty.

Thinking critically At what stage do you think intervention in the poverty cycle would be most effective? How might remedies applied to developing countries differ from those applied to poverty in Canada?

The Burden of Debt

How did the developing countries get into debt? The International Monetary Fund (IMF) and the World Bank were set up at the close of World War II as agencies of the United Nations. They were to provide loans and development assistance to help countries improve their standards of living through economic growth. The World Bank and IMF encouraged governments in developing countries to engage in megaprojects, such as dam building and agricultural irrigation, to promote economic growth. Many of these initiatives caused environmental damage and did not improve the countries' economies.

In the 1960s, Western banks were eager to lend billions of dollars for these projects to newly independent African countries, which were exporting minerals and agricultural products. Then, a world economic slowdown led to a collapse in prices for these commodities, making repayment of the debts difficult. Also, some of the loaned money had gone into the overseas bank accounts of corrupt dictators.

The Western banks and their governments encouraged the IMF and the World Bank to lend countries the money they needed to pay off their debts. The lenders had changed, but the debt remained. Today, African countries alone owe $227 billion. In return for the loans, the IMF told the debtor countries to restructure their economies to ensure repayment. The IMF wanted the debtor governments to agree to encourage foreign investment, grow cash crops for export, and have some government services run by private companies. These measures are called **structural adjustment programs** (SAPs). In the 1980s, a SAP in Zambia forced the government to stop paying the subsidy on maize meal (the staple food of most Zambians), which kept the price lower than the cost of production. Thousands of unemployed Zambians, who had lost their jobs, rioted.

Many debtor countries have few natural resources or receive low prices for them on the world market because there is an oversupply, or their resources are under the control of foreign **multinational companies** (MNCs). For example, Ghana, which produces 70 per cent of the world's

CASE STUDY

Kenya: Trapped in Poverty

Kenya is an example of a country where most people are caught in the cycle of poverty. This East African country is about 60 per cent of the size of British Columbia, but in 1999 was estimated to have a population of twenty-nine million. Its population had increased from 5.4 million in 1948 to 28.4 million in 1997. Nearly one million people are added to its population each year. Economic opportunities are limited, with education unaffordable for many, and few jobs, making employment prospects dim.

Kenya has three main geographic regions. The tropical coast has rainforests and sandy beaches that are now a destination for tourists from Europe. In the highland plateau region there are natural parks with abundant wildlife that form the basis of a tourist industry. About one-quarter of the northern interior plateau area is too dry for farming and has scrub vegetation that is poor grazing land. Another 37 per cent is tropical grassland, and is traditionally used by nomadic herders for grazing cattle. The highlands in the west have the one good farming area in the country, but it represents only about 7 per cent of the land. This area produces tea and coffee for export, as well as cut flowers to sell in Europe.

About 80 per cent of the population make a living from farming. There is now less food produced per capita than thirty years ago, partly because of the population increase, and partly because good cropland is being used to produce cash crops for export. Unemployment is estimated at 50 per cent. Less than half the population has access to safe drinking water, and nearly 30 per cent of children are underweight. Nearly two-thirds of its population are under eighteen years of age. Thousands are infected with HIV/AIDS, yet Kenya must provide basic medical and sanitation

Figure 14-11 Kenya's three main geographical regions.

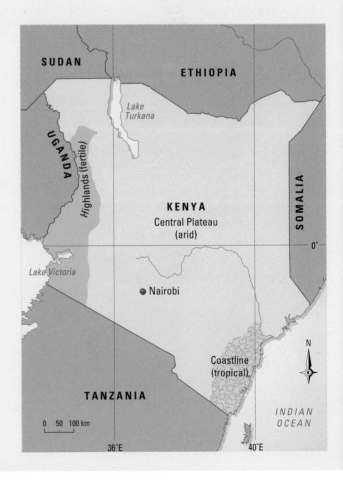

Figure 14-10 Kenya, a country in East Africa.

Reading a map

1. Match each of the photographs above with the appropriate region on the map.

2. Approximately what percentage of Kenya's land area is usable for agriculture?

	Total Population	Urban	Rural	Telephones (per 1000)	Personal Computers (per 1000)	Population per Doctor
Canada	29 000 000	77%	22%	590	193.0	465
Kenya	29 000 000	20%	80%	9	0.7	5954

Figure 14-12 Canada and Kenya: A comparison, 1995–1998.

services from a budget of $2.6 billion (U.S.). The per capita income is about $340 (U.S.).

Kenyans are leaving the countryside to move to shanty towns outside Nairobi, the nation's capital. Since 1990, about one million people have moved to the capital, which has industries and is the centre of tourism. In one of the shanty towns in the Mathare Valley, one-room shacks made of wood and cardboard are home to an estimated 400 000 people. The settlement has one paved road and no electricity, running water, or sanitation system. People live in a maze of lanes littered with garbage, which turn into rivers of mud in the rainy season. The shanty towns provide a pool of cheap labour for Nairobi.

Since 1978, Daniel Arap Moi has run the government as president and head of state. Corruption in government is widespread. The transients and migrants in the shanty towns have little influence on the government. The new arrivals from the countryside put added pressure on the few services available. All the problems facing Kenya are made worse by a crushing debt.

Questions

1. List the principal problems faced by Kenya as a result of the increasing population.

2. Which two of the factors in Figure 14-12 do you think most clearly illustrate the differences in development between Kenya and Canada? Explain your answer.

3. Make an illustration modelled on the diagram of the cycle of poverty in Figure 14-9 for people leaving the countryside in Kenya and moving to Nairobi.

4. What two strategies would you suggest to help Kenya break out of the cycle of poverty?

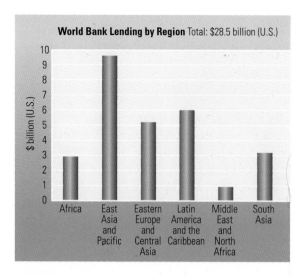

Figure 14-13 World Bank lending by region, 1998.

Thinking critically Why do you think the Middle East and North Africa received little funding?

cocoa, must sell the crop to four multinational companies who control the price. Very little of the profit filters back to the Ghanaian farmer. This makes it very difficult for farmers to earn the money to pay off their debts.

The debt burden of governments in developing countries means they are hard pressed to pay for services that could improve the standard of living of their people. Mozambique, for example, spends ten times more on debt repayments than on health care. As well, many African countries have suffered natural disasters, such as the devastating floods in Mozambique in 2000, or brutal civil wars like those in Rwanda and Sierra Leone.

Figure 14-14 The forty developing countries classified by the International Monetary Fund as being highly indebted poor countries.

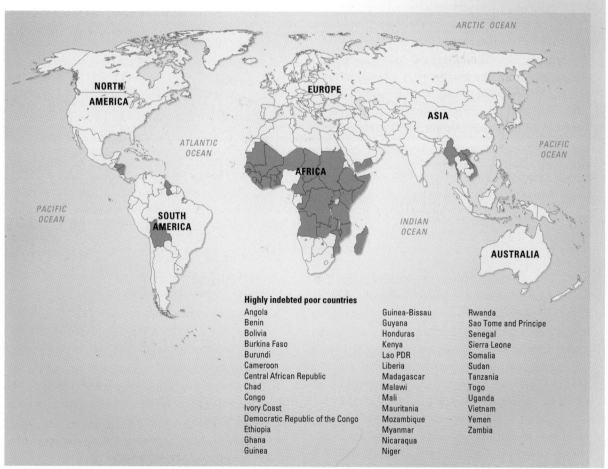

Highly indebted poor countries

Angola	Guinea-Bissau	Rwanda
Benin	Guyana	Sao Tome and Principe
Bolivia	Honduras	Senegal
Burkina Faso	Kenya	Sierra Leone
Burundi	Lao PDR	Somalia
Cameroon	Liberia	Sudan
Central African Republic	Madagascar	Tanzania
Chad	Malawi	Togo
Congo	Mali	Uganda
Ivory Coast	Mauritania	Vietnam
Democratic Republic of the Congo	Mozambique	Yemen
Ethiopia	Myanmar	Zambia
Ghana	Nicaraqua	
Guinea	Niger	

Some lenders have begun to act to reduce the debt. In 1999, an agreement was reached at an international summit to cancel about $111 billion of the $354 billion owed by the highly indebted poor countries. Mozambique became the third country (after Uganda and Bolivia) to be offered relief through the HIPC agreement. About half of Mozambique's $2.5 billion debt will eventually be wiped out, but only if Mozambique puts in place some harsh austerity measures. Critics claim that the HIPC initiative does not go far enough. For instance, Mozambique's relief will amount to only a 15 per cent reduction in its debt-servicing charges.

Canada has been in the forefront in calling for an easing of the debts owed by HIPCs. In 2000, the federal budget set aside $175 million for a debt reduction plan. The goal is to reduce the debt load of highly indebted countries so their scarce resources can go towards poverty reduction programs rather than to debt servicing. Canada has forgiven all overseas development aid debt to all the HIPCs except Myanmar, which is governed by a military dictatorship.

Since 1986, all *bilateral aid* for development (assistance from one government to another) has been in the form of grants, as opposed to loans. Also, ten Latin American countries have been allowed to repay debts by investing in environmental and other sustainable development projects in their own countries.

ACTIVITIES

1. How has the debt burden in developing countries prevented governments from looking after the basic needs of their people?

2. How is the HIPC program meant to help the poorest developing countries?

3. In a two-column chart, list the reasons for and against completely forgiving the debt of developing countries with the highest debt loads.

4. Write a letter to your member of Parliament explaining your point of view on debt forgiveness.

The Vulnerable Ones: Women and Children

The Position of Women

The burden of poverty creates particular hardships for women and children. Many developing countries have male-dominated societies where females and children have lower status than men. Women and children may have no legal rights, or the legal system may allow them to be treated as property. Women may even be killed to satisfy a family's honour. In some tribal societies, women and children may have to eat whatever is left after the men have finished their meals, which can lead to malnutrition.

A woman in a developing country may have to work for over twelve hours a day to ensure the survival of her family (see Figure 14-15). Women are often left to support the family when men migrate in search of work.

In much of the developing world, the rate of literacy is lower among women than among men.

Amina's Day

Activity	Hours Spent
Wake up at 5 a.m.	—
Walk to field with baby on her back	0.5
Plough, plant, hoe until 3 p.m. (taking meals in the fields)	9.5
Collect firewood and carry it home	1.0
Pound or grind grain	1.5
Carry water from the well or river	1.5
Tend the fire and cook meal	1.0
Serve food, eat, clean up	1.0
Wash herself, children, and clothes	1.0
Go to bed about 10 p.m.	—
Total	17.0

Figure 14-15 This Zambian woman's day during the planting season is typical of women in other parts of the developing world.

Making a graph Group the information into categories and present it in graph form. How would this workload prevent a woman from improving her status?

Education is often a luxury that is restricted to males. Only one-third of girls in rural India go to school compared to more than one-half of boys. The feeling is that education is wasted on girls. Many families will keep girls at home to look after the younger children and help with chores until they are married and move to their husband's village. Cultural tradition dictates that when a woman is married she is reborn into her husband's family, so there is an incentive for her to be married young.

Demographers agree that economic development and the fertility rate of countries are connected. A decline in the number of children a woman has in her lifetime frees her to improve her lot and that of her children. Study after study shows that better educated women have fewer children. They tend to marry later and bear children later. A World Bank report found that in places where women do not receive a secondary education, the average number of children was seven. When women have secondary school education, the figure drops to three. Because they are literate they have a better understanding of contraception, and may be able to resist family pressures to have more children.

Their children are also more likely to survive. Educated women know more about the importance of immunization, clean water, and good nutrition. A study in Peru showed that the infant mortality rate dropped for every year of schooling the mother had. When mothers are sure that their children will survive, they are less likely to have large families. The key to improving the status of women is education.

Women in Niger

The African country of Niger, which lies almost entirely in the Sahara Desert, is one of the world's least developed countries (see Figure 14-1). The life expectancy is under forty-nine years, literacy is 14 per cent, and 65 per cent of the population survive on less than $180 a year. A recent drop in the price of uranium, its only major export, has reduced the country's export earnings. As well, donor aid has been withheld until the military government returns the government to civilian rule.

Niger's women are taking a larger role in the economy, making pottery, selling firewood, cloth, and anything else that they can to keep their families from starving. Yet, in a traditional Muslim society, they are bound to obey the wishes of their

Women's Literacy Rates

Countries with 70%–79% of women illiterate	Countries with 80%–89% of women illiterate	Countries with 90% and over of women illiterate
Angola	Afghanistan	Burkina Faso
Bangladesh	Benin	Niger
Bhutan	Guinea-Bissau	Sierra Leone
Central African Rep.	Nepal	
Ethiopia	Somalia	
Gambia	Yemen	
Guinea		
Liberia		
Mali		
Mauritania		
Mozambique		
Pakistan		
Senegal		

Figure 14-16 Countries where 70 per cent or more of adult women are illiterate.

Interpreting statistics Colour and name these countries on a world map. Compare your map with Figure 14-2. What pattern is evident?

Figure 14-17 Women in Niger, one of the world's least developed countries, are forced into the economy to support their families, yet are still second-class citizens.

husbands, fathers, brothers, and other male relatives. Polygamy, or the practice of having more than one wife, is widespread, and the average marrying age for women is fifteen. The average number of children per woman is 7.4. When Niger ratified the U.N. convention on women's rights, there was criticism of those who supported this measure. Niger is an extreme example of the situation for women in many developing countries.

Children in Crisis

Children are often the first victims of underdevelopment. Famine, disease, war, and a host of other problems prey on society's most vulnerable dependents. Even if they survive the critical first five years, children in some developing nations have few educational opportunities and are all too often exploited as child labour. Some are even

trapped in the sex-trade. The high birth rates in many developing areas ensure that this problem will remain with us into the future.

Since 1990, the United Nations Children's Fund (UNICEF) has published an annual Progress of Nations Report (PNR) on the welfare of children. The PNR launched the twenty-first century with a new child-risk index that measures the risk of children in countries worldwide on a scale of zero to 100. The measure is based on five factors: the mortality rates of children under the age of five, the percentage of children who are moderately or severely underweight, numbers of children who do not attend primary school, risks from armed conflict, and risks from the disease HIV/AIDS.

Canada, the United States, Australia, Japan, and other highly developed nations had risk scores of five or below—differences that are of no consequence, according to UNICEF. Africa is the continent where children face the greatest risks. Africa's average score was sixty-one, compared to Europe's average of six, and the world average of thirty.

Top Ten Countries for Child Risk

Country	Rating
1. Angola	96
2. Sierra Leone	95
3. Afghanistan	94
4. Somalia	92
5. Ethiopia	85
6. Guinea-Bissau	80
7. Niger	76
8. Democratic Rep. of Congo	76
9. Burundi	74
10. Eritrea	74

Figure 14-18 These are the ten countries in which children are at greatest risk, according to UNICEF's Child-Risk Index.

Interpreting statistics Based on what you learned in Chapter 13 about how census figures are collected, how accurate do you think these figures are? Explain your answer.

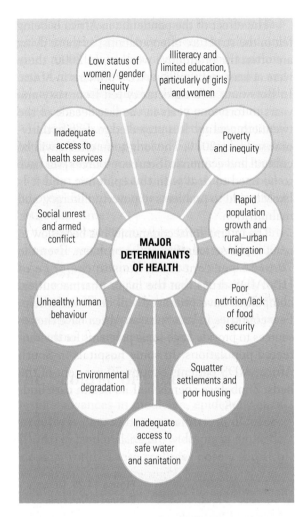

Figure 14-26 Major determinants of health in developing countries.

Thinking critically From what you have learned, identify the causes and effects that are linked in this web.

ACTIVITIES

1. Describe three difficulties in providing basic health care in developing countries.

2. Why should people in the developed world be concerned about the health of people in the developing world?

3. Research one of the diseases caused by contaminated water. Write a short report explaining what causes the disease, its effects, and how safer water supplies might contain its spread.

4. Predict how the loss of productive workers from the HIV/AIDS pandemic will affect the future of countries like Botswana.

Dealing with the problem of HIV/AIDS requires multilateral cooperation of many national and international agencies. Canada has been one of the leaders in the establishment of the Joint United Nations Programme on HIV/AIDS (UNAIDS). UNAIDS coordinates the work of such U.N. bodies as UNICEF, UNESCO, WHO, and the World Bank. It helps countries respond to HIV/AIDS, and helps health workers so they can educate people and limit the transmission of the disease.

Solutions

Since World War II, the developed world has been providing aid to the nations of South America, Africa, and Asia. A lack of political and economic stability in most of the newly emerging former colonies in Asia and Africa made the transition into independence a difficult one. Foreign aid programs were chosen as the way to foster development in these countries, while at the same time countering the growing influence of the communist bloc. As the volume of aid grew, the political and humanitarian motives of aid donors became interconnected.

The money spent on aid is still dwarfed by the amount spent on armaments in the world. In 1998, military spending was estimated to be $780 billion (U.S.), making it the world's largest industry. The United Nations aid agencies estimate that a fraction of this total would give universal access to basic social services in all developing countries. For $6 billion everyone could have a basic education, $9 billion would supply water and sanitation, and $12 billion would ensure reproductive health for all women. Basic health and nutrition could be achieved for $13 million.

Foreign Aid

The aid received by developing countries takes a number of forms. **Multilateral aid** is funded by a number of governments, and usually involves large-scale programs like dam building. Often, bilateral aid is **tied aid**, given with conditions attached. More than 30 per cent of Canadian bilateral and multilateral aid is tied to Canadian purchases. A criticism of Western aid projects is that they have been tied too much to the trade system that benefits the industrialized countries at the expense of the developing world.

Developing nations receive foreign aid from various sources. It can be provided to countries through international bodies such as the United Nations, national government agencies such as the Canadian International Development Agency (CIDA), and many non-governmental organizations (NGOs) representing religious groups, service organizations such as Rotary International, and other non-profit organizations, such as Oxfam.

Many agencies of the United Nations are dedicated to improving the living standards of people in the developing world. For example, UNICEF has been in the forefront in fighting iodine deficiency disorder, a disease that can cause mental retardation and stunt growth. The addition of a few grams of inexpensive iodized table salt to the daily diet prevents this disorder. In the early 1980s, more than 60 per cent of primary school children in Bolivia suffered from iodine deficiency. In 1996, Canada contributed 88 per cent of the budget for UNICEF's salt iodization program in Bolivia.

Canada's Foreign Aid Program

CIDA distributes aid projects through U.N. agencies, directly to governments, and through NGOs. It supports foreign aid projects in more than 100 of the poorest countries of the world. Its objective is to work with people in developing countries and to develop the tools for them to meet their own needs eventually. Yet, excluding emergency food aid, it is estimated that less than 20 per cent of Canadian development aid is spent on meeting basic human needs.

NGO aid projects often operate at the grassroots level, providing direct assistance to people. Initiatives range from well-known, large organizations such as the Red Cross and Doctors without Borders to smaller groups dealing with local

Figure 14-27 This eleven-month-old boy was buried under rubble for seven hours after an earthquake in Turkey, August 1999. He was the first patient to be treated at the Canadian Disaster Assistance Response team's medical aid station in the town of Serdivan.

Figure 14-28 The NGO World Vision is helping the village of Kasanga, Uganda, to build this new school. When the school is completed, students will be able to meet in classrooms instead of under trees.

projects. Often the development assistance of NGOs has been more effective than the large projects sponsored by governments, as the aid goes directly to the people who benefit from the projects.

Should Canada Link Its Foreign Aid to Human Rights?

Most Canadians would likely agree that the estimated 1.3 billion people living in extreme poverty in the world should benefit from our foreign aid programs. Yet, many of these people live under regimes that are regularly accused of abusing human rights. To what extent should Canadian aid be tied to the human rights records of governments?

Afghanistan, a landlocked country of about twenty-six million people, is one of the poorest countries in the world. Late in 1979, Soviet troops invaded the country. In the subsequent war, between one and two million Afghans, 90 per cent of them civilians, were killed. Six million became refugees. The Soviet invaders spread mines, slaughtered livestock, and committed atrocities such as rape. The United States supported the resistance fighters against the invaders.

When the troops left in 1989, civil war broke out. Gradually a group called the Taliban, or Religious Students Movement, took over two-thirds of the country. They confiscated all weapons and stopped the civil war in the areas they controlled.

The Taliban enforced their strict interpretation of Islamic law. The rules were harshest towards women, who were not allowed to appear in public without being covered head to foot in a *burqah*. They had to stay at home behind blacked-out windows. The only women allowed to work were doctors in women's hospitals. While some schooling for girls was tolerated, in 2000 the ban on female education remained in force. Women found guilty of adultery were stoned to death. Religious police patrolled the streets. People found guilty of offences such as failing to attend prayers, displaying photographs of living creatures, or possessing cassettes or videotapes could be publicly whipped. Thieves faced public amputation of hands and feet.

Figure 14-29 Many Afghan women lost their husbands during the twenty years of war and are without jobs because of the Taliban government's strict interpretation of Islamic law. Most widows must rely on donations from other community members to survive.

A U.N. Food and Agricultural Organization report in June 2000 warned that millions of Afghans had little or no access to food and that the situation would deteriorate because of a severe drought. This compounded problems in a country that had been ravaged and impoverished by more than twenty years of war. This situation clearly seemed to warrant Canada's immediate response with offers of aid. However, some claimed that the poor human rights record of the Taliban government of Afghanistan should be an issue in granting aid to that country.

The Universal Declaration of Human Rights and other U.N.-sponsored agreements, such as the Convention of the Elimination of all Forms of Discrimination against Women, call for protection of the political, legal, and social rights of women. CIDA's *Policy Framework for Women in Development* calls for women to be involved in planning and delivering aid programs in countries receiving aid. Should Canada insist that Afghanistan comply with these requirements?

The Case for Denying Aid

Those in favour of denying aid say that it is not enough for Canada just to support U.N. conventions and formulate policy, such as CIDA's regarding women's rights. The best way to change the practice of these governments is to deny aid whenever human rights violations occur. Also, there is no guarantee that the aid will get to the poor and underprivileged. In Afghanistan, the aid may not get to the women who need it.

The Case for Giving Aid

Those opposed to denying aid point out that different cultures have different interpretations of rights. They claim the U.N. Declaration of Human Rights represents a Western view of rights, a view not all framers agreed on when the declaration was written in 1948. People must be allowed to follow their own culture's teaching with regard to rights and toleration—including the treatment of women. Good causes are not made better by confusing needs with rights, these critics maintain, and change can be brought about more readily through dialogue.

There are some basic rights that can be agreed on by all cultures. According to Canadian author Michael Ignatieff, the purpose of the U.N. Declaration of Rights was "to put ... racism, sexism, and anti-Semitism for example, under eternal ban." A person supporting human rights could argue that capital punishment in the United States is as much an abuse of human rights as amputation or death by stoning in Afghanistan.

In supporting an increase in Canadian aid to Afghanistan, Maria Minna, Federal Minister for International Cooperation, claimed in June 2000 that working with the Taliban regime had brought little progress. A Canadian-financed maternal and childcare centre could help those most in need. The minister condemned the Taliban:

> ... for taking cultural traditions that discriminate against women to a new and intolerable level by enforcing them as official policy. However difficult dialogue is with the Taliban, it is only through dialogue that they will consider changes to their restrictive and harmful practices.

Analysing the Issue

1. In a two-column organizer, list the reasons for and against giving aid to countries where the government is a dictatorship.

2. Which side of the debate do you support? Explain your reasons.

3. Do you agree with Ignatieff's list of basic human rights that could be accepted by all cultures? Explain your answer. Name other rights that might be added to the list.

4. Write a letter to the Minister for International Cooperation outlining the precautions you would advise her ministry to take to ensure that Canada's development aid gets to poor and needy people.

5. Humanitarian groups have criticized developed countries for abuses of human rights, such as the disproportionate number of Aboriginal people in Canadian prisons, and the executions of mentally handicapped people in the United States. What is your reaction to the suggestion that Western countries should not impose standards for human rights on developing countries until all human rights claims against themselves have been dealt with? Explain your answer.

In Bangladesh, women—many of them landless labourers or wives abandoned by husbands—work on a CARE scheme repairing dirt roads for a three-year period. A portion of their wages of one dollar a day is held back and then given to them as a lump sum to invest. Some women buy engine-driven rickshaws or plots of land, or establish small businesses. Most are able to stop the cycle of poverty, improve their living conditions, and provide for their children's education.

In recent years, governments have followed the lead of NGOs in promoting small-scale, sustainable projects that are appropriate to the local environment and that can be maintained locally. Wells with simple pumps replace irrigation projects, tools are made from local or recycled materials, and local people are given the means to sustain their own development initiatives.

The amount Canada contributes to foreign aid has been decreasing for the past two decades.

The Canadian government in 1984 pledged to reach the U.N. aid target of 0.7 per cent of GDP by the year 2000. Since then, cutbacks in federal government programs have affected foreign aid contributions. By 1998, Canadian development assistance had reached a thirty-year low, dropping to 0.27 per cent of GDP.

ACTIVITIES

1. In an organizer, list the types of aid Canada sends to developed countries and comment on the pros and cons of each type of aid.

2. With a partner, make a list of the top three priorities Canada should follow in distributing aid to the developing world. Support each of your choices.

3. Make a list of reasons for and against a proposal to increase the amount of aid Canada gives to developing countries.

4. Organize a debate on the topic: *Resolved—Funding NGOs is the most effective way to get aid to the developing world.*

Global Problems, Local Solutions

It is clear that poverty is at the root of problems in the developing world. Women and children in particular are trapped in a cycle of poverty. High birth rates, high infant mortality rates, low levels of literacy, high instances of disease, and other problems are all linked. Too many of the world's people are still malnourished, in poor health, poorly housed, and without a secure economic future. An improvement in the status of women has been shown to reduce fertility and improve children's health.

Billions of dollars in aid have been spent in developing countries, much of it without improving conditions for the poor. Dictators or local elites are often the winners in the aid sweepstakes. The most successful forms of aid have come from programs that consult the local people and listen to their suggestions, giving the help of outside donor agencies if required.

Figure 14-30 This women's weaving cooperative in Banaue, Ifugao Province, Philippines was started with a grant and loan from a local development agency. Members pay a small annual fee, which goes towards the purchase of yarn. The weavers sell their products through local craft shops to tourists. To generate income in the months when there are few tourists, the co-op buys and sells rice. Membership in the co-op also entitles the weavers to small, low-interest loans.

LOOKING BACK

Develop an Understanding

1. Use a Venn diagram to compare and contrast the life of a child in a developing country suffering from civil war with that of a child you know in Canada. Summarize the similarities and differences in a paragraph.

2. Review the five factors measured by UNICEF's Child-Risk Index. Rank them in order of importance. Explain your choices.

3. As a group, list in priority the five most pressing problems facing Africa if standards of living are to be raised.

4. A Nigerian said: "If the developed world sends money it is only temporary. Send tools and technology and we will solve our own problems." In a group, brainstorm a mind map that shows the tools and technology that would be most useful in solving the developmental problems common to African countries.

Explore the Issues

5. The United Nations, International Monetary Fund, World Bank, and Organization for Economic Cooperation and Development have set a goal of cutting in half extreme poverty in the world by 2015. What steps do you think should be taken to achieve this aim by:

   a. these world financial institutions?

   b. the developing countries?

   c. Canada?

6. Almost 20 per cent of Canada's children are estimated to be living in poverty. With a partner, list in order of priority five steps the government should take to improve their standards of living. Display the list, with appropriate artwork, in a poster.

7. Role-play a conversation between a Canadian and a person from one of the least developed countries on the benefits of local development projects as opposed to large schemes.

8. With a partner, develop a Charter of Aid. Include in it the criteria Canada should use in deciding which countries will receive Canadian assistance.

9. In a group, develop a strategy to convince governments to divert 10 per cent of military spending to development aid to developing countries.

Research and Communicate

10. Research the effects of a structural adjustment program of the IMF. Report your findings to the class.

11. Develop a brochure for distribution in your community describing the five most pressing problems facing Africa, and indicating the international and government agencies and NGOs that Canadians could contact if they want information or wish to send donations.

12. Have each member of your group choose a country from Figure 14-16 (page 352). Research natural resources, demography, government, ways of making a living, culture, and other factors in the country that you feel may be relevant to explaining the statistic. Compare your findings with others in the group who have studied other countries. Compile a list of factors that are common to most countries where women's literacy rates are low.

13. Visit Craig Kielburger's Web site at **<www.freethechildren.org>**. Suggest a class project that could contribute in some way to the work done by Craig and his supporters to help child labourers.

14. Prepare a two-minute radio talk on the Human Development Index. In particular, address the question of why all but two of the bottom twenty-five countries in the Human Development Index are in Africa.

15. Use a two-column organizer to list the problems in one of the developing countries shown in Figure 14-2 on page 342. In one column, list the problems that come from within the country; in the other, list the problems that have come from outside.

16. Make a poster that informs Canadians of the connections between water and diseases in the tropical world.

15

Urbanization

Most people have mixed emotions about cities. Cities offer opportunity and excitement, but they can also be dangerous and threatening places. In the midst of their great wealth and beauty, there is also poverty and squalour. Cities are all these things—and much more.

Expressing ideas What do you like most about cities? What do you dislike? Explain your reasons.

Introduction

Think about what life was like for young Canadians in 1871, just four years after Confederation. For most young men, life revolved around their jobs on farms, in lumber mills, at quarries, or in fishing boats. The lives of young women centred on households, with chores such as preparing and preserving food, looking after children, and maintaining homes. Some women worked in their own houses, but many others worked as servants. In 1871, the majority of Canadians were rural dwellers, living in small communities or on isolated farms. Only 18.3 per cent of Canadians lived in towns and cities. By 1971, this percentage had changed drastically. Census figures showed that most Canadians—76.1 per cent—lived in towns and cities. In the first hundred years or so of its existence, Canada had become an urban nation. Such a movement of people to cities is referred to as **urbanization**.

Urbanization has happened all around the world. Most developed countries became urbanized during the nineteenth and twentieth centuries, and the shift from rural areas to urban centres in these countries is largely complete. The process of urbanization has now shifted to the developing countries of Africa, Asia, and Latin America. In Egypt, for example, less than 50 per cent of the population now lives in cities, while in Rwanda, in central Africa, only 8 per cent do so. These countries are currently experiencing, and will continue to experience, urbanization for some time to come.

The pattern of urbanization became an important global trend only in the twentieth century. In this chapter, you will examine some of the reasons for this trend, and the problems that it has created in cities and their surrounding areas. Why have cities grown up at certain sites, and why have some prospered more than others?

Global Urbanization

In 1900, less than 14 per cent of the world's people were urban dwellers. This reflects the fact that historically, humans have always been rural

dwellers, tied to the land that sustained them. The movement of people to cities was prompted by several key developments:

- *Mechanization*, or the use of machinery, displaced workers in mining, fishing, logging, and especially farming.
- *Industrialization*, or the switch to an economy dependent on manufacturing industries, encouraged the concentration of manufacturing at sites that had the right combination of raw materials, power, and transportation facilities. These sites became destinations for workers leaving the rural areas.
- *Technological change in fuel sources*—from firewood to coal and then petroleum—meant that energy supplies could be hauled long distances to cities, to be consumed by the factories and workers housed there.

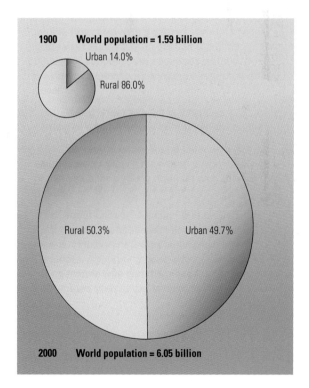

Figure 15-1 World urban populations in 1900 and 2000. The size of the circles is in proportion to the total population of the world.

Reading a graph How has the total urban population changed in this period? How has the ratio of urban population to rural population changed?

	1900	1920	1940	1960	1980	2000
Urban Population	223	360	570	1012	1807	3008
Rural Population	1367	1500	1725	1973	2567	3046
Source: United Nations Population Division, 2000.						

Figure 15-2 World urban and rural populations (in millions) for the twentieth century.

Interpreting statistics

1. Use the data in the table to construct a line graph showing the trends in world urban and rural population, 1900–2000. You will need one line to show rural population, and one to show urban population. Then, write a caption to describe the trends.

2. Calculate the percentage of the world's population living in urban areas in 2000. Predict, giving your reasons, whether this percentage will rise or fall by 2020.

The first countries to industrialize were the first ones to urbanize. The two trends worked together to transform societies. By the end of the twentieth century, almost half the world's people called cities their home.

You learned in Chapter 13 that world population growth rates in the past decades have been very rapid, particularly in developing countries. The rate at which urban areas are growing is 1.5 times faster than world population growth! So, while cities are experiencing population growth through births, they are also experiencing population growth through **in-migration**, or people moving into cities. Globally, urban areas are growing at an average rate of 2.5 per cent every year—about 3.5 per cent in developing countries and about 1 per cent in developed countries.

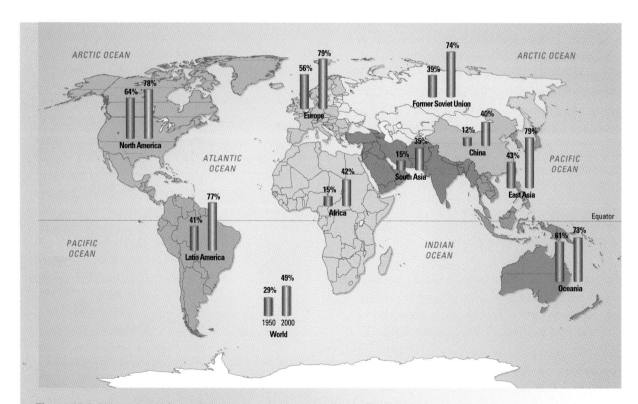

Figure 15-3 Urban share of populations in major regions of the world, 1950 and 2000, by percentage.

Interpreting statistics Which three parts of the world experienced the greatest change over this time period? Which two experienced the least change?

Millionaire Cities

The movement to cities has meant a dramatic jump in the number of cities having over one million people. In 1850, when only a small part of the world was urbanized, just London, Paris, and Beijing had populations of over one million. In 2000, fully 400 cities had over a million residents. With the exception of Australia, cities with over five million people can now be found on every

Figure 15-4 The world's largest cities, 2000.

Reading a map

1. Which continent had the largest number of cities with over five million people?

2. Which two countries had the largest number of "millionaire cities" (with over one million inhabitants)?

3. How would you explain the pattern you have identified?

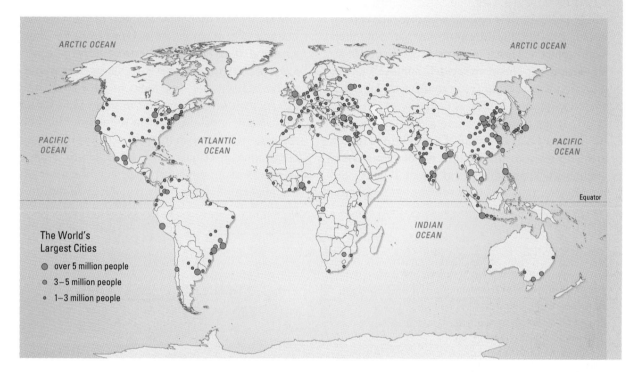

The World's Largest Cities

- over 5 million people
- 3–5 million people
- 1–3 million people

City	1950	City	1980	City	2000
New York	12.3	Tokyo	16.9	Mexico City	25.6
London	8.7	New York	15.6	São Paulo	22.1
Tokyo	6.7	Mexico City	14.5	Tokyo	19.0
Paris	5.4	São Paulo	12.1	Shanghai	17.0
Shanghai	5.3	Shanghai	11.7	New York	16.8
Buenos Aires	5.0	Buenos Aires	9.9	Calcutta	15.7
Chicago	4.9	Los Angeles	9.5	Bombay	15.4
Moscow	4.8	Calcutta	9.0	Beijing	14.0
Calcutta	4.4	Beijing	9.0	Los Angeles	13.9
Los Angeles	4.0	Rio de Janeiro	8.8	Jakarta	13.7
Source: Population Reference Bureau, 2000.					

Figure 15-5 The populations of the ten largest urban areas in the world, for 1950, 1980, and 2000 (in millions).

Using evidence

1. Use Figure 15-4 and an atlas to locate each of these cities. Which five cities listed in 2000 were not listed in 1950?

2. From what you know, how would you explain their rapid growth?

3. How would you account for London and Paris disappearing from the list by 1980?

continent. By 2015, population experts predict that twenty-seven cities will have populations greater than ten million. The number of huge cities in the developing countries demonstrates the rapid rate of urbanization in those parts of the world.

Dealing with Rapid Urban Growth

Large cities in developing countries are experiencing tremendous difficulties in managing their rapid growth. Most new arrivals find shelter by squeezing into the overcrowded homes of family and friends, and often resort to living on land that they do not own, which is called *squatting*, and constructing makeshift homes out of any materials that they can scrounge. These **shanty towns** grow up on vacant land that is not being used, such as the steep hillsides in Rio de Janeiro, and are often around the edges of large cities. Jakarta, Indonesia, has growth rates of 18 per cent per year in some parts of its shanty-town urban fringe, while half of the eight million people who live in Dhaka, Bangladesh, live in these makeshift neighbourhoods. Some newcomers to cities merely find a place on the street to live and sleep.

Cities in developing countries have few resources to accommodate these extra people. The many new arrivals tend to overload the existing infrastructure of the city. The demands of the exploding population put strains on water supplies, sewage facilities, mass transit, power grids, health and social services, policing, and fire protection. For example, roadways are so crowded in Bangkok, Thailand, that the average driver spends the equivalent of forty-four full days per year sitting in traffic jams. In India's capital city of New Delhi, the electricity is often turned off in some areas for up to six hours a day in order to reduce the load on the system. Efforts on the part of cities to improve conditions are usually futile because of the large numbers of migrants arriving daily. As a result, the growth of these cities is haphazard and unplanned.

Figure 15-6 The shanty town of Huaycan, on the outskirts of Lima, Peru. Shanty towns exist around large cities in most developing countries, though they are called different things. In Peru they are called *pueblos jovenos*, in Brazil they are *favelas*, in Argentina, *villa miserias*, in India, *bustees*, and in Indonesia people use the term *kampung*.

City	People per Room
Lagos, Nigeria	5.8
Guangzhou, China	5.7
Johannesburg, South Africa	5.0
Lahore, Pakistan	4.5
Bombay, India	4.2
Jakarta, Indonesia	3.4
Bangkok, Thailand	3.2
Ho Chi Minh City, Vietnam	3.1
Algiers, Algeria	2.5
Lima, Peru	2.3
Casablanca, Morocco	2.3

Source: *New Internationalist*, June 1999.

Figure 15-7 The number of people per room for some fast-growing large cities. Most North American cities have fewer than one person per room.

Thinking critically

1. Explain how the statistic about number of people per room is useful in showing crowding in urban areas.

2. What might be some problems in using statistics of this type? Which continents have the most crowded cities?

3. Suggest reasons for this pattern.

The Plight of Street Children

The flood of migrants to cities in the developing world has created an urban phenomenon—street children. An estimated 100 million children live on the street worldwide. In São Paulo, Brazil, they make up 10 per cent of the city's population.

The stresses of dealing with poverty, unemployment, inadequate and crowded housing, poor physical environment, and lack of services undermine the social and family structures in these cities. Children are frequent victims. Abandoned by families struggling with poverty, or fleeing abusive homes, the children have to make their own way, living on the streets. Lacking job skills, they turn to the informal economy—begging, peddling inexpensive goods like chewing gum, shining shoes, stealing, or prostitution. Often they become victims of street violence, sexual predators, or substance abuse. In some cities, the police have murdered street children whom they see as a nuisance.

Figure 15-8 On the left, a street child sleeps outside Rio de Janeiro's Central Station as others play, 1999. The lives of street children are often cruel, cold, lonely, and devoid of love and affection. They have been called the "lost generation."

ACTIVITIES

1. The percentage of the population living in urban areas in Canada has stabilized at about 76 per cent. Suggest two reasons that might explain why the rate has not gone much higher.

2. Outline reasons to explain why each of the three factors that are listed on p. 367 were important in encouraging urbanization.

3. Canada has street children living in its big cities, though not in the same numbers as in the cities of developing nations. From what you have learned in this chapter and Chapter 14, speculate on four reasons why the problem is less prevalent in Canada.

4. What solutions would you propose to deal with the issue of street children in **a)** the developing world? **b)** Canada?

Function and Form in Cities

People leave rural areas and go to cities because they are being both pushed and pulled there. They are driven by certain factors, called **push factors**, which encourage them to leave their rural homes. For example, they might find rural areas lacking in such things as adequate food supplies, jobs, education, and health care. They are drawn to cities because certain factors, called **pull factors**, attract them there. Most migrants think that they will be better able to meet their needs in urban areas. Cities are seen as places of opportunity, where dreams can be realized. While the reality of city life may not measure up to migrants' perceptions and expectations, people move there with high hopes. All the activities that they seek and that take place in cities are the functions of cities.

Important Early Functions	Example City
Defence — Sites that were easily defended were chosen for many of the oldest cities. Islands, cliffs, and mountains were used for their defensive and tactical advantages.	**Quebec City, Quebec** The cliffs and high land overlooking the St. Lawrence River at the point where the river narrows made the location defensible.
Transportation — Some sites were selected because they facilitated the movement of goods and people. Shallow spots on rivers where people could cross (fords), sheltered bays, mountain passes, and river mouths are important for transportation. These are good sites for setting up supply, repair, and coordination services.	**Halifax, Nova Scotia** The sheltered deep-water harbour on the east coast of North America made Halifax a natural place to prepare for the difficult journey across the Atlantic, or a place to rest after having endured the voyage.
Resource extraction — Communities were needed to house and provide services to people employed in extracting natural resources such as minerals, fishing, farming, or forestry.	**Thompson, Manitoba** The early community was constructed to provide services to the mining companies and miners who worked the vast mineral deposits in the area.
Head of navigation — At **break-of-bulk** points, goods have to be transferred from one method of transport to another. Services such as wharves or terminals are built to make the break-of-bulk work smoothly.	**Thunder Bay, Ontario** Larger vessels could travel westward on the Great Lakes only to this point. Here the cargoes had to be unloaded and transferred to methods that could handle the rugged overland trip.

Figure 15-9 Some original functions of cities. The spark that causes a city to be established in the first place is usually a particular need, such as a need for protection or a need to speed the movement of goods.

Gathering information

1. Which of these early functions apply to your community? Explain your answers.

2. Name urban centres in British Columbia for each of these categories.

3. Working in small groups, research the early functions of the ten largest urban centres in 2000 (see Figure 15-5). Which functions seem to be most important?

It is because of these **urban functions** that cities are established and grow.

Urban functions change over time. The original function of many cities may be long gone, but the city remains. Montreal is a good example. Its early function was to act as the central location for the fur trade in North America, an activity that has lost its importance for the modern city of Montreal. Changes take place, in part, because of changes in technology, such as the improvement of transportation services. Also, cities grow and expand, so that new urban functions emerge over time. Montreal, for example, has become a cultural centre, among other things. In general, the larger the population of an urban centre, the more functions it can offer.

Site and Situation

Most early communities developed because the *site* and *situation* of the place favoured certain activities, such as trade.

◼ **Site** refers to the physical characteristics of the land on which the city is built. Descriptions of site usually include details about landforms, drainage, and natural vegetation cover. For example, a person describing the site of Vancouver would point out the Fraser River and its delta, natural harbours at Burrard Inlet and False Creek, the mountains and valleys to the north and east, and the Strait of Georgia.

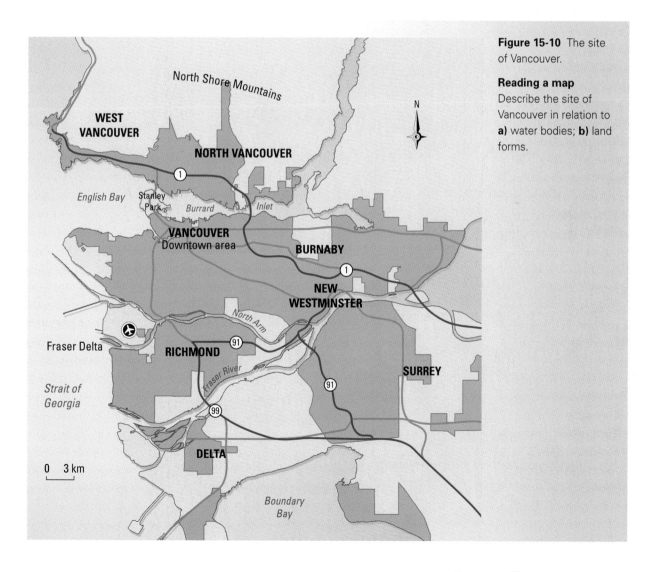

Figure 15-10 The site of Vancouver.

Reading a map
Describe the site of Vancouver in relation to
a) water bodies; **b)** land forms.

Situation describes the relationship between the city and its wider surroundings. Details about surrounding landforms may be included, as well as information about the population and economic patterns. A description of Vancouver's situation would make reference to its access to the interior of the province via the river valley, the proximity to the Canada–U.S. border, transportation connections to the Pacific region, and so on.

Figure 15-11 The situation of Vancouver.

Reading a map In two or three sentences, describe the situation of Vancouver referring to water bodies, land forms, and the international border.

Figure 15-12 Vancouver looking north. The city has both site and situational advantages.

Interpreting an aerial photograph

1. Locate Stanley Park; North Shore Mountains; Burrard Inlet.

2. How can you tell which area is downtown?

3. Locate on Figure 15-10 the area shown in this photograph (remember that the area will be like a pie slice). What do you learn from the photograph that you do not learn from the map? What do you learn from the map that you do not learn from the photograph?

Figure 15-13 Uranium city, Saskatchewan, is an example of a community that declined after its chief natural resource ran out and the uranium mine closed. When this picture was taken in 1957, the town had become a "ghost town."

If the site and situation of a location accommodate the kinds of activities that people want to engage in, a community may be established. For example, if there is fertile soil and access to other places for trade, a market town could grow up. If the site and situation remain favourable, the community will grow and prosper. Vancouver, for example, has grown much more rapidly than Victoria because its location puts it closer to raw materials, and it has a large harbour and land-based transportation systems. Because it is directly linked to large cities in the United States, such as Seattle and Los Angeles, and to the other cities of Canada, Vancouver also has a **locational advantage** over Victoria.

Some communities decline and even cease to exist because their sites and situations cannot sustain them. The once-busy mining town of Schefferville, Quebec, is a good example. Only a few hundred people currently live in this boarded-up community now that the mining company has stopped its operations. The area still has plenty of iron ore, but the company has determined that other ore bodies are more profitable to mine. Schefferville's location, far from cheap transportation routes and markets, puts it at a locational disadvantage.

ACTIVITIES

1. Identify three push factors and three pull factors that encourage the movement of rural people to urban areas.

2. Explain how the following technological innovations might affect the urban functions of a city:

   a) Air travel becomes fast, efficient, and cheap.

   b) Telecommunications connect most people using wireless technology (e.g., cell phones).

   c) Monorails are built for public transit, much improving speed and comfort.

3. Suppose you were asked by your city council to analyse the location of your own community.

   a) Describe the site and situation of the community.

   b) Identify one aspect of the location that has been most important in encouraging the growth of the community.

   c) Identify one aspect of the location that has been most detrimental to the growth and development of the community.

4. Use an atlas, as well as print and electronic sources, to research the site and situation of one of the largest cities in Canada or around the world.

Analysing Urban Functions

In general, urban functions can be grouped into two categories: *basic* and *non-basic activities*. **Basic activities** are also referred to as *town-forming activities*. In some cases, industries are the basic activities, such as mills, factories, and mines. Other examples of basic activities include tourism, military facilities, public administration, and transportation. These urban functions serve a larger population than just the community and bring wealth into the area.

Non-basic activities are *town-serving activities* because they exist to meet the needs of the local population. Grocery stores, places of worship, and municipal services such as parks are among these activities. Because these activities circulate the wealth that is within the community but do not generate new wealth, they seldom provide the impetus to begin a community. They are, nonetheless, important and necessary urban functions in a community.

As basic activities grow in a community, the additional wealth stimulates the expansion of the non-basic sector. For example, it has been estimated that for every job created directly in resource extraction industries, three jobs are stimulated elsewhere in the economy. This is called the **multiplier effect**. Earnings of workers in basic industries lead to expansion of the non-basic sector, for example, as more shops and

Figure 15-14 The pulp and paper mill at Powell River, British Columbia.

Developing understanding What makes this mill a basic activity for the nearby town?

services are provided. Unfortunately, the multiplier effect also works in reverse. Job losses in basic activities produce even greater job losses in non-basic activities within the community as stores go out of business and service workers are made redundant.

The multiplier effect leads to unequal growth among different communities. Communities that have a locational advantage enjoy growth in basic activities, and the multiplier effect produces even greater employment in non-basic sectors. These communities grow, and the increased services that are available become magnets for even more activities. Cities such as Toronto and Vancouver in Canada, and Bombay, Cairo, and Jakarta on other continents, have experienced rapid growth. These cities become the engines for the creation of wealth: for example, the city of Seoul earns 23 per cent of South Korea's gross national product, and Bangkok generates 43 per cent of Thailand's wealth.

Poor locations, perhaps in remote or resource-poor areas, result in few basic activities and services. These places do not attract new economic activities and may even lose those that they have to more vibrant communities. A community such as Sydney, Nova Scotia, struggles to maintain its services with the decline and closure of its principal industry, steel making. The growth of central Canada has left this Atlantic community far from the major markets for its products.

The success of large cities produces another problem as well—the depopulation of rural places. At one time, many rural areas in Canada supported active and vibrant communities, often centred on a church or school. Such organizations as the Women's Institute—a networking association for rural women—provided opportunities for geographically isolated people to come together for social and practical purposes. The drift of people to cities caused the rural population to decline, and many small communities ceased to exist. Schools and churches no longer had enough people to support them and were closed. Those people who remained in rural areas found themselves without the support of a close-knit community, making rural life more difficult.

City Forms

The interaction of function, site, and situation gives cities different shapes and appearances. While there is great variety, generally there are five patterns in city forms.

- *Political and religious cities* are designed to serve important religious or political functions such as being the national capital or a holy centre. The elements of the city are usually centred on a temple or place of great religious significance, or important public buildings, connected by grand boulevards arranged in a very structured way according to a model or plan.
- *Organic cities* have evolved quite naturally in ways that fit the physical landscape. Urban functions blend together, with shops, homes, and workplaces all close together.
- *Planned cities* are designed to keep urban functions apart, with separate places for homes, shops, and industries. The areas are linked through transportation connections.
- *Transit cities* are made up of sub-centres linked to a city core by transportation services. Urban functions arrange themselves in a linear fashion along the transit lines, sometimes for quite a distance.
- *Automobile cities* expand outward in all directions from the city core. Roadways link the urban functions that are separated into distinct zones. These cities typically sprawl outwards for many kilometres, adding suburbs to the original city.

Figure 15-15 Different city forms.

a) The Political or Religious City

These cities are often built using a rectangular street grid but based on a prominent axis. The city of Beijing, shown here, is a good example, with the Forbidden City, the former residences of the emperors, at its centre. Washington, DC, is another example.

Beijing

b) The Organic City

The close interaction of functions means that organic cities rarely grow very large. They are good cities to walk around in. Cities of this type are often at the core of older cities in many parts of the world, such as Amsterdam, pictured here.

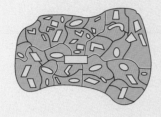

Amsterdam

c) The Planned City

These cities were usually laid out on a rectangular grid pattern because it is easy to design and separate the different functions. Many North American cities, for example, Vancouver, take this form.

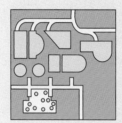

d) The Transit City

The development of high-speed transit systems spurred the growth of cities of this type. The sub-centres develop their own urban functions, but are all linked to the core via the transit connections. New York City is an example.

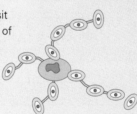

Vancouver

e) The Automobile City

The flexibility of travel allowed by the automobile means that the city can grow outwards in all directions. The prevalence of automobiles makes this the dominant form for cities in the world today. Los Angeles is a good example.

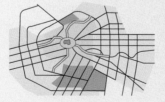

Interpreting a diagram

Decide, giving reasons for your choice, which of the city forms you think would be best for:

1. Developing a strong sense of community?
2. Encouraging industrial growth?
3. Accommodating recreational activities?
4. Adapting to life in the twenty-first century?

Los Angeles

The Automobile and the City

North Americans prefer a city form that allows people to leave the crowded, noisy city to go to homes in the *suburbs*—an environment that is in some ways reminiscent of the peaceful, rural countryside. The suburbs, which have sprung up around virtually every city on this continent, are a *low-density* approach to housing, that is, they have few people per hectare. By living in the suburbs, people avoid the *high-density* life in the inner city, where many people live close together. In the suburbs, most people live in single-family homes or townhouses that consume more land than apartments or condominiums. Many suburbs act as bedroom communities, because jobs are located elsewhere in the city where commercial and industrial activities are found. Cars have allowed us to separate work, home, recreation, and shopping. Unfortunately, they have also resulted in long commutes, daily traffic chaos, increased stress, polluted air, and looming petroleum short-

ages. The sprawling nature of suburban communities makes public transit expensive, further encouraging people to use private cars.

North Americans' dependence on the automobile has had profound impacts on their cities, including the shapes. About one-quarter of all the land in North American cities is used for transportation activities, with most paved over for roadways and parking lots. Every kilometre of expressway takes up about six hectares of land. Expressways give these cities their shape and form, serving as conduits that carry suburban commuters to and from the city.

Automobiles also affect the natural environment in and around cities. Water bodies are channeled and changed to make roadways efficient. Salt- and oil-laden runoff from roads and parking lots washes into streams, damaging their ecosystems. Cars are the largest single source of greenhouse gases that cause global warming (see Chapter 17). They also contribute to smog problems. The combination of paved-over areas and exhaust emissions helps create islands of heat within cities. Summer and winter, urban cores can be much warmer than surrounding areas.

Figure 15-16 Morning rush-hour traffic on Highway 99, northbound to Vancouver, near the George Massey Tunnel. North Americans value the personal freedom that automobiles give. Suburbs developed when cars allowed homes to be long distances from places of work.

ACTIVITIES

1. Develop a two-column list summarizing the benefits and disadvantages of the automobile in urban areas.

2. What options do people have for travelling and commuting to work in your region? What other options could be explored?

3. A new freeway has been proposed to go from the centre of a city to the outskirts. In a group of five students, take on the following roles:

   ■ an environmentalist

   ■ a commuter who wants to move outside the city

   ■ a resident of a quiet neighbourhood near the proposed highway site

   ■ a resident whose land may be expropriated (forcibly purchased) to build the highway

   ■ a member of the construction trade.

   In your group, discuss the benefits and drawbacks of the proposal, being sure to keep in your role.

Should There Be Land-Use Controls Against Urban Sprawl?

Cities transform the land on which they sit. Any large city, particularly one that is growing, if not limited by geography or regulations, spreads out into the surrounding countryside. Very often, the best land for suburban development is also the best agricultural land. This competition creates ongoing controversy as cities spread farther and farther into the rural environment.

In the Lower Mainland of British Columbia, farmland is at a premium. The Fraser Valley is less than 200 km long and 100 km or so at its widest and is hemmed in by mountains. The pressures, urban and agricultural, are considerable. Much of the land is in the Agricultural Land Reserve, a forward-looking 1970s policy meant to slow urban sprawl. Large tracts, however, are not covered by this land-use control. These areas are under development as cities such as Langley, Chilliwack, and Abbotsford grow to meet the needs of families looking for homes and jobs. Even some of the low mountains that fringe the valley are covered in subdivisions.

The Case Against Urban Sprawl

Many people are critical of the unchecked growth of cities, citing a number of areas where urban sprawl is considered a detriment to quality of life:

- The infrastructure that supports urban sprawl is expensive. For example, it costs about $10 million to build one kilometre of four-lane expressway. In the United States, the costs of providing the infrastructure for expanding suburbs is estimated at $45 000 (U.S.) per house. Water supplies and sewage treatment are also more expensive.

- Sprawl breeds more sprawl. Building more roadways is seen as the natural way to ease traffic congestion. Studies show, however, that within five years of building an expressway, it becomes clogged. Expressways encourage more people to move out to the fringes of the cities, so suburbs leapfrog outwards. A study in Toronto found that more than 160 000 commuters drove more than 30 km each way to and from work, with many spending in excess of one hour driving.

- Farmland is lost as suburbs expand. Through annexation of surrounding land, boundaries of large cities move outward. About 50 per cent of Canada's population live in urban areas that have been built on the best 5 per cent of the nation's farmland. In the United States, an estimated 400 000 ha of farmland are turned into strip malls, subdivisions, and freeways annually.

- Urban sprawl can be devastating to the social and economic health of a city. In some cases, the older core of the city decays because tax dollars and resources are used to develop the expanding fringe.

- The suburbs do not have the sense of place that characterizes small, vibrant, thriving communities. Land uses are segregated, with strip malls, recreational services, homes, and industries all in distinct zones. The car-based culture of the suburbs encourages shoppers to shift from patronizing locally owned stores and restaurants to patronizing large, regional malls and "big box" superstores.

The Case for Not Controlling Urban Sprawl

There are strong voices that present an alternative view of urban sprawl. These views are supported by the fact that people *choose* to live in suburbs. Suburbs continue to be built to meet a market demand from buyers who want to live in low-density developments on edges of cities. Arguments that support urban expansion include some of these ideas:

- Land costs are lower on the fringes of cities. Because of this, housing is more affordable and a greater number of families can afford newer, spacious dwellings. As an indicator of this trend, ownership of homes in suburbs averages 70 per cent, while in cities the average is 50 per cent.

- The construction of main roads creates natural locations for commercial development. Commercial activities then concentrate in these areas, leaving

Figure 15-17 The subdivision of Maple Ridge, British Columbia, in the Fraser Valley. Urban developments like this one have encroached on the region's fertile agricultural lands.

residential streets with relatively little traffic. In addition, the concentration of businesses in strip malls reduces overall travel, because customers do not have to drive long distances to shop.

▢ Homeowners in low-density housing developments plant trees and shrubs and grow lawns that help the environment. Trees and shrubs filter pollutants out of the air, and the lawns are green spaces that help create a more enjoyable landscape. These amenities are not found to the same extent in more densely populated urban areas.

▢ Jobs are being created in the suburbs. The assumption that people living in the suburbs all drive to work in the city is not accurate. For example, a study in Portland, Oregon, found that only 0.8 per cent of new jobs were created in the urban core. In Los Angeles, just 3 per cent of the region's jobs are downtown.

Analysing the Issue

1. Identify three groups who are likely to oppose suburban development. Who is likely to support the expansion of suburbs?

2. Often, as many as six different municipalities control the land use of areas surrounding a city. How could this situation contribute to further urban sprawl?

3. Suppose you had written a book looking at the whole issue of urban sprawl. What would be five of the chapter titles in the book? Give reasons to explain why you chose these titles.

4. Draw an editorial cartoon to show your views on this issue. Use your cartoon to make a humorous statement either in support of urban sprawl or against it.

5. Is urban sprawl occurring in your community? If so, give your opinion on this development.

Land Uses in Cities

Geographers are interested in how people use land. They categorize how land is used in cities based on the functions. In most cities, functions group together and create **land-use** patterns.

Figure 15-18 Urban land uses.

Developing understanding For each category in this chart, give one example from your local community.

Category	Urban Functions	Examples of Land Uses
Residential	Where people live	• single-family homes • townhouses and duplexes • apartments and condominiums
Industrial	Places that make goods	• light industry, often organized into "industrial parks" • heavy industry, including steel mills and automobile assembly plants
Commercial	Places that sell goods and services	• single shops, such as corner stores • strip plazas, usually along major arteries • shopping malls • central financial districts
Transportation	Land used to provide facilities to move goods and people	• roadways • railways and their stations • airports and terminals • harbours and port facilities
Institutional	Land used to support the culture of the people	• places of worship • educational facilities • libraries
Other	Uses to meet the various needs of people	• public administration uses, such as city hall • recreational areas • cultural facilities (e.g., art galleries) • health care facilities • open space

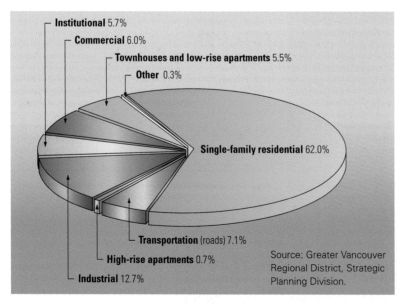

Institutional 5.7%
Commercial 6.0%
Townhouses and low-rise apartments 5.5%
Other 0.3%
Single-family residential 62.0%
Transportation (roads) 7.1%
High-rise apartments 0.7%
Industrial 12.7%

Source: Greater Vancouver Regional District, Strategic Planning Division.

Figure 15-19 Urban land use in Greater Vancouver (percentage of land area). The figures do not include parks, which are classified as either non-urban or vacant urban lands.

Reading a graph What percentage of land use in Greater Vancouver is residential? Suggest three reasons why so much of the land is used for homes.

Figure 15-20 Typical land uses in urban areas.

Using evidence Use the land-use categories in Figure 15-18 to identify the land use in each of these photographs.

17

Environment

FOCUS ON

• What are the principal international agreements concerning the environment?

• What is the concept of sustainability?

• How are resources, environment, and human populations interconnected?

• What are the environmental threats to water, air, soil, and forests in Canada and the world?

• How can we offset environmental threats at the local, national, and international levels?

Counterpoints Issue

• Should Canada treat water as a resource to be traded?

The moon landing in 1969 was a landmark event. For the first time, we saw our planet from another place in the cosmos. Earth appeared as a beautiful blue sphere alone in the vastness of space. For the first time, we could see for ourselves the limits of our world, a "spaceship" itself with its own life support systems. This was coupled with a realization that all parts of ecological systems are interconnected and affect the whole.

Expressing ideas Brainstorm a list of the ways in which your community is linked to the rest of the world. For instance, check where your clothes or other possessions are made. How many parts of the world can you list? Explain whether this does or does not make you feel a part of a global community.

Introduction

The Earth's resources, environment, and human populations are interconnected. People use the resources for energy and raw materials to sustain life and to create wealth. These activities have an impact on the natural and human-built environments. For example, agriculture has disrupted the natural systems of the Earth from the time it was first practised.

As the world's population has increased, the scale of human impact has grown. For example, in 1950, the harvest of fish from the world's oceans was nineteen million tonnes, rising to nearly ninety million tonnes by the end of the twentieth century. The same impact can be shown with water, soil, forests, minerals, and energy resources. We have caused harmful changes in the **biosphere**—the zone of earth, water, and air in which we live. It is from this thin zone that our livelihoods come, and it is back to it that all things, including people, return. In this chapter, we examine some of the changes in our environment, and look at some of the solutions that are being proposed for the problems these changes are creating.

Population and Resources

Each year nearly eighty million people are added to the world's population, putting ever more pressure on the Earth's natural systems. Yet much of the increase is in the developing world, so the impact is not as great as if it had occurred in the developed world. Nearly 85 per cent of the world's resources are being consumed by 20 per cent of the world's population, mainly in the industrialized Western countries (see Figure 14-5, page 344). If even a fraction of the increase in population in the developing world lived like most people in the industrialized world, pollution and waste levels could overwhelm the Earth's natural systems.

Sustainable Development

In 1992, 1700 concerned scientists from around the globe signed the World Scientists' Warning to Humanity:

> Human beings and the natural [environment] are on a collision course. Human activities inflict harsh and often irreversible damage on the environment and on critical resources. If not checked, many of our current practices put at serious risk the future that we wish for human society and the plant and animal kingdoms, and may so alter the living world that it will be unable to sustain life in the manner that we know. Fundamental changes are urgent if we are to avoid the collision our present course will bring about....
>
> WARNING—We the undersigned, senior members of the world's scientific community,

Figure 17-1 A landfill site in Ontario.

Using evidence
Canadian society is a "consumer" society. How does this photograph illustrate that description?

hereby warn all humanity of what lies ahead. A great change in our stewardship of the Earth and the life on it is required, if vast human misery is to be avoided and our global home on this planet is not to be irretrievably mutilated.

This concern is not new in Western society. Since 1962, when Rachel Carson published *Silent Spring*, there have been many international meetings that have discussed how to maintain economic growth without damaging the environment so much that it compromises the future of life on the planet. This concept is known as *sustainability*. The term came into common use following the findings of the United Nations Commission on the State of the Environment, also known as the Brundtland Commission.

In 1987, the Commission's report, *Our Common Future*, asked for people in the developed world to reduce resource consumption and develop a sustainable lifestyle. Economic development "must meet the needs of the present without compromising the ability of future generations to meet their own needs." The report said that the developing world would need to reduce population growth to allow for development that would not overwhelm the environment. The developed world would need to practise greater stewardship of renewable and non-renewable resources to ensure the needs of future generations and to reduce the impact on the environment. Canadians have looked to governments to take action. To date, our governments and international agreements have generally failed to live up to the challenge.

In 1992, the largest gathering of heads of state in human history met at the Earth Summit in Rio de Janeiro, Brazil, to look at ways of harmonizing economic growth and a safe environment. The conference produced a statement of action, called **Agenda 21**, to encourage the development of a sustainable world economy. Nearly a decade later, there has been little progress in slowing the environmental trends seen at Rio as a threat to the well-being of the planet.

Figure 17-2 The Dalai Lama, the Tibetan spiritual leader, gives a speech at the 1992 Earth Summit in Rio de Janeiro, urging world leaders to cooperate for the good of the environment.

Water: The Indispensable Resource

People cannot survive without water. Every person requires at least five litres of fresh water each day for good health. Many economic activities, particularly agriculture, rely on a regular supply of water. Yet, its value is often underrated. Many nations, particularly in the developed world, waste or pollute water resources.

Only 3 per cent of the water in the world is fresh water. Nearly 78 per cent of that is in the form of ice caps and glaciers, and much of the remaining amount is underground as **groundwater**. While there is enough water to supply the world's population into the future, the problem—as with many of the world's resources—is its uneven distribution. In Canada, we have a large share of the world's fresh water. The Great Lakes alone contain 18 per cent of all the surface fresh water on Earth.

Abusing an Underground Resource

Increasing populations are the main threat to the world's freshwater supply. Falling groundwater tables and diversion of surface supplies are the main causes of shortages. The Yellow River in China, the Ganges River in India, the Nile River in Africa, and the Colorado River in the United States are examples of rivers that run dry, or have little water left when they reach the sea. These shortages threaten world agricultural production. Forty per cent of the world's harvests comes from irrigated croplands. The United States, China, and India are all facing reduced groundwater supplies. These countries produce half the world's food.

Water Deficits in Selected Countries and Regions

Country/Region	Estimated Annual Water Deficit (billion m³ per year)
India	104.0
China	30.0
United States	13.6
North Africa	10.0
Source: Global Water Policy Project and Worldwatch Institute.	

Figure 17-4 A water deficit is a measure of how much more groundwater is being used than is being replaced. As the table indicates, the countries with the largest deficits are the two most populous countries in the world.

Thinking critically What are the long-term implications for India and China of these deficits?

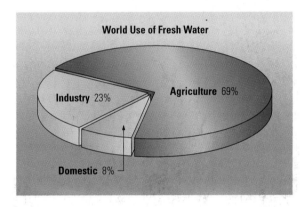

Figure 17-3 The demand for fresh water grew by 400 per cent in the latter half of the twentieth century.

Gathering information What is the main use of fresh water? Which parts of the world rely on irrigation for agricultural purposes?

In the latter half of the twentieth century, the amount of irrigated land more than doubled to over 250 million hectares. Using new technologies and techniques in well-drilling, farmers were able to tap the groundwater in **aquifers** beneath their land. Unlike erratic river flows or rainwater, the supply of groundwater is constant and can be pumped whenever the farmer needs it, and is cheaper to access than surface water. It does not need to be stored in costly reservoirs and is not subject to the high rates of evaporation found in hot, arid, or semi-arid lands. The problem is that, unlike surface supplies, aquifers do not recharge rapidly. The water in the aquifer comes from water slowly seeping into the surface through porous rocks such as sandstone or limestone. These are called *permeable* rocks. Sometimes the water in the aquifer is trapped between layers of *impermeable* rock, which does not allow water to seep through. The water table is the top of the saturated layer. There can be serious environmental and health consequences if the water table is allowed to fall too low.

Farmers in China, India, and the United States are witnessing the consequences of years of overpumping of groundwater sources. In India and China, groundwater was the fastest-growing source of irrigation water in the last quarter of the twentieth century. In the North China Plain, where most of that country's food is produced, the water table is falling by 1.5 m per year. Farmers are forced to drill deeper wells costing more money or to return to farming that relies on seasonal rains, which means lower crop yields. In India, water

building your skills

Identifying Causes and Effects

*I*dentifying causes and effects is an important skill that requires critical thinking. Sometimes it is too easy to "jump to a conclusion." A cause-and-effect sequence that appears to be straightforward at first glance can be much more complicated upon closer examination. You need to separate those causes that are clearly linked to the effect from those that are only marginal or have no connection. Your analysis should also distinguish between short- and long-term effects. A diagram or chart can be a good way to show the sequence of causes and effects.

Read the description below and decide on the causes and effects.

"Safe" Water and Sick People

In some areas of India, as wells are dug ever deeper in search of water, they tap into minerals such as arsenic and fluoride. These minerals affect the health of the people who use the water.

In the village of Hirapur, in the central state of Madhya Pradesh, the ill effects of wells put in to provide safe drinking water have begun to be noticed. During the United Nations International Water Decade of the 1980s, the Indian government was sinking up to 60 000 boreholes a year and analysing water from only a tenth of them. The rich mineral deposits of the area meant that the groundwater contained natural chemicals such as fluoride. The crippling effects of fluorosis (bone damage caused by high concentrations of fluoride in water) have made it difficult for people with deformed limbs to work or get to school. "The problem is enormous, unbelievable; in some villages, three-quarters of the population is seriously affected," says Andezhath Susheela of the Fluorosis Research and Rural Development Foundation in New Delhi. She estimates the number of people leading a painful and crippling life from fluorosis to be as high as sixty million, six million of them children. UNICEF and other agencies are testing water for fluorides and other chemicals, and geologists are mapping areas with safer sources of water. In the meantime, people continue to use the sources of water available, whether contaminated or not.

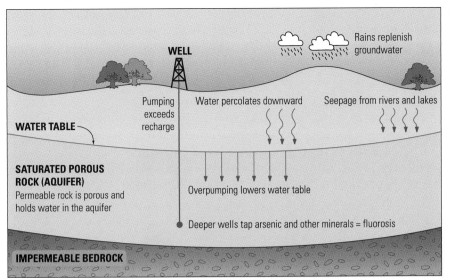

Figure 17-5 Groundwater depletion. Overpumping with diesel- and electric-powered pumps mines the water faster than it can be recharged by rains or seepage from surface sources. The falling water table means wells must be dug deeper.

WELL

Rains replenish groundwater

Pumping exceeds recharge

Water percolates downward

Seepage from rivers and lakes

WATER TABLE

SATURATED POROUS ROCK (AQUIFER)
Permeable rock is porous and holds water in the aquifer

Overpumping lowers water table

Deeper wells tap arsenic and other minerals = fluorosis

IMPERMEABLE BEDROCK

Figure 17-6 Fourteen-year-old Krishna suffers from the effects of fluorosis. She cannot walk to school because her legs are so bowed.

Developing understanding What other problems might Krishna face, now and in the future, as a result of her condition?

Applying the Skill

1. Copy and complete the flowchart below, using information from the description to fill in the principal causes and effects of the contaminated wells in India.

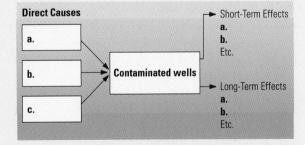

Direct Causes

a.

b.

c.

Contaminated wells

Short-Term Effects
a.
b.
Etc.

Long-Term Effects
a.
b.
Etc.

2. What other information would you want to know to be sure that the information in your chart is correct, and that you are not "jumping to conclusions"?

3. Complete a cause-and-effect chart for one of the other issues in this chapter, such as soil erosion, desertification, or global warming.

CASE STUDY

The Ogallala Aquifer

The United States faces difficulties as a result of groundwater depletion. The Ogallala aquifer is one of the world's largest sources of underground water. This huge underground reservoir underlies the Great Plains of the United States from just south of the Canadian border to Texas. It provides water for more than one-fifth of the irrigated land in the United States. Filled over thousands of years by runoff from the Rocky Mountains, it has taken a little more than half a century to reduce the aquifer by over half its volume. The U.S. federal government adds to the problem by allowing farmers to claim the depletion of groundwater on their income tax, giving them little incentive to conserve the resource.

Figure 17-7 The Ogallala aquifer.

tables are falling by one to three metres per year, and wells are running dry. Aquifer depletion could reduce India's harvest by one-fourth. With dwindling groundwater supplies, India will become more dependent on imported grain.

Abusing Surface Water

Surface waters—such as lakes, rivers, and coastal waters—are also being abused. They have been used for disposal of sewage and agricultural and industrial wastes. Tanker accidents and natural causes account for some of the pollution. But most pollution originates from municipal, agricultural, and industrial sources. Municipal wastewater may contain human effluents, detergents, and solvents. Farmers use agricultural chemicals in herbicides and pesticides. Industries such as oil refineries, pulp mills, and chemical factories discharge wastes into rivers and oceans. The effects of pollution in world oceans are confined mainly to coastal areas and enclosed waters that do not have the circulation of open oceans and seas (see Figure 17-18, page 434). Even whales and polar bears in Arctic regions have shown signs of toxic wastes, such as mercury, in their systems.

Figure 17-8 The Arkansas River cuts through the irrigated fields of western Kansas. Irrigation, above all other uses, places the biggest demand on the Ogallala aquifer in western Kansas. The river is almost the only surface water in that part of the state.

Questions

1. What is the Ogallala aquifer, and why should its depletion be of concern to Canadians?

2. Prepare a pamphlet for farmers who use water for irrigation from the Ogallala reservoir. Explain sustainable development and what farmers must take into account to ensure that they use the water resource in a sustainable way.

Many of the world's great rivers and lakes, such as the Thames in England and Lake Baikal in Russia, were so badly polluted by industrial and chemical waste that they could no longer support life. Life has returned to the Thames as a result of strict environmental controls. Waterways in the USSR were badly polluted during the communist regime; since its fall, the economic crisis has made the cleanup of lakes and rivers a low priority.

On Canada's east and west coasts, Victoria and Halifax dump untreated wastes into surrounding waters. Beluga whales in the St. Lawrence River and sturgeon in the Fraser River are threatened by waters polluted by industrial, agricultural, and human wastes. Interior pulp mills provide 50 per cent of the industrial discharge in the Fraser River; 90 per cent of the municipal waste in the river originates in the Fraser Valley and Vancouver areas. In Canadian lakes near populated areas, agricultural and industrial chemicals and wastes promote the growth of algae and weeds that deplete the lakes' oxygen supply for life forms and affect recreational use. In British Columbia's Okanagan lakes, it is a constant battle to prevent the spread of milfoil weed, which threatens a multimillion-dollar tourist industry.

Figure 17-9
Ducks swim among garbage here in the polluted waters of the Fraser River.

counterpoints

Should Canada Treat Water As a Resource to Be Traded?

Water Exports: Drinking Canada Dry

As world freshwater shortages grow, business people from Vancouver Island to Newfoundland have been quick to suggest ways to take advantage of Canada's abundant supply of pure water. In 1995, the British Columbia government banned the export of bulk water and was sued by a California company under the North American Free Trade Agreement (NAFTA) for compensation for lost opportunity. The Ontario government was forced by public outcry to cancel permission to export Lake Superior water to Asia. In Newfoundland, a plan to export lake water to the United States and the Middle East raised questions about Canada's water export policies.

Some Canadians argue that Canada's fresh water should be treated like other resources and be exported for gain. They point out that the revenues and jobs created in areas of high unemployment, such as Newfoundland, would justify the export policy. Others, however, claim

that water is in a different category. Maude Barlow of the Council of Canadians, a nationalist lobby group, strongly opposes exports, claiming: "Once you turn on the tap, you can't turn it off again." Nationalists claim that under the terms of NAFTA, if any bulk water is exported, all water will then be treated as any other trade good. Canada would lose control of its water.

Some water experts think that the whole issue of bulk water exports is overblown. They claim that transporting bulk water over long distances may not be profitable. A report to the Quebec government pointed out that desalination plants could turn salt water into fresh water for less than the cost of transporting it long distances by tanker. U.S. studies show that conservation methods such as low-flush toilets and drip irrigation make far better economic sense than massive water import schemes. However, rich countries like the United States and Canada do not always adopt the obvious or low-cost solutions to resource issues. Political pressure from southwestern sun-belt states for a quick solution to water shortages, and Quebec's reluctance to agree to federal policies, could also affect the outcome.

Few Canadians pay attention to the export of bottled water. These exports have been growing steadily, in particular to the United States. Canadian per capita consumption of bottled water is one-quarter that of the average U.S. consumption. A study by the International Joint Commission, a Canada–U.S. body that oversees water resources shared by the two countries, found that Canada is the biggest supplier of bottled water to

Solutions

The trend in water development programs is to conservation and efficient small-scale supply systems. U.S. environmentalist Dr. Peter Gleick, in his book *The World's Water: Biennial Report on Freshwater Resources, 1998–1999*, is optimistic in his belief that sustainable water management can be realized with present technology. Large-scale projects can be replaced by micro-dams, hydro systems that run with a river's natural flow, shallow wells, and more efficient rainwater harvesting. As technologies develop, he sees an increase in the use of reclaimed or recycled water and, to a lesser degree, of desalinated seawater.

Low-energy sprinkler systems and drip irrigation, which directs water to plant roots, are used extensively in water-scarce Israel, and could be used in agriculture worldwide.

In industrialized countries, industrial and domestic use can be reduced using the same thinking. For example, new toilet design has led to high efficiency and low flow, reducing by 70 per cent the amount of water needed to flush millions of toilets.

Canada, the United States, and India have no national policies to regulate the use of groundwater. Taxes or user rates could be introduced to encourage users to conserve water.

---

the United States, where the market is growing at over 10 per cent a year. The low cost of the Canadian dollar, close access to the market, and the perception of many Americans that Canada has an unspoiled environment, have all favoured Canadian exporters.

Province	Volume (litres)	Share (%)
Quebec	246 558 496	90.7
Ontario	16 710 533	6.1
British Columbia	7 679 841	2.8
New Brunswick	474 160	0.2
Alberta	258 127	0.1

Source: International Joint Commission Report, cited in "Bottled water gushing south," *Globe and Mail*, September 22, 1999.

Figure 17-10 Bottled water exports to the United States in 1998 for selected provinces.

Canadian provinces have issued licences to businesses for the extraction of thirty billion litres of water a year from Canada's springs, lakes, icebergs, and aquifers. British Columbia is the only province that charges a fee for the use of the resource, which brings only $25 000 a year in revenue. In British Columbia, licences are granted for life. Heather Smart, a water policy expert at the B.C. Environment Ministry, claimed in 1999 that "this is a problem right across Canada, that water is undervalued." Water bottling companies point to the jobs they create and the taxes they pay. They would agree to pay user fees if all other users of groundwater had to do the same. Environmentalists claim that a fee based on market worth would give the provinces needed revenue. They also note that the extraction of water over a period of time could affect an area's water table.

What is certain in the issue of water exports is that shortages will increase, putting added pressure on Canadian export policies. The basic question remains to be answered: Is water a special resource to be treated differently from other resources?

Analysing the Issue

1. What changes, if any, would you make in government regulation of the bottled water industry in Canada?

2. Do you agree with Heather Smart's opinion that fresh water in Canada is undervalued? Give examples to support your opinion.

3. Why might Quebec be opposed to regulation of the export of water supplies?

4. With a partner, script and act out a short dialogue between a Canadian opponent of water exports and a Texas farmer whose wells are running dry.

5. Do you think Canada should allow the export of bottled water? Bulk water? Both bottled and bulk water? Or no water? Give reasons for your answer.

6. Write a 200-word opinion piece that could be featured on an Internet site, entitled "Three Good Reasons to (or Not to) Export Canada's Water." Include a suggestion for an appropriate picture to accompany your opinion piece.

1. Do you agree that increasing populations are the main threat to the world's freshwater supply? Explain your answer.

2. In a two-column organizer, list the benefits and problems associated with groundwater use.

3. Which of Dr. Gleick's solutions to water management do you consider to be the most practical? Explain your choice.

4. Make a list of some of the sources of water pollution in your community. Find out what action is being taken to deal with the worst examples of pollution.

5. Do you think provincial governments in Canada should have regulations governing groundwater use? Why or why not?

Change Is in the Air

The Hole in the Ozone Layer

The ozone layer is a thin layer of ozone (O_3), a special kind of oxygen, in the atmosphere 15–50 km above the Earth's surface. Ozone is the only gas in the atmosphere that can block the ultraviolet (UV) rays of the sun. UV radiation can cause skin cancer in humans, and can damage other animal and plant species. Plankton—microscopic organisms that are at the bottom of the marine food chain—are particularly vulnerable, as UV radiation can penetrate up to 20 m below the ocean surface.

In the 1980s, it became apparent that the ozone layer was thinning. Ozone depletion is most evident at the northern and southern poles where holes open in the layer, especially in the spring. As much as 60 per cent of the layer has disappeared over Antarctica.

Chemicals, particularly chlorofluorocarbons (CFCs), which have done 80 per cent of the damage, are destroying the ozone layer. CFCs have been widely used since the 1930s in coolants for refrigerators and air conditioners, in foams, solvents, and aerosol spray cans. The United Nations Environmental Program (UNEP) has been working on phasing out the use of ozone-depleting chemicals. In 1987, all industrial nations agreed to

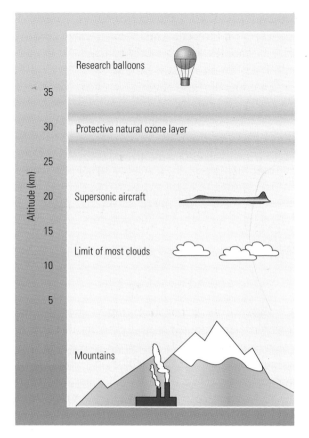

Figure 17-11 The ozone layer.

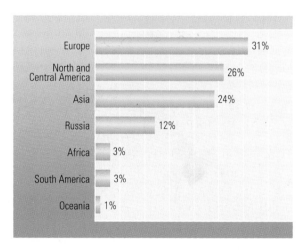

Figure 17-12 Emissions of CFCs (percentage of world total).

Reading a graph What was the combined percentage of CFCs emitted by Europe, North and Central America, and Russia?

cut their use of CFCs in an agreement known as the Montreal Protocol. The Protocol allowed countries of the developing world to use CFCs until 2000, as substitutes are expensive. Meanwhile, the amounts of these chemicals released into the air are increasing.

Only the complete elimination of CFCs and the recapture of those already in use will begin to halt the damage to the ozone layer. The U.S. Environmental Protection Agency claims that even if all ozone-depleting chemicals are phased out, it could take a century for conditions in the atmosphere to return to what they were in the 1980s.

Things Are Warming Up

The gases in the atmosphere trap the heat energy from the sun like glass in a greenhouse. They make it possible for life on Earth to exist. Natural factors, such as volcanic explosions and meteor impacts, have caused vast climatic changes in the past. Since the Industrial Revolution and the subsequent massive burning of fossil fuels—coal, oil,

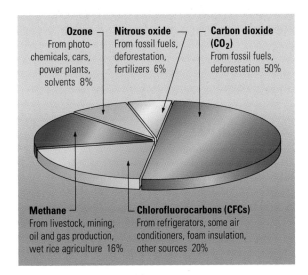

Figure 17-13 The greenhouse gases that contribute to global warming.

Reading a graph Which are the two main greenhouse gases? What percentage of greenhouse gases comes from burning fossil fuels and deforestation?

Figure 17-14 How the greenhouse effect works. Excess carbon dioxide accumulations trap heat that would otherwise be radiated back into space.

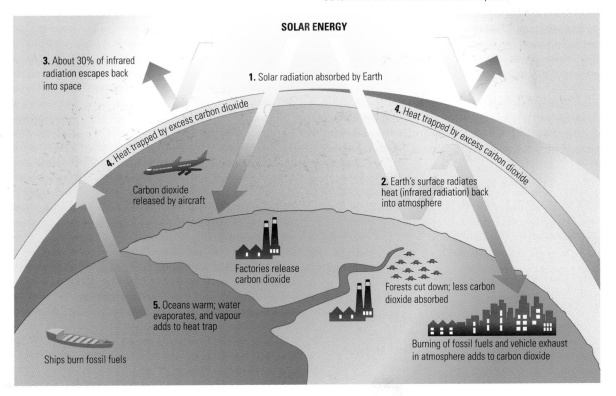

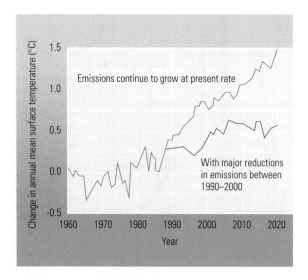

Figure 17-15 Predicted temperature changes due to the greenhouse effect.

Reading a graph What is the least amount of change that is predicted for 2010? What is the maximum?

and natural gas—scientists have detected much more carbon dioxide (CO_2) in the atmosphere. This could cause the temperature to rise by an additional one to three degrees Celsius by the year 2050. Even minor increases in the Earth's temperature can have profound effects on life on Earth.

Effects of Global Warming

There are consequences to the trends towards global warming. Scientists agree that the increased number of heat waves and the rising incidence of violent storms are linked to global warming. Above-average temperatures in polar regions are melting glaciers, and sea levels are rising as a result. Other effects cannot be directly linked. These include diseases extending their ranges because of warmer temperatures, and the earlier arrival of spring in many parts of the world. Shifting plant and animal ranges have been observed as species try to adapt to changing temperatures by moving to different habitats. Coral reefs are losing their colours in over thirty countries as the microscopic algae that give them these colours fail to adapt to warmer water temperatures.

Threats to Canada

It can be difficult to convince Canadians that rising temperatures are a problem. Yet in Canada's Arctic regions, the sea ice is shrinking and the seasonal melt is occurring weeks earlier than in previous years. Polar bears are slowly starving because they cannot use the ice to hunt seals. Since the 1980s, the bears' birth rate and average weight have fallen. Arctic communities are facing sinking shorelines as a result of the melting of **permafrost**, the permanently frozen subsoil.

The survival rate of spawning salmon in British Columbia is one-third of what it was in the early 1990s. Warmer ocean waters may have depleted the phytoplankton that salmon feed on, resulting in smaller fish that can't survive the swim upstream to spawn. Scientists also warn of the ripple effect of shrinking salmon stocks on the ocean food chain and the economies of coastal fishing communities.

Winter recreation and skiing areas close to populated areas in central Canada could be devastated by warmer winters. Freak weather conditions, such as the ice storm that devastated eastern Ontario and Quebec in January 1998, are more likely.

Warmer weather brings more droughts that make forest fires more likely. A benefit may be that the tree line could be extended farther north and higher up mountains. Global warming could also lengthen Canada's short growing season, helping farmers. This benefit could be offset by increased drought in prairie areas, such as the semi-arid Palliser Triangle in southern Saskatchewan and Alberta.

Doing Something About It

In 1997, Canada was among the countries that agreed to sign the **Kyoto Protocol**, promising to reduce greenhouse gas emissions by 6 per cent of our 1990 level by 2012. Countries not meeting their reduction targets could buy credits from other countries, likely less developed, that had emissions below their allotted levels.

Canada is among the top global emitters of greenhouse gases. Despite modest reduction targets, greenhouse gases emitted in Canada have continued to increase. In the 1990s, the fossil-fuel industry campaigned against the Kyoto

The Kyoto Commitment

Year	Greenhouse Emissions	Per Cent Increase/ Decrease Since 1990
1990	601 million tonnes	*
1997	682 million tonnes	+13.5
2010	565 million tonnes	−6.0
*Base year for Kyoto Protocol reductions.		

Figure 17-16 Canada's actual greenhouse gas emissions for 1990 and 1997. The 2010 figure shows the emission levels that Canada agreed to at Kyoto. By 2000, Canada needed to reduce emissions by approximately 27 per cent to achieve this target.

Figure 17-17 Wind turbines would be effective in windy locations such as along the coast of British Columbia or in the Alberta foothills, shown here.

Gathering information What would be the advantages and drawbacks to this form of energy?

Protocol standards. They claimed that meeting them would involve high costs and possible loss of jobs. Another problem is that the federal government signed the agreement, but provincial governments must regulate polluting industries. Reports in 2000 listing Ontario as North America's second-worst polluter support the claims of critics that the Ontario government has not taken the issue of global warming seriously.

There are many sustainable sources of energy that could be used to lessen dependence on fossil fuels. These include wind turbines, solar power panels, tidal power, ground-source energy or geothermal power, which uses heat from underground sources where available. The environmental group Greenpeace claims that within twenty years, wind power could provide 10 per cent of the world's electricity requirements. Although all these alternative sources of energy have drawbacks, they are without harmful emissions. The British Columbia company Ballard Power predicts that its hydrogen- or methanol-fuelled power cells will be in automobiles by the year 2003. The new, smaller fuel cells are adaptable for cars, buses, and other stationary uses in the home or in industry.

Can Canada make a difference? Canadians consume over forty times as much energy as people in developing countries, and our high standard of living means we consume resources at a much higher rate. Our small population can have as much impact on world energy and resources as a less developed country many times our size.

ACTIVITIES

1. **a)** What is the ozone layer, and why is it thinning?

   b) Why is this a threat to life forms on the planet?

2. Suggest ways to convince the public to phase out ozone-depleting chemicals.

3. **a)** What is global warming?

   b) Use a mind map or an ideas web to organize the principal and secondary causes of global warming.

4. Describe a major threat that Canada faces from global warming. What solutions to global warming can be found in Canada?

5. Which forms of sustainable energy would be practical in your area? Support your choices.

Agriculture and Soil

Soils

One of our primary resources is soil. It is the basis of the biosphere, and provides survival for plant and animal life. The formation of soil is a very slow process, taking hundreds of years in some places. The removal of soil by wind or water erosion can take place in a fraction of that time.

Only about 11 per cent of the land area of the Earth can be used for growing crops, yet soils are being lost and degraded around the world. Figure 17-18 shows areas of the world where **desertification**—that is, land turning to desert—is taking place. In the area south of the Sahara Desert in Africa, the area called the Sahel experienced years of drought in the 1970s. Cattle, the

people's main livelihood, overgrazed the sparse grasses that held the soil. Desperate people gathered what firewood was available. Gradually, the desert spread. In North America, the lessons of the "dust bowl" of the 1930s led to improved farming techniques. Farmers planted trees to form wind breaks, adopted contour ploughing, and used wheat stubble and straw left after harvesting to return nutrients to the soil and help stop wind erosion.

Poor farming techniques in marginal areas are another problem around the world. Irrigation in many arid areas has made soils too salty to grow crops. Most soils in tropical countries are nutrient poor. If the vegetation is removed, as in the Amazon rainforest, the nutrients quickly disappear and are not replaced. Soil on slopes is washed away. The land can become a desert.

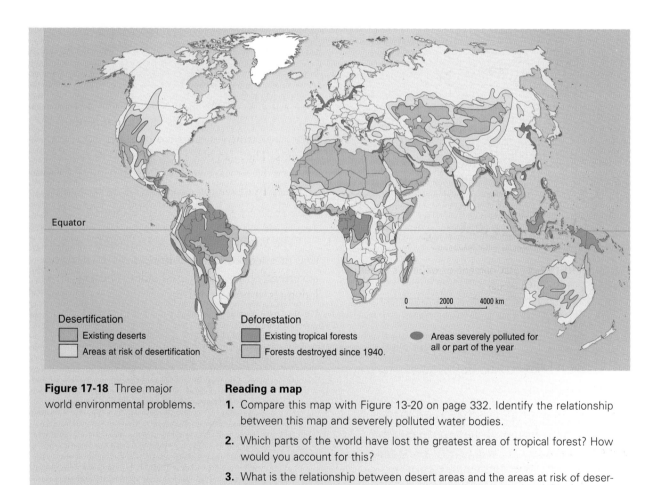

Equator

Desertification
- Existing deserts
- Areas at risk of desertification

Deforestation
- Existing tropical forests
- Forests destroyed since 1940.

- Areas severely polluted for all or part of the year

0   2000   4000 km

Figure 17-18 Three major world environmental problems.

Reading a map

1. Compare this map with Figure 13-20 on page 332. Identify the relationship between this map and severely polluted water bodies.

2. Which parts of the world have lost the greatest area of tropical forest? How would you account for this?

3. What is the relationship between desert areas and the areas at risk of desertification?

Figure 17-20 Soil erosion in Madagascar, following destruction of rainforest.

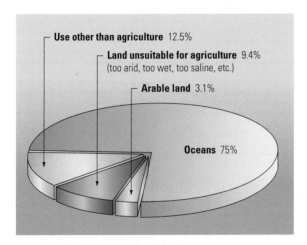

Use other than agriculture 12.5%

Land unsuitable for agriculture 9.4%
(too arid, too wet, too saline, etc.)

Arable land 3.1%

Oceans 75%

Figure 17-19 Only a small percentage of Earth's surface is suitable for growing crops.

A Rising Dependence on Chemicals

Rachel Carson wrote in Silent Spring: "For the first time in the history of the world, every human being is now subjected to contact with dangerous chemicals, from the moment of conception until death." The increasing use, in developed and developing countries, of pesticides and herbicides to control insects that attack crops and to kill weeds leads to toxic soils and residues in foods. In some forms of agriculture, the ground is sterilized so that only a single crop, such as cotton, survives, supported by heavy applications of chemicals.

Agricultural chemicals can be dangerous, as they eventually seep into groundwater and streams. They can also harm agricultural workers who are in contact with plants that have been sprayed. In developing countries, the safeguards available to Canadian workers often do not exist or are not enforced.

The World Wildlife Fund has profiled insects that are needed in agriculture but are being inadvertently poisoned by pesticides. These include ladybugs, a predator of aphids that destroy fruit trees; honeybees, needed for pollination of about one-third of human food; and dung beetles, which help decompose cattle dung on pastureland.

As of 2000, Canada restricted some pesticides, and these will be phased out completely by 2004. As Canadians become more aware of the harm chemicals can do to ecosystems and to themselves, many are willing to pay the higher costs of organically grown fruits and vegetables. These crops are grown without the use of agricultural chemicals. Most supermarkets now stock organically grown foods.

Figure 17-21 A single ladybug can eat up to 4000 aphids—insects that suck the juice out of plants and kill them—in a lifetime. The market for natural pest control is growing: Nature's Alternative at Nanoose, Vancouver Island, has developed a world market for "good bugs" such as the ladybug.

Genetically Modified Foods: Miracle or "Frankenfoods"?

Genetically modified (GM) plants are altered by splicing a gene from another organism into them. Some of these altered plants are more resistant to diseases or pests. Farmers claim that GM crops cost less because they require fewer pesticides and herbicides. Scientists supporting GM foods claim that in the next three decades, there will be another three million people to feed, and crop yields need to increase.

Controversy about genetically modified foods is growing. In Europe, supermarkets have had to remove GM products from their shelves because of consumer resistance. Two North American multinational companies have responded to this pressure. McCain Foods pledged in 1999 to ban genetically altered potatoes from its products, and the H.J. Heinz Company promised to ensure their baby foods were free of genetically modified organisms.

In Canada, the government has approved nearly fifty genetically modified foods since 1994, including corn, canola, soybeans, squash, potatoes, and cotton. The Canadian Food Inspection Agency (CFIA) estimates that up to 75 per cent of all processed foods are made with corn, soy, or canola products. In Canada and the United States, there are no labels on foods to show whether they contain genetically modified crops. This would be difficult to do, as harvested GM crops can be mixed with regular crops. As well, genetically modified seeds can be spread by wind, pollination by insects, and accidental transport by farm machinery.

Clash of Opinions

The issue of the safety of genetically modified foods has brought out impassioned arguments. Those in favour of GM crops claim they are little different from regular crops, and that in any case, people have been altering plants by breeding for generations. They point to careful testing by companies and assessment by government agencies before genetically modified organisms are approved for use. Those opposed to GM crops are concerned about the lack of long-term testing, and also about the possibility of GM crops crossbreeding with other crops. They claim that in less developed countries, use of GM seeds will make farmers reliant on multinational seed companies and eventually add to their costs of production. The following excerpts present arguments for and against this development.

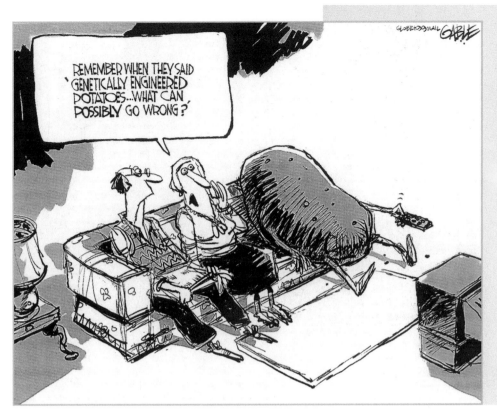

REMEMBER WHEN THEY SAID 'GENETICALLY ENGINEERED POTATOES...WHAT CAN POSSIBLY GO WRONG?'

Figure 17-22

Interpreting a cartoon What is the cartoonist's point of view about genetically modified foods? Give the cartoon an appropriate title.

For:

Professor Blumwald [of the University of Toronto] and associates identified the gene in a plant that determines tolerance for salty soils. By cloning the plant to overproduce the gene, the GM plant flourished in soil with a salt content that would kill non-GM cousins.

If this application can be safely extended to major agricultural crops, productivity in many salty-soil environments could grow by orders of magnitude. Because salty soils are a byproduct of irrigation, and because up to 40 per cent of the global harvest comes from irrigated land, the potential for gain is enormous. Many other potentially productive agricultural areas may also come into service.

Canada proposes that an international authority be charged with assessment of GM products and that countries be prohibited from barring imports of approved GM foods.

Source: Editorial, *Globe and Mail*, August 23, 1999, A10.

Against:

We are performing a massive experiment. The results will only be known after millions of people have been exposed to [these foods] for decades. Any politician or scientist who tells you these products are safe is either very stupid or lying. The hazards of these foods are uncertain. In view of our enormous ignorance, the premature application of biotechnology is downright dangerous.

At issue are fundamental laws of genetics. With genetically modified foods scientists are assuming that the behaviour of genes will be the same in different species. It is simply bad science to make that assumption. You have changed the context within which this new gene finds itself. Therefore what the behaviour of the new gene will be we simply cannot say.

Source: David Suzuki, quoted the *Globe and Mail*, October 14, 1999, A2.

Figure 17-23 Police faced demonstrators as thousands of environmental activists, wildlife conservationists, and students took to the streets of Genoa, Italy, in May 2000, to protest against genetically modified foods. Food scares such as "mad cow disease" in the United Kingdom have made Europeans more cautious about accepting GM foods than North Americans.

Figure 17-24 A growing number of people are attempting to maintain older or heritage varieties of fruits and vegetables. They hope to preserve the original strains, as these are the genetic record of today's food crops. Heritage strains can protect us in case of crop failure due to genetic uniformity.

ACTIVITIES

1. Explain why soil is an important resource.

2. How do North Americans differ from the rest of the world in their attitudes towards GM organisms? What are some possible reasons for the difference?

3. Use a two-column organizer to show the advantages and disadvantages of using pesticides and herbicides in agriculture.

4. Why have organic foods become more popular recently? Check your local supermarket and make a list of the variety of organic foods they stock.

5. All technologies have benefits and drawbacks. In a two-column organizer, list the principal benefits and drawbacks for the use of GM organisms.

Declining Forests

Almost half of the forests that covered the Earth before humans began to practise agriculture have been cleared or reduced to a degraded state. The remaining great blocks of naturally intact forests of the world are located in the Amazon Basin, Central Africa, islands of equatorial Asia, Russia, and Canada.

The Disappearing Tropical Forests

The rate at which the world's tropical rainforests are being destroyed has become a major issue for those concerned with sustainability. These forests

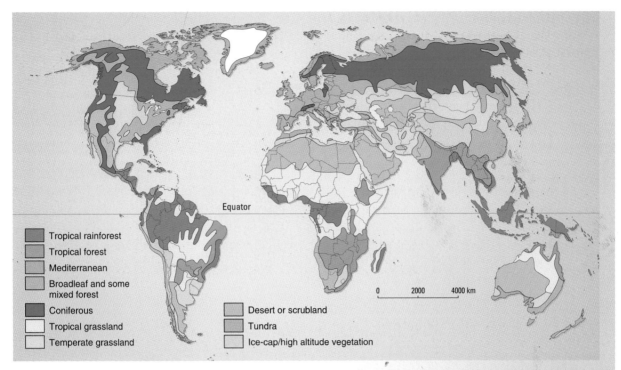

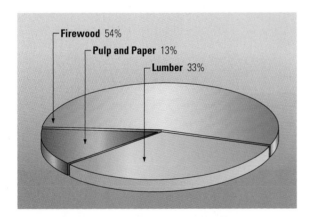

Figure 17-25 The map shows forested areas that existed under natural conditions. Much of the forested areas in India, China, western Europe, and eastern North America have been cleared. Figure 17-18 (page 434) shows the decline in the areas of tropical rainforest.

- Tropical forests contain 155 000 of the 250 000 known plant species
- 700 tree species were found in ten 1-ha plots in Borneo (equivalent to all tree species in Canada and the United States)
- One-fifth of all bird species are found in Amazon forests
- 90% of primates are found only in forest regions of Latin America, Africa, and Asia
- Panama has as many plant species as the whole of Europe
- Natives of North Amazonia use over 1300 plant species as medicines

Figure 17-27 Biodiversity in tropical rainforests.

Figure 17-26 How wood is used in the world.

are storehouses of **biodiversity** (Figure 17-27), or the variety of life on Earth. As well, they absorb carbon dioxide from the atmosphere and give off oxygen. This is why deforestation is a cause of global warming (see Figure 17-13, page 431). Forest removal can affect wind patterns, precipitation levels, and temperatures far beyond the forests themselves. As well, some of these forests are still home to indigenous peoples, whose way of life is being threatened.

The largest clearing of tropical rainforest is taking place in Brazil, where poor people are being encouraged to move into forests and clear land to use for farming. Huge cattle ranches have been set up. Previously remote highland areas of Ecuador, Colombia, and Peru have seen development by oil companies. Building roads to gain access to oil and mineral resources has opened up forested lands to settlement. Indonesia is another country that has undertaken huge clearances to resettle people from the main island of Java. Forests are disappearing at an alarming rate in other parts of Asia. Thailand's ban on the export of tropical hardwoods has been only partly successful because of illegal loggers, who make huge profits by sending timber across borders.

The wood of the forests is sought for industrial use, for specialty woods like teak and rosewood, and as fuel by local people. Once the forests have been cleared, reforestation is virtually impossible.

The forest's resources—timber, nuts, rubber, and plants used in medicines, all of which could be harvested selectively—have been lost.

The effects of forest clearance are far ranging. Most tropical soils are infertile; once the forest cover is removed, the few nutrients are used up, and wind and rains can erode the soil. What remains is an arid wasteland that is sometimes used for limited cattle grazing.

Damage is particularly severe on hillsides. Soil erosion leads to the silting of lakes and rivers, and clogs up hydro dams. Floods are more common, as the forests are no longer there to absorb the rainfall and release it slowly. Deforestation in the Himalayas has affected the regular flow of the Ganges, Brahmaputra, Irrawaddy, and Mekong rivers, disrupting farming downstream.

Figure 17-28 A girl fills a vessel with water during the devastating floods of 1999, when nearly one million people were displaced in Bangladesh. Deforestation in the Himalayas has increased the frequency of damaging floods from the Brahmaputra River.

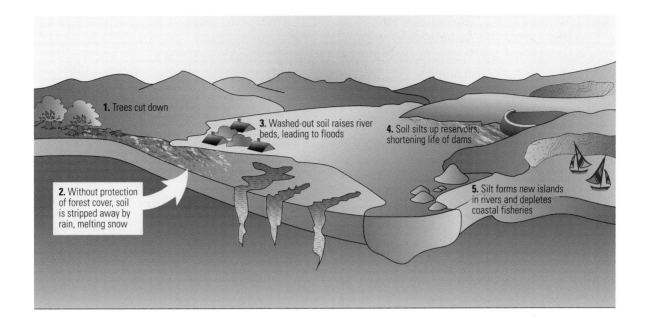

Figure 17-29 The immediate effects of deforestation are dramatic and wide ranging.

Temperate Forests

The temperate and northern forests make up approximately 20 per cent of Earth's land cover. Canada has one-quarter of the world's temperate coastal forest, one-third of the world's **boreal** (northern) coniferous forest, and virtually all of the world's old-growth red and white pine. These forests are used principally for logging and recreation. In the past few decades, some First Nations in Canada have claimed the forest lands they traditionally held as part of Aboriginal title.

Canada's forests stretch from the Pacific coast to the Atlantic. They include one of the world's largest assortments of lakes and wetlands, and are home to over 100 000 species of plants and animals. They provide over $70 billion worth of value to the economy.

This national treasure is threatened. In Alberta, only 9 per cent of the forest has not been degraded; in Quebec and Manitoba, dams and

diversions have damaged nearly one-fifth of the forests. Dr. David Schindler, of the University of Alberta, says that if we don't curtail industrial development and relieve the pressure on the system from acid precipitation and climate change, there will be no boreal ecosystem in fifty years. He warns that the boreal forest could be damaged faster than any other ecosystem in Canada by global warming.

In Northern Ontario in the last decade of the twentieth century, the temperature increased by 1.6°C; as a result, water loss by evaporation was accelerated by 50 per cent. Massive fires scorched the region and wiped out vast areas of boreal forest that show no sign of returning. Schindler's solution is to cut less of the forests and increase efforts to undo the harmful effects of acid precipitation.

Wildlife extinction will be one of the consequences of the decline of the boreal forests. Canada is home to one-third of the world's wolf population and brown and black bears, and more than half of the world's barren-ground caribou. It has now been recognized that ensuring the sur-

Figure 17-30 A silver birch displays the symptoms of acid rain damage. Acid precipitation results when emissions from the burning of fossil fuels combine with oxygen to make sulphur and nitrogen oxides. These raise the pH level of the snow and rain, which then can kill trees and make soil less fertile.

Figure 17-31 This erosion in British Columbia's _____ region resulted from the removal of forest cover.

Thinking critically From what you see in this photograph and know about the effects of running water, draw a cause-and-effect diagram to show the consequences of removing forest cover in this area.

vival of these species means preserving their habitat. In 1992, all governments in Canada endorsed the Tri-Council Commitment on Protected Areas, which planned to complete a network of protected areas representing all natural regions by the end of 2000. By July 1999, the protected areas of Canada had been increased from 3.2 per cent in 1989 to 6.4 per cent, half-way to the goal set in 1992.

Coastal Rainforests

The Western Mountain region has 14 per cent of Canada's forested land, but produces 40 per cent of its marketable timber. The forest industry is

the largest segment of the British Columbia's economy. The challenge is to balance economic growth with good environmental practice.

In recent years, concern has grown about the sustainability of British Columbia's forests. In 1993, the provincial government launched the Protected Areas Strategy (PAS), with a target of preserving 12 per cent of provincial land for parks, recreation, and wilderness by 2000. However, only a portion of the rich, coastal old-growth watersheds was included in the PAS. Since the 1980s, environmental groups have focussed attention on these old-growth watersheds. This reflects the changing attitude towards forests. Once consid-

Figure 17-32 This white spirit bear, also known as the Kermode bear, is a rare subspecies that lives only on the north coast of British Columbia. The total population of white spirit bears existing in the wild is believed to number fewer than 400. Because these animals depend on old-growth rainforest for food and winter shelter, environmental practices such as clear-cutting threaten their survival.

ered only as a source of revenue, they are now seen as a resource with many uses: recreation, research, industry, and—in the case of First Nations—culture. These diverse needs must be balanced with the principles of good stewardship. **Stewardship** implies careful management of resources so that they are sustainable.

Environmental groups such as the Sierra Club and Greenpeace refer to British Columbia as the "Brazil of the North." Those opposed to old-growth logging, which supplies the most valuable woods, have focussed international attention on the clearing of these forests. As you saw in Chapter 10, protests resulted in some logging being stopped.

Saving the Forests

Conserving paper and packaging can play a major part in the preservation of forests. Global paper use has grown 600 per cent since 1950. One-fifth of all wood harvested in the world ends up in paper, and nearly half of that is used for packaging. Paper makes up nearly 40 per cent of solid waste in the industrialized world. Canadians use over 300 kg of paper per person per year, compared to China's 27 kg and India's 4 kg. The U.N. Environmental Program suggested usage of 30–40 kg per person per year, and expanded recycling of used paper in the developed world.

ACTIVITIES

1. Define boreal; stewardship.

2. Give three reasons why efforts to stop the decline of tropical forests have not been successful.

3. In a flow chart, show how forest clearance in the Himalayas affects the lowlands of India and Bangladesh.

4. What arguments are offered by Dr. Schindler to support his claim that the boreal forest is threatened? What future does he see for the forest's wildlife?

5. Explain how the Protected Areas Strategy reflects the idea of stewardship. Do you agree with the amount of land being preserved? Explain.

6. How big a role might conserving paper and reducing packaging play in preserving our forests?

CASE STUDY

Ecotourism: Problem or Solution?

Some communities in Canada suffering economic hardship have turned to **ecotourism**. They use the fascination people have with the wonders of the natural world to promote tourism based on the environment. Fishers of coastal British Columbia have turned their fishing boats into charter boats for tourists who want to view marine wildlife, such as whales. Kayaking and paddling in wilderness areas have increased, as have wilderness hiking and forest tours. Ecotourism is one of the fastest-growing sectors of the Aboriginal economy, employing nearly 10 000 people and generating in excess of $250 million a year. It can provide jobs for young people that keep them in their home communities.

Figure 17-33 Many remote regions of Canada, such as Nahanni National Park in the NWT, have become destinations for ecotourists seeking wilderness adventure trips. In British Columbia, the tourist industry has grown steadily in recent decades, with revenues of $8.5 billion in 1999.

Ecotourism is also important for some countries in the developing world. Tourists from developed nations tend to favour places with a high degree of biodiversity, such as the Amazon, Costa Rica, or the game parks in African countries. The industry brings advantages for these countries. There is a transfer of wealth from the developed countries, and jobs are created in industries and services that cater to the tourists.

Problems

Unfortunately, ecotourism can accelerate the degradation of environments that attract tourism in the first place. Many places once considered "off the beaten track" have become overpopulated with visitors, accelerating the pace of social and environmental damage. In Nepal, more than three decades of intensive tourism has had an impact on the natural environment and the local Sherpa culture of this once-remote region. A local Nepalese who now runs a lodge recalled: "In 1970, when we first saw trekkers here, everybody went out to see the white people." Thirty years later, there had been almost a half million visitors. The government of Nepal was slow to deal with the effect of so many mountaineers and trekkers on the fragile mountain environment. For example, a trekking group uses ten times as much firewood a day as a local Sherpa family. Urged by local members of the World Wildlife Fund (WWF),

the government introduced tourist entry permits that bring in $500 000 (U.S.) a year for conservation of biodiversity and culture.

In the island societies of the Caribbean and South Pacific, the number of tourists can outnumber the local inhabitants. Fragile ecosystems can be threatened as the infrastructure of hotels, restaurants, and other services are established. Success as a destination for packaged tours may lead to overcrowding and increased pollution. An expert on sustainable tourism, Ted Manning, notes: "Tourists won't go where the economy, the society, the ecology is degraded. Not only that, they won't go where they think it's degraded." Complete reliance on tourists can result in great hardship should tourists stay away.

Sustainable Tourism Strategies

The development of a sustainable approach to tourism must be based on strategies that protect and strengthen both natural and cultural diversities. Sustainability includes recognizing the rights of local communities to use and manage natural resources, and applying any profits from tourism towards the benefit of local people and the local environment. For example, the indigenous peoples of the rainforests in the state of Amazonas in southern Venezuela reacted with outrage when insensitive tour operators brought tourists through their villages without permission. With advice from the Canadian embassy, they formed their own organization to promote ecotourism, using their traditional knowledge of geography, plants, and animal life.

Questions

1. In a three-column organizer, list the main benefits and drawbacks of ecotourism for the communities involved and for the environment.

2. Make a list of what you would hope to see if you took an ecotour with the indigenous people of Amazonas or some other remote area.

3. What advice would you offer the government of Nepal in its efforts to encourage economic development through tourism while at the same time protecting the environment?

4. With a partner, describe a sustainable tourist opportunity that could be developed somewhere in your region. Indicate why you think it can be successfully integrated into the local economy.

Figure 17-34 In the 1990s, the first Nepali-organized clean-up of trash left by mountaineers in climbing camps around Mt. Everest brought out 500 yak-loads of garbage.

One Step Forward, One Step Back?

Since the 1992 Earth Summit in Rio de Janeiro, Canada has attempted to make its economy more responsive to environmental concerns. In some areas, forest practices have improved significantly; waste recycling has been adopted by many communities, and Canadians have become innovative in such areas as turning sewage into fertilizer and developing more energy-efficient cars and buildings.

We've been less successful in reducing the use of pesticides and herbicides, and in cutting down on packaging and paper consumption. The rate of depletion of Canada's boreal forests, groundwater supplies, and other resources continues to be a concern if sustainability is to be achieved. Greenhouse gas emissions in Canada have increased, despite our agreement to reduce them after signing the Kyoto Protocol. In some respects, we seem to be at an ecological crossroad. The 2000 report from the United Nations Environmental Program stated that our "present course is unsustainable, and postponing action is no longer an option." Canadians, in particular, will ignore this warning at their peril.

LOOKING BACK

Develop an Understanding

1. How successful has the world been at living up to the goals of Agenda 21 in the past decade? Give specific examples from this chapter.

2. Summarize, in a short paragraph, what steps Canadians need to take to make sure that freshwater supplies in this country are used in a sustainable way.

3. **a.** Why is global warming an environmental problem?

   b. Why is international cooperation needed to deal with this problem?

4. Of the environmental problems you have read about in this chapter, which one do you consider most likely to affect your lifestyle if it is not addressed? Explain your answer.

5. Make a list of the types of information you would require if you were sent to determine the causes of the destruction of the tropical rainforests.

Explore the Issues

6. This statement was issued by British and U.S. scientists in 1997:

   It has often been assumed that population growth is the dominant problem we face. But what matters is ... not only the number of people ... but also how many natural resources they utilize, and how much pollution and waste they generate. We must tackle [the problems of] population and consumption together.

   a. What is the "problem of consumption"? How would you tackle this problem on a personal level?

   b. Why is it difficult to solve the "problem of consumption"?

   c. Do you agree with the scientists' statement? Explain your answer.

7. Stage a class debate on the topic: *Resolved— Technology is the Earth's best hope for the future and worst enemy today.*

8. Determine the amount of paper used in your school and how much of it is recycled. Brainstorm with your class on ways to reduce paper use and packaging in your school and homes.

9. Use an atlas to check which rivers in Canada could be easily diverted into the U.S. Southwest. Evaluate the difficulties and consequences of such diversions.

10. How many of the causes of global warming can be found in Canada? Suggest actions that could be taken to deal with the emissions in your area.

11. Have the class contact political parties and ask them to send you their policies on the environment. Evaluate the policies in a class discussion, and decide which one is the most practical in its efforts to protect the environment.

Research and Communicate

12. Send an e-mail, or a letter, to the federal minister of the environment explaining why that department should give the highest priority to addressing the problems of the boreal forests.

13. Research the use and state of groundwater resources in your region. The British Columbia Department of the Environment and Resources is a good place to start.

14. Choose one of the major rivers mentioned in this chapter and research the problems of water management, including problems that arise because of different political jurisdictions. Write a short essay on this topic, illustrating it with a map.

15. Compose a ballad that tells the story of a farmer who supports, or is opposed to, the use of genetically modified crops. (Many ballads begin with the line, "Let me tell you the story about….")

16. With a group, script and perform a magazine-style feature for a local news broadcast dealing with an issue such as global warming, water exports, or genetically modified organisms.

17. Research some ways in which British Columbia's First Nations share their environment and culture with tourists.

18. Design a poster or collage to illustrate the consequences for the Earth of the depletion of forests.

19. In a group, develop a proposal for a film on one of the issues in this chapter. Submit a story outline, cast, setting, soundtrack, and working title.

20. In a small group, write and perform a TV spot feature called "Forest Minutes" (in the style of "Heritage Minutes"), promoting the benefits of rainforests.

18

Looking Forward

FOCUS ON

• How will increasing diversity and regionalism affect the future of Canada?

• How will the impact of the new economy, technology, and biotechnology change the way you live?

• Can local cultures survive globalization?

• Will Canada be able to maintain a separate identity in the face of increasing Americanization?

• What impact might changes in the environment have on your future quality of life?

• Should Canadians work to make the world become more democratic? Would this lead to a more peaceful world?

The Child, The Future,

The Child, The Future by Aboriginal artist George Littlechild. At the end of the twentieth century, many Canadians were optimistic about the coming millennium. At the same time, many others felt great uncertainty about the future of their country and of the world as a whole.

Expressing ideas Why does the artist focus on a child in this work? Do you find this painting optimistic about the future? Give reasons for your view.

Introduction

Many writers have tried to predict the future. Most conclude that the only certainty is uncertainty. Yet there are some predictions we can safely make. The pace of change in technology and communications will continue to speed up. World population will continue to grow and put increasing pressure on the environment. Economies around the world will become more closely linked. Any wars are likely to be fought differently from the two world wars of the twentieth century.

In this chapter we will examine some of these trends, first in Canada, and then in world issues.

The Future for Canada

What will Canada be like in the census year of 2021? Will it still have the same number of provinces and territories? Will issues such as western alienation, multiculturalism, Quebec separatism, and Aboriginal self-government be satisfactorily resolved? Will we be able to afford our social services? What will be the basis of our economy? What will be our role on the international stage? It is impossible to know the answers to these questions, or to know what events will take place in the coming years. By observing current trends, however, we can get an idea of what issues could shape our future.

Federal–Provincial Relations and Multiculturalism

One challenge that Canada might well face in the future is increasing tension between the federal and provincial governments. During past decades, both levels of governments have disagreed over many issues. Spending for health and education, control of natural resources, powers of taxation, economic and development policy, the fairness of equalization payments, recognition of Quebec as a distinct society, and privatization of social services were all subjects of debate. As you have seen, provinces and regions became more frustrated with Ottawa's response to their specific concerns. Some formed their own political parties, such as the Bloc Québécois in Quebec and the Canadian Alliance, formerly the western-based Reform Party. In the federal election of November 2000, the federal Liberal party won a majority of seats in Parliament for the third time in a row as votes were split among the other four political parties.

Future leaders and citizens will also face the challenge of accommodating the needs and rights of other groups of citizens as well. Many land claims by Aboriginal peoples have yet to be resolved, and the shape of Aboriginal self-government is still being defined. As new immigrants continue to make Canada their home, the debate over multiculturalism could continue. The chal-

Figure 18-1 More than 2000 people prepared to take the oath of citizenship to become Canadian citizens in Toronto on Canada Day, July 1, 2000, in the largest citizenship ceremony ever held in Canada. Over fifty similar ceremonies were held across the country on that day, adding 5551 citizens to the population.

lenge that lies ahead, according to Governor General Adrienne Clarkson, is "how we adapt a huge immigrant population to what we consider to be the Canadian way of life.... [T]he challenge is to make Canada as rich and varied as possible while maintaining the structures that we know are very, very good and have worked for us."

Impact of New Technology

New technology will continue to change the society in which we live. By the 1990s, communications had already changed drastically. Cable and satellite broadcasting meant television viewers had the choice of hundreds of channels. New satellite links also allowed for cheaper long-distance telephone calls. By the year 2000, more than half of all Canadian homes had a personal computer, and the numbers continue to grow as costs fall. Many household computers have Internet access, allowing Canadians to communicate with distant family and friends, and to use a range of on-line information and consumer services.

The impact of computers has changed the way we live and communicate with each other and the rest of the world. It has also drastically changed the world of work. In some cases, robots—computer-programmed machines—have replaced humans, working at a fraction of their cost. In certain industries, new technology caused layoffs. In other cases, it created new jobs for those with the right training. A "new economy" has emerged in which a person's knowledge, skills, and ability to adapt to new situations are valuable assets. In order for Canadians to be competitive in an increasingly demanding world, they will have to learn new skills and be better informed than ever before. Educators in the twenty-first century will need to prepare students for an information-based economy in which knowledge will be the most critical resource.

Advances in Science

Many advances have also been made in **biotechnology**, the "engineering" of genetic material in plant or animal cells to change some of their characteristics. For the most part, biotechnology has been used to modify food production such as grains or vegetables. But experiments in genetic engineering have also led to **cloning**—the artificial reproduction of living things from genetic material. For example, "Dolly," the first sheep to be successfully cloned, was identical to her mother. Herds of identical sheep can be created this way. At various medical institutions, researchers are also looking for ways to modify genes in the human body, hoping to develop treatments for diseases such as Parkinson's and Alzheimer's. Other medical breakthroughs have been made. Organ transplants, as well as surgery that uses lasers or robotics, have helped to improve and prolong the lives of a growing number of Canadians.

Biotechnology also raises a number of concerns for the future. If sheep and cows can be cloned, why not humans? Do people have the right to create life in this way? Do we have the right to prolong life with sophisticated medical technology? Many of the new medical techniques are expensive: will the technology be available to

Year	Cost of call	Typical unskilled worker's wage	Work time to earn cost of call
1965	$4.50/3 min	$2.50/h	108 min
1999	$0.42/3 min	$10/h	2.5 min

Figure 18-2 Cost of a telephone call, Canada to Britain, typical unskilled worker's wage, and work time to earn cost of call, 1965 and 1999.

Interpreting statistics

1. Make a bar graph to show the cost of a call and a line graph to show the work time necessary to pay for it in 1965 and 1999.

2. Make a list of five changes that you think would result from cheaper phone calls. Do you think these changes are on the whole positive or negative? Why?

Figure 18-3 Assembly-line workers in car manufacturing plants are being replaced by robots and skilled workers who maintain the robots.

all or limited to only the rich? How much further will technology go in the new millennium?

Maintaining Our Cultural Identity

What of Canada's national identity and the "Canadian way of life"? During the last century Canadians were greatly influenced by U.S. cultural trends, ideas, and entertainment. Canadian governments responded to this growing U.S. influence by regulating radio and television to ensure that Canadian talent was heard and seen by Canadians across the country. Government subsidies are given to Canadian artists and artistic institutions to help Canadian culture and entertainment grow. But the impact of the Internet and increased access to information could pose a serious threat to Canada's cultural identity. Research by the Canadian Radio-television and Telecommunications Commission (CRTC) found that, between 1989 and 1999, 71 per cent of all Web sites were American and only 5 per cent of the content on the Internet was Canadian. The chairperson of the federal government's Information Highway Advisory Council has remarked that "if we wish to tell our own stories, sing our songs, or see our own theatre, we have to ensure that there is a place on that great [information] carriageway [highway] for Canadians."

Figure 18-4 *Napoli*, by Peter Jermolow, is a digital work created while the artist was a high school student in Aurora, Ontario. Using his computer, Jermolow manipulated the photograph to resemble a watercolour painting, then added the woman (from another photo) and text.

Expressing ideas What does this photograph suggest about tradition and change? Give reasons for your view.

Trends in the Global Economy

Canada is not the only nation concerned with the growing influence of U.S. culture. The presence of U.S. television, movies, music, and, increasingly, the Internet is being felt in almost every country in the world. Many individuals welcome the availability of U.S. culture, products, and technology. They enjoy the entertainment, the consumer goods, and the "gadgets." Others, however, resent this trend towards a dominant world culture. They object to being exposed to the U.S. way of life, which they feel promote values different from their own cultures.

Concern over U.S. cultural dominance is only one of many issues that have emerged in the global economy. Some countries, particularly smaller ones, fear **globalization** will force them to give up some of their political independence, as well. More and more countries are becoming part of large trading blocs such as the North American Free Trade Agreement (NAFTA), the European Economic Community (EEC), and the Asia–Pacific Economic Co-operation (APEC). Member countries benefit from the trading bloc. They have larger markets in which to sell their goods and services, and there is an unrestricted flow of foreign goods and services crossing their borders.

On the other hand, trade agreements limit the amount of control a government has over its trade, economic, and even social policies. Once a country becomes part of a trading bloc, for example, it loses the ability to protect local businesses through tariffs or other protective measures. In some cases, it loses control of how to manage its resources.

Most of the businesses that benefit from unrestricted trade in goods and services are from the developed world. Many operate worldwide, owning plants and resources in countries around the world, as well as such assets as the transportation facilities they need. These companies are called **multinational corporations** (MNCs). Some of these multinationals have assets and incomes greater than those of many developing countries.

Corporation	National Ownership	Estimated Assets (US$billions)	Revenues (US$billions)	Profit (US$billions)
General Motors	USA	273.9	173.5	6.0
Mitsubishi	Japan	78.9	117.7	2.3
Royal Dutch/Shell Group	U.K./Netherlands	113.8	105.3	8.5
McDonalds	USA	21.0	13.2	1.9
George Weston Ltd.	Canada	6.9	14.0	0.2

Figure 18-5 Examples of multinational corporations, 1999.

Figure 18-6
Protesters were sprayed with a mixture of water and cow dung by police in Davos, Switzerland, in January 2001 when the World Economic Forum was held there. They were objecting to the impacts of globalization on the developing world.

Theo-Ben Gurirab, the foreign minister of the African country of Namibia, expressed his concerns about globalization:

> Globalization is seen by some as a force for social change, that it will help close the gap between the rich and the poor, the industrialized north and the developing south. But it is also being seen as a destructive force because it is being driven by the very people, the colonial powers, who launched a global campaign of imperial control of peoples and resources in what we now call the third world. Can we trust them?

Source: *New York Times*, Sunday, September 3, 2000, 4.

The Future for Developing Countries

How will developing countries manage to compete in the new economy and information age? In order to participate in a global economy, people need a certain level of education, a functioning infrastructure (such as a power grid), and a good communications system, including computers.

For many people in the world, these conditions are impossible to meet. Decent incomes for most of the population, resources, and wealth are still concentrated in the developed world. For example, countries belonging to the Organization for Economic Cooperation and Development (OECD) have only 19 per cent of the world's population, yet they have 71 per cent of global trade in goods and services, and 91 per cent of all Internet users.

Small steps were taken in 2000 to reduce the debt burden of some of the highly indebted countries in the world. Still, for many of these people, their best hope for a higher standard of living in the future is to try to emigrate to one of the developed countries.

The Future of Our Planet

You have learned that, in the last decades of the twentieth century, the growth in population and economic output put tremendous pressure on world resources. We may be reaching the limits of the Earth's carrying capacity. Increasing use of fossil fuels has led to global warming and pollution. Life forms are threatened by the hole in the ozone layer. Manufactured chemicals have entered food chains. Species of plants and animals are becoming extinct in record numbers. Whether or not we can support the growing numbers, most scientists agree that, as one of the developed nations that consumes a disproportionate amount of natural resources, Canadians must look for ways to reduce their impact on the environment.

Our Ecological Footprint

One way to examine the carrying capacity of the Earth is to calculate how much impact one person has on the planet. Two Vancouver scientists, William Rees and Mathis Wackernagel of the UBC Healthy and Sustainable Communities Task Force, attempted this calculation. They used the concept of **"ecological footprints"** to measure the "load imposed by a given population on nature." They estimated how much in resources each person needed to support his or her present lifestyle, and expressed their findings as a land area. At present levels of consumption, the average Canadian requires almost 4.3 ha, or about three city blocks, of land. They calculated, for instance, that 0.1 ha of forest land is required to produce paper for an average Canadian's reading materials in a year. By this reckoning, the nearly two million people in Greater Vancouver and the Lower Fraser Valley, who live on approximately 400 000 ha of land, would require an area nineteen times larger, or 7.7 million hectares, to support their present consumer lifestyle.

Rees and Wackernagel have estimated that there are about 8.9 billion hectares of land available for human exploitation. With a population of six billion people on Earth in 2000, it is clear that the present ecological footprint of Canadians cannot be duplicated throughout the world. In comparison, the ecological footprint of an average person living in India is 0.4 ha, and the world average is 1.8 ha.

The closer people in developing countries approach the standard of living of the developed world, the more the carrying capacity of the Earth will be taxed and possibly exceeded.

1. Reread the quote from Theo-Ben Gurirab. Form a thesis sentence about the effect of globalization on developing countries.

2. **a)** Research three ways that globalization could reduce the gap between rich countries and poor countries.

   b) Research three ways that globalization could be a disadvantage for developing countries.

   c) Use your research to write a short paragraph essay defending your thesis. Your essay should include both sides of the argument.

3. **a)** One hectare is an area of 100 m by 100 m. A Canadian football field is about 100 m long. Try to visualize the area that the average Canadian needs to maintain our existing lifestyle.

   b) Draw a simple bar graph to compare the area required by a Canadian with the area required by an Indian.

   c) Evaluate your family's ecological footprint. Suggest three areas in which your family could reduce its impact on the environment.

Is World Peace Possible?

Until 1991, the world lived with the confrontation of the two superpowers, the USSR and the United States, each armed with weapons of mass destruction. With the end of the Cold War, nuclear tensions declined dramatically. The world's arsenal of nuclear weapons dropped by half, from a peak of 70 000 warheads in 1986 to about 37 000 in 1997. The number of countries with nuclear weapons, however, increased. It is believed that the United States, Russia, Britain, France, China, India, Pakistan, and Israel all have nuclear arms. Of these countries, India, Pakistan, and Israel have not signed the Non-Proliferation Treaty, an agreement that limits the spread of nuclear weapons. A number of other countries such as Argentina, Brazil, South Africa, and Iraq are thought to have started the development of nuclear weapons, but stopped voluntarily or were forced to stop, as was the case with Iraq.

Figure 18-7 Two lanes are carved through the wreckage of an Iraqi convoy, still sitting on a six-lane stretch of highway north of Kuwait City in March 1991. In February, Iraqi troops retreating from Kuwait during the Persian Gulf War were destroyed by superior missiles fired by the U.S.-led United Nations forces.

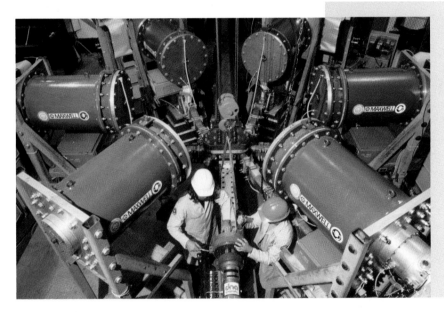

Figure 18-8 Technicians working on the U.S. Strategic Defence Initiative ("Star Wars") align a rail gun—a device that uses electromagnetism to accelerate particles to very high speeds—towards a target.

With so many countries possessing nuclear weapons, what are the world's chances for maintaining peace? Historian Gwynne Dyer believes the spread of democracy is a significant factor in the prevention of war. He argues that democratic countries tend not to fight wars with one another and that the more democracies there are in the world, the less likely it is that there will be war. If Dyer's argument is correct, then, according to the trend in the last century, the world should be moving towards greater peace. Research from the U.S. institute, Freedom House, shows that by the end of the twentieth century, there were 192 sovereign states (states with their own governments) in the world. Of this total, 120 states, with approximately 60 per cent of the world's population, were democracies. This figure represents a significant increase in the number of democratic countries since the beginning of the twentieth century, when nearly 60 per cent of the world

Figure 18-9 Millions across South Africa lined up in June 1999 to cast their vote in the country's second democratic elections. Freedom to vote for governments secretly and without intimidation is one of the marks of a democratic society.

Thinking critically What other features would you consider necessary for a state to be considered a democracy?

lived under some form of authoritarian government and 30 per cent were under colonial rule.

Many of the world's conflicts in the last years of the twentieth century, however, occurred between ethnic or religious groups within a country or a region. The conflicts in Bosnia, Rwanda, Chechnya, Kosovo, Kashmir, Somalia, Congo, and East Timor are all are examples of internal conflict. The victims in these wars are mostly civilians—people killed because of their beliefs, or driven out of their homes by an ethnic or religious majority.

Ralph Peters, a retired U.S. colonel, refers to this current trend as a "new age of conflict." Peters argues that wars with trained armies are largely gone. He describes many armies now as "half-trained killers in uniform, tribesmen, mercenaries, criminals, children with rusty Kalashnikovs [old Soviet-made machine guns], shabby despots and gory men of faith." These forces commit atrocities against civilians more often than they fight against other troops. According to Peters, it takes only a small force of these fighters to destroy peace in a fragile society. He thinks the power of Western armies should be used to maintain peace. But he cautions that the Western powers must decide which conflicts are worth fighting.

Acting Globally

Often, people can feel powerless when faced with issues such as government repression or threats to peace. There are many ways, however, for individuals to become involved in global issues. Organizations such as Amnesty International, for example, use letters from individuals to help raise awareness of violations of human rights by governments worldwide. These letter-writing campaigns help expose abuses such as torture, imprisonment without trial, rape, and murder of people who speak out against their government's policies.

One country that has been the focus of many human rights campaigns is Myanmar, formerly known as Burma. In 1988, a military government crushed pro-democracy movements, and some people were killed. That same year, the National League for Democracy (NLD) was formed with Daw Aung San Suu Kyi as the general secretary. The following year, the military regime put her under house arrest for five years. Although the NLD won the 1990 national election with an overwhelming majority of 82%, the government refused to acknowledge Aung San Suu Kyi as the new leader. While in detention, she was awarded the Nobel Peace Prize. Only after a concentrated

Figure 18-10 Aung San Suu Kyi, leader of the opposition forces in Myanmar, has refused to leave her country, even when her husband was dying in England. By staying in Myanmar, she is an effective opposition to the military government.

Developing understanding In what ways might Aung San Suu Kyi be more effective in opposing the military government?

Figure 18-11 A young girl collects and sorts rocks for a road-building project in Myanmar. The military regime uses forced labour to build roads and other projects. This regime has been in power since 1962, and Myanmar has become one of the poorest countries in the world.

effort by several governments, international organizations, and individuals writing letters, was she released from house arrest in 1995. Her high profile has helped prevent the military government from taking further action against her, although it continues to abuse the human rights of the citizens of Myanmar. In its 1999 annual report on Myanmar, Amnesty International noted that

> ...89 prisoners of conscience [were imprisoned] throughout the year. Hundreds of people were arrested for political reasons. Political prisoners were tortured and ill-treated, and held in conditions that amounted to cruel, inhuman and degrading treatment. Members of ethnic minorities continued to suffer human rights violations, including extrajudicial executions, torture, [and] ill-treatment....

Source: www.amnesty.org

Canada's International Role

As a middle power, Canada has had a degree of influence in international matters. It continues to participate in peacekeeping missions throughout the world. In 1996, Canada helped raise awareness of the issue of land mines by challenging countries from around the world to sign a treaty banning their production and use. In 1997, 134 countries and organizations signed the treaty, known as the Ottawa Process. The fight against the use of land mines has had some success. Since 1997, 20 million stockpiled land mines have been destroyed. As well, the number of countries pro-

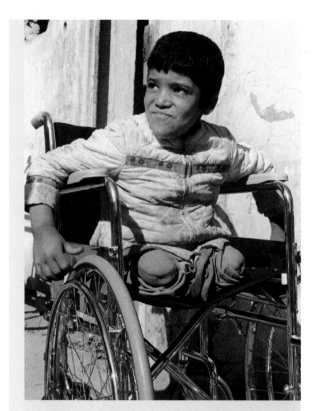

Figure 18-12 Thousands of civilians have been killed or injured in areas where land mines have been laid by warring forces. In some instances, injuries and deaths have occurred years after hostilities have ended. This boy was injured in Afghanistan, where millions of land mines were laid during the war against the former Soviet Union and in the civil war that followed the Russian withdrawal.

ducing land mines has gone from fifty-four to sixteen. Canada's minister of foreign affairs at that time, Lloyd Axworthy, was a driving force behind the Ottawa Process. He believes that the land mines treaty is an example of a new kind of global politics, "one where governments, civil society, and non-governmental organizations work together to effect positive change for people."

Canada has also become more involved in helping define the role that the United Nations should play in world conflicts and the protection of human rights. Canada supports a U.N. policy that recognizes a "human security agenda." This policy goes beyond the banning of land mines to cover the outlawing of child labour and the prosecution of political leaders for war crimes and crimes against humanity. It also focusses on "protecting people [in war-torn countries] from acts of violence and helping build a greater sense of security for the individual."

The international community faces many challenges in the future. Some of these include finding agreement among its members on when and how it should take action to protect civilians from abuse; establishing a permanent world court that will try those responsible for war crimes and crimes against humanity; and protecting the rights of children. Canada's influence will, undoubtedly, continue to be felt as these and other international issues evolve.

LOOKING BACK

1. a. Summarize the views of Gwynne Dyer and Ralph Peters about the future of war.

    b. Check recent editions of newspapers and magazines for reports from areas of conflict in the world. Give examples of wars today that meet these descriptions.

    c. Use this information to construct a collage depicting Peters's description of warfare. Include a map and annotations to inform the viewer of locations and other background information.

2. Research the history of nuclear arms reduction agreements since 1945. Do a PMI on the value of such agreements as a way to control the spread of nuclear weapons.

3. Find the Web site for the Canadian Department of Foreign Affairs and International Trade. Research the steps taken in organizing the Ottawa Process, the treaty banning land mines. What are some of the organizations involved in the Ottawa Process? Where were some of the planning conferences held? How long did Canada and other participating countries have to organize the treaty?

4. Organize a class debate on the topic: *Resolved— The world is safer today than it has been at any time since 1945.*

5. With a partner, make a collage with images that reflect the benefits of democracy.

6. What is your assessment of the future of democracy in the world? Use information from this text and from your own research to make a list of political systems that have tried to replace democracy in the twentieth century. Where do you think the next challenge to democracy will come from, and why?

7. Read about the major world issues at the United Nations Web site at <**www.un.org.cyberschoolbus**> under the heading Briefing Issues. What global issues are listed? Find one issue that you would like to understand better. Research that issue and present your findings to your group.

Glossary

aboriginal title   Claims by Aboriginal people to lands that their ancestors inhabited.

age structure   The composition of the population of a country based on the age groups of the population.

Agenda 21   The statement of action to promote *sustainable development* agreed to by heads of state who met at the Earth Summit in Rio de Janeiro in 1992.

agglomeration   A concentration of industries or other *economic activities* in one place.

agribusiness   An agricultural business where operations include growing, storing, processing, and distributing food, and may be owned by a business corporation, a family, or an individual.

Allies   In World War I, Britain, France, and Russia. In World War II, the term was applied to Britain, France, the countries of the British Commonwealth, and after 1941, the USSR.

amending formula   The process by which changes can legally be made to the Canadian Constitution.

appeasement   The granting of concessions in order to maintain peace.

aquifer   A underground layer of rock that allows water to flow through it. If the flow of water is stopped by a layer of *impermeable* rock, the aquifer holds underground water supplies (see *groundwater*).

arable   Land that is used for farming.

armistice   An agreement by warring parties to end hostilities.

assimilation   Adoption, often by a minority group, of the customs and language of another cultural group so that the original culture disappears.

autonomy   The power to govern oneself and make one's own decisions.

Axis   The alliance of Germany, Italy, and Japan during World War II.

baby boom   The increase in *birth rate* that occurred after World War II.

balance of power   The situation, especially before World War I, in which the strong nations of Europe attempted to remain of equal strength militarily and in their alliances.

basic activities   Economic activities such as the mining of ore or public administration that support a community and serve a larger community outside the local area.

Battle of the Atlantic   The struggle during World War II between the *Allies* and *Axis* powers to control the supply route for the Allies across the Atlantic Ocean.

biodiversity   The variety of living forms or species on the planet.

biosphere   The area of Earth that supports life. It consists of two parts: the atmosphere, the thin layers of gases and water vapour that surround the Earth; and the lithosphere, or Earth's crust, the layer on which we live.

biotechnology   The use of biological processes, particularly the "engineering" of genetic material in plant and animal cells, for industrial, agricultural, or other purposes.

boreal   The coniferous or needle-leaf forest that lies between the treeless tundra and the mixed deciduous and coniferous forest to the south.

branch plants   Factories, offices, or other operations set up in Canada but owned or controlled by U.S. or other foreign companies.

British Commonwealth An association of nations that were formerly colonies in the British Empire. The British Commonwealth of Nations is now known as the Commonwealth of Nations.

Cabinet The group of ministers chosen by the prime minister who decide government policy. Cabinet members usually have responsibility for particular departments of government, such as Foreign Affairs, Defence, and Justice.

cabinet solidarity The custom that cabinet members must not show public disagreement with government policies.

capitalist A person who practises or believes in capitalism. This is an economic system in which the production and distribution of goods are owned privately or by shareholders in corporations who have invested their money in the hope of making a profit.

carrying capacity The number of people (or animals) that can be sustained by an area of land.

caucus A group of representatives in legislatures who belong to the same political party. Caucus meets behind closed doors to discuss policies.

census The collection of statistics about people and activities. In Canada, a census is held every ten years, with a less complete compilation every five years.

central business district (CBD) The downtown area of a city or town where most of the important commercial and government activities take place.

civil disobedience The refusal to obey or follow laws one believes to be unjust or unfair; the intentional breaking of the law to gain the attention of government.

civil law The branch of the law that deals with relations between private parties such as individuals and corporations.

cloning The process of reproducing an organism asexually using DNA. The reproduction (the clone) is identical to the organism from which it was reproduced.

cohort An age group in a population, for example, the numbers of people between the ages of 13 and 19.

Cold War A period lasting approximately from 1945 to 1989 when there was tension and hostility between the *communist* Soviet Union and its allies and the *capitalist* and democratic United States and its allies.

collective bargaining Negotiation of a contract between unions and management regarding such things as wages and working conditions.

collective security The military support and cooperation provided by member states within an international organization to ensure that each will help the others in the event of aggression.

common law Law that is based on rulings made by judges in court cases.

communism A social and economic theory that property and production and distribution of goods and services should be owned by the public, and the labour force organized for the benefit of all. The application of the theory in the Soviet Union, China, and other countries resulted in dictatorships by members of the Communist Parties; forcible confiscation of property, including land; state-owned enterprises, such as collective farms and factories; and suppression of political dissent.

comprehensive claims Assertion of the right of Aboriginal nations to large tracts of land because their ancestors were the original inhabitants.

conscientious objector A person who refuses military service on the grounds of religious or moral opposition to war.

conscription Compulsory service in the armed forces.

constitutional monarchy A government in which the monarch has only the powers laid out in the nation's constitution and laws.

consumer society A *capitalist* society in which individuals are encouraged to spend money on new products and services so as to benefit the economy.

Crown corporation Businesses and industries owned by the Canadian government.

crude birth rate A figure obtained by dividing the number of births in one year by the population and multiplying the result by 1000.

crude death rate A figure obtained by dividing the number of deaths in one year by the population and multiplying the result by 1000.

crude density A figure arrived at by dividing the population of a country by its area. This figure can be misleading in a large country like Canada, where there are large areas with few people and small areas where many people live.

cut-off lands Lands taken from *reserves* without consent of the Aboriginal peoples.

decentralization The process of moving industries and services from the *economic core* to the *periphery*.

deficit The difference between expenditures and revenues that results when a government spends more than it takes in.

democracy A system of government in which people freely choose in elections who will govern them. It also refers to the principles and ideals of such a government, such as freedom of speech and the *rule of law*.

demographic transition model A model that shows the changes in a population's birth rates and death rates, and growth based on its technological development. Like all models, it is based on theory.

demography The study of population numbers, distribution, trends, and issues.

dependency ratio The ratio between the number of people in the work force and those who are retired or under the age of 14.

depression A downturn in the economy. The most severe economic depression of the twentieth century in the 1930s is sometimes called the Great Depression.

desertification The spreading of desert areas in regions of low rainfall, largely as a result of vegetation clearance, overgrazing by livestock, and farming.

developed country A country with a highly developed *economy*, with a strong service sector and often an industrial base. Citizens have the highest standards of living in the world, with high levels of literacy, health services, and food supplies.

developed economy An *economy* like Canada's that has a large service sector, manufacturing, trade, and diverse sources of income.

developing country A country with an economy that depends more on *primary industries*, and where citizens have a lower standard of living than those in developed countries.

developing economy An *economy* that is moving from a *traditional economy* by adopting more mechanized production methods and more services.

direct democracy A way in which people exercise control over political decision making. In a state with a large population like Canada, a referendum is one way that direct democracy can be exercised.

doubling time The period of years that it takes a country to double its population at its current birth rate.

ecological footprint A way of measuring the total impact that people have on the planet's environment.

economic activities   Processes that help produce wealth and maintain quality of life.

economic core   A region that leads in economic growth and attracts other economic activities, often from the *periphery*.

economic disparity   A situation where there is a large gap between people who have low incomes and those who are rich.

economy   The total of all *economic activities* such as production and consumption in a society.

ecotourism   Tourist industry that is based on the observation of natural ecosystems and the natural environment.

ecumene   The populated area of the world.

emigration rate   The rate at which people emigrate, usually based on the number of people per thousand who leave a country.

equalization payments   Payments made by the federal government to some provinces so that the standard of living will be more uniform across Canada.

ethnocentric   The belief that one's own culture is superior, and that other cultures should be judged by its values.

executive power   The power to make decisions in government and set policies.

exponential rate   A rapid rate of increase as each generation doubles in size.

fascist   A form of authoritarian government that was set up in Italy and Germany before World War II. The government in fascist states is *totalitarian* and *nationalist*.

feminism   A belief that women should have equality with men in political, social, and economic fields, and not be discriminated against on the basis of their sex.

first-past-the-post   The system in which the candidate who has more votes than any other candidate wins an election.

Free Trade Agreement (FTA)   An agreement signed in 1989 between Canada and the United States to allow goods produced in each country to cross the border tariff-free.

Geographic Information Systems (GIS) An integrated software package for the input, management, analysis, and display of information, especially for maps.

globalization   The process by which regions and countries of the world are becoming interconnected. Globalization has been speeded up by modern communication technologies.

gross domestic product (GDP)   The total value of all goods and services produced in a country, and excluding transactions with other countries, such as income from overseas investments.

gross national product (GNP)   The dollar value of all goods and services produced in a year in a country, including income from foreign investments.

groundwater   Underground water that is stored in *aquifers*.

habeas corpus   The protection that citizens who live in a democracy have to guard against unlawful detention. It requires that a person who is being detained be brought into court within twenty-four hours of arrest, where a judge or other official will decide whether the detention is lawful. In Canada, habeas corpus was suspended when the War Measures Act was invoked.

head tax   The fee that Chinese immigrants were required to pay after the Chinese Immigration Act was passed in 1885 when they entered Canada.

highly indebted poor country (HPIC)   A country that is so in debt to *developed countries* that most of its gross domestic product is used to pay interest on those debts. Such countries rate the lowest on the U.N. Human Development Index.

Holocaust The genocide committed by the fascist Nazi government in Germany against Jews and other peoples during World War II.

immigration rate The rate at which people immigrate to a country, usually based at the number of people per thousand who enter a country.

imperialism The building of empires by taking over new territories.

impermeable The quality of a substance, such as rock, of not allowing water to pass through it.

indictable offence A serious offence, such as armed robbery or murder, that can lead to a person's arrest.

industrial heartland An area where manufacturing and other industries are concentrated.

infilling The process by which *population density* in an urban centre is increased by building on waste land or underused land.

inflation The rise in prices for goods and services that increases the cost of living and triggers the demand for a rise in wages.

infrastructure Structures such as roads, railways, power grids, and communications links that are basic to the functioning of a modern economy, as well as buildings such as schools and hospitals.

in-migration The movement of people into an area, such as a city.

International Monetary Fund (IMF) An agency of the United Nations set up to help nations experiencing difficulty paying their debts. Its aim is to keep the world economy stable.

internment camps Government-run camps where people who are considered a threat are detained.

isolationists People who hold the belief that one's country should keep separate from the politics and disputes of other countries.

judicial power The power to interpret and administer the law.

Kyoto Protocol The agreement negotiated by 159 countries in 1997 to lower emission of gases that contribute to global warming.

laissez-faire A government policy of not interfering in the working of the market economy by regulations or economic policies.

land use How land is used in an area, such as for housing (residential) or for business (commercial).

legislative power The power to make, change, and repeal laws.

life expectancy The average number of years that a person or population can expect to live.

lobbyist A person who is hired to represent the interests of a *pressure group* by influencing policy decision makers in the group's favour.

locational advantage The advantage that one place has over others in terms of access to resources and transportation routes.

megaproject Large-scale construction projects that require a huge capital investment. The construction of the St. Lawrence Seaway is an example.

merchant marine Civilian ships and sailors. In wartime, they transport food, weapons, and munitions.

militarism A nation's policy of enlisting, training, equipping, and maintaining armed forces ready for war.

minority government A government in which the ruling party has less than half the seats in the legislature.

multiculturalism A policy of fostering the expression of the cultures of many ethnic groups that make up a country's population.

multilateral aid Foreign aid given by a group of countries through an organization like the United Nations.

multinational corporation (MNC) A large company that operates in more than one country. MNCs have more assets and annual income than *developing countries*, and have both economic and political power.

multiplier effect The chain reaction by which the growth or decline of an economic activity results in the creation or lessening of wealth.

national identity A sense of, and pride in, the character of one's nation.

nationalism A strong attachment to one's nation.

nationalist A person who has a strong feeling of attachment to his or her nation.

natural increase The difference between the number of births and the number of deaths, often given per thousand people.

net migration rate The difference between the number of people immigrating to a country and the number of people emigrating.

newly industrializing country A country in the transition stage between developing and developed nations. Most have rapidly growing economies.

non-basic activity An economic activity, such as a shopping mall, that meets the needs of the local population.

non-governmental organization (NGO) A non-governmental, non-profit organization that runs aid programs and lobbies for people's rights around the world. Some NGOs receive money from governments and work in partnership with them. Examples are Save the Children and Oxfam.

non-renewable resources Resources that do not renew themselves naturally, such as iron ore.

North American Air Defence Agreement (NORAD) This agreement in 1957 integrated the air-defence forces of the United States and Canada under joint command. The agreement was renamed the North American Aerospace Defence Command in 1981.

North American Free Trade Agreement (NAFTA) The agreement signed in 1992 and implemented in 1994 between the United States, Mexico, and Canada to create a free trade zone among the countries.

North American Treaty Organization (NATO) The mutual defence organization set up to protect fourteen Western European countries, Canada, and the United States from possible aggression from the USSR after World War II.

notwithstanding clause The clause in the Canadian Constitution (Section 33 [1]) that allows Parliament or the legislature of a province to allow an act to stand even though it contravenes the Charter of Rights and Freedoms.

nutritional density A measure of how much nutrition can be produced from land. An area with fertile soil and adequate temperatures and precipitation for plants to grow will have a higher nutritional density than an area like Canada's North.

official plan A plan for growth and development drawn up by an urban centre.

out-migration The movement of people out of an area.

patronage A favour, often a government position, given in return for political support.

peak-value intersection (PVI) A part of a city where major traffic arteries intersect and land costs are high because many businesses want to locate in that area.

per capita GDP The average income figure for each person in a country that is calculated by dividing the *gross domestic product* by the population.

periphery Areas that are outside the *economic core*. Areas in the periphery have fewer services and less variety in economic activities than core areas.

permafrost Ground that does not completely thaw in the summer.

permeable A substance that allows water to flow through it. For example, sandstone is a permeable rock.

plebiscite A direct vote by electors on an issue of public importance. The outcome of the vote may not be binding on the government.

population density A figure calculated by dividing the total population of a region by the area of the region.

population distribution The pattern of where people live in an area.

population pyramid A bar graph that depicts the population of an area by age groups and sex.

pressure group An organized group of individuals with common interests and concerns who attempt to pressure political decision makers. Pressure groups are also known as interest groups.

primary industries Industries dealing with the extraction or collection of raw materials, such as mining or forestry.

private member's bill A bill introduced into the legislature by a member of Parliament who is not a member of the cabinet.

productivity A measure of the effectiveness of effort that goes into producing goods. For example, a farmer can improve productivity by using mechanized tools.

propaganda Information usually produced by governments presented in such a way as to inspire and spread particular beliefs or opinions.

proportional representation An electoral system in which members of legislatures are chosen in proportion to the numbers of votes their parties receive.

protectionism A system of using tariffs to raise the price of imported goods in order to protect domestic producers.

pull factors Factors that attract people or industries to an area.

push factors Factors that result in people or industries leaving an area.

recession A decline in the economy, resulting in lower levels of employment and production.

referendum The process of referring a political question to the people for a direct vote.

regional disparity Differences in income, wages, and jobs in one area compared with another.

regionalism A concern for the affairs of one's own region over those of one's country.

renewable resources Resources such as trees and fish that, if managed in a *sustainable* way, will renew themselves.

representative democracy A democratic system in which citizens vote for representatives who are empowered on their behalf to make decisions.

reserves The designated areas of land set aside for Aboriginal peoples.

residential schools Government-authorized schools run by religious groups set up to educate Aboriginal children in Canadian culture. The children lived at the schools apart from their families.

residual powers In Canada's Constitution, any powers that are not specifically listed are held by the federal government or the Crown.

rule of law The principle that people are governed by laws, and that no person is above the law.

sanctions Penalties, such as restricting trade, applied by a group of nations to try to force an offending nation to end aggression or an offensive policy.

scarcity The idea that resources, including human labour, are in limited supply, and that these resources should be used in the most efficient way possible.

secondary industries Industries dealing with manufacturing or construction.

self-government The right of a colony or cultural group to define the structure, laws, and policies that will govern its own affairs.

shanty towns Makeshift communities that have grown up around rapidly growing urban centres in *developing countries*, and built by squatters on land they do not own from whatever building materials they can find.

site The characteristics of an area, such as landforms, on which a building or city is constructed.

situation The relationship between a city and the area surrounding it.

socialist A believer in a political and economic system in which the means of production and distribution in a country are publicly owned and controlled for the benefit of all members of a society.

sovereignty-association A proposal by Quebec nationalists that Quebec have political independence yet retain close economic ties or association with Canada.

specific claims First Nations' claims to land based on the belief that the government did not fulfil its obligations under a treaty or other agreement related to money, land, or other assets.

status Indian An Aboriginal who is registered with the federal government according to the terms of the Indian Act.

statutory law Law that has been passed as legislation by federal, provincial, or municipal governments.

stewardship The management of resources in a careful and sustainable way.

structural adjustment program (SAP) A program that requires an indebted country to restructure its economy by encouraging foreign investment, increasing exports, and turning government services over to the private sector in return for loans from the World Bank and *International Monetary Fund*.

subsistence agriculture A form of agriculture in which crops or livestock are raised for consumption by the farmers rather than for sale.

suffragists People who advocated that women should have the right to vote.

summary offence A less serious criminal offence than an *indictable offence* that carries in Canada a maximum imprisonment of six months.

sunset industries Industries that are no longer efficient.

superpowers Term used to refer to the United States and USSR in the post-World War II period when both were engaged in building up powerful weapons of mass destruction as deterrents against aggression.

sustainable cities Urban centres where decisions made do not degrade the quality of life for future inhabitants.

sustainable development A method of using resources and land without negatively affecting their future use.

tertiary industries Industries that provide services such as banking.

tied aid Assistance given by one country to another that requires the receiving country to buy goods and services from the donor country.

totalitarian state An undemocratic state in which the government demands total obedience from citizens and controls all aspects of society.

trade union A group of workers who unite to achieve common goals in discussions with owners and management of businesses and industries.

traditional economy An *economy* in which most people work in *primary industries* such as farming and fishing.

Treaty of Versailles The treaty that ended World War I.

Triple Alliance The alliance of Germany, the Austro-Hungarian Empire, and Italy prior to World War I.

Triple Entente The alliance of France, Russia, and Great Britain prior to World War I.

urban functions The activities and services that are provided by towns, such as cultural activities and financial services. In the past, walled cities provided a protective function.

urbanization The process by which an area changes from rural to urban.

vertically integrated business A situation in which a company owns and operates every step in the manufacture and distribution of its products.

War Measures Act An act of the Canadian Parliament that gave the federal *Cabinet* emergency powers, especially during wartime. It included the right to suspend *habeas corpus*.

Warsaw Pact A post-World War II military alliance involving the USSR and the Soviet-bloc countries of Bulgaria, Czechoslovakia, East Germany, Poland, and Romania.

western alienation The feeling on the part of western Canada that federal policies favour central Canada. It has led to the rise of several regional parties, of which the latest is the Canadian Alliance Party.

Index

Credits

Documents

Page 44

From *A Social History of Canada* by George Woodcock. Copyright © 1988 by George Woodcock. Reprinted by permission of Penguin Books Canada Limited.

Pages 206–207

From *Selling Illusions* by Neil Bissoondath. Copyright © 1994 by Neil Bissoondath. Reprinted by permission of Penguin Books Canada Limited.

Page 298

From *The Concubine's Children* by Denise Chong. Copyright © 1994 by Denise Chong. Reprinted by permission of Penguin Books Canada Limited.

Visuals

AP: Associated Press
Corel: Corel Picture Library
CP: CP Picture Archive
CTA: City of Toronto Archives
GA: Glenbow Archives
NAC: National Archives of Canada
TRL: Toronto Reference Library
VPL: Vancouver Public Library

Chapter 1

Page 4 *Tanoo, Queen Charlotte Islands* by Emily Carr, B.C. Archives, PDF-2145; Fig. 1-2 Source unknown; Fig. 1-3 Archives of Ontario #S-9745; Fig. 1-6 GA, Calgary NA-748-83; Fig. 1-7 VPL #30625; Fig. 1-9 NAC/PA-48475; Fig. 1-10a TRL T11245; Fig. 1-10b Provincial Archives of Manitoba #N2438; Page 14 Corel; TRL Picture Collection; Archival Collection, A.G. Bell National Historical Site, Baddeck, N.S.; Corel; Corel; Public Works & Government Services Canada; Fig. 1-11 CTA #SC244-136A; Fig. 1-14 NAC/C-30621

Chapter 2

Page 20 *For What* by Fred Varley, © Canadian War Museum; Fig. 2-2 Source unknown; Fig. 2-3a NAC/C-29484; Fig. 2-3b NAC/C-95378; Fig. 2-4 NAC/PA-66815; Fig. 2-5 City of Vancouver Archives #MIL.P.206.N96; Fig. 2-6 GA, Calgary NC-54-4336; Page 29 Corel; Source unknown; NAC/PA-1012; NAC/PA-928; Source unknown; Fig. 2-8 NAC/PA-2468; Fig. 2-9a Guelph Civic Museum, McCrae House; Fig. 2-9b Source unknown; Fig. 2-10 CP/NAC; Fig. 2-11 NAC/PA-988; Fig. 2-12 NAC/PA-122515; Fig. 2-13 *Canada's Answer* by N. Wilkinson, #8934, © Canadian War Museum; Fig. 2-15 VPL #NA-1870-6; Fig. 2-16 NAC/C-57358; Fig. 2-17 CTA, James #2451; Fig. 2-20 NAC/PA-2279; Fig. 2-22 NAC/PA-60562; Fig. 2-23 © Bettmann/CORBIS/Magma Photos; Fig. 2-24 GA, Calgary NA-3452.2

Chapter 3

Page 48 *October, 1928–1933*, by Clarence Gagnon, 1881–1942, mixed media on paper, 17.7 x 20.0 cm, Gift of Col. R.S. McLaughlin, McMichael Canadian Art Collection, 1969.4.29; Fig. 3-1 *Mail & Empire*; Fig. 3-2 Provincial Archives of Manitoba #N2762; Fig. 3-3 *Glace Bay* by Lawren W. Harris, 1925, Art Gallery of Ontario. By permission of the family of Lawren S. Harris; Fig. 3-4 GA, Calgary *Grain Growers Guide* Feb 3/26; Fig. 3-5 NAC/C-9055; Fig. 3-7 VPL #8135; Fig. 3-8a City of Vancouver Archives #BU.P.613; Fig. 3-8b GA, Calgary #NA-3229-88; Fig. 3-9 NAC/C-21562; Fig. 3-10 CTA #SC-244-1902; Fig. 3-11 NAC/PA-88191; Fig. 3-12 Whyte Museum of the Canadian Rockies #NA 33-882; Page 64 CTA #SC-244-8054; Source unknown; TRL; NAC/C-1350; Musée J. Armand Bombardier 1B7M2; Fig. 3-13 *Solemn Land, Algoma* by J.E.H. MacDonald, National Gallery of Canada; Fig. 3-14 NAC/PA-151007; Fig. 3-15 GA, Calgary #ND-8-397; Fig. 3-16 VPL #8956-D; Fig. 3-17 Reproduction by Preston Microfilm Services, Toronto

Chapter 4

Page 74 *Recluse* by Bertram Brooker, 1939, Musée des Beaux Arts de Montréal; Fig. 4-2 VPL #12749; Fig. 4-3 NAC/C-29397; Fig. 4-4 GA, Calgary #NA-2496-1; Fig. 4-5 *Winnipeg Free Press* (Apr. 14/31); Fig. 4-6 CTA #SC244-1682; Fig. 4-7 Source unknown; Fig. 4-8 GA, Calgary #NA-4868-181; Fig. 4-9 *Winnipeg Free Press* (Apr 14/31); Fig. 4-10 City of Vancouver Archives #CITYP.21; Fig. 4-11 NAC/C-52832; Fig. 4-12 NAC/C-7731; Fig. 4-13 NAC/PA-203126; Fig. 4-14 CP; Fig. 4-15 © Bettmann/CORBIS/Magma Photos; Fig. 4-16 © CORBIS/Magma Photos; Fig. 4-20 NAC/PA-119013; Fig. 4-21 CP

Chapter 5

Page 100 *Maintenance Jobs in the Hangar* by Paraskeva Clark, #14085, © Canadian War Museum; Fig. 5-1 TRL #T31373; Fig. 5-2 NAC/PA-108174; Fig. 5-3 NAC/PA-116586/Donald Grant; Fig. 5-4 Western Canadian Pictorial Index #A-1279-383112; Fig. 5-5 Canada Department of National Defence #RE-12378; Fig. 5-6 TRL, BDS 1939-45 Ind. Prod. #16; Fig. 5-8 © CORBIS/Magma Photos; Fig. 5-9 Remember Hong Kong poster, #19700036-024, © Canadian War Museum; Fig. 5-11 NAC/C-14160; Fig. 5-12 NAC/PA-112993; Fig. 5-13 NAC/PA-142415; Page 112 Source unknown; Source unknown; Corel; University of Arizona; Corel; Source unknown; Corel; Source unknown; Fig. 5-14 Canada Department of National Defence; Fig. 5-16 NAC/PA-163938; Fig. 5-18 NAC/PA-145972; Fig. 5-19a © Bettmann /CORBIS/Magma Photos; Fig. 5-19b © Reuters/Bettmann/ COBIS/ Magma Photos; Fig. 5-21 TRL BDS1939-45, Espionage #5; Fig. 5-22 *Montreal Gazette*/NAC/ PA-107910; Fig. 5-23 CTA, #SC 488-6408; Fig. 5-24 NAC

Chapter 6

Page 130 *Horse and Train* by Alex Colville, courtesy Ann Kitz; Fig. 6-1 NAC/PA-129625; Fig. 6-4 Andrew Medichini/AP/CP #0DHRB; Fig. 6-5 Canada Department of National Defence #15C-86-NA 753; Fig. 6-6 United Nations, NY; Fig. 6-7 P. Almasy/WHO 16739; Fig. 6-8 NAC/C-94168; Fig. 6-10 National Aviation Museum, Ottawa; Fig. 6-11 NAC/PA-127292; Fig. 6-12a NAC/PA-128280; Fig. 6-12b *Contact* by Edward F. Zuber, © Canadian War Museum, photo by Wm. Kent; Fig. 6-12c NAC/PA-170294; Fig. 6-13 Reprinted with permission, The Toronto Star Syndicate; Fig. 6-14 CP/Fred Chartrand; Fig. 6-15 CIDA/ACDI; Page 148 NASA 69-HC-680; NASA; Fig. 6-16 CP/Frank Lennon/*Toronto Star*; Fig. 6-17 CP/Bill Grimshaw; Fig. 6-18 CP/AP/Thomas Kienzle; Fig. 6-19 CP/Hans Deryk; Fig. 6-20 CP/Tom Hanson; Fig. 6-21 CP/Daniel Morel; Fig. 6-23 CP/Fred Chartrand

Chapter 7

Page 160 *Expo Walking Woman, 1967* by Michael Snow, Art Gallery of Ontario; Fig. 7-1 Public Archives of Nova Scotia #G1066-2; Fig. 7-3 John Henley/First Light; Fig. 7-4 © CORBIS/Magma Photos; Fig. 7-5 Archive Photo/Express Newspapers; Fig. 7-6 NAC/PA-112691; Fig. 7-7 © CORBIS/ Magma Photos; Fig. 7-8 Al Harvey/The Slide Farm; Fig. 7-9 CP; Fig. 7-10 CP; Fig. 7.12 NAC/C-123991; Fig. 7-13 Reprinted by permission, The Toronto Star Syndicate; Fig. 7-14 Reprinted by permission, The Toronto Star Syndicate; Fig. 7-15 Courtesy Mike Cranny; Fig. 7-16 CP/Peter Bregg; Fig. 7-17 CP/Tom Hanson (04G8Y); Fig. 7-18 CBC; Fig. 7-19 CP; Fig. 7-20 CP; Fig. 7-23 CP/Tom Hanson; Fig. 7-24 CP/Brian Schlosser; Page 188 Hulton Getty/Liaison; Source unknown; Sony Canada; CP; Tom Luff; Garmin International

Chapter 8

Page 190 *Unit Rally III*, Montreal by Evangeline Murray, Photo courtesy of Donald Murray. Fig. 8-1 *Montreal Gazette*; Fig. 8-2 CP/ *Montreal Star;* Fig. 8-3 Pearson Education Archives; Fig. 8-4 Roy Peterson; Fig. 8-5 CP; Fig. 8-6 CP; Fig. 8-7 Roy Peterson/*Vancouver Sun*; Fig. 8-8 Canada Wide; Fig. 8-9 Mayes; Fig. 8-10 CP/Wayne Glowacki; Fig. 8-11 Peter Jones/Reuters; Fig. 8-14 CP/Tom Hanson; Fig. 8-15 CP/Fred Chartrand; Fig. 8-16 CP; Fig. 8-17 CP/Shaney Komulainen; Fig. 8-18 Ian Smith/*Vancouver Sun*; Fig. 8-19 Canadian Museum of Civilization; Fig. 8-20 Canadian Museum of Civilization CMC#589-1736; Fig. 8-22 CP/Tom Hanson; Fig. 8-23 CP/Kevin Frayer

Chapter 9

Page 220 *Confedspread* by Joyce Wieland, 1967, National Gallery of Canada; Fig. 9-1 CP/Tom Hanson; Fig. 9-2 © Bettmann Archive/CORBIS/ Magma Photos; Fig. 9-3 CP/Ron Poliing; Fig. 9-4 National Capital Commission/D. Drever; Fig. 9-6 CP/Frank Gunn; Fig. 9-7a CP/*La Presse*/Bernard Brault; Fig. 9-7b CP/Chuck Stoody; Fig. 9-7c CP/Fred Chartrand; Fig. 9-9 CP/Tom Hanson; Fig. 9-11 CP/Fred Chartrand; Fig. 9-13a Roy Peterson, *Vancouver Sun*; Fig. 9-13b CAM, Ottawa Citizen (appeared in *Regina Leader Post*, 1993); Fig. 9-15 Photo by J.M Carisse, Courtesy of the Office of the Prime Minister; Fig. 9-16a Toronto Fire Services/ Scott Cowden; Fig. 9-16b © Chip Henderson/Image Network Inc.; Fig. 9-16c Canadian Food Inspection Agency; Fig. 9-18a CP/Tom Hanson; Fig. 9-18b

15-28 © Marcus Wilson-Smith/RETNA Pictures/ Ponopresse Int'l; Fig. 15-30 Al Harvey/The Slide Farm

Chapter 16

Page 394 Dr. B. Lynne Milgram; Fig. 16-3 L.T. Webster; Fig. 16-10 Dr. B. Lynne Milgram; Fig. 16-14 © Jeremy Horner/CORBIS/Magma Photos; Fig. 16-16 © Stephanie Maze/CORBIS/Magma Photos; Fig. 16-17 UNESCO/Dominique Roger; Fig. 16-19 © Stephanie Maze/CORBIS/Magma Photos; Fig. 16-21 © Bill Varie/CORBIS/Magma Photos #75641; Fig. 16-22 © Owen Franken/ COBIS/Magma Photos; Fig. 16-24 © Gunter Marx/CORBIS/Magma Photos; Fig. 16-25 © Lowell Georgia/CORBIS/Magma Photos; Fig. 16-26 © Roger Ressmeyer/CORBIS/Magma Photos; Fig. 16-29 *Vancouver Sun*

Chapter 17

Page 420 NASA; Fig. 17-1 Ontario Ministry of the Environment; Fig. 17-2 © Robert Maass/COR-BIS/Magma Photos; Fig. 17-6 © Fred Pearce; Fig. 17-8 Canadian Press/Orlin Wagner; Fig. 17-9 © Images B.C./Image Network; Fig. 17-17 Russ Heinl Group, Sidney, BC/Image Network Inc.; Fig. 17-20 © Walt Anderson/Visuals Unlimited; Fig. 17-21 © Bill Beatty/Visuals Unlimited; Fig. 17-22 Reprinted with permission from *The Globe and Mail*; Fig. 17-23 CP/AP/Luca Bruno; Fig. 17-24 © D. Cavagnaro/Visuals Unlimited; Fig. 17-28 CP/AP/ Pavel Rahman; Fig. 17-30 © Sally A. Morgan/ Ecoscene/CORBIS/Magma Photos; Fig. 17-31 © Gordon J. Fisher/Image Network Inc.; Fig. 17-32 Ron Thiele/Looking Glass Design Inc.; Fig. 17-33 © Tim Matheson/Image Network Inc.; Fig. 17-34 © Ecoscene/CORBIS/Magma Photo

Chapter 18

Page 448 *The Child, The Future* by George Littlechild; Fig. 18-1 CP/Aaron Harris; Fig. 18-3 CP/Fred Lum; Fig. 18-4 Peter Jermolow; Fig. 18-6 CP/ AP/Michele Limina; Fig. 18-7 CP/AP/Greg Gibson; Fig. 18-8 © Roger Ressmeyer/CORBIS/ Magma Photos; Fig. 18-9 CP/AP/Themba Hadebe; Fig. 18-10 CP/AP/ Grant Peck; Fig. 18-11 Reprinted by Permission, The Toronto Star Syndicate, photo by Martin Regg Cohn; Fig. 18-12 CP/AP/Zaheeruddin Abdullah